Irwin Book Team

Publisher: *Tom Casson*
Senior sponsoring editor: *Rick Williamson*
Developmental editor: *Christine Wright*
Marketing manager: *Michelle Hudson*
Project editor: *Beth Cigler*
Production supervisor: *Laurie Sander*
Prepress buyer: *Charlene R. Perez*
Designer: *Matthew Baldwin, Lucy Lesiak*
Photo research coordinator: *Keri Johnson*
Compositor: *Carlisle Communications, Ltd.*
Typeface: *10/12 Cheltenham Light*
Printer: *Times Mirror Higher Education Group, Inc., Print Group*

Times Mirror Books

Library of Congress Cataloging-in-Publication Data

Cats-Baril, William L.
Information technology and management / William L. Cats-Baril, Ronald L. Thompson
p. cm.
ISBN 0-256-17618-3
1. Information technology—Management. 2. Management information systems. 3. Information technology—Management—Case studies.
I. Title.
HD30.2.C42 1997
658.4'038—dc20 96-20202

Printed in the United States of America
1 2 3 4 5 6 7 8 9 0 WCB 3 2 1 0 9 8 7 6

Competition. Competition is a fact c
strategies of lower cost, differentiat
obtaining a market advantage. Info
and commonly used tool for implementing organizational strategy.

World Wide Web site: http://www.irwin.com/mis/catsbth

Information Technology and Management

William L. Cats-Baril

University of Vermont
School of Business Administration

Ronald L. Thompson

University of Vermont
School of Business Administration

IRWIN

Chicago • Bogotá • Boston • Buenos Aires • Caracas
London • Madrid • Mexico City • Sydney • Toronto

To the four cardinal points of my emotional compass: Amanda, Deva, Lucette, and Dédé.
Thank you for being such magnificent people. I love you.
WCB

To Jen, my inspiration; to Betty, for always being there;
and to the memory of Alan.
RLT

About the Authors

William L. Cats-Baril

is Associate Professor of Management Information Systems in the School of Business Administration at the University of Vermont. He holds a Ph.D. from the University of Wisconsin–Madison. He has held a variety of visiting appointments including stays at INSEAD and the London School of Economics. Willy has published more than thirty articles and book chapters on a variety of topics in information technology and decision making. He has taught a variety of audiences around the world ranging from first-year undergraduate students to senior executives, and has received various awards for teaching excellence. He has an international consulting practice. A former waterpolo player for the Mexican national team, Willy now enjoys skiing, bicycling, trekking and scuba diving.

Ronald L. Thompson

is Associate Professor of Management Information Systems in the School of Business Administration at the University of Vermont. His background includes experience in farming, banking, and academe. Ron has published in a variety of academic journals and has presented papers at national and international conferences. He also has taught a wide range of students and has won awards for excellence in teaching. His interest in the use of teaching cases was obtained while completing his Ph.D. at the School of Business Administration at the University of Western Ontario (London, Canada). Ron enjoys a variety of sporting and outdoor activities, including his latest hobby, rock climbing.

Preface

The authors of this textbook were given the opportunity—and challenge—of developing a meaningful first course in information systems that would address the unique needs of business students. After teaching the course for the first time, we found that our biggest hurdle was locating appropriate teaching material; none of the textbooks, articles, or cases we previewed or used seemed to work as well as we wished. This book grew out of our efforts to develop lecture notes, cases, and assignments that would help us achieve the following goals:

1. Provide a meaningful introduction to organizations and how they function and to the current philosophies on how to manage them.
2. Provide a clear understanding of the role of information technology in managing organizations, both now and in the future.
3. Facilitate the learning of concepts, frameworks, and approaches to apply information technology to managerial challenges that are technology independent.
4. Present the material in an interesting, informative, and useful format for the intended audience.

We believe that this first edition of *Information Technology and Management* is a new approach to the study of information systems. It is not just an introduction to information technology—it is an introduction to business processes and how information technology can make these processes more effective. The book covers the traditional topics of information technology, information system components, and information systems development. But it goes beyond this traditional coverage, showing first how businesses function and then how information systems enable businesses to function more effectively. Our goal is for the student to gain not only an understanding of information systems, but also an understanding of the role of information systems in helping organizations achieve greater effectiveness.

The conceptual backbone of the book is the notion that organizational responsiveness is the key to strategic success. Organizations need to respond quickly—or at least adapt more quickly than their competition—to changes in customer expectations, technology, supplier relations, and so forth if they are to remain viable entities. We define organizational responsiveness in terms of being constantly aware of customers' preferences and the availability of inputs and in terms of ensuring the flexibility and efficiency of the transformation process. We argue that organizational responsiveness in today's world is virtually impossible without information technology.

Every chapter of the book is brought back to this notion of responsiveness. For example, Chapter 4, "Organizational Communication," includes a discussion of how an information overload for managers slows down the responsiveness of organizations. Chapter 5, "Information Systems Concepts," includes a discussion of how to build an effective information technology architecture to deliver the least amount of information necessary to support managers and workers in their jobs, by minimizing overload and distortion. The logic is the following: If you want an organization to react quickly to changes in the environment, then managers cannot afford to sift through tons of irrelevant data, nor can they be constantly checking the credibility of the data, nor can they afford to be confused as to how and to whom to transmit information.

In the same vein, Chapter 6 "Information Technology," addresses the components of a computer system from the point of view of increasing responsiveness to the environment. Input devices are presented as tools to providing better service to customers (e.g., faster transactions, fewer errors) or providing greater control over inventories (e.g., point-of-sale scanners, electronic linkages to suppliers). Input devices are also discussed as the first line of defense against garbage (as in "garbage in, garbage out") coming into the system and, therefore, are presented as playing a critical role in keeping the organization responsive to its environment by ensuring the integrity of incoming information.

THE TARGET MARKET

The market for this book is the introductory information systems course for business students. Under the proposed ACM/DPMA curriculum for information systems, this course is taught after (or concurrently with) any computing skills course or labs. At four-year colleges and universities, this course is found at the undergraduate level in schools of business, often during the first or second year. It is normally required of all business students and is designed to introduce information systems in a business context.

This course is also found in MBA programs, where it is often required of incoming graduate students who do not have the equivalent undergraduate preparation. It may also be required of students concentrating in business computer information systems, in which case it is designed to provide a foundation for more specialized courses. At two-year colleges, this course may be required of students planning to transfer to business programs at four-year schools.

One of the major complaints from faculty teaching this type of course is that other books that have targeted this market have not provided adequate background for the student. These books usually focus on technology, explaining in detail how the hardware and software operate and describing how information systems support specific business functions. However, these textbooks do not explain the purpose, activities, and interplay of these business functions. Many competing books do not relate the management trends in the workplace (such as cross-functional teams and activities becoming the norm) to the need for a new approach to developing information systems.

This book overcomes the limitations of existing texts by concentrating first on organizations and their functions. Information systems are introduced only after discussing the dynamics of organizational performance, decision making, and communication. By then the student understands the crucial importance of information processing to organizational performance.

The book takes the view that the design of an information system starts with the definition of clearly specified goals and includes the collection of data (broadly defined to include data, images, and sound) from a variety of internal and external sources, the transformation of the data to generate output that is *acceptable* and *useful* to the users, and the communication network needed to distribute that output to the appropriate receivers. The concept of user acceptance is at the center of information systems design; the idea is to provide information that is *necessary* (i.e., accurate, timely, relevant) and *sufficient* (i.e., to avoid overload) to support effective decision making within the organization.

This perspective on information systems design is carried throughout the book; all information systems need to be justified in terms of accomplishing a goal. An information system does not just work with the organization's systems but is integrated with external information systems that exist locally, nationally, and internationally. The interorganizational and international perspectives are given significant emphasis throughout the book.

An emphasis on end-user involvement in information systems is also carried from the beginning. Chapter 1, "Introduction to Information Technology and Management," sets the context for the book and provides examples of companies in which end-users from different organizational levels (from line workers to senior managers) use information systems to improve organizational responsiveness. Module I, "Managerial Challenges," discusses many situations in which individuals can improve their communications and decision making skills through the use of information systems. Module II, "Information Systems Development," covers computer hardware and software topics that are of direct relevance to end users. Module III, "Applications and Management of I/S," emphasizes the role of end users in developing their own applications and in the development and management of organizational information systems. Module IV, "Information Technology and Society," addresses many implications of the application of technology, such as the Internet, to individual lives.

The book examines information systems in all types of organizations. Systems found in small and large businesses are discussed, those for businesses that operate locally and globally are described, and systems for nonprofit businesses and government agencies are explained. The objective is to present a wide range of information system examples.

Although the coverage is broad, this book does not attempt to cover the entire "waterfront" of management information system (MIS) issues in detail. Instead, it focuses on providing the student with an understanding of business processes and how information technology can help make those processes more efficient and effective. Although many issues surrounding information systems are introduced, only those considered important for the target audience are discussed and examined at length. We recognize, however, that needs vary substantially among different educational institutions. For that reason we have included an appendix (Appendix A) on data modeling and a second appendix (Appendix B) on systems development techniques.

PEDAGOGICAL FEATURES

Our package is not just a textbook. It is an integrated set of tools designed to support our teaching philosophies. The content of the book reflects what we consider to be the crucial issues that students need to understand to realize the importance of information processing to all organizations. The variety of pedagogic tools is designed to support the most effective ways to help students to *learn* rather than memorize. These tools and features include the following.

Chapter objectives begin each chapter and provide a quick overview of what the student should gain from reading the chapter.

The body of the chapter is written with a blend of theory and application. Rather than listing all possible theories addressing a specific topic, one or two prevalent theories are provided and discussed at an appropriate level of detail. For more important or complex concepts, relevant examples are used.

Business Briefs are short articles and stories obtained from a variety of sources that illustrate the concepts discussed in the chapter. These real-world applications are interspersed throughout the text, located near the corresponding course material.

Art and photographs have been carefully prepared and selected to support and enhance the text material. The photographs, figures, tables, charts, and other visual aids are designed specifically to facilitate understanding.

Organizational responsiveness, competitive strategy, and *ethical and international* examples are included throughout most of the chapters. These short examples illustrate managerial issues related to these important topics.

Connective Cases are used to illustrate the application of the material presented in the chapter. Analysis of the cases for the first four chapters only is provided, allowing students to compare their analysis to the solution suggested by the authors. The analysis for the Connective Cases in Chapters 5–13 is included in the Instructor's Manual, as this provides instructors with more cases to select for student assignments.

End-of-chapter aids include a brief chapter summary, a list of relevant concepts and terms, review questions, discussion questions, group assignments, application (hands-on) assignments, and a case assignment. The objective is to provide a variety of material to suit the needs of most instructors. Files (spreadsheets, databases, etc.) for the application assignments are available via the Internet on the book's home page.

Chapter references provide additional resources for those readers who wish to pursue a specific topic in more detail.

End-of-module cases involve cases that are longer and more complex than those offered at the end of the chapters. The end-of-module cases provide an excellent opportunity to review and reinforce material presented in the chapters of a given module. The module cases for Modules I, II, and III are three installments from the same company. Dakin Farm is a real organization in the gourmet food-by-catalog business, and the installments describe actual situations and decisions faced by its president. The module case for Module IV describes the development and implementation of the first large videotex system in the world, the French Minitel system. The Minitel case illustrates the pervasiveness of information technology applications in society and provides an interesting comparison to the Internet.

Theme icons represent the major themes in the book. The icons are introduced in Chapter 1. From then on, the Business Briefs and many cases have been "stamped" with the icons of the themes that they illustrate.

A *glossary of terms* for the entire text is included at the end of the book. The glossary provides brief, working definitions of the key concepts and terms used throughout the text.

Additional cases are supplied in the *Instructor's Resource Manual* and contain some short and other longer, more complex cases. The short cases are particularly suited for take-home assignments or exams, and the longer ones may be suitable for more advanced students (including upper-class undergraduates or MBA students).

The real-world cases present actual business situations taken from articles published in professional publications, published cases, and cases specifically developed by the authors. There are also a number of short fictitious cases that are based on real organizations but contain situations that are an amalgamation of events from multiple firms. Questions following each case ask the student to analyze the situation using the concepts presented in the chapter.

INSTRUCTIONAL SUPPORT

Recognizing the need for a variety of teaching preferences and approaches, we have put together a package of support materials that accommodates a broad spectrum of pedagogies. The *Irwin Advantage and Effective Series* application lab manuals can be packaged with this text for those instructors wishing to have more of a hands-on emphasis.

The *Instructor's Resource Manual,* prepared in collaboration with the authors, contains an introduction with alternative course syllabi. The material for each chapter includes an outline, a suggested teaching approach, and answers to questions posed in the chapter. In addition, the manual contains additional short cases, with questions and solutions, that can be used for take-home assignments or examinations. The *Instructor's Manual* is also provided electronically, so the instructor may modify material to match his or her needs.

An additional feature of the *Instructor's Resource Manual* is the inclusion of teaching notes for the cases. These notes provide suggestions on how to lead the case discussions, as well as some "inside" information for the instructor. Where relevant, the Instructor's Manual also includes "B" cases, which describe "what happened" and possibly lead to another decision situation. These cases are suitable for copying and distributing to the students following a discussion of the "A" case in class.

PowerPoint presentations have been prepared for each of the chapters. These can be used to generate overhead transparencies, or to provide the basis for classroom PowerPoint presentations. The presentations may also be modified by the instructor.

Video Case Installments are useful supplements to the written cases included in the text. The video installments are designed to augment the cases by presenting short clips related to the case material.

The videos were created concurrently with the written cases and are related *directly* to the case material. They bring the company and key players into the classroom and make the material much more salient for the students.

In addition to these two book-specific videos, the *Irwin Information Systems Video Library* contains 12 videos, each approximately 10–12 minutes long, on various I/S concepts like multimedia, business process reengineering, and client-server computing.

The *Test Bank,* prepared by Richard Herschel, of the University of North Carolina at Greensboro, of true/false, multiple-choice, and short answer questions is also provided, both in written form and on diskette.

The *WWW home page* contains updates to cases and Business Briefs, along with related topics and links to other sites of interest. The page is updated on a regular basis.

Author support is an area where we believe in practicing what we preach. If you have questions, comments, or suggestions as you consider adopting this package or as you use it in your teaching, we encourage you to contact us. Our electronic mail addresses are listed in the *Instructor's Manual;* send us a note, and we will respond as quickly as possible. We will incorporate suggested improvements and customize teaching materials as much as possible to meet your specific needs. Our goal is to continually improve this product, implementing advancements in theory, practice, content, and delivery as quickly and effectively as possible.

We look forward to hearing from you, and hope that you find this material as useful as we have.

ACKNOWLEDGMENTS

The authors would like to acknowledge the assistance of the following reviewers, whose constructive comments and suggestions helped shape the text in many ways:

Lyne Bouchard, Laval University
Michael K. Bourke, Houston Baptist University
Jane M. Carey, Arizona State University–West
Cathi Chambley-Miller, Aiken Technical College
Katherine M. Chudoba, University of Virginia
Drew Cobb, Johns Hopkins University
Duncan G. Copeland, Western Business School
Roger J. Deveau, University of Massachusetts–Dartmouth
Margaret Edmunds, Mount Allison University
Raymond D. Frost, Central Connecticut State University
Virginia Gibson, University of Maine
Mark Gruskin, University of Michigan–Dearborn
John W. Gudenas, Aurora University
Richard T. Herschel, University of North Carolina–Greensboro
Betsy Hoppe, Wake Forest University
Chris Jones, University of Washington
Kenneth Kozar, Univ of Colorado–Boulder
William L. Lomerson, Hardin-Simmons University
Jane Mackay, Texas Christian University
Gordon E. McCray, Wake Forest University
Nancy Paule Melone, University of Oregon
Rajesh Mirani, University of Baltimore
Shahdad Naghohpour, University of Southern Mississippi
Henry L. Novak, Saint Xavier University
Michael R. Padbury, Arapahoe Community College
H. R. Rao, SUNY–Buffalo
Dick Ricketts, Lane Community College
Jill Y. Slater, University of Denver
Maureen Sprankle, College of the Redwoods

The authors would also like to thank Gino Sorcinelli, who led a focus group of students in discussion of this text. Students who participated were as follows:

Ian Allison, Barbara Bruce, Allison B. Feinstein, Darren Flanagan, Randy James Harris, Cherry A. Jenkins, Gina Mandato, Michelle Miney, Pramila Pandey, Nathan Parmelee, Mary Lynne Rivera, Paul Tropeano, and Sandra Wright.

Much of the credit for this text goes to several individuals of the Irwin team. Our special thanks to Rick Williamson, the senior sponsoring editor, who believed in the project; Christine Wright, the developmental editor, who kept us on track; Beth Cigler, the project editor, who managed the production details; Matt Baldwin and Lucy Lesiak, the designer who gave the book its look; Michelle Hudson, the marketing manager; Laurie Sander, the production supervisor; Keri Johnson, the photo research coordinator; and Charlene Perez, the prepress buyer. Our thanks also to Laurel Anderson of Photosynthesis, who managed to locate the photos and screen shots we wanted. Obviously, we are solely responsible for any errors or omission in this book.

We would like to acknowledge the assistance of two special CEOs: Sam Cutting of Dakin Farm and Pam Linton of Pollution Solutions. Both gave of their time generously, both were willing to open their organizations to us, and allowed their companies to become live case examples for many of the concepts and principles we wished to illustrate. We also acknowledge the contribution of the many individuals and organizations who are the subjects of the numerous cases and examples which help make this book come to life, and the contribution of the hundreds of students that were submitted to earlier versions of the material presented here.

Finally, this book was written during a time of deep personal and professional transitions for me (WCB). At times, I felt like I was writing the book while shooting through white-water rapids. Through all the turbulence some individuals gave me stability and hope. This book could have never been finished without them. My gratitude for their support and love is deep and everlasting. Thank you Max Baril, Robby Barnett and Susan Mandler, Paul Davidoff, Santiago and Hebe Gutierrez, Silvia Llorens, and Chad Munger.

Willy Cats-Baril

Ron Thompson

Contents in Brief

Contents

Information Technology and Management

CHAPTER 1 Introduction to Information Technology and Management

CHAPTER OBJECTIVES

After reading this chapter, you should have a clearer understanding of how information technology and management issues interrelate. More specifically, you should be able to:

- Describe the pervasiveness of information technology in today's society and the impact of information technology on individuals and organizations.
- Provide working definitions of information technology and information systems.
- Explain the major themes of the book, which include the role of information technology in (1) organizational responsiveness to change; (2) organizational competition; (3) international (global) issues; and (4) ethical considerations.
- Explain current trends in managing today's organizations, including (1) the focus on satisfying customers as a primary organizational goal; (2) the emphasis on *how* we do business (processes) and not only *what* business we do (products and services); (3) the increased complexity of relationships among companies; and (4) the critical role of an appropriate information technology infrastructure for implementing organizational strategy and operations.
- Appreciate the method of case analysis for learning and understanding management issues.

What is this book all about, and why am I reading it?

MAJOR THEMES OF THE BOOK

As we know, the world is changing and changing fast. Some of these changes are social and political, others are ecological. Some are evolutionary, others revolutionary. No matter where you plan to live or what you plan to do, you can expect that constant and rapid change will be a normal part of your life.

Technology, especially **information technology (I/T)** and **communication technology,** is playing a large part in these changes. Advances in computer systems have facilitated advances in entertainment, in medicine, in military capabilities, in the collection and dissemination of global news reports, in the **management** of **organizations.** Continually evolving computer hardware and software have allowed organizations to significantly change their work processes; new products and services have been developed, new industries have emerged, old companies and industries have failed. And the technologies continue to converge in their capabilities and applications. Communication systems are no longer distinguishable from computer systems; educational systems look more and more like entertainment systems.

To be an active member in today's society, you need to be aware of, and participate in, many of these changes. In your personal life, you will increasingly be required to interact with other segments of society in new ways. From filing your income taxes to renting a movie, you will use information technology–based tools and systems that 20 years ago might have sounded like science fiction. Also, the days of landing a job with a large organization and working comfortably as a middle manager for the remainder of your working life are gone. Most large organizations have removed layers of management and with them many traditional career opportunities. Although these rapid technological advances have eliminated many career opportunities, the good news is that they have created many others.

Throughout history, technological advancements have created new jobs while eliminating old ones. The development of the automobile reduced the need for carriage builders and farriers (who fit and replace horseshoes), but increased the need for skilled manufacturing workers and automotive designers. Photos courtesy of The Underwood Photo Library.

Information technology may be viewed as a computer-based system that has the ability to accept, process, store and output information. Courtesy of Texas Instruments.

In our time, the changes brought on by technological advances happen *daily.* To take advantage of these changes, it is necessary to understand and appreciate them. This book is designed to give you such an understanding and appreciation.

At this point we should briefly explain what we mean by information technology; we will leave formal definitions until later (Chapter 5). For now, think of information technology as any form of computer-based system that has the capability of collecting, processing, and outputting information (which may include data, graphs, still images, sounds, and video images). A personal computer with word processing software would be considered one type of I/T. A bar code scanner, which reads the Universal Product Code (UPC) label on an item in a retail clothing store and translates it into computer-readable data, would also be considered information technology.

Another term we will use frequently is **information system (I/S),** which is also defined in more detail in Chapter 5. For now, just think of an information system as the use of I/T for a specific purpose. As mentioned, we could consider a personal computer with a spreadsheet package as an example of information technology. Now assume that a department manager in a company uses the personal computer and spreadsheet software to develop a budget that shows anticipated sales figures and expenses for the next month. She then stores the budget (as a spreadsheet model), so that it can be used from now on to compare actual expenses and revenues to the budgeted amounts. When we combine (1) the manager, (2) the personal computer and the spreadsheet package, (3) the monthly budget data, (4) the procedures the manager uses to update the budget, and (5) her goal of obtaining an accurate budget on time, we have an information system.

Before we discuss the impact of I/T in more detail, let's briefly consider the current situation for organizations and individual careers. Gone are the days when an individual could plan a career as a mid-level manager with a large, successful organization. Organizations can no longer afford to pay people to simply supervise

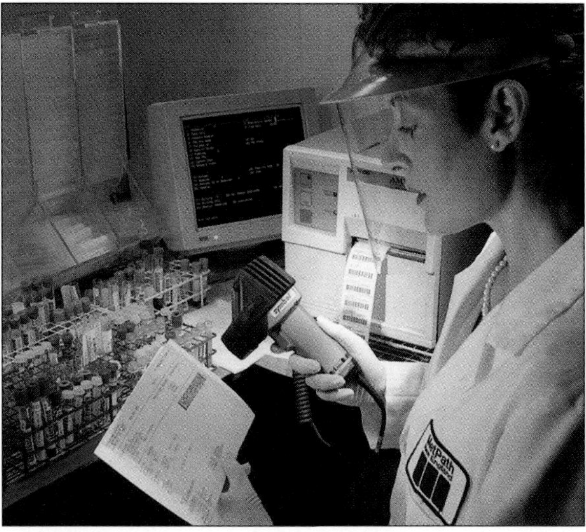

An information system involves the use of information technology by one or more people, using defined procedures, to perform a task or accomplish a goal. Photos courtesy of Tony Stone Worldwide (left) and MetPath (right).

others and to pass information up to the next level in the hierarchy. In fact, many organizations do not adhere to a well-defined hierarchical **organizational structure,** and **organizational communication** is often conducted extensively through the use of information technology.

Increased competition continues to drive the need for organizations to operate as efficiently as possible. When your competitor can provide the same product you do at 80 percent of your production cost, you either reduce costs, persuade your customers that your product is worth more, or go out of business. Companies that are growing rapidly one year may find themselves shrinking the next, so decisions to add more employees are made only very carefully, since people tend to be a very expensive resource. Many companies have found the need to reduce the number of employees and layers of management to decrease their operating costs. The Document Company (Xerox) went from 125,000 employees in 1985 to 90,000 in 1995, while IBM shrank from over 400,000 employees to just over 200,000 during the same period. AT&T, Delta Airlines, American Express, AlliedSignal, and numerous other organizations also reduced their number of employees significantly without reducing—in some instances even increasing—the level of business.

How do these organizations achieve such great gains in productivity? In many cases, it is by systematically implementing two approaches: (1) **empowering employees,** and (2) installing an **information technology infrastructure** to support the information needs of their employees. Empowering employees basically means allowing (or requiring) them to take more active roles in decision making, which reduces the need for organizational structures involving many layers of managers. Many organizations have been successful in empowering their employees by implementing computer-based systems (such as centralized databases and electronic mail) to help process and distribute information. The information technology infrastructure is the combination of computers, networks, software applications, and data used to process and distribute information. Information technology plays a large

BUSINESS BRIEF 1-1 POWER TO THE PEOPLE: COLOR ME ROSE

Puzzled, Charles Chaser scanned the inventory reports from his company's distribution centers one Wednesday morning in mid-March. According to the computer printouts, stocks of Rose Awakening Cutex nail polish were down to three days' supply, well below the 3½ week stock that Chesebrough-Pond's, Inc., tries to keep on hand. But Chaser knew his Jefferson City (Missouri) plant had shipped 346 dozen bottles of the polish just two days before. Rose Awakening must be flying off store shelves, he thought. So Chaser turned to his terminal next to the production line and typed in instructions to produce 400 dozen more bottles on Thursday morning.

All in a day's work for a scheduling manager, right? Except for one detail: Chaser isn't management. He's a line worker—officially, a "line coordinator"—one of hundreds who routinely tap the plant's computer network to track shipments, schedule their own workloads, and generally perform functions that used to be the province of management.

Although information technology is altering work patterns for all employees, the changes are greatest at the lowest levels of organizations. Workers are now being asked to analyze and act on data that previously were parceled out to them by jealous marketing departments or their own supervisors.

QUESTIONS

1. How is Chaser's job different than that of a traditional line worker? Do you think his job as a line coordinator would be more rewarding? Why?
2. Describe the inventory information that Chaser needs to make production-scheduling decisions. Do you think someone physically counts the inventory? How else could the information be compiled and transmitted to Chaser?
3. How might the work of (*a*) a truck driver or (*b*) an administrative assistant, be changed through the use of information technology?

Source: James Treece, "Breaking the Chains of Command," *Business Week*/The Information Revolution, July 12, 1994, pp. 98–99. Reprinted from May 18, 1994 issue of Business Week by special permission, copyright © 1994 by the McGraw-Hill Companies.

role by providing employees with the information they need to perform their job tasks. The example provided in Business Brief 1–1 illustrates how information technology can empower employees. As you read it, consider the information support that is required for Charles Chaser to do his job properly.

Information technology is also affecting the way decisions are being made in the public sector. Are you interested in serving in a public office, perhaps helping to write and pass legislation to combat crime? In the United States, one favored approach is to get tough on crime by locking up criminals. As a result, the United States has a larger percentage of its population in jail than any other country. Some individuals argue that U.S. legislators should consider the economic impact of the laws they pass—in this case, how many additional prison beds will be required and how much it will cost to provide them. By using computer programs that simulate the effects of different policies, lawmakers in some states can now obtain estimates of how much it will cost to implement new laws.

Also, many voters in North America believe that government departments and agencies do not provide adequate benefits to justify the resources (tax dollars) they consume. The national Republican party in the United States swept into power in 1994 on the promise of a smaller, more efficient government, as did the provincial Progressive Conservative party in Ontario, Canada, in 1995. One option for improving the efficiency of government offices is to apply information technology in appropriate ways. This is the approach that was undertaken by the provincial government of

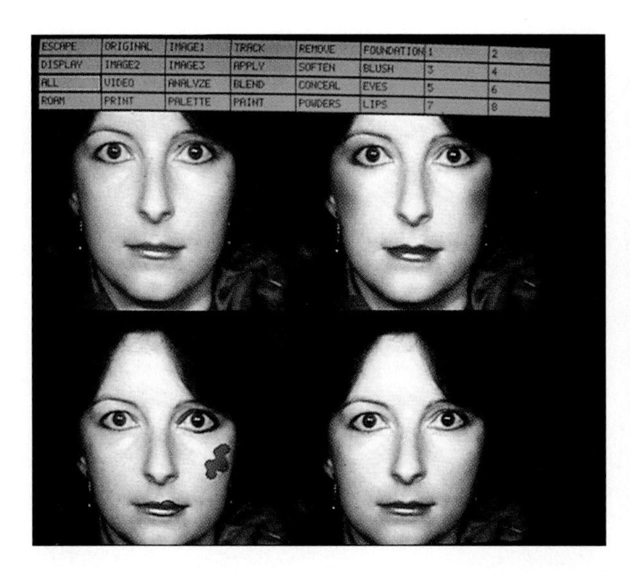

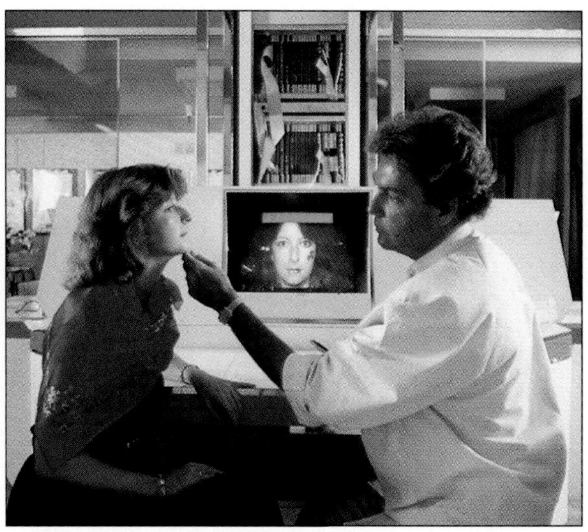

Information systems allow users to view alternatives before making a decision. Here a computer shows a client a step-by-step rendering of a makeover, and then a make-up artist for Elizabeth Arden uses the system to complete the makeover. Photos courtesy of Hank Morgan/Rainbow.

New Brunswick, Canada, which hired an information systems consulting firm to help them develop and implement a strategy for using information technology to improve government efficiency. Although this collaborative project is still in progress, the initial results are very promising.

Now let's look at more examples of the opportunity side of information technology. Are you interested in filmmaking? Ever since the breakthrough use of computer-generated images in the movie *Tron,* information technology has played a much larger role in the development and delivery of movies and related forms of entertainment. The changes enabled by I/T have profound implications for the entire film industry. It is now possible to use and manipulate video footage from the past (e.g., *Forrest Gump*), to electronically generate realistic images rather than filming them (e.g., *Jurassic Park*), to intersperse real and animated characters (e.g., *Who Framed Roger Rabbit?*) and to otherwise enhance movies in ways that were previously not possible. This capability enables casting agents to use actors who are deceased, it enables directors to use props or settings that don't exist, and it generally expands the options for film development exponentially. The first full-length feature film completely generated by computer (Disney's *Toy Story*) was produced in 1995.

Are you interested in clothing design? No longer is it necessary to create prototype (sample) articles of clothing using sketch pads, mannequins, and real cloth. Increasingly, designers use **computer-aided design (CAD)** systems to test combinations of style, cut, pattern, and material, without ever putting scissors to cloth. More sophisticated systems employed by companies such as The Gap feed the specifications from the CAD-generated design directly into a **computer-aided manufacturing (CAM)** system, which determines the best way to cut bolts of material to produce the least wastage. These companies also have systems that keep track of the inventory of raw material, the work-in-process and finished goods, and so on. Along similar lines, information systems are being used to help customers envision how they look in clothing they are considering buying, by watching a

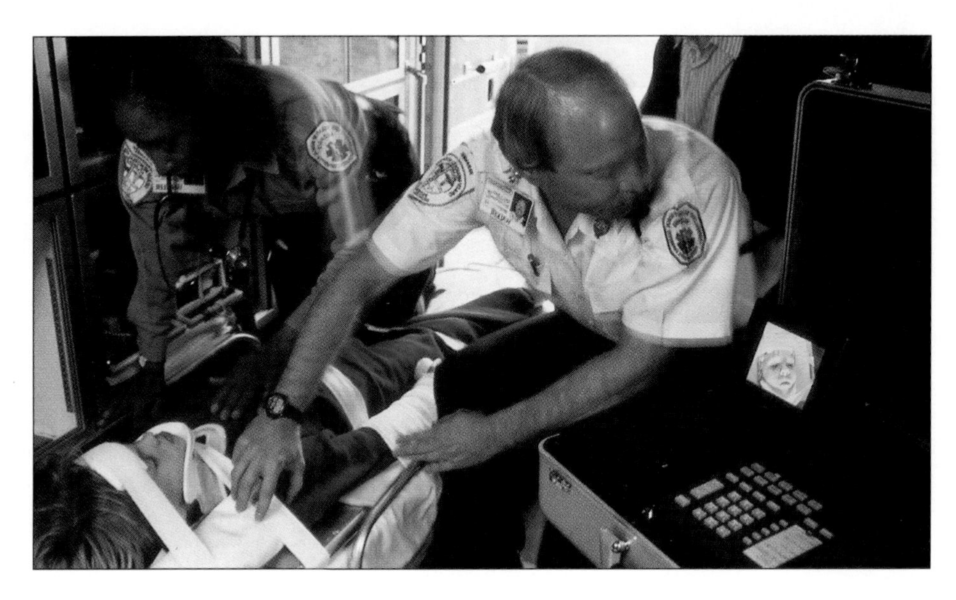

As telecommunications capabilities expand, geographic distances become immaterial. Here an emergency response team member sends an image of an injured person from an accident scene to a distant hospital. Photo courtesy of Frank Moscati.

computer-generated mannequin with their exact measurements. Another application of information technology lets potential home owners view a new house in a variety of ways, from modifying blueprints to allowing interactive "walkthroughs" using a "virtual house." To make the experience even more realistic, the customer can be treated to the simulated smell of chocolate cookies wafting from a simulated oven. Information systems are being used to help customize sports equipment for individuals. And there are many other applications.

Advances in information and communication technology have altered our concepts of time and distance. Business negotiations may be conducted in a "face-to-face" environment, even if one face is in Japan and the other in Germany. Similarly, information systems allow 24-hour trading on financial markets around the world. The continually expanding capabilities of information technology have implications for the management of organizations as well as for broader societal issues. We will explore these implications throughout this book.

Now that we have introduced a few examples illustrating the pervasiveness of information technology, we will discuss the four major themes of the book.

Organizational Responsiveness and Information Technology

What do dinosaurs, Pan American Airlines, American Motors, the Soviet Union, and Osborne Computers have in common? They're all extinct. Why? They did not adapt well enough to changing environments. Regardless of our personal views on change, it's important to recognize that *change is constant.* The physical environment changes, consumer tastes change, technology changes, regulations change, societal norms change, and so on. For businesses and nations alike, recognition of these changes is the first basic step to survival. The earlier changes are recognized, the greater the opportunity to adapt to these changes.

If you had been a senior executive at a major ski manufacturing company in the late 1980s, could you have predicted the growth of snowboarding? Most ski companies did not, and as a result they were very late in entering the snowboard market. Although the switch of customer preferences to snowboarding didn't kill ski companies, many lost market share in the winter sports leisure industry.

If you were an executive at a major publishing company, would you invest in a project that diverts funds to electronic publishing from traditional paperback products? What if you lose market share in the paperback business, and the electronic publication business doesn't develop the way you anticipate? Although the availability of electronic publications continues to expand, some indicators point to a rise in the purchase of hardcopy paperback books at the same time. Understanding these changes and trends is a difficult task.

For organizations to survive and thrive, they need to be responsive to the critical elements in their environments. These elements include customers, suppliers, competitors, governing agencies and regulations, and so on. **Organizational responsiveness** implies not only being aware of environmental changes, but doing something about them. This book stresses the role of information technology in achieving organizational responsiveness. For example, companies such as Otis Elevators and IBM have installed monitoring devices in the products they sell (elevators, computers), which keep track of the way customers use those products, and which send messages to service headquarters of any operational problems that may develop (long before the customer notices them). These devices allow the companies to react quickly to changes in customer needs.

Many organizations use information technology in a **proactive** way to keep informed of changes introduced by competitors, government agencies, and other parties external to the organization. For example, Dell Computer uses the Internet[1] to help communicate with customers and to keep track of competitors. Dell is only one of many companies with employees whose full-time job involves searching through the Internet, looking for comments about their products, services, or competitors.

The basic principle here, is that organizations need to constantly monitor their environment. The corollary to that principle is that monitoring the environment is an information intensive activity. That is, organizations will be at risk of failing and disappearing unless they have the necessary capability to process information. The better that capability, the better the ability of the organization to know what is happening in its environment, and therefore the better the chances of doing something about it.

Now that we have introduced the overriding theme of the book—*organizational responsiveness*—we call your attention to another important theme: the realities of organizational start-up, growth, and survival.

Competitive Strategy and Information Technology

The increasingly competitive environment for most organizations is forcing enterprises to change the way they operate and/or to change the products and services

---

[1] The Internet (discussed in detail in Chapter 12) is a loose, international "network of computer networks." It allows users to communicate, to share resources, to access and transmit data, sounds, video, computer programs, and so forth.

they provide. A second theme running throughout this book is that information technology enables these changes in operations and products.

What is **competition?** In the context of business, we need to recognize that consumers have limited resources, and they make choices about the products and services they will buy. Since monopolies (i.e., situations where one company has 100 percent of the market and no competitors) are disappearing, and since almost every product and service we use is provided by multiple companies, organizations need to convince customers to purchase from them. Now that the economy is essentially a global one, and consumers can buy products and services from companies around the world, the competition among organizations has increased substantially.

Competition is certainly not limited to profit-making organizations. Universities compete for good students, nonprofit institutions compete for private donations, government agencies compete with other agencies for the allocation of tax-generated funds. Although this book tends to focus on for-profit enterprises, keep in mind that the principles and concepts we introduce apply equally to other types of organizations.

For some enterprises, the need to improve is driven by forces that may seem to be outside of their control. At least on the surface, they appear to be **reacting** to threatening changes in their environment. One such threat could be technological obsolescence; a new technology might emerge that could make a company's product or service obsolete, or at least reduce demand for it substantially. Just as the telegraph replaced the pony express, the digital transmission of information (such as facsimile technology and the use of electronic mail) has greatly affected the transmission of business correspondence (e.g., mail and courier services).

Another threat is simply that of losing competitive advantage and being forced out of the marketplace. Most organizations go through a life cycle which is tied to the success of their primary goods and services. Although the length of the cycle varies, a typical success story starts with a small, entrepreneurial company that grows rapidly. As the organization grows, individuals within the company must make decisions about how it will compete, how it will be structured internally, how communications will flow within the company and between the company and external parties, and so on.

Let's use the early years of Compaq Computer as an example. Compaq copied ("cloned") IBM's popular personal computer (PC) to introduce a high-quality PC.[2] Consumers liked the idea that an underdog could take on the giant IBM, and they liked the high-quality product. Sales improved rapidly, and the company experienced explosive growth during the 1980s. At one point Compaq was the fastest growing company in American corporate history, and it was the fastest company to reach $1 billion in sales. Between 1985 and 1990 sales rose from about $1 billion to almost $4 billion.

The growth of Compaq's sales was matched by growth in the number of employees. Formal departments were developed, with formalized reporting relationships and communication channels. The organization began to look and operate more like a large bureaucracy than a small start-up organization. As the company grew stronger, it introduced new products that were no longer just clones of the personal computers offered by IBM. The company was a market leader generating large profits, and the future seemed rosy.

---

[2] In this book we use the term *personal computer* to refer to the broad category of microcomputer-based systems designed primarily for individual use, rather than as reference to a specific brand.

Unfortunately, the early years of high profits for Compaq were fleeting. By 1991, the company was no longer viewed as an underdog with great products. Some of their product offerings failed, and new companies entering the market eroded their market share. One such entrant was Dell, who used the innovative distribution technique of supplying direct from the factory to the customer (rather than using retail outlets). Compaq believed the reputation they had developed for high-quality products would enable them to charge higher prices and retain their profits. History proved they were wrong. As nimbler rivals undercut Compaq's prices, sales dropped to just over $3 billion, and their net income plummeted from over $400 million in 1990 to just over $100 million in 1991.

In 1991, Eckhard Pfeiffer took over from Rod Canion as the chief executive officer (CEO) for Compaq. His recovery strategy was simple: cut costs to the bone, then try to drive out the smaller "clone" makers, which (at that point) were capturing 60 percent of the market. After restructuring the manufacturing facilities and reducing staff, Compaq introduced a new range of personal computers in 1992 that were priced 30 percent lower than Compaq's previous line of products. That touched off a price war, as other companies also struggled to lower their costs. By operating more efficiently, Compaq continued to be a price leader, cutting their prices 20 to 30 percent each year. The company managed to recover from potential disaster and by 1993 was once again onto a new cycle, generating strong profits. Figure 1–1 shows Compaq sales and profits for the years 1985 to 1995.

The objective behind competitive analysis is to help us determine ways to improve customer satisfaction, and ultimately to improve our competitive position. Without some type of formal analysis, we tend to rely on intuition and guesses that may be incorrect. In Chapter 10 we discuss these formal approaches to competitive analysis in detail. We advocate using a variety of techniques to help identify competitive threats and opportunities. Once the threats and opportunities have been determined, the next step is to identify ways to address them, which is referred to as determining a competitive **strategy.** The next section briefly discusses how competitive strategy and the use of information technology are related.

Competitive Strategy. One of the most widely cited authors to address competitive strategy is Michael Porter. He argued in the late 1970s and early 1980s that companies could use one or more of the following strategies to compete: (1) be the low-cost producer, (2) differentiate the product and services, or (3) obtain a market niche. In the face of competition, Compaq initially attempted to differentiate its products by representing them as being of higher quality and more technologically advanced than its competitors', and charging a premium for it. This strategy began successfully, but competitors soon countered by matching Compaq's quality and level of technology, while lowering their own operating costs and the prices they charged to customers. Compaq discovered that in today's market, customers expect high quality, low prices, and excellent service at the same time.

The Compaq chronicle is the story of a company that, after introducing an innovative change (the idea of developing IBM clones at lower prices), found itself reacting to changes in its environment. Compaq started with a *proactive* stance, by anticipating a changing need in the personal computer market and making that change happen. As competitors began to drive additional changes in its environment, Compaq had to take a series of *reactive* steps.

Just as theories on how to manage organizations have changed, so have theories on organizational strategy. Some companies were not satisfied with offering a quality product at a reasonable price; they went on to offer products that were customized

FIGURE 1–1 Compaq Computer Sales (in $Billions) and Net Income (in $Millions)

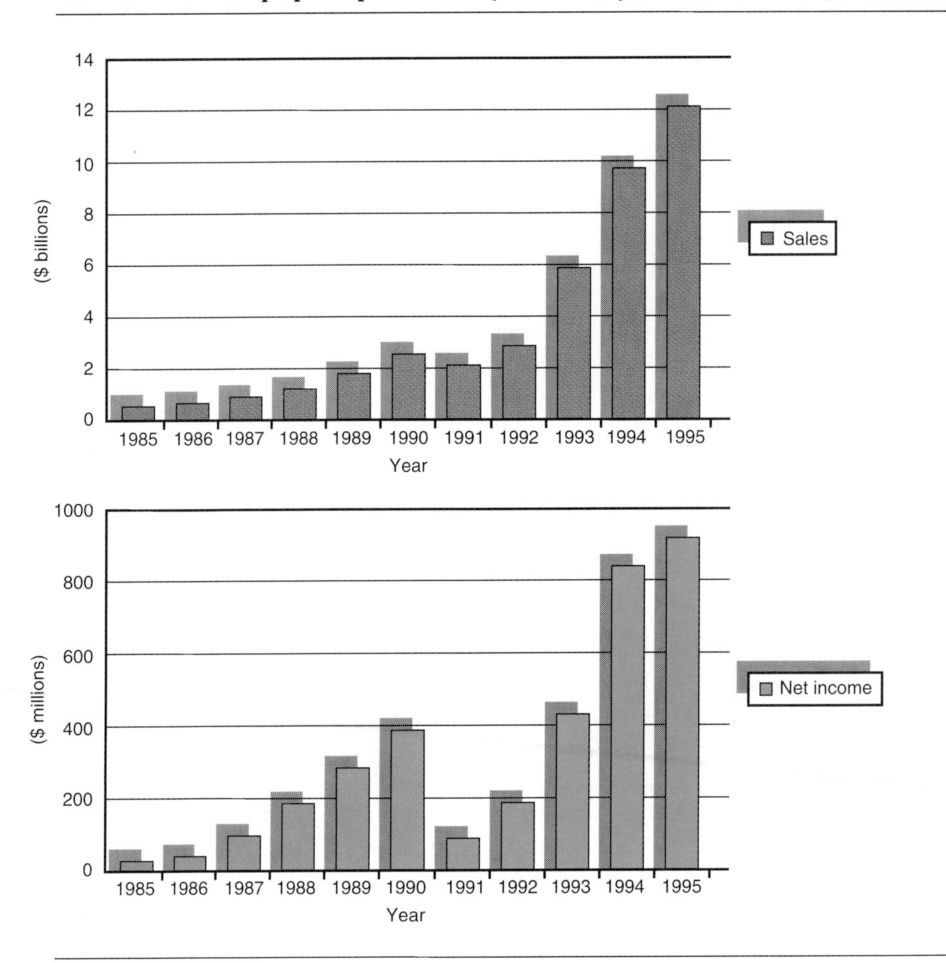

as well. **Customization** means giving individual customers a choice in how they want their product configured, rather than forcing them to select from products that are already assembled.

Consider the purchase of an automobile. If you want one quickly, you can go to a dealer and select among those in stock on the dealer's lot. If you can't find one that suits you (e.g., you want an unusual color with a larger engine, manual transmission, and so on), you can special order it, but normally that type of customization takes a relatively long time before your vehicle is available—perhaps 10 or 12 weeks, depending on the model. Most automobile manufacturers produce identical vehicles in large quantities, adding customized features to a few vehicles as part of a normal production run. An exception to the rule is Saturn, a division of General Motors. Saturn can make a car to your specifications and have it delivered to a local dealer within three weeks.

Many organizations are moving to a strategy of providing customized products or services in a timely fashion. **Mass customization** is a strategy that attempts to take advantage of the economies of scale achieved through high volume while providing customized products. Burger King will serve you a hamburger "the way

Combining mass production techniques with customization has become a very effective strategy. Here Dell employees quickly build a personal computer to satisfy the specifications provided by one of their customers. Photo courtesy of Dell Computers.

you like it"; Dell Computer Company will deliver a personal computer to your door with the exact configuration you are looking for. Burger King, Dell, and Saturn have adopted a business strategy that allows customers to select from numerous options and still promise to deliver the finished product within an acceptable time frame for the customer (for example, a maximum of 10 minutes for fast food, five days for a personal computer, three weeks for a car).

To illustrate how one strategy has been implemented, consider the description of a typical sale for Dell Computers. As you read through Business Brief 1–2, consider the information necessary to allow Dell workers to assemble the personal computer.

The Role of I/T. How do Burger King, Saturn, and Dell Computers do it? With great help from information technology. Consider the type of information that must be stored, manipulated, and transmitted for Dell's (or Saturn's) mass customization customer order operation. As the questions listed in Business Brief 1–2 suggest, there must be a complete and accurate inventory count—an inventory database—which is updated as soon as a new order is placed or when new supplies are retrieved. It is necessary to obtain detailed and accurate information from the customer concerning exactly what items (hardware components, software packages) are desired for each computer and also to keep track—in an *open-order* file—of each item on the order as the computer is being assembled. Since the assembly involves different people working at different stations, each must have access to the information stored in the open-order file and also be able to enter new information (specifically, the item each person added to the computer). Information is also needed on the method of payment (e.g., VISA or MasterCard number), credit authorization, customer balance outstanding (if any), and so on.

After the computer has been delivered and paid for, Dell will maintain a record of any service calls required for every computer it has sold. This will allow Dell to determine when service should be covered by its warranties, and to obtain

BUSINESS BRIEF 1-2 MASS CUSTOMIZATION: MR. COZZETTE BUYS A COMPUTER

Wednesday, 10:49 AM (Central time): Dave Cozzette, an accountant at Rothfos Corp., White Plains, New York, calls in his order for a Dell Dimension PC. At Dell's order center, sales rep Cassye Ewald promises that the PC will arrive within five business days.

12:50 PM: Dell's financial services unit verifies the charge with Cozzette's credit card company, and the details of his $2,700.22 order print out on the production floor across the street at Dell's factory. Laquita Lister checks the information sheet (called a *traveler*) listing the 60 items that Cozzette's computer must include, from cables to software. The order is branded with a serial number that will identify the PC for life.

1:00 PM: The assembly process starts with the installation of an Intel chip onto the machine's main circuitboard (the motherboard). A worker across the room is readying the diskette drives and hard disk for installation later.

1:55 PM: Rhonda Peña applies a sticker bearing the PC's serial number (3C9TQ) to the chassis and then lays in the motherboard, fastening it with screws.

2:01 PM: Anthony Garcia inserts Cozzette's fax modem (a device that can send documents created on the PC to fax machines or other computers via telephone lines).

2:10 PM: Manuel Brito installs the floppy drive that was prepared earlier, along with a tape backup unit (it will enable Cozzette to make up-to-date duplicates of his hard disk files in the event his machine has a breakdown).

2:20 PM: The power supply, a transformer that converts electrical current for use in the PC, goes into the unit, and Ronnie Hines affixes the PC's faceplate with the Dell logo subtly displayed.

2:26 PM: Shena Galvan scans the computer's bar code to update Dell's inventory. The components that have been installed in Cozzette's PC are now listed as removed from the company's storage facility in another area of the plant.

2:27 PM: The PC gets its first quality inspection. Steve Geil checks the traveler to make sure his co-workers have installed every component the computer should have. Then he creates a test diskette that will keep track of which software Cozzette has ordered and which components will need to be tested.

2:28 PM: The PC powers up for the first time during a *quick test* that checks memory, video circuits, and floppy and hard disk functions. If the test diskette finds a bad sector on the hard disk (a portion that cannot properly store data), Sophia Finney will install a new hard disk. The test diskette sets the computer's clock to Central time.

2:40 PM: Engitt Brooks slides on the PC's hood (cover).

2:45–7:45 PM: Cozzette's computer sits on a rack for an extended test called *burn in.* Before it starts, Aaron Whitley plugs the PC into the factory's network. For five hours the diskette runs the PC's components through grueling tests that simulate heavy use. Only 2 percent of the PCs fail. Finally, the test diskette uses the network to download the programs Cozzette has ordered, such as Microsoft Windows, and installs them on the hard disk.

8:20 PM: Jaye Mireles shoots a 25,000-volt charge into the PC's power supply. If the PC handles the jolt without going haywire, it earns a Federal Communications Commission Class B certification that it is safe to use in homes and offices.

8:32 PM: During the PC's final test, the system is hooked up to a monitor and keyboard and operated without its test diskette, just as Cozette will use it. Lonnie Gilliland looks for glitches in the newly installed software.

8:35 PM: Julie Goodman puts the PC through *wipe-down,* a cosmetic inspection that includes scrubbing off grubby fingerprints.

8:37 PM: Ramon Lopez puts Cozzette's computer in a box with its keyboard, manuals, and warranty papers; Darrell Arvie slaps on Rothfos Corp.'s address.

9:25 PM: Airborne Express worker Eric Foster loads the PC onto a truck. If Cozzette had called Dell a few hours earlier, his PC would have made it onto the truck before the 7 PM deadline for next-day delivery. Instead, he'll get it on Friday.

Friday, 10:31 AM (Eastern time): Airborne's John Baker drops off the package at Cozzette's office. He plugs in his PC, and Dell's greeting software offers its congratulations. It's up to Cozzette to reset the computer's clock to Eastern time.

QUESTIONS

1. How does Anthony Garcia know that Mr. Cozzette's PC should have a modem?
2. When Cassye Ewald is taking the order over the phone, how does she know that Dell has all the parts needed to assemble Mr. Cozzette's PC?
3. In what way does being able to quickly customize PCs help Dell compete?

SOURCE: S. Losee, "Mr. Cozzette Buys a Computer," *Fortune,* April 18, 1994, pp. 113–16.

information concerning common customer complaints which it can then use to help improve its products and customer service in the future. Without extensive use of information technology, it would be impossible for Dell to provide this type of mass customization.

Information technology can enable an organization to monitor changes in customer preferences immediately, allowing it to react quickly, and increasing its flexibility. I/T can also be used to improve the internal operations of the organization, lowering costs (increasing efficiency), and making better decisions (improving effectiveness). In short, information technology can be used in many ways to help an organization function better and satisfy customer needs more fully.

Not all instances of companies applying information technology result in success stories, however. In fact, many failures and near disasters have occurred and continue to occur. And as companies become more dependent on information systems, they become more vulnerable to systems that may contain errors or may "crash."

Take the case of Hopper Specialty Co., located in Farmington, New Mexico. In ten years, Hopper grew to become the largest distributor of industrial hardware in Northwest New Mexico, catering primarily to oil and gas drillers. Hopper purchased an inventory control system (an information system) called Warehouse Manager from the NCR company in 1988. Warehouse Manager was supposed to keep track of the thousands of items in Hopper's inventory, keep their prices current, warn when items were running low, produce invoices in seconds, and even balance the monthly financial statements. The system would help achieve the company's goals of reducing costs and improving internal efficiency and customer service.

Unknown to Hopper management, however, the Warehouse Manager system had to be converted to work with Hopper's computer system and the conversion didn't go well. During sales demonstrations, Mr. Hopper (the owner of Hopper Specialty) was impressed that the computer terminals could bring up a customer invoice in a fraction of a second. But when the Warehouse Manager was installed at Hopper, the response time ranged from half a minute to several minutes. This slow response time caused long delays for customers attempting to check out. Even worse, Warehouse Manager couldn't be relied upon to keep prices accurately. For example, a piece of industrial hose that should have been listed at $17 per foot showed up as $30 per foot. The clerks at the counter wouldn't know it was the wrong price; typically the customer would pay, but then would not return for any future business.

The errors in the computer system had a devastating effect on Hopper Specialty. Although still in business, the company shrank dramatically; between 1988 and 1994 the annual sales dropped from $3.5 million to $1.9 million. The company now keeps so little inventory stocked, it doesn't need an extensive information system to keep track of it. Hopper sued the computer company (NCR), but even a favorable verdict in the arbitration proceedings will not help much. Hopper has effectively lost several years of growth and its competitors have lured away many of its formerly loyal customers.

The Hopper case is discussed in more detail in Chapter 11. At this point we simply introduce the idea that, as with other technologies, I/T is no panacea. You must be aware that along with the numerous potential benefits from applying information technology to organizational processes, there are many risks and potential downfalls.

International Issues and Information Technology

A third major theme of this book is the inexorable march toward global markets. Do you view China or Argentina as being part of the same world you belong to? You should. The application of information technology has changed the way many individuals and organizations view the world and their role in it. Many organizations who thought they only had to worry about local competitors have found themselves competing with **international** ones. Many other organizations are discovering unexpected opportunities by expanding their scope of operations to extend beyond national boundaries. Taken to the extreme, there now exist organizations (such as ABB, Inc.) who do not have a "head office" located in any one country, nor do they consider themselves to have a specific national identity. By using information technology for communication and information dissemination, such organizations are able to operate in numerous countries without being solely affiliated with any specific one.

In this book we will study examples of organizations that have adopted information technology, or are considering adopting it, in ways that enhance or develop international operations. Just as we stress that organizations must be responsive to changes in their environment, we argue that advancements in the capabilities and application of I/T are driving a need to redefine environments from a *domestic* (national) focus to a *global* (international) focus. Through the use of satellite and fiber-optic communication systems, business people and government officials in Beijing, China, can watch the Cable Network News (CNN) broadcasts live from Atlanta, U.S.A. Automotive designers in France can transmit designs and specifications to manufacturing facilities in Taiwan in seconds. Tourists vacationing in Vancouver, Canada, can use an automated teller machine to easily withdraw funds from their bank account located in Frankfurt, Germany. Technical support staff working for Hewlett-Packard (HP) in Australia have simultaneous access to the same customer information as HP's support staff working in Great Britain. Today, through sophisticated networking and communications, information moves around the globe almost unimpeded.

At present, some developing nations are purposely trying to leapfrog over their more developed neighbors by investing heavily in communication and information technologies. In a developed nation such as the United States the effort and cost required, for example, to remove all existing copper telephone wire and replace it with fiber-optic cable is exorbitant. In a less developed nation with limited telephone service, installing fiber optics directly will actually be less expensive and less time consuming. The same logic applies to replacing information systems. Businesses in developed countries have been replacing mainframe computers with networks of personal computers at great cost and difficulty while businesses in developing countries never went through a mainframe "phase" and have been implementing networks quite rapidly.

Ethical Issues and Information Technology

The fourth theme woven throughout the book is the importance of **ethical** considerations in the use of information technology. Are you interested in debates concerning the rights of individuals versus the rights of organizations and society? The application of I/T has opened up tremendous concerns on this issue. For example, more and more individuals find themselves the subject of **computerized monitoring.** Systems that count and time keystrokes, systems that track physical

BUSINESS BRIEF 1–3 COMPUTERS WATCH PEOPLE: THE BOSS IS LOOKING

U.S. workers are among the world's most watched. But electronic monitoring of workers is spreading in developing countries such as India, Singapore, the Philippines, and in Caribbean nations, according to a new report on work surveillance around the world by the International Labor Organization in Geneva. The biggest reasons employers give for electronic monitoring: to check on productivity and investigate theft and industrial espionage. Other reasons: to prevent harassment, find missing data or illegal software, and stop personal work during company time.

Among the most monitored industries are telecommunications, retail sales, banking, and finance. The rights of northern European workers are the best protected. Sweden bars hidden cameras. Norway offers workers' rights against monitoring by letting the issue come up for union votes. German courts have granted workers the right of "informational self-determination."

QUESTIONS

1. What is meant by electronic monitoring of employees? Describe ways in which the activities of employees could be monitored, whether or not the monitoring is done electronically.
2. If an employee of a U.S. firm is working in Germany, should they be covered by U.S. laws (which allow greater monitoring of employees), or German laws?
3. Can you think of any situations where monitoring employees could improve employee morale?

SOURCE: *The Wall Street Journal*, August 2, 1994, p. A1. Reprinted by permission of *The Wall Street Journal*,

location (so that a person's whereabouts is always known), systems that monitor electronic mail communications, are all becoming widespread. These systems raise various concerns, such as the possibility of infringing on an individual's right to privacy. Business Brief 1–3 takes a further look at the situation.

Monitoring systems are only one example of ethical dilemmas that have been raised by the application of information technology. The new capabilities of I/T (such as the ability to detect and remove computer games from the computers of employees, or to keep track of the types of movies rented by individuals) strain the existing organizational policies and societal laws. As new I/T capabilities emerge, we need to continually reexamine and adjust corporate policies, societal norms, and laws.

The area of copyright and intellectual property protection gives another example of how I/T can cause ethical dilemmas. Computer programs are very easy to physically copy and distribute; thus, we have seen an explosion of illegal copying of everything from business programs to computer games. As the Internet developed and expanded during the mid-to-late 1990s, it became a ready conduit for everything from unreleased software to digitized pornographic images and videos. For example, a copy of a new release of IBM's OS/2 operating system for personal computers was stored on the Internet in October of 1994, and made available for illegal copying even before the software was officially released or made available for purchase by IBM. Some estimates place the percentage of illegally obtained software in American organizations as high as 50 percent. In China, estimates are that 90 percent of all software has been illegally copied.

At some point, most of us find ourselves facing a decision that has an ethical dimension. As the capabilities of information technology continue to expand, we encounter these situations more frequently. Although this book's sole focus is not the issue of ethics, it is important to have a framework for considering ethical situations. In Chapter 5 we introduce such a framework.

As organizations expand their scope of operations through information technology, domestic and international networks play a larger role. Here the Global Control Room at Electronic Data Systems allows employees to monitor electronic connections among dispersed computers. Photo courtesy of EDS Corp.

To highlight the four major themes we have discussed—organizational responsiveness to change, competitive use of information technology, global issues, and ethical considerations—we use an icon to represent each. The icons appear with the Business Briefs and cases, enabling you to quickly identify the major theme. Table 1–1 presents the icons, the themes, and a summary description of each.

Now that we have provided a sense of the pervasiveness of information technology in society and discussed the four major themes of the book, we wish to shift our focus to organizational management. Indeed, before discussing how I/T can be used to help manage organizations, we need to examine the current philosophies of organizational management.

MANAGING TODAY'S ORGANIZATIONS

What are the major trends in managing organizations today? The term *management* refers to the act of keeping an organization alive and functioning. After all, an organization does not operate by itself, without direction. Rather, an organization is composed of individuals who cooperate (to a greater or lesser extent) to accomplish a series of common goals. Management consists of keeping individuals working together to achieve a series of tactical and strategic objectives.

TABLE 1–1 Major Themes of the Book

Icon	*Theme*	*Relationship to Information Technology*
	Responsiveness to Change	Like a chameleon, an organization must respond to rapidly changing environments. Information technology may be used in diverse ways to facilitate responsiveness to change.
	Competitive Strategy	Competition is a fact of life for organizations; most pursue strategies of lower costs, differentiated products and services, and obtaining market advantages. Information technology is an effective and commonly used tool for implementing organizational strategy.
	Global View	Information and communication technologies facilitate the integration of markets, suppliers, customers, and competitors, reducing organizational and international boundaries.
	Ethical Issues	Rapidly advancing capabilities of information technology stress our existing laws and societal norms, leading to many ethical concerns, such as potential breaches of individual privacy and questions of intellectual property rights.

Theories of how to manage are numerous, and they change frequently. Some theories appear radical when first proposed; others seem to be enhancements to existing theories or, possibly, formalizations of what some might refer to as common sense. Some theories start as fads that last a couple of years before disappearing. In Chapter 3, we discuss how organizations are structured (*organizational structure* is one important manifestation of management philosophy), and we also examine the functions of managers in more detail. At this point, we just want to briefly introduce some current trends concerning the management of organizations.

One trend is the change from formal, hierarchical structures to more temporary, process-based structures. This trend is called *task-based management.* Traditionally, a common form of organizational structure was the *functional hierarchy,* where individuals with common expertise and responsibilities were grouped together in departments. For example, a group of marketing analysts would report to a marketing manager who would report to a vice president for marketing, and so on. Figure 1–2 shows a sample functional organization chart. Other ways to structure organizations are by division (for a company that operates in somewhat different industries), by product (where each major product or product group has its own mini-organization), and so on.

Under a task-based management structure, companies organize individuals with diverse skills into work groups. The work groups may be responsible for one or more major business processes (such as product development). Other groups may be brought together to focus on a specific project or problem, and then disbanded and reassembled into different groups to work on new projects. This constant reorganization has certain drawbacks, but one of the primary advantages is the ability to draw upon expertise from different functional areas without the usual communication difficulties.

Intel Corporation, which develops and manufactures microcomputer chips, is one organization that has embraced task-based management. At Intel, one task-based group was organized to focus on an $80 million (in U.S. dollars) marketing

FIGURE 1–2 Partial Organization Chart—Functional Hierarchy

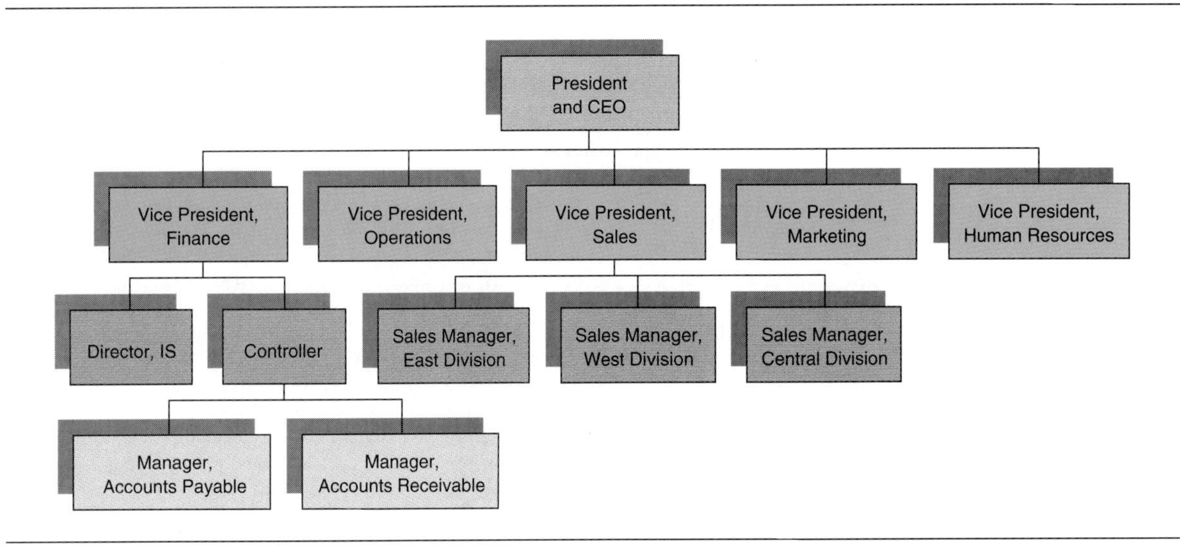

campaign. The objective was to develop an effective campaign to advertise the advantages of using a personal computer powered by Intel's Pentium chip when it was first introduced. The group was composed of individuals drawn from disciplines as diverse as legal and advertising, and was disbanded once the campaign was underway.

Pushing the team approach further, current management philosophy suggests breaking the entire organization (not just special projects) into teams of about six to eight individuals. Experience has shown that the tendency to add more people doesn't work very well. As teams get larger and larger, employees must spend more time communicating what they already know and less time actually applying that knowledge. Even if a large number of people is required to accept similar responsibilities, it is often possible to assign a subset of the responsibilities to smaller teams.

For example, consider the responsibility of responding to customer complaints. One approach is to have all customer queries handled on a first-come, first-serve basis by whichever customer service representative is available. A different approach is to assign a subset of customers (perhaps those located within a specific geographic region) to a specific customer-response team. This gives the customer-response team a feeling of accountability to their customers, which tends to encourage better service. Customer satisfaction levels can be measured and tracked, fostering some competition between teams. Employees at Microsoft, the largest company that develops and sells popular software for personal computers, have used the team approach extensively within their organization.

Another trend is the fairly recent change in management philosophy to emphasize *customer satisfaction* as the major driver of business strategy. Historically, many organizations focused on producing a set of products, and then used innovative marketing and sales techniques to sell their products to as many customers as possible. Although there have always been some organizations that made customers the center of their strategy, it is relatively recent that so many organizations have become **customer driven.** This trend actually represents a reversal of philosophy: first find out who your customers are and what they need (perhaps by involving them in the design of the product and service you are offering), and then do whatever is necessary to provide the best quality, at the best possible price, in the quickest way to satisfy their needs. Customer-driven companies realize that the product or service they provide customers is only one component (although clearly a major one) of the business relationship they have with those customers.

Some companies even recommend a strategy of finding out who your most difficult customers are and then focusing on their needs. The philosophy behind this approach is that if you can satisfy your most difficult customer, you can satisfy anyone. Silicon Graphics, Inc. (SGI), producer of high-powered, specialized computer workstations, has employed this strategy for some time. In the early 1980s the U.S. military was SGI's most demanding customer, and the company spent considerable time and effort working with military personnel to design products for specialized military applications. During the 1990s this focus for SGI changed, and its most demanding customer became Walt Disney's Imagineering group, which creates attractions for the famous theme parks. For example, SGI worked with Disney engineers to develop a virtual-reality ride where tourists strap on special headgear with visual displays that give them the illusion of flying on a magic carpet through the desert scenery from the animated film *Aladdin.* Once the technology was developed for Disney, SGI could apply it to products for other customers.

A third management trend results from the increase in cooperation between organizations (specifically with customers, suppliers, and even competitors), and is referred to as **co-opetition.** We discuss this trend in more detail in Chapters 3 and 10. For now, simply note that it is often just as important to manage relationships *between* organizations as *within* organizations. Indeed, today many companies cooperate in certain market segments and compete in others. For example, IBM and Apple Computers joined forces with Motorola to develop the PowerPC microprocessor chip, even though IBM and Apple compete directly in the sale of personal computers.

The fourth and final trend we will note here is the trend toward spreading information more widely throughout organizations. Efforts are being made in many organizations to make information available as quickly and accurately as possible to the people that need it (e.g., to answer customer requests, to decide on resource allocations, to make personnel decisions). This is in direct contrast to more traditional situations where managers often hoard information, knowing that the sole possession of information can lead to power.

Processing and disseminating information widely throughout an organization is not a simple task. The larger and more complex the organization, the more difficult it becomes. To address this challenge, organizations need to carefully plan and implement an information technology infrastructure, which incorporates all required processing and communication capabilities. Development and management of such an infrastructure is a prerequisite for implementing a management philosophy of wide information dissemination.

Table 1–2 summarizes the four noted managerial trends.

STRUCTURE OF THE BOOK

This book is organized into four modules which are to some extent self-contained. Module I introduces some of the major challenges faced by managers today, and

TABLE 1–2 Trends in Managing Organizations

Trend	*Description*
Task-Based Management	Reduces reliance on hierarchical organization structure; forms temporary groups of individuals with diverse skills and expertise to address specific tasks and responsibilities.
Customer-Driven Management	Focuses on satisfying customers as a driving organizational strategy. In the long run, satisfied customers are essential for survival and growth.
Co-opetition	Organizations that compete on some markets may still cooperate, if it is mutually beneficial. Co-opetition is growing rapidly.
Information Dissemination	As employees take on more responsibilities, they need access to relevant information. Organizations are developing the I/T infrastructures needed to deliver such information.

illustrates how these challenges are related to the ability to process information effectively. Module II introduces important issues in the development of information systems to support managers in dealing with the managerial challenges identified in Module I; it also discusses information technology resources. Module III describes the role of information technology in improving individual productivity and organizational competitiveness, and how information systems can be used to help improve the effectiveness and efficiency of business processes. Module IV discusses electronic commerce and public networks (such as the Internet) which will serve as the foundation of the information systems of the future, and then concludes with a discussion of broader issues of information technology and society.

Each chapter of the book introduces a set of major concepts. Chapter 2 focuses on organizational responsiveness by offering the analogy of organizations as systems operating within changing environments, needing to acquire inputs from the environment, to transform them, and to generate outputs. We concentrate our discussion on the necessity of organizations to process information quickly and effectively in order to understand and act on changes in their environment that may threaten their survival.

However, information processing within organizations is fraught with problems. Chapter 3 describes the limitations that human beings face in processing information. Very often, individuals and groups have poor communication and decision-making skills, and these cause serious information-processing problems in organizations. In order to ensure organizational responsiveness, we need to know how to overcome these problems.

Another major problem is that many organizations have structures and reporting relationships that slow down or distort the transmission of important information. Chapter 3 also gives examples of organizations that have moved away from rigid, hierarchical structures to more flexible ones that can be rapidly modified as needed.

Chapter 4 focuses on the challenges presented by organizational communication. In many organizations, the distortion of communication is often the rule rather than the exception. Chapter 4 addresses the basic paradox of organizations being required to process information effectively to survive, but at the same time being ill-equipped to do so.

Chapter 5 introduces the notion of an information technology architecture. This concept is central to visualizing information technology as part of the basic infrastructure of an organization. Chapter 5 also introduces the notion that information systems consist of several components, including a business goal, people, procedures, information, and information technologies. Four of these components of information systems are discussed in Chapter 5. Chapter 6 concentrates on the fifth component, information technology. We can think of information technology as consisting of three major components: hardware, software, and telecommunications (or networking). In the past, these three components were distinct and separate, but today they are converging. Chapter 6 discusses the issues managers face because of this convergence.

A powerful strategy to help managers address the organizational challenges discussed in Chapters 2 through 4 is to use the components of information systems described in Chapters 5 and 6 to develop effective information systems. Effective information systems are those that help managers achieve specific organizational goals. Chapter 7 discusses a process for designing and implementing effective information systems. Chapter 7 presents the information systems development process as being iterative and cyclical in nature, and suggests that there are more ways than one to proceed through the development cycle, each managerial problem requiring a slightly customized design approach.

Information systems should be developed in response to a well-defined organizational need for improvement. One approach to improvement is to reexamine the business processes that are currently in place and then determine the critical information needs requiring information systems support. Some changes to business processes will be gradual, focusing on continuous improvement of existing processes that are working well; others may require radical changes in the processes themselves before any automation takes place. Chapter 8 discusses the challenges of removing and redesigning ineffective processes, and the role of information technology in making that redesign possible.

Once the need for process improvements has been defined, information systems must be developed, or acquired, to fill the critical information-processing needs of the organization. One approach is to focus on the productivity needs of individuals and groups; by improving individual and group productivity, organizational productivity should improve as well. Numerous information technology tools are available to improve individual and group productivity, and Chapter 9 describes the use of these tools.

In Chapter 10, we move from the individual and workgroup level to that of the organization. Chapter 10 focuses on the ways information technology can be used to provide a competitive advantage for organizations. Two major concepts especially warrant emphasis. The first is the need to create customer value as a basic organizational strategy—customer value is what drives customer satisfaction. The second is that organizations are using information technology to establish tight links with their customers and suppliers. In the extreme, organizations form what are called *virtual organizations,* that is, organizations that technically do not exist. The organization, its suppliers, and its customers are all separate legal entities, but their processes (e.g., order fulfillment) are so tightly coupled that they behave as one organization.

Chapter 11 addresses the issues that arise when actually implementing information technology projects to achieve competitive advantage. The development and implementation of information systems involve major commitments of resources and therefore require a systematic and careful project management approach. Unfortunately, almost 80 percent of all information systems development projects run behind schedule and over budget. As information systems become more prevalent in an organization, more resources are invested in development and the organization becomes more dependent on the systems. This greater dependency increases the organization's vulnerability to systems failure and raises complex operational and ethical issues. These issues require substantial managerial attention and Chapter 11 discusses these.

The last module of the book moves from the discussion of the use of information technology within organizations in the previous three modules to the broader issues of public networks and the potential impact of information technology on society. Chapter 12 presents a discussion of public (value-added) networks, with a special focus on the Internet. The discussion deals with issues such as intellectual property and first amendment rights, as well as business opportunities.

We close with a brief look at the broad issues of information technology and society in Chapter 13. We suggest possible implications of the pervasiveness of this technology for education, entertainment, human interaction, world relations, and the environment. In our treatment of these issues, we do not try to provide answers, but rather to raise critical questions, as we consider to what extent the advancement of information technology is positive (or negative) for human society.

So why should managers worry about information technology? Simply put, because they have to. Without an effective information-processing capability, an organization will lose touch with its environment and eventually die. Improving the capabilities of an organization to process information means redesigning the business processes, improving the communication systems, and developing the information technology infrastructure (hardware, software, data, etc.) to sustain them. These activities require close managerial attention, because (1) as organizations apply I/T to more processes they become more dependent on it, and (2) managing I/T involves very complex tasks.

Throughout the book, we avoid the temptation to focus too much on the specifics of present-day information technology. The reason: by the time you read this, major changes in technology will already have occurred. Memorizing details about today's computer hardware and learning the quirks of current productivity software (e.g., wordprocessing or spreadsheet packages) is a good thing, but by itself it is inadequate to prepare you to be an effective manager or entrepreneur in tomorrow's rapidly changing technological environment.

Instead, we employ *concepts, themes and frameworks* that are much more enduring in their usefulness. For example, communication will *always* involve at least one sender and one receiver, and will *always* need to address the concerns of distortion and overloading the receiver, regardless of which technology is applied to the communication process—be it drums, smoke signals, or personal videoconferencing. You will naturally need to be aware of new information technologies as they emerge, in order to determine whether they can improve your individual, and organizational, productivity. You will also need to watch for trends in organizational management and operations to determine which new structures and techniques can be of help to your company.

We applied this same philosophy—the focus on enduring concepts—to our treatment of the convergence of information and communication technologies in Chapter 6. Although a certain amount of base knowledge is essential, we focus more on enduring features of hardware, software, and telecommunications (networking) technology. We will always be concerned with the ease of use, reliability, and accuracy of input devices, and, at least for the present, we all have to contend with issues of compatibility (of software with hardware, or between software packages).

The Use of Case Examples. One final note. This book uses many examples to illustrate the concepts and theories discussed in the text. Also, each chapter provides two cases and a few short Business Briefs. The first case, which follows the chapter summary and is titled a "Connective Case," is designed to help you connect selected concepts from the chapter to a real-world situation. The second case follows the review and discussion questions, and is intended to provide you with a more challenging assignment. The Business Briefs are very short actual situations about organizations that help illustrate concepts from the chapter.

There are a variety of cases in the book. Some cases and Business Briefs are quite simple, and are not meant as exercises requiring detailed analysis and recommendations. The descriptions in these provide insufficient information concerning competitors, customers, and so on to conduct much of a formal analysis. This type of case is intended to illustrate how a manager has successfully integrated the use of I/T to complement his or her management philosophy and to support the organizational structure. Beginning in Chapter 2, we also provide a selection of more extensive cases requiring more formal and comprehensive analyses.

The Case Analysis section below provides a quick introduction to reading and analyzing cases. Typically, case questions tend to be quite open-ended, requiring you to apply some structure to your analysis. To illustrate how to answer open-ended questions, we have provided sample case analyses for the Connective Cases in the first module. We strongly recommend that you attempt to analyze the cases yourself *before* reading our suggested analyses. Proficiency at case analysis helps prepare you for effective decision making in real situations, but it does take time. Practice makes perfect, so be patient, and ask yourself questions such as these: What are the critical events and facts in the case? What are the important concepts from this chapter? How do they apply to the situation described in the case?

The Connective Cases provided in the chapters are an example of short descriptive cases. There are taken from popular sources, and are intended to illustrate one or more points. These descriptive cases generally do not require extensive, in-depth analysis. Although questions are added to help focus attention on certain issues, this type of descriptive (or illustrative) case is provided primarily to help make the link between theories and concepts in the chapter to actual situations in the real world.

Real-life situations are rarely as simple and straightforward as those presented in brief case descriptions. In an effort to provide a better sense of the complexity of issues and alternatives facing decision makers in real organizations, some authors have adopted a style of case description that results in longer, more comprehensive cases. These cases may have multiple issues requiring consideration, may involve multiple individuals providing diverse viewpoints, and may contain material that seems extraneous to the primary issues at hand. Frequently, the reader is required to take a global or "big picture" perspective, balancing the values and priorities of various stakeholders and dealing with considerable uncertainty in arriving at a set of recommendations.

In this book, we have made a conscious effort to keep most of the cases more focused, and have removed much of the extraneous material. This has the effect of reducing the overall length of the cases. To provide a better sense of the complexity of issues facing the primary decision maker, however, we have also written a series of cases about the same company, Dakin Farm, which are included at the end of the first three modules. We have added videos for Dakin Farm which show the actual decision makers and the actual company. Over the course of viewing multiple video segments and analyzing multiple case installments, we believe you will obtain a better appreciation of the complexity and realities of managing a real company.

Keep in mind, however, that even "realistic" cases are not real. They are representations of a real situation. The case is provided in a relatively neat form, and the case writer has made judgments about what information to include and exclude. Case writers gather information by conducting interviews, reading memoranda, analyzing quantitative data, and so on. Although they generally attempt to be objective and unbiased, the case writer may inadvertently miss important information or alter it as they go through the case-writing process. Also, although you may be asked as a student to make a decision, you obviously don't have to live with the consequences of that decision. The result is that although a good case can help us learn, it does not substitute for decision making in real situations.

CASE ANALYSIS

Some of the longer cases in this book have sufficient complexity to allow for more in-depth analysis. In this situation we will typically ask questions requiring you to "use the concepts from the chapter to analyze the situation" or "use concepts from the chapter to provide recommendations. . . ." This type of case requires you to go beyond a common-sense response, and apply frameworks or concepts that have been introduced in the chapter. If you analyze each case as you read it, you will most likely find yourself doing the same when you read newspaper articles, or listen to news reports, or as you interact with real organizations as part of your day-to-day life. This is the ultimate goal of case analysis: to help form the way we think and act.

The reason for using nondirected questions is quite simple: we want you to develop skills needed to assess a situation and to ask insightful questions. A business leader once commented that 90 percent of the task of a top manager is to ask useful questions. Answers are relatively easy to find, but asking good questions is the more critical skill.

There is no single way to analyze a case since the analysis depends on the purpose for which the case is being used. One general approach that might serve as a good starting point is as follows:

1. Quickly skim through the case to get an overall sense of the organization, the main players, and the main issues. Don't worry about the details at this point; ask yourself what basic concepts and issues seem to be involved.
2. If it hasn't been specified for you, identify the perspective you wish to take for analyzing the case. Should you put yourself in the shoes of one of the primary players in the case? Should you consider yourself a consultant to senior management? Often recommendations will differ, depending on the perspective you adopt.
3. Now read through the case carefully, underlining key facts and noting key issues as you go. Refer back to course material, and use the frameworks and concepts in the chapter (or from previous chapters, if appropriate) to prepare a set of recommendations supported by your analysis of the case.

We hope that by the end of this book, you will have developed not only a good appreciation of management and information technology, but also a good grounding in approaching and analyzing business cases.

SUMMARY

Information technology (I/T) is becoming widespread throughout society. Advances in information technology are changing the way we as individuals communicate, learn, and function in our everyday lives. Information technology continues to change our entertainment options, our shopping, our career choices. Indeed, the ongoing advancement of I/T and communication facilities provides infinite opportunities for leisure and for business. On the other hand, the increased capabilities of I/T continue to raise many ethical issues. From a global or international perspective, geographic and time distances are becoming immaterial as I/T communication technologies virtually open up and shrink the world.

Philosophies of how to manage organizations are also changing. Many forward-thinking managers are organizing their employees around tasks and responsibilities, rather than around the traditional functional disciplines like finance and marketing; these organizations construct a team around a verb (e.g., fulfilling a customer order) rather than a noun (e.g., sales). Managers are becoming more like coaches, working to lead teams and remove obstacles that prevent team members from accomplishing their goals. There has been a renewed focus on identifying and satisfying the needs of customers every opportunity.

Organizations operate within a very competitive environment, and one important consideration of management is how to compete effectively. At one point the dominant strategy options were to become a low-cost producer, to differentiate the product, or to obtain a market niche. Recently, some organizations have focused on trying to accomplish all three. The term mass customization has been used to describe the strategy of providing products that are configured (assembled) to the needs of each individual customer, but doing so for a very large customer base.

Long-term survival and growth require an efficient and effective organization that satisfies all the needs of its customers. Information technology plays an important role in the internal functioning of organizations, as well as in their ability to respond to change and to satisfy their customers' needs. Although it is possible for some organizations to thrive without the effective use of I/T, it is becoming more and more unlikely.

The business opportunities emerging through the development and application of I/T are enormous. But to take advantage of these opportunities requires a basic understanding of the changes I/T can bring to individuals, organizations, and society. Countering the opportunities are many risks. As organizations become more dependent on information systems, they also become more vulnerable to system failures, abuses, or errors. As with any other powerful tool, I/T needs to be managed carefully. The effective use of I/T requires time and resources and, in today's world, needs to be a top priority for management.

KEY CONCEPTS AND TERMS

KEY CONCEPTS

- Change is constant. To survive, organizations need I/T to be responsive to change. (7)
- Organizations need I/T to compete effectively. (11)
- I/T alters perceptions of distance and time; the environment for organizations is global, not regional or national. (14)
- The application of I/T raises many ethical concerns. (14)
- Computing and communication technologies are converging. (1)
- Satisfying customer needs drives competitive strategy. (18)
- Organizational structures are less permanent; there is an increasing use of task-based management teams. (17)
- I/T is being used to empower employees and redefine job tasks and roles. (3)

KEY TERMS

communication technology (3)
competition (10)
computer-aided design (7)
computer-aided manufacturing (7)
computerized monitoring (16)
co-opetition (21)
customization (12)
customer-driven (21)
employee empowerment (5)
ethics (16)
information system (4)
information technology (3)
information technology infrastructure (5)
international (16)
management (3)
mass customization (12)
organization (3)

organizational communication (5)
organizational responsiveness (9)
organizational structure (5)
proactive (9)
reactive (10)
strategy (11)

REFERENCES

Cash, J. I.; F. W. McFarlan; J. L. McKenney; and L. M. Applegate. *Corporate Information Systems Management: Text and Cases.* 3rd ed. Homewood, Ill: Irwin, 1992.

Deutschman, A. "The Managing Wisdom of High-Tech Superstars." *Fortune,* October 17, 1994, pp. 197–206.

Geyelin, Milo. "Doomsday Device: How an NCR System for Inventory Turned into a Virtual Saboteur." *The Wall Street Journal,* August 8, 1994, p. A1.

Hammer, M., and G. E. Mangurian. "The Changing Value of Communications Technology." *Sloan Management Review,* Winter 1987, pp. 65–71.

Haynes, Peter. "A Survey of the Computer Industry." *Economist,* September 17, 1994, pp. 2–22.

Kallman, E. A., and J. P. Grillo. *Ethical Decision Making and Information Technology: An Introduction with Cases.* (2nd Ed) New York: McGraw-Hill, 1996.

Porter, M. *Competitive Strategy: Techniques for Analyzing Industries and Competitors.* New York: Free Press, 1980.

Wiseman, C., and I. C. MacMillan. "Creating Competitive Weapons from Information Systems." *Journal of Business Strategy,* Fall 1984.

CONNECTIVE CASE: Frito-Lay Crunches Rivals

Threading his way around stainless-steel conveyor belts transporting fried Cheetos, Doritos, and Tostitos to tumblers where salt and seasonings are applied, Frito-Lay plant manager Steve Smith grabs a tempting sample and pops it into his mouth. Smith, who runs the 22-year-old plant in Rancho Cucamonga, California, says his efforts at turning factory management over to workers have required "no magic, no pixie dust."

He started in 1990, when Frito-Lay, PepsiCo's most profitable unit and the nation's leading manufacturer of salty snacks, began encountering stiff competition from Anheuser-Busch's Eagle Snacks and Borden's Wise and Old London foods. The salty-snack war pressured prices and shrank margins. PepsiCo Vice Chairman Roger Enrico cut 1,800 jobs, reorganized the company around leaner headquarters, and directed factory managers to empower workers in search of productivity gains.

For the 38-year-old Smith, one of the first steps in transforming hourly workers into business people was an educational campaign aimed at demonstrating why and how their involvement could improve the balance sheet. To strengthen the tie, PepsiCo inaugurated a program called SharePower that distributed Pepsi stock to every full-time employee.

Today, Smith estimates that about half the plant actively contributes to managing the business. Teams of workers evaluate their performances by feeding data—such as how many pounds of corn were used—into a computerized information system. The computer system spits back calculations that rate each shift against a business plan and a more ambitious target. When the numbers are disappointing, teams brainstorm how to improve them.

Rancho Cucamonga's performance has exceeded Frito-Lay's expectations: customer complaints are down by 50 percent and the plant fills orders promptly 99.5 percent of the time. The bottom line is strong. Rancho Cucamonga has cut costs by $5 million over the past three years, and Smith estimates savings will total $1.5 million for each of the next three years.

Frito-Lay's future looks bright. Veteran machine operator Richard Montanez, 37, became so energized by Smith's new operating style that after listening to salesmen he developed a new ethnic-food concept aimed at the Hispanic market. After testing recipes and outlining a marketing strategy, Montanez burst forth with a kernel of an idea: Flamin' Hot Popcorn will soon make its debut.

Case Question

1. In what way(s) does this case example illustrate the concepts and issues raised in this chapter?

CASE ANALYSIS

Although brief, this case description illustrates many of the points we wish to stress in this book. Like most organizations, Frito-Lay found that its environment changed. Competitors (Anheuser-Busch and Borden) began to encroach on its sales, decreasing profits. A short-term response to this change in the environment was to reduce operating costs by laying off many employees. The longer-term strategy was to involve employees directly in the management of the organization, restructuring the organization around multifunction teams rather than using a bureaucratic hierarchical structure.

The change in structure and management style was facilitated through the effective use of information technology; although mentioned only briefly in the case, a computerized system provides current information that helps the teams monitor their performance and make changes on the fly if necessary. The adoption of task-based teams and the application of information technology has enabled the company to operate more efficiently, reducing the inputs (raw materials and labor) required to produce the same level of outputs. This lowered the costs, which enabled the company to lower the price charged to customers.

The company has also reduced customer complaints dramatically, and its products are being delivered on time. In addition, the change in management philosophy has enabled the company to take better advantage of the knowledge and expertise of its employees, as illustrated by the new popcorn product envisioned and championed by Mr. Montanez, a machine operator. It appears that information technology has been applied effectively to implement the company's strategy.

SOURCE: David Hage and Linda Grant, "How to Make America Work," *U.S. News & World Report,* December 6, 1993, p. 52.

IT'S YOUR TURN — END OF CHAPTER MATERIALS

REVIEW QUESTIONS

1. Briefly define the term *information technology,* and provide an example of an information technology that does not appear in this chapter.
2. Distinguish between information technology and an information system.
3. List three examples of how information technology has become more pervasive in your personal life over the past 10 years.
4. Briefly define the term *organizational responsiveness.*
5. What are some of the reasons that organizational competition is increasing?
6. In what ways can information technology help organizations be more competitive?
7. How can information technology enable companies to expand their operations beyond the boundaries of their home country?
8. List three examples of ethical issues arising from the use of information technology.
9. List the four management trends identified in this chapter.
10. Define the term *co-opetition.*

DISCUSSION QUESTIONS

1. Is it possible to have an information system that does not use information technology? Explain.
2. Select a retail store you are familiar with (a sporting goods store, a bookstore, a clothing store, etc.). Who are the primary competitors? What strategy(ies) does the organization use to compete? In what ways (that you know) are information systems used to help the store compete? Can you think of other applications of information technology that could help the store operate?
3. Describe the mass customization strategy (as employed by Saturn and Dell Computer Co.). How could employing this strategy apply to an organization that provides a business school education?
4. Identify an organization that is structured as a functional hierarchy. How does this differ from a process-based (task-based) organizational structure?
5. Discuss how the work of a trucker might be changed through I/T. How might the work of an officer at the Welfare Office be changed through I/T?
6. The authors of this book believe that most (if not all) productive members of society will need to employ information technology in their personal and professional lives. To what extent do you agree with this argument? Why?

GROUP ASSIGNMENT

Divide your group into two. Consider the issue of having pornographic material available on the Internet. Have one team argue why such material should be made available, and the other team, why it should be banned. As a group, propose a public policy that would address this issue.

Use a wordprocessing package or a presentation package (e.g., PowerPoint) to prepare three overhead slides: (1) listing arguments in favor, (2) listing arguments against, and (3) your joint position. Be prepared to make a five-minute group presentation.

APPLICATION ASSIGNMENTS

1. Access the Internet, and locate the home page for this book. Print the home page, and bring it to class. Keep track of how long it takes you to find the home page.
2. Send an E-mail message to your instructor. Briefly describe your expectations for this course. Comment on how easy (or difficult) it was for you to use the E-mail system.
3. Using a wordprocessing package of your choice, write a two-paragraph memo to a family member explaining one of the management trends introduced in this chapter.

CASE ASSIGNMENT: General Electric Motors

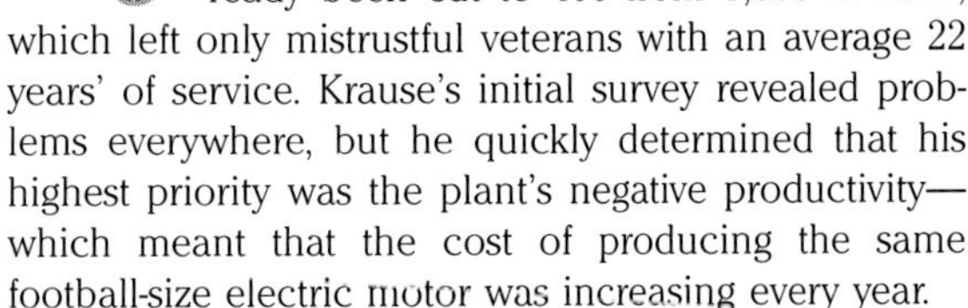

When Dick Krause took over management of a faltering General Electric Motors plant in Fort Wayne, Indiana, two years ago, his mandate from headquarters was clear: orchestrate a turnaround, or the steadily shrinking business would be moved abroad or sold. The factory's unionized workforce had already been cut to 400 from 1,000 in 1983, which left only mistrustful veterans with an average 22 years' of service. Krause's initial survey revealed problems everywhere, but he quickly determined that his highest priority was the plant's negative productivity—which meant that the cost of producing the same football-size electric motor was increasing every year.

Before Krause, 54, began to solicit ideas on how to reorganize the plant, he approached International Union of Electrical Workers' representative Ron Fee for advice. Fee's counsel: "Go to the plant floor every day, listen and talk to the hourly workers." Krause followed the advice. Today his workers hold him in high esteem. And despite further job cuts, which have lowered the head count to 265, morale is on the rise.

To help fix the Fort Wayne plant, Krause negotiated with the union to improve quality and increase flexibility. Equipment was rearranged and computerized reporting systems upgraded so that newly formed teams could monitor a part's progress from beginning to end. Everyone attended classes on group dynamics, while Krause disseminated facts and figures about GE competitors and, more important, customers.

There has been a profound payoff. The cost of producing GE motors has dropped by 16 percent in two years. Quality has improved from 2,300 rejects per million two years ago to just 150 today, a rate considered nearly perfect by manufacturing measures. And elapsed time from order to shipment has dropped from 55 days to 16. An informal poll of workers suggests that about 80 percent support Krause's sweeping changes. Says 28-year veteran Dave Wilkin: "Krause doesn't think management is necessary in manufacturing; he thinks we can do it."

Case Questions

1. What was the environment like for GE's Fort Wayne plant prior to Krause's arrival? What was GE's short term reaction to the changes in the environment?
2. What was Krause's primary goal upon taking over control of the plant?
3. Discuss the relative importance of management philosophy, organizational structure, and information technology in aiding the turnaround at the GE plant.
4. What strategy(ies) did Krause pursue for the Fort Wayne plant?

MODULE I Managerial Challenges

The three chapters in this first module provide the background necessary to understand the key challenges facing managers and entrepreneurs. These chapters also introduce the ways information technology can be used to address these challenges.

Chapter 2 focuses on the primary theme of this book: organizational responsiveness. In Chapter 2 we argue that organizations that respond more quickly to changes in their environment are more likely to be successful. Examples illustrate how information technology can be used as environmental scanners to help organizations be more responsive, and as feedback mechanisms to help managers control operations.

Chapter 3 introduces the critical issues of decision making within organizations, and describes how information systems can be used to improve decision making by individuals and work groups. Chapter 3 also introduces important concepts of how organizations may be structured, and discusses ways information technology can be used to support alternative (more responsive) organizational structures.

The final chapter of this module, Chapter 4, focuses on organizational communication. We describe some common weaknesses in organizational communication, and we propose ways to address these weaknesses using information technology. In general, Module I provides the foundation for understanding how information technology can be used as an effective managerial tool.

CHAPTER 2 Organizational Responsiveness

CHAPTER OBJECTIVES

After reading this chapter, you should have a clearer understanding of why it is important for organizations to be responsive to changes in the environment and of the role that information technology can play in promoting that responsiveness. More specifically, you should be able to:

- Describe an organization as a system that processes inputs acquired from the environment into a series of outputs (i.e., products and services), which are then sent out into the environment.
- Use General Systems Theory (GST) as a framework to understand the interactions between the organization and its environment.
- Identify the responsibilities of management to achieve organizational responsiveness, by ensuring (1) the availability of inputs from the environment necessary to keep an organization going, (2) the acceptance of an organization's outputs by one or more components of the environment, (3) the flexibility and efficiency of the transformation of inputs into outputs, (4) the effectiveness of decision making, and (5) the accuracy and timeliness of information processing in the organization.
- Understand why the organization's need for environmental awareness and scanning increases as the turbulence of its environment increases.
- Explain the dynamics of organizational responsiveness and how organizations attempt to stay in equilibrium with their environment by developing feedback and feedforward capabilities, and by using buffers.
- Understand the role of I/T in facilitating organizational responsiveness.

Given that change is constant, how can my organization keep pace? I know that information technology can help us, but where do we start?

INTRODUCTION TO ORGANIZATIONAL RESPONSIVENESS

The focus of this chapter (and the conceptual backbone of this book, for that matter) is the notion that **organizational responsiveness** is the key to a firm's long-term success. Organizations need to respond quickly—at least more quickly than their competition—if they are to remain viable entities, and there are two components to such organizational responsiveness. The first is being aware of change, and the second is doing something about it.

Why focus so much on organizational responsiveness? After all, it makes sense that organizations should keep a close watch on their environments and adapt to any changes. How difficult can that be? Well, consider this for a moment: Very few companies have been around for more than a century; and the number of companies that have failed in the last 25 years is staggering. Companies like American Motors, Osborne Computers, and Pan American Airlines have disappeared. Companies like General Motors, Chrysler, IBM, Sears, TWA, and AT&T have gone through major transformations after being scarred by a substantial desertion of customers. And the last decade has seen the emergence of some fast-growing companies, such as Compaq, Microsoft, Intel, Wal-Mart, MCI, MTV, CNN, and Starbucks Coffee. How long are these newcomers going to be around? Only time will tell.

One of the excuses poorly performing companies use is that nobody can predict the future. However, some companies have done very well creating a future rather than reacting to it. Companies like GE, 3M, Motorola, Microsoft, Intel, Dupont, and Merck have acted proactively to shape their future. The managers in these companies identified the key trends of social, ecological, technological, political, and economic change and understood how the impact of these trends would affect their companies. This **environmental scanning** enables organizations to develop contingency plans and actions which reduce the response time needed to address an environmental opportunity or threat.

To achieve organizational responsiveness, managers have to minimize the uncertainty that exists in their environments. The key to minimizing uncertainty is having accurate and timely information about the critical aspects of the environment. In *turbulent* (rapidly changing) environments, the quantity of data and the speed at which the data changes are such that managers cannot keep track of all meaningful events without using information technology.

Information technology has become a strategic tool for companies to keep pace with their environment. Information technology helps companies by, for example, tracking the tastes and desires of customers through point-of-sale (POS) systems, by allowing management to stay in close touch with suppliers through electronic matching of production schedules, and by providing flexibility to the production process through computerized manufacturing systems. Having a fast response capability is critical in today's markets, where products and services have shorter and shorter life cycles, and where customers' tastes change quickly. To help illustrate this point, we turn to the example of a well-known retail company.

From humble beginnings in a single shop in Venice, Italy, to over 5,000 shops in 75 countries by the late 1990s, Benetton has become one of the premier global marketers. Bypassing wholesalers and retailers in favor of designing its own tightly controlled distribution system, Benetton has become the quintessential quick change artist. By integrating information processing capabilities with manufacturing technology, Benetton is able to respond in lightning fashion to changes in customer demand anywhere in the world where it has a store.

The company's strategy of leaving sweaters undyed and waiting for "just-in-time" information on which colors are needed by retail stores around the world allows it to rapidly adjust the product mix to fit the configuration of the market. This speed and coordination happen through an intricate communications system, high-speed computers, and a $20 million computerized warehouse that services the company's seven factories in Italy. When a customer purchases a sweater in Portland, Oregon, the details of the sale (product size, color, etc.) are captured with a point-of-sales bar code scanner and transmitted electronically to the centralized computer system in Italy within seconds.

Details of each specific sale are combined with other transactions from outlets around the world to determine daily production runs (dyeing of sweaters) at each of the seven factories. Finished goods are shipped directly from the centralized warehouse to retail outlets, with quantities of different products determined by the recent sales transactions. Similarly, items that are not selling in each retail outlet are monitored closely and removed on a regular basis.

As Harvard's James Heskett says, Benetton has

> pioneered a retailing approach throughout Europe that promises to influence a number of other retailers worldwide; it substitutes information for assets. Because its first retail outlet offering knit outerwear in colorful fashions was very small, the Benetton family developed an approach to retailing that makes effective use of small spaces. Unlike its more traditional competitors with stores of perhaps 4,000 square feet, a typical Benetton outlet is not more than 600 square feet. Little space is wasted on floor selling or back-room storage.
>
> An electronic communications system is supported by a manufacturing process that allows for dyeing to order and for rapid replenishment of the items in greatest demand during a fashion season. The result is a higher rate of inventory turnover in the store and a level of sales-per-square foot that is often several times that of Benetton's competitors. Benetton's assets support many more sales because it has injected both communications and flexible manufacturing into its service. In fact, Benetton can make changes in inventory in 10 days that take most retailers months.[1]

Benetton could not be as responsive to changes in its environment without information technology. Neither could The Limited, Dell Computers, L. L. Bean, Otis Elevators, Mrs. Fields' Cookies, and many other companies. Information technology is so central to these companies' ability to respond to changes in their environment that it has become a strategic concern of management.

General Systems Theory is a useful framework to determine the information-processing capabilities that organizations need to develop to stay in touch with their environment. We turn to this framework next.

---

[1] Quoted in Cavateri, S. and K. Obloj, *Management Systems: A Global Perspective,* Belmont, CA: Wadsworth, 1993, p. 162.

Many retail companies use sophisticated computer and communication systems to respond quickly to changes in customer preferences. Photo courtesy of Bonnie Kamin.

A FRAMEWORK TO ACHIEVE ORGANIZATIONAL RESPONSIVENESS

General Systems Theory (GST) is a framework to help management identify the critical aspects of a company's environment and the areas where information technology can play an important role. In this section, we introduce and discuss its major concepts.

GST provides a simple yet powerful approach to understanding how organizations interact with their environment. It also illustrates why organizations need to be proactive and responsive to changes in their environment in order to survive. GST is a particularly useful approach for individuals interested in studying information systems because it emphasizes the critical importance of information processing to the survival of an organization.

Charles Darwin, the 19th-century naturalist, proposed his theory of the evolution of the species by observing how specific animal species had adapted to changes in their environment. His theory was based on the observation that those species that were able to change to meet changes in their environment had survived and thrived, while those that were not able to adapt perished and disappeared.

General Systems Theory is a Darwinian approach to understanding the evolution of organizations. The philosophical underpinning of GST is the *need to adapt to environmental changes in order to survive* (i.e., to remain a viable and functional

Darwin proposed that as the environment changed, some species—those that could adapt to address the changes in their environment—would be more successful than others. Photos courtesy of Chip Clark/Offshoot Stock (left) and Jim Brown/Offshoot Stock (right).

entity). Although in this book we will use GST only to understand the relation of responsiveness to the long-term survival of companies, GST is generic enough that it can also be used to understand the behaviors of organisms and mechanisms.

Indeed, GST can be applied to the behavior of mechanisms like a combustion engine (the more adaptable the engine to changes in the quality of fuel and the oxygen and humidity levels, the better the performance of the engine over time), of animal organisms and populations (the more adaptable animals are to changes in their environments, the bigger their populations will become), and to social organizations (a for-profit organization needs to produce goods and services that are constantly evolving with the needs and preferences of its clients in order to grow; a nonprofit organization needs to pursue goals perceived as important by its constituencies and adapt its goals and strategies in order to remain viable as these perceptions change).

However, GST differentiates humans and social organizations from animals and mechanisms by recognizing the ability of humans and social organizations to imagine the future and to be **proactive** toward potential changes in the environment. Although mechanisms cannot (yet) reinvent themselves, and animals only adjust reactively, social organizations are capable of changing their structure and processes to match actual or *forecasted* changes in the environment.

A System and Its Environment. Basically, General Systems Theory describes the relationships between an organization, or **system**, and its **environment**. The system acquires **inputs**, **transforms** them, and generates **outputs**. These outputs are exchanged with the environment. If the environment accepts the outputs, the cycle continues. If the environment does not accept the outputs, the system must change the outputs it produces or it will fail and disappear.

Systems have **goals** (the most basic one is to remain a viable entity), and consist of a series of interrelated components called **subsystems**. The major subsystems are the transformation subsystem (e.g., manufacturing), the decision-making subsystem (upper-level management), and the information-processing subsystem (the infrastructure for processing and disseminating information). Each of these subsystems

The oil refinery system acquires crude oil inputs, transforms them, and generates diesel and gasoline products as outputs. Photos courtesy of Bryan & Cherry Alexander (left), Russ Shleipman/Offshoot Stock (center), and B. Daemmrich/The Image Works (right).

can be broken down into more specific and narrowly defined subsystems; for example, management can be broken down into marketing, finance, and so on and manufacturing can be broken down into inventory management, quality control, scheduling, and so forth.

An oil refinery (system) acquires crude oil (input), distills it (the transformation process), and produces gasoline, diesel, kerosene, and other products (outputs) to increase the wealth of its shareholders and provide meaningful jobs for its employees (goals). The individuals running the refinery (the decision-making subsystem, or management) need to decide what the best product mix is and what volume to produce, where to acquire the necessary crude oil, and how to price the products. In order to make these decisions, management needs information on what its competitors are doing, on how much fluctuation there will be in the future prices of oil, and on what the potential demand is. This information is provided by the information system subsystem (which in turn could be broken down further into the collection of data, the storage of data, the transmission of data, etc.).

Anything that is outside of the system can be considered its environment. However, from a managerial perspective and an organizational responsiveness point of view, we will define the environment of a system as those factors that (1) have an impact on the behavior of the system, and (2) over which the system has little or no control. The environment consists of all those factors the system needs to consider for decision making that are outside of its control. For business organizations, elements in the environment include competitors, customers, suppliers, government agencies, unions, technology, and demographic and economic trends.

Since defining where the system ends and the environment begins is often difficult, a good rule of thumb is to ask, "Does the system have control over this component?" If the answer is no (as in the case of interest rates or the price of oil), then the component is part of the environment. If the answer is yes (as in the case of proprietary technology), then the component is part of the system. If the answer is more or less (as in the case of the level of impurities in the gasoline or water used in a manufacturing process), the component straddles the boundary and belongs partly to the environment and partly to the system.

Subsystems and Local Rationality. Systems can be subdivided into parts, or subsystems. Systems have different degrees of complexity. In general, *the more complex a system, the greater the number of subsystems it has.* These subsystems perform functions that are required of the system by certain aspects of the environment (e.g., having customers requires a sales function; paying taxes requires having an accounting function; having competitors requires a strategic management function). Typically, as a system grows and evolves it starts to differentiate its functions. For example, in an entrepreneurial small business the functions of accounting, marketing, sales, and strategic planning are usually shared by a handful of people and are often performed by only one or two individuals. As the small business grows and the number of interactions with the environment increase (more customers, more inquiries, more invoices) those functions are assigned to different individuals and eventually departments (or subsystems) are formed to organize their work.

Ideally, these subsystems work together in harmony to achieve a specific set of goals. If we look at the human body as a system, it is composed of various subsystems: the skeletal subsystem, the cardiovascular subsystem, the immune subsystem, the digestive subsystem, and so on, all working together to keep the person alive and healthy. When the subsystems do not work in unison, a person becomes sick. The difference between a social system and the human body is that, under normal circumstances, the subsystems of a social system or organization do not necessarily work in total unison and harmony. Subsystems in social organizations tend to develop their own goals, which at times conflict with the overall goal of the system as a whole. This phenomenon is called **local rationality.**

Local rationality requires constant negotiations among the different subsystems. For example, consider the following conversation. The participants were the vice president of manufacturing (Vijay) and the vice president of finance (Michelle). Michelle started the conversation.

"Vijay, I just noticed that you ordered an additional 5,000 components from Quinbee Electronics. What's going on?"

"Well Michelle, I'm anticipating a couple of big orders, and I don't want to run the risk of having to stop the production line while we wait for more parts."

"That's all well and good, but Quinbee requires us to pay cash right away. As you know, we are expanding our Malaysian factory and we need the money there. This is not the time to speculate on possible orders by holding excess inventory."

"Okay, Michelle, but if I have a shortage and the orders are late, I'll let you explain it to our customers."

From the manufacturing department's point of view, Vijay is acting rationally (ordering inventory to avoid stopping the production line). However, from an overall systems point of view, the high inventories are tying up cash that is needed somewhere else, and Vijay's actions would not benefit the organization as a whole. Information technology could be used to improve this situation. Vijay might ask for an information system that connects him directly to his customers' scheduling and ordering systems. Such a system would provide him with notification of orders as soon as they are placed. Similarly, an electronic linkage with his suppliers would enable him to order the parts he needs immediately and have them delivered quickly, thus reducing the need to stockpile parts (this approach to inventory management is called *just-in-time.*) Such a system would be good for manufacturing (by minimizing order delays and production line stoppages) and good for finance (by minimizing the financial resources needed to keep inventory).

Active watchfulness means monitoring and evaluating all parts of the environment that can affect survival. Photo courtesy of Tony Stone Worldwide.

Another example of local rationality is when manufacturing departments argue with marketing departments about the merits of having a diverse product line. Manufacturing typically argues that less diversity in product options is better because efficiencies (a main goal of manufacturing) are easier to achieve when producing larger volumes of a smaller number of standard products. Conversely, marketing argues that not all customers have similar needs, and that adding options may lead to gains in market share (a main goal of marketing). An information system that tracks customer preferences might help the organization determine what level of customization would provide the maximum market share with the greatest manufacturing efficiency, and therefore maximize financial returns (a main goal of the organization as a whole).

Strong local rationalities that are not resolved can have a detrimental effect on an organization's ability to match changes in the environment. Within all subsystems there must be a clear understanding of the overall goal of the organization, and all should do their part in making sure the goal is achieved. If subsystems either pursue their own goals at the expense of the overall goal, or spend too much time negotiating with other subsystems to agree on a course of action, the organization may lose the opportunity to act or react to a change in the environment.

Environmental Scanning. The fact that an important component for the survival of an organization is outside of its control does not mean that it should be ignored. The organization should never take a passive view of the environment, and should constantly battle the view of "Why should I worry about it if I can't do anything about it?" The attitude of the organization toward the environment should be one of active watchfulness; this is the process we referred to as *environmental scanning.* Also, the organization needs to develop contingency plans to address changes in the environment. Organizational responsiveness implies not only recognizing a change in the environment, but doing something about it.

Consider, for a moment, the interactions between an organization and a government. Some companies might assume they have little control over the federal government of the country in which they have established their primary operations. They are constantly in a reactive mode; when the government passes legislation dictating that they must contribute a certain percentage of total employee wages for unemployment insurance benefits, they believe they have no option but to do so. When the government passes legislation on pollution standards, they assume that the only alternative is to comply. Other companies might take a different approach. Banding together in groups, they collect and analyze information that shows the effects of such legislation, and with that information they lobby government officials in an effort to convince them to modify the legislation or have it stopped before it is put in place.

The process of environmental scanning consists of at least three important steps. First, it is important for an organization to know what variables in the environment affect its survival and performance. Second, it is important to determine whether or not those variables are changing (is customer demand changing?), what direction the change is taking (is the demand increasing or decreasing?), and the speed and rate of change (how fast is it increasing, and is the growth in demand constant or is it slowing down?). And third, it is important to assess the magnitude of the change to decide whether to develop plans of action to counteract these changes (is the increase in customer demand large enough to require extra production capacity?).

The need for environmental scanning is driven by the intensity of the interactions between the environment and the system (discussed in the next section) and the degree of **turbulence** of the environment (that is, the rate of change of the environment). The greater the turbulence, the greater the need for the system to monitor its environment.

For example, the baby food industry can be considered an industry where changes occur slowly and can be predicted fairly well, and the critical variables in its environment are fairly stable. After all, the birth rates change slowly, those rates can be predicted with a high degree of accuracy, brand loyalty is high (most people feed their babies what their parents fed them—whether out of revenge or good memories is not clear), technologies and consumer tastes evolve slowly. On the other hand, industries such as automakers, computer hardware, construction, financial services, and fashion have a highly turbulent environment where changes

Some industries, such as fashion, are very volatile and change rapidly. Photo courtesy of The Underwood Photo Library.

occur quickly across a wide range of variables: technology, economic conditions, consumer preferences, type of products and services, and others.

As the need for environmental scanning increases, the information-processing capability of the organization needs to be greater and faster. You would naturally expect baby food companies to spend less resources on information-processing technology than companies in the financial services industry.

As the economy goes global, environmental scanning must include considerations of the sociopolitical climate. Suppose, for example, that the Canadian firm Nortel (Northern Telecom) was considering investing in a joint partnership with ENTEL, one of the six major state-owned firms in Bolivia. ENTEL is a long-distance telecommunications company that requires some infusion of capital and technology to help expand the domestic telephone and communications infrastructure in Bolivia. Nortel would need to assess the political system (how stable is the representative constitutional democracy under the leadership of President Gonzalo Sanchez de Lozada?), the legal system (two justices were recently removed from Bolivia's Supreme Court for alleged corruption—is this an indication that corruption has been brought under control, or that it is becoming more widespread?), and so on, before deciding what level of investment to make.

The process of environmental scanning requires a constant monitoring of all critical elements of the environment. Once these elements have been identified, it is often possible to design information systems that provide this monitoring function. For example, an information system can be put in place that records each change as it occurs, as in the case of Benetton. It can then generate reports showing how customer preferences change from one product to another, without any time lag between when the change occurs and when the organization knows about it.

Open versus Closed Systems. The need for environmental scanning depends on the level of interaction and interdependence between the organization and its

Environments can change quickly and sometimes in very unexpected ways. The dismantling of the wall between East and West Germany created great opportunities for some organizations, and spelled the demise of many others. Photo courtesy of Peter Burhle/Black Star.

environment. Organizations can be classified on a continuum of the type of interactions they have with the environment. This continuum runs from organizations that have few, well-controlled, and predictable interactions with their environment (**closed systems**) to organizations that have many, unpredictable, and frequent interactions with their environment (**open systems**).

The rigid definition of a closed system is an organization that has all the resources it needs within it and therefore does not need to interact with the environment to survive. A closed system is a self-contained system. In the context of social organizations, such systems seldom exist; when they do, they don't tend to last very long. Examples of closed systems included the utopian, self-sufficient communes of the 19th century, and the political systems of Albania and China during parts of the 20th century.

It is helpful, however, to think of organizations being on a continuum, from organizations that are very dependent on interactions with their environment (e.g., those in very competitive industries where the environments are fast changing and unpredictable) to organizations that are not very dependent on interactions with the environment (monopolies and highly regulated industries with few competitors and slow-changing environments).

One variable that changes along the open-closed systems continuum is the need for environmental scanning. On the one hand, closed systems are, by definition, internally focused and worry little about changes in the environment. Closed systems do not need to maximize organizational responsiveness, since changes in the environment affect them little or not at all. Open systems, on the other hand, have to be very much aware of the changes in their environment, since they interact so much with it. Therefore, it is less critical for organizations toward the closed end of the continuum to have a good environmental scanning capability than for organizations that are more open.

THE ELEMENTS OF ORGANIZATIONAL RESPONSIVENESS

The primary objective of managers in an organization is (at minimum) to maintain the organization as a viable entity, and to make it thrive if possible. General Systems Theory identifies the areas to which managers should devote their resources, energy, and time to ensure maximum responsiveness. When it comes to assessing organizational responsiveness, managers need to ask the following questions:

- Are inputs *available?*
- Are outputs *accepted?*
- Is the transformation process *efficient* and *flexible?*
- Is decision making *effective?*
- Is information about our internal operations and external environment *accurate* and *timely?*

Figure 2–1 illustrates these elements graphically; we discuss them in more detail next.

Inputs

Systems, by definition, transform inputs into outputs; without inputs a system cannot exist. Without inputs there is no transformation process, and therefore outputs cannot be produced. Inputs might include materials (oil for a refinery; silicon wafers

FIGURE 2-1 The Key Elements of Systems Theory and Their Managerial Concerns

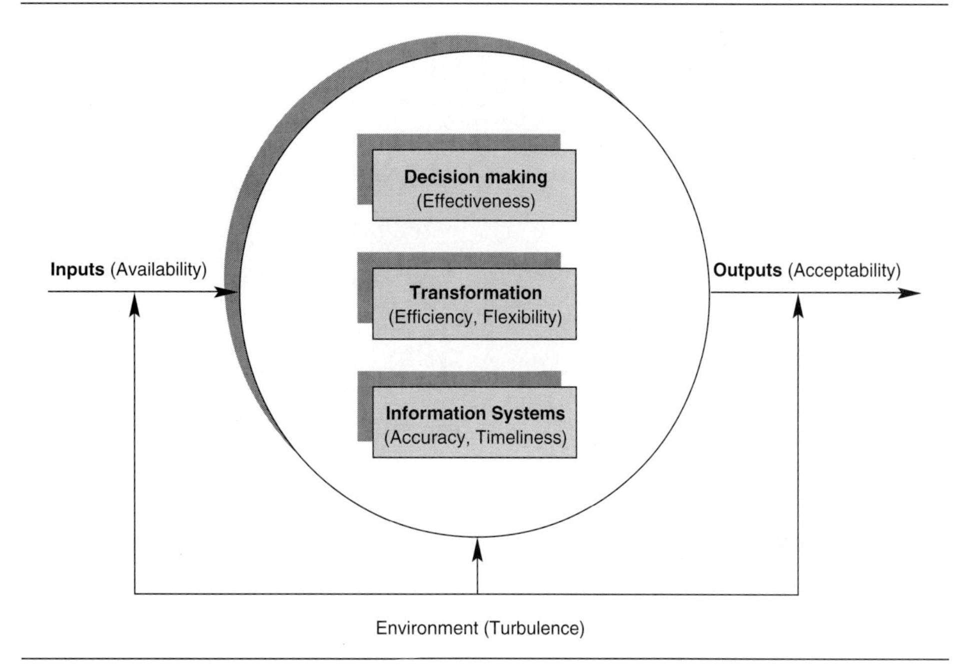

for a computer chip manufacturer), human resources (students for a university; patients for a hospital), money (deposits for a bank), data (sales reports for management), and/or energy (electricity for an aluminum producer).

The central concern of management with respect to inputs is their acquisition. The quality of the inputs often determines the quality of the outputs and the need for a more or less complicated transformation process.

An inability to acquire inputs on time can have dire consequences. On occasion, automobile manufacturers have to stop their production lines because a supplier did not deliver a needed part in sufficient quantities. Shutting down the line may cause losses of several million dollars, even though an individual part might be worth only a couple of dollars or less. In continuous manufacturing environments (e.g., refineries and certain chemical manufacturers), inputs are so important that suppliers have become key strategic partners. For a service organization such as a consulting firm, entry-level consultants (recent graduates of a business school, for example) could be considered inputs to the system. If the consulting firm is unable to hire a sufficient number of qualified applicants, they will be unable to fill the positions left vacant when other consultants leave or those required when new consulting contracts are signed.

Predicting the availability of inputs and ensuring their acquisition is one of the key elements in achieving organizational responsiveness. Information technology may be used in numerous ways to help ensure the availability of inputs. For example, many manufacturers are linking their production schedules to the computer systems of their suppliers. This electronic linkage allows the supplier to plan how many parts will be needed and when, avoiding costly shortages, and smoothing the production schedules of the supplier, which lowers the costs of the parts. Also,

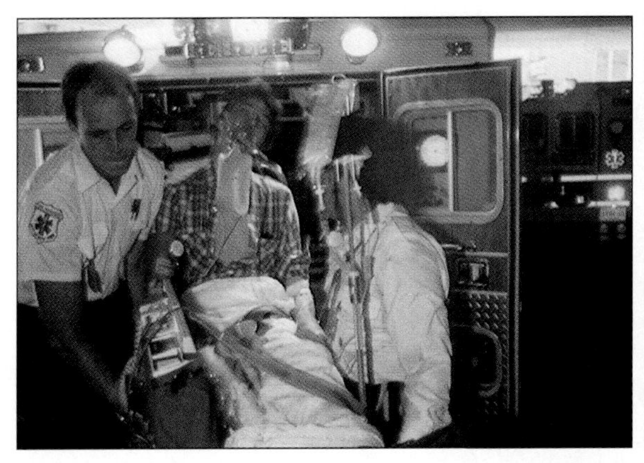

Without inputs a system cannot exist; a hospital needs patients, and a shipping company requires cargo. Photos courtesy of David Harvey/Woodfin Camp & Associates (left) and Ed Kashi (right).

global electronic markets (where companies solicit bids for components from around the world by posting their requirements on specialized electronic bulletin boards) have been instrumental in identifying suppliers of parts on short notice and/or at lower prices. Business Brief 2-1 gives a quick example of what happens when a firm runs short of essential inputs.

Outputs

Without outputs a system has no reason to exist. The purpose of a system is to transform inputs to outputs, and then exchange those outputs with the environment to acquire the necessary resources to continue the cycle. Outputs can consist of products (computers, shoes, cars), services (legal and medical advice), data (reports from a computer system), and/or energy (electricity from a nuclear plant).

The concern of management with respect to outputs is their acceptance by the environment; without this acceptance, the organization cannot survive for long. A university cannot go on for long if its graduates do not find employment (i.e., graduates not accepted by employers); an automaker cannot go on for long if its cars are not bought (cars not accepted by consumers); a hospital cannot go on for long if the patients treated in that hospital are—assuming they leave the hospital alive—dissatisfied with the resulting level of health (health outcomes not accepted by patients and insurance companies). The challenge to management is that the expectations, the standards, and the tastes and desires of consumers change over time and sometimes change quite rapidly.

Determining what the outputs of a firm are or should be is a critical decision. Take, for example, the case of a university. What are the outputs of a university? One would probably suggest graduates, and might discuss issues of acceptance of outputs in terms of the percentage of graduates who obtain jobs within their chosen field of study and the percentage of undergraduates who go on to graduate school. But is the only goal of obtaining a university education to obtain a job? What about concepts such as "learning how to learn" and "becoming a more enlightened member of society?" Deciding on the answers to these questions will determine what type of faculty the university will hire, what type of student programs it will develop, how it will market itself, and how it determines its success.

Other questions that need to be answered to determine the success of a university are, for example, how to measure the attributes of graduates that the

BUSINESS BRIEF 2-1 NO INPUTS MEAN NO PROCESS: PARTS SHORTAGE HALTS PRODUCTION

DETROIT—Ford Motor Corporation said a parts shortage at its Wixom, Michigan, luxury-car assembly plant resulted in 1 1/2 days of lost production for the automaker. A Ford spokeswoman said that a shortage of instrument panel parts halted production on Tuesday and Wednesday this week at its factory that builds the Lincoln Mark VIII, Town Car, and Continental models.

QUESTION

1. Comment on the plant closure for Ford Motor Corporation. Consider such issues as the logistics required to ensure that a sufficient quantity of all necessary parts is on hand, and the advantages and disadvantages of relying on suppliers to provide relatively small quantities of parts on short notice.

Just-in-Time

SOURCE: *The Wall Street Journal*, August 5, 1994, p. A4.

university believes are important. Should we use annual surveys of alumni? If a university has a low job placement rate but receives high marks from alumni, does it constitute reasonable acceptance of outputs? To the extent that testimonials from satisfied alumni help persuade prospective students to attend the university, alumni evaluations might be considered one measure of acceptance of outputs. But if the primary determinant factor for prospective students is job placement, then placement rates become a more compelling measure of output acceptance.

Two key managerial issues in achieving organizational responsiveness are understanding what the outputs of the organization are (or should be) and what characteristics those outputs must have to achieve high acceptance by the environment. Information technology can be used to track the acceptance of products. Many companies (such as Benetton and other retail and supermarket stores) collect sales data using point-of-sale (POS) systems. These information systems collect information directly from the cash registers of stores across a country, or around the world, as the products leave the store. Some systems not only track the customer acceptance of specific products but also generate strategies to affect future acceptance of those same products by triggering adjustments to inventory levels, orders to suppliers, coupons for future purchases, and data to determine whether a price promotion is called for.

Transformation Process

The **transformation process** is the series of activities that organizations use to turn inputs into outputs.[2] The transformation process is the key to the long-term survival of an organization. Developing a process that is flexible and efficient, and that produces goods and/or services that represent value to the organization's customers, is a critical strategic concern for management.

The transformation process includes the activities involved in making, packaging, and delivering a product or service. We cannot speak of a "best" or "optimal" transformation process for a whole industry. The appropriate transformation process

[2] The term *transformation* has recently been used to represent major structural changes within an organization. In this section, we use the term in the more traditional sense of a sequence of activities required to process inputs into outputs.

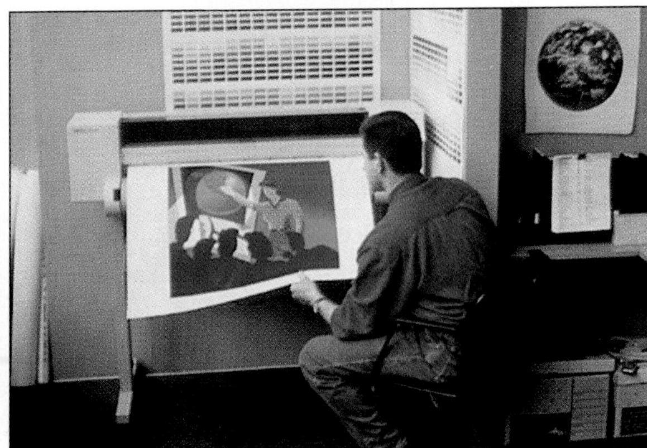

Outputs define why systems exist; they may take a variety of forms. Photos courtesy of Bonnie Kamin (top left), Ben Barnhart/Offshoot Stock (top right), Jim Brown/Offshoot Stock (bottom left), and Tony Stone Worldwide (bottom right).

is a function of the type of product or service you sell, and the type of market you are after. The process to produce and sell a Rolls-Royce is significantly different than the one used to produce a Ford Mondo; the products and experience of shopping at Wal-Mart are quite different from the products and experience of shopping at Neiman-Marcus; airlines "transport" first-class passengers differently than coach passengers; a top Ivy League business school uses a different process to educate MBA students than does a correspondence school. Specifically, Rolls-Royce produces a relatively small number of automobiles, the manufacturing process is very labor intensive, the cars can be customized to a large extent, and the salesrooms are plush; the Ford Mondo is produced in very high numbers, the manufacturing process is highly automated, the possibilities for customization are few, and the salesrooms are simple.

However, no matter what process you have in place, two critical characteristics of that process are its efficiency and its flexibility. The issue of **efficiency** involves the relationship between inputs and outputs; how many inputs (such as hours of labor) are required to produce a unit of output (such as an automobile or an insurance policy). The more efficient a company is, the fewer inputs it requires to produce the same level of outputs. Requiring less inputs is particularly important, since the availability of inputs is at times uncertain. The fewer the inputs (raw materials, number of employees, energy) the system needs to produce a given level

Companies such as Levi-Strauss analyze sales patterns daily to readjust production and inventory levels almost continuously. Photo courtesy of Levi-Strauss co.

of output, the lower is its dependency on the environment. Also, greater efficiency of the transformation process means lower costs.

The **flexibility** of the transformation process refers to the ease or difficulty of changing the outputs, both in terms of type and quantity. A manufacturer, for example, can improve flexibility by reducing the time it takes to alter the manufacturing line to assemble a different product or by increasing the number of products that come out of the same line.

Large automakers such as GM and Chrysler can change their production line to produce a new model in about one week. A decade ago, the changeover would have taken much longer. Toshiba has trained its workforce and automated its manufacturing for consumer electronics to the point where different products can be assembled on the same production line. Toshiba is able to alter the production levels of specific products without having to reset a whole production line or retrain its production employees.

Information technology facilitates the increased automation of production lines. More specifically, computerized machine tools that can be programmed with several different sequences of operations are a key to flexible manufacturing systems. These computerized machine tools read a bar code on the side of the parts to be worked on, which invokes the proper sequence of operations. Flexible manufacturing systems not only allow a greater number of options and variations in product, but also shrink the time needed to respond to customer demands.

Another example of I/T supporting the transformation process is that of a customer order fulfillment system. This type of system, which coordinates commitments from the sales department (such as price, volume, and delivery dates) with the production schedules of manufacturing departments, and at the same time manages inventory, can greatly improve the efficiency of the process and reduce the turnaround time on customer orders.

The products shown here come from the same production line at Toshiba. This flexibility allows Toshiba to react very quickly to changes in demand for any of these products. Photos courtesy of Toshiba.

Striving for a flexible and efficient transformation process should be a major concern of managers in their quest to achieve organizational responsiveness. It is important to note, however, that having a wonderfully flexible and efficient transformation process that generates products nobody wants will still lead to failure. Efficiency and flexibility in the transformation process are necessary, but not sufficient, characteristics to ensure responsiveness. Effective decision making on what to produce, when to produce it, and how to market it is just as important.

Decision Making

The primary criterion we are concerned with when we look at the decision-making subsystem of an organization is its **effectiveness.** Effectiveness means making the right decisions. Right decisions about what? Well, decisions about what products to make or what services to provide, and in what quantity. Decisions about how to price those products and services and whether or not to enter specific markets. Decisions about how to manufacture products or how to offer services.

The **decision-making subsystem** is the subsystem in charge of understanding the past and looking at the future. It is the subsystem that positions the organization in its environment and "reinvents" the organization, if need be. It is the subsystem responsible for organizational responsiveness, and ultimately the subsystem responsible for the success or failure of an organization.

Information technology plays a critical role in supporting the decision-making function in organizations. From sales reports to inventory management systems, to performance appraisal systems, to customer databases, I/T provides the input to the decision-making subsystem. Effective decision making is impossible, on a consistent basis, without timely and accurate information. More and more, effective decision making means making decisions fast, and acting before the competition does. As the amount of information increases and the sources of that information are spread around the globe, quick analysis of business threats and opportunities is possible only with some sort of I/T support in collecting, transmitting, and understanding data.

Information System

Knowing what the environment has been doing, is doing, and will be doing is critical to organizational responsiveness. There cannot be responsiveness without awareness. There cannot be awareness without information. Information about factors such as changes in customer preferences, about competitors' prices, and about the availability of raw materials is critical to an organization's functioning. Effective decision making requires information that is accurate, relevant, and timely. The responsibility of feeding such information to the decision-making subsystem falls on the information system (I/S) subsystem.

As part of its role in giving information to decision makers, the I/S subsystem provides **feedforward** and **feedback** support to the organization. Providing feedforward support means forecasting changes in the future and setting up goals, or planning. Providing feedback support means reporting on an event that has already happened and determining whether or not that event was predicted. This dual role of the I/S subsystem is also called search (for opportunities and challenges) and surveillance (or control) of events to check whether or not they occurred in ways that were planned.

Feedforward and feedback essentially keep managers informed as to whether the organization is understanding its environment and taking appropriate actions to stay in touch with it. We discuss these topics in more detail below.

THE DYNAMICS OF ORGANIZATIONAL RESPONSIVENESS

Organizations vary in their ability to adapt to changes in the environment. The degree of adaptability is a function of (1) the organization's understanding of its environment, and of (2) its learning how to modify internal processes to deal with those changes. Adaptability can be determined by assessing the organization on its homeostatic, feedback, and feedforward capabilities, and on its use of buffers to manage environmental change.

Homeostasis. Organizations strive for survival by addressing the major sources of uncertainty in their environment. Organizations tend to be in equilibrium with their environment, and when that equilibrium is broken they will try to reestablish it. The process of constantly attempting to be in equilibrium with the environment is called **homeostasis** (from *homeo,* meaning *almost like,* and *stasis* meaning *no change*).

The principle of homeostasis states that when the environment changes, the organization, once it is aware that the change has occurred, tries to match the change.

FIGURE 2–2 Homeostasis

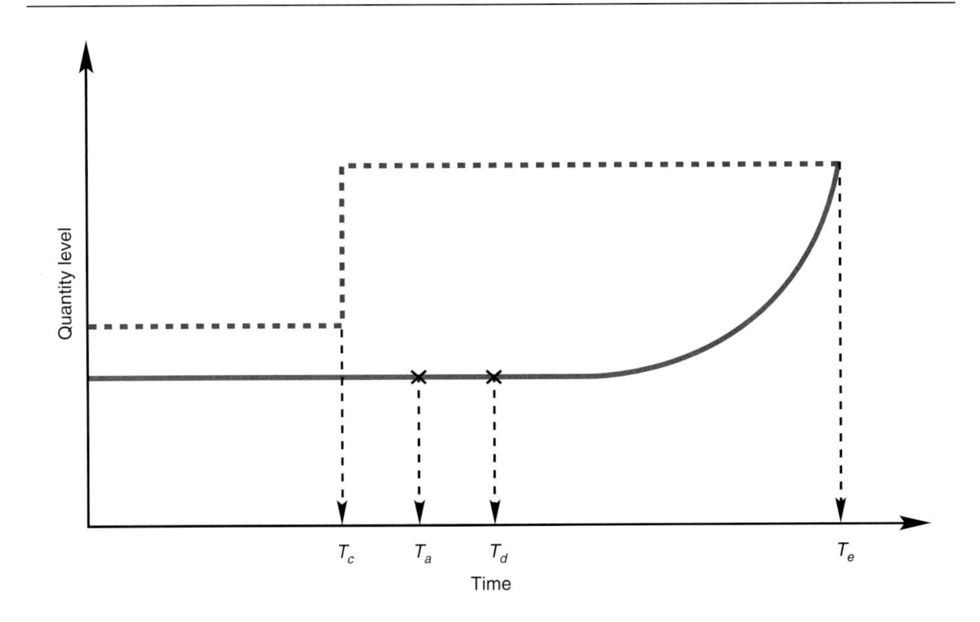

Organizations are not always successful in matching changes, and when they are, they usually match the change with a delay, or **time lag** (see Figure 2–2). The lag (the elapsed time between T_c and T_e in the figure) is a function of (1) the speed with which the change is recognized by the organization (the elapsed time between T_c and T_a in the figure); (2) the speed with which decisions are made on whether and how to match the change (the elapsed time between T_a and T_d in the figure); and (3) the time it takes the organization to match the change once the decision has been made to do so (the elapsed time between T_d and T_e in the figure). This last component of the lag represents the **inertia,** that is, the resistance to change inherent in the organization.

General Systems Theory argues that those organizations that respond with the shortest lag to changes in the environment have a better probability of survival. This means that organizations should attempt to minimize the time elapsed between T_c and T_e in Figure 2–2. Organizations can do it by constantly scanning their environment to recognize changes sooner (reducing the elapsed time $T_a - T_c$). Options include the use of point-of-sale systems, having contingency plans ready to minimize the decision time (reducing the elapsed time $T_d - T_a$), and having a flexible production system, with slack resources, to reduce the time necessary to match a change once the decision to do so has been made (reducing $T_e - T_d$).

Figure 2–2 shows an organization that reacts to a change in its environment. When an organization is in a *reactive* mode, a lag is inevitable no matter how responsive the organization is. Even when an organization manages a fast recognition

FIGURE 2–3 Homeostasis with Forecasting

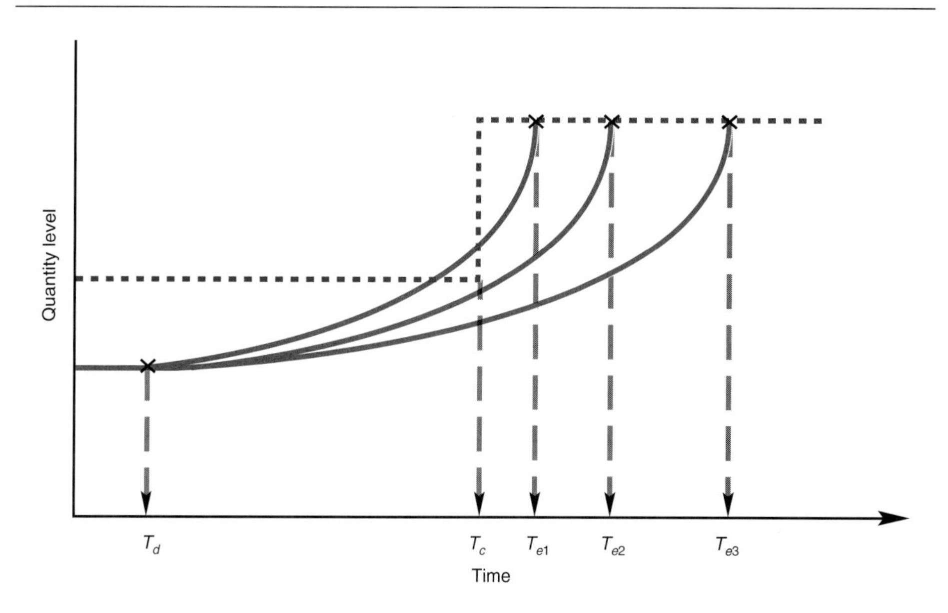

Demand level
Supply (system's output)
T_c = Time at which change in demand occurs
T_d = Time at which system has made a decision to act to match the change
$T_{e1,2,3}$ = Times at which the system is back in equilibrium with the environment depending on the inertia in the system

of the change, a quick decision time to do something about it, and a quick implementation of the chosen action, a lag will exist. The only way to banish the lag is to *forecast* the change in the environment and start the internal adaptation process some time before the change occurs.

Feedforward. When an organization is in a reactive mode, there is an obvious advantage to having the ability to quickly implement change (i.e., having low inertia). The same advantage exists when the organization is in a *proactive* mode. Figure 2–3 shows a hypothetical situation where an organization uses a feedforward system to forecast that a change will occur at time T_c , and decides to introduce the necessary internal changes. The three curves that start at T_d represent three levels of inertia in the organization. When the inertia is lowest, the organization reaches the new level of output just after the environment changes (T_{e1}); as the inertia increases, the organization reaches equilibrium with the environment with a substantial lag (T_{e2} and T_{e3}) even though it had an early forecast of the need to change.

Forecasting changes is difficult and risky. An inaccurate forecast can lead to situations such as excess capacity or large inventories of goods for which there is little demand (Figure 2–4). It is particularly difficult to forecast accurately far in advance of the event one is interested in; typically, the longer the forecast time horizon or lead time, the more uncertain the forecast is.

Another advantage of a flexible, responsive organization with low inertia is that it can wait longer before committing to an action to match a forecasted event. By

FIGURE 2–4 Flexibility and Forecasting Horizon

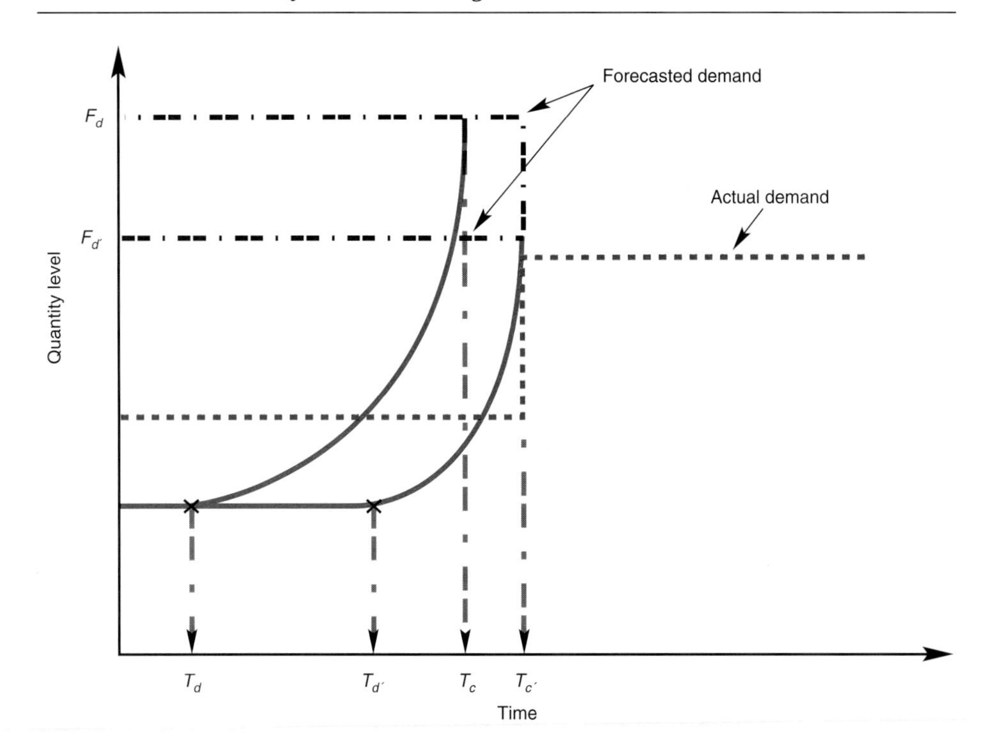

Actual demand level
Supply (system's output)
T_d = Time at which system makes a decision to adjust output and predicts change will occur at time T_c
F_d = Necessary output level forecasted at time T_d
T_c = Time at which change was forecasted to occur
$T_{d'}$ = Time at which system makes a decision to adjust output and predicts change will occur at time $T_{c'}$
$F_{d'}$ = Necessary output level forecasted at time $T_{d'}$
$T_{c'}$ = Time at which change was forecasted to occur (and actually does)

waiting longer, the time horizon of the forecast is shortened and its accuracy tends to increase. This is also shown in Figure 2–4, where you can see that $T_{d'} - T_{c'}$ is much shorter than $T_d - T_c$, reflecting a more flexible, responsive organization.

Consider the Kao Corporation, Japan's biggest soap and cosmetics company and the sixth largest in the world, with sales of over $5 billion annually. Kao's distribution system is based on an information system that allows the company and its wholly owned wholesalers to deliver goods within 24 hours to any of 280,000 shops, whose average order is just seven items. Kao's network virtually eliminates the lag between an event in the market (e.g., Mrs. Wanatabe buys a bar of soap) and the arrival of the news at the company. That makes Kao less dependent on sales forecasts and buffer inventory.

Business Brief 2–2 illustrates some of the opportunities, and dangers, of relying on forecasting. Electronic Arts decided that they were willing to gamble on the demand for CD-ROM video games expanding rapidly, while their competitor Acclaim Entertainment decided on waiting to see how the market developed. If Electronic Arts was correct, they could get a jump on the competition and capture a larger

BUSINESS BRIEF 2–2

ENVIRONMENTAL SCANNING: ELECTRONIC ARTS SHIFTS FOCUS TO CD-ROM

San Mateo, California—Electronic Arts Inc. is leaping into unchartered waters, and some of its shareholders are afraid of getting wet. The maker of entertainment software rode the home video-game cartridge boom to glory. But now that the business appears to be cresting, Electronic Arts is gambling that the next big wave will be games that use compact disk drives.

Retreating from the cartridge games that provide three-quarters of its revenue, Electronic Arts is pouring much of its effort into making titles for a new generation of game players equipped with CD-ROM drives. It says half of the 100 to 110 new titles it plans to release during the fiscal year ending next March [1995] will be made for CD-ROM, and that those CD games will account for 15 to 20 percent of its sales [about $400 million in 1994] compared with 5 percent in the latest year. By 1996, it expects CD-ROM games to account for nearly half of its sales [forecasted to be about $500 million].

The move is risky mainly because it could be premature. The size of the CD-ROM market still pales with that of the current generation of cartridge-based players found in 30 million homes. The cartridge player "is what's driving the business now," says Roger Goddu, executive vice president at Toys Я Us, the Paramus, N.J.-based retail chain.

Although most analysts believe the CD-ROM game market will begin exploding in two or three years, fewer than two million of the machines are now in use worldwide. And while the number of personal computers containing CD-ROM drives is expected to reach 11 million by the end of 1994, studies show many PC customers don't buy software not already included.

CD-ROM machines are also still much slower than the ones that use cartridges, which makes them less able to run the action games that dominate the video-game market. While advances are being made to increase their speed, analysts say computer microprocessors will have to gain radically in performance to attain the instant response time of a cartridge. They say this is likely to take at least two years.

Lawrence F. Probst II, Electronic Arts' chairman, says Electronic Arts is moving into CD-ROM quickly to get a head start on the competition. "Our strategy is to get there early, be prolific, and carve out market share," he says. Other analysts think Electronic Arts is doing the right thing by pulling back in the $6 billion cartridge market before it craters. Adds Michael Stanek, analyst at Piper Jaffray Inc. in Minneapolis: "If you're willing to overlook a topsy-turvy year, I think Electronic Arts has tremendous prospects for the next three to five years."

Electronic Arts' strategy is more ambitious than its competitors, who seem determined to milk the cartridge market. Acclaim Entertainment Inc. says less than one-fifth of its games will be written for CD-ROM machines in the next year. The Oyster Bay, N.Y., game maker says it, too, plans to eventually switch to CD-ROM, but only when the market is big. "Worst case, it means you are second to the party as opposed to first," says Robert Holmes, Acclaim's president.

QUESTIONS

1. Use Figures 2–3 and 2–4 to discuss the situation described above. What quantity levels are being forecasted by Electronic Arts? How lengthy are the lead times involved?
2. The listed price for Electronic Arts common stock dropped from a high of nearly $30 per share in January, 1994 to a low of about $14 in June, 1994. In September, 1994 it was trading at about $17.50. Would you have advised purchasing shares at that price, at that time? What is the share price for Electronic Arts today?
3. Assume you were the portfolio manager for a large mutual investment fund focusing on growth stocks at the time the article was written, and you were looking to beef up your technology holdings. If you had to select between Electronic Arts and Acclaim Entertainment, which would you have chosen? What additional information would help you make a choice?

Source: Jim Carlton, staff reporter, *The Wall Street Journal*, September 7, 1994, p. B4. Reprinted by permission of *The Wall Street Journal*, © 1994 Dow Jones & Company, Inc. All rights reserved worldwide.

BUSINESS BRIEF 2-3 THE RISKS OF FORECASTING DEMAND: IBM SELLS OUT NEW APTIVA PC

Just three weeks after announcing its new Aptiva home computer line, International Business Machines Corp. (IBM) is sold out through year end and can't fill all of its holiday orders.

The shortage, which IBM attributes to conservative forecasting, means the company could forgo tens of millions of dollars in revenue in the all-important fourth quarter, when home PC sales are hottest. It shows that IBM has yet to solve its chronic problem of miscalculating demand for its personal computers, which contributed to IBM's drop in U.S. market share to fourth place this year from a near tie for No. 1 in 1993.

For the Aptiva launch, IBM had planned to ship up to 125,000 PCs by the end of the year, industry executives say. But retailers now are believed to have ordered well over 200,000 units. That means IBM may be giving up potential revenue of more than $100 million. IBM has had similar supply problems with its popular ThinkPad series of portable computers, with the highest-priced models in short supply since their introduction two years ago.

G. Richard Thoman, the senior vice president in charge of IBM's personal computer unit, said he imposed a conservative plan for the Aptiva rollout. IBM last year was burned by overly aggressive forecasts for the ValuePoint line, which bloated its inventory to about $700 million in unsold PCs and forced it to resort to steep discounts. The fire sale is part of the reason why IBM's PC unit hasn't been profitable this year, analysts say.

Industry analysts say IBM also shipped too many of the predecessor model of the Aptiva, called the PS/1, in last year's fourth quarter, giving it another reason to be cautious this year. In addition, the PS/1 oversupply strained relations with some retail chains, which were stuck with unsold machines. That may have led retailers to place smaller advance orders when IBM was planning the Aptiva launch months ago, said Richer Zwetchkenbaum, an analyst at International Data Corporation..

Now that dealers have seen the Aptiva line and tasted the initial response from consumers, orders have suddenly surged. Some of the demand may stem from retailers who, fearing a shortage, sent in double orders. But it will take a few months to step up production. IBM's Mr. Thoman said in an interview that IBM should be able to catch up with Aptiva demand by January, which he said is a strong sales month for consumer PCs though not as strong as the fourth-quarter holiday season.

IBM's cautious planning contrasts sharply with that of Compaq Computer, the rival that has jumped past IBM this year to take the top spot in PC shipments. Compaq has built up a huge inventory of computers in anticipation of a strong holiday sales period. At the beginning of the third quarter, Compaq's inventory was at a daunting $2.2 billion, alarming some analysts.

But Mr. Thoman said he views Compaq's strategy as too risky. Building up inventory can force a manufacturer to discount prices if sales don't meet expectations, which can anger consumers who bought at the higher prices only months earlier. "The downside of producing too much is you cheapen the brand" through price cuts, he said.

QUESTION

1. Use concepts from this chapter to contrast the strategies of IBM and Compaq with respect to their use of finished-goods inventories.

SOURCE: Bart Ziegler, *The Wall Street Journal,* October 1, 1994, p. B4. Reprinted by permission of *The Wall Street Journal,*

portion of a growing market. If their forecasting was incorrect, they could have lost ground in their existing market. With hindsight, Electronic Arts was accurate in their forecast; at the time, however, their decision was quite risky.

Feedforward systems are designed to scan the environment for changes that may have some influence on, or present some opportunity for, the organization. Feedforward systems are forecasting systems that support the creation of different scenarios about future environmental conditions.

Forecasting is a particularly risky proposition in turbulent markets. Consider the situation IBM found themselves in, as they attempted to forecast demand for their Aptiva personal computers (see Business Brief 2–3).

On the other hand, good forecasting can provide a competitive advantage to a firm by allowing that firm to position itself favorably to take advantage of changes in the environment. For example, the development and introduction of video-on-demand (VOD) services could have major implications for the video rental business. VOD is a service where feature-length movies are stored on a computer database system, and distributed through cable to individual homes. The customer selects a movie from a menu, and it is copied into a special box attached to their television set. They can then view the movie with the same options as they could with a videotape (pause, reverse, etc.). At the time of writing, this service was being offered on a test basis to a limited number of homes in a small region of the country.

If you are the owner of a video rental store, how important is it for you to be aware of VOD? Among other things, your feedforward system could involve reading business magazines that discuss the development of the VOD technology, or belonging to an industry (video rental) association that publishes periodic newsletters. If you are aware of VOD as it develops and moves into the market, you should be able to plan accordingly. For example, if you believe that VOD is going to remain very expensive for the next decade, you might decide to continue to stay with video rental and compete on price. If you believe that VOD is going to destroy the video rental industry within your geographic region within the next two years, you might decide to sell your entire stock of videos to a competitor who doesn't have a feedforward system.

Feedback. The simplest definition of feedback is providing information about a past event. A more interesting and useful definition of feedback is providing information about a past event to determine whether the event was better or worse than expected. Effective feedback is a message that either confirms that the conditions are as expected or, if they are not, a message that allows the organization to understand how it needs to change its behavior to adjust to those conditions.

Providing useful feedback requires a definition of the critical variables of performance to be monitored, a set of conditions or limits around those variables, and the appropriate measures or indicators of those variables of interest to the organization (e.g., market penetration and share, customer loyalty, innovation, financial resources, profit, productivity). Providing feedback also implies understanding the internal workings of the organization to know to whom the feedback should be provided.

To provide feedback, **sensors** must be in place to detect changes in those indicators. **Standards** or **goals** and **tolerance levels** must be developed to determine whether those changes are significant. The measure taken by the sensor is compared to the goal to determine if there is a difference and whether the difference is significant or not. A plan of action has to be specified in response to significant deviations from the standards. This plan of action may or may not be automatically invoked. An "owner" has to be identified. Owners are the individuals responsible for the corrective action being taken, or those managers whose areas are affected by the corrective action.

Figure 2–5 describes the components of a feedback system. In the figure we have assumed that the inventory level for a product has been fluctuating between its preplanned limits of acceptability for some time, but then at time T_o, the level goes beyond the predetermined upper tolerance level. Note that we have also assumed that the feedback system is not scanning continuously, but at regular intervals. After comparing the measurement to the predetermined limits, the system reports that the level of inventory is out of control at time T_i, when the inventory is now well beyond the upper tolerance limit. A certain time passes ($T_c - T_i$) before a corrective action

FIGURE 2–5 Feedback

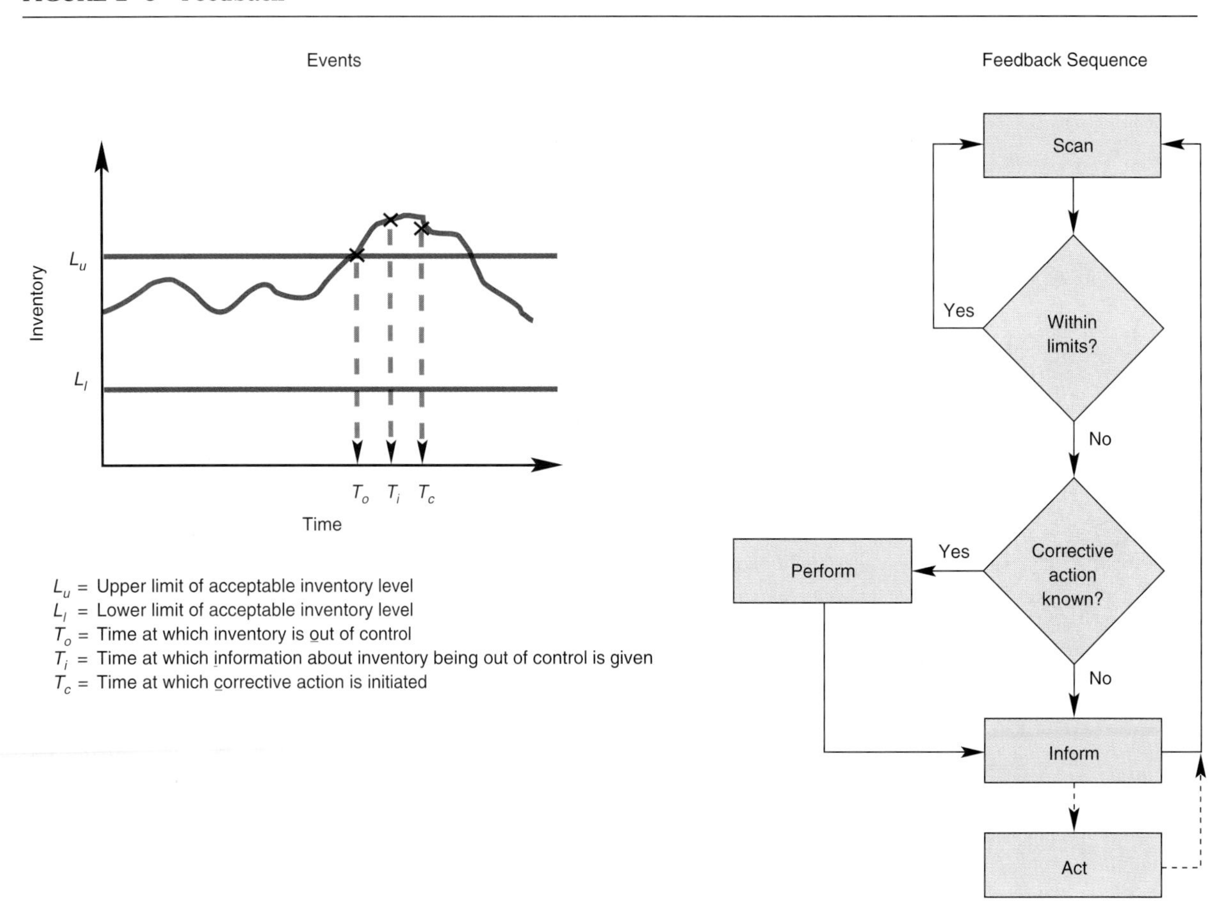

is taken at time T_c. The corrective action is effective and the inventory level starts to fall back to an acceptable level.

With this example in mind, we can start designing a feedback system. First of all, we need to determine how we are going to measure the inventory level. This decision includes the method, the frequency, the accuracy, and the time at which we are going to take that measure. Then, we need to determine what are unacceptably low and high levels of inventory. After the measurement has been taken, it has to be compared with the predetermined tolerance levels. If the measurement is within those levels, then the feedback system goes back to scanning and measuring. However, if the measurement is outside of the levels, then a corrective action has to be taken.

The next step depends on the "intelligence" of the feedback system. If the system has a database of rules, or knowledge-base (e.g., a rule could be the following: if inventory of blue shoes with red heels reaches upper limit, then lower the price by 25 percent), then it can take corrective action automatically without human intervention. After taking the corrective action, the system informs a predetermined set of managers. The advantage of building such a knowledge-base is that the speed of response can be higher (e.g., no need to track down a human decision maker). However, building such databases takes time, and requires the ability and expertise to build a variety of scenarios. If the system does not have such

The law of requisite variety says that for every action, there needs to be a specific reaction. Photos courtesy of Bonnie Kamin (left) and Ben Barnhart/Offshoot Stock (right).

a knowledge-base, or if it does but the set of circumstances is not in the knowledge-base, then the feedback system informs the predetermined managers so that the necessary corrective action can be taken.

In designing a feedback system, we should keep in mind the **law of requisite variety.** This law says that, in order to have an effective feedback system, the system needs to recognize every possible event of interest and know how to respond to it. To illustrate the law, let's use a sport analogy. In football, the defensive team needs to "read" the offensive formation of the opponent team to adjust its own formation (and vice versa). Defensive coordinators spend the whole week before the game identifying the different formations or "looks" that the opponent uses. They then instruct the defensive team that when a certain formation occurs, they should adjust accordingly. The law of requisite variety implies that the defensive team should have at least as many specified actions as the offensive team has formations, otherwise there may be situations when the defensive team does not know what to do. This same principle applies to the opening moves in chess games.

In short, the design of a feedback system includes not only decisions on how often, how quickly, and in how much detail the sensing must be performed, but it also includes a knowledge-base and the identification of a different set of managers to be informed of the situation, depending on the circumstances.

An everyday example of a feedback system is a classroom thermostat coupled to a furnace. The temperature of the classroom is set to stay at 70 degrees Fahrenheit. If the room temperature falls below this target temperature, the thermostat sends a signal to the furnace to heat the room. When the temperature rises above the target, the thermostat shuts off the heat.

This example of a feedback system may sound trivial, but it's not as simple as it seems. Consider the following issues. Where should the sensor be placed? Should it be by the door, by a window, in the back of the room? Should we have only one sensor or several? How accurate should the sensors be? If the temperature is outside the desired range, who should be informed?

The answers to these questions are obviously linked to the goals you want to achieve. For example, the number and accuracy of the sensors would be higher if, instead of a classroom, we were talking about a laboratory where experiments needing a constant temperature are conducted. The ideal situation is to put an infinite number of sensors to capture the most detailed information possible.

However, that tends to be very expensive. In general, one would place sensors (whether temperature sensors, customer satisfaction questionnaires, or sales-tracking systems) in locations representative of the universe you are interested in measuring. It is advisable to install several sensors (not only to get a fuller picture of the situation you are interested in controlling but also to eliminate the vulnerability of relying on only one sensor), and average their readings.

The decisions on how accurate and how many sensors to install in a given situation should be based on a cost/benefit analysis, in which the frequency and accuracy of those measurements are a function of cost. The more frequent and accurate the measurements, the more expensive the measuring device and overhead; however, the benefits can certainly overcome the costs (e.g., temperature fluctuations could spoil experiments in a lab and be very costly).

Another consideration is the goal you are trying to achieve. For example, if your goal is to maximize people's comfort, then the place to put the sensor of the thermostat is where people are sitting. If, on the other hand, your goal is to minimize costs, then the sensor should be placed in a spot where the temperature changes the least.

These questions of placement, accuracy, and frequency of measurement are also applicable to business settings. A feedback system might involve computerized inventory records with programmed reorder levels, point-of-sale recording of sales with automatic reduction of inventory levels, and automatic reordering of stock. Some of the issues that will need to be settled include the following: If we wish to track sales of a particular product, how are we going to do it? Are we going to track sales in every store that sells our product, or just in a handful of stores we believe are representative of the rest? How often should we track sales—every day, once a week, once a month?

Hydro-Quebec (a major electric utility) has developed a sophisticated monitoring system that keeps track of 40,000 pieces of equipment at all times. Each piece of equipment has a sensor that sends a message concerning the status of the equipment every second. This data is stored in a centralized database, and is monitored constantly by an operator at Hydro-Quebec headquarters using a computer system. When a breakdown occurs, say a storm brings down some power lines, up to 15,000 alarms can be triggered in the first few seconds.

These alarms used to appear on the operator's screen in chronological order. The display was overwhelming, and not very helpful to the operator who then needed to make sense of all that data to identify a probable cause for the breakdown. Today, Hydro-Quebec has installed a diagnosis system that interprets the data for the operator and selectively displays on his/her screen the relevant alarms and suggests alternatives to bring the system back up. The rules used by the system have been proposed by the most experienced operators and engineers at Hydro-Quebec. The system behaves, in effect, as if this group of experienced operators and engineers were available to the operator at all times. This type of system is called an *expert system* because it follows the rules of experts. It is also an example of an intelligent feedback system.

Buffers. Traditionally, organizations have protected themselves from changes in the environment by developing **buffers.** These buffers can take the form of long-term contracts with suppliers or customers, of slack resources (such as excess capacity), or of inventories of raw material or finished product. Buffers can also take the form of strategies to absorb the impact of changes in demand, price competition, or

Hydro-Quebec has developed a sophisticated monitoring system that keeps track of 40,000 sensors that send messages about the status of the equipment every second. Photos courtesy of Hydro-Quebec, Montreal.

availability of resources. One such strategy is vertical integration (buying suppliers) or horizontal integration (buying competitors), which is an attempt at redefining the boundaries of the organization to eliminate a source of uncertainty (variable prices of supplies; tough competition). Developing and implementing buffers allows a system to buy time before a change in the environment actually affects its operations. In a way, buffers move the system toward the "closed" end of the classification of systems continuum.

In the past, the process of protecting the business from changes in the environment was seen as an effective way to run an efficient operation. However, management theory has changed its views on attempts to close the organization to the environment. The current view is that you cannot close the organization forever, and that closing the organization (i.e., using large buffers) is at best a temporary solution. Using buffers can induce a false sense of security, and can inhibit the organization in making necessary improvements of increased responsiveness and efficiency.

Today's management philosophy is that closing the organization to the environment is not the way to create a viable enterprise in the long run. The best way is to be open to changes in the environment, and to deal with those changes with greater organizational responsiveness through greater flexibility and better assessment of the customer's needs.

An interesting example of the negative effects of creating buffers to protect a firm from environmental turbulence is the policy of devaluating the currency in

Inventories are common buffers in manufacturing. Photo courtesy of Russ Schleipman/Offshoot Stock.

certain countries during the last decade. These countries, whose industries were under pressure from global competition, would devaluate their currency on a regular basis to keep those industries afloat and to avoid the social disruptions from the resulting unemployment if those industries went bankrupt.

Although the devaluation brought temporary relief to their industries, more often than not it also lulled them into complacency. The industries, rather than invest in their transformation process and R&D to become more competitive, would just wait for the next currency devaluation. In addition, the devaluation (1) created inflationary pressures that accelerated the erosion of the buffer, and (2) forced the competitors from other countries to become more efficient. The currency devaluation, though effective in the short term, was counterproductive in the long term. And so it is with many buffers.

SUMMARY

This chapter introduced the primary concept of organizational responsiveness. It also introduced General Systems Theory (GST), which is a framework for understanding how organizations operate and try to stay in touch with their environment.

An organization adjusts to, and sometimes anticipates, changes in the environment. Organizations may operate on a continuum from open to closed, with open organizations being much more vulnerable to environmental change or turbulence, and closed organizations being self-contained entities that can afford to be more lax about changes in the environment. The concepts of General Systems Theory are useful in understanding the critical need for organizations to process information quickly and accurately.

Buffers (e.g., long-term contracts and large inventories) help organizations protect themselves from changes in the environment. Previously, organizations attempted to become less vulnerable (more closed) to changes in the environment by building buffers. Current management philosophies recommend using flexible transformation processes and effective feedback and feedforward systems to be more open and responsive to environmental change.

GST can help identify areas for information system development, such as sources of uncertainty and targets for surveillance (feedback) and search (feedforward). GST can also be used as an analogy for designing an effective information system (inputs must be available, the transformation process must be efficient and flexible, decision making must be effective, and outputs must be accepted, i.e., useful).

To achieve organizational responsiveness, managers have to reduce the uncertainty that exists in their environment. The key to reducing uncertainty is having accurate and timely information. In turbulent environments, the quantity of data and the speed at which the data changes is such that managers cannot keep track of it without information technology. One example could be a point-of-sales system which records transactions as they occur, updating inventory records and alerting managers to unexpected sales trends.

KEY CONCEPTS AND TERMS

KEY CONCEPTS

- Organizations need to adapt to changes in their environment. (33)
- More responsive organizations are more successful. (33)
- Responsiveness implies both awareness and action. (33)
- Managerial energies should focus on ensuring the availability of inputs, the acceptance of outputs, the effectiveness of decision making, and the efficiency and flexibility of the transformation process. (42)
- Information technology plays a key role in helping organizations be responsive to their environments by supporting feedback and feedforward systems. (51)

KEY TERMS

buffers (58)
closed system (42)
decision making (48)
decision-making subsystem (48)
effectiveness (48)
efficiency (46)
environment (36)
environmental scanning (33)
environmental turbulence (40)
feedback (49)
feedforward (49)
flexibility (47)
General Systems Theory (35)
goal (36)
homeostasis (49)
inertia (50)
input (36)
law of requisite variety (57)
local rationality (38)
open system (42)
organizational responsiveness (33)
output (36)
proactive (36)
sensor (55)
standard (55)
subsystem (36)
system (36)
time lag (50)
tolerance level (55)
transformation process (45)
transforms (36)
turbulence (40)

REFERENCES

Cavaleri, S., and K. Obloj. *Management Systems: A Global Perspective.* Belmont, Calif.: Wadsworth Publishing Company, 1993.

Churchman, C. W. *The Systems Approach.* New York: Dell Publishing, 1968.

Kast, F. E., and J. E. Rosenzweig. "General Systems Theory: Applications for Organizations and Management." *Academy of Management Journal,* December 1972, pp. 447–65.

Mockler, R. J. "The Systems Approach to Business Organization and Decision Making." *California Management Review* 11 (2), 1968, pp. 53–58.

Schoderbek, P. P.; C. G. Schoderbek; and A. G. Kefalas. *Management Systems: Conceptual Considerations.* 4th ed. Homewood, Ill: BPI/Irwin Publishing, 1990.

Young, S. "The 'Total Systems' Approach." *California Management Review* 11 (2), 1968, pp. 21–32.

CONNECTIVE CASE: Creative Aerospace, Inc.

Creative Aerospace, Inc. (CAI) employs 10,000 people worldwide, including those located at its headquarters in California. CAI specializes in small airplanes and related products for two primary markets: For the defense market, CAI produces reconnaissance planes. For the airline market, it sells commuter planes for trips covering distances shorter than 500 miles.

CAI interacts only minimally with its customers. Its strategic plans are created every five years, and managers and engineers stick to them through thick and thin. The plans are formally reviewed every two years. The saying at CAI is that if the world and the strategic plan do not match, the world must be wrong. Although the company has enjoyed strong profits and a good reputation for quality during most of its 70-year history, the last three years have shown losses.

CAI did not have very good working relationships with its suppliers, and has had problems in the past obtaining the necessary raw materials. Consequently, CAI had resorted to ordering parts and raw materials in large quantities because of coordination problems. CAI had very high on-hand stock of parts and a high rate of waste—currently many parts become obsolete and need to be discarded. Even with the large inventories, in the last year the production line had to be stopped five times because of a lack of parts.

For years CAI made the best airplanes, and had a dominant share in its market segments. Though CAI was never known for being close to its customers, engineers raved about CAI products. For many years price was not an issue. The end of the cold war, however, brought drastic reductions in defense spending. Similarly, deregulation of the domestic airline industry resulted in price wars, mergers, and consolidations which slowed down the spending on new airplanes. As a result, CAI found itself in a market where pricing had become extremely aggressive. CAI was also facing increased foreign competition, as more airplane manufacturers fought over a temporarily shrinking market.

Government regulations played an important part in this industry. For one thing, the U.S. government, a large customer of CAI, raised the quality standards in the mid-80s on all of its aerospace projects. CAI responded by instituting a major quality movement in 1991 which had improved the quality of its manufacturing process and products for its customers, including the U.S. government. However, the government could change the required specifications and standards at any time, and often did so without much lead time.

Other examples of regulations were the constraints and restrictions CAI faced in selling its products to foreign countries, and environmental regulations. Environmental regulations had hit CAI pretty hard, since its main manufacturing plant was less modern and more polluting than those of its competitors. The only way CAI could fulfill the regulations was by running its plant at less than 80 percent of capacity.

CAI was one of the last aerospace companies to implement computer-aided design (CAD) and computer-aided manufacturing (CAM) software. CAD/CAM software provided the flexibility to make modifications to original plans and assess the impact on manufacturing and scheduling very quickly. There were a number of reasons for the slow implementation. First, the company did not actively look for ways to improve their design process. It was a year after sophisticated CAD/CAM software was introduced before anyone at CAI was even aware of it.

The CAI managers at the time didn't have any knowledge about the new technology. Some believed that CAD would not be a major quality improvement over their existing drafting systems, and so they didn't believe it would affect their business. It took almost six months to get managers to attend a meeting to discuss whether a change in technology was needed. It was a full 14 months after they became aware of CAD software that they actually decided to use it. Once the decision was made, it took another eight months to evaluate different systems on the market, and then acquire a CAD system and integrate it into their existing operations. Another three months went by before the required level of quality was reached. At this point, many of their competitors had been using CAD/CAM systems for more than a year and had been able to respond to their customers' needs much better.

Case Question

1. Use the concepts of General Systems Theory to comment and analyze the situation at Creative Aerospace, Inc. Be thorough.

CASE ANALYSIS

Creative Aerospace, Inc. is operating in an *environment* that has become increasingly *turbulent*. Government regulations are changing more quickly, it has more foreign competitors to deal with, new technology is being introduced to the industry, and customer preferences are changing. When customers began demanding higher quality and lower costs, CAI was slow to respond. As a result, its products (*outputs*) were no longer being readily *accepted*.

CAI does not have a very *flexible* production (*transformation*) process. As a result, it tries to use inventories of parts as a *buffer* against changes in customer demands. This strategy doesn't work very well, as inaccurate forecasts lead to the need to dispose of stock that has become obsolete. We are also told that it has to run its main production facility at less than 80 percent of capacity, which is not a very *efficient* use of resources.

CAI's *environmental scanning* also appears to be inadequate. Managers were slow to realize that computer-aided design (CAD) and computer-aided manufacturing (CAM) systems were being adopted by their competitors. The *time lag* between when they realized that CAD/CAM systems might be useful (time T_a from Figure 2–2) and when they actually began using such systems productively (time T_e from Figure 2–2) was a little over two years, putting CAI behind its competitors. This suggests a high level of *inertia* in the organization, making it slow to react to changes.

There are a number of ways that CAI might attempt to improve. Management needs to institute some type of *feedback* system that monitors customer preferences. This might be accomplished by building closer links with customers, perhaps even having customers become part of the design process. To improve the *flexibility* and *efficiency* of its *transformation* process, CAI might need to consider investing in new production facilities.

Building closer ties to its suppliers is also important, so that CAI can reduce the costs of carrying excess inventories and avoid production shutdowns. Rather than attempting to build *buffers*, managers need to improve their *forecasting* capabilities.

SOURCE: This case was written by Associate Professors Ronald Thompson and William Cats-Baril of the School of Business Administration, University of Vermont. It is loosely based on Harvard University's "Aerospace Technology Manufacturing, Inc." This case is an amalgamation of situations found in several firms, rather than a representation of a specific company.

IT'S YOUR TURN | END OF CHAPTER MATERIALS

REVIEW QUESTIONS

1. Briefly explain the concept of organizational responsiveness.
2. What is the relationship between the level of environmental turbulence and the need for an effective feedforward system?
3. Give four examples of elements in the environment that most companies need to be aware of.
4. Explain the concept of local rationality.
5. Briefly describe what is meant by environmental scanning.
6. Differentiate between open and closed systems. Give an example of an organization that is very open and one that is very closed, and explain why you would classify them as such.
7. Give three examples of buffers that can be used by an organization.
8. List the primary elements of a system, as described in this chapter.
9. List the questions managers need to ask themselves to assess organizational responsiveness.
10. List the elements of a feedback system.

DISCUSSION QUESTIONS

1. In what way(s) does General Systems Theory provide a useful framework for understanding organizations?
2. Describe in detail an example of a feedback system (other than those provided in the chapter). Draw a diagram of the system.
3. How does the addition of "intelligence" (decision rules) change a feedback system? Who would you involve in developing those decision rules?
4. Compare the first 25 companies in the Fortune 500 lists from 1980 and today.
   a. Pick two companies that have disappeared and research and comment on the reasons for their failure.
   b. Pick two companies that have burst onto the lists and research and comment on the reasons for their success.
5. The argument has been made that General Systems Theory is too general to be of much use. Comment on this statement.
6. The Benetton example at the beginning of the chapter describes its inventory control system to keep track of sales around the world. Identify another type of organization that could use a similar system, and discuss how such a system would work (what information would need to be collected, where the information would originate and where it would need to be transferred, and so on).

GROUP ASSIGNMENT

As a group, select a company that, after being successful for a certain period of time, got into serious financial trouble or lost major market share and then recovered. Use the Internet and your library resources to obtain additional information concerning the company. Use a wordprocessing system to prepare a brief description of the history of the company (its initial success, its decline, its recovery) using General Systems Theory terminology (see the CAI analysis in this chapter for suggestions).

APPLICATION ASSIGNMENTS

1. Select one of the following companies: Burger King, McDonald's, Kentucky Fried Chicken, Taco Bell, or Wendy's. Obtain annual sales and profit information for each of the past five years (your school library and company home pages on the Internet should be able to help you obtain this information). Using an electronic spreadsheet package, enter the data and then print a graph showing

sales versus profits. Use your word processor to write a one-page memorandum discussing the environmental factors involved in explaining the sales and profit graphs.

2. Use a presentation package (e.g., PowerPoint) or word processor to prepare three overhead transparency masters. The first should introduce the organization you selected for question 1, and contain an image from the company's home page or web site (copy the image and import it into your word processor or presentation software). The second should briefly describe the company using the elements of General Systems Theory (see Figure 2–2); the third should show the graph created in question 1.
3. Send an E-mail message to your instructor that identifies the company you selected for question 1 and its World Wide Web address.

CASE ASSIGNMENT The Norris Company (A): Keeping Up with the Competition

At approximately 7:30 AM on June 23, Sherry Craig, manager of the Norris Company's central plant, swung her car out of the driveway of her suburban home and headed toward the plant located some 10 miles away just inside the city limits. It was a beautiful day. The sun was shining brightly and a cool, fresh breeze was blowing. The trip to the plant took about 20 minutes and sometimes gave Sherry an opportunity to think about plant problems without interruption.

Sherry Craig had started with the Norris Company as an expediter in its Eastern plant in 1982 just after she graduated from Ohio State. After three years Sherry was promoted to production supervisor and two years later was made assistant to the manager of the Eastern plant. Early in 1993, she was transferred to the Central plant as assistant to the plant manager and one month later was promoted to plant manager, when the former manager retired.

The Norris Company owned and operated three quality printing plants. Norris enjoyed a nationwide commercial business, specializing in quality color work. It was a closely held company with some 350 employees, nearly half of whom were employed at the Central plant in Ohio, the largest of the three Norris production operations. The company's main offices were also located in the Central plant building.

Although the company had been successful over its 30-year history, the past two years had seen declining profits, and the forecast for the current fiscal year was not promising. The company prided itself on providing very high-quality, customized products, which was important in the commercial printing industry. Most customers demanded very high quality, and the introduction of increasingly sophisticated printing machines made it easier for printing companies to respond to these demands. Innovations such as six-color printers (instead of four-color) and the electronic storage of typeset images had changed the industry significantly.

By storing images electronically, printers could now respond to customers' requests for changes to previous jobs by retrieving the previous image electronically, rather than starting from scratch. This feature also helped with quality control, since customers could view an electronic image of the final product and approve it or request modifications. Previously, printers had to print a "proof," provide it to the customer for approval, and possibly go through two or three iterations before reaching a satisfactory proof to be put into production. This process was time consuming and expensive, but was still used by those printers who had not invested in the newer, computerized printing machines. The new technology also removed the advantage of firms that were physically close to their customers. Firms could now download proofs onto the customers' systems for review and feedback even if they were three time zones away. Norris found itself competing with five or six new printing companies that had never encroached on its markets before.

The customers' expectations of quality and service had been changing continuously for the last decade. Currently, those expectations were driven by rapid response to requests and by receiving accurate price quotes. As the printing industry became more sophisticated with computerized printing machines and computer-based job-tracking and job-estimating systems, competitors of Norris attempted to gain market share by providing better service and higher-quality products. The industry norm changed from charging on a "cost-plus" basis (adding a profit margin after the job was done) to providing a "plus-or-minus" quote (a specific amount with a small percentage for margin of error) up front. If the printing company underestimated the cost of a job, it would have to take the loss.

The customers' emphasis on the quality of the printing jobs had reached a level that caught Norris somewhat off guard. Over the past three years more jobs were returned because of unsatisfactory printing quality, and Norris had to absorb the lost revenue when it improved the quality and ran the jobs again. Unfortunately, rerunning the jobs took extra time, which also dissatisfied the customers. At this point the company had established no clear procedures on how often or at what points in the production process the jobs should be inspected; it was pretty much up to all foremen to decide for themselves.

The rate of technological innovation for the industry seemed to be increasing, with new systems and printers becoming available on a regular basis. It was frequently difficult for Norris Company to keep up with all the new possibilities, let alone decide whether to adopt them. A good example was the introduction of electronic (as opposed to mechanical) typesetting. As personal computers and software matured during the 1980s, some customers began doing simpler document set-up tasks on their own. Eventually many customers had the in-house capabilities to do fairly sophisticated typesetting, and were no longer willing to pay printing companies to do this for them. In addition, the customers expected the printing companies to have systems that would allow them to accept the electronic versions from the customer on diskette, and then print the jobs. This trend affected smaller printing companies first, but as customers became more sophisticated and gained more in-house expertise, the larger companies had to respond as well.

Norris was one of the last national printing companies to accept electronically typeset documents and proofs from customers. There were a number of reasons for this. First, the company did not adopt personal computers internally very quickly, and employees of Norris did not keep up on the rapidly changing capabilities of personal computer–based software. It was a full year after Apple Computer Company introduced reasonably sophisticated publishing software for the Macintosh computer before anyone at Norris was aware of it. Second, even after the plant managers at Norris became aware of the personal computer trends they were slow to react. The managers at the time didn't have any knowledge about the new technology. Some believed that electronic typesetting with personal computers could never come close to matching the quality of their existing commercial systems, and so they didn't believe it would affect their business.

It took almost six months to get managers to attend a meeting to discuss whether a change in technology was needed. It was a full 18 months after they became aware of PC-based typesetting that they actually decided to accept jobs from customers rather than insist on doing all of the typesetting themselves. Once the decision was made, it took another eight months to evaluate different systems on the market, select those that would be compatible with most of Norris's customers, and then acquire the systems and integrate them into the existing operations. Another three months went by before the typesetters were able to reach the required level of quality. At this point, many competitors had been offering similar services for more than a year.

Another change in the industry revolved around supplies and suppliers. As customers asked for more fast-turnaround, high-quality, customized jobs using nonstandard materials, it became more difficult to forecast demand and to stock supplies. Norris managers had a policy of buying supplies in large quantities two or three times a year in the open market, that is, buying supplies from whatever company had the lowest prices. However, now they frequently found themselves frantically calling suppliers to try and locate specialized materials on short notice, and on four instances during the last quarter they had to delay production for lack of the necessary materials.

Sherry was in reasonably good spirits as she relaxed behind the wheel. Despite some recent hardships, it seemed that the company might be on the road to recovery. She began to mentally run through the day's work, first one project, then another, trying to establish priorities. One issue that needed attention was finding a way to do a better job of keeping tabs on competitors and customers. Norris had been very late in accepting electronically typeset images from customers; the delay had seriously damaged relationships with some customers, and Sherry wanted to make sure that fiasco wasn't repeated.

Questions

1. Use the concepts of General Systems Theory discussed in this chapter to analyze the situation at Norris. Be thorough; use the CAI analysis as a guide.
2. Put yourself in the position of Sherry Craig. Use the concepts of General Systems Theory to help describe what you believe Norris needs to do to survive and grow in the future.

SOURCE: This case was written by Associate Professors Ronald Thompson and William Cats-Baril of the School of Business Administration, University of Vermont. It is loosely based on Northwestern University's "The Case of the Missing Time." This case is an amalgamation of situations found in several firms, rather than a representation of a specific company.

CHAPTER 3 Decision Making Within Organizations

CHAPTER OBJECTIVES

After reading this chapter, you should have a better understanding of the complexities and difficulties of making decisions within an organizational setting, as well as an understanding of the ways that information technology can be used to address some of these difficulties. More specifically, after reading this chapter you should be able to:

- Discuss the roles of managers within organizations, including their decision-making responsibilities.
- Describe the rational decision-making process.
- Identify factors that limit and constrain human decision making.
- Provide alternatives to the rational view of how managers make decisions in organizations.
- Explain the issues involved in group decision making.
- Describe different models of organizational structures.
- Discuss how I/T can be used to improve the decision-making process and to facilitate more flexible, responsive organizational structures.

Why is it so tough to make the right decision?

INTRODUCTION TO DECISION MAKING

In this chapter we explore the concept of decision making in detail to set the stage for a discussion of how information technology can help improve decision making within organizations. For those who have not studied organizational decision making elsewhere, the chapter will provide a useful introduction to the topic. For those who have, the linkages we make to the role of information technology should provide a useful complement to previous knowledge.

The chapter begins with a discussion of decision making from an individual manager's perspective; since one of the primary emphases of this book is on management, it seems reasonable to examine first what managers do. Not surprisingly, many managerial functions involve making decisions, both as an individual and as a member of a group. After examining the ideal rational approach to decision making, we modify it by discussing some of the actual complexities and difficulties of decision making in a real organizational setting. The difficulties include the limitations of human beings as information processors. These limitations are major constraints on our ability to assimilate and manipulate information and therefore to follow the rational approach (assuming we wanted to). Other complexities include the role of stress, time pressures, and making decisions within a group situation.

The remainder of the chapter is devoted to a discussion of organizational decision making and the role of information technology in aiding decision making within organizations. We examine three alternative models of organizational decision making—rational, administrative, and political—as well as different perspectives on how organizations operate. The chapter closes with a brief discussion of alternative organizational structures, and the connective case, ABB, provides an example of an international organization which has used information and communication technologies to implement a very flexible, lean, and effective structure.

WHAT DO MANAGERS DO?

The day-to-day management of an organization or department is frequently not very glamorous. Most decisions that managers need to make on a daily basis seem on the surface to be quite trivial. Take this example: we have all experienced the frustration of standing in a long line at the checkout for a grocery store. Why aren't there more checkout clerks available at that particular time? At some point, a manager decided how many clerks to schedule for the shift. Although it might not seem very exciting, this decision is necessary to keep the grocery store operational, and it has a substantial impact on customer retention. One of the responsibilities of the store manager (or shift manager, in a larger store) is to balance the need to provide an adequate level of service to customers against the need to keep costs lower.

Different theories have been developed to describe and explain the functions of managers. A somewhat traditional perspective suggests that managing can be defined as the process of accomplishing (or attempting to accomplish) organizational goals through planning, execution and control.

Determining how many employees should be scheduled for a work shift is a typical decision for a manager or supervisor, which influences customer satisfaction. Photo courtesy of Tony Stone Worldwide.

Planning. **Planning** refers to the activities involved in defining the goals of the organization and describing how it will accomplish these goals. When an individual wants to borrow money from a bank to help start a new business, the bank will ask him or her to prepare a business plan. Within an established business, managers are generally required to prepare plans and budgets for their departments. Government agencies and not-for-profit organizations also prepare plans, to help them set priorities to use later as a benchmark to ensure that the organization is accomplishing what it set out to do. In the grocery store example, the store manager may have set a goal of having fewer than 5 percent of all customers wait more than a given time period, perhaps five minutes, in a checkout line. This goal could be part of a plan to improve customer service to make the store compete more effectively.

A plan is the product of a planning *process.* A plan is usually accompanied by a budget. The budget is just an allocation of resources to activities that reflect the priorities set out in the plan. Planning takes place in all organizations, although it is much more formalized in some than in others. In some instances planning is conducted in a very simplistic fashion; one approach is to assume that the priorities for this year are the same as for last year, and then to take last year's budget and add 5 percent to every item (revenue or expense) to generate a budget for the next year. Though an easy way to generate a budget, the effectiveness of such an approach is questionable.

Typically, people involved in a planning process require large quantities of information, drawn from multiple sources. To prepare a useful plan—a plan that tells you where you are, where you want to go, and how—it is necessary to consider, in most organizations, issues such as what competitors are doing and what they will be doing in the near future, how customer preferences have changed and how they will evolve, what the cost position is compared to the competitors', what new legislation has and will be proposed by different governments, and so on. This means that in order to prepare a useful plan, relevant, accurate, and timely information about past events and the likelihood of future ones must be available to the individuals responsible for the planning process. Therefore, all other things being equal, the better the information available from the organization's information systems, the better the resulting plans.

Execution. **Execution** is the process of assigning responsibilities and resources to accomplish the plan. (Note that some people use the term *organizing* rather than execution. We believe that the terms *organizing* and *organization* are employed too frequently, so to prevent confusion we use the term *execution* instead.) In the grocery store example, the process of determining schedules for employees, and perhaps calling in part-time employees on short notice to help cover a busy period, would be considered execution. Execution involves not only a good understanding of the business but also excellent interpersonal skills and the ability to react to the unexpected.

Execution is where good managers shine. Though planning comes first and determines the general direction for a firm, it is execution that makes it happen or fail to happen. The store management may set an objective that "no customer will wait more than 5 minutes in line," but it is a shift manager that needs to find ways to make it happen. And generally, plans tend to be overly "clean," assuming that most things will go smoothly. But, typically, reality is much messier and requires that managers execute the plans by being creative and resourceful. As Lawrence A. Bossidy, the CEO of AlliedSignal has said, "Strategies are intellectually simple; their execution is not."

As we discuss later in this chapter, for decisions with many variables involved, managers need help in deciding how best to allocate resources. They particularly need this help if there are tight deadlines and heavy time pressures. Fortunately, information systems (I/S) can be used in numerous ways to facilitate the execution of plans. For example, specialized I/S are readily available to help allocate resources—systems that determine the best delivery routes for truck drivers, or that identify which customers are most valuable and therefore should be served first when production capacity cannot meet overall demand, or that identify suitable employees for a new project team.

Control. The process of monitoring activities to make sure they are developing as planned and making corrections when necessary is referred to as **controlling.** In a production process, control could involve sampling products on an assembly line and ensuring that the number of defects is below a certain predetermined level. Another example of control could be that of a regional sales manager who receives sales reports from all salespeople within the region, uses the reports to ensure that sales figures are above the minimum planned levels, and takes action if the figures are of concern. The example that people identify more often with control is the activity of ensuring that one is within a predetermined budget.

Information technology is often used in control situations. Here a manager compares budgeted and actual figures using a spreadsheet. Photo courtesy of Hewlett-Packard.

In Chapter 2, we discussed the important role of feedback systems, which are essentially designed to aid in control functions. A manager (or management team) sets broad goals (perhaps to increase market share) and more specific objectives (perhaps to have each salesperson increase their total number of customers by 10 percent). Once the objectives have been established, measuring methods and devices (sensors) can be put in place, such as periodic reporting of visits to existing and potential customers by all salespeople. These periodic measurements can be then compared to the goals. The critical role of the manager in controlling organizational activities is not so much to supervise that "things are OK" but rather to be an effective surprise-handler, that is, someone who can react quickly to unexpected events and circumstances and implement, alone or through a team, an appropriate corrective action.

Information technology and information systems can very productively support managers in performing control tasks. Rather than having the salespeople report verbally or in handwritten form, records of sales calls and sales could be entered into a database, which could then be queried to produce the desired sales reports. The sales manager could extract data from the database and move it to an electronic spreadsheet, allowing for a quick and accurate comparison of actual versus planned numbers. More and more often, information systems are becoming an integral part of all control activities within organizations.

Most functions performed by managers involve decision making, and information systems can be used in many ways to aid the decision-making process. Before we discuss particular ways of using I/S to aid decision making, however, we need to examine decision making within organizations in more detail.

DECISION MAKING IN MANAGEMENT

In an ideal world, managers would behave perfectly rationally all the time. Rational behavior from a formal decision-making perspective means that managers would ask all the right questions, obtain all necessary information, discuss the problem with all the interested parties, and weigh all factors carefully and accurately *before* making decisions. But in real life, this description of how decisions should be made is more the exception than the rule. Indeed, if one uses those criteria to define rational decision making, then most decisions made by managers (and other organizational members) appear to be irrational.

This section of the chapter is devoted to exploring the ideal of **rational decision making,** the impediments that stand in the way of reaching that ideal, and alternative models of decision making that are a better description of how people actually do make decisions. Specifically, this section addresses three questions: (1) How do managers behave in making decisions? (2) What are the limitations (cognitive, administrative, cultural) that interfere with their information processing? (3) How can information systems help managers make more rational decisions?

The obvious starting point is to examine the concept of rationality itself. In a somewhat simplified form, rational decision making is based on the *logic of optimal choice;* that is, the assumption that a decision maker will always choose the option that maximizes value for the organization (or individual). The manager is assumed to be an objective, totally informed person who would select the most efficient alternative, maximizing whatever amount and type of output he or she values.

Decision making can be described broadly as consisting of two phases. One is the information collection phase; the other is the information analysis and synthesis phase. Rationality in decision making can be broken down into **content rationality,** which refers to knowing how to collect and focus on only the relevant information to make decisions, and **process rationality,** which refers to combining that information to make choices optimally. Rationality assumes the *unbiased* processing of all relevant information. Objectivity and comprehensiveness are both required to make rational decisions. This definition of rationality implies that managers have a clear and constant purpose and are unwaveringly consistent.

Unfortunately, this idealistic view of managerial decision making is not very accurate. In the next section we examine a more realistic perspective.

The Realities of Decision Making

When theoreticians in decision analysis, behavioral decision theory, and cognitive psychology warn about human shortcomings in decision making, some people dismiss the cautions as academic extrapolations from studies of university students (like you) doing irrelevant tasks in unrealistic settings. But enough evidence has been gained in real settings for managers and designers of information systems to accept the pervasiveness of *cognitive limitations*—and the need to compensate for them by using information systems.

Table 3–1 provides a list of standards of rational decision making and the shortcomings that most managers have with respect to those standards. Basically, these observations suggest that many decision makers fall substantially short of following the ideal rational decision-making process.

After a decision has been reached, the decision maker must then make detailed provisions to implement or execute the chosen action. Furthermore, it is advisable to develop contingency plans to deal with risks that have been identified. Here, too, many decision makers fail to adequately address these issues, assuming that once a decision is made, the implementation will somehow follow more or less automatically.

We now know that many decision makers fail to employ a rational decision-making process. If we want to design or acquire information systems that improve the decision-making process, we need to know *why* managers sometimes fail to follow the rational approach. We now address this issue.

TABLE 3–1 Characteristics of Rational Decision Making

Characteristic	*Observation—Many Decision Makers:*	*Potential Role of I/T*
Accumulating information before making a decision.	Do not search intensively for new information, and fail to gather contradictory information; do not explore what is known and unknown, or organize the available information into a coherent picture.	Facilitate access to multiple data sources.
Collecting information that is problem centered and goal directed.	Collect the wrong kind, or amount, of information.	Facilitate access to multiple data sources; appropriate tools for manipulating and reporting information.
Documenting the existence of a problem, the need to solve it, and the benefits to arise from its solution.	Refuse to believe that a problem exists at all; or identify the wrong problem, the wrong causes, or both.	Documentation and communication tools; idea generation (brainstorming) tools.
Considering several alternatives for reaching the goal or solving the problem.	Develop too few alternatives; apply old solutions without determining whether they fit the problem.	Tools for decision support; weighing of multiple attributes, etc.
Proposing logical and consistent cause–effect relationships.	Are misled by apparent correlations in data, and do not investigate alternative explanations for the correlations.	Tools for statistical analysis.
Assessing the value of costs and benefits of various alternatives.	Fail to weigh the costs and benefits of each alternative adequately; do not reexamine the positive and negative consequences of the alternatives, before making a decision.	Tools for decision support, including financial analysis of multiple alternatives.
Determining the individual and organizational values behind the data and interpretations being used.	Have difficulty articulating their own values and beliefs, and even more difficulty understanding the values and beliefs of the information sources they are using.	Unknown

Alternative Views of Management

Not everyone agrees with the traditional view of management described earlier in this chapter. Although the traditional view describes the functions performed (plan, execute, and control), it doesn't say much about *how* these functions are completed. Behavioral theorists argue that the traditional view is too simplistic. Though decision makers go through all of the functions, they do not do so in any linear, rational manner. Managers tend to be issue oriented, spending attention on events, disturbances, crises that are important at the moment. Their schedules tend to be fragmented, their deadlines tight, and their work sessions constantly interrupted. Though they have access to written reports and electronic data, most managers prefer to use their large and complex web of personal contacts and be informed through verbal interactions.

A manager's work consists of tasks which are brief, fragmented, and varied. Information technology can help organize the work and allow the manager to be more productive. Photo courtesy of Stephen Agricola/Stock Boston, Inc.

After observing managers in their day-to-day activities, the behavioral theorists point out that managers perform high-volume, high-speed work involving a large number of topics. Managers are very often under **stress** working against tight deadlines. They have frequent meetings and constant telephone, E-mail, and fax communications with both internal and external parties. Their work is characterized as being (1) brief: they rarely spend more than 30 minutes on an activity; (2) fragmented: they deal with a number of problems in a day and deal with a particular problem sporadically over a long period; and (3) varied: they deal with many types of problems and decisions. Basically, managers have very little time to sit back and think.

These observations undermine the validity of the rational decision model. Job realities being what they are, managers are involved in several activities simultaneously and divide their time and attention among several problems and issues. Also, the amount of information initially available on a problem is seldom sufficient to solve it. Sometimes additional information is available at a cost; other times it is totally unavailable. These situations force managers to make one more decision: whether or not to spend the time and money to collect additional information. Clearly, managers do not devote unlimited time and resources to collect all the relevant information on every problem to develop optimal solutions every time.

These observations also support the notion that managers make extensive use of simplifying strategies—shortcuts—to reduce the time burden of making decisions. In the short run these strategies save time and other resources, but they tend to produce solutions with less than maximum quality. The use of these shortcuts increases when stress increases or when time and other resources decrease.

One of the implications of the way managers work is that the design of information systems needs to be driven by the realities of managerial decision

BUSINESS BRIEF 3-1 USING I/T TO FIND INFORMATION: THE MIDS SYSTEM AT LOCKHEED-GEORGIA

Lockheed-Georgia, a subsidiary of the Lockheed Corporation, is a major producer of cargo aircraft. Senior executives at Lockheed-Georgia are hands-on users of the Management Information and Decision Support (MIDS) system. MIDS is used to access on-line information about the current status of the firm. The system is graphics oriented and draws upon communications, data storage, and retrieval methods. Over the past eight years, MIDS has evolved to where it now offers over 700 displays (screens) for 30 top executives and 40 operating managers, including the president. Consider two examples of how the system is used:

- The president is concerned about employee morale, which for him is a critical success factor. He calls up a display that shows employee contributions to company-sponsored programs such as blood drives, United Way, and savings plans. These are surrogate measures of morale, and the president discovers that recent contributions are substantially lower than he would expect.
- The vice president, human resources (HR) returns from a trip and wants to review the major developments that took place while he was gone. While paging through the displays for the HR area, he notices that labor grievances rose substantially.

Both the president and the VP, human resources come to the same conclusion: Something is causing a decline in employee morale.

QUESTIONS

1. Consider the situation before the implementation of the MIDS system. How long might it have taken for the president to obtain information concerning employee contributions to several different programs? How likely is it that the VP, human resources would have discovered the labor grievances so quickly?
2. Discuss how the MIDS system could be a factor in terms of accumulating information in the first phase of a decision-making process. In what ways could MIDS support rational decision making?

SOURCE: Adapted from G. Houdeshel and H. Watson, "The Management Information and Decision Support (MIDS) System at Lockheed-Georgia," *MIS Quarterly,* March 1987, pp. 127–140. Reprinted by special permission from *MIS Quarterly.* Copyright 1987 by the Society for Information Management and the Management Information Systems Research Center at the University of Minnesota.

making. Indeed, information systems, in order to truly enhance the decision-making process, should provide support not only by delivering data but by helping analyze and process the data and by helping the manager avoid bad habits and shortcuts as s/he goes through the different phases of decision making. For example, an information system that reduces the effort needed to search for information—by providing easy access to a large number of centralized databases—could reduce the tendency of managers to cut short the information-gathering phase. Consider the case at Lockheed-Georgia in Business Brief 3–1.

In addition to situational factors such as time constraints, human beings have limitations, such as cognitive biases, that interfere with rational decision making. We now briefly discuss some of these and suggest ways that I/S may be used to address these limitations. Keep in mind that our overall goal is to provide managers with the best possible support in making decisions.

The Limitations of Rationality

Researchers in decision making and experienced observers of management agree that managers need help processing information. However, we must first understand where help is needed—where the weaknesses are—in order to design tools to provide it.

The economist (and Nobel Memorial Prize winner) Herbert Simon proposed the concept of **bounded rationality** to describe how humans deal with complex decision-making situations. Bounded rationality basically means that people consciously or unconsciously construct simplified (bounded) models of real situations, based on their understandings and beliefs. They then behave rationally with respect to their **model,** even though their behavior may not be even close to optimal with respect to the real world. To understand or predict how people will behave, we have to understand how they construct their models of reality.

Before we begin detailing limitations of humans as information processors, we should emphasize that humans also have a great number of strengths. We are able to use heuristics to sift through extraneous information, we can reach logical deductions with imperfect information, we have a tremendous memory capacity. Having said this, however, we need to note that humans also have numerous weaknesses which, in most cases, can be overcome through the appropriate use of information systems.

The **first limit on rationality** stems from the fact that the human perceptual system is not all-powerful. Experiments have shown that certain characteristics of human information-processing capabilities are fixed across individuals and tasks. These characteristics include the size and access speed of the different types of memory (short- and long-term), the mode of processing, and the ability to deal with overload of environmental stimuli. Briefly, we know that humans assimilate and process information relatively slowly and that they compute and remember poorly, though the human capacity for information storage seems to be unlimited. Our information-processing system is limited by low capacity in short-term memory (e.g., experiments have shown that people cannot remember more than 9 numbers in a row, a phenomenon called the magical 7+/–2 number). Other limitations are slow storage in long-term memory, slow serial (as opposed to parallel) processing, and the use of sometimes inappropriate but familiar patterns when analyzing new information. We can process and integrate information at a limited rate when making business decisions, and we are overloaded fairly easily.

Information systems can be used to address these limitations. For example, it would be unreasonable to ask a human to remember details such as the price and quantity on hand of thousands of parts. By storing this information in a database, and making it readily available to the decision maker, we are essentially expanding the short- and long-term memory available to him/her. Also, modern operating systems allow multitasking, which means the decision maker can quickly flip from task to task or pull information from multiple sources to apply to a specific decision task.[1] Finally, information systems can help reduce overload by using filters to screen out irrelevant data, select important messages by identifying key words, and format and highlight particularly significant events.

The **second limit on rationality** is the extensive use of overly simplistic strategies, and the interference of **personal biases.**[2] Decision makers perform a lot of tasks when they process information: They must sift through a lot of data, integrate contradictory opinions, assess the causalities and interconnections of events, evaluate the value of outcomes, and collate information from several sources before selecting a course of action. Unfortunately, research shows that managers do all these tasks less than optimally. Pervasive biases interfere with tasks like making inferences, predictions, diagnoses, evaluations, and choices.

---

[1] An operating system is a computer program that controls the basic operations of computer hardware. Operating systems are discussed in more detail in Chapter 6.

[2] The term *bias* is used here to mean not only a set of values that colors the way one sees events but also a strategy to process information.

People are often overwhelmed with work because they have limited information-processing capabilities. Photos courtesy of Jim Brown/Offshoot Stock (top) and Peter Southwick/Stock Boston, Inc. (bottom).

For example, the *frequency* bias misleads managers in the assignment of probabilities to events. The frequency bias causes people to remember rare but impressive events and to assume they occur more frequently than they really do, while underestimating the frequency of more common but rather mundane events. People tend to overestimate the likelihood of winning the lottery, or of a plane crashing, because of the attention that the media gives to such events (the media does not usually cover stories on the millions of people who buy lottery tickets and never win or the thousands of flights that arrive safely to their destination every day). Another related cognitive limitation that affects the assignment of probabilities to events is the *availability bias:* People assign a greater likelihood to events that are easier to retrieve from memory than others, independent of the actual frequency of occurrence. The *recency effect* is a bias that interferes with the evaluation of alternatives. The recency effect describes the phenomenon that occurs, for example, when a manager is reviewing candidates for a job. The manager's judgment of a given candidate will be affected by the application that the manager reviewed just prior to the current one. If the previous application was inferior, the one now being reviewed will be seen as better than it actually is, and vice versa.

In general, people have trouble making comparisons across large sets of data, particularly when computations, specifically ratios, are involved. This weakness causes people to tend to overlook significant differences in results. For example, some people would evaluate the performance of two different salespeople where one sold five units and the other eight, as being similar, though there is a 60 percent difference between them. The notions of probability, variance, and correlation versus causality are not intuitive notions, and managers often use them incorrectly in making decisions.

Another finding is that a person's training colors the way s/he sees and structures problems. Such *selective perception* also predisposes people to seek information consistent with their views, and to downplay contradictory evidence. As a person becomes an expert in a subject area, these types of biases may occur less frequently. However, most managers are not experts in one subject and thus need help in identifying and overcoming such biases.

Once again, information systems can be used to help compensate for these cognitive limitations. For example, an expert system (described in more detail in Chapter 5) might be designed to help determine whether a request for a credit card purchase should be approved. Having access to the expert system can help a novice decision maker avoid taking short cuts and can reduce (or remove) the influence of personal biases. Table 3–2 summarizes the essential needs from an information system, to compensate for human cognitive limitations.

TABLE 3–2 Cognitive Limitations and Implications for Information Systems Design

Limitation	Implications for information system (I/S) design
Bounded Rationality	I/S should attempt to expand the limits of bounded rationality, helping managers to maximize value by reviewing and analyzing several alternatives and avoiding premature closure.
Magical Number 7+/–2	Codes for human use should not exceed five to nine symbols, or else they should be divided into segments of five or less. I/S should avoid having humans do significant, unaided processing or avoid assuming the accuracy of data retrieved from the user's memory.
Overload	I/S should be designed to filter out irrelevant data and to provide increased filtering when decisions are being made under time pressures.
Humans as Intuitive Statisticians	I/S should provide statistical analysis of data: sample size, variance, correlation, probability estimates, etc. Data formatting and presentation should be designed to assist in eliminating frequency, availability, and recency cognitive biases.
Difficulty in Noticing and Assessing Differences	I/S should compute and highlight significant differences rather than assume that humans will notice them.
Difficulty in Reformatting Data	The information needed should be displayed in the format most appropriate to support the decision to be made. No added processing or reformatting should be required.
Desire for Context	I/S should present summarized data whenever possible (to avoid overload), and should also allow the user to browse through the raw data.

As an aside, certain environments can make biases more or less acute. As mentioned, managerial work is characterized by time pressures, frequent interruptions, attention to numerous diverse tasks, limited information, and high stakes. Such stressful environments tend to magnify biases and promote the use of simplistic heuristics. Each distraction and pressure has been shown to impair information handling and to increase the likelihood of managers falling prey to cognitive biases. The relevance of this discussion for designing information systems is that, under certain circumstances, decision makers become more erratic and bias prone. Identifying these circumstances can help us determine what sort of support is needed, and when.

The **third limit to rationality** includes the limitations caused by personality characteristics. **Cognitive style** (the method of collecting and evaluating information), dogmatism (the resistance to considering information that differs from a preconceived view), risk propensity (the willingness to make decisions with only partial information), creativity (the ability to absorb input from many sources), all affect the efficiency and effectiveness of information processing. (See Table 3–3.)

The role of I/T in addressing individual differences is to complement personal preferences and overcome individual weaknesses. For example, individuals tend to use only information that is displayed, and then only in the form in which it is displayed. This tendency causes individuals to discount or ignore information that must be inferred, or transformed from the display. Therefore, when we design information systems we must consider very carefully how to display information so that it easily and quickly communicates the intended meaning. As an example, since some people prefer to have numerical information displayed in graphical form (charts) while others prefer tabular form (see Figure 3–1) an information system should have the capability to let the user select whichever form of report they prefer. In general, individual preferences should be identified and explicitly accommodated whenever possible through a flexible system interface.

With the exception of time pressures, so far we have only considered sources of bias and distortion that are internal to the manager. It is important to remember that managers operate more often than not as members of committees and teams. We now turn our attention to group pressures that increase the potential for biases and distortions in information processing. We also discuss how organizational structures restrict information flows, and how standard operating procedures bias people toward exclusive use of certain types of information. This discussion will serve as a transition to Chapter 4, which introduces (among other things) the variables affecting the relationships between message senders and receivers, and the variables influencing the content of those messages and the direction in which they flow.

GROUP DECISION MAKING

Most decision making in organizations occurs in teams. Seldom does a manager make a decision without input from other members of the organization, clients, and/or suppliers. When individuals in a group are asked to reach decisions, the decision situation becomes more complex. It is no longer appropriate to consider each decision maker as an individual unit; we now have to consider issues such as group dynamics. Just as individual biases can affect individual decision making, group characteristics can influence **group decision making.**

Some major differences between group and individual decision making are found in the time needed to seek consensus and the resolving of conflicts among

TABLE 3–3 Individual Differences and Their Effect on Information Processing

Individual Differences	*Explanation*	*Effects on Information Processing*
Cognitive Style	People have strong preferences for the type of evidence they use in solving problems and the format they want the data to be in.	People will overlook or misinterpret data presented in formats that do not fit their styles.
Dogmatism (low–high)	Extent to which person is positive about beliefs and opinions and integrates information contradicting them.	Low dogmatism related to more information search activity, more deliberation, and less confidence in decisions.
Risk-taking propensity	Extent to which person is willing to take risks.	High risk-taking propensity related to less information search activity.
Locus of control (internal–external)	Extent to which events are perceived to be controlled by oneself (internal) versus by other forces (external).	Internal locus of control related to more information search activity than external locus of control.
Extroversion–introversion	Extent to which person is concerned with external physical and social environment versus own feelings and thoughts.	Extroverts have quicker long-term memory and information retrieval, better retention over short intervals, and less retention over long intervals as compared to introverts.
Tolerance for ambiguity (low–high)	Extent to which person needs clarity and specificity versus vague, unclear rules, directions, procedures, etc.	Lower tolerance for ambiguity related to preference for concrete information and for more information.
Intelligence (low–high)	Measured by ability to perform well on intelligence tests.	High intelligence related to faster information processing, more effective information selection, better retention, faster decisions, and better organization of information.
Quantitative abilities	Extent of ability to perform computations, follow algorithms, and use numeric reasoning.	High quantitative abilities related to more use of short-term memory and less use of long-term memory.
Verbal abilities (low–high)	Extent of vocabulary development and use in expressing thoughts.	High verbal abilities related to more effective short-term memory.
Experience in decision making	Extent of experience in formal decision making.	Experience related to more effective information selection, greater flexibility, and less confidence.
Task knowledge (low–high)	Extent of knowledge of how to perform the task.	High task knowledge related to less information search.
Age	Chronological age.	Older subjects use more information search, select information more effectively, are more flexible, and require more decision time than younger subjects.

group members. One must evaluate carefully when to use groups and when not to. The benefits of group decision making include having greater knowledge available, greater creativity, increased acceptance once the decision has been made, and better understanding of the objectives and criteria behind the decision. These benefits are to be weighed against the potential liabilities of involving a group in decision making, which include the process taking longer, possible domination of the group by an individual, the group being sidetracked with a different agenda,

FIGURE 3–1 Greenway Ltd. Regional Fall and Winter Sales

Information systems need to address personal preferences of users. Here the same information is displayed in two different formats.

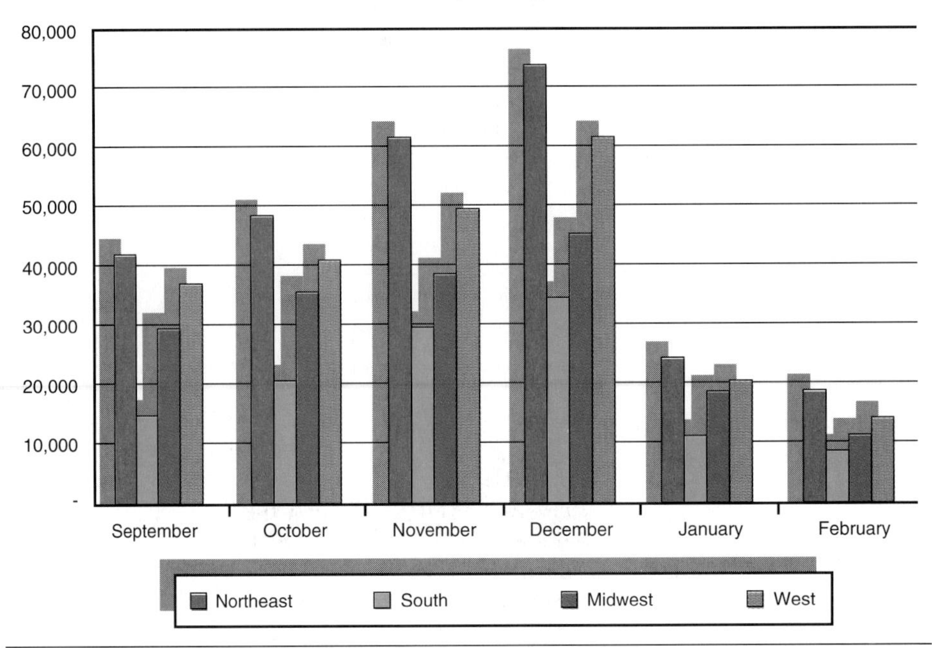

	September	October	November	December	January	February	Total
Northeast	43,000	48,000	62,000	74,000	24,000	18,000	$269,000
South	15,000	21,000	29,000	35,000	11,000	8,000	$119,000
Midwest	29,000	35,000	38,000	45,000	18,000	12,000	$177,000
West	36,000	41,000	49,000	61,000	21,000	15,000	$223,000
Total	$123,000	$145,000	$178,000	$215,000	$74,000	$53,000	$788,000

expecting consensus and not reaching it, and having the peer pressure in the group suppress dissent (i.e., **groupthink**).

The Vroom-Yetton model (shown in Figure 3–2) helps determine whether or not to use a group. Consider the problem facing Jane Lovett, vice president for human resources at MayFair Suites, a hotel chain oriented toward the budget-minded business traveler. Jane is faced with a problem of high turnover of cleaning-room workers at one of her properties—about 200 percent a year, at least twice the average in the industry. She investigated the problem and found that employee satisfaction is low because of a recent company policy regarding pay. In this situation, group acceptance will be important in devising a solution to the problem. The Vroom-Yetton model indicates that Lovett can meet with all cleaning-room workers individually (style 3 or 4) or meet with the entire group at once (style 5). Lovett should choose style 3 or 4 if she believes there is likely to be conflict among the workers concerning the preferred solutions (situation H in the figure). Lovett should choose style 5 if she believes that all workers share her concern to solve the problem (situation G in the figure). In this case, Lovett probably would choose style

Decision making by groups involves many interpersonal variables and dynamics. Photo courtesy of Hewlett-Packard.

5. Meeting with the entire group of workers at once would clearly be the least time-consuming way to approach this problem.

The old adage, "If you want to kill an issue, create a committee to study it" reflects the fact that very often groups tend to be ineffective. To be effective, groups must have a clear understanding of their mission and objectives, and have guidelines and procedures to make decisions. Their members need to achieve good communication, learn how to give and receive help, and learn how to deal with conflict. The composition and size of groups affect their performance. For example, a heterogeneous group (e.g., a group whose members come from various departments in an organization) will usually be more creative in generating alternative solutions to a problem but will take more time to agree on a course of action.

The process of group decision making can be considered to roughly follow that of individual decision making. For convenience, we can divide the process into four general phases:

1. Inception of a project (e.g., choice of goals). This phase includes collecting information.
2. Solution of technical issues (e.g., deciding on how the tasks will be accomplished, such as group roles).
3. Resolution of conflict (e.g., resolving conflicts of viewpoints and interests, such as political issues.
4. Execution of the performance requirement of the project.

Assume, for a moment, that you have been assigned to a project team composed of four individuals in a college course. Your group assignment involves researching a specific organization, and producing a report that (*a*) describes the organization (history, products, etc.), (*b*) details the competitive strategy it employs, and (*c*) discusses how a specific information system or application of information technology has helped the organization implement its strategy. A typical project

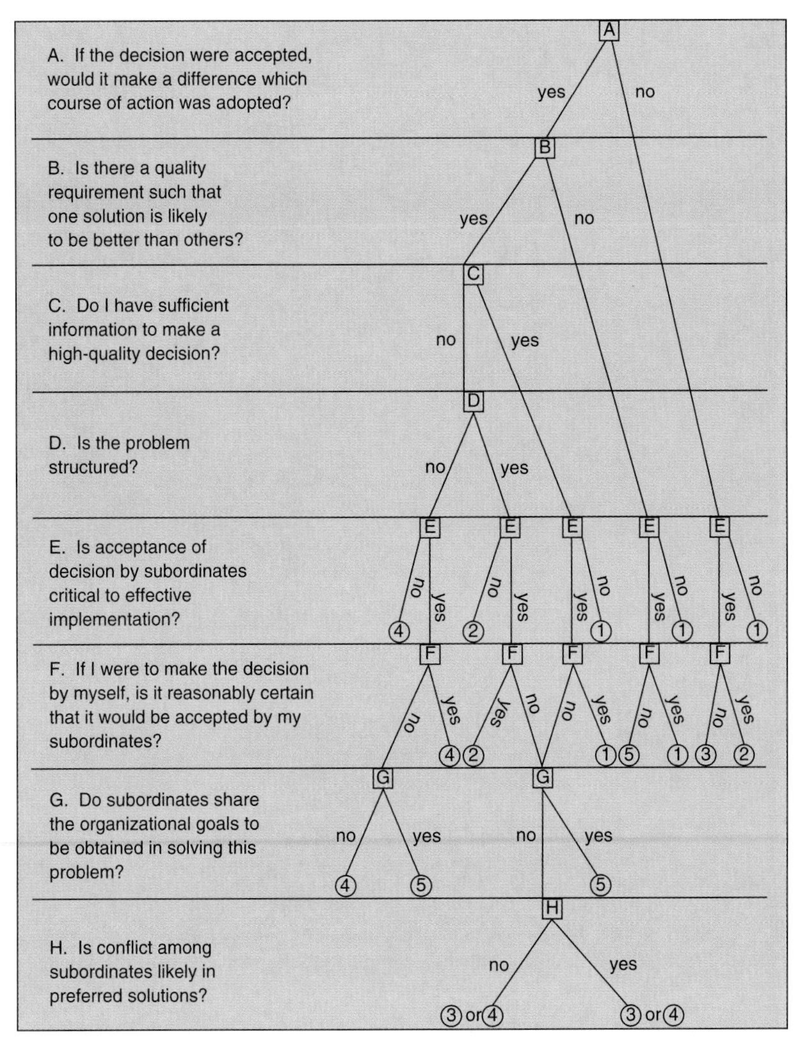

FIGURE 3–2 Questions from the Vroom-Yetton Model to Determine When and How to Involve Others in a Decision-Making Group

Degree of subordinate participation encouraged by managers	Recommendation
Low (Autocratic) ①	• You solve the problem or make the decision yourself using information available to you at that time.
②	• You obtain the necessary information from your subordinate(s), then decide on the solution to the problem yourself. You may or may not tell your subordinates what the problem is in getting the information from them. The role played by your subordinates in making the decision is clearly one of providing the necessary information to you, rather than generating or evaluating alternative solutions.
③	• You share the problem with relevant subordinates individually, getting their ideas and suggestions without bringing them together as a group. Then you make the decision that may or may not reflect your subordinates' influence.
④	• You share the problem with your subordinates as a group, collectively obtaining their ideas and suggestions. Then you make the decision that may or may not reflect your subordinates' influence.
⑤ High (Participative)	• You share a problem with your subordinates as a group. Together you generate and evaluate alternatives and attempt to reach agreement (consensus) on a solution. Your role is much like that of a chairman. You do not try to influence the group to adopt "your" solution, and you are willing to accept and implement any solution that has the support of the entire group.

SOURCE: Reprinted by permission of publisher from "A New Look at Managerial Decision-Making," by Victor H. Vroom, *Organizational Dynamics*, Spring 1973. © 1973 by AMACON, a division of American Management Associations. All rights reserved.

might focus on a company such as Saturn or Dell Computers, and their use of information technology to implement a strategy of mass customization.

Assuming that you are initially unfamiliar with the other members of your group, part of the group process will be devoted to getting to know one another. The inception of the project will be facilitated by the course instructor, although the group might be required to select the organization to serve as the focus of the project. Issues such as schedules and the expectations of different group members (e.g., grade expectations) must be addressed and dealt with. One group member might want to dominate the group process; another might be very busy with outside activities, such as varsity sports; a third might have little or no interest in the course or the project; and so on. The technical issues of assigning tasks and the resolution of group conflicts must be handled. Finally, effort must be expended to actually accomplish the task at hand (execution): producing a report that satisfies the requirements of the project assignment.

A concept that comes into play in group decision making is that of **information richness.** Information richness refers to how much the information contains surplus meanings, beyond the literal symbols used to express it. As you read these written words, you are restricted to the literal symbols (alphanumeric characters) used to express information. If, on the other hand, the authors were speaking these words to you through the use of an audio tape, you would receive additional meaning through our accents, voice inflections, and so on. With the addition of video, there would be the added meaning of body language. If our discussion of information richness took place in a face-to-face meeting, additional meanings would be added far beyond the alphanumeric characters used to represent words.

The importance of information richness to group decision making (and to a lesser extent, individual decision making) is related to the task and the phase in the project. If the focus is on generating ideas or plans, there is less need for information richness; a medium such as electronic mail allows the expression of ideas adequately. As the task moves to negotiation and conflict resolution, the information richness of face-to-face communication becomes much more important. It is therefore important to match the medium to the task, and subsequently to match the type of I/T to the task (since different technologies provide different levels of information richness).

Our intent in this section is not to make you an expert on group decision making, but rather to introduce you to some of the concepts that are important to consider when designing I/S support. In addition to information richness, it is important to consider such issues as the status differential (group members with lower status defer to members of higher status) and need achievement of group members (some members will try to dominate and/or manipulate the group).

Group decision support systems are information systems that have been designed specifically to facilitate group decision making. These systems vary substantially in their capabilities. The systems enable electronic meetings, which are generally facilitated by a person familiar with both the technology and group decision-making processes. The systems consist of tools that enhance the verbal interaction among the participants.

One such tool is *electronic brainstorming.* All ideas generated at individual workstations appear on each participant's screen; thus one person's idea may stimulate a new idea from another person. Once the ideas are generated, additional tools facilitate creating categories, establishing priorities, and assigning tasks. The computer interaction is anonymous (which encourages those less outspoken to

Group decision support systems are designed to improve group decision-making processes. Photo courtesy of the University of Arizona.

contribute), and done in parallel (vastly reducing the duration of the meeting). Other tools include prioritizing and voting software as well as software that allows groups to jointly compose and write documents.

MODELS OF ORGANIZATIONAL DECISION MAKING

When we speak of rational behavior, we should remember that our focus in this discussion is not on making decisions, but rather on how to support the process of making decisions. Managers are *change agents,* not just decision makers, so the steps before and after a decision are as important as the actual choice of action. Preparatory steps include creating tension for change, understanding the positions of the various constituencies, and developing political support for a chosen action. Steps after the decision include naming the change monitor and identifying the monitoring methods. Therefore, the mission of a good information system is broader than just collecting data to make a choice. Designers of information systems must understand not only how managers think but also how the decision process will be implemented in the managers' environment. An information system that is well designed is an information system that is used. Thus, an information system, in order to be useful, must be implemented. To understand the implementation process better, we review three models of organizational decision making—rational, administrative, and political.

The Rational Model. The **rational model** of decision making was introduced earlier in this chapter. It is based on the logic of optimal choice: the choice that would maximize value for the organization. The manager is assumed to be an objective, totally informed person who would select the most efficient alternative, maximizing whatever amount and type of output s/he values. We can summarize the rational choice process as follows:

1. An individual is confronted with a number of known alternative courses of action.

2. Each alternative bears a set of possible consequences. These consequences are known and are quantifiable.
3. The individual has a system of preferences or utilities that permits him or her to rank the consequences and choose an alternative.

There is no empirical support for the contention that these three phases are actually used. In reality, managers seldom have the time or money to analyze all alternatives or envision all consequences. If rationality were ever-present among members of an organization, the organization would appear as a coherent and rational policy-making entity that maximizes the attainment of a unique set of goals and has no internal conflicts. In other words, a rational decision process implies a rational organization. A rational organization is an organization that has (1) centralized power, (2) harmony and consistency of goals across boundaries, and (3) members who are objective, fully informed, and inclined to choose alternatives that maximize the common good of the organization.

The rational model represents a sanitized vision of how organizations make decisions. In reality, organizations often seem more like complex groups of coalitions fighting for shares of limited resources, and using multiple sources of information with varying reliability to achieve a set of fluid goals. Individuals within organizations typically have widely divergent perceptions and goals and act to maximize their own gains, not necessarily those of the organization. Because of this disparity between the rational model and reality, we prefer to accept the rational model primarily as a benchmark for comparing the remaining two organizational decision-making processes. In searching for a more realistic description of how organizations make decisions, we turn to the **satisficing,** or administrative, model.

The Administrative Model. The quest for a more realistic description of organizational decision making produced a variation called the **administrative model.** This model sees decision makers as people with varying degrees of motivation who are besieged by demands but have little time to make decisions and thus seek shortcuts to find acceptable solutions. Under the administrative model, a decision maker does not try to optimize but instead "satisfices"—treats objectives as loose constraints that can tighten if there are many acceptable alternatives that fulfill those constraints. While optimization would require choosing the alternative with the highest value, satisficing requires finding the first alternative with an acceptable value, that is, an alternative with a value above a minimally acceptable level on a given constraint.

Assume you had a car you wanted to sell. If you listed your car for $2,500 and had 10 offers, you could choose with either method. With the rational method, you would determine which offer had the highest value in terms of conditions and price. With the satisficing model, you would accept the first offer that met your lowest acceptable price. Satisficing may lead to a reduced decision quality, but it saves time and effort. Satisficing is a dynamic construct: the aspiration levels of the manager and the number of alternatives determine what is a "feasible, good enough solution."

It has been pointed out that satisficing is an appropriate (i.e., rational) strategy when the cost of delaying a decision or searching for further alternatives is high in relation to the expected payoff of the supposedly superior alternative. When you take into consideration the costs related to extended search, it is questionable whether the optimum procedure is to search for the optimum value.

When a decision has been reached and the solution to the problem implemented and found to be acceptable, then the organization institutionalizes the procedure used to solve the problem into a **standard operating procedure (SOP).**

SOPs are rules, programs, and routines that are invoked by managers to gain time and to avoid the task of solving a problem from scratch each times it appears. Sometimes managers invoke those SOPs when the organization is facing a similar but not identical problem to the one that the SOP originally solved. Since SOPs are often processes that worked once but nobody is quite sure why or whether it was the best way to solve the original problem in the first place, SOPs are not always the time-savers they are supposed to be.

One implication of having rationally bounded decision makers in organizations is that organizations cannot be seen as single entities. Rather, problems are broken down and assigned to specialized units within the organization that develop their own priorities and goals. These goals, sometimes termed *subgoals*, may not agree with the organization's overall goals. This phenomenon has been called *local rationality.*[3]

Using this perspective, organizations could be viewed as constellations of loosely allied units, each having a set of SOPs and programs to deal with its piece of the problem. As time passes, these units become more distinct and their subgoals more entrenched. These divergences are enhanced by increasingly distinct perceptions of priorities, information, and uncertainty; they are further reinforced by recruitment, rewards, and tenure. When these tendencies are very strong, the loose alliance of organizational units breaks down into "organized anarchies." In the extreme case, coalitions are created with conflicting interests.

This leads us to the political model of rationality. You should note that the term political does not imply that this model is only relevant in the public (government) sector; rather, the term applies to a type of organization that may exist in any industry or industry sector.

The Political Model. In contrast to the rational model, players in the **political model** (often referred to as incrementalists) do not focus on a single issue but on many intraorganizational problems that reflect their personal goals. In contrast to the administrative model, the political model does not assume that decisions result from applying existing standard operating procedures, programs, and routines. Decisions result from bargaining among coalitions. Unlike in the previous models, power is decentralized. This concept of decision making as a political process emphasizes the natural multiplicity of goals, values, and interests in a complex environment. The political model views decision making as a process of conflict resolution and consensus building and decisions as products of compromise. The old adage, "Scratch my back and I'll scratch yours," is the dominant decision-making strategy.

When a problem requires a change in policy, the political model predicts that a manager will consider a few alternatives, all of them similar to existing policy. This perspective points out that decisions tend to be incremental—that managers make small changes in response to immediate pressures instead of working out a clear set of plans and a comprehensive program. This incrementalist approach can be seen as the simplest or most extreme form of satisficing.

The incremental approach of the political model allows managers to reduce the time spent on the information search and problem definition stages. Incremental decision making is geared to address shortcomings in present policy rather than consider a superior, but novel, course of action. In the political model, the

[3] A discussion and some examples of local rationality was presented in Chapter 2.

stakeholders have different perceptions, priorities, and solutions. Because stakeholders have the power to veto some proposals, no policy that harms a powerful stakeholder is likely to triumph even if it is objectively "optimal."

Our purpose in reviewing these models of organizational decision making is to highlight the realities of decision making that must be recognized when developing or acquiring information systems. If the designer of an I/S assumes that the rational model is a valid representation of the way a given organization is being managed when in fact the political model is a more valid description, s/he may encounter serious implementation problems. For example, access to information can be a very sensitive issue, since in politics, "information is power." If managers discover that once a new information system is implemented they will no longer have access to certain data, it is quite possible they will resist the implementation effort.

When we consider the issue of organizational decision making, it is important to recognize that the structure of the organization has a strong influence on how and when information is communicated and who gets involved in what decisions. We now turn our attention to the issue of organizational structure.

STRUCTURE OF AN ORGANIZATION

When we speak of the structure of an organization, we are referring to aspects such as reporting relationships, working relationships, and communication channels among departments within the organization. The organization chart describes the formal structure of an organization. **Organizational structure** is a logical concept rather than a physical one. Most organizational structures exist only on paper, but they act like switches on train tracks: They direct the flow of information and decision making in organizations. The major purpose of creating a structure in an organization is to provide stability, regularity, and predictability to the organization's internal workings.

The traditional view of organizational structure is that of a **hierarchy.** An individual (or very small group) resides at the top of the structure, with increasing numbers at each successive layer below. Consider a fairly simplistic, five-level organization for a moment. Employees at the lowest levels of the structure perform the actual day-to-day operations of the enterprise, and report to supervisors. The supervisors oversee the activities of the low-level employees, reporting in turn to mid-level managers. The managers compile information from the departments they are responsible for, and pass the summarized reports up to the vice-presidential level. The vice presidents use the summarized reports to develop strategies for the organization, under the direction and oversight of the president.

Functional View of an Organization. When people think of the structure of an organization, they also tend to think of a hierarchical organization chart which is divided on the basis of functions or disciplines. A typical structure modeled in this way might have a president and/or chief executive officer at the top of the hierarchy, with numerous vice presidents (to keep it simple, we'll assume only one level of vice presidents). Each VP is responsible for one or more major functions of the organization, such as production, marketing, finance, accounting, distribution, information systems, and human resource management. Figure 3–3 charts this type of **functional organization.**

There are many alternatives to a completely functional hierarchy. Some organizations are structured initially by geographic region, and then by function within the

FIGURE 3–3 Functional Hierarchy—Partial Organizational Chart

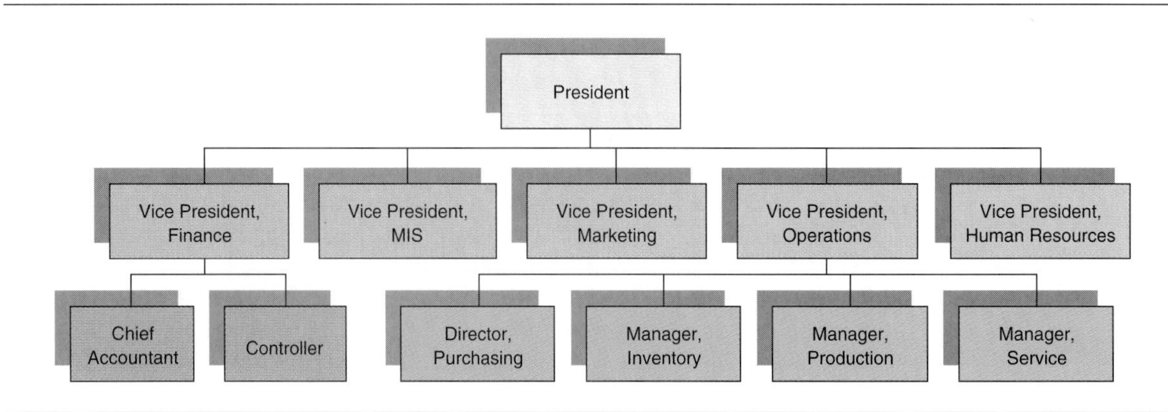

region. Some are structured around product categories; there could be a director of marketing reporting to a product manager for each of the major products. Some structures combine geographic and product responsibility to form what is known as a *matrix organization*. For example, a salesperson will have two supervisors; a country supervisor who is responsible for the performance of the company within a country and oversees the salesperson in selling all company products within that country, and a product supervisor who is responsible for the performance of a certain product worldwide and oversees the salesperson in selling a given product.

In addition to the functions performed by individuals, another structural consideration is the degree of formality. An organization that has a high degree of formalization and where much of the decision making is centralized at the top is known as a **bureaucracy.** Bureaucracies are characterized by (1) a hierarchy of formal positions, (2) formal positions with clear roles defined by strict rules and regulations (e.g., standard operating procedures), and (3) a specialized division of tasks.

As mentioned before, SOPs can reduce the need for decision making. In the airline industry, the reservation agents no longer price tickets. The agents would be overwhelmed by the thousands of different fares to choose from. Today, when you make a reservation, computerized models price the ticket automatically using hundreds of SOPs. Airlines update and fine-tune these SOPs, and the resulting prices, daily, a job that would be impossible if computer models based on specific rules were not available.

A bank might institute SOPs (and other types of decision rules) relating to the granting of personal automobile loans. An example of a SOP could be, "If the person requesting the loan has an income of at least $30,000, has a perfect credit rating, and the car payments are less than $150 per month, then grant the loan without asking for a review from your superior." The actual decision is not made by the loan officer; the decision on whether the loan is granted is based on the SOP, and the loan officer only gathers information from potential clients. This formalization of decision making increases consistency among all loan officers, saves time, and, by allowing fewer and possibly less well-paid loan officers, also saves money (the caveat being that the SOP is a good one). However, this formalization creates a certain rigidity in organizational decision making and may lead to problems in highly turbulent environments where constant adjustments to the SOPs are needed, or where exceptions, improvisation, and customization are required.

An alternative to the centralized structure is a *decentralized* organization, where decision making is handed down to individuals lower in the organizational hierarchy. This could involve, for example, giving the marketing manager for a specific geographic region complete control over all product advertising within that region. A decentralized organizational structure tends to be more responsive to customers and changes in the environment, but it also tends to increase the need for coordination and communication. The tendency to give lower-level employees more and more discretion in decision making has been called *empowerment.*

The functional view of organizations is deeply ingrained in society, partly because of the development of functional specialization within the educational process. Many current managers of organizations received their education in business schools that emphasized functional specialization. Students were encouraged to specialize in disciplines such as finance or accounting, taking as many courses as possible in their chosen area. The argument was that with the increasing complexity of decision making within organizations, it was necessary for specialists to receive increasing *depth* of knowledge within a relatively narrow field.

This educational focus produced managers who became accustomed to viewing organizational issues from a somewhat narrow focus. The VP of finance was concerned about the management of investments and decisions relating to the financial implications of planned capital expenditures, while the VP of production might focus on reports detailing the efficiency rates of various departments within the production facility. The VP of marketing might concentrate on alternative advertising media, while the VP of information systems attempted to acquire new computer hardware and software as soon as it became available on the market.

One problem with the functional approach to structuring and managing an organization is that it can lead to ineffective decision making. It is possible (and highly probable) that the best decisions made from the perspective of individual functions (departments) may not be the best possible decisions for the overall organization. This functional approach to decision making can lead to problems of local rationality, discussed previously.

Although we will always need some level of functional specialization (either internal to the organization or available externally, possibly through consultants), too much emphasis on the functional approach can impose severe limitations, delays, and obstacles to dealing with and responding to customer needs. A firm should be organized in the way that serves the customer better; organizational structure should be an enabler of customer satisfaction, not an obstacle. Customers, after all, do not care who in the organization works where, as long as they get good products representing good value in the promised quantities at the promised prices.

Process View of an Organization. An alternate way to view organizations is to look at them as a set of interrelated processes; this is **process organization.** A process is determined by a series of inputs and outputs; it is a clearly defined and structured set of activities designed to produce a specified output for a particular client. Since every process has an output, it means that every process has at least one customer. Therefore, a process is a composition of activities for satisfying a customer need. In other words, a process is a set of rules that help deliver, in a systematic and measurable way, a service or product to a customer, internal or external.

Typically, processes cut across traditional departmental or functional lines. Indeed, taking a process view of organizations implies an emphasis on *how* work is done—it implies looking at what an organization does in terms of verbs (selling,

FIGURE 3–4 Two Examples of Processes which Bridge Several Functional Areas

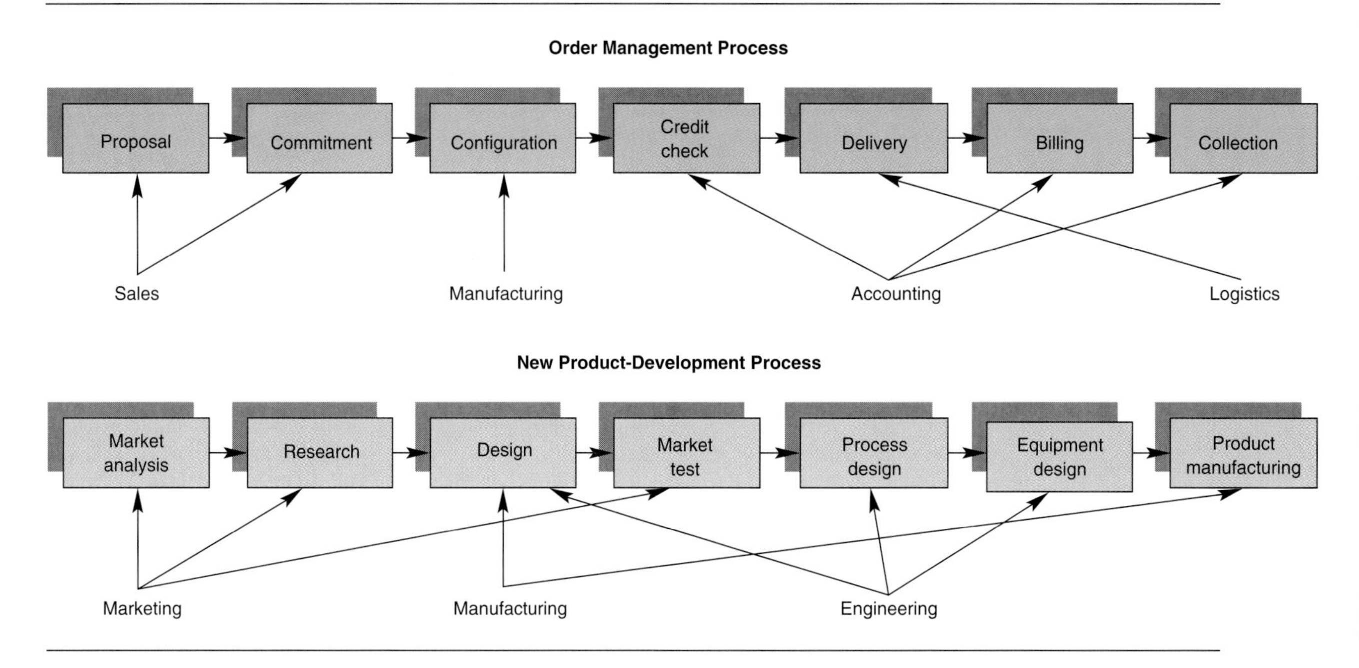

producing value, keeping customer happy, billing, etc.) rather than nouns (production, sales, finance, accounting, etc.). A process orientation forces a company to think about its capabilities. Organizations today look at how they are performing—what their capability is—in the product delivery process (how long is it taking us to bring products/services to market?), in the market-to-collection process (when the customer orders, how quickly do we fulfill that order and collect for it?), in managing the supply chain, and in servicing the customer. Clearly, these processes bridge several functional areas and require tight integration among them (see Figure 3–4). Therefore, a process orientation implies looking at organizations from a **horizontal structure** rather than a **vertical structure**.

Viewing organizations as a series of processes that cut across functional areas differs profoundly from the traditional view of organizations as hierarchical structures of authority, responsibility, and reporting relationships. A functional view of organizations presents the internal structure of the business in terms (e.g., reporting relationships) that are clear to the people working within the organization but that may be foreign to the needs and interests of the customer. A process orientation, on the other hand, generates an understanding of how the organization delivers value to a customer.

A process orientation does not mean abandonment of all functional area expertise; rather, it implies coordinating the expertise to accomplish the common goal of satisfying customer needs. Establishing a process orientation within an organization that has traditionally been structured around functions can be difficult. Typically, there are prejudices, misconceptions, and rivalries to be overcome. Marketing specialists might view accountants as "boring bean-counters," while the accountants might perceive marketers as having no concept of fiscal responsibility. Also, traditional measurement and reward systems for governing hierarchical,

BUSINESS BRIEF 3-2 I/T AND JOB RESPONSIBILITIES: THE NATIONAL BUILDS A NEW STRUCTURE

The National & Provincial Building Society, the United Kingdom's 12th largest bank, has been undergoing a radical transformation since 1990 when Mr. David O'Brien joined as chief executive. Mr. O'Brien describes what he has been doing at N&P as process design rather than process reengineering. The decision was taken to focus on becoming a true bank assurer: the kind of organization a customer can approach easily for advice and guidance about his or her unique financial circumstances.

Mr. O'Brien, drawing on his experience as managing director for Rank Xerox (U.K.) and particularly with its Japanese ally Fuji-Xerox, decided to start from scratch. Some 18 processes within the bank were reduced to 10. New names reflect new approaches. There is no longer a marketing department; instead, there is a customer requirement process. There is no sales department. It has been replaced by a customer engagement process.

"Our staff no longer have jobs, they have roles. They do not have job descriptions, they have responsibilities," says Mr. O'Brien. He believes that process design encompasses a whole range of activities that are often described as being discrete. So empowerment, de-layering, and total quality management are all elements in his design process rather than ends in themselves.

Note that computer systems are the final part of the operation. They are mapped onto the new organizational structure rather than being used to automate existing processes. The society is working with Unisys, the U.S. computer manufacturer, on hardware and software as it moves from mainframe-based systems to a modern client-server approach.

Now four years into the program, Mr. O'Brien believes he is about two-thirds of the way through the transformation. He measures several parameters to test how successfully the new organizational structure is working. A key measure is the strength of N&P's relationship with its customers. Put simply, the society draws up a profile of the financial services each customer could benefit from, and compares it with the services they actually use. Mr. O'Brien says there are now no obsolete, low-interest accounts where neither the society nor customer benefits.

QUESTION

1. In your own words, briefly explain the main elements of the organizational change program undertaken at N&P. How will the new organizational structure affect the ability of N&P employees to help satisfy their customer needs?
2. At what point in the process were information systems brought into the picture? What advantages might there be in defining responsibilities and roles before designing information systems to support those responsibilities?

SOURCE: "Using Computers in Business," *Financial Times*, September 26, 1994, p. IV.

functional organizations often disempower teams charged with executing cross-functional processes.

Refer to the example of the National & Provincial Building Society described in Business Brief 3–2. N&P replaced the marketing and sales departments with a customer requirement process and a customer engagement process. A customer requirement process implies determining what customers really need. This probably involves the use of many techniques that would be viewed as marketing techniques: focus groups, customer surveys, and so on. The customer engagement process attempts to work with customers, and potential customers, to effectively match N&P product offerings with customer needs.

Although to some people this may just seem like putting different labels on the same old thing (and in some organizations that may be what it is), it is really an attempt to change how employees view their roles within the organization. Instead of asking themselves "what will sell," members of the customer requirement group ask, "What do our customers really need?" Instead of asking, "How can I get this person to buy a short-term certificate of deposit?" a member of the customer engagement group asks "Does this customer need a certificate of deposit?" Employees have to adjust their mindset to that of working *for* the customer, whether it is the ultimate consumer or another group within the company.

The Virtual Organization. When talking about a process orientation, we describe employees from a number of departments working together as a team to achieve an objective (e.g., customer satisfaction) that cuts across functional areas. In some cases the members on the team may be in different physical locations, even in different countries, rarely meeting face to face, sharing information using electronic mail and similar communication facilities. This has been referred to as a *virtual team*; rather than having a physical departmental space with a group of people conveniently confined to it, this virtual team exists "only" in cyberspace. Virtual teams exist only as activities; they have E-mail addresses but not a physical space of their own.

Some organizations have moved not only to a process orientation but also to a project focus. Project teams are assembled and disbanded as necessary, bringing together individuals with diverse backgrounds and areas of expertise while the project is in progress. In this type of environment, a specific individual might belong to multiple virtual teams at the same time.

Some organizations have taken the process orientation further, and have blurred the boundaries between customers, suppliers, and even competitors. Some companies have created their virtual teams consisting of their employees and also the customers' and supplier's organizations. Other companies move part of their infrastructure to their customers' locations, while some other companies take on customers' facilities and manage them for the customers. The American Hospital Supply put computer terminals in the offices of their customers, the hospitals and medical centers. Customers can now check for the availability of products by accessing AHS's inventory databases directly (through the computer and communication links), and even place the order themselves. Similarly, automobile manufacturers such as Ford, Chrysler, and many others are linked electronically with their suppliers, and coordinate their mutual production schedules to ensure delivery of parts just in time. Another example is the contract that Federal Express has with many companies to manage their inventories of parts and finished goods, under which Federal Express sometimes moves its own personnel to ship products directly from the customers' locations.

This type of linkage and cooperation between organizations has continued to evolve into something that is now known as the **virtual organization,** which can be viewed as an extension of the virtual team or department. The virtual organization involves cooperation on projects between members of multiple organizations, using information technology to facilitate communications. In this way, an employee of one company might have responsibilities with his or her organization, but also have responsibilities with one or more virtual organizations that have been put in place. Figure 3–5 illustrates how two processes might be approached through a virtual organization.

Part of the impetus for movement toward virtual organizations has been the emergence of what some people have termed *co-opetition.* The basic idea is that, rather than being secretive about all internal decisions, some companies have begun to cooperate enthusiastically with the same hated rivals they confront on a daily basis in a range of markets. The incentive for such cooperation might be to

FIGURE 3–5 The Virtual Organization (Coupling of Different Companies through I/T)

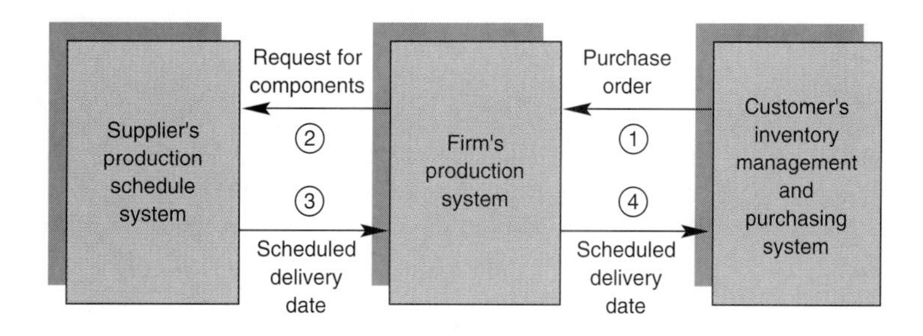

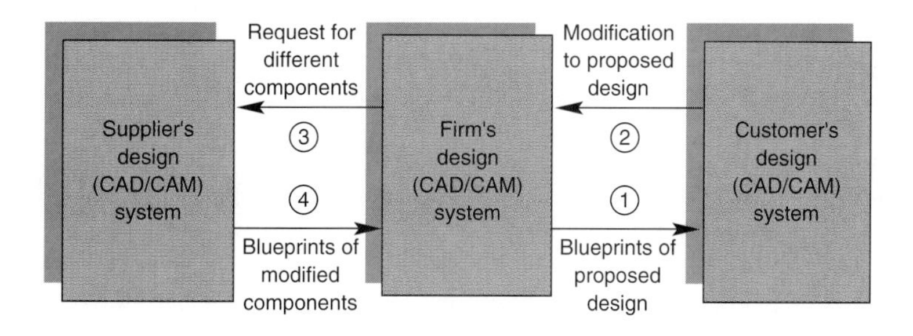

allow one group of companies to compete more effectively in a certain market, or even for one industry to gain an advantage over another. For instance, railroad companies might decide to actively collaborate in order to compete more effectively against trucking firms. As part of the cooperation, the competing firms might establish virtual organizations during the life of the cooperative effort.

The reporting relationship is one aspect of organizational structure that needs precise examination. What form of communication is required from the subordinate to the supervisor? How easy or difficult is it for two individuals in different departments to communicate? Do they need to report formally through their respective supervisors, or is it possible for them to use informal channels such as a meeting at the water cooler or an exchange of E-mail messages to settle business-related issues? How are standard operating procedures enforced? It is impossible to consider organizational structure without also considering organizational communication. In fact, as virtual organizations become more and more common, the organizational communication patterns will be the de facto organizational structure.

Business Brief 3–3 raises a number of interesting issues concerning the close relationship between organizational structure and communications. In terms of formal reporting relationships, the traditional medium for communications was written reports that were passed from level to level. All persons who handled the information as it passed up the ladder had the opportunity (and in many cases, the incentive) to alter information to suit their personal needs. Changing the medium

BUSINESS BRIEF 3–3 NETWORKS AS DISTORTION BUSTERS: ONE, TWO, THREE . . . YOU'RE WIRED

Executives claim three major benefits from working in a wired organization. The first is time and money saved. News that once waited for Monday's staff meeting goes out today. When SynOptics Communications, a supplier of systems used for network integration, audited its work practices, the company learned that electronic delivery of mail and files can speed product development projects by as much as 25 percent. Says CEO Andy Ludwick: "It takes hours or days for information to go from an out-box through the mailroom to an in-box, while the project is idle. E-mail is instant."

Second, networks provide easy links across functional boundaries, the old walls between departments. That short-circuits what Lotus Development's CEO Jim Manzi calls "the slowest cycle in any company, the vertical processing of information"—up the chain, across, and down again. Says he: "If you move information laterally, you've saved a long round-trip."

Even more important, multidisciplinary teams are smart. Says John Manzo, VP of engineering at Pitney Bowes: "To develop complex products, you need lots of people with specialized knowledge, working together in a little virtual department." It is simple to troll for such experts; the most common phrase on computer bulletin boards is probably, "Does anyone know . . .?"

Working in a wired company provides a third benefit; nets catch raw information. For example, Lotus receives more than four million phone calls a year—an invaluable source of information not only about bugs but also about customers' wants. Before electronic networking, technical support people used a costly and cumbersome process to collect and catalogue the data, passing them on to sales, marketing, and product development. Now information goes directly into a database, available on demand. Anyone with access to the data can search according to her needs, rather than accept someone else's idea of what is important.

QUESTION

1. In what ways has Lotus Development used I/T to improve decision making?

SOURCE: Thomas Stewart, "Managing in a Wired Company," *Fortune*, July 11, 1994, pp. 46–47.

(through the use of electronic mail, for example) can drastically alter the content of the messages as well as the reporting relationships.

Not all uses of communication systems such as e-mail are positive, however. As we will discuss in Chapter 12, the capabilities of computing and communication systems have also been used for illegal and unethical purpose. Business Brief 3–4 describes one such situation.

THE ROLE OF INFORMATION TECHNOLOGY

The transition from function to process structures and the changing roles of managers have required a change in the role of information technology. Table 3–4 provides a quick overview of some of the changes in managers' roles.

The new team-based organizations incorporate an entirely new set of assumptions about the role of a manager. Rather than being a traditional "boss," the new manager acts as a facilitator for self-managed teams who can *employ technology effectively* to store, manage, transform, and communicate information. To create a shared vision for the team, the new manager can use technology-based channels to *influence* people who then solve problems and make decisions. Unfortunately, little thought is generally given to training managers as to *how* to incorporate I/T as a mechanism for enhancing leadership efforts.

BUSINESS BRIEF 3-4 UNCLE SAM IS WATCHING: E-MAIL TAP NETS CRIMINALS

The first court-approved wiretap of an E-mail account has resulted in the arrest of three people charged with running a sophisticated cellular-fraud ring. The alleged mastermind, a German electrical engineer, advertised his illicit wares on CompuServe, where they caught the attention of an engineer at AT&T's wireless unit. The Secret Service and the Drug Enforcement Agency then got into the act, and obtained the Justice Department's permission to intercept E-mail messages between the alleged perpetrator and his accomplices. "This case represents the challenges in the future if we can't get ahead of the curve in technology," says a U.S. attorney, whose office is prosecuting the case.

QUESTION

1. Discuss the pros and cons of allowing U.S. Federal agencies to monitor international electronic mail messages.

SOURCE: *The Wall Street Journal,* January 2, 1996, p. 16. Reprinted by permission of The Wall Street Journal,

TABLE 3-4 Traditional versus Team-Based Managerial Roles

Traditional Managerial Roles	*Team-Based Managerial Roles*
Thinks of self as a manager or boss; follows the chain of command.	Deals with anyone to get the job done.
Works within a set organizational structure.	Changes organizational structures in response to market change.
Makes most decisions alone.	Invites others to join in decision making.
Hoards information.	Shares information.
Tries to master one major discipline, such as marketing or finance.	Tries to master a broad array of managerial disciplines.
Demands long hours on the part of subordinates.	Demands results (focuses on output, not input).

SOURCE: Adapted from B. Dumaine, "The New Non-Manager Managers," *Fortune,* Feb. 22, 1993, pp. 80–84.

In fact, one fundamental problem facing managers is that they are generally not well educated in the use of information technology as a leadership tool. Most of the executives of large organizations are over 40 years old, and they completed their education before computers became part of the curriculum. Although many have taught themselves how to use I/T effectively, many others still struggle with it. In addition, many leadership training courses emphasize a certain set of traits and behaviors, and virtually ignore information technology as a viable vehicle for implementing or supporting organizational leadership. As "virtuality" (i.e., teams, departments, companies that exist only as a set of activities taking place through a series of electronic information exchanges) becomes the norm rather than the exception in a company's standard mode of operation, using information technology creatively to manage people will become a requirement of an effective manager.

SUMMARY

Managers' decision making does not meet the standards of classical rationality, and managers frequently operate within a stressful environment of tight deadlines, multiple interest groups, and many issues. Consequently, they often use shortcuts in decision situations.

Significant obstacles confront managers who wish to behave rationally. The multiple demands for their attention and time, the shifting coalitions, the constraints on memory, the biases in information processing, and the sources of distortion in communication make the classical model of rationality an almost unreachable ideal. These limitations on rational behavior represent an opportunity for information systems to make an important contribution in organizations. By designing information systems to overcome the managers' cognitive limitations, they can improve the quality of information processing in organizations.

Though the classical model of rational decision making is not a good description of how managers make decisions, it is a useful benchmark for designing information systems. The administrative and political models describe how managers think, choose, and solve problems more accurately than the rational model and, therefore, are better guides to identify areas where information systems can help.

Most decisions are either made or implemented through teams, committees, and workgroups. It is important to know the benefits and liabilities of using groups. Before involving a group in decision making, one must think about the potential dysfunctional effects of groups. When used appropriately, a group can increase the quality of the decisions and their acceptance by the members of the group. There are more and more electronic tools to help groups be more efficient and creative. These include electronic brainstorming tools, prioritizing and voting tools, and software to write jointly create documents.

The structure of a company refers to the way employees are organized, and is formalized by defining job functions and reporting relationships. The traditional view of organizational structure is that of a hierarchy. A bureaucracy is an organization with a high degree of formality in job descriptions and communication flows. Bureaucracies may be efficient in terms of internal information processing, but they are rigid and slow to change. In some organizations, including bureaucracies, most of the decision making is centralized at the top. In others, the decision making is decentralized, which means that employees at lower levels of the organizations can make decisions on their own. Information technology, by allowing centralized information to be displayed simultaneously in multiple locations wherever and whenever it is needed, has had a tremendous impact on reshaping organizational structures.

An organization may be structured around functions (marketing, finance, etc.), geographic region, product supplied, and so on. In contrast to a functional view of organizational structure, a process view recasts the structure of the organization as a series of processes performed to fulfill a customer need. This approach to organizing work brings about greater integration across functions. Some organizations have become very flexible in their structure, creating and dissolving teams and organizational units by assigning individuals to projects as required. Through electronic communications, virtual organizational units have emerged. These units do not have a physical location; they exist only as set of relationships in cyberspace. When customers, suppliers, and/or competitors are also involved, virtual organizations are created.

The use of process and team-based structures has led to new roles for managers. Rather than viewing him/herself as a traditional boss who makes decisions alone and then controls subordinates as they complete assigned tasks, team-based managers share information and invite others to join in decision making. Information technology can be used in numerous ways to facilitate these new roles, through applications such as centralized databases, group decision support systems, and advanced communication systems.

KEY CONCEPTS AND TERMS

KEY CONCEPTS

- Rational decision making is an ideal that is often difficult to apply in real situations. (70)
- Information systems can help bring a decision process closer to the rational ideal. (94)
- The administrative and political models are usually a more accurate description of organizational decision making. (85)
- Designers of information systems need to be aware of the organizational context in which the systems will be implemented. (87)

KEY TERMS

administrative model (85)
biases (75)
bounded rationality (74)
bureaucracy (88)
cognitive style (79)
control (69)
content rationality (71)
execution (69)
first limit on rationality (75)
functional organization (87)
group decision making (80)
groupthink (81)
hierarchy (87)
horizontal structure (90)
information richness (83)
leadership (000)
model (75)
organizational structure (87)
planning (68)
political model (86)
process organization (89)
process rationality (71)
rational decision making (71)
rational model (84)
satisficing (85)
second limit on rationality (75)
stakeholders (87)
standard operating procedure (SOP) (85)
stress (73)
third limit to rationality (79)
vertical structure (90)
virtual organization (92)

REFERENCES

Andrews, P. H., and R. T. Herschel. *Organizational Communication: Empowerment in a Technological Society.* Boston: Houghton Mifflin, 1996.

Byrne, J. A. "The Horizontal Corporation." *Business Week,* December 20, 1993, pp. 76–81.

Deutschman, A. "The Managing Wisdom of High-Tech Superstars." *Fortune,* October 17, 1994, pp. 197–206.

Drucker, P. F. "The Coming of the New Organization." *Harvard Business Review* 66, 1988, pp. 45–53.

Dumaine, B. "The New Non-Manager Managers." *Fortune,* Feb. 22, 1993, pp. 80–84.

MacGrimmon, K. R., and R. N. Taylor. "Decision Making and Problem Solving." In *Handbook of Industrial and Organizational Psychology.* ed. M. Dunette. Chicago: Rand McNally, 1976, pp. 1397–1453.

Mintzberg, H.; D. Raisinghani; and A. Theoret. "The Structure of 'Unstructured' Decision Processes." *Administrative Sciences Quarterly* 21, June 1976, pp. 246–275.

Mintzberg, H. *The Structuring of Organizations.* Englewood Cliffs, N.J.: Prentice Hall, 1979.

Simon, H. A. *The New Science of Management Decision.* New York: Harper & Row, 1960.

Vroom, V., and P. Yetton. *Leadership and Decision Making.* Pittsburgh: University of Pittsburgh Press, 1973.

CONNECTIVE CASE: Frugal Shopping for ABB

When ABB Inc., the U.S. arm of the global provider of products and services for power plants, industry, and transportation, initiated a new strategy in 1993 to "shop the globe" for its manufacturing needs, we faced many challenges. They ranged from the complex logistics of coordinating supply purchases among hundreds of businesses for thousands of technically complex products to analyzing commodity markets and understanding the movements of foreign exchange. But the challenge that proved most difficult and the one that affects all companies embarking on change was the emotional response of people. We had to change not only how people viewed their jobs, but how they viewed themselves.

We first tried to confront their resistance with data. We had a strong argument. In the United States, ABB's expenditure for supplies amounted to 50 percent of its cost of doing business, yet our worldwide structure offered an unusual advantage in reducing these costs. ABB has a presence in 140 countries, half in soft currency markets, and can use its local contacts to buy more where the dollar is strong.[4]

But, although the economic data and rationale supporting our new strategy were compelling and clear, we were not persuasive. Information rarely catalyzes change—people do. How were we going to reorient hundreds of purchasing managers, training them to be as comfortable purchasing components from Finland as from Fort Wayne? We had to craft a process to deal directly with their emotional reactions and basic response to change.

We witnessed the rejection stage as soon as we began to talk about new procedures. Our early meetings were peppered with examples of both national and corporate resistance—questions such as "What about buying American?" or "We're making money, so why change?" and statements like "We've done business our way for years and we can demonstrate price decreases

[4]A soft currency is one that is not widely accepted outside of the country in which it is issued, and cannot be readily converted into a "hard" currency such as the U.S. dollar or German deutsche mark.

from our domestic suppliers," "Language barriers prevent quality products," "Time zones prohibit efficiency," "Different countries have different rules."

Our purchasing managers were resisting two major changes in their job responsibilities. First they had to reconfigure their jobs in the United States, and then they had to identify supply sources around the world. We knew their greatest discomfort and sense of loss was the sinking realization that they had to start up the learning curve again, starting from scratch in their jobs. So we introduced the changes in stages, while simultaneously providing training and a personal support network.

First, we created an information network for purchasing agents to help them communicate among themselves about supply management issues and the problems adjusting to change. Not only was there an immediate leveling of individual discomfort, but we generated a new camaraderie. No one was in it alone. This support enabled some managers to move on to the acceptance stage. We saw positive results fairly quickly. New network contacts provided new opportunities.

For example, as purchasing managers were learning how to reduce costs in soft currency markets, they began to use the same process with their domestic suppliers. Managers in two different ABB companies, through our network, identified eight other ABB companies in the United States who were using similar components for different products. The product was being supplied by more than 24 suppliers, and thus the new colleagues, working as a team, arranged to purchase from a single supplier. By widely communicating these results, we enabled people to begin to move to the next level: the global market.

But many questions still remained. How can a supplier of a specific commodity be identified? How do you deal with currency differences and the logistics of making the call, securing accurate estimates on shipping, and handling many more complex arrangements?

To deal with these international issues, we developed a network that we hope will grow to 2,000 supply managers worldwide, who can learn from each other, communicate successes, facilitate the use of suppliers in their local markets, and develop teams relevant to specific projects. Within the network, we have created a process to help managers purchase in soft currency countries. This includes procedures for supplier selections and quality assessment standards. ABB supply managers in every soft currency country provide local eyes, ears, and support to peers who are buying materials several time zones away.

In this process ABB supply managers are now expected to have the expertise of a commodities broker and the experience of a foreign currency trader. ABB Treasury Center provides them needed guidance, education, and resources. Our network and internal education are enabling purchasing agents to analyze data from both the commodities and currency exchange markets, to bypass outmoded patterns of purchasing, and then to select either another ABB company in the global network or an ABB-recommended supplier in a soft currency country.

ABB Power T&D Electric Metering Business in Raleigh, N.C. was one of the first to put its new skills to use. After analyzing the cost of components, it decided to buy materials from Latin America, providing a savings of 18 percent. And success breeds success. ABB managers continue to identify credible suppliers in soft currency countries and to communicate success constantly among themselves.

As people in the network communicate about significant results, perceptions of what is attainable are altering as well, both for themselves and their companies. Without the learning process—people to people, peer to peer—our strategy could not have been launched. We are still in the early stages of culture change. But it is clear that even in an engineering company, it is people who drive and sustain fundamental change more than numbers ever will.

Case Question

1. Use concepts from this chapter to discuss the changes instituted in the buying process for ABB, Inc.

CASE ANALYSIS

1. The purchasing managers at ABB Inc. were presented with quantitative data showing that the company would be able to save money if they were to collaborate with their colleagues at other ABB companies around the world, combining their purchase requests and finding suppliers in other countries. The managers discounted this information, however, since it was inconsistent with their perceptions (mental models) of reality. They believed that purchasing outside of the United States would be too complicated and risky to be worth the effort. In essence, they were operating in a situation that could be described as "local rationality"; their decisions made sense from their individual perspective, but from the perspective of the overall company they were missing many opportunities to save money and other resources.

With respect to the rational decision-making model, the ABB purchasing managers refused to believe that a problem existed. They did not search for new information, they developed too few alternatives, and they failed to weigh the costs and benefits of each alternative. In general, they were operating under the "If it ain't broke, don't fix it" philosophy.

Under the previous organizational structure, the purchasing managers at ABB in the United States reported to the senior executives within that company, and had little interaction with their peers in other ABB facilities. The introduction of the communications network, within the United States and eventually throughout the world, facilitated a move to process (task-based) management and the development of teams. The purchasing managers do not have to clear every decision with their bosses within ABB; they are given the responsibility of working with their peers to make purchasing decisions. Without the information provided by their international counterparts, and the communication network required for fast, accurate communications, these international teams could not operate.

By developing contacts with purchasing managers around the world, the managers from ABB in the United States were able to take advantage of the knowledge and contacts of their peers, and at the same time share their own knowledge and contacts. As the teams develop and the skills (such as a better understanding of soft currencies and foreign exchange markets) of the purchasing managers improve, they are able to investigate far more alternatives and pursue options that are more consistent with the overall goals of ABB Inc.

SOURCE: Keith, Bonnie J. "A Support System to Engineer Change," *The Wall Street Journal*, July 24, 1995. Ms. Keith is the director, supply management, at ABB Inc. Reprinted by permission of *The Wall Street Journal*,

IT'S YOUR TURN — END OF CHAPTER MATERIALS

REVIEW QUESTIONS

1. What are the three primary functions of managers?
2. Describe the "ideal" rational decision-making process.
3. Provide a definition of the term *satisficing*, and give an example of satisficing in reaching a decision to (*a*) purchase a used car, and (*b*) make a plan for Friday night with your friends.
4. List the three models of organizational decision making.
5. List some advantages and disadvantages of a bureaucracy.
6. Behavioral theorists argue that managers are rarely able to follow a rational decision-making approach even if they want to. What are some of the realities of management that interfere with the ideal rational decision-making process?
7. What is the difference between a function-oriented and a process-oriented organizational structure?
8. How do the administrative and political models of organizational decision making differ from the rational model?
9. Briefly define the term *frequency bias*, and give an example of a situation where frequency bias might occur.
10. List the benefits and liabilities of using groups in decision making.

DISCUSSION QUESTIONS

1. What is a virtual organization? Describe how a virtual organization could be formed.
2. This chapter has argued that managers of teams need to adopt different roles than those traditionally attributed to managers. Discuss how a centralized database of information and electronic mail could be used to support the new roles.
3. Consider the situation of a college student who has decided to purchase a personal computer for use at home and at school. Assume that the student wants to choose the best possible combination of hardware, software, and communications capabilities. Describe a *process* that could help the student make a rational decision.
4. Refer to the decision situation in question 3. Now assume that a group of faculty members has been charged with the task of recommending a standard configuration for personal computers for incoming students. Identify some of the issues the group would need to deal with, and describe how the process they would go through might differ from the process you described in question 3.
5. In many colleges and universities, departments have been established to deal with different aspects of the administrative tasks relating to students. For example, there might be an admissions department which decides if a student should be accepted; a financial aid department; a residence and/or housing department; a registrar's department; and so on. Students are required to deal with many different people and departments, some of which may not share information or share common goals. Describe how the experience for a student would differ if they were provided a single point of contact within the university for all administrative functions. Also describe what this would mean with respect to how

the college would be organized, and the roles performed by administrative staff.

6. Refer to question 5. Consider the implication for establishing databases (stores of information records concerning students) under (*a*) a functional department structure with little information sharing, and (*b*) a team-based, process structure with a single point of contact for students. Under which arrangement would the need for centralized databases be greater?

GROUP ASSIGNMENT

As a group, identify a local company that has at least 100 employees. Arrange to interview a manager within the company, and focus your attention on (1) the organizational structure, and (2) decision making. Obtain a copy of the organization chart (if available), and ask the manager to describe the extent to which the organization is structured around processes and/or functions. Determine the extent to which teams are a part of the organization. Also ask the manager to identify the types of decisions s/he is involved with, and classify them as being primarily group or primarily individual decisions. Use a word-processing package to prepare a five-page report describing the findings of your interview.

APPLICATION ASSIGNMENTS

1. Assuming that you have been assigned to a group for this course, use your e-mail package to create a group containing the E-mail addresses of all of your group members. Send a message to the group, asking for an acknowledgment in return. Use their responses to ensure that you established the group properly (you should now be able to create a message and send it to all group members simultaneously, without typing each member's E-mail address individually).
2. Susan Gross, the sales manager for ACME, Inc. is trying to remember which of her company's customers have been ordering the most products, so that she can offer special discounts to generate even more sales to them. Susan remembers a very large purchase from Bayridge, and she believes that they have been one of the top customers over the past year. Access the internet, locate the home page for this book and open the ACME database on the student diskette you received with this textbook. Perform a query to list all purchases over the past one-year period, and then create a report that groups the purchases by customer and shows the total for each customer.
3. Use a wordprocessing package to write a business memo to Susan Gross. Provide her with the list of the top three customers over the past year. Explain the concept of frequency bias to Susan, and describe how the database can be used to counteract a frequency bias.

CASE ASSIGNMENT Norris Company (B): Decisions, Decisions

Sherry Craig was about half way to the Norris Company Central plant on her drive to work. Trying to set priorities for her day, she was anxious to set in motion some way of keeping tabs on customers and competitors. She had decided, however, that the establishment of company procedures for inspecting job quality was probably the most important; certainly the most urgent. She frowned for a moment as she recalled that on Friday the vice president of operations had casually asked her if she had moved the project any further. As plant manager for the printing company's largest facility, it was one of her responsibilities. Sherry realized that she had not been giving it much thought lately. She had been meaning to get to work on this idea for over three months, but something else always seemed to crop up.

A blast from a passing horn startled her but her thoughts quickly returned to other plant projects she was determined to get under way. She started to think through a procedure for job quality inspections. Visualizing the notes on her desk she also thought about the inventory analysis she needed to help her identify and eliminate some of the slow-moving stock items, the proposed employee-tracking system, and the need to settle on a job printer to do the simple outside printing of office forms. She also decided that this was the day to confer once again with the Eastern plant manager about a competitor who had recently begun encroaching on Norris's territory from the competitor's facility in Montreal. There were a few other projects she couldn't recall offhand but she could tend to them after lunch if not before. She said to herself, "This is the day to really get rolling."

EXHIBIT 1 Norris Company (B)—Partial Organizational Chart

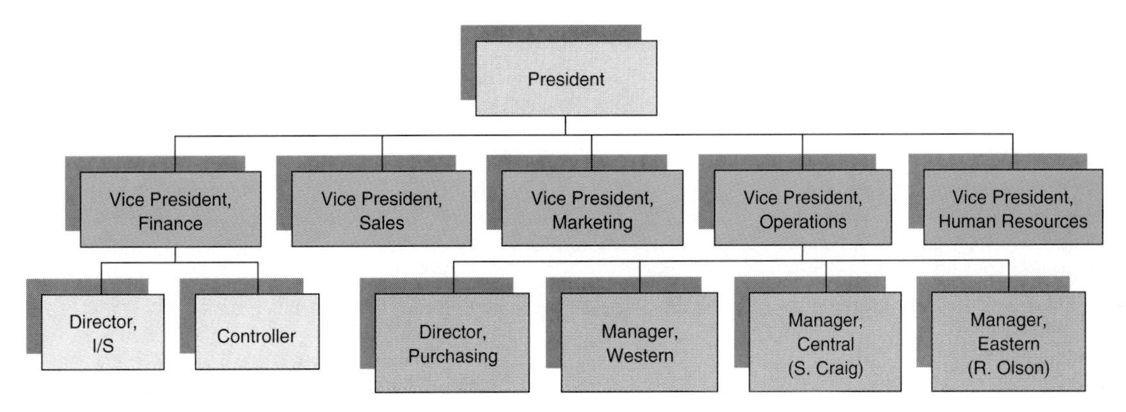

The Norris Company was somewhat traditional in terms of management philosophy, and this was also reflected in their organizational structure (see Exhibit 1 for a partial organizational chart). The head office, which was physically located at the Central plant in Ohio, housed the senior executives and the head office staff. The company was organized along functional lines, with vice presidents overseeing the major functions (finance, marketing, operations, human resources, and sales). The Executive Committee, which formalized strategies for the firm, was composed of the vice presidents and chaired by the president. The controller and the director of information systems both reported to the vice president of finance, who exerted quite a bit of power within the Executive Committee.

The three plant managers reported to the vice president of operations, who was widely recognized within the company as being second in command to the president. He and the vice president of finance both had very strong personalities and differing views of the direction the company should be moving in; the Executive Committee meetings were frequently quite contentious. Although Sherry reported formally to the vice president of operations, she found that her own views of the future of the company were more aligned with those of the vice president of finance, and she occasionally consulted with him on an informal basis.

Although the plant managers were responsible for the day-to-day operations of the printing facilities, they had little input into the strategic planning process for the company. For example, the decision to accept electronically prepared and stored typesetting jobs from customers had been made by the Executive Committee. Sherry had been acting as the assistant to the Eastern plant manager during the time when the move to accepting electronic typeset jobs from customers was being discussed, and she had been an early supporter of the idea. She was one of the first Norris employees to obtain an Apple personal computer, and she became an advocate for the company to embrace the newer technology and assimilate it into their operations.

The manager of the Eastern plant, Bobby Olson, showed little interest in electronic typesetting or Sherry's early experiences with the Apple personal computer. In fact, he had originally vetoed her request to purchase the Apple computer; Sherry had to "sell" the personal computer as a tool to help her prepare reports for him. Olson was a strong proponent of the old saying, "If it ain't broke, don't fix it." He had risen through the ranks in the Eastern plant during the era of mechanical printing presses, when typesetting and printing were highly skilled trades requiring experience and creativity. He refused to believe that computers could ever rival the quality of jobs that his typesetters and press operators could produce.

Furthermore, Bobby Olson was a very busy man. He believed in a hands-on management style. Since he had worked in virtually every department during his time with the company, he knew the operations inside and out. He spent his time talking with all of his supervisors and workers, getting involved in even the most routine decisions. He wanted to know everything that was going on, and became annoyed when someone made a decision without him. Although Sherry was his assistant at the time, her tasks had evolved into providing Olson with routine reports and keeping him aware of emerging industry trends. He seldom seemed to listen to her advice, however, which Sherry had found very frustrating.

When Sherry had discovered how some of their customers and competitors were using personal computers and electronic typesetting, she had told Olson and offered the opinion that Norris should get involved. Olson had thanked her for her opinion, but then did nothing with the information. Sherry didn't drop it completely, however; about a month later she had an opportunity to meet the vice president of finance for the company when he was visiting the Eastern plant, and she had discussed the matter with him. The vice president of finance was much more receptive to her views than Olson, and had asked her to keep him informed of any further details she obtained.

The vice president of finance was the one who eventually championed the move to electronic printing presses and the acceptance of typeset jobs from customers. He managed to persuade the vice presidents of sales and marketing to support him, and when it came to a vote in the Executive Committee, they were able to outvote the vice presidents of operations and human resources. The president had remained somewhat aloof in that particular decision, and had not cast a vote.

Sherry spotted a large pothole in the street before her, and swerving to avoid it brought her back to the present. Her old boss at the Eastern plant was still there; he had been considered for the position of plant manager for the Central plant, but was close to retirement and decided he didn't want to move from Massachusetts to Ohio. Also, although the vice president of operations supported Olson, the vice president of finance believed he was somewhat of a dinosaur and had opposed any effort to move him to the Central plant facility. He had been the one to suggest Sherry for promotion.

Sherry had received a call from her old boss about two months ago. Their working relationship was reasonably good, although Sherry believed him to be too slow to change, while Olson in turn had difficulty treating her seriously as a colleague. The issue he had raised surprised her; apparently his sales people in New England were losing some customers to a competitor, Superior Printing, that was operating a facility out of Montreal. When he had pressed for more information, Olson discovered that Superior was completing jobs in a facility in Montreal and then trucking the completed jobs from Montreal to customers in northern New England. He couldn't understand how Superior was able to produce and distribute the jobs at a lower cost than Norris's Eastern plant in Massachusetts, and had asked Sherry for help. He knew that she was more up to date than he was on new technology, and thought that the technology might be a factor where she could give some advice.

Sherry had done some investigating on her own, and had discovered that Superior sales representatives were actually typesetting consultants, who would call on customers in New England and work with them to develop the typeset images. Superior was focusing on lower-end jobs, which required less sophisticated typesetting equipment. The sales representatives used portable Apple personal computers and software to develop the job with the customer, and then transmitted the images and job details electronically to the Montreal printing facility. The Montreal facility was highly automated, requiring fewer workers than Norris' plant. Superior also took advantage of the exchange rate difference between the Canadian and U.S. currencies, which enabled them to purchase more printing supplies in Canada with fewer U.S. dollars. The result seemed to be that Superior could actually deliver the completed jobs at a total lower cost than Norris.

When Sherry had called Olson back to give him this information, he had sounded worried. He couldn't see any easy way to cut the operating costs at the Eastern plant, short of laying off employees and trying to work the remaining staff harder. He had thanked Sherry for her information, and told her he would probably decide to leave the lower-end jobs to Superior and try to focus Norris's efforts in the eastern markets on the higher-end jobs where there were larger margins.

This decision had bothered Sherry somewhat, as she thought there must be other options he could consider. Also, although the problem seemed to be focused in the Eastern region for the moment, she expected similar situations could crop up elsewhere, affecting the entire company. Sherry was somewhat bothered by her conversation with Olson when she learned of his probable decision, but she was also very busy, and besides, that was more his problem than hers. Sherry had her own crises to manage. For example, yesterday she had discovered that an order for supplies submitted the previous week had been way off the mark relative to what they had actually needed. The stockroom supervisor had been so busy helping unload trucks that he had just made a not-so-educated guess. This had resulted in shortages of some needed materials, and an oversupply of others. Maybe she wouldn't call Olson today, after all.

Questions

1. Describe Olson's decision to let Superior take over the lower-end printing jobs in the New England region, using the "realities of decision making" framework introduced in this chapter.
2. Which of the three organizational decision models (rational, administrative, political) seems to be most effective in describing Olson's decision? Why?
3. Consider the decision reached by the Executive Committee to move to the use of electronic typesetting and the acceptance of typesetting images from customers. Given the limited information provided in the case, which of the three organizational decision models seems to describe the decision-making process? Explain.

SOURCE: This case was written by Associate Professors Ronald Thompson and William Cats-Baril of the School of Business Administration, University of Vermont. It is loosely based on Northwestern University's "The Case of the Missing Time." This case is an amalgamation of situations found in several firms, rather than a representation of a specific company.

CHAPTER 4 Organizational Communication

After reading this chapter, you should have a clearer understanding of organizational communication and its potential problems, and the ways that information technology may be used to address those problems. More specifically, after reading this chapter you should be able to:

- Explain why good (i.e., undistorted), communication is key to organizational responsiveness.
- Discuss the different types of communication within organizations.
- Describe the main components of the most basic communication link, a communication dyad.
- Understand the major causes of message distortion in the communication process, in particular of information overload.
- Explain two general strategies for improving organizational communication consisting of first reducing the need for processing information, and then increasing the capacity for processing information.
- Discuss the potential roles information technology can play in improving various aspects of the communication process.
- Understand the need to align organizational structure, organizational climate and incentives, and information technology strategy to effectively reduce distortion in communications.

I know you heard me, but did you understand me?
Also, does anybody really read all those reports?

INTRODUCTION

Communication is the glue that holds an organization together. Communication is the means by which an organization creates a common vision and a common culture among all its different parts. Communication allows the organization to move as a unit. Communication is also the means by which the organization interacts with all the elements of its environment: with customers, suppliers, competitors, government agencies, and any other parties. This communication is a two-way exchange: the organization *collects* information *from* others on their needs and future actions and *provides* information *to* them on its needs and to generate a certain image. In today's organizations, information technology is a major enabler of communication.

In the process of collecting information from the environment, analyzing this information to determine what actions are needed, and providing information to the environment about themselves, organizations tend to generate a large number of detailed reports. Typically, a large proportion of these reports have questionable value in terms of enhancing the decision-making processes of managers and employees.

Managers and other decision makers often find themselves literally overloaded with data. Many managers spend so much time trying to check and assimilate all the data they get, that by the time they want to use it, they have very little time left to analyze it and act. Indeed, overload slows managers down and reduces their effectiveness. In most cases, problems created by ineffective organizational communication stem not from a lack of data but from an excess of it.

As managers lose effectiveness and fall behind in their decision-making responsibilities, the responsiveness of their organization suffers. Therefore, key concerns to enhance the responsiveness of organizations are to ensure that the reliability of the data collected for decision making is high, to identify what pieces of data are important to communicate immediately to whom and which ones to overlook, and to organize and format data to facilitate analysis *before* the data are transmitted to the manager.

In this chapter, we call the process of collecting, formatting, analyzing, and transmitting data to generate an organizational action, *organizational communication.* One of the major points of the chapter is that effective communication is at the center of achieving organizational responsiveness. We define effective communication as the process of delivering reliable and undistorted data, in a timely fashion and through an appropriate format and channel, to the individual that needs it to keep the organization in touch with its environment.

Chapter 1 provided two examples of manufacturing plants—Frito-Lay and General Electric—that experienced problems resulting from changes in their environments, and responded by making significant changes to their internal transformation and decision-making processes. During the period between the time the environment changed and the time their internal changes were fully operational, both companies experienced hardships that led to employee layoffs and the threat

Ineffective organizational communication stems not from a lack of data but from an excess of it. Photo courtesy of Jim Brown/Offshoot Stock.

of plant closures. Nevertheless, these companies succeeded, to a large extent because of the extensive and open communication philosophies of their management.

Those two examples illustrate that to move an organization from the status quo to some new, desired state requires energizing all organizational members to change. Energizing the organization means communicating the need for change across all the units of that organization. The clearer that communication is, the quicker that communication takes place, and the faster the organization will be able to move and implement change.

Therefore, distortion in organizational communication can lead to poor responsiveness. A major source of distortion in communication is the transmission of information that is perceived by the recipients, rightly or wrongly, to be flawed (data are false or biased, credibility of the source is low, etc.). If information about the need to change actually is flawed, two possibilities exist: either (1) the organization is unaware that the information is distorted and acts on it, running the risk of making poor decisions; or (2) the organization realizes the information is flawed, determines where the distortion occurred and corrects it, and then acts on that corrected information—but only after losing precious time to start implementing the desired changes. In either case, organizational responsiveness suffers.

The purpose of this chapter is to create an understanding of the factors that interfere with effective communication, that is, what factors foster the distortion of communication, so that you (or someone operating on your behalf) can design a communication network that supports maximum organizational responsiveness by minimizing distortion. Module II, beginning with Chapter 5, will explain the design, development, and management of information systems (including communication networks) in more detail. At this point we want to stress that you cannot design effective information systems without a clear understanding of the potential distortion problems in the communication process that those systems will be part of.

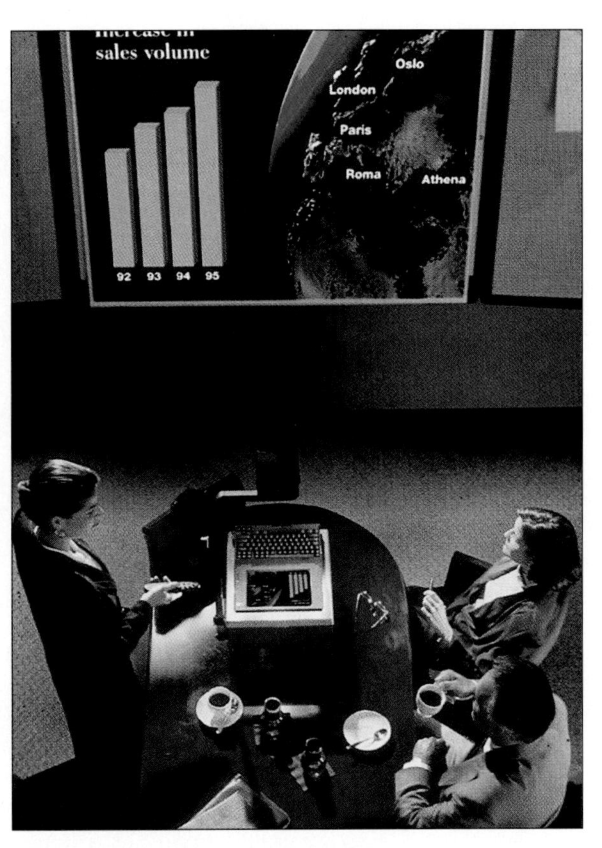

Communication is best thought of as a process comprising the collection, analysis, and transmission of information. Photos courtesy of Hewlett-Packard (left) and IBM (right).

ORGANIZATIONAL COMMUNICATION

Communication is the sharing of information between two or more individuals to create a certain meaning, a meaning that will be common to the sender and the receiver (common and communication have the same etymological root). Organizational communication is the sharing between two or more individuals or organizational units, of information related to an organizational activity. Sharing of information implies the collection, analysis, and transmission of information. Therefore, organizational communication is best thought of as a process. In today's organizations, this process takes place quite often over both formal and informal networks (some of which are electronic in nature).

Formal and Informal Communication. Organizations have a formal structure to create stability and predictability in reporting to facilitate the coordination of purposes and tasks. **Formal communication** consists of explicit messages that are recognized as official by the organization and tend to follow the formal organizational reporting structure. These messages are typically in written form (though more and more videos and voice messages are being used), and take a vertical, top-down direction.

In addition to its formal structure, every organization has an informal structure consisting of interpersonal communication flows that do not follow formal channels

Informal communications are an important part of the overall organizational communications network. Photo courtesy of Bonnie Kamin.

but rather follow the social structure in the firm. **Informal communication** consists of spontaneous messages distributed through an individual's networks of friends and acquaintances based on self-interest. These messages tend to be less precise and to contain less evidence than formal communication. For these reasons, informal communication has a tendency to move faster than formal communication and is an important component of organizational responsiveness. However, the informal communication structure is generally a breeding place for rumors (a rumor is an unconfirmed message); these can sometimes weaken the strength of formal messages and therefore slow organizational responsiveness.

One of the purposes of organizational structure is to determine communication behavior; for example, formal communications tend to follow formal reporting relationships. Once organizations settle on a structure, however, they tend to keep it for longer than they should. Ideally, organizations should reorganize themselves to match changes in the environment and as the goals of those organizations evolve. As the environment changes, often the patterns of organizational work and communication also change.

In an ideal situation, communication needs determine organizational structure. As communication needs change, so should the structure of the organization, that is, the patterns of communication. Some organizations, recognizing the fluid state of their environments, have structured themselves as webs of relationships, expertise, and resources sometimes extending beyond their own boundaries to include suppliers and customers. The terms used to describe organizations that attempt this type of responsiveness include **adhocracy,** *network organization,* and *cluster organization.* Figure 4–1 depicts in a simplified manner how communication needs should determine organizational structure.

Upward, Lateral, and Downward Communication. Organizational communication can take place in three directions: up, down, and laterally. **Upward** communication occurs when subordinates inform superiors about the results of a particular action

FIGURE 4-1 Communication Patterns in Different Organizational Structures

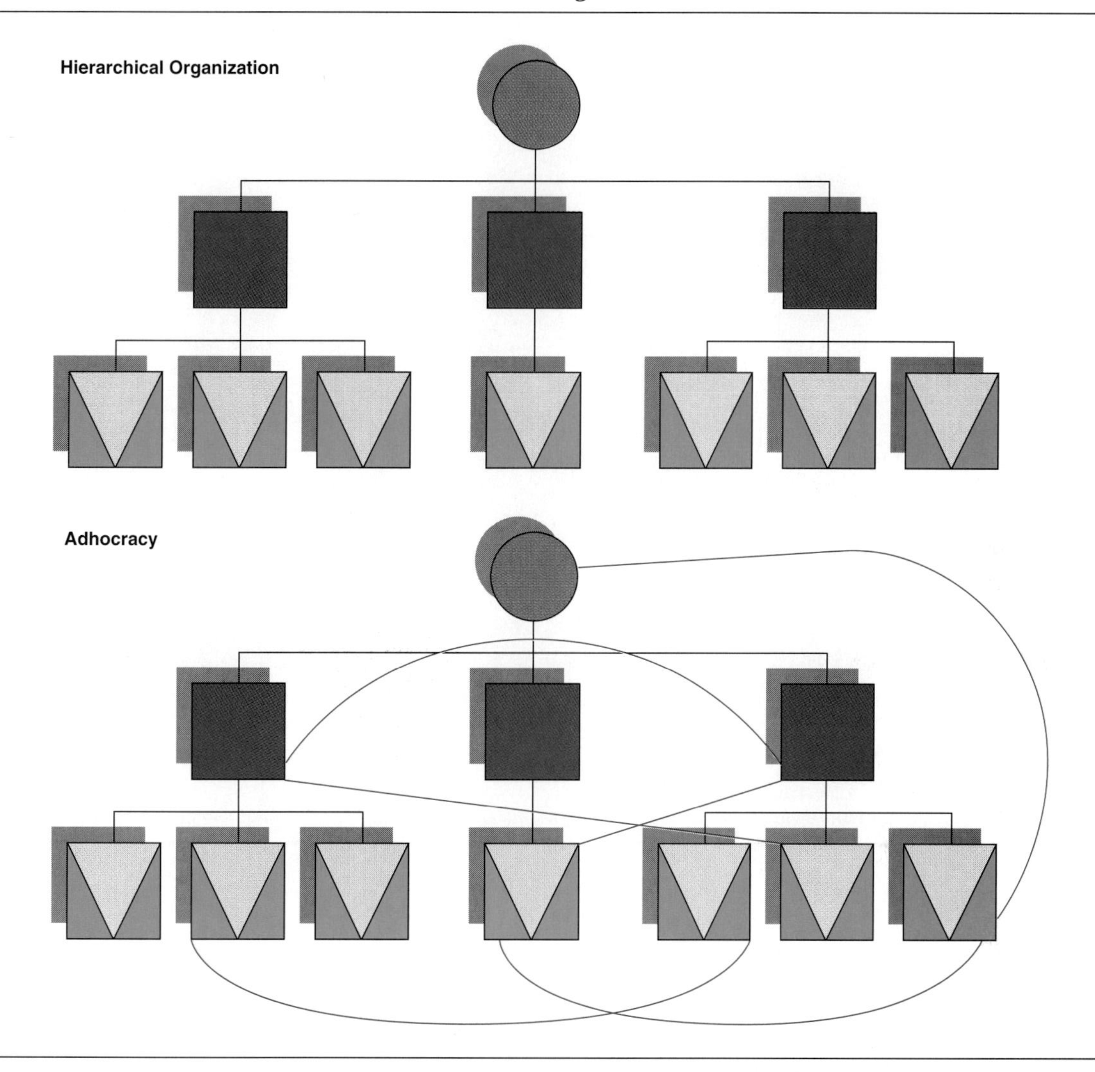

or the occurrence of a business event, or provide feedback on a previously given command. **Downward** communication refers to superiors transmitting information to subordinates. Most of the downward communication consists of the three Cs: command, coordination, and control information. When there is contact between individuals of different status, downward communication takes place more easily than in the reverse direction.

Lateral, or horizontal, communication is when individuals at the same hierarchical level exchange information. Individuals tend to communicate more openly and effectively with their peers than with their superiors because there is less pressure and they share a common frame of reference. Hence, horizontal communication flows in an organization are more frequent than vertical flows.

Upward negative feedback is often very scarce in an organization. The content of the message going upwards from subordinates to superiors tends to be positive, rather than realistic. This has been described as the *MUM (minimize unpleasant*

Lateral communication flows in an organization are more frequent than upward flows. Here a woman uses a videoconferencing system to communicate with peers. Photo courtesy of AT&T.

messages) effect. The result of this distortion behavior is that inaccurate information about existing conditions is often sent to the top. One consequence is a slowdown in organizational responsiveness, since upper management will be informed only after a delay (if at all) about a problem (e.g., a customer complaint, a delay in a product launch, a budget overrun). Another consequence of this type of information distortion is that top-level managers will not have an accurate picture of the operational situation of the firm, may misread the environment, and allocate resources suboptimally, again affecting organizational responsiveness.

Downward communication tends to be summarized every time it goes through a layer of management. Studies have found that the message content of a communication that was initiated at the board of directors level is reduced an average of 80 percent—and by as much as 95 percent—by the time it reaches employees four levels below. This reduction of information is due to a misperception of managers that subordinates may not be interested in the message, and by a preference of those managers to spend their time and energy communicating with their superiors. However, in order to achieve organizational responsiveness, employees at all levels of the organization need to have a full understanding of the goals and strategies of the firm.

Consider the process of evaluating someone's performance. In a typical hierarchical environment, a boss evaluates his or her subordinates; the boss's evaluation is

FIGURE 4-2 Communication Dyad

Communication relationship between two individuals, called a *communication dyad,* is a process that over time builds a set of idiosyncratic characteristics (language, format, meaning, code, etc.).

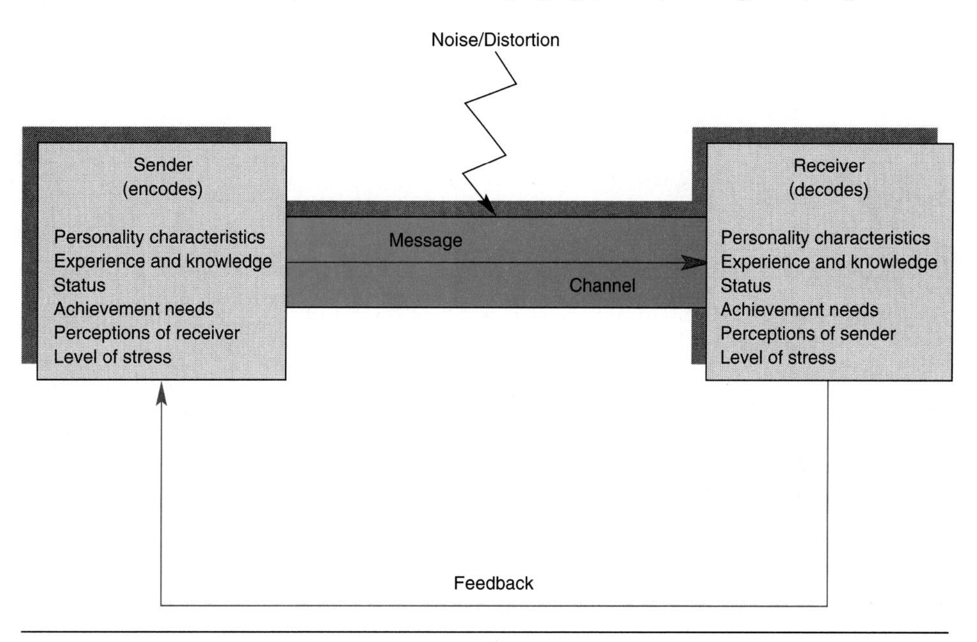

communicated downward, to the employee. Another approach, which has been termed 360 degree evaluation, also requires the employee to rate the boss, and peers (colleagues) also rate the employee. In this situation the communication is flowing downward (boss to employee), upward (employee to boss), and laterally (peer to peer), giving everybody involved a much better idea of the contributions, strengths, and weaknesses of the employee, and eliminating evaluations that are overly influenced by personality likes or dislikes. This type of evaluation may seem cumbersome. But, by including information from several sources and perspectives, it leads to a more satisfied employee and a better organizational climate—and therefore, a more motivated employee who will show, in all likelihood, greater productivity—making the extra time spent on the performance assessment well worth it.

Communication Dyads. A communication network is made of a series of communication **dyads.** A dyad consists of a **sender** (source), a **receiver,** a **message** delivered through a **channel**(s), a **medium** connecting the sender and the receiver, and **feedback** from the receiver to the sender (see Figure 4-2). The communication process consists of the sender collecting data, encoding the data to form a message, and sending the message to the receiver, who decodes it. Communication is the process through which data, information, or an idea is transferred from a source to a receiver with the intention of changing the receiver's understanding of his or her environment.

Good communication is defined as a message that gets decoded in the manner and with the meaning that the sender intended. Note that this definition is independent of the content of the message (good communication is independent of whether news is good or bad). The litmus test to assess the quality of communication in a dyad is whether or not the receiver understood the message and its purpose as the sender intended, that is, whether the message got distorted or not. In every communication, there is a certain amount of background noise: data that are not directly relevant to the intended message but that somehow were transmitted with the message. In order to maintain an effective communication dyad, efforts have to be made to minimize distortion and keep the level of noise as low as possible when transmitting messages. Regularly asking for and giving feedback is the best way to verify that the communication dyad is functioning effectively.

DISTORTION IN ORGANIZATIONAL COMMUNICATION

The quality of decisions made in organizations is affected not only by the values and beliefs of the individuals in the organization but also by the validity of the information coming through the organization's communications system. The communications system consists of the processes through which information is collected, stored, analyzed, and transmitted. Since these processes are responsible for communicating, among other things, information about the environment and about the availability of inputs and acceptance of outputs, and for allowing the organization to move as a unit, these processes are key to achieving organizational responsiveness.

Unfortunately, organizational communication is fraught with problems. Studies have shown that 70 percent of the communication taking place in an organization is bound to be distorted, misunderstood, rejected, forgotten, or disliked. One researcher, in studying team decision making by managers, found that 90 percent of the individuals showed inefficient and mutually inconsistent communication patterns.

Communication distortion is the transformation of the meaning of a message by altering (intentionally or not) its content. This transformation includes any instance where information gets lost or destroyed, is modified or altered in a misleading manner, is sent to the wrong place, arrives late, or cannot be understood by the receiver. In most instances, communication distortion is preventable.

Noise consists of any disturbance in the communication process that interferes with the intended effect of the message. Noise is defined as any part(s) of a message that the sender did not intend to send but somehow became part of the message by the time the receiver got it.

For example, the sender's clothing, looks, or language may distract the receiver while s/he is processing the content of the message the sender is delivering. A manager interviewing an applicant for a job might be distracted if the interviewee's appearance is outside the norm for the organization (such as an individual interviewing for a Wall Street job wearing a nose ring). Other distractions like stress, biases, and external stimuli (actual loud noises or a bad telephone connection) can also interfere with the processing of a message. Noise is not synonymous with distortion but correlates with it: the higher the level of noise around a message, the higher the probability that the message will be distorted.

Since clear and undistorted communication is key to achieving organizational responsiveness, it is important to reduce distortion and noise in all organizational communication.

The perceptions between sender and receiver are an important component of the quality of the communication between them. The way you dress becomes part of the message you are sending. Photo courtesy of Bonnie Kamin.

Sources of Distortion. Why are we interested in understanding the sources of distortion? Because distortion affects the responsiveness of organizations. By understanding what the causes of distortion are, we will be able to develop strategies and systems to counteract them and enhance organizational responsiveness.

There is considerable evidence that the quality (i.e., the amount of distortion) of communication in dyads is affected by five different factors. These factors, which relate directly to the components of a communication dyad described in Figure 4–2, are:

1. The *structure* of the organization—how rigid and hierarchical it is. These characteristics affect the "distance" (in terms of organizational levels) between sender and receiver and the possibility of shortening that distance.
2. The *interpersonal variables* of the individuals communicating with each other—their similarity on certain attributes like gender, beliefs, background, and personality, their relative status (peer, subordinate, or superior), their location (internal or external to the organization), and their history of communication (e.g., perceived credibility).
3. The *content* of the message (e.g., good versus bad news) and its perceived relevance by the sender.
4. The *channel and medium* being used to communicate the message.
5. The type of *feedback* that the receiver gives the sender.

Organizational Structure. Organizational structure guides communication flows. Organizational structure is supposed to facilitate the exchange of information among individuals in organizations by creating stable and regular patterns of communication.

However, several studies have linked structural variables to dysfunctional communication. For example, as an organization grows, the departments in it increase in number and specialization. Over time these departments develop their own rules, jargon, and standards, creating coordination and information exchange problems.

As an organization grows, it also tends to become more formal and hierarchical, adding layers of management and control. These additional layers increase the number of links in the communication chain, slowing the transmission of information, increasing the probability of distortion, and therefore decreasing organizational responsiveness.

Rigid hierarchical structures can be efficient for filtering and funneling information from lower levels upward and back, but they can lead to different types of unintentional as well as intentional distortion due to the large number of links in the chains of communication. In organizations where only a few people can make decisions, information channels tend to be clogged with routine questions on how to act or react. This centralization of decision making inhibits the rapid processing of information and slows the responsiveness of the organization. Also, as the message travels, its relevancy changes: the level at which the message originates has often a different reality (i.e., local conditions make the message more or less relevant or urgent) than the level that receives it. In general, the more a message is relayed, handled, and transmitted, the higher the probability of that message being distorted.

Consider the My Lai massacre of Vietnamese civilians by American troops in 1968. Newspaper reporters in Vietnam at the time observed that army orders tended to be interpreted quite broadly as they passed from one echelon to another down the chain of command. A war correspondent was present when a hamlet was burned down by the U. S. Army's First Air Cavalry Division. An inquiry showed that the order from division headquarters to the brigade was: "On no occasion must hamlets be burned down."

The brigade radioed the battalion: "Do not burn down any hamlets unless you are absolutely convinced that the Vietcong are in them." The battalion radioed the infantry company at the scene: "If you think there are any Vietcong in the hamlet, burn it down." The company commander ordered his troops: "Burn down that hamlet."

One type of organization having a very high degree of formalization, i.e., rules controlling communication behavior, is a bureaucracy, of which most government agencies are a prime example. As discussed in Chapter 3, the purpose of a bureaucratic structure is to achieve a high degree of efficiency by classifying situations that can be faced by the organization and developing rules, or standard operating procedures (SOPs), to deal with them. As long as the demands on the organization fit within these standard operating procedures, bureaucracies are indeed very efficient. However, when the demands do not fit the SOPs, bureaucracies are very slow to respond, since communication along hierarchy lines tends to be delayed and often distorted to support the status quo. In fast-changing environments, where demands change rapidly and flexibility and openness is key, bureaucratic organizations tend to be overwhelmed.

Flexible organizational structures are more able to cope with changing environments. Flexible organizational structures require an efficient and effective communication network to allow teams to form, dissolve, and re-form as required. However, flexible organizations that use electronic networks for communication channels experience more than just changes in communication patterns. The science and economics of networks encourage direct, me-to-you talk regardless of position, pay, or power. This can result in a change in office culture. In an article from *Fortune,* Warren Bennis of the University of Southern California states: "The beauty of bureaucracy is that it makes relationships more proper—bureaucratic etiquette is easy to understand. In networks, informality inevitably increases."

Bureaucracies can be efficient for processing information, but they tend to be slow to change in response to an exception or a change in the environment. Photo courtesy of Peter Menzel/Stock Boston, Inc.

Interpersonal Variables. **Interpersonal variables** also affect the amount of message distortion in a communication dyad. The sender, or **source,** is the originator of the message in the dyad. It may be an individual, a group (e.g., a committee), or an institution (e.g., a government agency). The source is responsible for encoding the message and, as such, is typically responsible for choosing the format, channel, and destination of the message. The choice is (or should be) driven by the identity and location of the receiver. As such, the sender is the most influential element in the communication process. Having an experienced, reliable, and credible source is a critical component in minimizing distortion.

The **receiver** is the target and destination of a message. The receiver ultimately determines whether the dyad is working effectively or not. Unfortunately, senders often overlook the receiver's needs and preferences and do not adjust the format, content, and level of the message, as well as the channel used, to fit those needs and preferences.

The interpersonal variables that have an impact on the distortion of a message include:

- The status differential of the dyad (e.g., superior/subordinate/peer).
- The achievement needs of both (e.g., ambition and motivation).
- The functional perspective (e.g., department and professional training).
- The trust between sender and receiver (driven by their communication history, habits, and past credibility).
- Differences in culture and gender.

As the similarity of the individuals in the communication dyad increases across the variables listed, so does the efficiency of the dyad.

The personal interests and concerns of the individuals in the sender–receiver dyad often determine whether information is added, modified, or eliminated—in a word, distorted—before transmission. In general, if the sender perceives a high material or psychological cost, the probability of distortion is high. For example, a subordinate's accuracy in upward communication is inversely related to his/her desires for advancement, leading to distortion of any matter that could harm the subordinate's career. Also, if the sender mistrusts the receiver he or she will suppress unfavorable but relevant information while increasing the flow of favorable but possibly irrelevant information to the receiver.

Functional location in an organization also fosters distortion. Several studies have found that depending on the area they work in (engineering, marketing, human resource management, accounting, etc.), people develop localized acronyms and terms that are effective ways of speeding intradepartmental communications but complicate and slow down communication across departments. Also, depending on where they work, individuals not only have different perceptions of a given piece of information—even one with the same source—but also react differently to it. For example, the finance and human resources departments will have different reactions to a statement from the CEO announcing a 15 percent cut in the workforce. These different interpretations, which can lead to misunderstandings, are due to the socialization process within functional areas whereby their members develop their own jargon and values, and give priority to their own goals and procedures. This effect is particularly acute when the members of a department share similar professional training and backgrounds.

An illustration of this potential distortion is a situation that occurred at the Cummins Engine Company. The information systems manager wanted to implement a series of formal systems and procedures. Information systems managers, after all, are trained to think in terms of formal systems. However, his systems ran counter to the organizational culture of most other departments, which valued operating informally and without systems. Rather than adapting his message to the culture of the users, the I/S manager tried to impose his message—a message that to him had an inescapable logic—coming across as a zealot and straining his department's relationships. Soon not even his phone calls were returned. By not recognizing the values of his customers, the I/S manager cut off his communication links and lost his effectiveness.

The two other important variables mentioned that affect organizational communication are the culture and the gender of the individuals communicating. **Cultural differences** and **gender-based differences** tend to be based on stereotypes. When people hear "culture" as a barrier to communication, they most often think of the transcultural communications between Eastern and Western traditions (e.g., Eastern cultures tend to be more formal, more opaque when it comes to emotions, to value silence and listening; Western cultures tend to be more informal, more open about emotions, uncomfortable with silence, and to value talking). These differences are real and can be major barriers to communication.

However, another important cultural barrier to communication is not based on differences in nationalities or ethnic backgrounds but on differences in corporate culture. For example, when Lou Gerstner left American Express to take over IBM, he changed the way executives made presentations to him. Before his arrival, top executives at IBM would make decisions based mostly on information presented in meetings through a series of overhead transparencies and in a "bullet point" format. Gerstner instructed that for any presentation he was going to attend, a position paper explaining in detail the background, issues at hand, and decisions to be made should be forwarded to him before the presentation. Painful as it was, this change was instituted.

Several books have documented the difficulties that men and women have in communicating with each other. For example, Deborah Tannen, in her best-selling book *You Just Don't Understand,* argues that men (because they value independence and success in competition) and women (because they value close relationships and cooperation) use different approaches and focus on different information when they communicate.

The content of a message influences the probability of distortion; news about winning an award will be transmitted differently than that of breaking a window. Photos courtesy of John Curtis/Offshoot Stock (left) and Bonnie Kamin (right).

Message Content. The content of the message affects the probability of the message being distorted. Its timeliness, perceived relevance, and ambiguity, its actual versus its desired content, and whether it is bad news or good news, all affect the likelihood of message distortion. Researchers have found that repression of types of information differs according to the direction of flow and the power relationship between sender and receiver. For example, they have found that favorable information moves upward much faster than unfavorable information; and that trust has a bigger impact on upward transmission than on downward or lateral transmission. Also, the amount of favorable information transmitted is directly correlated to the sender's belief that the receiver has a lot of influence over the sender's future.

Channels and Media. **Encoding** a message is the second step in the communication process. After the data have been gathered, encoding is the process of translating data, information, or ideas into a language that the receiver will understand. When there are no standards of communication (such as forms to be filled in a specific way), the sender needs to judge (and sometimes guess) the receiver's capability to **decode** the message and then choose the channel, medium, and format to facilitate the decoding task.

As mentioned earlier, the **channels of communication** are the means by which a sender conveys a message to a receiver. Channels can be verbal, written, or

In today's work environment choosing what media are most effective for a specific message is not a trivial matter. Photo courtesy of Bonnie Kamin.

nonverbal. The **medium** (plural **media**) is the actual path chosen to physically transmit the message. Media are the actual vehicles of communication such as letters, electronic mail, the telephone, face-to-face meetings, and video-conferencing. Depending on the importance of the message, multiple media may be used to convey it.

The medium chosen to deliver a message is so important to the way the message gets interpreted that some organizational theory scholars have proposed that the "medium is the message." Media have a set of characteristics that affect the likelihood of a message being distorted. Among these characteristics are the medium's accessibility, reliability, formality, and cost. The more accessible and easy to use a medium is, the more often that medium will be used, regardless of how appropriate the medium might be to send the message at hand. Many managers, for instance, continue to use telephones extensively, even if electronic mail might be more efficient. In general, as the costs of transmission through a medium go up (e.g., time, resources) the likelihood of using that media for transmission purposes decreases. Some media have been noted to cause shorter response times. For example, people react faster to electronic requests than to written ones.

The formality or informality of a medium can also affect the way people read the message. In an article from *Fortune*, Lee Sproull, a Boston University sociologist and co-author of *Connections*, a book about behavior in networks, has stated: "People are always surprised to discover that if you give human beings a chance to talk, they'll talk. And sometimes they'll say things you wish they hadn't said." It's been true since Babel, and electronic mail makes it worse. E-mail is fast and efficient—and can be highly inflammatory. At a big newspaper, one manager was so taken aback by the impudent tone of his incoming E-mail that he had the system changed so that he alone could send messages, and everyone else merely read them.

Some people blame the media itself. Something about E-mail releases inhibitions, just as something about the telephone encourages teenagers to share confidences. In an article from *Fortune*, Bill Raduchel of Sun Microsystems states: "E-mail looks like an exchange of letters. In reality, it's a form of speech—it's conversation." But it's speech without gestures. No smiles to take the edge off tough statements, nods to say, "Yes, I get it," or raised eyebrows to warn the other person away from dangerous ground. Result: not sure she has made her point, a writer MAKES IT VERY EMPHATICALLY and appears angry; jokes are misread as insults; "flame wars" erupt.

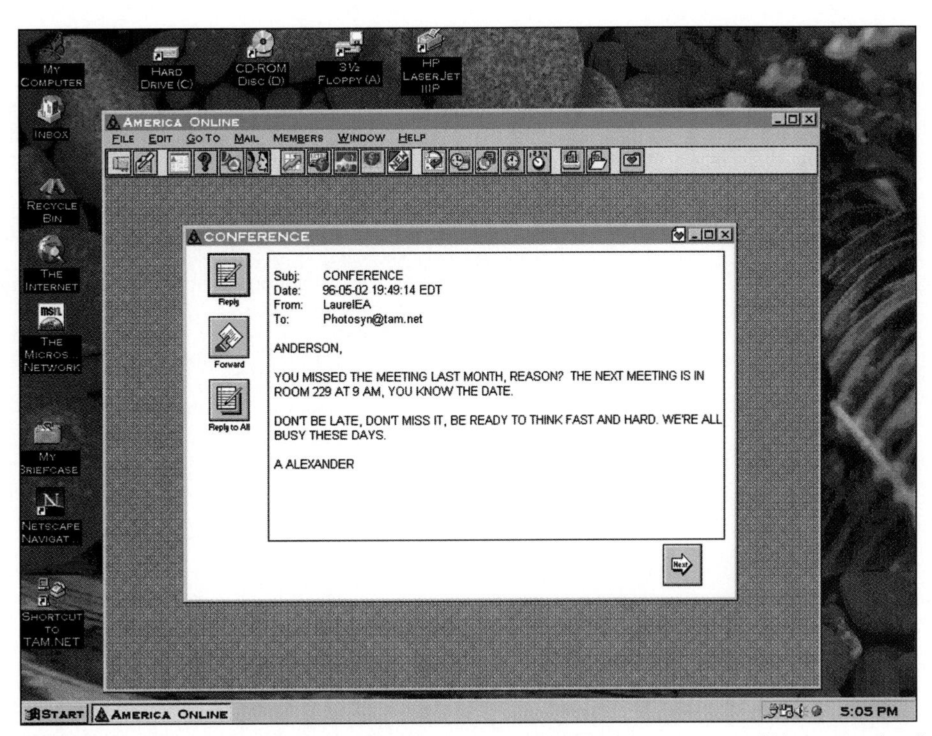

The medium influences the message. Here the recipient of an E-mail message would be uncertain of whether the sender was angry, joking, or neither.

Quality of Feedback. **Feedback** in a communication dyad is defined as the response by the receiver to the sender's message. Feedback is crucial to ensure good communication, because through it the sender knows whether or not the receiver got the message. Indeed, the likelihood of future messages being distorted decreases as the quality of the feedback on past messages increases. Lack of feedback in a communication dyad is like bowling on an alley with a curtain across it, hiding the pins from the bowler.

To be effective, feedback should be given by the receiver often and as quickly as possible after receiving the information. The sooner the sender gets feedback about the appropriateness of the communication (i.e., its timeliness, format, and content), the more effective that feedback will be. The more detailed and clear the feedback is, including specific examples of which communications were good and which were not, the more effective it will be.

Also, the more formal the feedback (e.g., feedback given at a meeting purposefully set to discuss the quality of communications) the more effective that feedback will be. Though feedback is given informally most of the time (e.g., students looking bored or confused during a class let the professor know informally that they are lost), the importance of systematic and formal feedback needs to be underlined (e.g., formal and systematic written student evaluations to inform the professor on which approaches work and which don't).

Finally, feedback is most effective when it is given frequently and at regular intervals.

Table 4–1 summarizes the major concepts introduced in this section.

TABLE 4–1 Sources of Communication Distortion

Sources of Distortion	*Effect*
Organizational structure	Hierarchy and large number of organizational levels increase the likelihood of messages being distorted.
Interpersonal variables	Status, achievement need, trust, culture, and gender affect the type and frequency of messages sent.
Message relevance	The content of the message affects the likelihood of distortion.
Channel and medium	The utilization of a certain medium to communicate a message depends on the medium's costs, accessibility, reliability, and formality.
Quality of feedback	The timeliness, frequency, and content of the feedback from the receiver to the sender impact the level of distortion between them.

Types of Distortion. Not all types of distortion are the same, and different types will require different measures to correct or avoid them. Therefore, it is important to understand what type of distortion can potentially affect a communication dyad so as to develop the appropriate preventive measures. Since the sender typically chooses the channel, the message content and length, and the list of receivers, the quality of communication is highly dependent on him/her. However, it's important to remember that distortion is not always related to a flaw on the sender's part and that it can occur due to the channel, the amount of noise, the receiver, or the feedback.

Distortion can take four different forms: **Routing** information to the wrong individual (or not routing it at all); **delaying** the message; **modifying** (from slight changes to the total destruction of the message); and **summarizing** the message (leaving out important data items). Distortion can also be **intentional** (fostered by aspirations to climb the hierarchy: e.g., purposefully delaying bad news) or **unintentional** (caused by cognitive limitations and increased by stress, time pressures, etc.), giving us eight types altogether, as shown in Table 4–2.

Examples of distortion in organizational communication are easy to find. Take organizations you are familiar with, such as universities. Students frequently move, and sometimes there is a delay between the time they move and the time they notify the university of a change of address. Also, many universities do not have centralized databases of student information; records such as addresses are maintained by different departments (registrar's office, financial aid, career development, accounts receivable). If a student notifies one department (say the registrar's office) of a change of address, other departments may not be notified quickly (or at all) of this new information. If the accounts receivable department sent a bill to the most recent (but incorrect) address they had on file for a student, it would be an example of unintentional routing distortion.

There are numerous ways to reduce distortion in organizational communications. Take the case of Spaulding Sports Worldwide. Spaulding is an international manufacturer of sports equipment that faces a fast-moving market where quick response to customer trends is critical to success. Yet the company found that it took a year and a half from an initial product design to availability at its stores—even if

TABLE 4–2 Examples of the Eight Types of Communication Distortion

	Routing	*Delaying*	*Modifying*	*Summarizing*
Intentional (Political, financial reasons)	Sending message to the wrong person; leaks	Purposely waiting for a deadline to go by	Changing the message; destroying data	Leaving negative data out
Unintentional (Fatigue, stress, overload)	Not knowing where to send message; sending to the wrong address	Not being able to send message due to overload	Forgetting to include material	Not having time to integrate all available material

the design was simply a change in logo and color. A good part of the problem was in getting copies of the design specifications to the right people for approval and modification—a problem, common to many organizations, consisting of information being constantly delayed by having to relay images or documents back and forth (and every time incurring the risk of sending the information to the wrong individual, etc.).

Spaulding implemented a document and image management system to streamline the design/implementation process. New design specifications are now stored in a centralized data repository where authorized users anywhere in the world can examine, comment, and access them instantly. The design/implementation process has been reduced by almost one year to about six months. Spaulding's initial software investment of $100,000 paid for itself almost overnight, according to a manager in their operations research group, since the company had been spending $85,000 a year just in copying, mailing, and distributing product specifications.

Information Overload. **Information overload** is a major contributor to communication distortion. The concept of information overload is comparable to the overload of an electrical circuit. A circuit, when overloaded, will blow a fuse. A communication network, when overloaded, will first suffer a deterioration in its performance and then stop functioning altogether. Information overload refers to the inability of an organizational unit or individual to decode the information and data inputs and recode them for transmission to a receiver. This inability can be due to the number of inputs, their frequency, and/or their complexity. It can also be due to a time constraint or other environmental pressures that makes the usual task of decoding and encoding data particularly difficult. Figure 4–3 illustrates what can happen as the number of inputs or the degree of overload increases.

An overloaded unit cannot decode, read, and analyze all the messages it receives. Under conditions of overload, organizational units use coping mechanisms to manage the inflow and outflow of messages. These coping mechanisms include queuing, prioritizing, and eventually overlooking incoming messages; reducing the time spent analyzing those messages; reducing the quality of the analysis; choosing the format and channel that take the least amount of time rather than those that best fit the needs of the receiver; reducing the number and quality of outgoing messages; and eventually, stopping outgoing messages altogether (e.g., missed deadlines). Although these mechanisms are effective in delaying the breakdown of a unit due to overload, they can have an immediate negative effect on the responsiveness of the organization.

FIGURE 4–3 Information-Processing Performance under Various Levels of Overload

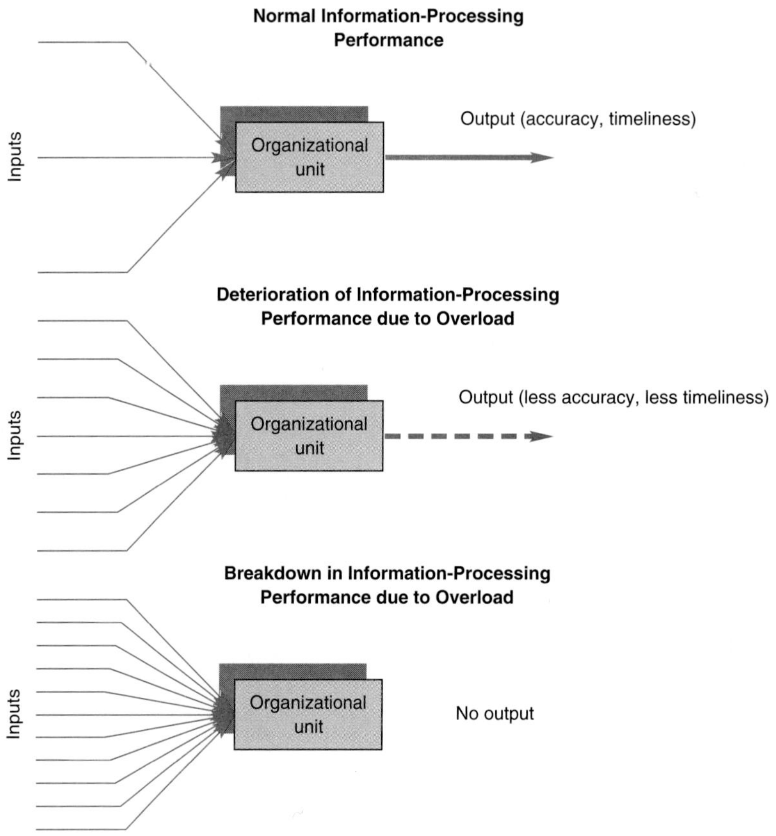

Normal Information-Processing Performance

Inputs

Organizational unit

Output (accuracy, timeliness)

Deterioration of Information-Processing Performance due to Overload

Inputs

Organizational unit

Output (less accuracy, less timeliness)

Breakdown in Information-Processing Performance due to Overload

Inputs

Organizational unit

No output

Information technology can certainly help in reducing overload but sometimes information technologies can also contribute to the overload. This situation is described in Business Brief 4–1.

STRATEGIES TO REDUCE DISTORTION

Two points should be clear by now. The first is that a good communication network is one that minimizes organizational distortion. The second is that the less distortion there is in communications, the better the responsiveness of the organization will be. We now turn our attention toward ways to overcome distortion.

Two effective strategies to minimize the distortion of organizational communications are (1) to reduce the need for information processing in the organization, and (2) to increase the organization's capacity to process information. These two strategies are generic and can be applied to all organizations. Let us look at each more closely.

Reduce the Need for Information Processing. The less information flows back and forth in an organization, the fewer the opportunities for the information to be distorted. We suggest applying the principle of "less is more" to the management of

BUSINESS BRIEF 4-1 INFORMATION OVERLOAD: THROW ME A LINE, I'M SINKING

Mark Rosenker, VP of public affairs for the Electronic Industries Association, loves to give statistics about, say, sales of electronic pagers or, better yet, his quick take on the state of U.S. electronics manufacturers. "The business," he'll observe, "is smoking."

But ask him how well he's handling the amount of information that comes through his office every day and you get a new, frustrated Rosenker. "Let me put it this way," he begins. "E-mail is an incredibly valuable service, but when you become inundated, it gets to be just like junk mail. It's reaching the point where I'm spending an hour a day going through junk, or using a keyboard to respond to junk, or thinking about junk, or reading junk."

Over the past decade, technology and downsizing, at least two horsemen in the apocalypse of corporate efficiency, have combined to turn today's office into a quagmire of information. Computer manufacturers promised the paperless office. Companies bought computers—and shipments of office paper have risen 51 percent since 1983.

Want to get out of the office to escape the paperwork? Forget it. Since 1987 we've added over 130 million information receptacles. Americans now possess 148.6 million E-mail addresses, cellular phones, pagers, fax machines, voice mailboxes, and answering machines—up 365 percent, from 40.7 million in 1987. Throw in 170 million standard-issue telephones, and you've got the picture of what we'll dub the Infobog: a pervasive, invasive information infrastructure that is as much a part of our lives as religion was for medieval serfs. Let starry-eyed fantasists and smooth marketers dream of sailing on some futuristic Infobahn. The rest of us just want to avoid drowning in the Infobog.

The quality of what we're getting, and creating, has not necessarily improved. Harvard economist Juliet Schor has seen an extraordinary growth in self-publishing among academics. As a result, she says delicately, "the range of quality is much greater." Adds management guru Tom Peters: "I'm concerned that this global cacophony will in fact be garbage at the speed of light."

QUESTION

1. E-mail is here to stay. Some people literally spend hours each day reading and responding to it. What would you suggest to make the situation more manageable?

SOURCE: Rick Tetzeli, "Surviving the Information Overload," *Fortune,* July 11, 1994, p. 60.

data in organizations: *Less* meaningless data floating in the system means *more* time to analyze and understand the essential data. The point is that in most organizations the major communication problem is not a lack of information, but an excess of irrelevant information.

Reducing the need for information processing does not imply restricting flows of information. It implies analyzing what information needs to be where, when, and in what format, and then delivering it in the most efficient manner possible. It implies eliminating unused, unwanted, and superfluous data from the communication system.

A basic assumption behind this strategy is that every time a message is exchanged, there is a probability of distortion; therefore, the less exchanges a message goes through, the less likely it is to be distorted. Another assumption is the need for quick response. The shorter the path between sender and user of the information, the quicker the information will be used and the sooner a decision will be made. Finally, the less information that flows to an individual, the less the chances of that individual being overloaded.

There is a muddy trade-off between the need to know and overload. On the one hand, you want to provide filtering mechanisms (which can be administrative assistants or managers, and/or intelligent computer programs to screen out irrel-

Information systems can be used to increase the capacity for information processing. A document scanning system with optical storage media can be used to replace paper files. Photo courtesy of Steve Weber/Stock Boston, Inc.

evant or unimportant messages) to reduce the potential for overload. Secretaries can screen telephone messages for their bosses. E-mail systems can screen incoming messages on the basis of key words, the name of the sender, and so on. This capability enables the recipient to review incoming messages in a prioritized sequence.

Some approaches to reduce the need for information processing include automatic decision making (e.g., automatic reordering of inventory based on prespecified levels); reporting events by exception only; and decentralization of decision making to keep the chains of communication short. Another approach is to establish clear, unambiguous operating procedures, standards, decision rules, and formats for information. This reduces the tendency to add more "information" to a message than is necessary, eliminates questions about who is supposed to make a decision or how to deliver information, and to decreases the amount of inconsistency and confusion caused by variable reporting formats.

Increase the Organizational Capacity for Information Processing. Once the relevant information has been identified, we can determine whether or not the organization is deficient in its capacity to process information. If *after* reducing the amount of irrelevant data, some organizational units continue to be overloaded by their data-processing needs (i.e., quantity and speed), then ways to *augment* their information-processing capability should be explored.

Therefore, efforts to increase the information-processing capacity of the organization should be implemented *only* after efforts have been made to reduce the need for information processing. Increasing the capacity for information processing includes supporting individuals and groups with computerized aids, and using or redeploying resources to overcome information-processing bottlenecks (e.g., reassigning employees from slower departments to others where employees are overloaded).

Oticon A/S of Copenhagen, a large hearing-aid manufacturer, was facing a serious customer service problem. Because most of its customers were elderly, and all were hard of hearing, few service requests came in over the telephone. Most came in by mail. Tracking down letters often became problematic since more than one person was typically involved in addressing the customer's request.

Oticon first determined what customer information was really critical. Then, using an imaging and workflow system, Oticon completely changed the way it handled incoming mail. Rather than delivering the mail when it arrives, all mail is now scanned in the mail room and delivered electronically. Then all the paper (except "critical" documents) is shredded. To demonstrate the benefits of the paperless office, Oticon went as far as installing a transparent tube from the shredder that goes through the cafeteria, so employees can see the volume of paper being shredded. Meanwhile, the important customer requests are always available in an electronic file cabinet to anyone who needs them.

As a result of the group management system, Oticon has achieved some impressive results. The company estimates that paper storage has decreased by 70 percent, productivity has increased by 30 percent, costs have been cut by 15 percent, and sales have increased by 20 percent. These changes have contributed to a significantly improved bottom line.

Business Brief 4–2 provides an illustration of how one organization has used computerized decision aids to help increase their information-processing capacity. As you read through the case description, consider what it would be like to try and assign flight attendants and pilots to schedules *without* using some type of specialized information system. The system developed by Decision Technologies has substantially increased the capacity for information processing of that organization.

GENERAL RECOMMENDATIONS

There is little disagreement that by reducing the data overload and communication problems of managers we can achieve greater organizational responsiveness. However, there is a common misconception about how to solve communication problems in organizations. We call it the *plumber syndrome.*

Imagine a series of communication dyads as sinks connected by a series of pipes. The plumber syndrome views the main problem in organizational communication as clogged pipes, and the solution as the ripping out of all those old pipes because they are too narrow, and replacing them with the latest technology pipes with much greater capacity.

What we suggest as a good first step in improving communication is to reduce the amount of garbage flowing through the pipes and then see if they still get clogged. Remember that, more often than not, freeing the flow of information results in the receivers being flooded—that is, overloaded. Indeed, the problem usually resides not only in the "pipes" but also in the "sinks" (i.e., the sender and the receiver are overloaded with messages and work). There is no point in increasing

BUSINESS BRIEF 4-2 COMPUTERS AS COMPLEXITY BUSTERS: I'D LIKE NEXT FRIDAY OFF

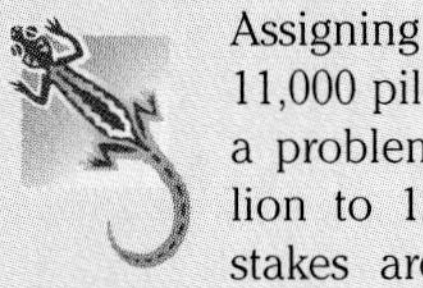

Assigning 21,000 flight attendants and nearly 11,000 pilots to 681 airplanes in 201 cities is a problem that can generate some 10 million to 12 million possible solutions. The stakes are huge: American Airlines crew costs exceed $2 billion annually. And because labor contracts often require American to pay pilots and flight attendants who are on duty but not actually flying, the airline estimates that a 1 percent increase in crew utilization saves it $13 million a year.

Two years ago, Decision Technologies (the American Airlines division devoted to using computers to schedule crews) achieved a computing breakthrough that allowed it to raise its computing power from 10,000 variables to 20 million variables and generate crew schedules that are close to perfect. The result? American estimates it saves $40 million to $50 million annually by reducing wasted crew time. This is still small change for American, which had revenues of $14.4 billion last year, but it is symptomatic of the way the fast-growing U.S. airline industry has tapped technology in an effort to stay on top of breathtaking expansion.

The problem tackled by Decision Technologies is a "typical" scheduling problem, in that there are known resources to allocate and known constraints to work with. The difficulty posed by the situation was the sheer number and complexity of variables that were involved. It is not hard to develop a schedule for such a situation, but developing one which is efficient is rare. By using computing power to apply known rules and scheduling techniques, Decision Technologies has drastically reduced the number of people required to complete schedules, and has dramatically improved the outcome of the scheduling process.

QUESTION

1. Discuss how this example illustrates the concepts of reducing the need for information processing and increasing the capacity for information processing.

SOURCE: Adapted from *U.S. News & World Report,* December 6, 1993, pp. 48, 49.

the capacity of the pipes if the sink hole cannot debit the necessary volume; the sender and the receiver might be the bottlenecks, not just the transmission channels.

As shown in Figure 4–4, we see the design of a series of information filters that provide less quantity but deliver more quality information as a major component of the solution to the problems of overload and distortion. However, filters are not the only means to cope with these problems. Organizations have several choices to overcome distortion. We list some of them next and categorize them as propositions, under the general headings of Organizational Structure, Management, and Information Technology.

We propose that the most effective strategy to minimize distortion in organizational communication is based on three components: (1) A well-designed organizational structure, (2) an effective incentive system that creates a climate of trust and openness, and (3) the necessary information technology to support flexibility and fast access to information. Although our emphasis throughout this book is on the third component, keep in mind that all three components need to work together to be effective. If any of the three components is not well designed, then the effectiveness of organizational communication will be compromised. For example, implementing a state-of-the-art electronic mail system won't improve vertical communications if subordinates do not trust their supervisors—no matter how great the mail system is.

FIGURE 4–4 A Plumbing Analogy of Information Processing Organizations

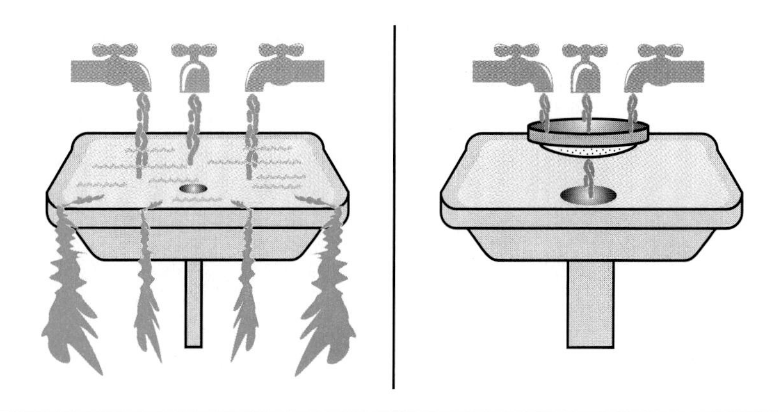

Reducing overload means reducing the amount of unnecessary data (filtering information flows), augmenting the manager's capacity to process information (bigger sink hole), and transmitting it faster (larger pipes).

Organizational Structure

A good communication system is one that ensures that the correct people get the correct information at the correct time. Designing an organizational structure to foster good communication is like designing a highway system. In linking two parties (e.g., two cities) for communication purposes, how fast and direct do you want that link to be? That is, do you want a dirt road (snail mail) or a paved road (E-mail)? How many lanes (capacity of the communication channel) should the highway have? Where do you put access ramps (who should have connections, access to the electronic network), exits (who should receive output from the network)? When? And so on.

In order to ensure organizational responsiveness, efficient and undistorted collection and transmission of information should be an integral part of the design of the organizational structure. Table 4–3 presents some propositions dealing with the organization's structure.

Management: Climate, Incentives, and Staffing

In addition to organizational structure issues, there are numerous opportunities to improve communication by focusing on the organizational climate, incentives, and staffing of positions in the communication network. Basically, distortion can be reduced by creating a climate of trust and cooperation, by empowering individuals to make decisions, and by reducing the level of and ambiguity about the expected communication performance. Table 4–4 shows propositions relating to management issues.

Information Technology

The goal in designing a communication system is to minimize all sources of potential distortion in the collection, processing, and transmission of relevant data. One important cause of the deterioration in organizational communication is how rapidly decision makers can be overloaded. Since most managers do not suffer from a lack of information but rather from a lack of knowing what information is relevant

Designing an effective communication system shares many challenges with designing an effective highway system. Photo courtesy of Woodward Payne/Photo 20–20.

TABLE 4–3 Propositions for Using Organizational Structure to Improve Organizational Communication

	Proposition
ST1	Keep distance between source and receiver as short as possible. A potential drawback: there may not be enough filtering.
ST2	Provide multiple independent sources for important messages. A source is more likely to pass information when the receiver is likely to hear it from another source. A potential drawback: redundancy may cause overload. Use redundancy selectively (critical messages, unreliable channels, etc.).
ST3	Delegate decision making to lower levels to avoid overload of upper levels, to reduce the probability of clogging communication channels, and to improve responsiveness. A by-product: an increase in participation and fulfillment and therefore less distortion.
ST4	Develop flexible communication patterns. Rigid hierarchical communication causes distortion in the direction of the status quo. A potential drawback: sources not knowing who to communicate with.
ST5	Increase lateral communication. Lateral communication is as effective as an error-reducing approach (assuming a noncompetitive environment among peers).

and how to use it, we believe that I/T should act as a filter to keep "garbage" and noise—irrelevant data—out. This implies that in order to improve communication, I/T should provide not more information but more appropriate information and guidance on how to use that information. As mentioned before, in designing information systems, very often *less* (data) is *more* (analysis and information).

However, the quality of the data that a decision maker utilizes in addressing a given issue or task is determined to a large extent by the transmission mechanisms used to deliver that data. Therefore, the use of information technology to reduce distortion should go beyond supporting an individual with better decision rules and

TABLE 4–4 Propositions for Using Management Techniques to Improve Organizational Communication

	Proposition
MT1	Define objectives and organizational relationships; explain them to subordinates to avoid ambiguity. This will reduce insecurity and therefore reduce distortion. It will also minimize unintentional misrouting.
MT2	Create a climate of cooperation; increase participation of low-status individuals.
MT3	Define standards and criteria for performance, and provide regular and formal feedback. Effectiveness, trust, and cooperation will increase.
MT4	Reward on basis of correct decisions (not on decisions based on information received).
MT5	Reward collection and transmission of high-quality information (appropriate, timely, accurate). Note: risk of overload as more information than needed is transmitted.
MT6	Rotate individuals to reduce the probability of a source of information being preconceived and stereotyped. Note: risk of increased anxiety caused by new environment.

TABLE 4–5 Propositions for Using Information Technology to Improve Organizational Communication

	Proposition
IT1	Use decision rules–based *normative* models (such as models to determine the optimal level of inventory to maintain, or the optimal quantity of raw materials to order).
IT2	Summarize and combine information dealing with statistical data.
IT3	Use standard data-entry screens and prefilled, standardized input forms.
IT4	Provide flexible, customized report formats.
IT5	Report on a "by-exception-only" basis.
IT6	Route messages automatically on the basis of key words and findings; provide selective access (shortcuts) to upper levels of the chain of communication on specific issues.
IT7	Create a centralized database and provide access to it from all hierarchical levels in the communication chain.

mathematical models, and provide support of the organizational processes to collect and transmit information.

Electronic tools like E-mail and groupware like Lotus Notes and computer conferencing, by providing quick, customized, and simultaneous access to information, are having a tremendous impact on the design of communication systems. These tools have affected the efficiency and effectiveness of communication in two ways. They have increased the speed at which people interact with each other, and they have increased the number of subordinates that a manager can oversee effectively (what is called the manager's **span of control**). This increase in span of control has led to flatter organizations (fewer levels) and, therefore, more responsive organizations.

Table 4–5 shows propositions relating to the use of information technology to overcome distortion.

BUSINESS BRIEF 4–3 ACCELERATING RESPONSIVENESS: FOLLOW THE SUN

There were networks before there were computers; old-boy networks, loose contacts that led you to your job, the tangled connections and communications of the "informal organization" which gets things done and fills out the paperwork later. What's new is the deliberately networked organization, made possible by less expensive and more functional information technology. Communications capabilities and patterns will never be the same.

Take Hewlett-Packard's customer-response network, for example. When a customer reports a problem, the call (or electronic message) goes automatically to one of four hubs around the world, depending on the time of day. Operators get a description of the problem and its urgency, typing the information into a database and zapping the file to one of 27 centers where it might be picked up by a team specializing in, say, operating system foul-ups.

The database is shared by all of the centers and is "live"—that is, whenever an employee works on a file, it is instantly updated, so every center has identical information about each job at all times. If the first center can't solve a problem quickly, it follows the sun: at 6:00 PM in California, for example, the action shifts to Australia, to be picked up by a crew a third of a world away. The file, of course, is already there.

"With the ability to share information broadly and fully without filtering it through a hierarchy, we can manage the way we always wanted to," argues Robert Walker, Chief Information Officer. Every month Hewlett-Packard's 97,000 employees exchange 20 million E-mail messages, 70,000 messages with entities outside the company; share three trillion characters of data, such as engineering specs; and execute more than a quarter of a million electronic transactions with customers and suppliers.

QUESTIONS

1. Comment on how the system used by H-P's customer-response technical support staff addresses the types and sources of distortion discussed in this chapter.
2. Describe the system used by H-P's customer-response technical support staff using the concepts of feedback and homeostasis from General Systems Theory from Chapter 2.

SOURCE: Thomas A. Stewart, "Managing in a Wired Company," *Fortune*, July 11, 1994, pp. 44–46.

Business Brief 4–3 describes the ways Hewlett-Packard has used I/T to improve internal and external organizational communications. As you read through the example, consider what it would be like for Hewlett-Packard if they had no electronic communication capabilities, or if they did not have the centralized database of customer problems.

Now let us illustrate how the propositions discussed in Tables 4–3, 4–4, and 4–5 can be applied to actual situations. Consider the example where a single source (say, a subordinate) is communicating with a single receiver (the boss) as shown in Figure 4–5. In this situation, many of the types of distortion discussed previously can interfere with the quality of the communication. Interpersonal variables could come into play, such as the aspirations of the subordinate and the previous history of communication between the two. For example, the boss could question the reliability of the information given that there were some issues with the credibility and objectivity of the subordinate in the past.

One way to address this situation would be to add one or more independent sources to provide the same information. Since adding one more source could result

FIGURE 4–5 Building Selective Redundancy and Filters

Situation: One source; reliability and credibility are questionable.

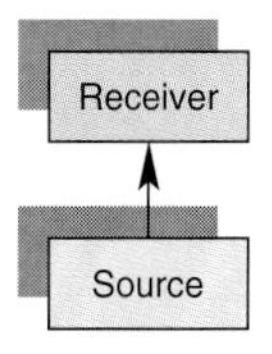

Solution: Add redundant source, build filter to check information from both sources, and present two versions only if discrepancies occur.

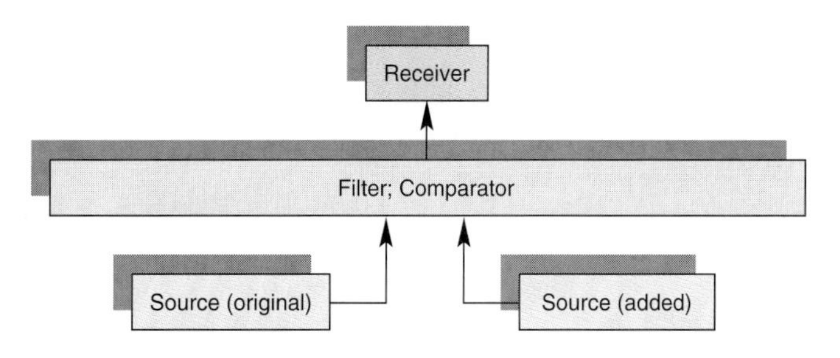

in information overload, a filter should be added to compare the information from the two sources. If both sources agree, then only one report is produced. If the sources disagree, then the system notifies the boss (receiver) of the discrepancy and two reports are produced.

Consider now the transmission of information through a typical hierarchy (Figure 4–6). In this example, messages have to flow from one level to the next, without any opportunity to skip levels or for different levels to share information simultaneously. The fact that information goes through numerous steps in the process of being communicated along the hierarchy slows down the organization's response and increases the probabilities of distortion.

One way to improve this situation is to create a database of information and provide access to anyone (assuming they have the appropriate security and confidentiality clearances) within the chain of command. Figure 4–6 illustrates the example of a director having direct access to information deposited in a database by a lower-level employee without needing to go through two intervening layers in the management hierarchy. This type of bypassing can reduce the potential lag in the director being informed about an important event, and therefore, can enhance organizational responsiveness. Also, subordinates—knowing that their supervisors have access to the same raw data—are less likely to intentionally distort the messages they send upward summarizing that data.

Another important benefit of implementing centralized databases with broad and decentralized access to them, and information filters to keep irrelevant data out, is the ability for a supervisor to communicate effectively with more subordinates. As mentioned, this increase in the supervisor's span of control leads to a flattening of the organization and, eventually, to greater responsiveness.

FIGURE 4–6 Using Centralized Databases and Decentralized Access

Situation: Hierarchical transmission of information.
Subordinates inform supervisors. If supervisor has a question, the supervisor will query the subordinate, who in turn will question the next level subordinate, and so forth.

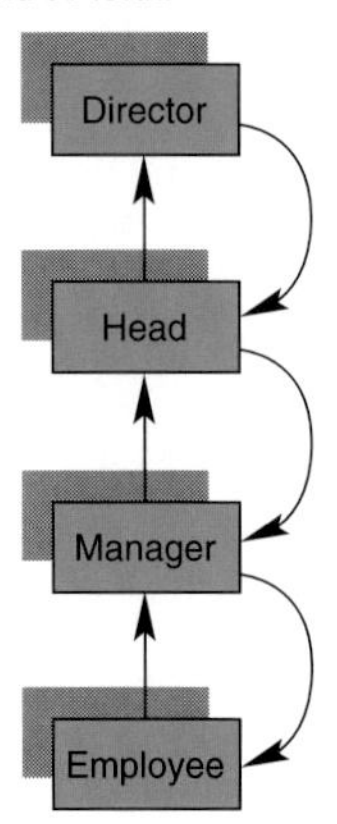

Solution: Create a database that can be accessed by anyone on the chain of command and allow for selective access up the chain of command.

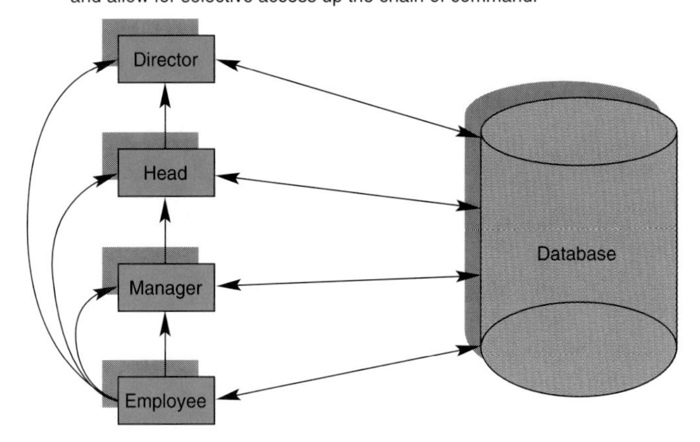

SUMMARY

Communication is the glue that holds an organization together. Communication allows a company to adjust to changes in its environment by providing information to make decisions and coordinate activities. Ineffective communications—communications that are distorted—slow down organizational responsiveness.

Communication networks can be viewed as a series of dyads. Each dyad is defined as a process in which a sender, after analyzing some data or event, decides to encode a message, and transmits the message to a receiver through a channel using a specific medium; the message is then decoded by the receiver, and the receiver provides feedback to the sender about the message. A message can be distorted during transmission by noise. Noise consists of any disturbance in the communication process that interferes with the intended meaning of the message (the clarity of the channel, the distraction level of the receiver, etc.).

Within an organization, communication flows upward, laterally, and downward. The direction of the communication affects the content of the message. Formal communication follows the established communication lines within the organizational structure, while informal communication flows along personal relationships. Ideally, organizational structure should reflect the communication needs of the organization and adjust as these needs change. Organizations that have achieved this level of flexibility are called *network* organizations or *adhocracies*.

Communication becomes distorted in numerous ways. Based on the components of a communication dyad, we identified five specific *sources* of distortion: Organizational structure, interpersonal variables, message content, channel, and type of feedback. We then classified distortion into eight distinct *types*: Intentional and unintentional cases of routing, delay, modification, and summarization of messages. Knowing what type of distortion may interfere with a communication dyad is important because the type of distortion determines what type of solution we need in order to avoid it.

One result of badly designed organizational communication networks is information overload. Information overload can cause a node in a communication network to operate inefficiently or even break down completely. Information overload is a major culprit behind the distortion of organizational communication. Two generic strategies to reduce distortion are (1) to reduce the need for information processing, and (2) to increase the capacity for information processing.

Managers have a series of tools at their disposal to overcome distortion in organizational communications. These include the design of appropriate organizational structure, climate, and incentives, and the use of information technology. The I/T that can be used to alleviate distortion includes centralized databases accessible from a variety of locations, "smart" software to create filters that prioritize information and screen out irrelevant data, groupware that allows individuals in different geographical locations to work together simultaneously, and E-mail systems that shortcut the long, formal reporting chains.

The design of an appropriate organizational structure, the implementation of a positive climate and incentives, and the use of information technology need to be aligned—they need to be consistent and to reinforce each other—to be effective. If any of these components is not well designed, then the effectiveness of organizational communication will be compromised, and ultimately, organizational responsiveness will suffer.

KEY CONCEPTS AND TERMS

KEY CONCEPTS

- Communication is the glue that holds organizations together. (105)
- Effective communication is key to organizational responsiveness. (106)
- Communication is the process of transmitting a message with a certain meaning through a specific channel from a source to a receiver with the intention of having the receiver respond and provide feedback to the sender. (111)
- Distortion in organizational communication can be intentional (e.g., caused by self-promotion) and unintentional (e.g., caused by fatigue). (112)
- Most problems of communication within organizations are not due to a lack of data but to an excess of it. (121)
- An overloaded receiver not only becomes bogged down but, as part of a communication network, s/he also becomes a bottleneck, creating inefficiencies in others and affecting organizational responsiveness. (121)
- Reducing the amount of unnecessary data and increasing the capacity for processing information are two effective strategies to reduce distortion in communication. (122)
- Organizational structure should reflect the communication needs driven by the imperative of being responsive to changes in the environment. As those needs change, so should the structure of the organization. (127)
- Information technology can be used effectively to counteract causes of distortion. (127)
- Designing an effective communication network means designing an organizational structure, climate, incentive program, and information technology strategy that work together. (126)

KEY TERMS

adhocracy (108)
channel (111)
communication (107)
communication dyad (111)
cultural differences (116)
decode (117)
delaying (120)
distortion (112)

downward communication (109)
encode (117)
feedback quality (111)
formal communication (107)
gender-based differences (116)
informal communication (108)
information overload (121)
intentional distortion (120)
interpersonal variables (115)
lateral communication (109)
media (118)
medium (111)
message (111)
message content (117)
modifying distortion (120)
noise (112)
quality of feedback (119)
receiver (111)
routing distortion (120)
sender (111)
source (115)
span-of-control (129)
summarizing distortion (120)
unintentional distortion (120)
upward communication (108)

REFERENCES

BusinessWeek. "The Horizontal Corporation." December 20, 1993, pp. 76–81.

Deutschman, A. "The Managing Wisdom of High-Tech Superstars." *Fortune*, October 17, 1994, pp. 197–206.

Fortune. "Can We Talk? Can We Ever?" July 11, 1994, p. 54.

Fisher, D. *Communication in Organizations*. Minneapolis/St. Paul: West Publishing Company, 1993.

Rogers, E., and R. Rogers. *Communication in Organizations*. New York: The Free Press, 1976.

Tannen, D. *You Just Don't Understand*. New York: William Morrow and Co., 1990.

CONNECTIVE CASE: Wisconsin Department of Health and Social Services

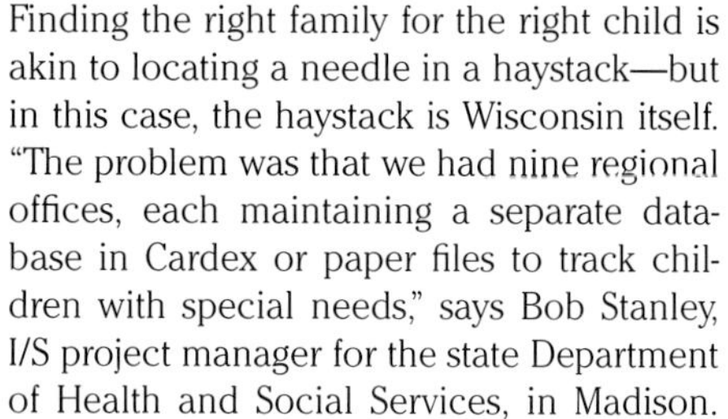

Finding the right family for the right child is akin to locating a needle in a haystack—but in this case, the haystack is Wisconsin itself. "The problem was that we had nine regional offices, each maintaining a separate database in Cardex or paper files to track children with special needs," says Bob Stanley, I/S project manager for the state Department of Health and Social Services, in Madison. "And each region had its own list of potential families for these children."

Such a system might be adequate for placing young, healthy children. But finding a home for special-needs kids requires more investigation. Social workers need to be able to look in every part of the state for potential foster homes and adoptive families. Under the old system, it was necessary to send messages through all the offices, asking the social workers to look through their files. Sometimes the messages would be lost or delayed. Occasionally the message would contain incomplete information, requiring the social worker who received the message to make educated guesses to try and fill in the blanks. Also, since most of the records were kept in paper files, a social worker might miss an important opportunity if a folder with a potentially matching family was on someone else's desk.

The challenge for a new system was how to allow a social worker in one region to search through the files looking for prospective families in other regions, without requiring an inordinate amount of time and effort. Tom Seeliger, the network manager for the department, considered several alternative ways of connecting the offices together. He knew that a central database of information would make sense, but it would also be necessary for each regional office to access and update the database. A consultant was hired to help generate and evaluate alternatives, and he assisted Seeliger in managing the implementation of the chosen alternative.

The solution that was settled on was to have a centralized database that was maintained on a mainframe computer, using the DB2 Database Management System (DBMS). Social workers in the various regions access the database using personal computer–based workstations, which are connected through modems and dial-up connections. The Windows NT network software was employed, so that when a workstation at a remote office dials in (using a standard 28.8 Kbps modem), it becomes an extension of the network. Another software package, StarSQL, was also required. The StarSQL program acts as an interface between the social workers and the DB2 database on the mainframe computer. Using StarSQL, social workers are able to pull information from the database relatively easily, and can then use spreadsheets or other programs if they wish.

Setting up and operating the system was no easy task. There were many different pieces that had to be put together, from making sure the personal computers would all run the required software to getting the data loaded from paper files onto the mainframe database. Once the system had been developed and the pieces put together, procedures had to be defined to make sure that the data would remain current and accurate. It was also essential that the system be secure, since much of the data is sensitive and must be kept confidential. All of the social workers had to be taught how to use the system, and how to follow new procedures so that the system would continue to operate effectively.

The results are in. The new system came on-line in the middle of 1995, and it has helped the state's social workers communicate efficiently and share information. The state placed more than 300 children with special needs over the previous year. The new system also helps the social workers deal with the heavy administrative responsibilities that accompany the important adoption procedures, freeing them up to spend more time on their key tasks. The bottom line is that the system is helping achieve one of the organization's key goals: finding happy homes for kids who currently don't have homes.

Case Questions

1. Identify three potential sources of distortion in communications using the old way of locating homes for children with special needs in Wisconsin. Use Table 4–2 to classify each potential source on each of the two dimensions.
2. Briefly describe how the new system within the Wisconsin Department of Health and Social Services (WDHSS) can help reduce the potential sources of distortion you identified in question 1.
3. Use Tables 4–3, 4–4, and 4–5 to identify which propositions match the changes employed by WDHSS with their new system.

CASE ANALYSIS

1. The three potential sources are as follows:
Unintentional delay—request for information sent from one social worker to another in a different office was occasionally lost or misplaced.
Unintentional modification—request from one social worker to another in a different office is missing information; recipient may guess or ignore missing components.
Unintentional modification (or delay)—missing information on a prospective family for a child if the family's folder was not filed in the proper place in the filing cabinet.

2. The centralized database, with remote access for social workers at each of the offices, will eliminate the possibility of files being misplaced (assuming proper procedures are put in place to ensure records aren't accidentally deleted). Since the social workers access the database directly, it removes the possibility of a message between social workers being misplaced, delayed, or incomplete.

3. The primary proposition is IT7, creating a centralized database and providing access to it from all hierarchical levels in the communication chain. Although not mentioned, it is also probable that WDHSS has employed proposition IT3, using standard data-entry screens and prefilled, standardized input forms. This would ensure that the database records are consistent in the information they provide and would reduce the possibility of data-entry errors. The new system also uses proposition ST1, keeping the distance between the source and receiver as short as possible. Although the social workers may not be any closer (physically) to the database, they do not have to go through the intermediary of another social worker to access the information.

SOURCE: Paul Karon, "Client/Server System Helps Find Homes for Special Kids," *InfoWorld*, January 15, 1996, p. 60.

IT'S YOUR TURN END OF CHAPTER MATERIALS

REVIEW QUESTIONS

1. Define organizational communication.
2. What is the difference between formal and informal communication?
3. What are the differences among upward, downward, and lateral communication?
4. List the elements of a communication dyad and draw a picture of one.
5. What is meant by communication distortion?
6. List five potential sources of distortion in organizational communication.
7. Enumerate the eight types of distortion and give an example of each.
8. Give two examples of factors that might lead to intentional communication distortion and two examples that might lead to unintentional distortion.

9. Explain the two basic strategies for reducing distortion in organizational communication.
10. List the three categories of recommendations to overcome communication distortion and give an example of each.

DISCUSSION QUESTIONS

1. Comment on the importance of effective communication to achieve organizational responsiveness.
2. How can information technology help minimize distortion in organizational communication?
3. Give an example of each of the eight types of distortion shown in Table 4–2 (use your answers to Review Questions 7 and 8) and then design a communication system to overcome each of your examples by using the propositions summarized in Tables 4–3, 4–4, and 4–5.
4. Give an example from an actual company to illustrate the strategy of reducing the need for information processing and one example to illustrate the strategy of increasing the capacity for information processing.
5. Write an essay on your thoughts about gender and cultural differences affecting the way people perceive and communicate information. Do you believe those factors are major or minor influences on how people understand each other? Can information technology mitigate their influence?
6. Some companies have a policy classifying all E-mail messages from and to an employee's desktop at the office to be the property of the company and, therefore, auditable. Given the importance of informal communication in organizations, comment on the pros and cons of such a policy.

GROUP ASSIGNMENT

Select an article from the front page of today's *The Wall Street Journal* or this week's *BusinessWeek* or *Fortune*. Have one member of the group summarize the article in approximately one-third of the length of the original article. Another member of the group should then take that summary and in turn reduce it to one third of its length. Continue to do this until you run out of group members or the length of the last summary is one paragraph.

As a group prepare a one-page memorandum comparing the meaning of the original article to the final summarized version. Comment on how each member made the decision of leaving material out. Finally, put yourselves in the position of a CEO getting the summarized version rather than the original article. Do you think that the CEO would be as well informed? What are the implications for designing an effective communication network?

APPLICATION ASSIGNMENTS

1. Access the internet, locate the home page for this book, and open the ACME spreadsheet for Chapter 4. Make a recommendation on the number of units to be produced for July 1998 without changing the spreadsheet and record the time it took you to make the recommendation.

   Now make a copy of the spreadsheet, and modify it to facilitate the same task. Write a couple of paragraphs on how designing formats to display data can affect the ease of information processing.
2. Select an article from the front page of today's *The Wall Street Journal,* or this week's *BusinessWeek* or *Fortune.* Summarize the article into three PowerPoint slides. Each slide should not contain more than three bullets. Make a fourth slide depicting a graphical representation of the article.
3. Access the Internet. Use a search facility to get a listing of Web sites of companies offering computer services and products. How many sites did you retrieve? Assume that you want to purchase the least expensive color laptop computer with a built-in CD-ROM in the market and purchase a maintenance contract. How useful is the list you just retrieved to help you in your purchase?

CASE ASSIGNMENT:
The Norris Company (C): Sherry's Day at the Office

Sherry Craig's thoughts were interrupted as she pulled into the parking lot for the Norris Company's Central plant. She greeted the group of workers huddled around John, the office manager, who was discussing the day's work schedule with them. As the meeting broke up, John picked up a few samples from the clasper, showed them to Sherry, and asked if they should be shipped that way or if it would be necessary to inspect them. Before she could answer, John went on to ask if she could suggest another operator for the sealing machine to replace the regular operator who was home ill. He also told her that Gene, the director of production, and Al, the stockroom supervisor, had called and were waiting to hear from Sherry.

After telling John to go ahead and ship the samples, she made a note of the need for a sealer operator for the office and then called Gene. She agreed to stop by Gene's office before lunch. She then called Al. "A great morning, Al," Sherry greeted him cheerfully. "Not so good, Sherry; my new worker isn't in this morning," Noren growled. "Have you heard from him?" asked Sherry. "No, I haven't," replied Al. "Have you asked Human Resources to call him?" Al hesitated for a moment before replying. "No, Sherry. I thought you could help me find someone to replace him. I have five trucks to unload today." Sherry said, "I'll call you in half an hour, Al, and let you know."

She then went over each supervisor's report about the types and volumes of orders they were running, the number of people present, how the schedules were coming along, and the orders to be run next. Sherry had found some of the reports to be unreliable in the past. She shook her head, realizing that she couldn't trust the information contained in the daily reports. After all, it was information critical to the satisfaction of customers, and necessary for her to be able to detect problems sooner rather than later.

Although Norris had finally caught up with their competitors in terms of the use of newer, computerized printing press equipment, their internal administrative systems were woefully inadequate. The supervisors still completed their daily reports by hand. Every one of the supervisors had complained that the reports took too long to complete and that under the day's pressure they sometimes had to skip some entries, give an approximate answer, or quickly, and very often incompletely, summarize the status of an order. Also, the handwriting was often difficult to read and Sherry had to get the supervisor on the phone to go over the figures.

There were other problems. One supervisor seemed to be always reporting he was running behind. The grapevine said this was to avoid getting new orders and also to work overtime and thus get better pay. Another supervisor was reputedly covering for absent workers in exchange for part of that workers' pay. Sherry knew she needed to address these issues but she had been too busy to do anything about them.

She helped the folding-room supervisor find temporary storage space for consolidating a truckload shipment; discussed quality control with a press operator who had been running poor work; arranged to transfer four people temporarily to different departments, including two for Al in the stockroom, talked to the shipping supervisor about pickups and special orders to be delivered that day. As she continued through the plant, she saw to it that reserve stock was moved out of the forward stock area; talked to another press operator about her requested change of vacation schedule; had a "heart-to-heart" talk with a press helper who seemed to need frequent reassurance; and approved two type and one color order okays for different press operators.

Returning to her office, Sherry reviewed the production reports on the larger orders against her initial projections and found that the plant was running behind schedule. She called in the folding-room supervisor and together they went over the lineup of machines and made several necessary changes. She asked him why he had not informed her earlier about the problem. He answered that he had left a message for the night supervisor, asking that the information be passed on to Sherry. The night supervisor had been sick for a couple of days and the message was on his desk waiting for his return.

During this discussion, the composing-room supervisor stopped in to cover several type changes and the routing supervisor telephoned for approval of a revised printing schedule. The stockroom supervisor called twice, first to inform her that two standard, fast-moving stock items were dangerously low; later to advise her that the paper stock for the urgent Dillon job had finally arrived. Sherry made a mental note that inventory management had to be improved. The report of on-hand raw materials was consistently out of date because the stockroom supervisor was just too busy manually entering and deleting items in inventory. Also, most of the time nobody knew when a supplier was delivering an order, which made production planning very difficult.

Sherry then began to put delivery dates on inquiries received from customers and salespeople (90 percent of all the inquiries were routine, and John handled some of the routine inquiries, but all inquiries were reviewed by Sherry). While she was doing this she was interrupted twice, once by a sales correspondent calling from the West Coast to ask for a better delivery date than originally scheduled; once by the vice president of human resources asking her to set a time when she could hold an initial training and induction interview with a new employee.

After dating the customer and sales inquiries, Sherry headed for her morning conference in the executive offices. At this meeting she answered the sales vice president's questions in connection with "hot" orders, complaints, the status of large-volume orders and potential new orders. For these meetings, which occurred three times a week, Sherry had to transcribe information from the supervisors' daily reports into a different format. She then met with the vice president of operations to discuss a few ticklish policy matters and to answer his questions on several specific production problems. She did not feel as prepared as she should have been but the morning had just been too busy. Before leaving the executive offices, she stopped at the office of the purchasing director to inquire about delivery of cartons, paper, and boxes, and to place a new order for paper.

On the way back to her own office, Sherry conferred with Gene about two current engineering projects concerning which he had called earlier. Meetings with Gene were always difficult. Sherry had asked Gene to use written reports for their meetings, but he resisted the idea and insisted on verbal reports at face-to-face meetings. Gene had been a candidate for Sherry's job. Ever since Sherry got the promotion, Gene's manner toward her had been gruff, and she suspected he resented reporting to someone who was much younger and, even worse, a woman. She had heard Gene, who was excellent at his job but had only gone to a vocational school, complain that "these college kids think they know everything."

Since her appointment as plant manager, Gene had been going over her head to coordinate equipment purchases with the Eastern and Southern plants. Sherry had not said anything, thinking that the practice would stop, but it had not. Gene was very influential with the production staff, and Sherry did not want to antagonize him too much. But three times he had provided her with wrong information about equipment capacities and when she used that information in a presentation to the vice president of operations, Gene stood up to correct her. At first she thought it had been an innocent mistake, but now she wondered if there was more to it.

It was 10 minutes before lunch, just time enough to make a few notes of the details she needed to check in order to answer knotty questions raised by the sales manager that morning.

After lunch Sherry started again. She began by checking the previous day's production reports; did some rescheduling to get out urgent orders; placed appropriate delivery dates on new orders and inquiries received that morning; consulted with a supervisor on a personal problem. She spent a very frustrating 45 minutes on the phone and the fax machine going over problems with the Eastern Plant. Each plant had a different classification system for jobs and when a customer order came through that required two plants' involvement to fulfill it, the coordination was a nightmare. Proofs had to be produced, and twice in the last month a project had to be stopped when the proofs from the two plants did not match.

By mid-afternoon Sherry had made a tour of the plant after which she met with the human resources director to review with him a touchy personal problem raised by one of the clerical employees, the vacation schedules submitted by the supervisors, and the pending job evaluation program. Following this conference, Sherry hurried back to her office to complete the special statistical report for Universal Waxing Corporation, one of Norris's best customers. The report took a long time to finish. The format of the report had been developed by the vice president of operations and was difficult to use for Sherry's purpose. She had to recalculate most of the data she needed from the production reports because the format presented the data per type of product rather than per customer order. She was being extra careful checking her calculations at least twice because last month she had made an embarrassing mistake in a report to another good customer, Generic Polishing Corporation.

Questions

1. Use concepts introduced in this chapter to comment on the communication between Sherry and Gene, and to provide recommendations to Sherry.
2. Identify four instances of distortion in organizational communication within Norris, excluding communications between Sherry and Gene. Use terms introduced in this chapter to analyze each of them and to suggest ways to reduce them. At least two of these solutions should involve the use of information technology.

SOURCE: This case was written by Associate Professors William Cats-Baril and Ronald Thompson of the School of Business Administration, University of Vermont. It is loosely based on Northwestern University's "The Case of the Missing Time." This case is an amalgamation of situations found in several firms, rather than a representation of a specific individual operating within a specific company.

MODULE I CASE

DAKIN FARM (A): MAIL ORDER PROCESSING

On a cold February morning, Sam Cutting Jr., the president of Dakin Farm, took some time to contemplate the evolution of his business. The company had grown from total sales revenues of $10,000 in its first year, to over $2.5 million in the previous year. The line of business had changed from selling syrup at a roadside stand to being primarily a specialty foods mail order business with two retail stores. Sam had developed three major strategic goals for Dakin Farm: (1) to produce moderate growth (double sales revenues over the next 10 years), (2) to improve efficiency in the business processes, and (3) to control business costs.

As Sam considered how to achieve these goals, he was concerned about the mail order processing system and its limitations. During the most recent Christmas season Dakin had to turn away customer orders; the existing system was restricting growth and constraining some of his business options.

COMPANY BACKGROUND

The Dakin Farm business began in 1960 when Sam Cutting Sr. brought his family to Vermont after a tour in the U.S. Air Force, on a quest to buy a Vermont farm with potential for improvement. Sam Sr., originally from Connecticut, had learned to appreciate Vermont while studying Agriculture at the University of Vermont. Sam Sr. finally decided to purchase Dakin Farm in Ferrisburg, 20 miles south of Burlington, Vermont. The 130-acre working farm, 1792 farmhouse, and small roadside stand that sold pure Vermont maple syrup to tourists appealed to Sam and his partner, Helmut Lenes.

Dakin Farm had gross revenues of about $10,000 during its first year of business, although the roadside stand was open only for about six months during summer and fall. The company had been growing ever since. The introduction of Dakin Farm's Vermont Mountain Shop at the Ferrisburg location was successful and later sold to Sam Sr.'s partner, Helmut Lenes. Lenes moved the Vermont Mountain Shop to Burlington to compete with the introduction of Eastern Mountain Sports and renamed it Climb High.

Later a successful clothing business was started at Dakin Farm, with such lines as Pendleton, Woolrich, Lady Thompson, Sero, and more. In 1980, when Sam Cutting Jr. graduated from the University of Vermont with a bachelor of science degree in business administration, he went to work full time for Dakin Farm. Sam Jr. had a clear vision of where he wanted the company to go—the mail order business. The clothing line was liquidated almost immediately, and the focus set on mail order.

This change in business focus was swift, but Dakin Farm was not without experience. Before Sam Jr. joined Dakin Farm full time, a small mail order catalog had been sent out every year in the Fall to about 5,000 customers. The customer data were kept on a rolodex file, and every transaction was processed manually. The customer order labels were typed by hand, and every time the catalog was sent, 5,000 names and addresses were typed and manually updated.

The specialty foods industry was quite competitive, ranging from local Vermont businesses (Cold Hollow Cider Mill, Harrington's) to national companies such as Hickory Farms. Most of the customers were individuals who purchased packages or baskets of products to send to friends and relatives for special occasions. Some customers were tourists who stopped in at the retail store while visiting Vermont; others responded to the direct mail advertising consisting of catalogs and flyers. Dakin Farm relied quite extensively on repeat business.

Some smaller competitors produced the specialty foods themselves, and then packaged them for shipment. Most regional or national companies purchased packaged goods for resale, but might also acquire some raw materials (such as butchered hogs) and then finish and package the final products. Regional and national companies had the advantage of being able to purchase in large quantities, which tended to reduce their cost of goods. They also tended to locate their retail outlets in shopping centers and other locations that received a lot of consumer traffic, providing a great deal of exposure to the buying public. The smaller competitors (including Dakin Farm) were generally located outside of metropolitan areas, relying on reaching potential customers through tourist traffic and mail order.

BUSINESS OPERATIONS

Sam Cutting Jr. became president of Dakin Farm in 1992, and had been running the business since that time. The company was still located in Ferrisburg, Vermont, al-

EXHIBIT 1 Dakin Farm (A): Partial Organization Chart

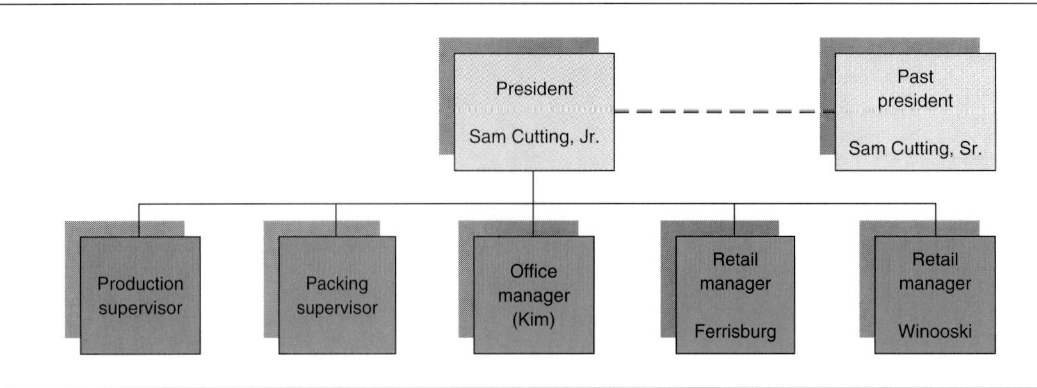

though the farm was no longer associated with the business. Sam had taken charge of all marketing functions, focusing on expanding mail order operations. The company sent a major catalog, flyer, double postcard or newsletter in the mail about once every three months. By last year, over 350,000 pieces were mailed annually to regular customers, and additional names of potential customers were rented or exchanged from other companies. Dakin Farm also advertised on a regular basis with direct response ads in nationally published periodicals such as *Yankee Magazine, Gourmet,* and *Bon Appetit.*

Dakin Farm did not produce its goods from scratch, but rather performed valued-added processes. For example, maple syrup remained an important product in their offering; they sold about 60,000 containers of maple syrup last year. Dakin produced some of this, but purchased most of its supply in bulk from local suppliers; it was tested (for clarity, color, specific density), graded, and then packaged into Dakin containers. Quality control was important, and Dakin had the capacity to enhance the quality to some extent by blending syrup from different sources to achieve more desirable traits. Similarly, by operating its own smokehouse operation Dakin could use its own ingredients to smoke cheese and meats, producing goods that could not be readily imitated. Dakin advertising stressed high quality, with made-in-Vermont products and a family-owned and -operated company.

With the success of Sam's mail order strategy, the company was able to open a second retail store in the Champlain Mill, a medium-sized mall located in Winooski, just outside of Burlington, Vermont. At that store, customers could purchase food or fill out mail order forms for gifts to be sent to almost any destination. Typical volumes of orders would be 50 to 80 per day during the summer, with 800 to 1,000 per day during the peak season in December. About 80 percent or 90 percent of Dakin's annual sales occurred during a four-week period. Dakin Farm's sales revenue for the previous year was slightly more than $2.5 million, and was expected to keep rising. During the most recent Christmas season, however, Dakin was unable to handle all of the orders it received, and had to turn away an estimated $30,000 to $50,000 of business.

Between the two stores, Dakin Farm employed from about 15 people in the summer to as many as 50 people during their busy season in the late fall and early winter. Sam Jr. acted as the president, and he used a hands-on management style. He had an office manager, Kim, who supervised the customer service representatives and ran the operations when Sam was unavailable. There was a packing supervisor (one for each shift, during the busy season) for the packers who filled and shipped the customer orders, as well as a supervisor who ran the production operations (smokehouse, cutting room, etc.). There were also two store managers, one for the Ferrisburg and one for the Winooski Mill retail outlets, who supervised the store operations (see Exhibit 1 for an organization chart).

Although Kim was theoretically in charge when Sam wasn't in his office, in reality most decisions were made by Sam. Kim focused more on keeping the office functions (such as accounting and order processing) running smoothly. It was not unusual for her to leave messages for Sam on his desk, informing him of some recent activity or requesting a decision on some issue. If the production supervisor wanted to know what flavor of smoked ham to produce during a shift, he would question Sam. If the store manager at the Winooski outlet was running low on one-quart maple syrup containers, she would call Sam. If the packing supervisor couldn't handle the volume of orders requested for his shift, he would notify Sam. Sam was obviously in great demand, and frequently decisions were delayed while he was being located. He also found himself overloaded with requests during the busy season, and often had to reach decisions based more on intuition than any analysis of data.

Communications between the Winooski store and the main office were handled by telephone and personal delivery. Customer orders (for gift sales) were recorded on a form that was signed by the customer. These forms were collected, and each day at the close of business the store manager would drive to Ferrisburg and drop them off. These orders were then added to those completed by the staff at Ferrisburg. Requests for products to replenish the Winooski store inventory were also handled by completing a form that was taken to Ferrisburg with the customer order forms. Any emergency requests were transmitted by phone; the store manager would call the Ferrisburg office and indicate that she needed more of a certain product before the regular delivery. Someone at the Ferrisburg plant would load the required products and deliver them to Winooski, if time permitted.

Trying to determine how much of any given product to stock in inventory was a difficult decision, especially for the more perishable items. Sam had to order some products far in advance of the busy season. With the maple syrup, for example, Sam had to order in February for the following Christmas. The production process also required forecasting demand for certain products, although there were more opportunities to modify the process as required. For example, if Dakin appeared to be selling a large number of maple-glazed hams, production could cut back on some of its smoked turkey flavors and increase the production of maple-glazed ham.

THE MAIL ORDER SYSTEM

With the company growing in the mail order business, its success demanded the implementation of an efficient method for generating and processing mail orders. The rolodex file system required manual input and maintenance, which made it very inefficient. The manual storage and processing of customer orders also slowed the process substantially, leading to errors and delays. Sam knew a computer programmer who had written a mail order software package intended for another company, but the product had been scratched before completion. He negotiated with the developer, and eventually acquired the package for Dakin Farm. Sam also purchased a used Digital Equipment Corporation (DEC) PDP 11/73 minicomputer with four dumb terminals for about $3,000 in 1983. The software was supposed to be an on-line order-entry system that would allow customer service representatives to service customers with any required information while they were on the phone. The system was sluggish, littered with bugs, and could not respond fast enough for people who were trying to order over the phone. Some improvements were obviously needed.

The programmer was hired to modify the software by dropping some modules and rewriting others, and eventually it looked nothing like the original software package that was purchased. Rather than being on-line, the mail orders were processed manually on paper, and then entered in batch mode into the computer. The system was inefficient, but marginally sufficient for the volume of business that Dakin was doing in the late 1980s to early 1990s.

The Mail Order Process

The mail order process began with the completion of an order form in one of the retail stores, or with the ringing of the telephone in the Ferrisburg office. When the phone rang, any available customer service representative (CSR) answered. The CSR asked the customer a series of questions necessary to complete the telephone order form (see Exhibit 2). After writing customer information and order details, the shipping date and the form of payment were completed. The CSR totaled the order manually after the phone call. If the customer requested the total purchase amount before the call was ended, they either waited on the phone until it was calculated by hand, or a CSR called back after totaling the order.

Once the order form was completed, it was filed with all other orders waiting to be processed for that day. Any order received after 11:00 AM was held for packing the next business day (Monday through Friday). The reason for this was that orders received after 11:00 AM could not be processed and packed before the UPS daily pickup. Orders could be processed early, but not packed, because of the perishable nature of the product. Many of the products had to be stored in large coolers in the packing room; although there was a cooler for packed orders in the basement, it had a limited capacity.

After the orders were written and collected, they were entered into the mail order information system using the dumb terminals in the mail order offices. This was a batch style entry that included entering all of the information from the written telephone order form. The order entry screen was similar to the telephone order form. This was no accident; the form was designed to facilitate speedy order entry. There was still room for data entry errors, however, since the CSR could make a mistake entering the information into the computer system.

The Batch Processes

When all of the orders were entered for that business day, the batch processes began. While the following

EXHIBIT 2 Telephone Order Form

Telephone Orders

Date ______________ Clerk ______________
Customer # ______________ Source Code ______________

From: ______________
____
____

Telephone #

To: ______________
____
____

Telephone # Ship Date: ______________

Cat. #	Qty.	Description	Total Price
		Sub Total	______
		Shipping	

Gift Card: Other Side Total ______________
Grand Total ______________

Visa MC AE Exp Date ______________

batch jobs were performed, the system terminals could not be used. The batch jobs had to be finished before the system terminals could be used again.

The first batch process was printing the packing lists from the minicomputer to the printer in Sam's office. (Exhibit 3 shows a floor plan for Dakin Farm's Ferrisburg operation.) The packing list had two parts, a packing list and an address label, separated by perforation.[1] When the packing lists were all printed, the CSRs were responsible for retrieving them from Sam's office, and then verifying all of the information on them by comparing them with the original written telephone order forms. Once the packing lists were verified for accuracy, they were assigned a ship date. Lists with same-day shipping dates were given immediately to the packers in the packing room. Packing lists with future ship dates were filed according to ship date for future packing. At this point the information flow diverged.

After all of the packing lists were printed, all of the invoices associated with them were also printed.[2] The invoices were printed on an impact printer, in duplicate, using carbon forms. One of the copies was filed and one was mailed to the customer. Before the invoices were mailed, however, a CSR carried all of the invoices that were associated with a credit card purchase into Kim's office. Kim then downloaded the credit card information from the minicomputer to a desktop personal computer and used a communications software package to communicate electronically with Dakin Farm's bank. Assuming all credit card orders were approved, the process continued.

After mailing the proper invoices to customers, the CSRs filed the invoices by date and the next batch process began. Kim ran another software program on the minicomputer to generate the "posting summary." The posting summary was a daily sales summary for all of the orders processed that day. Once it was printed, the total sales for the day were verified against the

[1]A *packing list* is a list of all items that are to be included with a specific order; it is used by the employee who pulls the required items from storage and packs them.

[2]The invoice copy acted as a receipt for the customer.

EXHIBIT 3 Dakin Farm, Ferrisburg Floor Plan

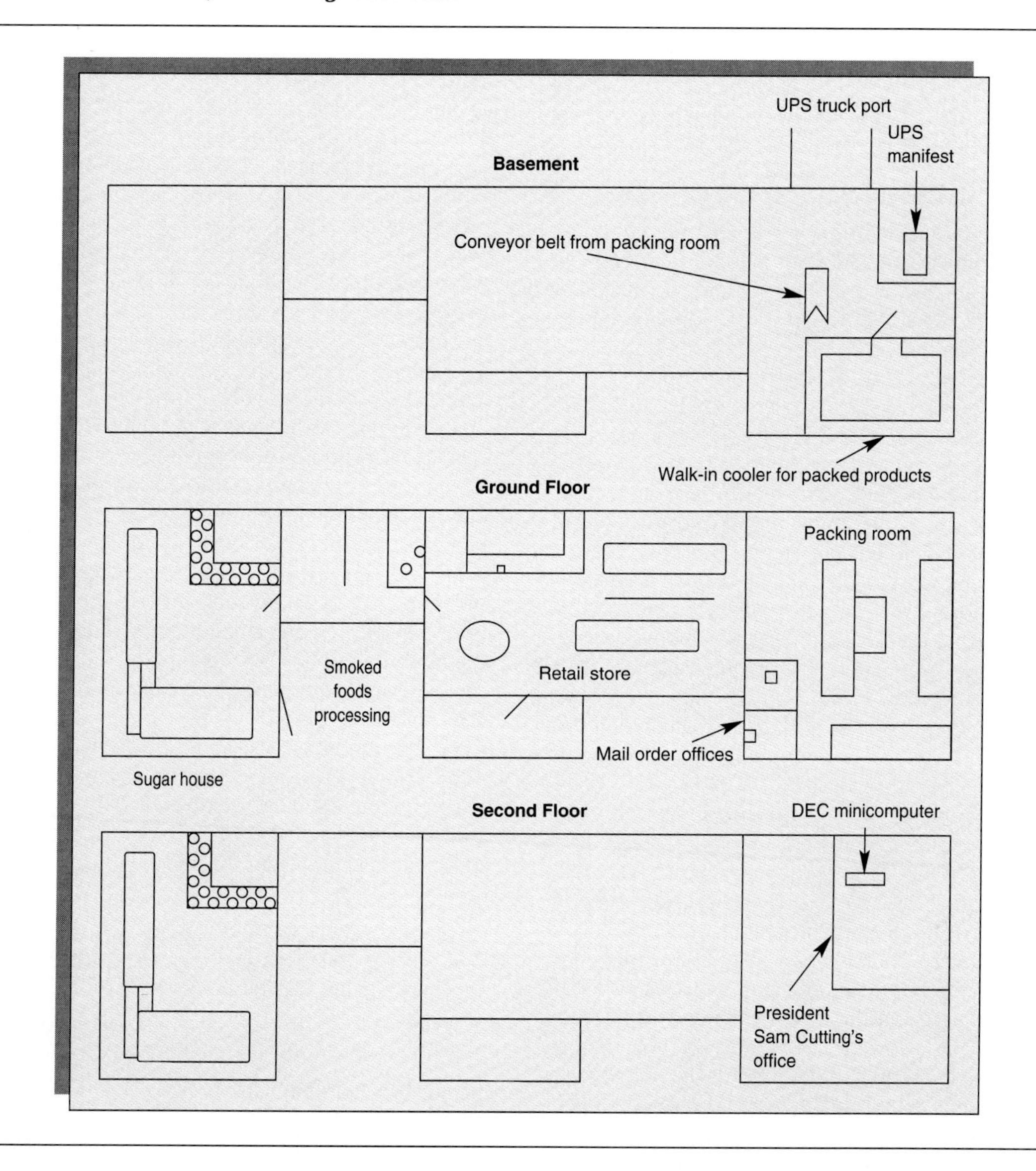

manual tally (addition) of all the telephone order forms, which one of the office staff prepared.

The final step in the mail order process was to produce the "source-tracking" report, which was another batch-style process. The source-tracking report detailed where the sales for the day originated. The different sources (which included catalogs, fliers, advertisements, etc.) were identified as codes on the telephone order form. An office staff member flipped through the order forms, tabulating the number of orders from each source. This was an important marketing tool for Sam, as it identified which promotions were successful for him.

While the batch operations were being performed, the packers used the packing lists to pick items from the storage coolers and pack the orders. The finished packages, with a packing list in the box, and the address label on the box, were put on a conveyer belt to the basement. In the basement all of the packages were weighed and entered into the UPS manifest computer, which was also in the basement. The information that was captured by the manifest computer included weight, destination, and cost of shipment. When all of the orders to be shipped were entered into the manifest, the final tally was printed and the data stored on diskette. When UPS arrived for shipment the tally sheet was verified and signed and the packages left Dakin Farm destined for locations all over the world.

PROBLEMS WITH THE MAIL ORDER PROCESS

The manual order recording for telephone sales was time consuming and costly. Both the customer and the business lost money by using this system. The customer lost the money they paid for an extended toll call, and Dakin Farm lost important CSR time. Furthermore, this slow process could discourage customers from calling again. Additional problems occur when customers changed their minds or wanted to verify the status of an order. The person receiving a call for information about a previous order would have to go through literally hundreds or even thousands of paper order forms, looking for the correct one. During the busy season, Dakin lost much valuable employee time checking orders instead of processing new ones. In addition, the CSRs had no way of knowing exactly what was still in inventory at any given time. They might accept an order from a customer, only to discover later that the packer was unable to fill it. The CSR would then call the customer back, and ask if they would like to substitute an item.

Another problem existed with the credit card verification part of the process. If all of the credit card purchases were not approved by the bank, the credit card information was verified against the original telephone order form. If the information was correct and the credit card purchase was still not approved, Kim would go to the basement and pull the packing list or pull the package from the cooler where it was awaiting UPS pickup. The divergence of information flow created inefficiencies in the mail order process. If an order was associated with a bad credit card purchase, it might already be packed by the time Kim discovered it. If so, the time it took to pack the order was wasted, and the order had to be unpacked as well.

A third problem arose from the packing operation itself. There was no formal process for packing; it depended on the personal preference of the packer. Considerable time was wasted as the packers bustled about, often retracing their steps as they moved from one order to the next. For example, an order might come through that required a corn-smoked turkey, which was located at the end of the storage cooler, far from the final packing area. After packing this order, the packer moves to the next and discovers that it, too, requires a corn-smoked turkey. If he had known that in advance, he could have picked two turkeys at the same time, saving steps and time.

Another drawback was that the information for the source-tracking report was manually tabulated, kept on paper, and not directly accessible by Sam on demand. Also, CSRs occasionally omitted the source code, or made one up. When they were rushed during the busy season, it was quicker to jot something down and then move on to the next phone call. It also saved them the discomfort of asking the customer, who might not be interested in disclosing this information.

By February of this year, Sam Cutting Jr. knew that the existing order-processing system needed to be changed. As the company continued to grow and the number of mail orders increased, the backlog of orders to be processed grew and the turnaround time on orders also increased. Dakin Farm was not operating in a monopoly situation; competitors such as Hickory Farms were firmly established and smaller companies were entering the market as well. Just providing top-quality foods was no longer sufficient; customers wanted quality foods, at a reasonable cost, and with excellent service. Furthermore, customers who selected specialty food gifts had other options; Sam knew that he was actually competing with more than just the obvious companies. If Dakin Farm was to reach the goals he had set, updating the order-processing system would be critical.

Questions

1. Describe Dakin Farm in terms of General Systems Theory, using GST terminology.
2. Comment on the effectiveness of decision-making processes within Dakin as of the case setting.
3. Discuss communication flows within Dakin Farm, and between Dakin and its customers. Identify potential sources of communication distortion.

SOURCE: This case was written by Associate Professors William Cats-Baril and Ronald Thompson of the School of Business Administration, University of Vermont. The case is designed solely as the basis for classroom discussion, and is not intended to illustrate either effective or ineffective handling of an administrative situation. Jim Collins, Sean Harvey, Myles Kelman, and Denise Moore contributed to an earlier version of the case.

MODULE II Information Systems Development

The first module focused on challenges facing managers and the need to use information systems to address those challenges. This second module answers the "how" question—how to go about developing an information system.

Chapter 5 presents a formal definition of an information system by defining the five components that an I/S is made of. Chapter 5 discusses four of the five components (purpose, people, procedures, and data) in detail. The chapter also discusses three basic considerations in the design of information systems. Finally, Chapter 5 introduces the information systems (I/S) cube. The I/S cube is a framework for classifying information systems and explains why certain types of systems are more difficult to develop than others.

Chapter 6 discusses the fifth component of information systems: Information technology. Chapter 6 describes hardware, software, and telecommunications, and how these technologies are converging. The approach adopted for the chapter is to provide an overview of the different technologies, to show the need for each technology, and then to caution you about the issues that need to be considered when acquiring the technology.

Chapter 7 provides a framework for developing information systems. Suggestions are provided for how to reduce the risks inherent in developing information systems, including an overview of project management techniques. Chapter 7 also provides a discussion of the issues to consider when deciding what parts of an information system should be built internally, and what components should be purchased.

CHAPTER 5 Information Systems Concepts

CHAPTER OBJECTIVES

After reading this chapter, you should have a better understanding of the basic concepts underlying information systems. More specifically, after reading this chapter you should be able to:

- Define the notion of information technology architecture.
- Discuss the three basic considerations in the design of information systems: (1) to minimize overload of employees and distortion of communications, (2) to provide specific support for individuals, workgroups, and the enterprise, and (3) to assess the potential for ethical abuses.
- Describe a five-step process to design effective information systems.
- Understand the concept of by-exception-only reporting.
- Explain the different types of information systems by using a classification scheme called the *information systems (I/S) cube*.
- Describe the primary components of information systems, which are (1) purpose, (2) people, (3) procedures, (4) data and information, and (5) information technology.

How do I organize the hardware and software to make my organization more responsive? And, by the way, what exactly is an information system?

INTRODUCTION

This chapter is a transitional chapter. It is the hinge between the organizational issues and the technical issues that need to be addressed in designing information systems (I/S). This chapter links the three chapters in the first module on managerial challenges and organizational dynamics (Chapters 2, 3, and 4) to the next two chapters on information systems development (Chapters 6 and 7). The discussion of the technology components of an I/S becomes much more detailed in Chapter 6, while in Chapter 7, we provide a much more detailed discussion of the methodology to develop information systems applications.

In previous chapters, we have made a series of points which include:

- For organizations to be successful, they need to be responsive to change.
- Being responsive to change is an information-intensive proposition. That is, in order for organizations to understand the needs of their customers, the strategies of their competitors, the availability of supplies, and so forth, they must constantly collect and analyze data about them.
- As organizations face environments that have become more international, and therefore more turbulent, their information-processing needs have become more demanding and complex.
- Managers, and groups of managers, have trouble processing information given the tight deadlines, multiple issues, and many interruptions that characterize their work.
- Individuals have some inherent limitations and biases in processing information. These limitations are particularly acute when processing statistical information or when under conditions of stress.
- The process of communication between individuals in organizations includes the collection, storage, analysis, and transmission of data. Data can be distorted at each of these steps by a variety of elements in the relationship between the sender and the receiver.
- Messages sent through traditional organizational communication networks are often distorted and delayed. The main reason behind the distortions and delays is information overload. Two strategies that help alleviate overload are to reduce the amount of (irrelevant) data that needs to be processed, and to increase the information-processing capacity of the organization.

What these points lead us to conclude is that in today's organizations, being responsive to the environment involves being capable of processing information well and quickly, and that such a task is impossible without having a powerful and flexible I/T infrastructure.

ORGANIZATIONAL RESPONSIVENESS AND I/T ARCHITECTURE

The **information technology infrastructure** of an organization consists of the software, hardware, and telecommunications capabilities that are in place to collect, transport, store, and transform data. You can think of the I/T infrastructure as the inventory of information technology "parts" of an organization.

This infrastructure can take different forms depending on how the hardware and software are linked together; for example, the computers on the employees' desks may act mostly as dumb terminals connected to a centralized computer for most of their operations, or they may perform most of the operations independently and only connect to a centralized computer from time to time. The way the organization's hardware, software, and data are organized—how the information technology parts are put together—is called the **information technology architecture.**

The I/T architecture of an organization is basically a blueprint, a plan, that specifies the policies on *what* software and hardware to purchase, *how* the hardware and software are going to support business processes, and *who* is in charge of maintaining and securing the organization's software and data. The I/T architecture of an organization is a framework that links the decisions on information technology—what technology to buy, what data to collect, and where to store the data—to the organization's strategy (i.e., its objectives and the ways to achieve them). It is important that the framework be flexible to accommodate changes in strategy as well as in technology.

As they build their information technology infrastructure, organizations face technical issues which include the compatibility of hardware, the obsolescence of software, the security of data, and the definition of communication protocols to interchange information with external entities (e.g., customers, suppliers, government agencies). These technical issues must be addressed in the context of an overall plan, a plan that reflects management's philosophies toward the accessibility of data, the decentralization of decision making, and the role of customers and suppliers. The I/T architecture is that plan.

Therefore, we can think of the I/T architecture as the linkage, the bridge between management strategy and information technology. The I/T architecture is first a set of policies and philosophies to direct the use of information technology to

Just as a blueprint for a house represents the values and priorities of the owner, the I/T architecture represents the managerial values and priorities on the use of information. Photo courtesy of Bonnie Kamin (left) and Hewlett-Packard (right).

support management objectives and plans. Indeed, the I/T architecture describes, based on the organization's philosophy on the use of information, how data are to be managed (i.e., transported, stored, and transformed) and therefore what hardware, software, and telecommunications capabilities are needed.

Just as the architecture of a house first exists as a blueprint reflecting the priorities and philosophies of a given lifestyle and then as a physical reality embodied in a series of walls and spaces, the I/T architecture starts as a policy statement on how information technology needs to support the strategy of the organization and then is embodied in a series of specific I/T components and information systems applications. The I/T architecture is therefore a plan, based on an overall organizational philosophy and strategy, that guides the design and implementation of specific I/T applications. It is important to develop that plan carefully, since a badly planned I/T infrastructure can hamper the responsiveness of an organization by taking away options on how to react to the environment.

Consider the example of an insurance company that wants to be known as the company with the best service in the industry. To that effect, the company decides that every customer representative will be able to look at the customer's full record no matter where in the world the customer is calling from (e.g., you rented a car in Germany and just got in an accident and you call to find out whether or not you are covered) and where the customer representative is located (this will depend on whether it is cheaper to have a 24-hour service capability in a centralized location, say Lincoln, Nebraska, or a series of branches around the world). The company will need to build a database accessible from around the world that will house all the documents from a customer (e.g., policies, driving licenses, birth certificates, photographs, hospital records). In order for these documents to be accessible by any and all customer representatives, the documents must exist in an electronic format, which means that the insurance company will need to develop an advanced imaging and document management capability and the necessary telecommunication facilities. Therefore, the strategic objective "best service in the industry" implies a very specific I/T capability.

In this chapter, we discuss three considerations in the development of an appropriate I/T architecture. These considerations are: (1) to minimize overload of employees and distortion of communications, (2) to provide specific support for individuals, workgroups, and the enterprise as a whole, and (3) to assess the potential for ethical abuses in the systems. We then provide a formal definition of information systems and describe the different types of information systems. We also examine two classification frameworks that introduce the actual components of an information system.

THREE OVERALL CONSIDERATIONS TO DESIGN AN INFORMATION SYSTEM

A designer of information systems needs to think about how to collect, process, transmit, and format information in a way that supports a decision maker in addressing a given issue or accomplishing a given task. **Information systems support** means not only providing relevant information but also minimizing all sources of potential distortion.

In this section, we discuss three basic considerations in the design of information systems. We do this in the context of designing a new system; keep in mind, however, that in many situations one would actually be modifying existing systems rather than starting one from scratch. We also introduce a simplified five-step process of how to design a system, based on the managerial issues raised in Chapters 2 through 5. A more detailed information systems development process (explaining the "how-to" of every step) will be described in Chapter 7.

Consideration 1: Design I/S by Minimizing Overload and Distortion. Decision makers can rapidly be overloaded. Therefore, information systems should strive not to provide more information, but to provide *more appropriate* information. Since most managers do not suffer from a lack of information but rather from not knowing what information is needed and how to use it, effective information systems should act as filters, keeping irrelevant data out. The design process of an effective information system that follows this philosophy involves the following steps:

1. Understand the *objectives and business* **goals** (the purpose) of the information system.
2. Define the **information needs** that are to be fulfilled (data items, frequency, format, etc.), and who the user of the system is.
3. Map the *information flows* that will bring the necessary data into the information system (sources, routing, etc.) and get the reports from the system to the people that require them. Basically, this step identifies the communication network involved in fulfilling the particular information needs of the system.
4. Identify the *sources of distortion* that may affect those flows and develop a plan to overcome them.
5. Identify the *obstacles* to implementing the system and develop a plan to overcome them.

We now consider each of these steps in more detail.

Step 1: Understanding Objectives. Before developing a new information system or modifying an existing one, it is important to ask exactly what the *objectives* are that we are trying to accomplish. The overall goal of all organizations is to survive; but this goal is just too broad to be useful in directing the design of specific I/S applications. For a goal to be useful, it must be broken into measurable objectives. Stating that we need to be "more efficient in responding to a request for a price quote from a customer" is a much better purpose definition than "we want the organization to survive," but it is still not specific enough. A specific purpose would be, "we want to respond to a request for a price quote within 48 hours." Future chapters discuss the development and assessment of goals in more detail, but let's say at this point that the objective "within 48 hours" was determined by performing a competitive analysis, or *benchmarking* (This concept is discussed in Chapter 8), which showed that 48 hours is what customers want—and possibly already get from a competitor. We also need to develop a sense of the financial implications of providing the organization with that capability (e.g., How much business volume will we lose if we don't have that capability? How much new business will we gain because of that new capability? Is the investment worthwhile?).

A strategy of being responsive to changes in the environment is fundamental to all businesses, but we need to identify a set of detailed and measurable goals that operationalize a specific business strategy (e.g., best service in the industry, lowest cost, reachable from anywhere, anytime.) before we can design or acquire a cost-effective information systems capability. Before buying anyone in the company the latest personal computer on the market, we need to understand exactly what responsibilities individuals have, how they need to interact with others within and outside the company, and what goals they need to achieve before determining what the best hardware/software combination is to support them.

The questions that must be continually asked when designing and implementing an information system include: "What are the business objectives we are trying to achieve? How can I/T best support them? What is the specific role and **purpose** of this information system?"

Step 2: Assess Information Needs. The purpose of an information system will determine to a large extent what information is required. However, there is a tendency for managers to ask for more information than they really need. Indeed, the information a manager asks for is not only a function of the problem/opportunity he or she is facing, but is also a function of both the manager's experience and confidence. Generally, more experienced decision makers have a better sense of what information is truly relevant, and hence, they require less data than inexperienced managers and know better how to use it.

As we have discussed previously, the design of information systems should be guided by the principle of **minimizing overload.** If the decision maker is provided with less raw data, he or she will have more time to perform analysis (generating and weighing alternatives, for example). Three common strategies to avoid overload are (a) to employ filters, (b) to summarize data, and (c) to implement systems that support the management philosophy of reporting by-exception-only (defined below).

Filters are mechanisms for screening incoming data. Filters work by invoking prioritization rules that rank the data in terms of their usefulness and urgency. These priority rules are created by the recipient of the data. Electronic mail programs, for instance, typically have the capability of screening incoming messages and sorting or destroying them on the basis of key words or the return address of the sender. All messages from our boss or a customer could go automatically to the top of the list.

Summarization is another common method for reducing overload. Typically, the president of a large company would not be interested in the details of a single customer purchase (unless of course the purchase is huge and represents a sizable percentage of total sales). The details of one sale would be combined with all others by a salesperson or computer program, and reported as part of a total amount to a sales manager. This total amount would be combined with the totals from other sales representatives who report to that manager, and this total forwarded to the regional sales manager. This type of summarization allows a busy senior executive to get a quick snapshot of different aspects of the organization, without being bogged down with unnecessary details.

The third method of avoiding overload is using a **by-exception-only (BEO)** reporting philosophy. BEO is a type of filter which, instead of prioritizing incoming information, only lets information through to a manager if the information is about an event that was not expected. BEO requires that a range of acceptable events be defined beforehand; information is then provided to a manager only if events happen outside of that range. Consider the example of an inventory control system. As long as the inventory level remains within a prespecified range, the decision maker doesn't receive any information about it. As soon as the inventory level rises above or drops below the specified levels, an exception has occurred and the decision maker is notified. This reporting strategy saves the decision maker's time and energy required to constantly monitor the inventory level.

Step 3: Map Information Flows. Having defined the purpose and business objectives of the information system, and the information required to fulfill those objectives, we can now proceed to map how that information is going to be collected, stored, processed, and distributed. Mapping information flows involves determining the **communication network** required to provide a decision maker with (a) the relevant data needed to perform his/her job; and (b) the list of individuals that need to be informed about his/her decisions.

The collection and transmission of information are integral parts of the design of information systems, just as data processing and formatting are. The quality of the information that a decision maker utilizes in addressing a given issue or task is determined to a large extent by the transmission mechanisms used to deliver that information.

Therefore, to design an effective information system we need to understand the flow of information in the organization to ensure that everyone stays informed. This means asking who and what the sources of information are; how the information moves from the sources to the recipients; when the information has to be somewhere and in what format. Think of the following analogy: Information (in the broader sense of the term, including text, graphs, sound, video, etc.) is the lifeblood of the organization, and the communication network is the circulatory system that feeds each cell (individual). Understanding how the circulatory system can be clogged, and how some cells can be cut off from the flow, is a prerequisite for keeping the organization healthy.

Consequently, before you design an information system, you need to have a good sense of how the information moves (or doesn't move) through the organization. Mapping information flows will give you an overall picture of the obstacles to overcome in collecting and disseminating the necessary information to fulfill the role of the information system.

Step 4: Identify Sources of Distortion and Develop a Plan to Minimize Distortion. With the map of information flows in your hand, you can start discerning the real and potential problems of distortion and delays in those flows. The fourth step of this methodology involves (a) the identification of all potential sources of distortion and overload, and (b) the development of a plan to eliminate them.

The identification of all the sources of distortion involves analyzing in detail how the required information is going to be collected, processed, stored, accessed, and transmitted. The development of the plan to **minimize distortion** at its sources requires the designer to consider solutions that involve organizational structure, management (e.g., rewards, incentives, climate), and information technology. If information technology is applicable (E-mail, data and rules bases, standardized forms), then one needs to think about the modes of information presentation (formats for outputs) and the data collection mechanisms (e.g., forms, screens, protocols), keeping in mind the need to avoid overload.

The final section of Chapter 4 introduced specific ways to use I/T to reduce the need for information processing and to improve communications. Consider these suggestions as possibilities for inclusion in an information systems plan. The first suggestion (proposition IT1 from Table 4–5) was to use decision rules–based normative models to help reduce the need for information processing, giving the manager more time to concentrate on issues where a normative model cannot be used. Although we have not discussed the use of normative models in detail, we have provided some examples—the economic order quantity model for determining the optimal size of an order to replenish inventory is a good one. When such a model is employed, the manager no longer has to go through the entire decision-making process for how many parts to order to replenish the inventory; this reduces his/her need for information processing and frees him/her to do other tasks.

The other I/T propositions offered in Table 4–5 also support the basic design consideration we have been stressing: Reduce overload and overcome sources of distortion. For example, summarizing and combining information (proposition IT2) reduces information overload. The use of standard data entry screens (proposition IT3) can help reduce distortion. Reporting on a BEO basis (proposition IT5) reduces overload. Routing messages automatically on the basis of key words and providing selective access and shortcuts to upper levels (proposition IT6) reduces distortion; when subordinates know that upper levels have access to raw data, there is less likelihood they will intentionally distort messages.

Creating a centralized database and providing access to all hierarchical levels (proposition IT7) reduces **overload** (by allowing decision making to be decentralized), and also reduces distortion (similar to proposition IT6, since upper levels will have access to raw data). The only I/T proposition we haven't mentioned yet (proposition IT4—providing flexible, customized formats) addresses the issue of individual cognitive biases; for example, some individuals process information better in graphical format rather than in table format. Even here, providing the flexibility to receive information in either format helps reduce distortion.

The product of this fourth step in the design process is a plan that identifies each and every source of potential overload and distortion at each step in the collection, storage, processing, and transmission of data and matches a solution to it; that is, a method of neutralizing that source.

Step 5: Identify Implementation Obstacles and Develop a Plan to Overcome Them. A successful and effective information system is an information system which is actually used. No matter how wonderful the technical specifications of a system are, if the participants needed to provide, analyze, and receive information from the system won't use it, the system will be a failure. Designing and implementing I/S may generate resistance from users, as the I/S may be perceived as a tool for organizational control (e.g., my supervisor knows my monthly results before I do). Users may also feel threatened by divulging personal decision rules (e.g., now that they know how I pick stocks, I'm expendable) and may feel that the system somehow violates their rights, such as a right to privacy (e.g., my supervisor can read my E-mail messages).

We won't pursue the issues involved in the implementation of information systems at this point; Chapter 7 will present them in more detail. For now, just recognize that part of designing an information system is the identification of *political* as well as *rational* considerations. Since one of the primary goals in designing I/S is to move organizational decision making away from the political model and closer to a rational model, we must realize that we will need to ask individuals for rules and sources of information they may not want to divulge. Indeed, it is important to remember that users of the system may have political agendas that could bias their responses, and personal and ethical concerns that may interfere with their willingness to use the system. Identifying the sources of resistance early on as the system design unfolds, and making a plan to overcome them, is an important step in implementing a system that will be accepted and used.

Finally, the implementation plan needs to address the technical difficulty of developing the information system. Systems that provide support to only one individual to perform a fairly simple and well-defined task with objective, numerical

Designing an information system to support an individual is like designing a home for a single family. There is usually a consistent set of requests and objectives. Photos courtesy of Craig Blovin/Offshoot Stock (left) and Hewlett-Packard (right).

data (e.g., calculating interest payments on a mortgage) are relatively easy to design and implement. On the other hand, systems that provide support to a workgroup performing complex and ill-defined tasks, with information that includes numbers, text, opinions, images, and sounds (e.g., developing a marketing campaign) can be very difficult to design and implement.

Consideration 2: Different Types of Support—Individual, Workgroup, Enterprise, and Inter-Enterprise. In developing an I/T architecture for the organization, one needs to think about all the activities that must be supported with information technology to make the organization an effective entity. The task may seem overwhelming at first. One way to approach the task is to think of organizational activities and requirements at four levels.

There are four levels of support that an information system can provide: An information system can support an individual, a group of individuals, an enterprise as a whole, and/or the transactions among several enterprises. It is important to differentiate information systems on this basis because the approaches to designing these systems are quite different. To illustrate, four analogies are helpful.

In developing an **individual support** system—one that will help an individual perform a given task better—the role of the designer is very similar to the role of an architect designing a family home. The bulk of the interviews are about the users' needs, preferences, and habits. How many bedrooms are required? Is an open-concept floor plan preferable? Should the home be multi-level or single-level? In designing the individual I/S, the questions include: What do you want your reports to look like? What level of accuracy do you need? How often do you want to enter data?

In developing a **workgroup support** system—one that will help a group of individuals perform a task requiring coordination and/or collaboration—a useful analogy is the design of a condominium: some decisions are made by the association of homeowners (e.g., common land and services), others by individuals (e.g., customization of personal spaces). Questions about common infrastructures might include type of heating source (oil, natural gas, electricity?) and external

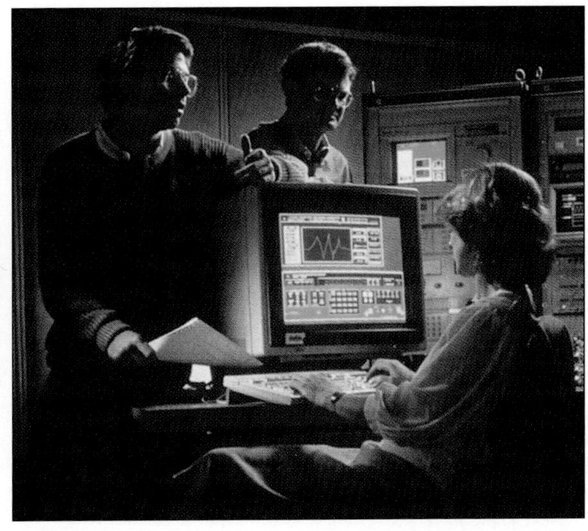

Designing an information system to support a workgroup is like designing a condominium complex. Some features are customized to the needs of individuals, and others are customized to meet the needs of the group. Photos courtesy of Jim Grove/Kamin Collection (left) and Tony Stone Worldwide (right).

siding of the buildings (vinyl siding, adobe, wood?). Decisions for owners of individual units could include selection of flooring (slate entranceway, hardwood in living area, wall-to-wall carpeting throughout?) and other customized features (a wood or gas fireplace?). For information systems that will support workgroups, standards must be created for the software packages to be used (e.g., which word-processing and spreadsheet software?), but individuals can choose how to customize their screens and program their own menus and default settings (e.g., icons, colors, alarms, etc.).

In developing an **enterprisewide support** system—one that helps the whole organization function better (e.g., a personnel system, a general ledger system, an order fulfillment system)—the I/S designer behaves more like a city planner figuring the best way to channel traffic around and through the city. One responsibility is to ensure a good road and highway system. A good I/S ensures that the correct people get the correct information at the correct time: in linking two or more individuals for communications purposes, how fast, how direct do you want that link to be? That is, how many lanes should the (communication) highway have? Where do you put "on and off ramps"? Who should have access to the highway?

In addition to roads and highways, the planner must consider other forms of infrastructure (water, sewers, power). Similarly, the designer of enterprisewide systems must consider more than the transmission of textual messages; what information (video, images, text) must be collected and stored? What types of I/S are required to support cross-functional decision-making processes? What mail system is to be used and supported in the enterprise? Should we standardize hardware as well as software?

The development of an **inter-enterprise support** system—one that links two or more organizations to perform a task better (e.g., a just-in-time delivery system, an electronic fund transfer system)—typically involves negotiations among I/S designers from the various organizations interested in creating an electronic link. In developing inter-enterprise systems (also called **inter-organizational systems,** or

Designing an information system to support an enterprise is like designing the infrastructure of a town. Decisions need to be made on where resources will be located and how they will be accessed. Photos courtesy of Bonnie Kamin (left) and Tony Stone Worldwide (right).

IOS), I/S designers behave like a team of politicians and civil engineers trying to build a bridge between two or more countries. In linking two or more countries, the issues that need to be addressed are the different construction safety codes and standards and the concerns about security, health, and sanitation. These same issues apply to IOS: Instead of construction codes, electronic communication protocols must be negotiated; the security and sanitation issues are translated as protecting sensitive information and ensuring that no computer viruses are introduced into the system.

Consideration 3: Ethical Issues in Information Systems Design. The designers of information systems must consider a broad set of issues in addition to the purpose of the system. An I/S could be designed to do a great job of accomplishing a business goal but fail to be implemented because some of the **stakeholders** (i.e., players) in the system refuse to use it. And one reason for not using it could be concerns for potential ethical abuses.

An example will help illustrate this concern. In the late 1980s, a medium-sized insurance company found they were losing market share and determined that their costs of operations seemed higher than their competitors. They evaluated many of their business processes, and decided that some needed substantial improvement in efficiency. One such process was the handling of insurance claims for customers.

Under the existing situation, claims processors would take the information from clients over the telephone (or from written requests), retrieve the customer's file, and then begin the process of determining what portion (if any) of the customer's claim should be paid. This process was occasionally time consuming, as the processor would have to look up company regulations in different procedure manuals. The claims processors were given some leeway to interpret the manuals and base their decisions on previous cases they had dealt with.

To improve the efficiency of this process, a new information system was purchased and implemented. With the new system, all of the procedures were available on-line in a rules database. All of the customer information was also stored in a database. When the claims processor received a claim from a customer, he or she typed in the appropriate information and the information system did everything after that. The system pulled up the customer information, applied the rules, and printed the check.

Unfortunately, this system was not accepted by the claims processors. When they saw how their jobs were going to change, they began to resist the implementation of

FIGURE 5–1 Inter-Enterprise System

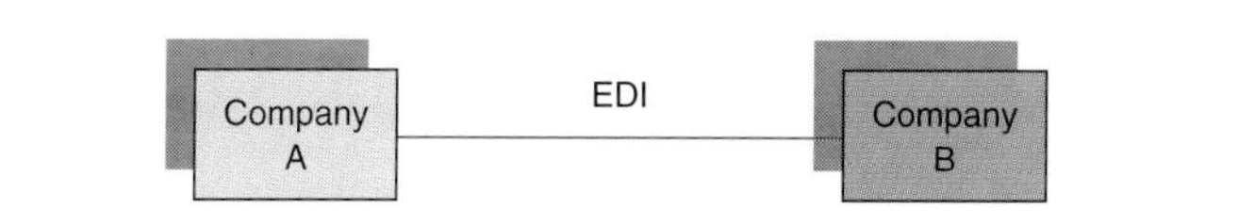

Designing an information system to support the exchange of information between two companies is like designing bridges, highways, railways, and airline routes between countries. Protocols are needed to exchange people or information. Photo courtesy of Ed Kashi.

the new system in subtle ways. They recognized that they were going to lose the decision-making function of their responsibilities, and their jobs would basically become that of data entry clerks. The claims processors refused to use the new system as it was originally envisioned; eventually the system was redesigned to retain some of the decision-making responsibilities for the claims processors, and implemented with more success.

The point of the story in Business Brief 5–1 is that it is important to consider the rights and responsibilities of the various stakeholders in the design and use of information systems. A system that maintains detailed records of purchases by people may help in direct-marketing efforts, but it may also violate the individual's right to **privacy.** To avoid unnecessary complications at the implementation stage, it is a good idea to consider potential ethical considerations up front.

One relatively simple framework for analyzing ethical concerns involves a four-step process:

1. Identify the ethical issue and the primary stakeholders involved.
2. Determine if any relevant guidelines exist to address the situation (e.g., policies, laws).
3. Consider any relevant rights and duties (e.g., privacy rights). If rights and duties of various stakeholders appear to conflict, attempt to weigh the consequences of one action against another.
4. Reach a defensible decision, recognizing that in some situations there may be no way to avoid violating the rights or duties of some stakeholders. Document your decision and inform those involved.

Too many individuals and organizations become enamored with I/T without considering how it will help them accomplish specific business goals. What we wish to stress in this section of the chapter is that you need to understand (a) the organizational goals, (b) decision processes, (c) communication needs, (d) level of support, and (e) ethical concerns *before* designing an information system.

BUSINESS BRIEF 5-1 I/T AND PRIVACY: EYES IN THE SKIES

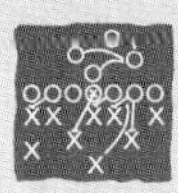

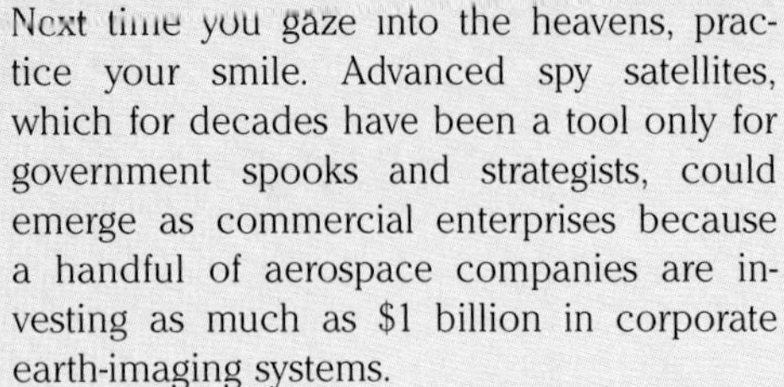

Next time you gaze into the heavens, practice your smile. Advanced spy satellites, which for decades have been a tool only for government spooks and strategists, could emerge as commercial enterprises because a handful of aerospace companies are investing as much as $1 billion in corporate earth-imaging systems.

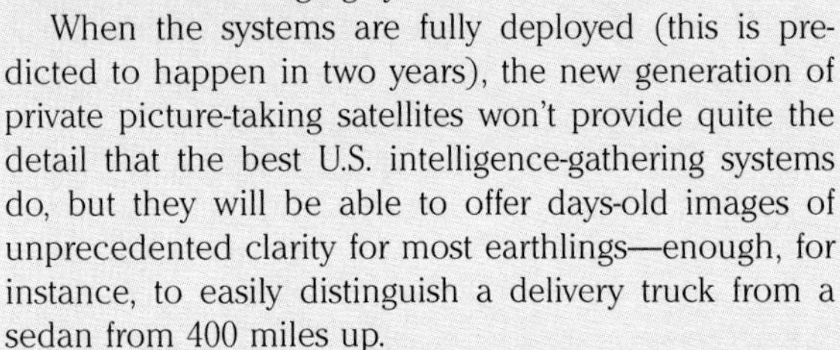

When the systems are fully deployed (this is predicted to happen in two years), the new generation of private picture-taking satellites won't provide quite the detail that the best U.S. intelligence-gathering systems do, but they will be able to offer days-old images of unprecedented clarity for most earthlings—enough, for instance, to easily distinguish a delivery truck from a sedan from 400 miles up.

These corporate systems use optical and digital technology that was freed up by the U.S. government for private use in 1994, and they worry some scientists and federal policy makers concerned about privacy invasion and a free-for-all expansion of espionage. For now, though, those questions are being overshadowed by excitement in fields ranging from forensic crime research to forestry.

Coldwell Banker Corporation is among those planning to offer real-estate shoppers pictures from space of homes, neighborhoods, and traffic patterns, as opposed to the more commonplace maps and ground shots. Television networks such as ABC expect to transform the new digital images into remarkably detailed "flights" over battle zones for the evening news. Urban planners foresee new ways to direct growth and update property-tax rolls by peering into backyards, while Pacific Bell is preparing to plot the laying of phone lines without the costs of sending crews to study the terrain. Before the end of the decade, consumers, too, should be able to summon fresh high-resolution pictures of far-flung vacation spots on their home computer screens.

QUESTION

1. Commercial companies (such as real estate firms) are anxious to begin using the satellite imaging systems to provide better products and services to their customers because they believe this will give them a competitive advantage. Identify and discuss one or more potential ethical considerations which may arise through the use of these systems.

Source: Jeff Cole, "Eyes in the Skies: New Satellite Imaging Could Soon Transform the Face of the Earth," *The Wall Street Journal*, November 30, 1995, p. A1. Reprinted by permission of *The Wall Street Journal*

Indeed, what the three overall considerations point to is that it pays to spend time, effort, and money in the design phase. Spending resources and time "up front" saves a lot of resources and time if changes need to be made later on. Just as it is much cheaper and easier to make changes on blueprints than to make changes on a building that is already built, so it is with information systems. It is easier, cheaper, and plain smarter, to spend time understanding the needs of users rather than patching up a software application once it has been programmed and implemented. It is the job of the I/S designer to make sure that the decision maker has considered all the relevant information required to make the specific decision now and in the near future. Otherwise, when the time comes for the decision maker to make the decision, she/he will have to spend valuable time looking for the necessary data that was not provided.

TYPES OF INFORMATION SYSTEMS

Classification schemes are useful ways of categorizing entities; a good classification enables us to identify and categorize members of a set on the basis of certain criteria or characteristics. We are then able to discuss different classes on the basis of shared understanding of common characteristics. For example, we have a common understanding that the class "mammal" includes animals that are warm-blooded, produce milk, and so on. By classifying elements of a set, we are able to simplify our subsequent discussions and considerations. In the context of information systems, a useful classification scheme also provides insight into design issues.

Traditional Classification Scheme. A widely used classification scheme has evolved over a period of years, mirroring to some extent the historical development of computerized information systems. Although variations exist on the actual titles used, the more common types of systems are typically described with the following labels and acronyms: transaction processing systems (TPS), management information systems (MIS), decision support systems (DSS), expert systems (ES), executive support systems (ESS), and office automation systems (OAS).

Transaction processing systems (TPS) are those that record actual transactions, such as an order for a product or a withdrawal from a checking account. These systems tend to have clearly defined inputs and outputs, and there is an emphasis on efficiency and accuracy (see Figure 5–2). TPS record data, but they do little in the way of converting data into information or knowledge. Early computerized systems were primarily TPS. Since TPS collect and store the basic operational data of a company, they are the foundation on which other information systems are built. Because they provide the basic building blocks for other systems, critical TPS in larger organizations tend to be fail-proof or **fault-tolerant,** meaning that the system has backup hardware and software so that, in case of a breakdown or failure in one of the systems (a power failure, a fire, a flood, an earthquake) the company can continue to collect data with the other (optimally, the backup system is in a different

FIGURE 5–2 A Point-of-Sale System as an Example of a TPS

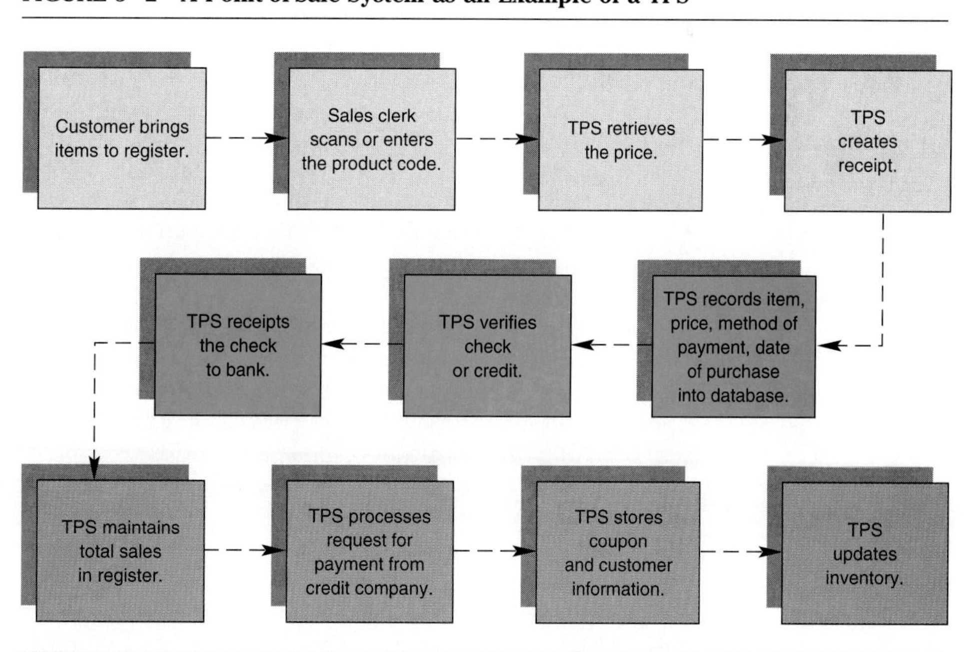

SOURCE: Adapted from *Information Systems: A Management Approach* by Stephen R. Gordon and Judith R. Gordon (Fort Worth, TX: The Dryden Press), 1996, p. 308.

location than the primary system). The extra hardware and software systems that serve as backups are called **redundant** systems. Redundancy is an effective way to ensure the reliability of the TPS. Typical TPS are point-of-sale systems, airline reservation systems, and general ledger systems.

Management information systems (MIS) take the data recorded by a TPS and convert them into management reports. You can think of an MIS as a set of computer programs that use data from recorded transactions from a TPS as input, and produce summary and routine reports as outputs. As Figure 5–3 illustrates, an MIS report allows a manager to review past performance. The reports follow standard formats, are produced on a regular basis, and typically are not interactive; the manager can look at screens and/or printed reports but cannot ask questions and change parameters on-line. A monthly sales report listing the total sales figures for each salesperson would be an output of an MIS. The emphasis in the late 1960s and early 1970s was on developing ever more complex and comprehensive reporting systems, and at one point the term MIS was broadened to include almost any type of computerized information system. Most people now use the term MIS in the more narrow (reporting system) sense. Examples of MIS are inventory reports, energy consumption reports, and attendance records.

Decision support systems (DSS) were the focus of a great deal of interest and conjecture during the late 1970s and into the 1980s. DSS typically focus on the future, and are designed to help decision makers with messy or unstructured decisions. The main feature of a DSS is its interactive nature. That is, it has the capability of allowing managers to ask "what-if" questions and to build various scenarios to understand better what the real problem or opportunity is as much as to come up with an action plan to address it. DSS are used on an as-needed basis. Figure 5–4 illustrates the contents of a DSS.

An example of a DSS might be a forecasting model used to predict demand levels for a product at different prices, inflation rates, and success rates of a marketing campaign. This type of DSS would allow the manager to change any of the rates and "see what happens." It would also have a variety of forecasting models to choose from, each of the models based on a different set of assumptions. Another example might be a spreadsheet model for budgeting purposes that enables the manager to ask questions such as, "What happens to our budgeted cost of capital if interest rates are 10 percent next year instead of 8 percent?" DSS have also been called **what-if systems** and for that reason many people immediately think of scenarios and contingency analysis when they hear the term *DSS*.

In the last few years, DSS software has been developed to support workgroups. These systems, called *group decision support systems (GDSS)*, serve the same function as DSS but allow members of a group to interact among themselves as they question each other's assumptions and estimates. Another type of software to support group interaction is called *groupware*. Groupware allows several members of a workgroup to *coordinate* their work (individuals work on separate and distinct pieces and those pieces then come together) and to *collaborate* on their work (individuals work together to produce the final result or set of conclusions). Typical uses of groupware are the writing, editing, and production of documents and presentations, the design of products, and consensus building.

Expert systems (ES) are generally considered a subset of **artificial intelligence (AI)**, which began to receive a great deal of attention during the 1980s (although examples of ES existed earlier). The intent of an ES is to try to capture the knowledge and reasoning capabilities of a human expert and transfer this expertise to a computer system. Although a number of different approaches are used, a

FIGURE 5-3 An MIS Report

Summary Operating Statistics
Store# 32
Week of 3/15/97

	Your store	Avg. PizzaCo
Seats	92	105.3
Customers	3 ,216	3,532.6
Customers/seat/day	4.99	4.79
Restaurant Sales	45,703	50,129
Sales/ customer	14.21	14.19
Sales/ seat/ day	70.97	68.01
Take-out sales	.	.
Total sales	.	.
Take-out/ total sales	.	.
Returns	.	.
Returns/ total sales	.	.
Employee-hours	.	.
Average labor rate	.	.
Emp-hrs/customer	.	.
Emp-hrs/sales	.	.
Emp-cost/customer	.	.
Emp-cost/sales	.	.
.	.	.

Sales Exception Report
Month Ending 3/31/97
Store #35

Prod #	Description	Code
202	Pizza, pepperoni	A,M
321	Manicotti, baked	M

Codes:

A: Sales of this product are at least 10% below that of the average PizzaCo store's sales as adjusted for total sales volume.

M: Sales of this product are at least 5% below that of last month as adjusted for total sales volume.

SOURCE: Adapted from *Information Systems: A Management Approach* by Stephen R. Gordon and Judith R. Gordon (Fort Worth, TX: The Dryden Press), 1996, p. 328.

common one is to have the ES contain a **knowledge base,** accessed through an *inference engine.* The knowledge base contains rules (usually of the type "*if* X happens *then* do Y") while the inference engine is the reasoning strategy used by the system to apply the rules. The system applies rules provided by a human expert or group of experts in making a decision. Figure 5-5 illustrates an example of decision

FIGURE 5–4 A Decision Support System

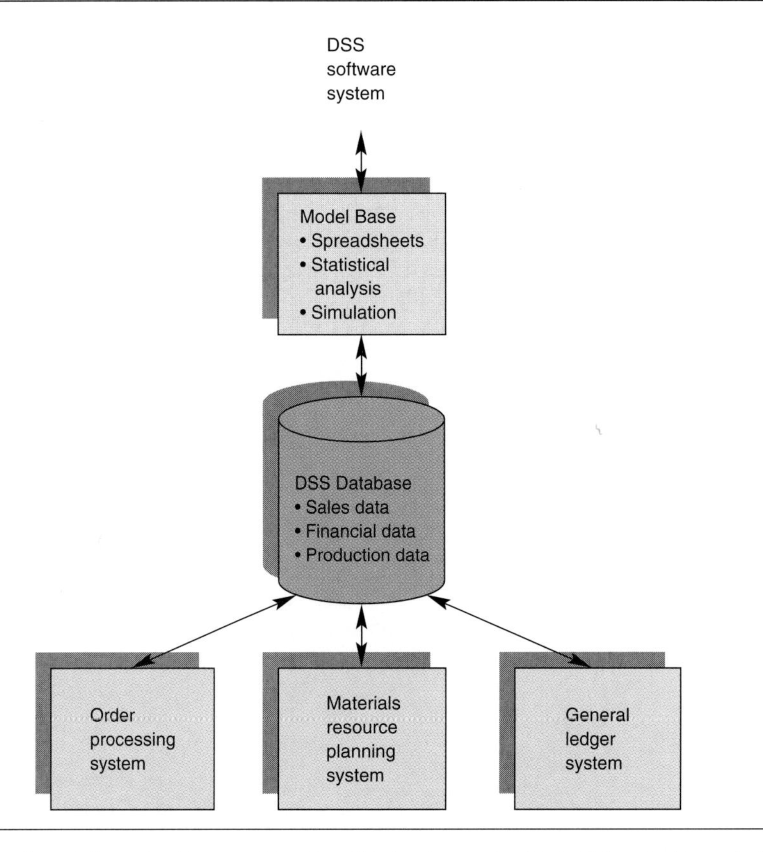

SOURCE: Adapted from *Information Systems: A Problem-Solving Approach,* Third Edition, by Kenneth C. Laudon and Jane Price Laudon (Fort Worth, TX: The Dryden Press), 1995, p. 599.

FIGURE 5–5 Decision Rules in an Expert System

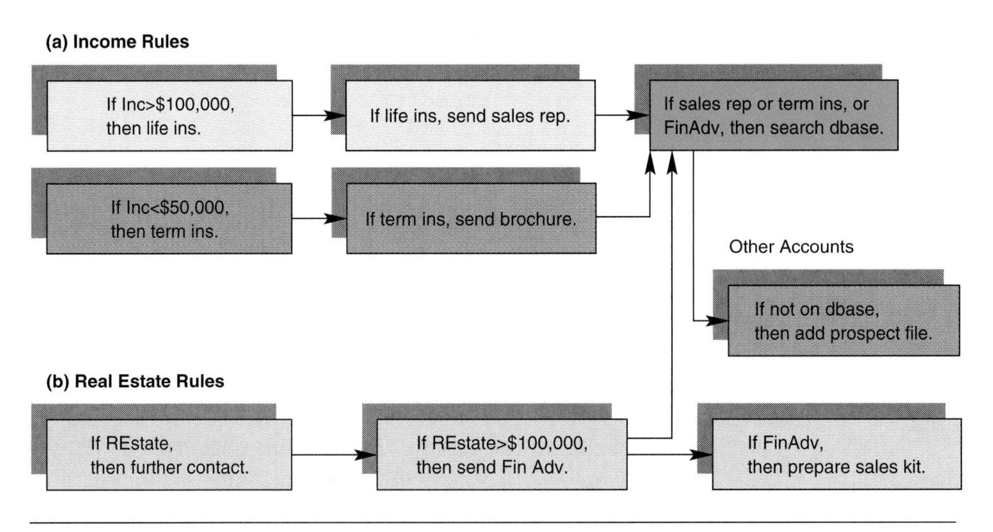

SOURCE: Adapted from *Information Systems: A Problem-Solving Approach,* Third Edition, by Kenneth C. Laudon and Jane Price Laudon (Fort Worth, TX: The Dryden Press), 1995, p. 562.

BUSINESS BRIEF 5-2 AUGMENTING KNOWLEDGE: EXPERT ANALYST AT AMEX

In the late 1980s, American Express (Amex) was having difficulty keeping up with the demand for authorizations. Some 300 employees worked at four authorization centers around the United States, responding to calls for purchase authorization. Unlike credit cards such as MasterCard, Visa, or Amex's Optima card, the original American Express has no predefined limit. Members can rack up charges as high as they like—as long as they pay the entire bill every month.

While this policy may be good for customer relations, it can be a headache for Amex employees (authorizers) who are responsible for determining whether to approve or deny any given purchase. Since there is no predefined limit at which credit will be denied to a customer, authorizers must rely on customer credit histories and bank account information supplied when the customer obtained the card.

The cost of making wrong decisions is huge. If an authorizer rejects an attempted purchase because the account has an unusually high balance or a history of late payments, for example, Amex loses the revenue it would collect from the merchant and also risks losing the insulted shopper as a customer. If the authorizer approves a purchase that should not have been approved, the company faces the risk of never receiving payment. Amex guarantees merchants that they will receive decisions on purchases within 90 seconds.

In 1988, Amex completed an expert system, dubbed the *Authorizer's Assistant,* to help lighten the authorizers' load. The system condensed the array of customer data needed during each transaction by the authorizers into a single screen. Using rules garnered through interviews with the company's most experienced authorizers, the expert system also formulates an approve-or-deny suggestion. The Assistant was combined with a second program that handles all routine transactions (about 95 percent of all credit requests are considered routine), allowing authorizers to focus only on borderline decisions.

QUESTION

1. What are the implications of using the Authorizer's Assistant for the jobs of the authorizers?

SOURCE: Adapted from D. Steinberg. "Amex Builds an Expert System to Assist Its Credit Analysts," *PC WEEK,* Nov. 17, 1987, pp. C1. Reprinted from *PC WEEK* with permission. Copyright © 1987 Ziff-Davis Publishing Company.

rules. Expert systems have been used successfully in a wide variety of fields including medicine, financial planning, loan granting, stock trading, mineral prospecting, tax assessment and abatement strategies, order picking and inventory control. Business Brief 5–2 provides a specific example.

While ES provide the ability to explore deeply into a very narrow domain, **Executive Support Systems (ESS),** also called **Executive Information Systems (EIS),** are designed to provide breadth as well. As the name implies, these systems were developed (initially in the late 1980s and early 1990s) to help support the information needs of top-level executives. These systems cut across functional areas of the organization and provide access to external databases. The interfaces and commands tend to be very easy to learn and use. A typical system provides access to sales information, production information, marketing information, research and development, and so on.

EIS generally have the capability to browse through information on all aspects of the organization, and then zero in on those areas the manager believes to require attention. An EIS might also have built-in features to report exceptions (such as a red light indicating a low inventory level), to allow more management by exception. The EIS can also allow the executive to check the price of the company's shares on the stock market, link to a news organization to see whether any articles have been

FIGURE 5–6 An Executive Support System

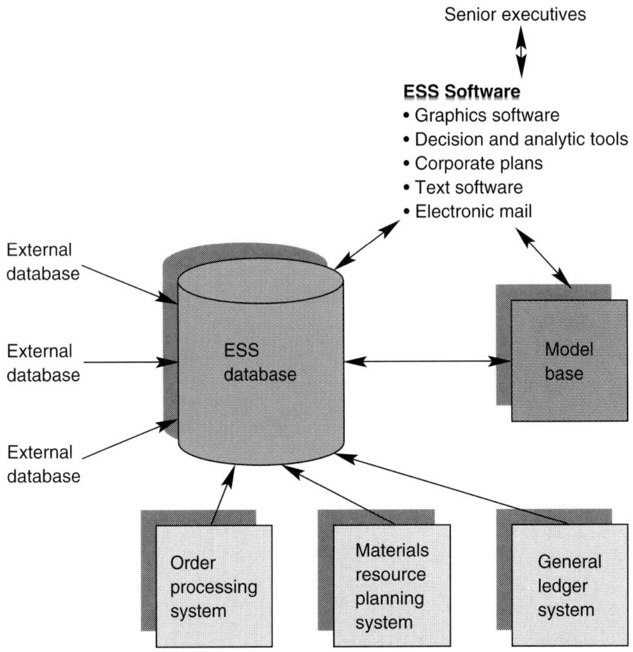

Senior executives

ESS Software
- Graphics software
- Decision and analytic tools
- Corporate plans
- Text software
- Electronic mail

External database
External database
External database
ESS database
Model base
Order processing system
Materials resource planning system
General ledger system

SOURCE: Adapted from *Information Systems: A Problem-Solving Approach,* Third Edition, by Kenneth C. Laudon and Jane Price Laudon (Fort Worth, TX: The Dryden Press), 1995, p. 608.

written on the company, and access industrywide databases to check market share information. Figure 5–6 illustrates how ESS can allow top-level management to have both a general overview of performance and a very detailed explanation of events.

Office automation systems (OAS) are those that combine various technologies to reduce the manual labor required in operating an effective office environment. The term OAS is typically applied to the technologies that include voice mail, electronic mail, local area networks, scheduling and word-processing software, scanners, shared on-line printers and photocopiers, facsimile (FAX), and so on. Just about every technology used in the operation of a modern office is considered part of OAS, and these separate technologies are merging. OAS tend to be the nerve centers of organizations; their main role is the management of documents and voice messages, and the coordination and scheduling of meetings (electronic and face-to-face).

Although this traditional classification of systems has been useful, it is beginning to outlive some of its usefulness: It is becoming more and more difficult to classify a specific information system. If we can no longer classify a majority of systems with a given scheme, then the benefits of having a classification scheme are no longer realized.

This is what is happening within the realm of information systems. Many systems now have multiple capabilities; no longer is a word-processing system just capable of creating and manipulating text within a document. For this reason, we believe that the scheme we have described is limited in its functionality, and it is time to develop complementary classification schemes.

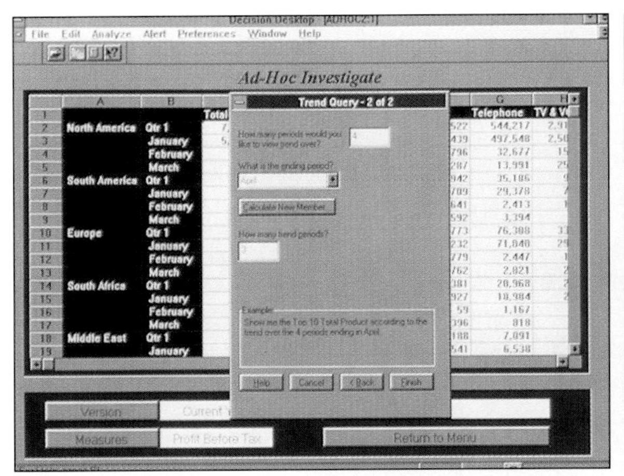

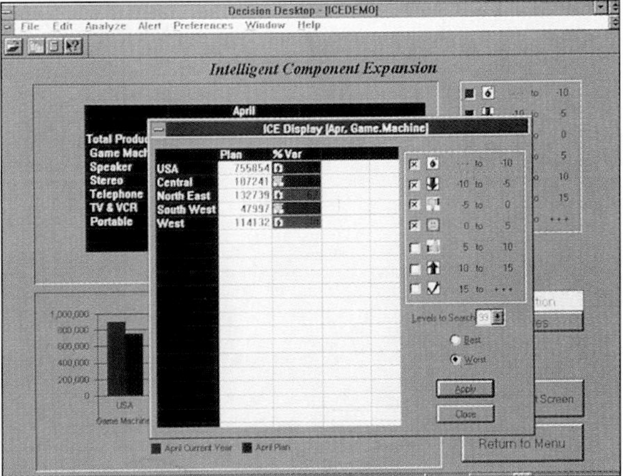

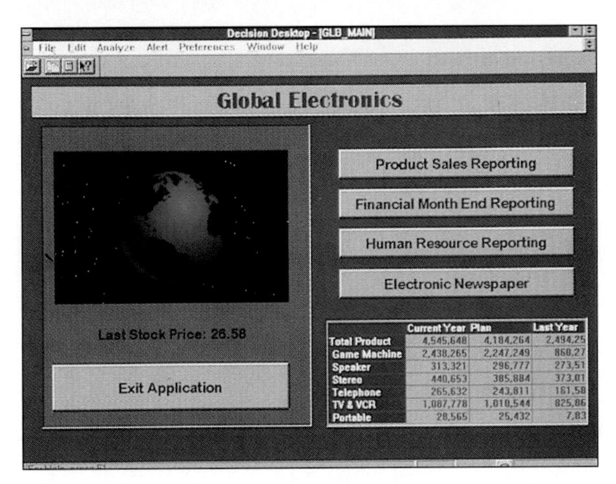

Executive support systems have a very easy-to-use interface, and provide a variety of options for information access and processing. Photos courtesy of Comshare, Inc.

The Information Systems Cube. The **Information systems cube** is a classification scheme based on the activities and tasks that are supported by information systems, rather than the specific capabilities of the systems themselves. We believe that although the technical capabilities of information systems will continue to change rapidly, the inherent functions that the systems are used for will remain basically the same. Figure 5–7 illustrates the I/S cube classification scheme pictorially.

The first dimension of the I/S Cube is the *scope* of the application being supported; the second is the **complexity** of the task, and the third is the *information richness* required. We now examine each of the dimensions in more detail, and provide examples of how to use the classification scheme.

Application Scope. **Application scope,** or simply **scope** refers to who (or what) the information system supports. A mailing list of previous customers of a real estate agent is used only by that individual agent; it is designed to achieve the goal of improving that individual's customer relations. At the other end of the spectrum, a system linking an organization with a supplier that automatically orders new parts when the inventory runs low would be an example of an interorganizational system. The broader the scope, the greater the impact on the organization and the harder the information system will be to design and implement.

Office automation systems are the nerve centers of organizations; they manage documents and voice messages, coordinate, schedule, and support meetings. Paper-based systems are generally much less efficient. Photo courtesy of Richard Palsey/Stock Boston, Inc.

We have used the end points of individual and interorganizational, but we could add others for additional precision if desired; for example, we could use:

1. Individual.
2. Workgroup (within workgroups we could further refine the classification to distinguish among tasks that require coordination but no collaboration; coordination and collaboration; and consensus at every step of the task).
3. Department (which contains multiple groups performing different functions).
4. Campus (which represents a single site of an organization, containing multiple departments).
5. Organizational or enterprisewide (containing multiple sites, including multinational offices).
6. Interorganizational (which could link customers, suppliers, collaborating organizations).

Task Complexity. **Task complexity** refers to the degree of **decision structure** inherent in the task being performed by the information system. The term *structure* is commonly applied to the realm of decision making. Specifically, a **structured decision** occurs when courses of action may be programmed under all possible circumstances. A structured decision is a decision for which a solution is readily available and the steps of which are well known. Consider, for example, the activities

FIGURE 5–7 The Information Systems Cube

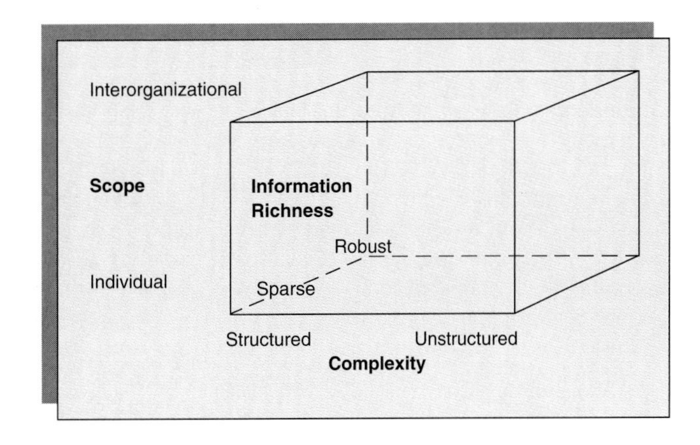

supported by an automated teller machine (ATM). The ATM does not support activities that require creativity in decision making; it only allows the user to perform functions that can be automated. When a user requests a withdrawal of funds from a savings account, the computer program retrieves the balance from the account, and compares it to the requested amount. If the requested amount is lower than the account balance, the transaction is processed and the funds are provided.

Unstructured decisions, on the other hand, require creativity or human judgment. If the bank customer wishes to obtain financing to start a new business, instead of making a simple withdrawal from his or her account, the situation is much different. There are many factors to consider in reaching a decision on the request, and there is no way to automate the decision-making process. Similarly, the selection of advertising artwork and copy for a new marketing campaign would be considered an **unstructured task,** and cannot be automated. As with application scope, task complexity is not an either-or concept; any given decision situation could range across a continuum from completely structured to completely unstructured. The more unstructured the task (i.e., the more complex it is), the harder the information system is to design and implement.

Information Richness. The concept of **information richness** was introduced in Chapter 3, in our discussion on group decision making. Information richness refers to how much surplus meaning the information contains, beyond the literal symbols used to express it. For example, spoken words contain much more meaning than written ones, because of voice inflections, accents, and so forth. Face-to-face meetings can add even more meaning to messages, through factors such as body language.

The end points on the information richness dimension of our cube range from sparse to robust. In the context of the application of information technology, *sparse* would refer to machine language (the basic symbols understood by a computer) while *robust* could be full sound and motion, real-time, interactive video conferencing. Once again it would be possible to add intermediate points along the continuum such as text only, graphics, sound, and so on. The greater the information richness required to accomplish a task, the harder the information system is to design and implement.

Referring to the example in Business Brief 5–3, we can demonstrate how the classification scheme would be used. The *application scope* is at the low end of the

BUSINESS BRIEF 5-3 INFORMATION IS MORE THAN DATA: DON'T LAY IT ON TOO THICK

On the horizon are potent new applications that marry computer maps from geographic information systems (GIS) with signals from global positioning satellites (GPS). The signals enable any vehicle equipped with a receiver to pinpoint its location as it moves. Eventually GIS and GPS could transform aviation and shipping—and even agriculture.

An Iowa farmer with technological know-how, Donald Larson has worked with tractor manufacturers on a system that brings some scientific accuracy to the process of mixing and spreading chemical fertilizer. Traditionally, soil samples are drawn from different locations in a field, the results are averaged, and one mix of chemicals is spread across the entire field. The problem is that soil quality varies, and not all parts of a field should get the same dose of fertilizer.

The software unites a GPS receiver right on the tractor with a Compaq PC showing a computerized map of the field and its various types of soil. As the tractor's position is continually updated, the PC makes sure the right amount of fertilizer is dispensed. The system primes the field for maximum yield and reduces harmful runoff because low-producing acres don't get too much fertilizer.

QUESTION

1. Consider the information system used by Donald Larson with respect to the three elements: scope, complexity, and information richness. What are the implications for designing this type of system?

SOURCE: Rick Tetzeli, "Mapping for Dollars," *Fortune*, October 18, 1993, p. 96.

spectrum, as the system is designed to support an individual (the person responsible for fertilizing the field). The *task complexity* lies also at the low end; the decision of what combination and concentration of fertilizer to use for a specific type of soil is fairly well structured. Some level of complexity is introduced by the variety of soil compositions that can exist in a given field or tract of land. Also, the degree of structure is somewhat dependent on the state of knowledge concerning fertilization. Finally, the system would probably be classified toward the middle of the *information richness* dimension. The information requirements include data that have been analyzed and interpreted, as well as geographic images, but there is no need for sound or moving images.

The information systems cube can be used to classify systems (i.e., to compare systems across its three dimensions) and it can also be helpful in developing an implementation plan. For example, a system that has a broad scope, deals with a highly complex task, and requires great information richness will be a system with a higher level of difficulty of implementation (i.e., delivering the system on time, on budget, and with the appropriate functionality) than a system with the opposite characteristics.

COMPONENTS OF AN INFORMATION SYSTEM

One definition of an information system is the following: an information system is an integrated, computer-user system for providing undistorted information to support the operations, management, and decision-making functions of an organization. The **components** of an information system are its *purpose, people, procedures, information,* and *information technology.* Although it is possible to have an information system without information technology (a manual accounting system, for example), the focus of this book is on systems that do involve I/T.

Information systems consist of a purpose, people, procedures, information, and information technology. Photo courtesy of Bruce Ayres/Tony Stone Images.

Purpose

The **purpose** is the reason for having the system; it is something we are attempting to accomplish. As we know, a major goal of most organizations is survival. When we look at information systems, it is usually possible (and desirable) to identify narrower, more specific objectives and purposes. For example, one goal of the order entry system for a mail order company might be to provide more personalized customer service, and a specific way of doing that is to retrieve customer order history data for the customer representative using the system within five seconds of the request being made. Let's assume for a moment that the system uses telephone numbers to identify customers. The service representative keys in the telephone number, which they have obtained from the customer, and the information system searches through a database and retrieves a record of sales transactions that match the customer telephone number.

Some people differentiate between goals and objectives. A fairly common way of distinguishing the two is to view goals as broader, more general statements of purpose, while objectives are specific and measurable. In the previous example, the goal would be to provide better customer service, and an objective would be to retrieve customer sales history within five seconds of request. By breaking broad goals into specific objectives, it is possible to measure how well the information system is performing. In this book we use the term *purpose* to include both general statements of intent (goals) as well as more specific, measurable objectives.

Every information system should be designed for one or more purposes. This seems like a relatively simple concept, but it is interesting to note that for many I/S development efforts that have run into difficulty, the purpose was not clearly specified up front. Also, unless the purpose can be clearly identified and described in measurable terms, there is no way to evaluate the effectiveness of the information system. Given the amount of resources information systems consume in most organizations—estimates suggest that 50 percent of all capital expenditures by organizations are, directly or indirectly, for information systems—it is imperative to have a clearly specified purpose.

People

People are an integral part of information systems. Sooner or later people are involved in using the information generated by the system. Therefore, we will always define information systems as having a "people component," though sometimes it may not be obvious.

To illustrate, consider an information system designed to facilitate inventory control. At a low level, we could identify computer software that runs on some type of computer hardware. The program accepts as input the amount of a particular item sold, calculates the quantity of the item on hand, compares this to a predetermined reorder level, and produces as output a line indicating the quantity of the item that should be reordered. This line is stored in a file, which will later be printed (by another computer program) onto a low-stock report.

This inventory program is really a subsystem of the overall inventory control system. At a higher level, a purchasing agent uses the low-stock report generated by the inventory control program to make purchasing decisions (how much to order, from which supplier). The purchasing agent who uses the report is considered part of the complete information system, and typically is referred to as the *user* of the system. People also play other roles with respect to information systems; someone has to design and install the system (the developer), someone has to keep it running and ensure its protection against disasters (the operator), and so on.

Procedures

Procedures, or work practices, are the human activities required to interact with other components of the information system. Procedures (which may or may not be written in a formal manner) describe *how* the people involved with the information system should interact with the information technology. For example, when you remove cash from your bank account using an automated teller machine (ATM), you follow a set of procedures. You need to insert your bank card, enter your personal information number, and so on. If you don't follow the procedures properly, the information system will not function and it will not accomplish its purpose (to satisfy your needs as a bank customer).

Data and Information

One important function of managers, acting as components of an organizational system, is making decisions. In organizations, managers seldom make decisions by themselves. They collect information from a variety of sources, analyze that information with others, and then transmit the information in order to coordinate their actions. Organizational decision making can be viewed as a transformation process requiring information as an input, and providing a decision as an output. Viewed in this way, it is easy to see that without good information, it will be difficult to reach a good decision. The key question on the input side is, "What is good information?" We can start answering the question by considering the difference between information and data.

Data is the term applied to unstructured facts which are gathered about some entity, event, or observation (in Latin, *data* is plural, while *datum* is singular). Data can be generated, stored, retrieved, filed, updated, deleted. It is also important to keep in mind that there are costs associated with capturing, storing, and manipulating data. In addition to obvious costs for physical items such as computer storage media and input forms (e.g., customer data sheets), there are usually very expensive human costs of employees required for tasks such as data entry. Data can become a marketable commodity, one that can be bought and sold. (Consider the willingness of organizations to purchase data such as past stock market quotations.)

Information, on the other hand, implies (1) that some structure has been imposed on the data (i.e., that the data have been processed and organized), (2) that the data have been evaluated for a certain purpose by a decision maker or a computer, and (3) that uncertainty as to what action to take has been reduced (i.e., an option has been chosen or at least some options have been eliminated). This latter point is critical. Information can be defined as a message or signal that changes, in the mind of the receiver, the probability that a given alternative will occur in a given situation. That is, the message reduces the receiver's uncertainty about how to act.

Information has a cost and a value associated with it. The **cost of information** is determined by the time and resources needed to collect and analyze the data. The **value of information** is determined by the difference between the expected result (e.g., monetary returns) of knowing what alternative is best and the alternative that one would choose without information.

Let's reconsider the purchase of stock market quotations for a moment. There is no incentive for someone to exchange money for these data, if they are not put to some use. If an investment analyst uses the data to predict future trends based on historical records, then the data have been converted into information. If the predicted future trends come close to what actually happens, one could say that the information was good. If the analyst invested differently because of the information and made more money, then the information had value. (Note that the value of information depends on its timing; obviously, information about an event is more valuable before it occurs than after.)

Consider another example. The staff of a company that manufactures and assembles tables from wood want to ensure that they don't run out of raw materials (wood). On the other hand, they don't want to keep more wood than necessary in inventory (there are costs associated with keeping inventories). To decide when and how much wood to order, the manager in charge of controlling the raw material inventory requires information concerning factors such as recent and projected sales figures, quantity of material on hand, the minimum size and cost of orders for different suppliers, the length of the delivery time, the length of time required for the manufacturing and assembly processes, and so on. Any specific fact (such as the cost of maple hardwood from supplier ABC) is a piece of data; when combined with other data and evaluated within the structure of the reorder decision process, it becomes information.

Therefore, data become information when they are evaluated for a *particular* decision, for a specified *individual* (or decision-making process), at a specific *time*, and for achieving a definite *goal*. Characteristics of "good" information (as compared to just data or noise) are pertinence (relevance), timeliness, accuracy, reduction of uncertainty faced by the user, and providing an element of insight and/or surprise.

In addition to decision making in the context of ongoing operations, most organizations deal with the development of new products and services, as well as the communication of product and service information to customers and potential customers. These activities require the generation and dissemination of *ideas*, rather than "hard facts." In this type of context, information can be considered to contain more than data or manipulated data; it may also contain sounds, graphics, other images.

This expansion of the concept of information has been reflected in the evolution of Xerox, now known as The Document Company. The organization realized that the name Xerox was associated with office equipment such as copiers and printers, but in the mid-1990s wanted to expand the scope of operations to include the communication of any type of information structure within or between organizations. To reflect this change in company strategy, the name of the company was changed to The Document Company (although the name Xerox is still attached).

Information Technology

Information technology includes the hardware and software used to store, retrieve, process, and transmit data. This could include computer hardware (personal computers, mainframe computers), telecommunications hardware (routers, multiplexors), software (operating systems, programmed applications), networking hardware and software (Local Area Network cards and operating systems), and so on.

Keep in mind that information technology cannot accomplish any goals by itself. The technology (which we discuss in detail in the next chapter) is simply a tool to be used for accomplishing a specific business goal. Information technology enables a vision—it does not provide it.

In this chapter, we have talked about information technology as the means to reduce overload and minimize distortion. There are four specific technologies that are particularly helpful in that role if used selectively and with discretion. These are (1) **networking**: the ability to interconnect different computers to exchange data no matter where the computers are; (2) **database management**: the ability to centrally store large amounts of data, images, and sounds and then provide decentralized access to anyone in the organization with the proper clearance; (3) **telecommunications**: the ability to transmit with high levels of speed, integrity, accuracy, and security large amounts of data, images, and sounds; and (4) **personal computing**: the ability for individuals to work on desktop and portable computers powerful enough to be independent of a central computer and therefore able to provide customized support. These technologies will be discussed in detail in Chapter 6.

SUMMARY

The design of a successful (effective) information system requires a five-step process that begins with defining goals, as the problems or opportunities to be addressed. Two important principles for guiding I/S design are to minimize distortion and to minimize overload. Techniques for reducing overload include (1) the use of filters, (2) summarizing data, and (3) implementing systems that support the by-exception-only management philosophy. A good I/S plan should include effective and efficient ways to collect, store, access, and transmit *necessary* information.

When designing information systems, ethical dilemmas can become important considerations. A system that is successful in addressing efficiency and effectiveness objectives can still fail if it does not adequately address ethical concerns.

Information systems may be classified along three dimensions: application scope, task complexity, and information richness. This classification scheme (the I/S cube) emphasizes the use or application, rather than the capabilities of the system. The cube is useful in determining the implementation complexity involved with each system.

An information system has five components: purpose, people, procedures, information, and information technology. The purpose should be specified as a measurable objective. People are the users of the system, and they interact with I/T using procedures. Information may include data and information in the form of text, graphics, sound, and images (still or motion). Information technology encompasses hardware and software, and communication technology. Advances in networking, database management, personal computing, and telecommunications can generate an overload of data. However, if used selectively and with discretion, they can be very helpful in addressing and overcoming sources of distortion in organizations.

KEY CONCEPTS AND TERMS

KEY CONCEPTS

- An information system should be designed to reduce distortion and overload. (150)
- The design of information systems needs to consider potential ethical abuses. (156)
- Information systems can be classified according to their function (TPS, MIS, etc.) or according to their characteristics (scope, complexity, information richness). (159)
- An information system is composed of a purpose, people, procedures, information, and information technology. (168)

KEY TERMS

artificial intelligence (AI) (160)
by-exception-only (BEO) (151)
application scope (165)
communication network (152)
complexity (175)
components (168)
cost of information (171)
data (171)
database management (172)
decision structure (166)
decision support systems (DSS) (160)
enterprisewide support (155)
executive information systems (EIS) (163)
executive support systems (ESS) (163)
expert systems (ES) (160)
fault-tolerant (159)
filters (151)
goals (150)
individual support (154)
information (171)
information needs (150)
information richness (167)
information systems cube (165)
information systems support (149)
information technology (172)
information technology architecture (148)
information technology infrastructure (148)
inter-enterprise support (155)
inter-organizational systems (IOS) (155)
knowledge base (161)
management information systems (MIS) (160)
minimize distortion (152)
minimize overload (151)
networking (172)
office automation systems (OAS) (164)
overload (153)
people (170)
personal computing (172)
privacy (157)
procedures (170)
purpose (151)
redundancy (160)
scope (165)
stakeholder (156)
structured decision (166)
summarization (151)
task complexity (166)
telecommunications (172)
transaction processing systems (TPS) (159)
unstructured task (167)
value of information (171)
what-if systems (160)
workgroup support (154)

REFERENCES

Alter, S. *Information Systems: A Management Perspective.* Reading, MA: Addison-Wesley Publishing, 1991.

Hicks, J. *Management Information Systems: A User Perspective.* 3rd ed. Minneapolis, MN: West Publishing Company, 1993.

Kallman, E., and J. Grillo. *Ethical Decision Making and Information Technology: An Introduction With Cases.* 2nd ed. New York: McGraw-Hill, 1996.

Lyons, P. *Applying Expert System Technology to Business.* Belmont, CA: Wadsworth Publishing Company, 1994.

Zwass, V. Management Information Systems, Dubuque, IA: Wm. C. Brown, 1992.

CONNECTIVE CASE: Oakland Housing Authority

Like a car buff who's attached to a vintage vehicle, Curt Beckman, I/S Director of the Oakland Housing Authority (OHA), in Oakland, California, spent several years nursing an aging minicomputer system while the rest of the world embraced sportier, faster networks and PCs. The system did something that none of the newer alternatives could do: run the entire housing agency in a way that nearly 200 users were familiar with.

Sure, it was painfully slow, requiring users to plan 24 hours ahead to decide which reports they wanted run overnight. It was also expensive; parts and software for the NCR Corp. minicomputer (running the proprietary ADDS software on the Pick operating system) were difficult to find. For newcomers to the agency, the Pick operating system was a step back to earlier days of computing. And the minicomputer simply wasn't able to communicate with either the new PCs and LANs or the systems being used by other agencies.

The Oakland Housing Authority is responsible for helping low-income residents of the city of Oakland find housing. It places these applicants in housing from both the private sector and its own properties. The computer system was used for the entire rental process, from applications keyed in by data entry clerks to follow-up letters to applicants and reports on vacancies. Each time the OHA rents an apartment, it takes on the duties of landlord, and the computer system tracks rent payments, work orders for fixing up structures, and a variety of social services that the OHA provides. In addition, the system has to provide daily reports on properties and applicants to its main funder, the Department of Housing and Urban Development (HUD).

With maintenance costs rising and the minicomputer's capacity diminishing, the agency had to do something about its computing system. Beckman created a strategic task force in May 1994 to develop a requirements list and study the agency's options. The task force came up with a total of 12 recommendations ranging from upgrading the infrastructure of the computing system to providing new applications and even constructing an Internet strategy. In addition, the agency was under pressure from HUD to improve its telecommunications links; HUD was switching to SprintMail as its method of collecting daily reports from housing agencies, and the old system simply couldn't support such a link.

The agency put out a request for proposals in late 1994, specifying what the new system should provide. The proposal from Edge Information Systems of San Jose, California was selected; Edge would provide systems integration, programming, and installation of the new network. The new system was switched on-line in July of 1995. It uses a Hewlett-Packard minicomputer as a database server, and two additional servers to run the network. The UNIX operating system is used, along with Novell Inc.'s NetWare network operating system. The Unidata relational database management system was selected, along with Wordperfect for UNIX and Lotus Development Corp.'s 1-2-3 for UNIX. The Novell NetWare network operating system was used to support the 175 client users who have a variety of personal computers and dumb terminals. The biggest challenge was migrating the ADDS system from the Pick operating system to UNIX, but the project went well.

All told, the new system cost about $750,000. Was it worth it? Beckman says absolutely. First of all, the network has reduced Beckman's overall support and maintenance costs. Supporting the network is vastly easier than supporting LANs, stand-alone PCs, and the aging minicomputer system. The second payback came through increased productivity. For example, the network is much more responsive than the old system. One application that used to run six hours takes only nine minutes on the Hewlett-Packard. Now, instead of having to schedule reports to print at night in a central location, managers and case workers do all their printing locally on one of the HP LaserJet printers. The change to using WordPerfect as a standard word-processing package (from several incompatible packages) has also helped improve productivity. Standard form letters are created and stored centrally, to be accessed by whatever employees need them. Training and support costs have also been reduced significantly.

Another benefit of the new system is that it can easily accommodate the SprintMail link to HUD, and the agency is also looking to add advanced E-mail capabilities and possibly an imaging system. Moving to the new network has opened a world of possibilities.

Case Questions

1. Use the framework from this chapter to identify the five components of the new information system described for the Oakland Housing Authority.
2. Using the case information provided and the description of the information systems cube from this chapter, classify the new system in terms of application scope, task complexity, and information richness. Make (and state) any assumptions you feel are necessary.

SOURCE: Adapted from Rachel Parker, "Client/Server System Puts Housing Agency into Overdrive," *InfoWorld,* January 8, 1996, p. 58.

IT'S YOUR TURN — END OF CHAPTER MATERIALS

REVIEW QUESTIONS

1. What is the information technology architecture of an organization?
2. List the three considerations behind I/S design.
3. List the five steps of a simplified process to design an information system.
4. What are three common strategies to minimize overload?
5. What are the components of a framework to identify ethical issues in the design of I/S?
6. Explain the analogies used in this chapter comparing the design of a single-family home, a condominium, and the layout of a town to the design of information systems supporting individuals, workgroups, and the enterprise, respectively.
7. List five different types of information systems. Give their acronyms and their definitions.
8. Explain the three dimensions of the information systems cube.
9. List the five components of an information system.
10. What is the difference between data and information?

DISCUSSION QUESTIONS

1. Why is it important to clearly define the goals for an information system before going further with its design?
2. Some people have argued that filters, summarization, and reporting by-exception-only (BEO) are all one strategy. Comment on that argument.
3. In your opinion, should businesses have the right to read the E-mail messages of their employees? Why or why not? Suggest a policy that would protect the interests of the business but yet protects the privacy of the employees.
4. What are some of the difficulties in developing a group decision support system? What are some advantages of GDSS? What are some disadvantages?
5. Consider the following three information systems:
   Information system A is a personal computer–based system developed by one sales manager to analyze sales over a period of 12 months. The system calculates the profit and margins of each of her accounts.
   Information system B is a personnel system that has all the information on employees of the firm. The database includes actual photographs of all of the employees and the public files of the employees can be perused by anybody in the firm. The system resides in the main computer, which is accessible by everybody in the firm.
   Information system C is an imaging system that allows an insurance company to take all the correspondence with clients, doctors, pharmacies, and hospitals and store them electronically in a database. The correspondence includes letters, bills, x-rays, photographs, and so forth. The database can be queried by all employees from anywhere in the company including the overseas branches. Clients, doctors, pharmacies, and hospitals can also access their own accounts from their computers.
   Place these three information systems on the I/S cube.
6. We have defined information systems as being made of five components. Comment on the importance of each of the components. Are any of the five components critical? Are they all necessary?

GROUP ASSIGNMENT

The group as a whole will design a system to choose what courses to take every semester. Assume that any information you want to include is somehow available: in electronic databases in the registrar's office and career placement, through the grapevine, from the professor teaching the course. Draw a blueprint for the system. Identify on your blueprint the different sources of information, how to acquire the data from those sources, and the format of the reports you are going to generate.

APPLICATION ASSIGNMENTS

1. Open the file named Chapter5.DAT. Produce a report that summarizes sales, revenues, costs, and profits.
2. Open the file named Chapter5.DAT. Develop a spreadsheet model that will allow you to assess the effect of an increase of 5, 10, 12, and 23 percent in the costs of raw materials on profits.
3. Develop a set of at least 5 but less than 10 "if-then" rules to decide what to do on a Saturday night. Program those rules (in Basic, Pascal, C, or whatever language you are familiar with) and try your program on a friend. Prepare two PowerPoint slides that comment on your experience. (How could you improve the system? How much time did it take you to build the system? Was the time invested worth it? What type of problems should be addressed with an Expert System?).

CASE ASSIGNMENT The Norris Company (D): One More Decision

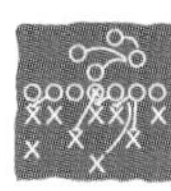

Sherry Craig, Manager of Norris Company's Central plant, rubbed her temples and grimaced at the pile of urgent messages still waiting for her. She had just finished a statistical report for one of their major customers. She glanced at the next item in her in-box, which was a proposal from the general manager of the plant. The personnel director had spoken to Sherry the day before, asking if she had given more thought to the proposal to install an employee tracking system. They would both be meeting with the Executive Committee to discuss the proposal, and the personnel director wanted to know what recommendation Sherry would support.

The tracking system was being offered by one of their computer vendors as a way of improving job estimation and quotes. It would involve issuing new badges to employees and installing small transmitters at numerous locations around the building. By tracking employees' movements Norris would get much better data on the labor component of job costs. This would enable them to be much more accurate when quoting prices on jobs. Sherry was concerned about the potential impact on employee morale, however, and had suggested they discuss the proposal further before the Executive Committee meeting. As she began to look through the proposal to refresh her memory, the telephone rang.

"Good afternoon, Sherry, this is John again. Order processing got an order for $250,000 from ALOP Systems. They are still late on payments and Joe from order processing called me yesterday for approval. I forgot to mention it to you earlier, and I wanted to get your approval before I let it go through."

"All right, John. Hmmmm. Have they made payments in the past few months?"

"Well, let me take a look at the accounts receivable report. Here it is. They've owed us $800,000 since August. They paid $119,000 in September and another $257,000 in October. Nothing in November or December. Without interest they still owe us $524,000."

"What does sales say about this?"

"Lisa says ALOP is doing better since their reorganization and the replacement of their CEO."

"What do you think?"

"It seems to me that Lisa wants the sale because she needs it to make her numbers this quarter, but I think she's shaky on it."

"Me, too. Can we take some time to look into the situation?"

"I don't think so. The order was urgent when it came in yesterday. If we wait any longer to respond, I think ALOP will go with someone else."

"Tell Joe we'll approve it conditional on the job being shipped COD. Ask Gene to schedule the job, and have Lisa tell ALOP we'll cut them off completely if we don't get a large payment this month!"

"OK, Sherry. Thank you, and good night."

"Keep me informed, John. See you tomorrow."

As she hung up the phone she discovered that it was 6:10, and she was the only one left in the office. Sherry was tired. She put on her coat and headed through the plant toward the parking lot; on the way she was stopped by both the night supervisor and night layout foreman for approval of type and layout changes.

With both eyes on the traffic, Sherry reviewed the day she had just completed. "Busy?" she asked herself. "Too much so—but did I accomplish anything?" Her mind raced over the day's activities. "Yes and no" seemed to be the answer. "There was the usual routine, the same as any other day. The plant kept going and I think it must have been a good production day. Any creative or special project work done?" Sherry grimaced as she reluctantly answered, "No."

With a feeling of guilt, she probed further. "Am I an executive? I'm paid like one, respected like one, and have a responsible assignment with the necessary authority to carry it out. Yet one of the greatest values a company derives from an executive is her creative thinking and accomplishments. What have I done about it? An executive needs some time for thinking. Today was a typical day, just like most other days, and I did little, if any, creative work. The projects that I so enthusiastically planned to work on this morning are exactly as they were yesterday. What's more, I have no guarantee that tomorrow night or the next night will bring me any closer to their completion. This is a real problem and there must be an answer."

Questions

1. Diagram the information flows in this case.
2. Based on the situation described, how could you design an information system to improve the decision-making process of whether or not to ship to a client?
3. Discuss the ethical dilemma facing Sherry Craig with the possible adoption of an employee monitoring system.
4. Provide recommendations to Sherry concerning the employee monitoring system.

CHAPTER 6 Information Technology

CHAPTER OBJECTIVES

After reading this chapter you should have a better understanding of information technology and the convergence of hardware, software, and telecommunications. More specifically, you should be able to:

- Be an intelligent consumer of information technology (computer hardware, software, and telecommunications technology) by understanding the basic operating characteristics of computer components.
- Understand that leading technology is not always better for a given application (cost-effective technology and latest technology are not always one and the same).
- Understand the trends in information technology that have an impact on business decisions.

I don't really understand how computers work, and there are so many different ones available; how can I possibly decide what type of I/T to purchase?

INTRODUCTION

Earlier in the book, we talked about the critical need of organizations to process information quickly and accurately in an effort to stay in touch with their environments. Information processing was described as a survival skill that all organizations need to acquire and master. Information technology plays a key role in supporting organizations in their quest to process information better. As such, information technology is crucial in achieving organizational responsiveness.

Objectives in Automating Information Processing. There are at least three objectives when automating information processing:

1. Provide information in a more timely fashion (e.g., quicker response to customer demands).
2. Provide more accurate information (e.g., avoid computing mistakes, sift through large amounts of data without overlooking anything).
3. Reduce the costs of performing information processing activities (e.g., automate repetitive tasks, eliminate intermediate processing steps, read data faster).

There is no doubt that computers help in processing information. For example, the U.S. Internal Revenue Service (IRS) has found that there are errors in only 1 percent of all the income-tax returns filed electronically versus errors in 17 percent of all paper returns. However, computers are expensive—even when talking about those that seem to be inexpensive. Indeed, the costs of training and maintenance outstrip the purchase price. And although the cost of hardware is decreasing, the overall cost of owning a computer is increasing. For example, in 1995 the estimated total five-year cost of buying, maintaining, and upgrading a personal computer was $41,000 per workstation, up from $19,000 in 1987 (this includes salaries for support staff, software upgrades, and so on).

Therefore, the basic management decisions on technology consist of choosing the appropriate hardware (computers, input/output devices, and telecommunication infrastructure), the configuration (centralized or distributed, micros or terminals, network topology), and the type of software (choice of applications and languages). However, these choices should be based on trade-offs between (*a*) human and machine productivity and (*b*) the performance of the technology and its cost.

You can always buy a faster microprocessor, more memory, a fancier printer, a bigger screen, or the latest version of a software package; the question that you need to ask is, "Is it worth it?" That is, what are the tangible benefits of a better system? Will the customer or upper management notice the difference? Remember that old technology does not always mean obsolete (useless) technology. When buying information technology you should think in terms of *appropriate* (cost-effective) technology and not necessarily in terms of *latest* technology.

Technical knowledge is obviously important when choosing the appropriate information technology platform to design an information system, but it is not critical. What is critical is understanding what you want to achieve with information technology, that is, understanding the business goal that needs to be fulfilled. Understanding the business needs will define a set of technical requirements. For example, determining what specific information you want to collect about your customers (which is determined by a business need) and also determining the number of customers you have will drive the size of the database and, therefore, the memory capacity you require. Determining the type and volume of data you need to exchange with suppliers and the frequency of the exchange (which are determined by a business need) will drive the type of communication medium, the speed, and the protocol you will use to communicate with those suppliers.

A given information technology configuration is only the vehicle that allows the enactment of a particular system design. Therefore, we should be more concerned with appropriate technology than with leading-edge technology (although sometimes the appropriate technology *is* the latest technology).

Upgrading technology for technology's sake rather than for fulfilling a specific business need is, from a cost-benefit point of view, very ineffective. The saying that "leading-edge becomes bleeding-edge" for most companies is not just cute; it is based on evidence that companies underestimate the costs associated with training and upgrades, the lower productivity that results from the lack of adequate documentation, and the risk of "bugs," which are typical of first versions of hardware and software products.

Information Processing Activities. There are four basic information processing activities: (*a*) the collection of data, (*b*) the storage of that data, (*c*) the manipulation of data, and (*d*) the transmission of data. Information technology can help in all four activities by automating all or part of them. Specific technology has been developed to support each of these activities. For example, optical and bar code scanners facilitate the collection of data; CD-ROMs have made the storage of sound and images commercially viable; faster microprocessors and spreadsheet software have made feasible the manipulation of large financial computations and scenarios; user-friendly software and hardware have made electronic mail a way of life in most organizations.

The purpose of this chapter is to give you an understanding of the questions you should ask vendors when they propose an information technology configuration to address your needs. The chapter is an introduction to the basic building blocks of I/T-based systems. At the end of the chapter, we expect you to understand the critical performance characteristics of input devices, microprocessors, storage media and disk drives, output devices, and networks. We don't expect you to be an expert in computer technology.

You can think of information technology as a three-legged stool. The legs are hardware, software, and telecommunications. These three "legs" are becoming more and more intertwined. For simplicity of presentation we first discuss each leg separately; then we comment on their convergence.

HARDWARE

Computer **hardware** consists of the following four elements: (*a*) the input devices; (*b*) microprocessors or the central processing unit (CPU), including primary memory (RAM); (*c*) secondary storage devices; and (*d*) output devices. Figure 6–1 illustrates the hardware components.

FIGURE 6-1 Computer Components

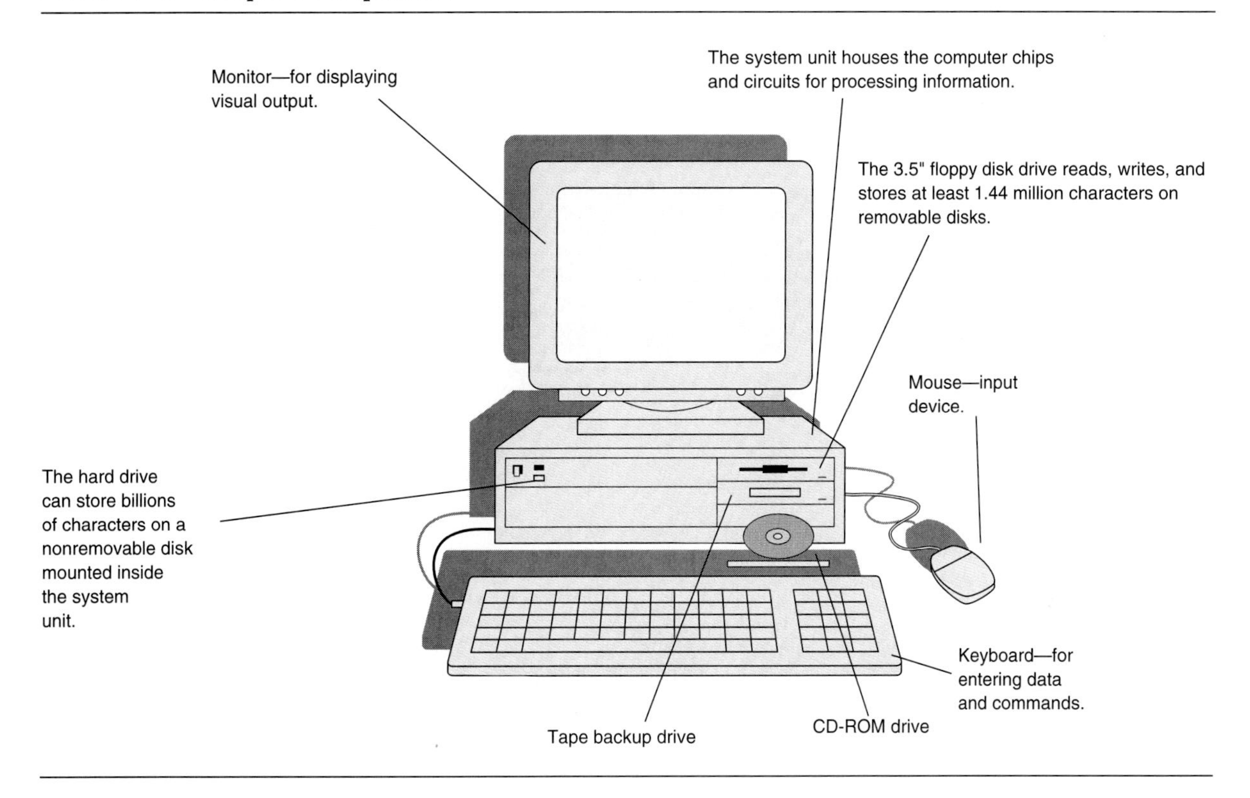

Input Devices

Input devices (e.g., keyboards, touch-sensitive screens, voice-activated devices, optical character readers, magnetic character readers) allow data to be entered into the system (see Figure 6–2). As such, they can play a major role in keeping "garbage" out of the system. An input device can be thought of as the first line of defense against information distortion. The best strategy to ensure high-quality data in the system is to check that "contaminated" or distorted data do not enter the system in the first place; input devices are the key to this strategy. The "smarter" the input device and the software associated with it (i.e., the more input validation is performed to keep erroneous data from entering the system), the higher the integrity and quality of the system. One of the most common sources of a mistaken analysis is basing the analysis on wrong data, and the most common root cause of wrong data is data-entry errors (as illustrated in Business Brief 6–1).

The main characteristics of input devices are as follows:

- Speed.
- Accuracy.
- Reliability.
- Capacity.
- Portability. (Can you take the input device with you to the field, such as the aisles of a supermarket?)

FIGURE 6–2 Input Devices

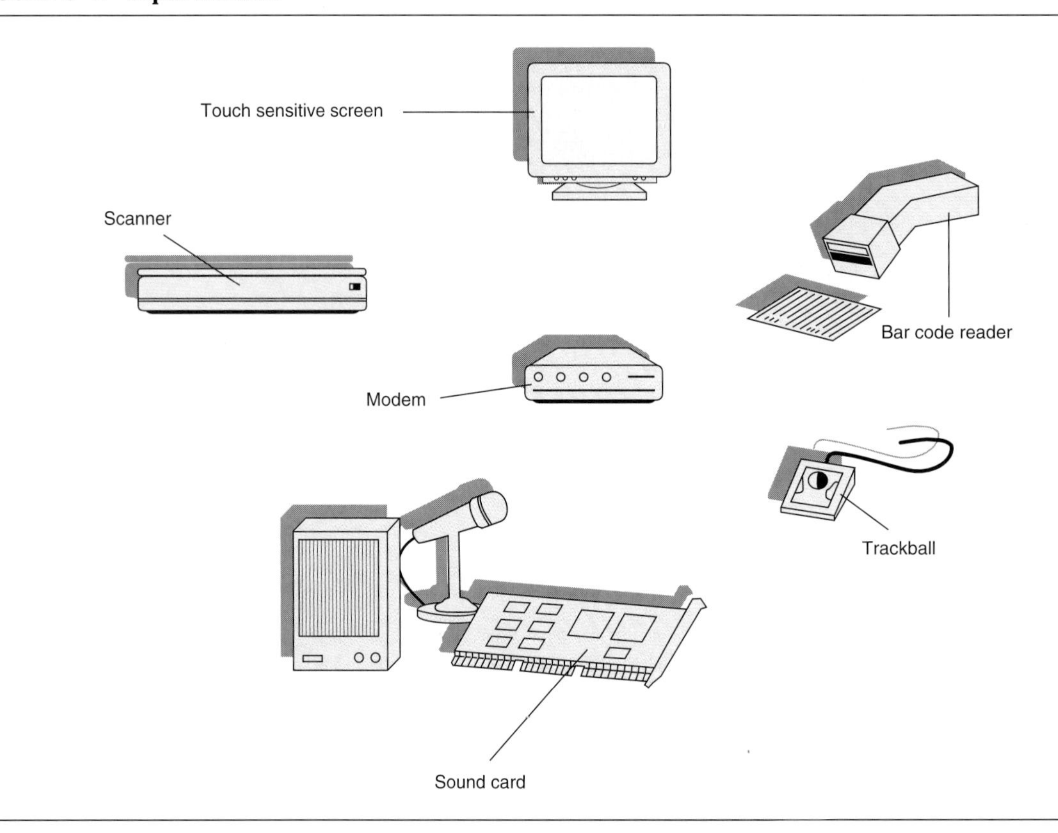

Central Processing Unit (CPU)

The **central processing unit (CPU)** is the engine or brain of a computer. The CPU is the component of the computer that actually processes data and instructions. It consists of a **control unit (CU),** an **arithmetic and logic unit (ALU),** and **primary memory** or primary **random-access memory (RAM).**

The CU's role is to be the traffic cop and captain; it decides what to do next and what to do with the data being processed. The ALU is the computer's calculator; it adds and subtracts and performs logic operations such as comparing numbers. RAM is the CPU's scratch pad for its instructions and data warehouse. Earlier in the development of computers the CU, ALU, and the RAM were on separate computer chips. Today, the CU and the ALU are on the same chip, called a **microprocessor.** RAM is on a set of chips affixed to a different, but contiguous, board.

All computers work on a fetch-decode-execute-store cycle (see Figure 6–3). The CU reads information from RAM (fetch). This information is then interpreted by the CU (decode), and the instruction is performed by the ALU (execute). The resulting information is stored in RAM by the CU (store). The CU then reads the next instruction and so forth. This cycle is performed millions of times per second.

BUSINESS BRIEF 6-1 FUND SNAFUS: INVESTOR GETS $320,000 'GIFT'

It might have been easy to grab the money and cruise away on the boat. But Massachusetts investor Roger Harris says he is an honest man.

Invesco Funds Group sent him a notice showing that an account he had closed in 1994 was reactivated April 4 with a whopping $320,000 mutual-fund purchase. Mr. Harris immediately phoned the Denver mutual-fund company to report the error.

"I don't lie, cheat, or steal—unfortunately," says the 63-year-old recent retiree. "I could have just headed for the Cayman Islands."

How likely is an investor to wind up on the flip side of such an error, with money meant for his or her mutual-fund account tossed into a stranger's account? What are the consequences? And can someone in Mr. Harris's shoes simply take the money and run?

If he were so inclined, Mr. Harris notes, he wouldn't have been the easiest person for Invesco to catch up with. Mr. Harris recently sold his home and his manufacturers-representative business and he is within days of taking up a free-floating residence on his boat.

Invesco and other fund companies say error money transfers and related mistakes are rare but inevitable given the sheer volume of transactions in the $3-trillion asset fund industry. "There is just too much information flowing," says Dave King, head of servicing for John Hancock Funds in Boston.

Although many investors believe wiring money to a fund company is more secure than mailing a check, that's not necessarily the case. If you send in a check with a preprinted stub from the fund company that stub is typically encoded with your account number. Such codes are read by machines at the fund company. And machines don't tend to make transcription errors.

Wiring funds, by contrast, requires human input. This opens the door to human error. On the positive side though, notes Mr. King of John Hancock, a wire transfer "Is more secure in that at least you can trace it."

Mutual-fund snafus come in lots of varieties, of course. For instance, the Lindner Funds group was embarrassed last year when a company it had hired to print and mail client statements put some of them in the wrong envelopes. One woman says her family's Lindner statement went to the next-door neighbor. Fewer than 10% of Lindner customers were affected, a firm spokesman says, and the mailing concern was dismissed.

Some errors involve account holders with the same name, says Mr. King of John Hancock. For instance, a John Smith who doesn't have his account number handy calls to request that $10,000 be redeemed from his account and a service representative accidentally clicks on the wrong John Smith. (John Hancock, besides fixing such errors, makes it a practice to give affected customers $25 as a "service guarantee," Mr. King says.)

Mistakes can be particularly tough to catch when an investor dies and family members and friends scramble to sort out that person's financial affairs. Fund-industry consultant Geoff Bobroff of East Greenwich, R.I., has a friend in New York who is trying to work out such a problem now.

After the death of the woman's husband a few years ago, two joint accounts were switched into her name. But an incorrect address was put on one account, and the woman didn't know this account even existed until recently. Unfortunately, the fund company, which Mr. Bobroff declined to identify, wound up forwarding the account balance to the state as abandoned property, and has so far refused to reinstate the woman's account and straighten out the mess by itself.

QUESTIONS

1. How much time and resources do you think Invesco Funds Group spends tracking the misplaced funds?
2. How would you design an input device that would avoid this mistake?
3. If you were Mr. Harris, what would you have done?

SOURCE: Adapted from Karen Damato, "Fund Snafus: Investor Gets $320,000 Gift," *The Wall Street Journal,* April 30, 1996, p. B1. Reprinted by permission of *The Wall Street Journal,*

FIGURE 6–3 Fetch-Execute Cycle

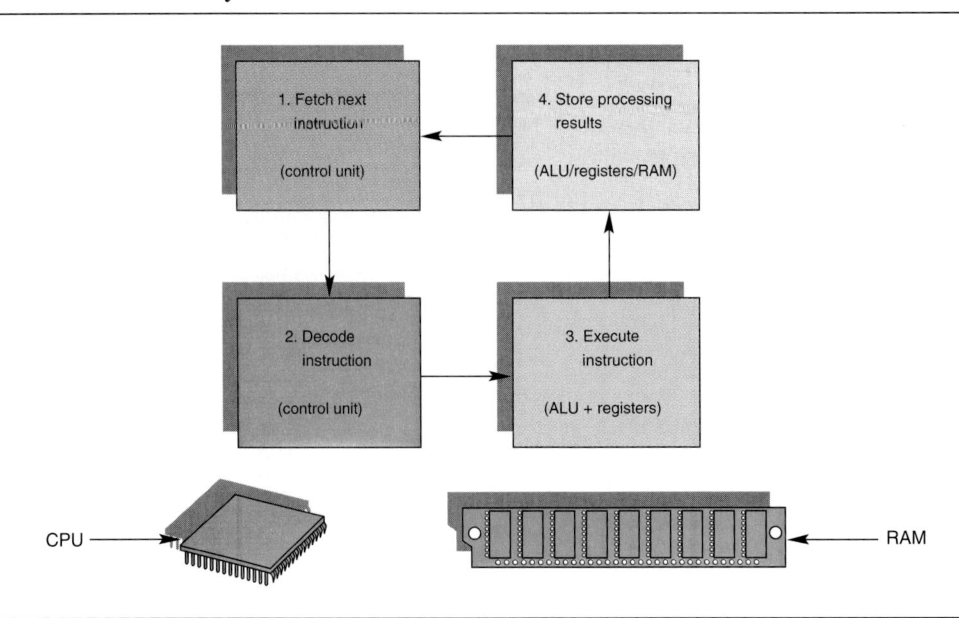

The timing for all systems operations is determined by a master clock. This clock emits pulses at a given rate to coordinate the operations (think of this clock as the aerobics instructor or the drum beater of the CPU). This rate, called clock rate or clock speed, determines the speed of the microprocessor; that is, it sets the number of instructions that can be performed in a given unit of time. The clock speed is measured in **megahertz (MHz).** A microprocessor that has a clock rate of 150 MHz is a microprocessor that can perform 150 million instructions—that is 150 million fetch-decode-execute-store cycles—in 1 second. Figure 6–4 illustrates the components of a CPU.

Data is represented in *bits* (*b*inary dig*its*). A bit can have a value of 0 or 1. Characters and symbols are uniquely represented by a string of (usually) 8 bits called a *byte.* Bits (information) are moved from one part of the CPU to another, and back and forth between external storage and the CPU, through a **databus** (see Figure 6–5). The databus is like a street or highway connecting the different parts of a computer. The wider the databus—that is, the more lanes on the highway—between secondary storage and the CPU, the faster the processing. The databus width typically ranges from 32 to 128 bytes.

The primary memory is usually called RAM (random-access memory) and can be used for any purpose and application. RAM is the short-term memory of a computer. You can think of RAM as a series of switches that can be either "on" or "off." Each character, number, and mathematical sign is represented in RAM by a specific pattern of on and off switches (represented respectively by 0's and 1's) (see Figures 6–6 and 6–7). In most computers, RAM is volatile, which means that whatever is stored in RAM (i.e., the patterns of on and off switches) disappears when the machine is turned off (or when there is a power outage).

FIGURE 6–4 CPU Components

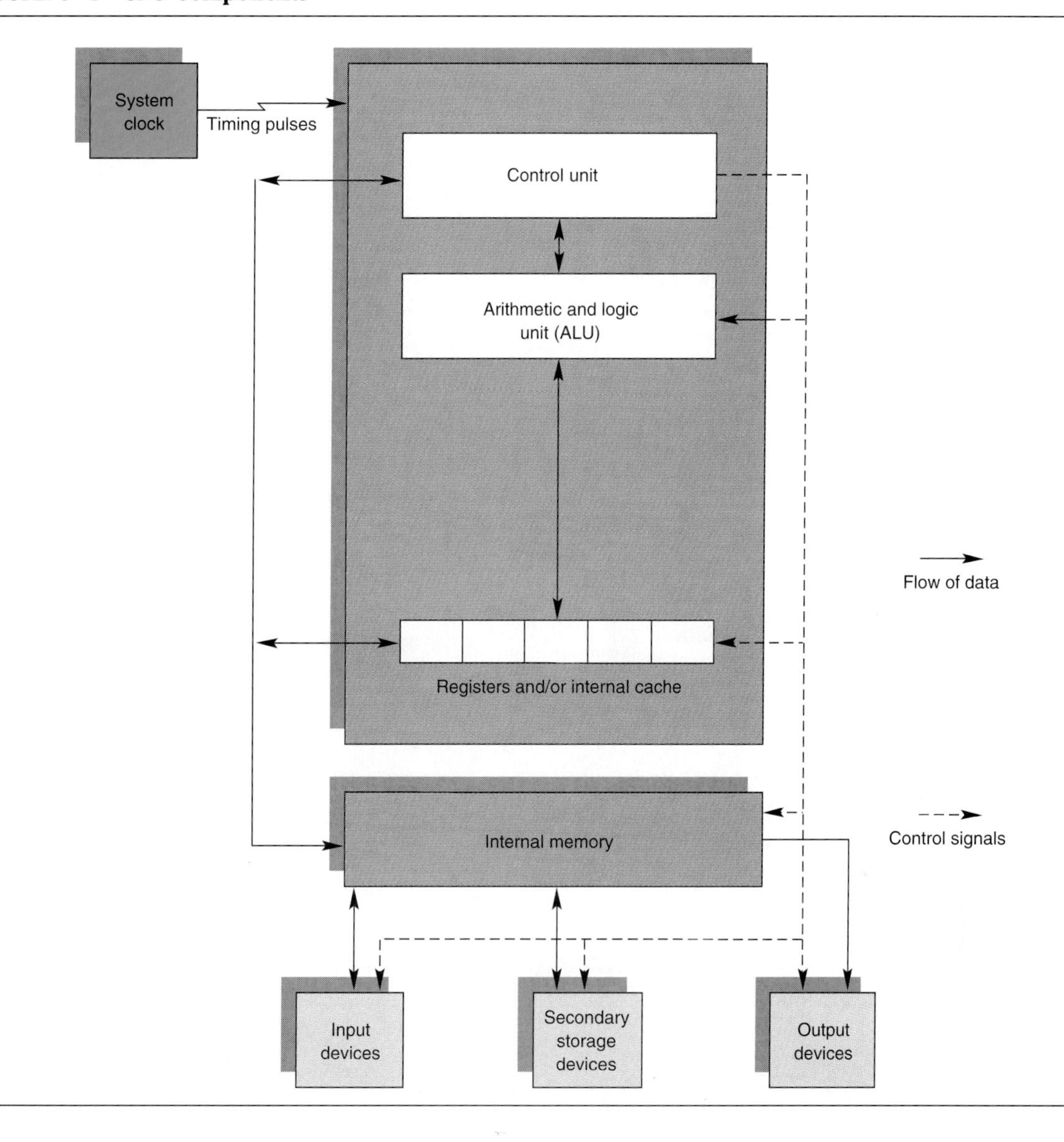

RAM functions as a scratch pad on which the computer is working. To store your work for later reference, you need to "rip" the "pages" from your "scratch pad" and store them into a folder (file) that you will then put in a file cabinet (secondary storage is discussed later). If you don't want to save the work on the scratch pad, just turn your computer off (basically ripping a page off your scratch pad and throwing it away).

Real computer speeds (the speed of processing that is noticed by the user) can be affected by the size of the RAM. The bigger the RAM (the bigger the scratch pad), the less time the microprocessor wastes looking for a free space on the scratch pad, and the fewer trips it makes back and forth to the hard drive, CD-ROM drive, or disk drive to retrieve the information it needs. The size or capacity of the computer's RAM

FIGURE 6–5 Databus

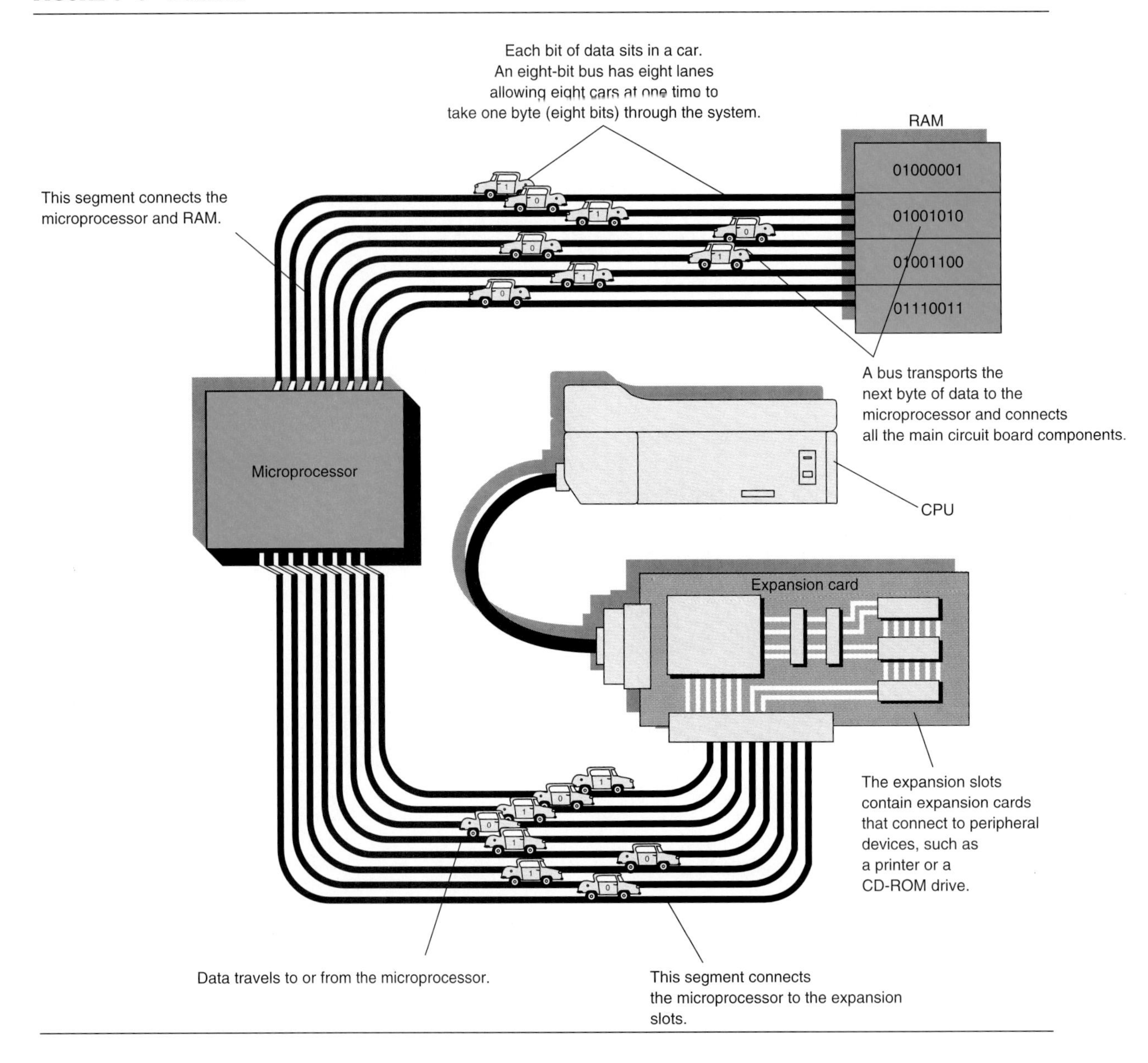

is measured in terms of how many millions of characters (megabytes) can be held in it at any one time.

RAM has dedicated sectors (chips) called **ROM (read-only memory),** where, as part of the manufacturing process, a subset of the switches have been permanently set to their on and off positions, and the user cannot alter them. ROM is used when you turn your computer on; it provides the necessary instructions to boot up the computer. Sometimes, the RAM also contains **PROM (programmable read-only memory)** chips. PROM allows the customization of ROM. This customization provides, for example, software vendors with the ability to perform certain functions

FIGURE 6–6 On and Off Switches

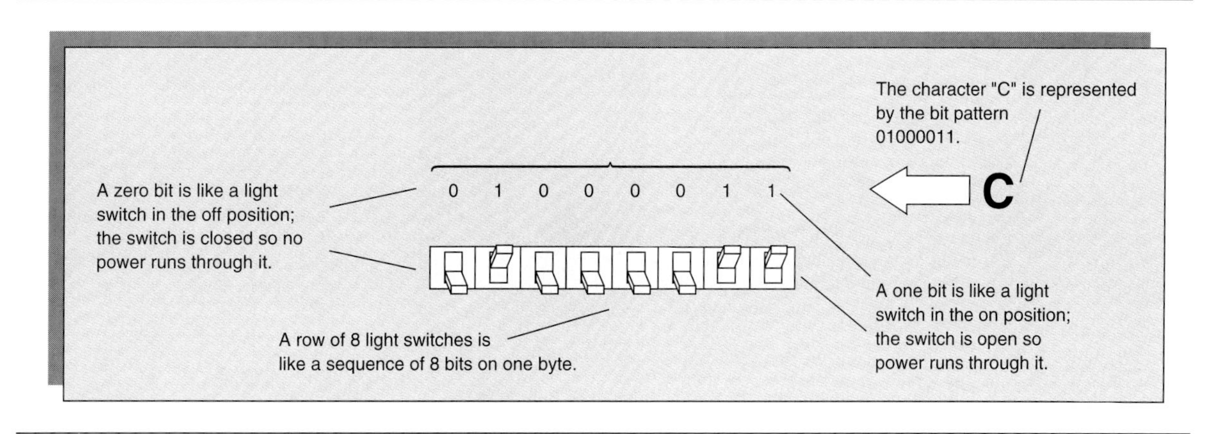

FIGURE 6–7 RAM

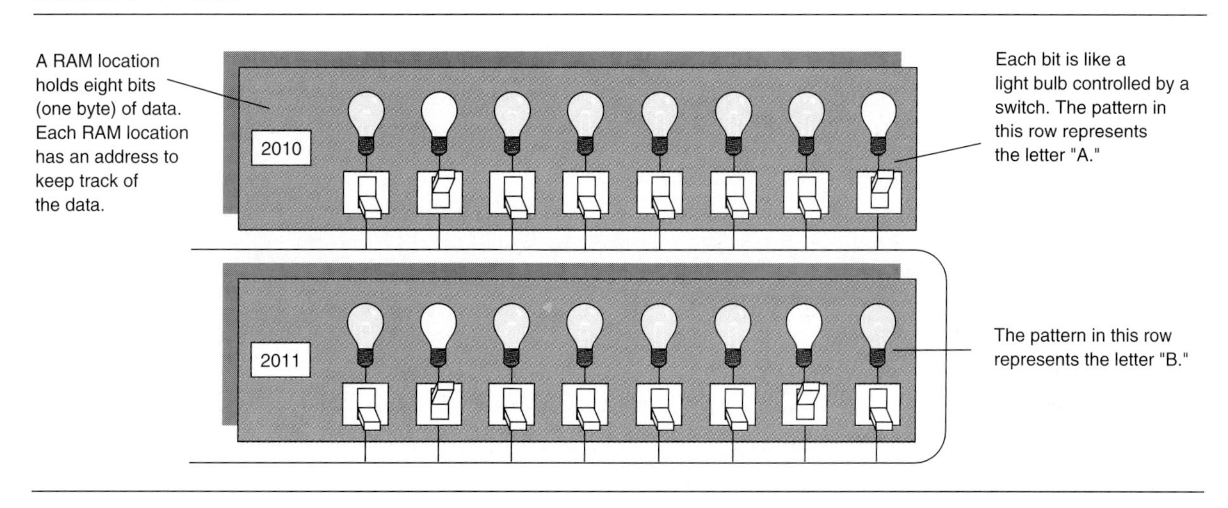

during the startup process of the computer. ROM and PROM are permanently stored in RAM, and the only way to disable them is to take the chips out.

There are some data that computers need to store when you turn the computers off (e.g., their configuration). There is a special type of memory chip (CMOS chips) which requires very little power to store data and can be powered by a battery, allowing for the permanent storage of the data (as long as your battery is working).

To review, the main characteristics of a CPU are as follows:

- Computing power (clock speed in megahertz).
- Processing speed (measured in millions of instructions per second).
- Databus capacity (measured in number of bits).
- Storage capacity of its primary memory (RAM) (measured in millions of bytes or megabytes).

FIGURE 6–8 Computer Board

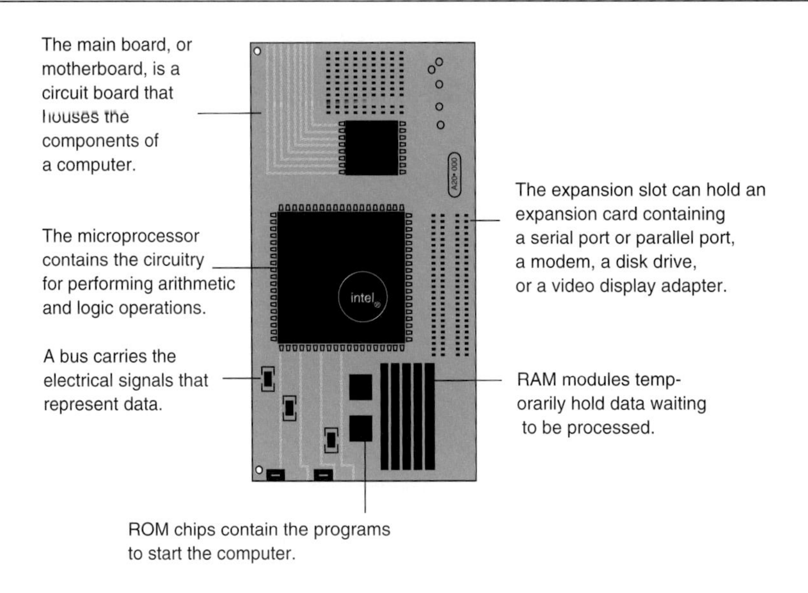

Compatibility between the hardware and software to be used is not a performance characteristic per se, but it is a key consideration since, depending on how compatible they are (i.e., whether the software was written to take advantage of the specific features of a given computer chip or not), the performance (e.g., response time to program instructions) will be affected. All the components of the CPU are attached to a motherboard (see Figure 6–8).

Secondary Memory (Secondary Storage)

Secondary memory has larger capacity, is less expensive, and is slower than primary memory. Secondary memory, or *external* (to the CPU) *memory*, is practically limitless; for example, you can buy as many diskettes as you want to store data. You can think of secondary memory as a series of folders or notebooks that you have filed away in a file cabinet. Typically, primary memory or RAM is called *memory*, while secondary memory or external memory is called *storage*.

The most common storage media are **magnetic disks,** diskettes, CD-ROM(compact disk/read-only memory), and tapes (see Figure 6–9). Magnetic storage media consist of a substratum made of metal or mylar, covered by an oxide-based coating, that can be polarized in one of two ways in order to store the specific bit value of 1 or 0. In the case of CD-ROMs, the surface is covered with a reflective coating that allows for two levels of reflection (shiny or opaque).

Secondary storage is generally accessed through disk drives. Drives are the devices that spin the storage medium and then read and write data onto the storage medium. You can think of the drives as "go-fors": they have a certain speed (some are faster than others in getting to the storage medium); some can find data faster than others; some can carry more data than others.

FIGURE 6–9 CD-ROMS, Diskettes, Hard Disks

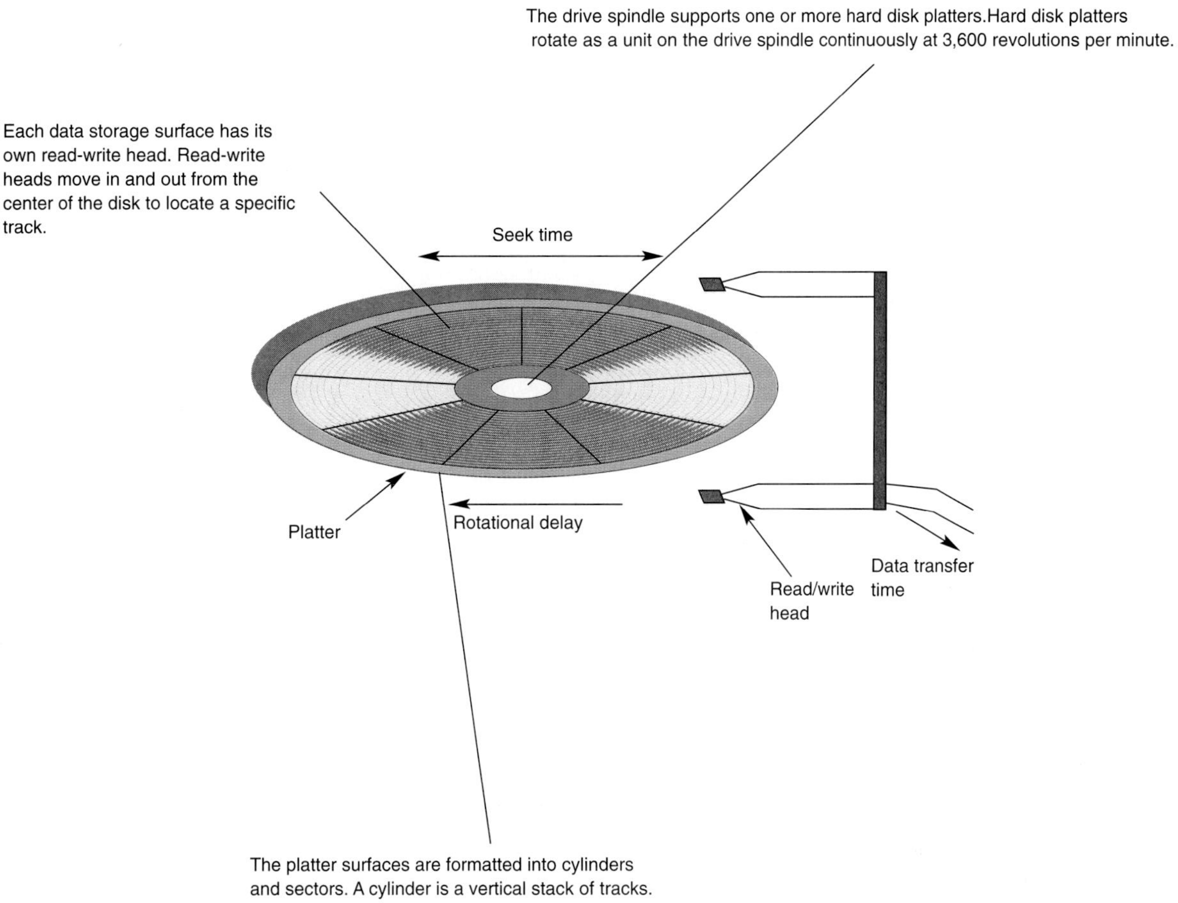

The drive spindle supports one or more hard disk platters.Hard disk platters rotate as a unit on the drive spindle continuously at 3,600 revolutions per minute.

Each data storage surface has its own read-write head. Read-write heads move in and out from the center of the disk to locate a specific track.

Seek time

Platter

Rotational delay

Read/write head

Data transfer time

The platter surfaces are formatted into cylinders and sectors. A cylinder is a vertical stack of tracks.

Reading or writing of data is done by an arm with a head that moves in and out across the surface of the storage medium. The reading head does not affect the polarity of the particles stored on storage medium. The time to read a specific location is called the seek and retrieve time. The shorter the time, the better, particularly in applications that are data intensive. Typically, faster times imply a more expensive disk. The speed, reliability, and capacity of storage media are affected by the rigidity of the storage device (e.g., hard disk's aluminum versus the mylar in 3.5-inch floppy diskettes).

Access to secondary storage can be of two types: random or direct access (e.g., CD-ROMs, hard disk) and *sequential access* (e.g., tape cassettes). Direct access means that the read/write head goes directly to a given location; sequential access means that the head has to sequentially go through the storage medium until it gets to the desired location. The method of access affects the speed of access. Speed of access is (*a*) the time required to position the head of the drive over the track where the desired data are, (*b*) the time required to position the head of the drive over the sector where the desired data are, and (*c*) the time required to transfer the data to RAM. When manufacturers give an access time of 10 microseconds, for example, they are giving an average of these three times.

The recording areas on the surface of a disk, diskette, or CD-ROM are concentric circles, or **tracks**, each subdivided into **sectors**. Most storage media are double-sided, which means that you can store data on both sides. There are also double-density or high-density storage devices.

Disk density refers to the size of the magnetic particles on the disk surface. A high-density diskette has double the number of tracks and sectors tracks as a single-density diskette. Although the number of tracks and bytes per sector changes, depending somewhat on the formatting process, most single-density diskettes have 40 tracks per side and 9 sectors per track, and each sector can hold 512 bytes (512 characters). Therefore, for a double-sided, high-density diskette, the total number of tracks would be 2,880 with a capacity of 1.44 megabytes or 1.44 million characters. Figure 6–10 illustrates the parts of a diskette. Figure 6–12 further describes these characteristics.

A hard disk is a common feature of all personal computers (PCs). You can think of a hard disk as a series of continually spinning stacks of double-sided diskettes whose surface, usually aluminum or glass, under the oxide-based coating is rigid (or "hard"). Hard disks can contain up to a couple of thousand stacks or cylinders, with each cylinder containing several diskettes or platters. The address of a particular record consists of a specific track, sector, and surface and, in multidisk packs, a specific cylinder.

CD-ROM (compact disk/read-only memory) media can hold a tremendous amount of data (several hundred megabytes), which allows for the storage of images, sounds, and text. However, CD-ROMs cannot (until now) be written over

FIGURE 6–10 Storage Devices: Disks, Tracks, and Sectors

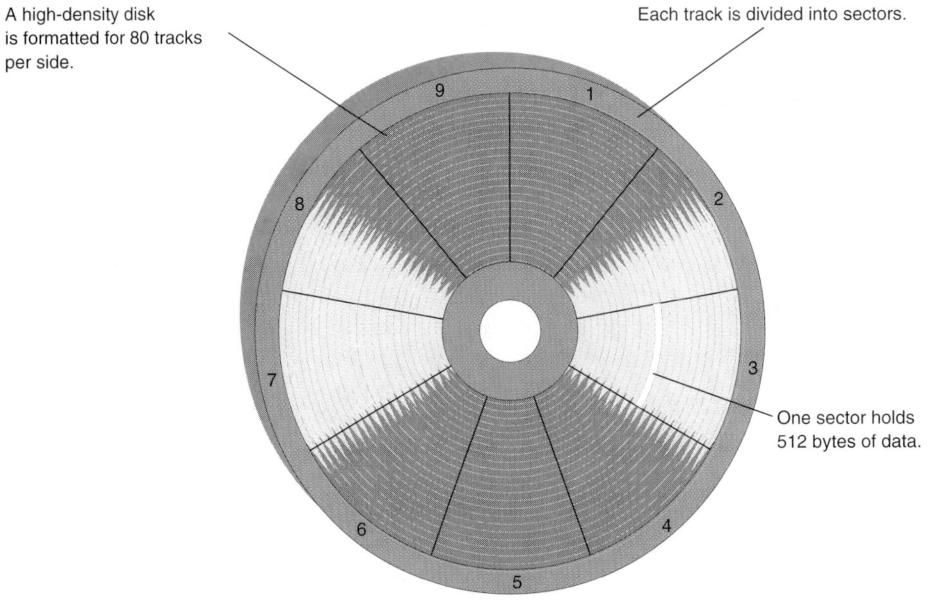

A high-density disk is formatted for 80 tracks per side.

Each track is divided into sectors.

One sector holds 512 bytes of data.

1 2 3 4 5 6 7 8 9

(the nonreflective areas on the surface are "written" on by actually creatingperma-nent minuscule pits). You can only read the data that has been originally stored on them (to protect the data, the disk surface is coated with a clear plastic cover). Because of this limitation, the main user applications of CD-ROM technology have been encyclopedias, catalogs, games, and for copying and distributing large software program applications. CD-ROMs are also used as archival backups for large amounts of data (e.g., accounting transactions). Figure 6–11 illustrates a CD-ROM disk drive. New technologies for storing data emerge constantly. A recent one, DVD (digital video disk), can hold 10 to 14 times the amount of data stored on a CD-ROM.

To review, the main characteristics of secondary memory are as follows:

- Capacity.
- Method of access.
- Speed of access.
- Transportability.
- Reliability (ability to retain data under changing environmental conditions—including sticky fingers!).

The key performance characteristics of disk drives are as follows:

- Access speed (the speed of accessing the location where the needed data reside).
- Transfer speed (the speed of reading and writing data onto/from the storage medium).
- Reliability [durability and ability to work in hostile (dust, vibration, change in temperatures) environments].

FIGURE 6–11 CD-ROM Disk Characteristics

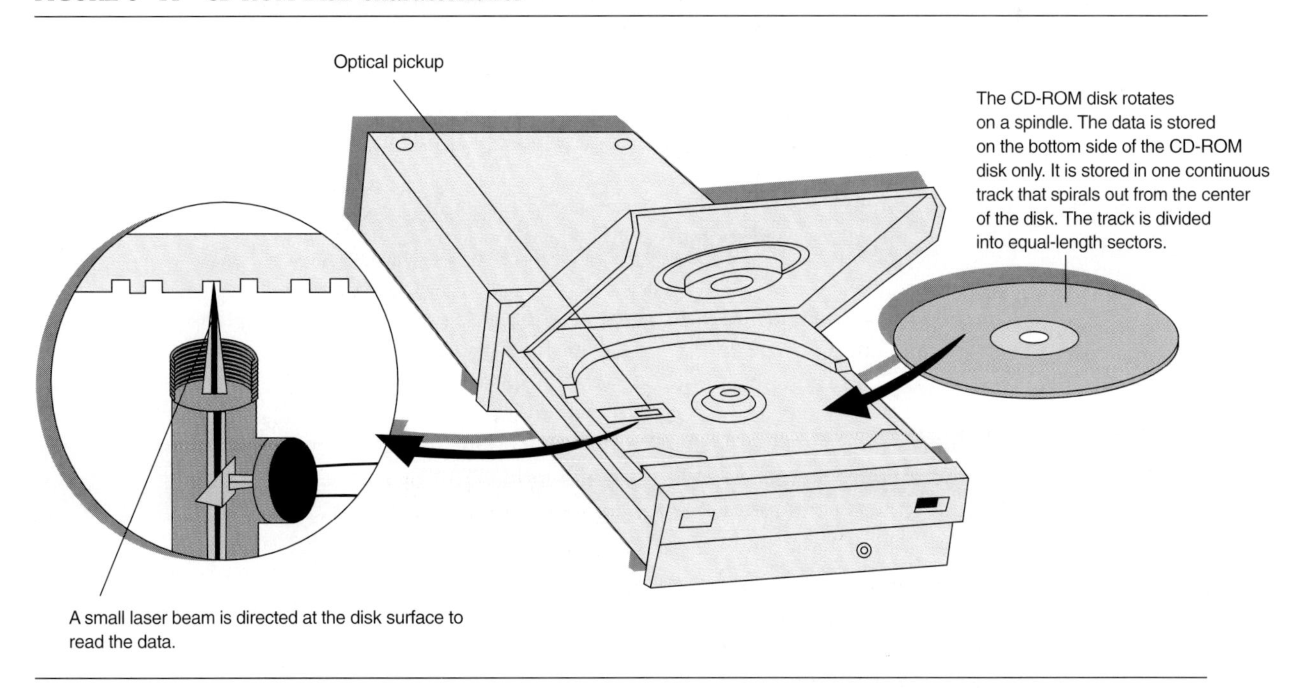

FIGURE 6–12 Floppy Disk Sizes, Features, and Capacities

Disk Size (Inches)	*Tracks*	*Sectors/Track**	*Capacity*
3.5	80	18	1.44 Mb
3.5	80	36	2.88 Mb
Floptical 3.5	1250+	varies	20 Mb-50 Mb

Floppy disk storage capacity is determined by the number of sectors and tracks, and the data stored on each track.

Output Devices

Output devices produce what is ultimately the most important aspect of computing: the reports and charts that users consult to make decisions. Output devices are the tools of the artist—they allow the user to convey the impact of his or her message or analysis. The greater the flexibility of the output device, the greater the opportunity to customize the report to the tastes of the message recipient. The degree of flexibility includes the ability for the output device to display color, the quality of resolution of the display (whether in the number of pixels in the case of a video display terminal or the quality of the characters in the case of a printer), its durability, and its portability. In the case of printers, speed is a very relevant performance characteristic since print time can become a bottleneck in a network. The speed of printers varies from a very slow 100 characters per second to a very fast 120 pages per minute.

Output can be classified as *human readable* (e.g., alphanumeric and graphic reports) and *machine readable* (i.e., electronic output, basically a stream of bits). Examples of output devices are printers (matrix and laser), plotters, video display terminals, sound cards and audio output devices, videos and microfiches, and electronic files on disk or tape (see Figure 6–13).

To review, the two main characteristics of output devices are:

- Speed.
- Quality of presentation.

Computer Generations and Types. There are four recognized generations of computers. Each generation is based on the technology used in designing and building the CPU. The first computer generation lasted through the 1950s and used vacuum tube technology. The second generation started in 1961 and was based on transistors. The third generation started in the mid-1960s and was based on monolithic circuits. The fourth generation started in the early 1970s with large-scale integration semiconductor technology and the invention of the microprocessor. By the late 1970s, although the technology was essentially the same, increased miniaturization led to **very large scale integration.** As integration technology advanced (more and more circuits in less and less space), so did performance (greater memory and logic capacity and speed), but prices decreased precipitously (since the chips were smaller, more chips could be manufactured at the same time).

FIGURE 6–13 Output Devices

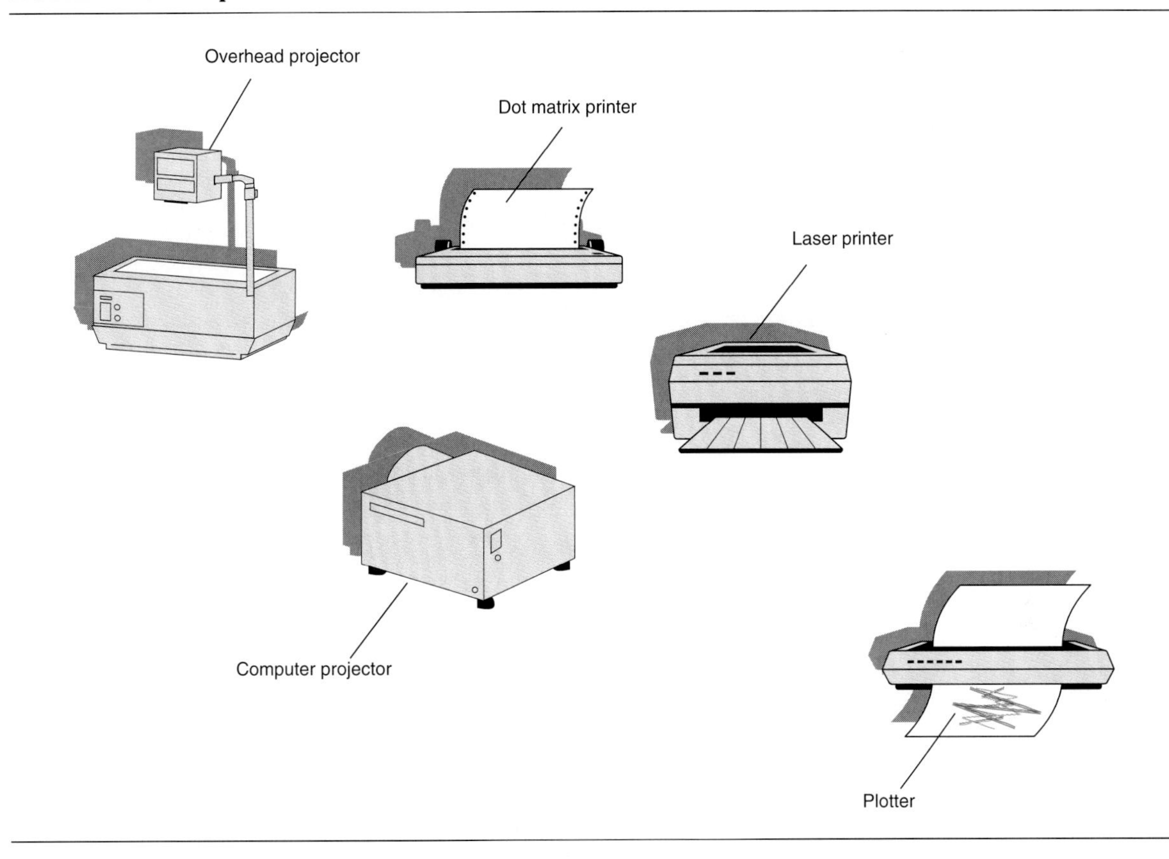

Figure 6–14 illustrates the four generations of computers. The number of transistors on a microcomputer chip has increased by a factor of 200 in less than 20 years as illustrated in Figure 6–15.

The silicon-based technology, on which the fourth generation of computers has been based, is reaching its limits—any more integration, that is, cramming of more circuits in the same space, is becoming impossible. The limitation is lack of heat dissipation. Research is under way to find materials that will dissipate heat better than silicon and therefore allow greater integration. However, the much-awaited fifth generation of computers is most likely going to be based on different methods of computing.

One of these different methods is the **reduced instruction set computing (RISC)** approach to computer design. Conventional chips—based on an approach called *complex instruction set computing (CISC)*—have many internal instructions embedded in them, although only 20 percent of the instructions are needed for 80 percent of the tasks performed by a computer. RISC chips contain only the most frequently used instructions, allowing the CPU to process information much faster. Other approaches that have the potential to bring about the fifth generation of computing involve what is called *massively parallel processing*. Massively parallel processing consists of hundreds of microchips working together to achieve very high information processing speeds.

FIGURE 6-14 Computer Generations

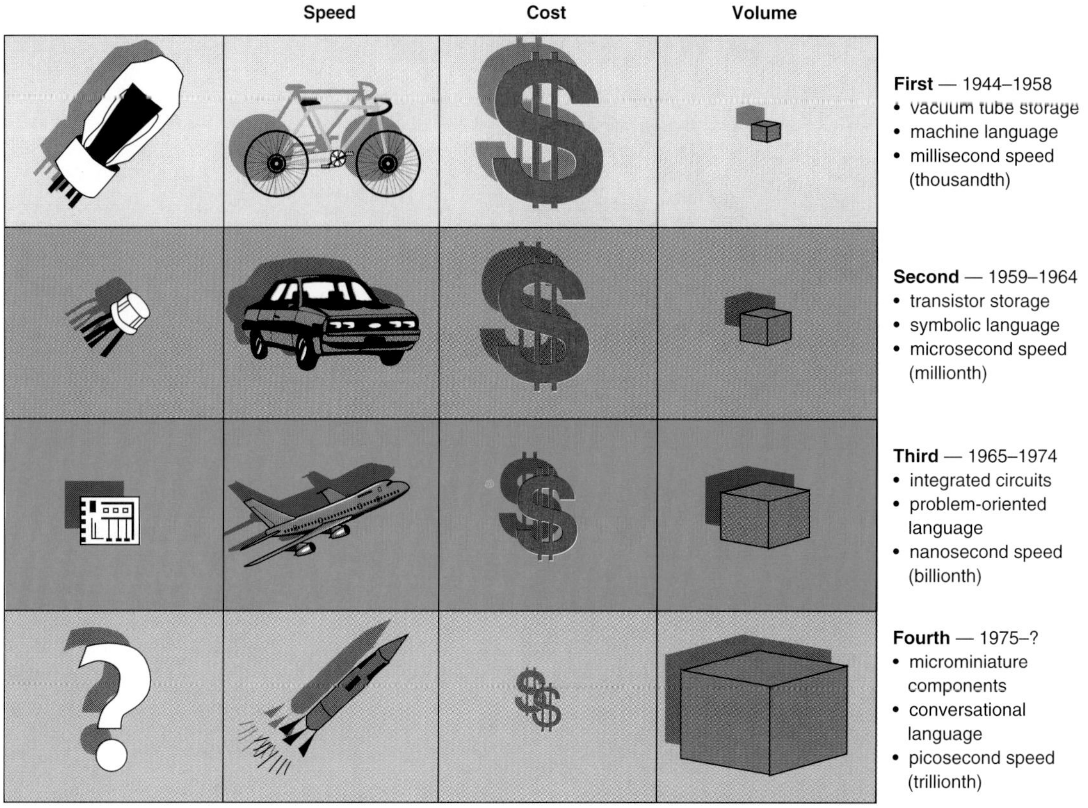

Speed Cost Volume

First — 1944–1958
- vacuum tube storage
- machine language
- millisecond speed (thousandth)

Second — 1959–1964
- transistor storage
- symbolic language
- microsecond speed (millionth)

Third — 1965–1974
- integrated circuits
- problem-oriented language
- nanosecond speed (billionth)

Fourth — 1975–?
- microminiature components
- conversational language
- picosecond speed (trillionth)

FIGURE 6-15 Intel's Microprocessor Generations

Product Name	*Date*	*Number of Transistors (in thousands)*	*Speed in MIPs*[1]	*Price per Unit*[2]
8086	July 1978	29	0.33	$ 360
286	Feb. 1982	134	0.9	360
386	Oct. 1985	275	6	299
486	April 1989	1,200	20	950
Pentium	March 1993	3,100	100	965
Pentium Pro	Sept. 1995	5,500	250	1,200[3]

[1]Millions of instructions per second of performance assumes a 32-bit operating system and application programs.

[2]Price at introduction in quantities of 100 or 1,000.

[3]Estimate.

BUSINESS BRIEF 6-2 THE COMPUTER CELEBRATES ITS 50TH BIRTHDAY

Fifty years ago, Army Major General Gadeon Barnes pushed a button in Philadelphia and turned on an incredibly bulky, maddeningly slow, and absurdly unreliable machine that would change the world.

It was called ENIAC (Electronic Numerical Integrator and Computer) and was the first electronic computer. While there are challengers for the title of the "first computer," the dedication of ENIAC on February 15, 1946, is widely accepted as the day the Information Age began. ENIAC is the direct ancestor of every PC and every electronic calculator. Plans for ENIAC began in June 1943, with a contract from the Army for the amount of $61,700. The final tab would be $486,800 (an amount close to $10 million in today's dollars).

Compared with the computers of today, ENIAC is a clumsy monster. It filled a 30-foot by 50-foot room and weighed 30 tons. It used 17,468 temperamental vacuum tubes, all of which had to be working if ENIAC's calculations were to be accurate.

Keeping it going was no picnic either. ENIAC's average running time between breakdowns was 5.6 hours. Operation required six technicians on each shift. For all its size, ENIAC was a computational weakling that would be unable to hold its own against a modern pocket calculator. ENIAC could process 1,000 instructions per second; a modern desktop computer is at least 50,000 times faster. It needed to be reprogrammed for each calculation by manually switching wires. At the time it was introduced, however, ENIAC was a wonder. It could calculate a 60-second trajectory in 30 seconds, compared with 15 minutes for a differential analyzer and 20 hours for a person with a desk calculator.

The first computer bug consisted of an actual bug that found its way into the computer's vacuum tubes because they were generating heat and got itself grilled in the process, creating a short circuit that brought down the computer.

The news media apparently didn't quite know what to make of ENIAC. A reporter for the *Philadelphia Inquirer* grasped the significance. "A new epoch in the history of human thought began last night," the story began. His editors ran the story deep in the paper, next to "Judge Frees 5 in Liquor Graft."

QUESTION

1. Compare the bulk and computing power of ENIAC to the bulk and computing power of a handheld calculator or a personal assistant such as an Apple Newton. Can you think of any other industry where the performance/price and performance/size have improved as much as in the computer industry?

SOURCE: Adapted from Michael Dresser, *The Baltimore Sun*, "The Computer Celebrates Its 50th Birthday," reprinted in *The News* (Mexico City), February 19, 1996, Living Section, p. 1. Reprinted by permission.

The driving force in making computer chips more powerful is microminiaturization and speed (which, of course, are related). The smaller you make the chip, the faster it runs (since the electrons have less distance to cover). The faster it runs, the more operations it can perform. The more operations it can perform, the more end-user features and functions can be provided in the software. Therefore, hardware enables more and more powerful and more and more user-friendly software. That is why software generations follow hardware generations so closely.

The range of computer sizes goes from micros to minis to mainframes to supercomputers. The size of computers can be determined by the capacity of the primary memory size in **megabytes (MB; millions of bytes),** the speed of the processor (in **millions of instructions per second, MIPS**), the **word size** of the databus, and the number of simultaneous users it can support. The number of simultaneous users goes from one to several hundred. Business Brief 6-2 describes the evolution of the computer.

FIGURE 6–16 Computer Power

Chips are the tiny silicon components of a computer's brain. As engineers squeeze more transistors onto the surface of each chip, computing power increases dramatically. In the chip that drives the computer's operations, the *microprocessor* or *central processing unit,* power means speed. Intel marketed the first microprocessor in 1971. Measured by ability to perform calculations, speed has increased with each new chip.

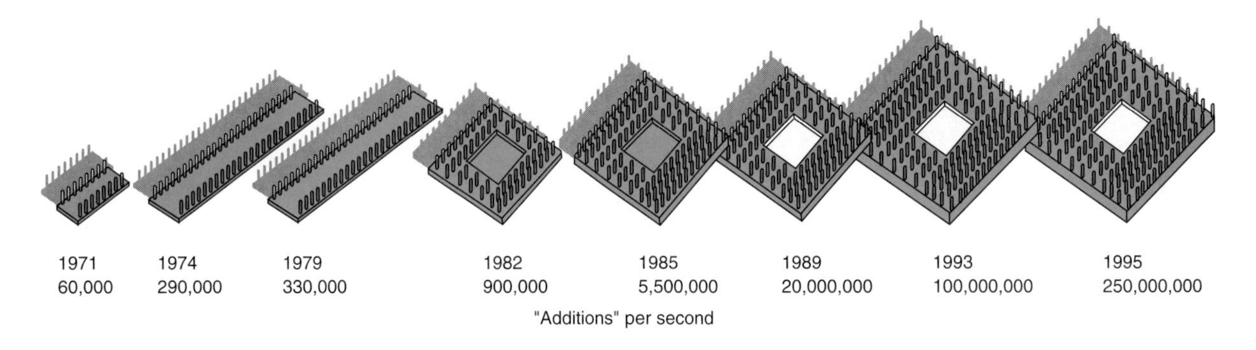

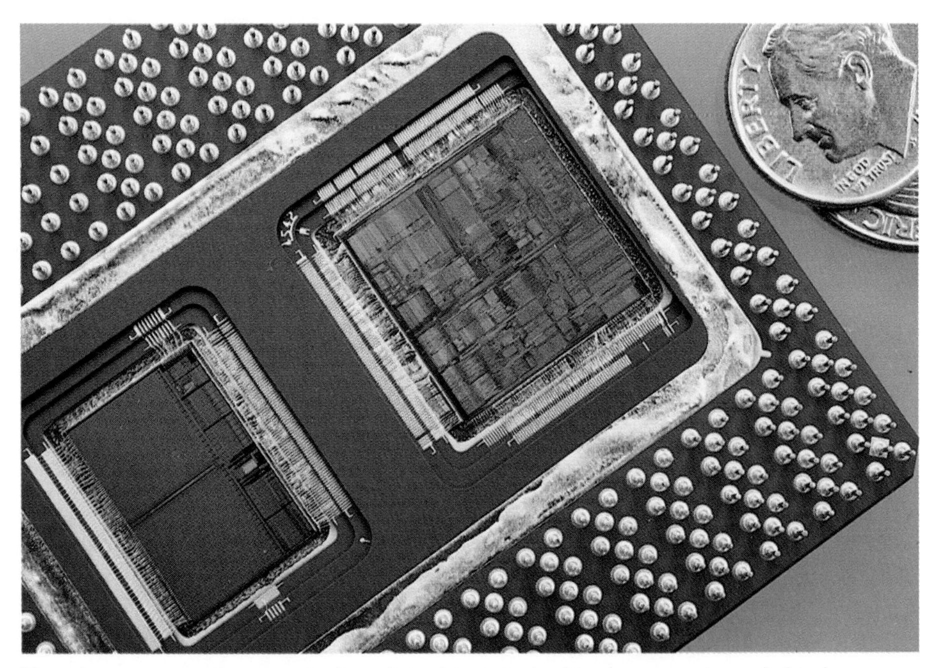

The microprocessor of a computer is contained in a single chip. A commonly used chip for microcomputers is Intel's Pentium chip. Photo courtesy of Bonnie Kamin.

However, size of computers is not much of an issue today since more and more user installations are based on networks and since PCs have become more and more powerful. Computing is becoming more "distributed" or decentralized; that is, more and more users have the computer power on their desk to perform all the computing they need and are less dependent on the computer *power* of a large processor.

Today, what is called the client/server architecture allows for very flexible computing capabilities. Client/server computing is a method of computing in which one computer (the server) acts as a central repository for data, files, messages, and programs shared among many user **workstations** (the clients). Part of the processing takes place on the server and part on the client. A **client/server architecture** consists of loosely coupled arrays of networks that can communicate with each other to share resources, that is, a series of client/server clusters. Although the implementation of the concept has been harder to manage than previously thought from a data management point of view, client/server architectures have provided great flexibility in the use of computer resources.

Computers can be used in two modes of operation:

- *Batch*, or *off-line*, when the user prepares data to be processed at a later time by the computer.
- *On-line,* or *real-time*, (and/or timesharing), when transactions are processed as they occur.

Hardware Horror Stories

Hardware horror stories usually involve tales of the hardware not being able to grow with a business's needs. Typically, the story is that computer speed and capacity are not enough to keep pace with the demands of customers and management. The horror comes when the company realizes that there is no upward compatibility in the hardware (a detail that the vendor forgot to mention or that you forgot to ask); that is, you cannot just upgrade the existing system but must buy a totally new one. This occurrence is common because of the difficulty in imagining future information needs.

Another typical story is the lack of compatibility across computer platforms (a *computer* **platform** is a series of computer models based on a specific computer chip), for example, printers that cannot be driven by a certain type of computer, or computers that have a different data transmission protocol, which makes the exchange of files, data, and E-mail difficult if not impossible.

The most serious problems with hardware are those that are practically invisible and, therefore, hard to document, particularly if they seem to occur randomly. For example, Intel introduced a new microprocessor, the Pentium, with great fanfare—touting it as a major improvement in performance over the existing (486-based) microprocessors. Customers flocked to buy PCs, servers, and workstations that used the Pentium microprocessor. Six months after the introduction of Pentium, customers reported the occurrence of random mistakes in calculations. Initially, Intel refused to publicly accept that the microprocessor was at fault. But as complaints started to accumulate, Intel recognized that the microprocessor had a flaw that could create errors in computation-intensive applications by rounding numbers incorrectly. Reluctantly, Intel offered to replace the original microprocessors and changed the design of Pentium.

Hardware Tips

1. Never buy hardware that is too small. Never buy hardware that fits OK today. Computing needs, like children's feet, grow, so allow room for expansion.
2. The computer technology market is very volatile. Promises of support and guarantees are not very useful if the vendor is not in business anymore.

Buy hardware from companies that are likely to be around five years from now. Check the vendor's long-term financial viability and not just the technical performance of its computers.
3. Compatibility is still an issue. Make sure that all parts (hard disk, CD-ROM, extra RAM, monitor, printer) work together well; whenever possible, buy them already "bundled" or installed.
4. Distinguish between obsolescence and the latest trend. Your applications may not require the latest computer chip to run effectively.
5. Prices of hardware tend to drop rapidly, and hardware reliability tends to increase over time. It usually pays to wait a couple of months (if you can afford to wait) before buying the latest piece of hardware. You may reap the benefit of fewer bugs for less money.
6. Choose software first, and then match the appropriate hardware to it.
7. Even if you are buying a standalone computer, buy it "network ready." You will find yourself using some sort of network service sooner rather than later.

SOFTWARE

Software is basically a translation system between human language (e.g., English) and computer language (i.e., machine language). Software is what makes a computer useful by letting humans command computers to perform tasks. You can command computers in their "own" language **(machine language)** very efficiently. However, learning and using machine language is time consuming and difficult. Powerful operating systems and application software eliminate the need for users to have to learn machine language. They can command the computer with Englishlike commands. Soon, software and hardware capabilities will be such that they will allow humans to command computers by voice in plain English (or French or Swahili). See Figure 6–17 for a depiction of the stages of software generations. When this level of user friendliness occurs, users will not have to learn a computer language at all. Software in computers can be of at least four types:

1. Operating systems (e.g., MS-DOS, Windows, OS/2, Macintosh, UNIX).
2. Application generators (e.g., spreadsheets, report generators, database management system software).
3. Specific applications (e.g., payroll, inventory control).
4. Languages (e.g., COBOL, FORTRAN, PASCAL, Visual BASIC, C++).

Operating systems are a set of programs that manage the operation of the computer hardware, including the input, output, and secondary storage devices. The operating system is always running in the background, ensuring that user applications are operating smoothly. Operating systems are composed of a supervisor program (which controls the flow of activities), utility programs (format disks; create, select, and delete directories; name and copy files; time clock; anti-virus programs), and language translators (to translate Englishlike commands or icon-based commands into executable machine language).

Application generators are also called *productivity tools.* They enable a user to write and edit documents (word-processing software); make complex computations and what-if analyses (spreadsheet software); build, search, and retrieve directories of records (database management software); and make use of video and sounds in making presentations (multimedia software). **Application software** is a program that

FIGURE 6–17 Software Generations

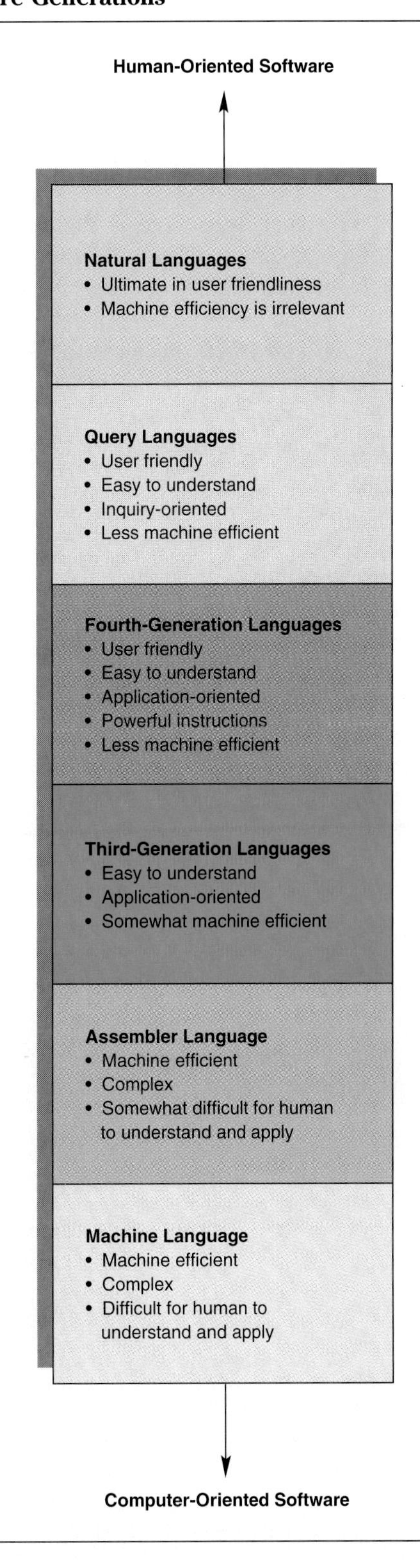

deals with a specific problem (inventory management), and only with that problem.

Computer languages are typically categorized as on a continuum from low to high level. Low-level languages refer to languages that require great knowledge of programming, whereas high level languages are very user friendly, approximating natural language, and, therefore, require less computer knowledge. The higher the level of the language, the easier it is to learn and use for programming. Higher languages have better, easier-to-use interfaces.

A **software interface** is the layer of software that allows users to command computers to perform certain functions. Examples of interfaces are the **graphical-user interface (GUI),** based on icons, where the user points and clicks with a mouse on a picture (e.g., the picture of a printer to start the printing of a document); **menu-driven interfaces,** where the user is given a series of choices and picks one by clicking or entering the choice with a keyboard; and voice recognition–based interfaces, where the user issues commands by speaking to the computer.

High-level languages, also known as fourth-generation languages (4GL) or nonprocedural languages, make it much more feasible for users to develop their own applications by "bundling" commands into ready-to-use functions (e.g., statistical analysis functions within spreadsheet programs). The trend of users developing their own applications rather than relying on professional programmers has been called *end-user computing.*

The increase in user friendliness in software comes at a cost in terms of hardware. High-level languages require much more memory and computer power than lower-level languages. In general, the friendlier the interface, the more overhead (amount of RAM and microprocessor speed) the software requires to run properly. For example, Microsoft's Windows 95 required at least 8 MB of RAM to run properly. The paradox here is that although the hardware is ever faster and more powerful, the software—by being more user friendly and, therefore, cumbersome—sometimes makes the hardware behave as if it is slower and less powerful.

The trade-off implicit in the use of high-level languages versus low-level languages (e.g., assembler, machine) is the increase in human productivity (e.g., reduced time in developing, debugging, and learning a software package) versus the added expense of extra primary memory storage and higher speed microprocessors. In most cases, the extra hardware cost is worth it.

When buying software, the main characteristics that need to be taken into consideration are as follows:

1. Functionality (i.e., what it does).
2. Memory requirements.
3. Speed.
4. **User friendliness** (ease of use and minimum required level of skills).
5. Available support. (What happens when something goes wrong with the software or when a feature is not clearly explained in the documentation? For example, is there a free, 24-hour, 800-number to call? Does the software vendor guarantee a two-hour response time in case of trouble?)
6. Compatibility with existing hardware platforms and other applications.
7. Upgradability. (Does it fit not only with the current business goals, but also with future ones?)

Software Horror Stories. "Bad" software means software that has mistakes, or bugs, and therefore does not perform as expected. Most bugs tend to create frustration and disappointment. Sometimes, however, bad software can cause

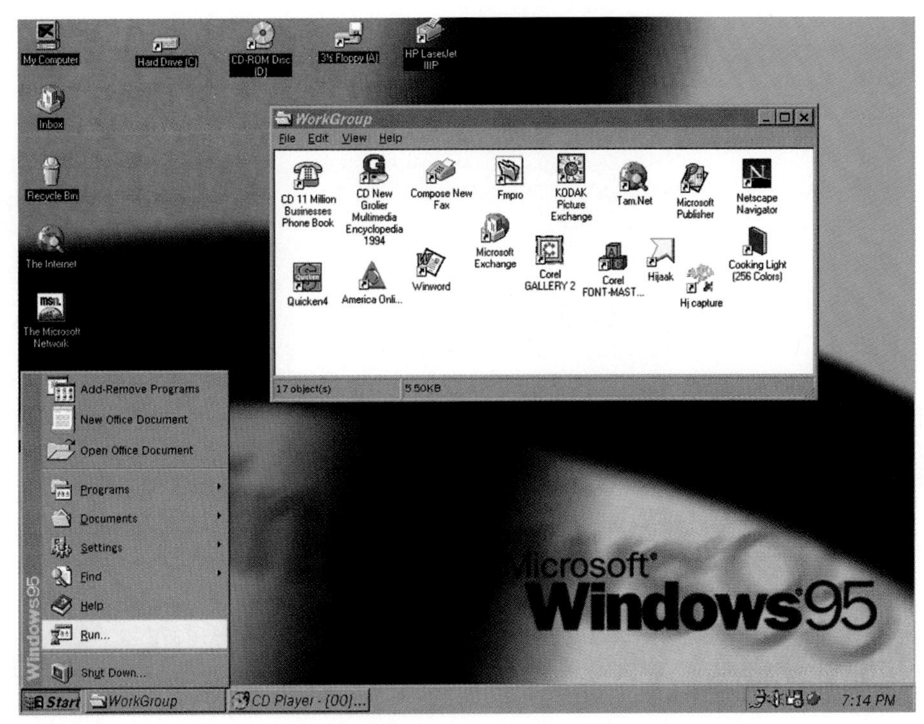

If hardware is the body, the operating system is the soul of a computer system. Photo courtesy of Microsoft.

profound havoc. In Chapter 1, we briefly told the story of a company that faced bankruptcy because of a malfunctioning inventory control software package (we will revisit in detail the Hopper Specialty Company debacle in Chapter 11). This is only one of many horror stories around.

Consider the software that was supposed to drive the baggage delivery system at the new Denver International Airport. The software was supposed to deliver passengers' bags from registering counters to loading docks and from loading docks to luggage pickup carousels. The system was based on bar-coded carts. The first test of the system saw the carts jet around the tracks so fast that the luggage was thrown off the carts. The luggage that made it to a destination was, in most cases, at the wrong destination. After many attempts at solving the software problems, a decision was made to build an alternative low-tech baggage system. The opening of the airport had to be delayed by two years with a cost of almost $2 billion.

Another well-documented software nightmare is the development and implementation of a new reservation system at the Greyhound bus company. The system was supposed to have been the central part of a totally reengineered reservation system that would allow the same capabilities as airline reservation systems (e.g., frequent fare changes, multiple fares per bus, frequent traveler programs, on-line analyses). The system was so slow and passengers were so angry at the long waits that clerks reverted to a manual system to write tickets. The system was such a failure it brought Greyhound to bankruptcy proceedings.

These cases of software problems are spectacular in that they have created multimillion dollar losses for the companies that implemented them. Clearly, these were large, complicated systems where the likelihood of something going wrong was

Some computer languages are easier than others and require much less training to use and understand them. Icons and pull-down menus facilitate computer use. Photo courtesy of Microsoft.

high. However, there are plenty of horror stories attached to software that was of low cost and performed what can be considered straightforward tasks.

For example, the Internal Revenue Service decided recently that individuals that made a mistake in filing their returns by using a software package—sold by a very reputable company—that had a bug were personally responsible for the penalties and fines due to those mistakes (the software company apologized, advertised that there was a mistake, but, until now, has yet to offer to cover the penalties and fines of the affected individuals).

Another example is a package sold nationally to write your own will (without the help of an attorney). One of the features of the package is the ability to write a power-of-attorney letter. Unfortunately, the boilerplate letter has a logic error that would make it useless in a court of law. Unless the user is somewhat familiar with a power-of-attorney, they might not catch the error.

Software Tips.

1. Make sure your hardware system can handle the software.
2. Get a demonstration version first.
3. Make sure you are buying the most recent version.
4. Check the return policy (if the return policy is quite liberal, make sure that you are buying an originally sealed software package).
5. Never buy used software; it could contain a bug or virus.
6. Find out about upgrades.
7. Determine what kind of support is offered.

8. Ask for references (i.e., other users), preferably references that have the same amount of experience and needs that you do.
9. Remember, you usually get what you pay for.
10. Whenever possible, buy rather than develop your own software.
11. Read the documentation *before* you buy the system (ask the vendor or the merchant for samples of the documentation materials).
12. Ask whether the data, documents, and files you may already have are transportable to the new system. Try it yourself before buying the new software.
13. Be a pest. The more questions you ask and the better you understand what the software package does, the happier you will be.

NETWORKS AND TELECOMMUNICATIONS

Basically, you need to think about installing a network when

- Two or more people need access to the same database or computer application (e.g., accounting program, personnel records, customer accounts).
- Several individuals are using the same software package (e.g., word processor, spreadsheet). You could save resources by buying a single network version of the package rather than many single user licenses.
- Office communications are frequent and cumbersome (employees are in and out of the office, work across time zones, or share work).
- You want to ensure good data hygiene (ensure that security, documentation, backups, and procedures to share consistent data are implemented).
- You want to share resources such as high-quality printers.

Computer networks are a subset of telecommunications. **Telecommunications** shrink distance, allow coordination, and compress time. Crucial aspects in the design of most information systems are the capability for a computer to communicate with remote devices and for physically separate, or distributed, computers to communicate with each other. Most distributed systems are organized in hierarchies (i.e., many micros communicate to fewer minis, which communicate to a couple of mainframes).

The components of a telecommunications network (and their function) are the following:

- Source device (creates data).
- Back-end processor (manages outgoing messages and data flows).
- Data communication device (converts/encodes data; e.g., modem).
- Switching system (determines the path of the data).
- Data channel (transmits the data).
- Data communication device (converts/decodes data; e.g., modem).
- Front-end processor (manages incoming messages and data flows).
- Destination device (receives data).

Figure 6–18 illustrates the components of telecommunications.

A number of devices (sources, receivers) can use the same transmission line by using a *multiplexor* at each end, allowing for a more efficient use of communication lines. In large networks, a small computer manages all data communications. This dedicated computer is called a front-end processor and/or back-end processor, depending on whether its role is to send (front) or receive (back) messages and data

FIGURE 6–18 Telecommunications Components

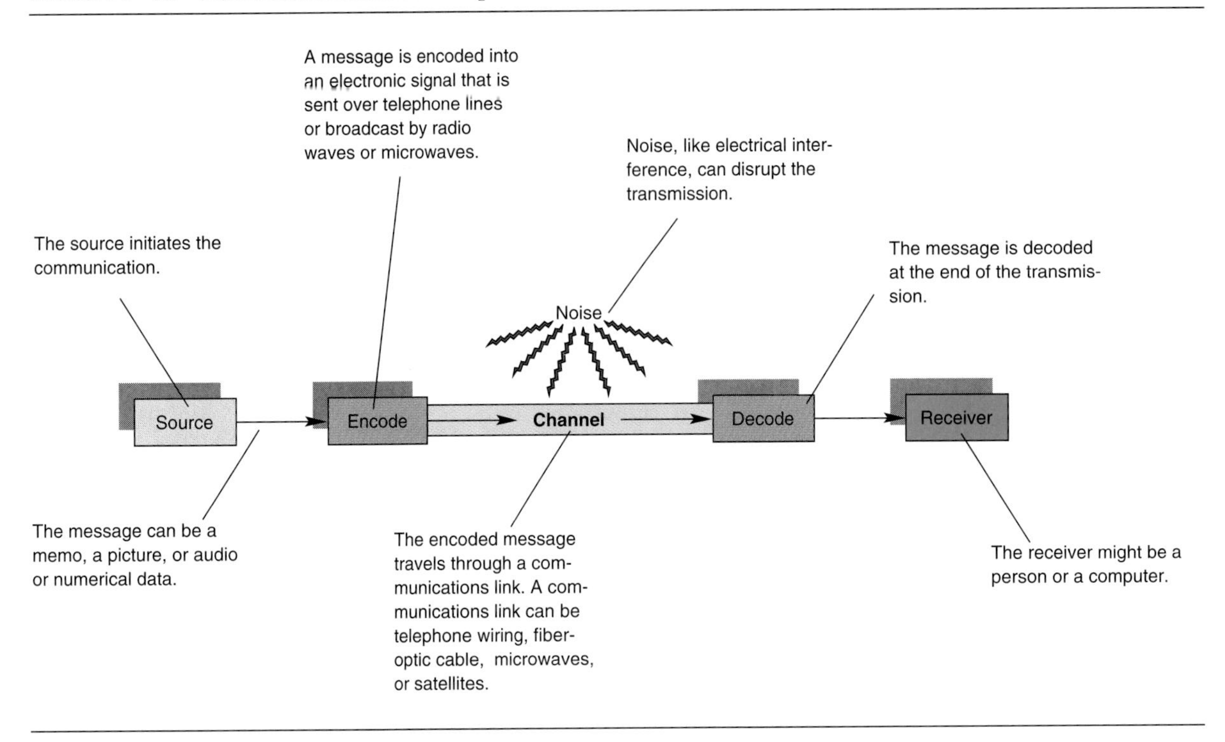

flows. When an analog transmission is used (e.g., in normal telephone lines), a device called a **modem** is used. A modem consists of a *mod*ulator to encode the (binary) data before transmission and a *dem*odulator that reverses the process.

The data channel can be of two types: cabled and wireless. There are three basic types of cables (twisted pair, coaxial, and fiber optic) (see Figure 6–19) and three types of wireless (radio, microwave, and satellite). The capacity of a transmission line is called its *bandwidth.* The bandwidth of a channel varies—the broader the band, the more data can be transmitted on it per unit of time. A broadband network can carry voice, data, and video signals simultaneously.

The transmission capabilities of a channel and modem are measured in baud rates, or characters per second. An analog phone line transmits data at about 2 million bits per second (bps). A *broadband transmission* refers to any transmission at a speed higher than 2 million bps (usually around 10 million bps). A protocol offered by telephone companies, called *integrated services digital networks (ISDN),* turns a standard copper phone line into a high-speed digital link that can send voice and data simultaneously. *Asynchronous transfer mode (ATM)* is a high-speed digital switching and transmission technology that allows data, voice, and video to be sent over a single line at speeds ranging from 25 million to 1 billion bps.

There are, broadly speaking, three *classes* of networks: a **local area network (LAN),** which is a network of interconnecting locations within a building or a set of buildings in close proximity; a **wide area,** or long-haul, **network (WAN),** which is

FIGURE 6–19 Different Types of Cables

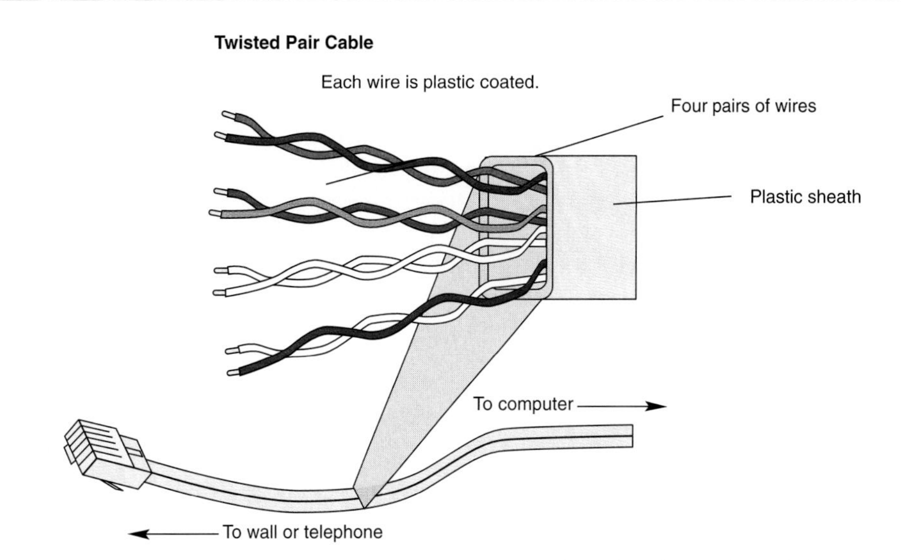

Fiber-Optic Cable

Glass fibers

Each fiber is a glass tube with a diameter less than that of a human hair.

Plastic coating

Metal wire to strengthen the cable

Plastic coating

The fiber is wrapped to help reflect the light that travels through the fiber.

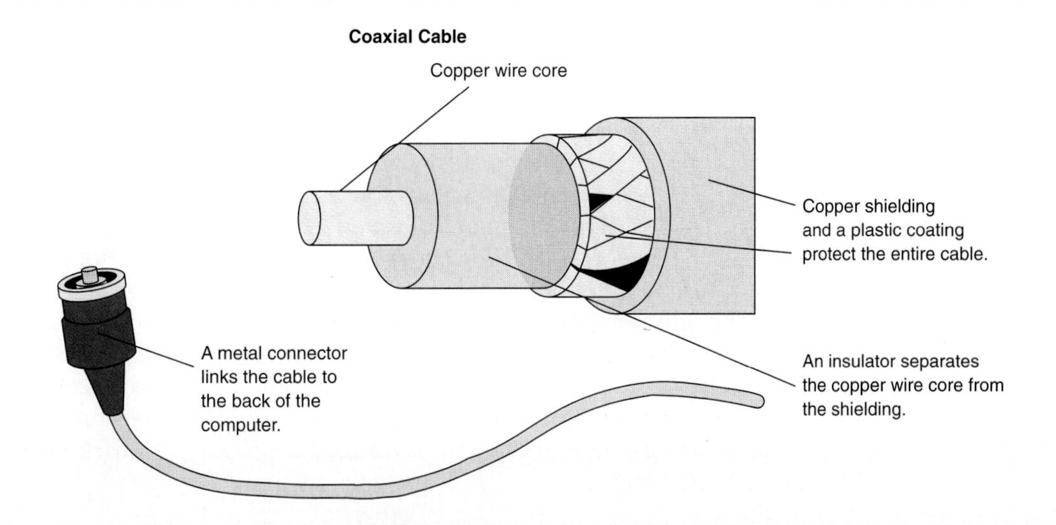

an enterprisewide network that links a LAN via public or private lines to other LANs in remote locations; and, **value-added networks (VAN),** which are private, carrier-provided, multisite telecommunications systems with, in many instances, access to external databases (e.g., Lexis/Nexis; Prodigy).

Generally speaking there are two types of network configurations: **server-based networks** and **peer-to-peer networks** (see Figure 6–20). Server-based networks use a fast, central computer (the server) as a central repository for data and software programs that can be shared among all the users of the network. Users talk to each other "through" the server. Peer-to-peer networks are networks where users interact with each other directly, often using each others' hard-disk space to share information. Peer-to-peer networks require less infrastructure and maintenance but tend to be slower. As the network grows, the server-based configuration is much more efficient.

LANs can have several configurations or **topologies**, but they are usually a variation of the star, ring, or bus (linear) network (see Figure 6–21). Each network configuration has its advantages and disadvantages. For example, the star topology is highly efficient but becomes inoperable if the center node is disabled. The linear topology affords great flexibility in adding nodes to the network but requires substantial message collision management (i.e., managing the traffic of messages in the line) and, therefore, is less efficient.

Networks can be evaluated on the following dimensions or performance characteristics:

1. Type and frequency of access. (How much traffic (volume) and what type of traffic (type of data, distance) can the network handle?)
2. Reliability. (Can the network transmit data always without loss or distortion; how often is the network down?)
3. Response time. (How fast is the network in supporting multiple queries?)
4. Capacity. (How many users and what type of traffic can be sustained by the network before it slows down substantially?)
5. Flexibility. (How easy is the network to maintain and upgrade; does it allow for easy addition of users?)
6. Security. (What are the available measures to protect the security and integrity of the data being transmitted back and forth on the network?)

An example of a network and its applications is shown in Figure 6–22.

Network Horror Stories. Most of the horror stories about networks deal with the increased vulnerability of companies to a network crash. This vulnerability is the result of the company becoming totally dependent on the work flow supported by the network. Standalone computing affects the productivity of the individual. Network computing affects the productivity of a whole team, department, or organization by not only changing the productivity of the individual but by changing the way the individual communicates and makes decisions.

Consider the case of the School of Business at Eastern Mountains University (EMU). To attract students by projecting an image of technological awareness and to teach students the latest job-related skills, EMU required students to purchase a PC. To make the requirement even more attractive, EMU decided to install a network exclusively for its students. Faculty were to exchange messages, homework assignments, and academic advice with students through the network. Students would have access to high-quality printers, scheduled events, and their peers in EMU through the network.

FIGURE 6–20 Network Configurations

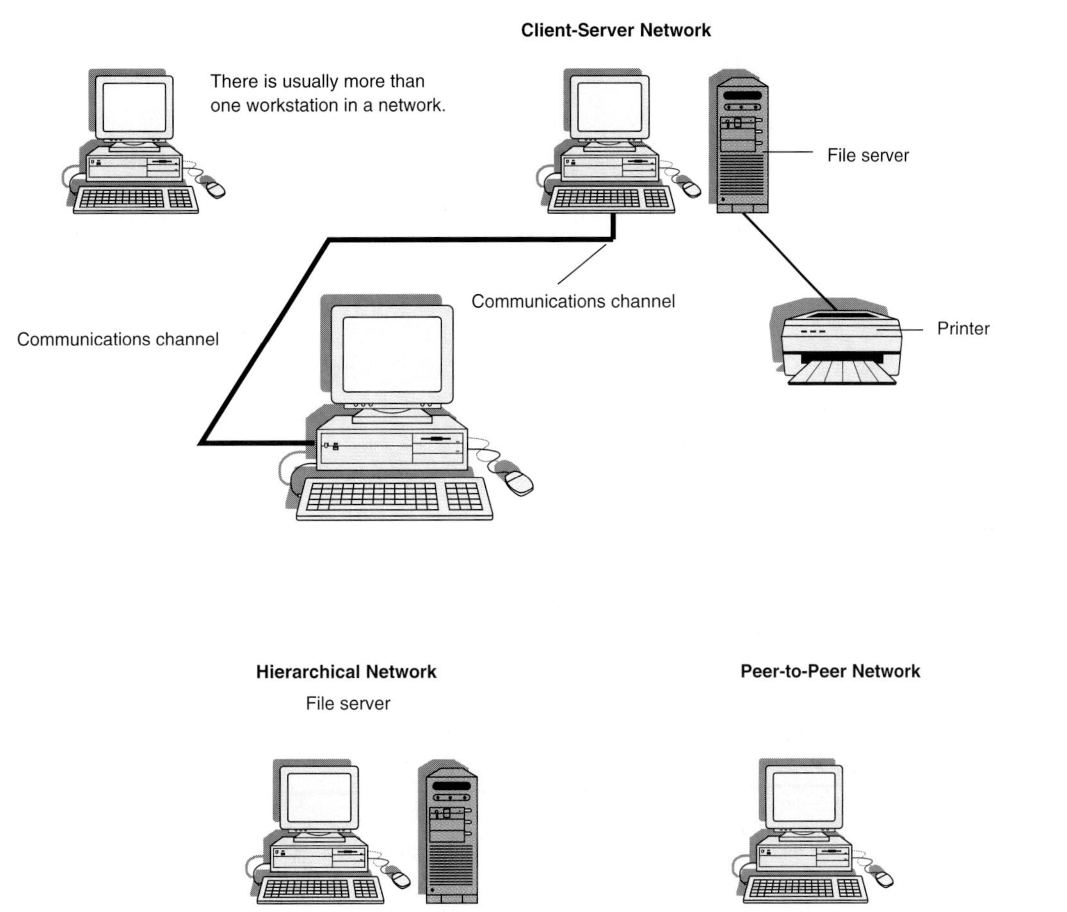

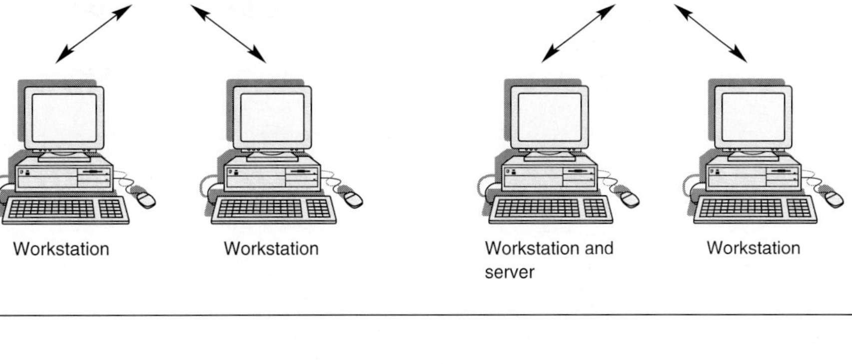

However, EMU, as with many other business schools in the country, was short on funds. Rather than wait to have the adequate resources, EMU decided to move forward with the network. The network that was implemented was a network that the school could afford; not the ideal configuration with the required level of technical support that was needed.

The network that was implemented was based on a client-server architecture with a server that was adequate for the predicted needs during the coming

FIGURE 6–21 Network Topologies

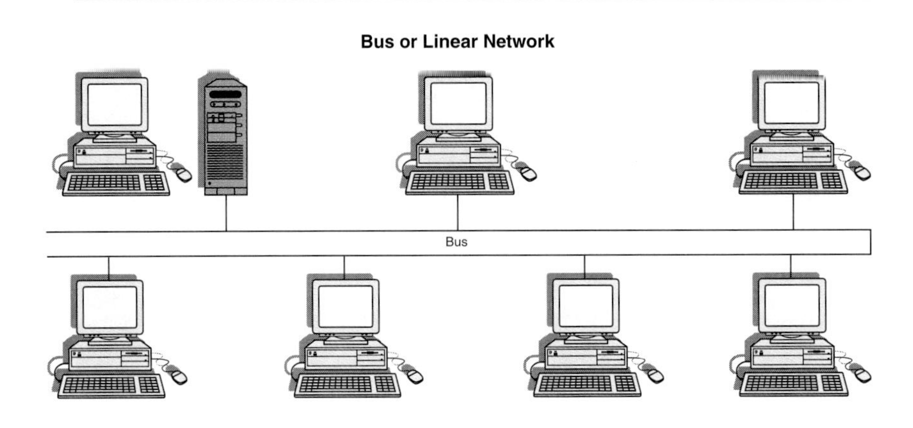

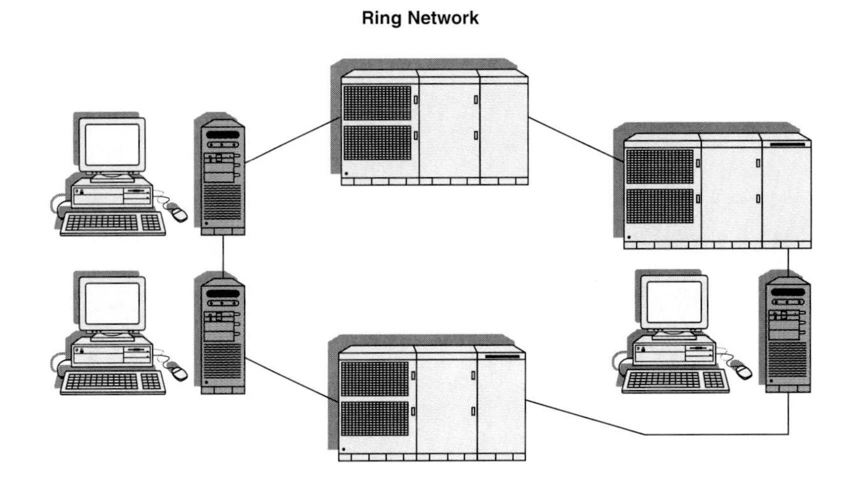

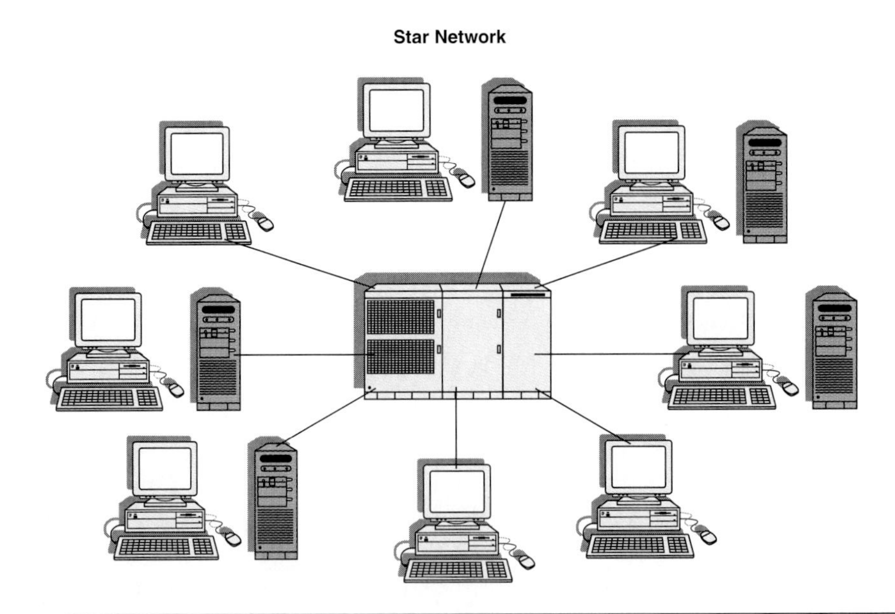

FIGURE 6–22 Anatomy of a Network

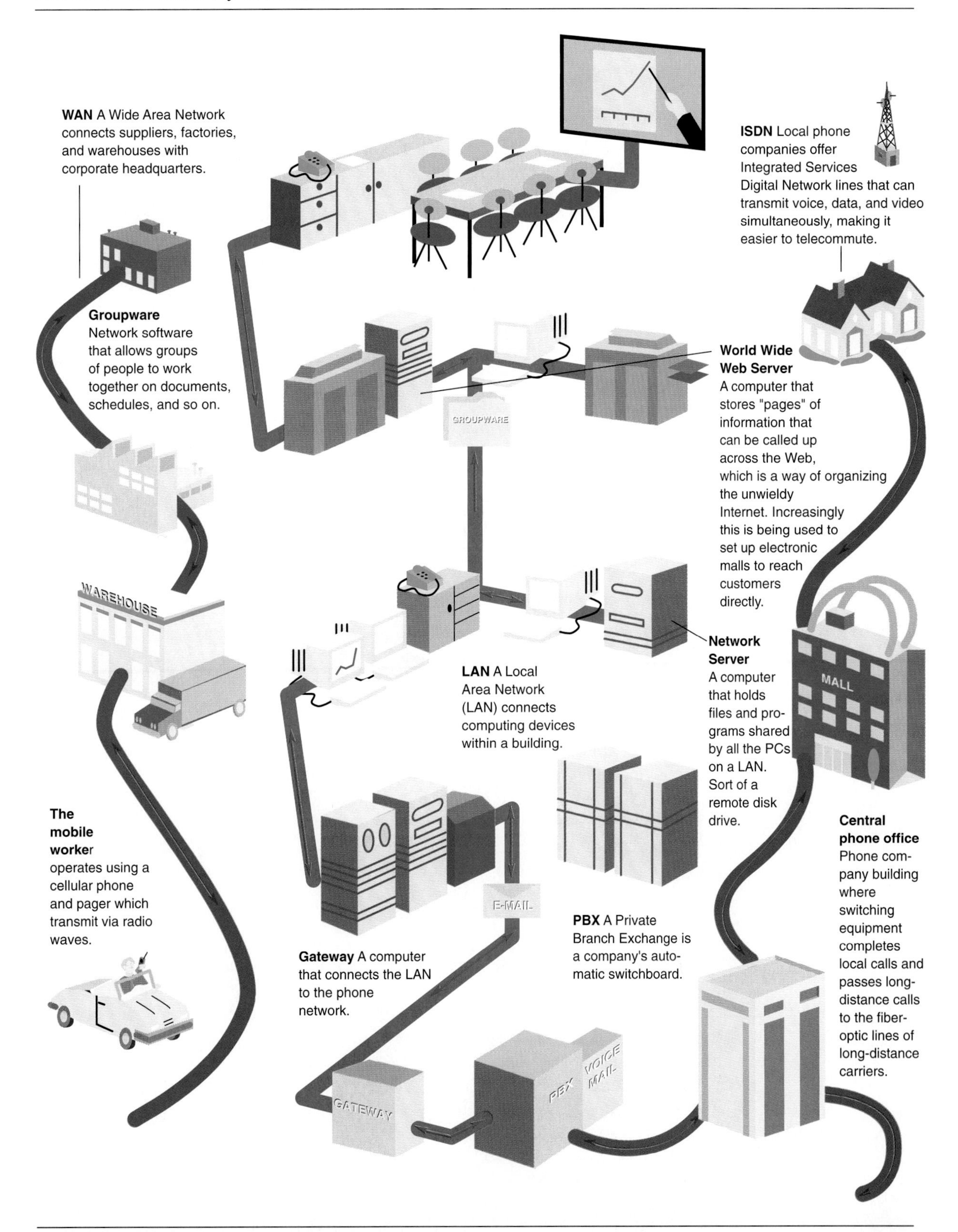

SOURCE: *Business Week*, June 26, 1995, pp. 90–91.

academic year but with no backup server. The technical staff was minimum, but the software running on the network was supposed to have been debugged and also very easy to use and maintain.

Unfortunately, the network was a great success. Not only did students use it but they used it much more than predicted. Faculty also found the network useful and started storing, among other things, exam and assignment grades in the server. As the final week of classes started, use of the network increased dramatically as students exchanged more and more messages with faculty and their peers and used the network to print their end-of-term papers.

The network crashed. A new server was brought in, but, for whatever reason, the network was still down. The technical expert of the school, a retrained executive secretary, was not able to diagnose the problem. After checking with the network software vendor, the staff attempted several remedies, none of which worked. The network had taken "hostage" students' papers and the faculty's ability to compute final grades. After two weeks of misery, the network problem was finally solved.

Network Tips.

1. Networks are expensive. If you decide you need one, a fast file server is always a good purchase.
2. Implementing a network increases the vulnerability of a company in case of malfunction. Therefore, don't skimp on training or backup procedures and systems. Over-engineer your backup systems. Make sure you have backup and recovery plans, and test them before you need them.
3. No matter what you think at first, you will eventually need a network administrator.
4. User guidelines on security are a must.
5. Keep the server "light;" that is, implement on the server only those applications that need to be shared.
6. Absolutely let a professional do the cabling.
7. Identical configuration of all the machines connected to the network make buying, upgrading, and maintaining software easier.
8. Check and recheck compatibility of the software applications with the network operating system.
9. You cannot be too thin, too rich, or have too much transmission capacity (i.e., go broadband if you can afford it).

THE CONVERGENCE OF TECHNOLOGIES

Although we have treated the topics of hardware, software, and telecommunications under separate sections in this chapter, there is an irrevocable convergence trend. It is becoming harder and harder to differentiate among the three "legs" of the information technology stool. Hardware, from computer chips to printers, has a greater software component in them. Software is more frequently being developed for sharing results and data with other remote users over networks and telecommunications systems. More and more business problems and applications are requiring an integrated solution.

Legislation is following suit. In the spring of 1996, the Telecommunications Act was signed into law by President Clinton. The bill deregulated the telecommunications industry, allowing communication companies to compete by offering and

BUSINESS BRIEF 6-3 THE COMING TELESCRAMBLE

"It's no longer a question of how large a share of the $76 billion long-distance market you can get," says an analyst. "It's a question of how big a share of the $500 billion converged or integrated market they will get."

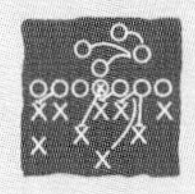

By dynamiting the walls that separated the telecommunications sector for the last six decades, the Telecommunications Act of 1996 tears down the regulatory walls that had prevented what many believe is the inevitable melding of telephone, computer, and entertainment technologies. In a world where phone calls and movies alike can be reduced to the digital language of 0's and 1's, the distinctions between phone company and cable TV carrier and between broadcast network and long-distance network are disappearing. Vice President Al Gore, a champion of technology, declared the signing of the bill tantamount to the fall of the Berlin Wall.

What comes next is a multibillion dollar dogfight for the hearts, minds, and checkbooks of the nation's businesses and consumers in a combination of electronic infrastructure building, corporate joint venturing and acquiring, and Madison Avenue marketing that will make the 1984 breakup of the Bell System seem like a minor event. New goliaths will emerge; old ones will fade.

Some suggest that AT&T, Sprint, and MCI (the giants of long-distance calling) are best positioned for the future. However, as competition heats up across the board, no company is expected to go it alone. AT&T bought McCaw Cellular for $12.6 billion and now offers long-distance, cellular, Internet access, and satellite TV under the AT&T brand and all billable to the AT&T Universal credit card.

MCI and Sprint are determined to match AT&T service for service. MCI sold 20 percent of its share to British Communications Ltd. in 1994 to finance its own diversification plans. Its first move was the spending of $2 billion for 13.5 percent of Rupert Murdoch's News Corp. MCI then went out and bid $682 million in January 1996 for a license to launch its own Direct Broadcasting System (DBS) service, which it will build in partnership with News Corp. The company recently spent a total of $1.2 billion to purchase a cellular phone reseller and computer systems integrator and teamed with Microsoft Corp. to develop Internet services.

Sprint, meanwhile is building one of the nation's largest wireless calling networks, using the new personal communications services (PCS) technology. PCS works much the same as cellular, delivering calls over radio waves, but it is all digital and cheaper to run. Sprint wants to combine its nationwide PCS network with cable TV systems that will have voice and video. Sprint's partners in the venture are three of the largest U.S. cable operators (Tele-Communications, Inc., Comcast, and Cox Communications), who reach a total of 39 million households. The grand scheme is to offer consumers a discount on wireless calling if they also sign up for local phone service, long-distance service, and cable TV, all under the Sprint brand name. Sprint also signed an agreement with a handful of foreign telecommunication companies, including France Telecom and Deutsche Telekom, to create a global telecommunications company.

Local service providers say the long-distance carriers have a leg up because of their branded names and nationwide coverage. Long-distance carriers say that Baby Bells are in the driver's seat because of their control of local lines and their large staffs of technicians. And everyone believes the cable companies will outpace them because 95 percent of the United States is wired for cable and because the thick lines run into houses are optimal for delivering the widest range of services including phone, data, and video.[1]

Besides, the cable TV operators and their emerging competitors need programming to shove through all those high-speed lines, and cable TV companies know how to compete on content. Witness Time Warner's willingness to pay $7.5 billion for Turner Broadcasting System, which owns CNN. Or Comcast's recent purchase of the Philadelphia 76ers basketball and Flyers hockey teams and Cox's one-third stake in Digital Domain, the company responsible for the visual effects in the movies *Apollo 13* and *True Lies*.

The aim of all these alliances is to win customers by offering the most attractive package of services at the most attractive price. As the alliances shape up, customers can expect a blitz of marketing and one-stop telecommunications shopping. "At some point in the very near future, we'll be receiving five or six sheets from companies saying, 'let me be everything to you'," said an analyst.

BUSINESS BRIEF 6-3 THE COMING TELESCRAMBLE–*CONT.*

QUESTIONS

1. Explain the statement, "The battle of telecommunications convergence is basically a battle on two fronts: content and distribution."
2. Update some of the alliances and competitive alignments described in this Business Brief.
3. What technologies have changed since the passing of the Telecommunications Act of 1996?

---

[1]If you've got cable television service, take a look at the cable plugged into your wall. Now look at the wire coming out of your telephone. Which one is bigger? The TV cable of course. It's a big, fat piece of coaxial cable. And it's not just bigger physically. Electronically speaking, it's gigantic, capable of carrying millions of bits of information every second, far more than wire phone lines. The trouble is that the overall design of cable systems relies on amplifiers that send traffic only one way. But optical fiber technology is not standing still. The latest technology can carry up to a trillion bits per second. That's enough to carry 12 million simultaneous conversations or download 100 two-hour movies in a second.

SOURCE: Adapted from Jon Auerbach; "Melding Media Firms Rush to a Revolution," *The Boston Globe*. February 11, 1996, p. A1; Haiawatha Bray, "Cable TV Wire Is Likely to Be Multimedia Pipeline," *The Boston Globe*, February 11, 1996, p. A5; Catherine Amst, "U.S. Giants Aren't Sleeping," *Business Week*, April 8, 1996, pp. 44–45, Ronald Grover with Elizabeth Lealy, "1 Way or No Way for Cable," *Business Week*, April 8, 1996, pp. 46–47, and Peter Coy, "Please Hold for New Technology," *Business Week*, April 8, 1996, pp. 48–50. Material from *Business Week* is reprinted by special permission, copyright © 1996 by the McGraw-Hill Coompanies.

bundling whatever services they want. The act ends government rules that had maintained barriers, which had become more and more artificial, between local and long-distance calling, cable TV, broadcasting, and wireless services. The short-term effect will be a series of mergers, alliances, and an overall restructuring of the industry. Phone companies, publishing companies, information technology firms, movie production studios, broadcasters, and cable TV operators will be competing with each other in the new communication arena of multiple, interconnected networks, delivering all kinds of services.

When the converged communications industry does emerge, who will the winners be? Experts suggest that when the dust settles in five years or so the new telecommunications arena will be dominated by a handful of "convergence conglomerates," which most likely will include the existing long-distance carriers. Business Brief 6–3 discusses this idea.

SUMMARY

The basic management decisions on technology consist of choosing the appropriate hardware, its configuration (centralized or distributed, micros or terminals, network topology), and the type of software (choice of applications and languages). These choices should be based on trade-offs between (*a*) human and machine productivity and (*b*) the performance of the technology and its cost.

Computer hardware consists of the following four elements: (*a*) the input devices (keyboard, mouse, scanner); (*b*) microprocessors or the central processing unit (CPU), including primary memory (RAM); (*c*) secondary storage devices (diskettes, disk drives, CD-ROM); and (*d*) output devices (printers, speakers, monitors).

One important distinction between computer processors is whether they are reduced instruction set computing (RISC), such as the PowerPC chip, or complex instruction set computing (CISC), such as the Pentium chip. CISC processors have many internal instructions embedded in them, although only 20 percent of the instructions are needed for 80 percent of the tasks performed by a computer. RISC chips contain only the most frequently used instructions, allowing the CPU to process information much faster.

Software is basically a translation system between human language (e.g., English) and computer language (i.e., machine language). Software is what makes a computer useful by letting humans command computers to perform tasks. Software in computers can be of at least four types: (*a*) operating systems (MS-DOS, Windows, OS/2, Macintosh, UNIX), (*b*) application generators (spreadsheets, report generators, database software), (*c*) specific applications (payroll, inventory control), and (*d*) development languages (COBOL, PASCAL, Visual BASIC, C++, Java).

Computer networks are a subset of telecommunications. Telecommunications shrink distance, allow coordination, and compress time. Crucial aspects in the design of most information systems are the capability for a computer to communicate with remote devices and for physically separate, or distributed, computers to communicate with each other. Most distributed systems are organized in hierarchies (i.e., many micros communicate to fewer minis, which communicate to a couple of mainframes).

Recently, the three main components of information technology (hardware, software, telecommunications) have been converging.

KEY CONCEPTS AND TERMS

KEY CONCEPTS

- Information technology includes hardware, software, and telecommunications. (182)
- Easy-to-use software requires more powerful hardware. (202)
- Outdated technology is not necessarily obsolete. (181)
- Hardware, software, and telecommunications technologies are converging. (212)

KEY TERMS

application generator (200)
application software (200)
arithmetic and logic unit (ALU) (184)
central processing unit (CPU) (184)
client-server architecture (199)
control unit (CU) (184)
databus (186)
disk density (192)
graphical user interface (GUI) (202)
hardware (182)
input device (183)
local area network (LAN) (206)
machine language (200)
magnetic disks (190)
megabyte (197)
megahertz (MHz) (186)
menu-driven interface (202)
microprocessor (184)
million instructions per second (MIPS) (197)
modem (206)
operating system (200)
output device (194)
peer-to-peer network (208)
platform (199)
primary memory (184)
programmable read-only memory (PROM) (188)
random-access memory (RAM) (184)
read-only memory (ROM) (188)
reduced instruction set computer (RISC) (195)
secondary memory (190)
sectors (192)
server-based network (208)
software (200)
software interface (202)
telecommunications (205)
topology (208)
tracks (192)
user friendliness (202)
value-added network (VAN) (208)
very large scale integration (194)
wide area network (WAN) (206)
word size (197)
workstations (199)

REFERENCES

Arinze, B. *Microcomputers for Managers.* Belmont, CA: Wadworth Publishing, 1994.

Davis, W. S. *Management, Information, and Systems: An Introduction to Business Information Systems.* St. Paul, MN: West Publishing, 1995.

O'Brien, J. A. *Introduction to Information Systems.* 7th ed. Burr Ridge, IL: Irwin Publishing, 1994.

Parsons, J. J., and D. Oja. *New Perspective in Computer Concepts.* Cambridge, MA: Course Technology, Inc., 1995.

CONNECTIVE CASE: Intranet Solution for Geffen Records

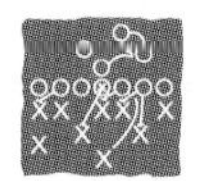

Guns 'N' Roses. Lisa Loeb. Sonic Youth. Elastica. Weezer. It's probably safe to say that the names of these rock acts don't immediately turn a person's mind to thoughts of client/server computing, cyberspace, and operating systems. Unless, of course, you're Jim Griffin, enthusiastic Internet surfer, Web cruiser, and director of technology for Geffen Records, the influential recording company that produces these and many other acts at the center of today's music scene.

To support the 225 employees who parlay these musicians into a $500 million operation, Griffin and his I/S staff at Los Angeles–based Geffen have created a company intranet that uses existing technology and solutions from an information environment that boasts Internet and other cyberspace solutions.

What Griffin envisioned was a fully networked, multimedia environment that would bring together the kinds of data that Geffen's employees need to do their jobs, including the music and videos of artists they represent and the financial data residing on mainframe and midrange computers at MCA, Geffen's parent corporation.

In the process, Geffen became one of the first companies to deploy Microsoft Corp.'s Windows 95 in a corporate setting and to put the operating system through its paces. The results, said Griffin, show that a combination of simple and inexpensive Windows 95 and Hypertext Markup Language (HTML) tools can be the basis of a highly flexible and robust enterprise information system, boasting communications and connectivity that rival more traditional—and, in many cases, far more expensive—approaches.

Griffin recognized the potential of the World Wide Web and the Netscape Communications Corp. Web browser to solve Geffen's needs to share information across platforms (the company uses a mix of about 60 Macintoshes and 170 PCs). The decision to build a Geffen intranet marked the inception of what Griffin and his employees came to call Geffen World, the company data crossroads that blends internal and external data resources under a single umbrella. Data could be generated either internally, as with Geffen's album release dates, or externally, as with radio airplay statistics collected by a separate company that studies the entire music industry and makes its data available on-line via modem.

"In the past, people would go to their computer and dial up various services by modem several times a day," Griffin says. Now, users only click on a button on Windows 95 and the Geffen World system accesses the information without requiring the user to know whether it resides on a company server, the Internet, or someplace else. Less flashy but equally important data, such as phone and E-mail lists, are maintained by the various users in each department, who need to learn HTML or have a suitable word processor to modify the database.

One other thing: The Geffen World intranet cost only about $10,000, Griffin says. Much of the cost went to the $40-per-seat Netscape licences; although now, with competitors giving away Web browsers for free, Griffin says he could put together Geffen's intranet for next to nothing. As for security issues, Griffin says he felt comfortable using Netscape's Secure Commerce Server, which restricts system access.

The Geffen World intranet does more than support the information needs of the company's employees. Using the internal Web pages also gives them expertise in the most important new realm of Geffen: cyberspace. As the on-line multimedia marketplace hungers for new content, Griffin also sees marketing advantages in providing Geffen's employees with Web and Internet skills. Ultimately, Geffen hopes to not just advertise in cyberspace but also create and sell music and other media content over the Internet.

Case Questions

1. How does an intranet, similar to the one employed by Geffen, differ from a local area network?
2. What are some of the advantages to Geffen of using their intranet rather than a LAN?

SOURCE: Paul Karon, "Intranet Solution Makes Geffen Shake, Rattle, and Roll," *InfoWorld*, February 12, 1996, p. 65.

IT'S YOUR TURN END OF CHAPTER MATERIALS

REVIEW QUESTIONS

1. What are the objectives of automating information processing activities?
2. What are the most important characteristics of input devices?
3. What are the most important characteristics of output devices?
4. What are the most important characteristics of a microprocessor?
5. What are the most important characteristics of secondary storage?
6. When selecting a vendor to purchase hardware from, what factors should you take into consideration?
7. What are the most important characteristics of computer software?
8. When selecting a vendor to purchase software from, what factors should you take into consideration?
9. What is a local area network?
10. Under what conditions would it make sense to implement a LAN?

DISCUSSION QUESTIONS

1. Why is it not always necessary to purchase the latest, most expensive software (e.g., word-processing package) available?
2. Researchers continue to push forward in the development of systems that can translate speech into text. Discuss the implications of this type of application for software and hardware developments.
3. The chapter cites an example of a software package that creates legal documents but that contains a logic error in the creation of a power-of-attorney (which transfers power from one person to another to conduct their affairs, such as banking transactions). Discuss some implications of this type of error. Should the software developer be held liable if an error causes financial losses for a customer?
4. Wireless networks allow devices (such as personal computers) to interact with a local area network without physically attaching cables. Discuss some advantages of using wireless networks. Why do you think that wireless networks have not taken over completely from those requiring wires?
5. The chapter cites an example of a university in which a local area network crashed, leaving students and faculty members unable to access or process much of their work. Describe how your life would be affected if you were unable to use a computer or computer network for *(a)* one day; *(b)* one week; *(c)* one month.
6. Explain what is meant by the convergence of information technologies (hardware, software, and telecommunications).

GROUP ASSIGNMENT

Individually, research the latest multimedia PC systems offered (select one vendor each). As a group, create a table that compares the different systems oncriteria you select (such as processor speed, size of RAM, input devices supported, etc.).

APPLICATION ASSIGNMENTS

1. Use PowerPoint to create a slide that contains sound, an image, and animation.
2. Identify the latest versions of a common database package (such as Microsoft's Access), a word-

processing package (such as Word), and a spreadsheet (such as Excel). Determine the minimum hardware requirements to run the packages (RAM, hard-disk storage space, etc.). At the same time, find out what the minimum hardware requirements were for the previous versions of each package. Use a word-processing package to create a table that compares these requirements.

3. Use the Internet to research the price and specifications for a personal computer you might like to own. Create a PowerPoint slide that provides the highlights of the system you identified.

CASE ASSIGNMENT: Videoconferencing: Hardware, Software, and Telecommunications

By the mid-1990s, electronic companies and telecom operators were scrambling to forge alliances to feed a market that was expected to grow rapidly in the next few years: desktop videoconferencing. Industry analysts believed the sector had reached a landmark similar in its development to the one that fax machines had reached some years earlier. Indeed, in the late 1980s, fax machine sales took off after being available for more than a decade. The critical factor was agreement on industrywide standards that enabled fax machines to communicate with each other, no matter who made them. Customers were no longer locked in to one supplier, and prices fell quickly.

Desktop conferencing enables users to dial up a colleague or customer from the PC screen; the connection is made in the same way as a conventional telephone call. The caller's and receiver's pictures are picked up by small cameras, some with a wide angle lens, on top of the PC. Users can share data and images, which can be copied and downloaded for printing onto any of the PCs participating in a conference call. Or, within local area networks, several people can be called to take part in an internal conference (some systems would do more, but the size of the screen picture became smaller). Each user appeared in a window on everybody's PC. The mix and sizes of those pictures could be changed by the participants.

For example, law firms were using live data exchange that enabled simultaneous editing of legal documents, and medical teams were using the technology to look at and exchange notes on x-rays and other images and data across the globe. Users could type or write with electronic pens on shared documents, changing text, annotating documents, or working on spreadsheets together. Manufacturing and engineering design teams in different offices around the world were working on draft designs on-screen; insurance companies could take a customer's signature for a legally binding policy approval without the two having to be in the same place—they were able to share the document on PCs at home, in the office, or in a kiosk.

Agreement on standards was driving the videoconferencing market. Intel, the world's biggest chip maker and a producer of personal conferencing equipment, agreed to fall in with the rest of the industry on a sectorwide standard. This agreement followed a year-long battle in which Intel was accused of trying to create a market for its next generation of PC chips.

The standard—known as H320—governed the technology needed to compress and decompress (codec) the images, sound, and data to be transmitted on telephone lines to enable live electronic meetings. The industry had agreed on H320 in 1992, but Intel produced its own standard, called Indeo, which the company argued was more efficient. Both are algorithms, or mathematical formulae, for compression and decompression.

Intel's argument was that since videoconferencing needed very high processing power, the best approach was to use powerful microprocessors and to allow the conferencing applications to be driven by software. Many producers, including market leaders PictureTel, Compression Labs, and GEC Plessy Telecommunications (GPT), believed that a better approach was to slot extra processing power on a card into computers to deal with video compressing. This method would not slow down or interfere with other applications. This approach won.

Intel's motivation to be in the market was clearly to sell and create a market for the next generation of PC chips. Intel made the 486 chip, which was being copied by other chip makers at the time. Since chip makers were soon to match Intel's more powerful Pentium chip in performance, the company wanted to plug the gap by finding a market for yet more powerful chips.

Intel denied it had been trying to skew the market in its favor and said it was committed to cross-industry standards. But Intel still argued that the future lay in increasingly powerful chips and that, as such, it was well-placed in an expanding market. "We are not shy about saying that videoconferencing is an application that will drive the demand for high-performance microprocessors well into the next decade," said Michael Sullivan, an Intel public relations manager. "Given that we are a leader in microprocessors, that is good for us." Other vendors include AT&T, Compression Labs, GPT, VTEL, and the BT/IBM joint venture.

Prices in the desktop sector were falling rapidly, and analysts believed the equipment was starting to look affordable for the mass market of business users. "The H320 standards were the basics on which the market was moving forward, but users wanted to see prices come down further," said an expert consultant. "Prices needed to head for about $1,000 to $1,500 (in 1995 dollars) for the add-ons that enable videoconferencing (excluding PCs). That was the sort of price at which users said it was no longer a difficult decision."

Other factors besides standards were driving the market. PCs and networks were so widely used that an aversion to appearing live on screen was disappearing. The technologies were improving so that pictures were clearer, and some companies were reducing sound echo and poor synchronization between sound and pictures.

In addition, digital telephone lines were becoming more available, particularly in Germany, Great Britain, and other parts of Europe, although the cost was still relatively high. In the United States, digital lines were cheaper but less available. Conventional analog telephone lines lacked the capacity of digital ISDN (integrated services digital network) to transmit the quality of images, data, and audio needed for multimedia.

The view was that desktop videoconferencing would replace telephone calls rather than business meetings. Therefore, telecom companies, which, along with software makers, were forging alliances with the electronics sector to provide videoconferencing, started to cut their charges for rental, connection, and calls on ISDN lines. The market's highest growth rates were shifting toward desktop systems—PC-based ISDN—and away from the large, expensive studio- and room-based systems that dominated the market at the time.

However, the technology and standards that would bring the greatest potential for business users was yet to come. In the mid-1990s, standards covered only some basics of transmission and interpretability. There was still no agreement on standards across different systems that would allow users to share and exchange data, enabling users to work on documents jointly from remote points on different PCs. Data sharing was possible only between systems from the same manufacturer. The industry was optimistic that a standard (T120) governing data exchange was to be agreed upon through the International Telecommunications Union, the standard-setting body.

Although the industry's estimates were at the time that the worldwide market for videoconferencing systems was to grow from less than $400 million in 1994 to $550 million in the year 2000, some observers still said that videoconferencing was looking for a market rather than responding to a need. On the flip side, suppliers said that face-to-face contact, even if not television quality, would greatly improve business communication as well as cutting the time and expense of business travel in increasing global markets.

Questions

1. Is videoconferencing a software application? A hardware application? A telecommunications application?
2. Who in the Information Technology Department of an organization should be responsible for choosing a videoconferencing system and managing it?
3. Do you think that videoconferencing is a good idea? Give examples of situations where videoconferencing capabilities would be useful.

SOURCE: The story has been adapted from an article by Sheila Jones in the *Financial Times,* May 16, 1995, p. 14.

CHAPTER 7 Information Systems Development

After reading this chapter, you should have a better understanding of the process required for building, implementing, and maintaining an information system. More specifically, you should be able to:

- Provide a brief history of the changes in methodologies for information systems development, including the evolution of I/S development techniques.
- Understand how information systems development may be viewed as a problem-solving activity, using the rational problem-solving approach.
- Describe the different roles within the I/S development process: user, analyst, designer, programmer, project manager, and database analyst.
- Describe a generic I/S development process consisting of six phases: definition of goals, definition of information requirements, generation of alternatives, design of the chosen alternative, implementation, and evaluation.
- Explain the variables involved in the decision to build software in-house versus buying from an external vendor.
- Explain how the I/S cube may be used to aid I/S development and I/S project management.

Okay, I agree that there is a need for a new information system. Now what do I do?

INTRODUCTION

An information system is composed of the business goals to be supported by the system (the *purpose*), the *people* that run and use the system, the *procedures* needed for the system to be successfully integrated into the organization's flow of work, the *information* being processed and communicated by the system, and the information and communication *technologies* used to implement the system. Deciding what specific combination of these components to use for any given information system can be a very complex, time-consuming task. There are usually a vast number of options available, not only in the different components of an information system, but also in the design and development process itself. After all, since information systems are different, why should the development process used to build them be the same?

In this chapter, we argue that the development process should be custom tailored for the type of information system being developed. Nevertheless, although the processes may differ, the development phases are the same; it is the specific activities within each of the phases that vary from system to system. Furthermore, it helps to keep in mind that the development of an information system is essentially a problem-solving activity; we have a specific problem or opportunity that we believe can be best addressed by implementing an information system. Before we explore this notion too much further, it is first useful to examine the development of information systems from a historical perspective.

Historical View of Information Systems Development. The development of information systems has changed dramatically over the relatively short life span of information technology, and we can expect this change to continue. Forty years ago, computers were very expensive and only a few companies had them. Since computers were a rarity, relatively few individuals possessed the knowledge and skills required to effectively program and use them. At that time, **computer programs** were developed by a handful of computer vendors and the companies who purchased the computers. The programs were written in machine or assembly languages and were difficult to use and modify. Typically, the focus of those programs was on accounting applications. Accounting applications consist of repetitive tasks with very clear and quantifiable rules. In those days, accounting required a great deal of manual processing of data, and therefore the cost justification for computerization was straightforward. Most of the applications were custom designed for a specific organization, even though the applications had a lot of generic aspects to them. For example, each organization developed its own accounts receivable program, although the programs were very similar.

As computers decreased in cost and proliferated to more and more organizations, many recognized that the development of numerous, similar programs for the same application (such as accounts receivable) represented an expensive and unnecessary duplication of effort. Companies emerged that focused on the development of software (computer programs) for specific applications and industries.

Computer vendors also increased the scope of their product offerings, bundling computer programs and support with their hardware. There remained a great deal of duplication of effort, but most organizations now found they had options as to whether to develop the programs themselves or hire another firm to do the development for them.

By the late 1960s and into the 1970s, the number of computers and computer applications was growing rapidly. The emergence of third-generation languages (e.g., FORTRAN, COBOL, BASIC) made it easier to write computer programs, and computer-programming skills spread. As computer programming proliferated, software developers recognized the need for more organized and efficient development procedures.

Methodologies started to emerge that used the philosophy of breaking complex programs into smaller, self-contained modules. These methodologies were referred to as **structured analysis and design.**[1] By copying and re-using existing program modules that were designed for common functions, programmers were able to reduce some of the duplication of effort, shorten the time needed to complete new programs, and increase the reliability of the programs. The use of a modular program design also made it easier to correct errors or make changes at a later time. If there was an error or a modification in a computer program, instead of checking or rewriting the entire program, it was only necessary to revise the module that was affected.

In addition to the increased availability of prepackaged software (programs designed to address the needs of numerous organizations), the 1980s saw the expansion of **end-user computing.** This term is applied to describe situations where the ultimate user of the system (a financial analyst, for example) is also the developer of the system. It has been argued that the introduction of electronic spreadsheet software for personal computers was the single most important event in the subsequent explosion of personal computer adoption and use. This was because electronic spreadsheets were so easy to learn and use that non-information systems personnel could quickly develop small applications on their own. Since it was no longer necessary to have a computer science degree to get a computer to create a financial model or produce a report, individuals from all business disciplines (e.g., marketing, finance, accounting, etc.) began to use computer systems to create their own applications.

In addition to easily customized packages and electronic spreadsheets, the 1980s and 1990s saw rapid growth in the development and use of what was termed *fourth-generation languages* (4GL) or *nonprocedural programming languages* and tools. These tools (such as FOCUS, RAMIS, and the application development part of many database management systems, or DBMS) were so easy to use and provided so many prewritten functions (e.g., report-generating routines) that they shortened considerably the development time required to build an information system.

These tools also encouraged the use of a **prototyping** development approach, where the developer (who might also be the final user) would rapidly create a small working model, or prototype, of a system. Since the fourth generation tools allowed the computer programs to be changed quickly and easily, a user could provide feedback on the prototype to the developer and see the changes almost on the spot. The design of information systems became a highly interactive and iterative process.

[1]Appendix B describes systems development tools and techniques in detail.

The IBM microcomputer and electronic spreadsheet software were the major drivers of the use of computers by nontechnical individuals. Photo courtesy of IBM.

Information systems specialists not only applied their skills to developing new information systems, but also to improving the tools they had available to support the development process. This new software, termed **computer-aided software engineering (CASE),** was designed to store diagrams and descriptions of the user requirements and make them available to all members of the development team. CASE tools also provided some prototyping capabilities, and could be used in a limited capacity to generate computer programs.

By the mid 1990s, many I/S professionals were beginning to question the continued reliance on structured analysis and design techniques. Indeed, prepackaged software was now available for most common applications, and it was much easier to customize it to suit any particular organization. Many companies no longer developed major new applications internally, but instead hired outside consulting firms (including computer and software vendors) to do the development for them (a decision called *outsourcing*). These consultants typically had expertise in a given type of application and industry, and could modify existing programs quickly to meet a specific organization's needs.

Another development during the 1980s and 1990s was the creation and use of what were termed **object-oriented programming (OOP)** languages, and the subsequent change to object-oriented design (OOD) techniques. An object is a self-contained piece of programming code that exhibits certain characteristics. For example, a car (the object) can be defined by a series of characteristics, like a brand, a color, the number of doors, weight, and so forth. For programming purpose, a document is an object with a set of characteristics: its contents, its length, its format, its location, its medium.

In an object-oriented approach, the developer first defines the objects that are needed in a new (or revised) information system. If the needed objects already exist, they are re-used. If they don't exist, the developer selects objects that are close (e.g., you want the object *truck* rather than *car*), and then modifies them as needed. The original CASE tools and database management systems were not designed to support OOP or OOD; this was a factor to consider when developers had to decide whether to stay with their more traditional approaches or to embrace object-oriented approaches. Soon, as object-oriented techniques gained popularity, fourth-generation languages, CASE tools, and DBMS were developed to support the object-oriented approach.

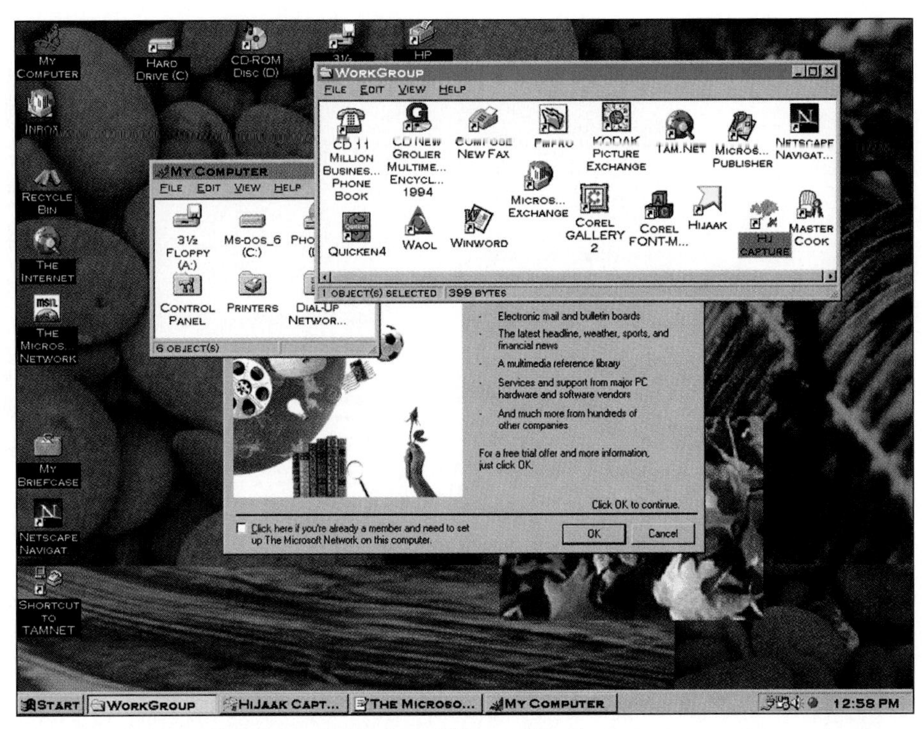

Icon-driven interfaces like Microsoft's Windows 95 have allowed users to concentrate on *what* they need to do, rather than *how* they do it. Photo courtesy of Microsoft.

The development of easy-to-use software interfaces—such as the Apple Macintosh operating system, IBM's OS/2, or Windows from Microsoft—coupled with the explosion in networking and the easy access to external databases brought the latest change in user behavior. Today, users want to pull data and information from a variety of sources and computers using one common interface. And they do so without having to write a single line of computer code. Users can concentrate on *what* they want and need to do with computers rather than on *how* to get the computers to do it.

Three decades ago, a captive computer user was forced to select from a few, not very attractive software options, and work through a technician that often did not understand his or her needs. Today, a user can roam freely through cyberspace, using highly sophisticated and friendly packages to cut and paste information from a variety of databases. The flexibility and power available to a computer user has come a long way, and so have the tools to design information systems.

In addition to the changes in the information systems development software and processes during the last 30 years (e.g., 4GLs, CASE tools, end-user computing, etc.), the hardware environment changed as well. From the large mainframes of the 1960s and 1970s, to the minicomputers of the 1970s and 1980s, to the microcomputers of the 1980s and 1990s, the changes have been dramatic. Although all types of computers (often referred to as *platforms*) were still in use in the 1990s, the trend continues toward using the smaller, less expensive, but ever more powerful desktop and portable machines.

The availability of these highly powerful computers, which were sold at reasonable prices and could do an enormous amount of independent processing, led to the development of the **client-server configuration.** In this configuration, many personal computers and workstations (*clients*) are attached to one or more computer *servers* (these could be powerful personal computers, minicomputers, or mainframes, depending on the application). The server contains a variety of programs that can be shared by the clients as well as being a repository of data and files. This node computer is called a *server* because it serves, or delivers, programs and files to the networked computers.

The move to a client-server environment was difficult for many organizations, since their internal I/S departments had little or no experience with such arrangements. For three decades, I/S departments had worked within an environment where all computer power was centralized in large mainframe computers, and where most applications were developed by them. Later, I/S departments developed expertise working on standalone personal computers. But the client-server configuration requires knowledge of telecommunications and networking, and an information architecture based on decentralization and flexibility—distributed databases and so forth—and few companies had that vision and expertise. As a result, many companies called in consulting firms to help them make the transition to a client-server environment.

The broad availability of software and the range of consulting services caused I/S departments to change their focus from being a shop to develop software applications to a shop in charge of implementing the proper information technology architecture. Basically, the role of the I/S department went from being the main provider of software solutions to being an internal consultant and facilitator, implementing the I/T infrastructure necessary to maintain the organization's competitiveness. Today, the major responsibilities of the typical I/S department are:

1. Developing an information technology plan to support the strategic objectives of the business.
2. Developing, operating, and maintaining existing inter-enterprise and enterprisewide information systems and databases.
3. Installing and maintaining local and wide-area networks.
4. Evaluating, acquiring, and integrating new hardware and software products (workstations, office communication systems, operating systems, productivity tools).
5. Training and supporting internal customers (including defining their I/S needs).
6. Negotiating with and overseeing outside I/S consultants in the acquisition and development of new information technology and systems.

Table 7–1 provides a quick overview of the historical perspective of changes in I/S development discussed in this section.

Despite all of the changes we have seen, many of the concepts and techniques associated with structured analysis and design are still useful and applicable today. Few people would argue that structured techniques should be used to develop information systems in all situations. However, an understanding of the structured analysis and design methodology provides a good starting point for examining ways to reduce the difficulties in developing and acquiring information systems. With an understanding of the structured analysis and design methodologies, we can identify ways to reduce risks in the development process—risks of being over-budget or late, or of delivering a nonperforming system—through project management techniques.

TABLE 7-1 Historical Perspective of I/S Development

Decade	*Development Methodology*	*Role of I/S Department*	*Who Provides*	*Number of Providers*	*Hardware*	*Development Software*
1960s	Varied and haphazard	Implementors	Computer vendors	Few	Mainframe	Assembly
1970s	SA&D	Developers; central role	Computer and software vendors, I/S departments	Several	Mini, Mainframe	3GL
1980s	SA&D, prototyping, End-user computing	Developers; diminishing role	Computer and software vendors, I/S departments, end-users	Many	PC, mini	3GL, 4GL
1990s	SA&D, prototyping, end-user computing, Outsourcing	Consultants; peripheral role	Computer and software vendors, I/S departments, end-users	Multitude	PC, client-server	4GL, OOPs

CHOOSING AN APPLICATION DEVELOPMENT STRATEGY

In Chapter 5, we introduced a three-dimensional scheme to classify information systems and entitled it the *information systems cube.* The three dimensions were the *scope* of the information system (ranging from individual to interorganizational), the *complexity* of the task being supported (ranging from well-structured to unstructured), and the necessary *information richness* (ranging from sparse to robust) to provide the required support. The I/S cube (repeated here in Figure 7-1) can also help in determining how best to manage the development process for a specific information system.

On the one hand, the easiest system to develop and manage is one that addresses a situation we would find at the lower left-hand corner of the cube: an application for *one user,* where the inputs necessary to carry out the task and outputs from the task are very *well understood and structured,* and the information richness required is *sparse* (textual information only). Consider the example of an information system designed to list accounts receivable by date (i.e., the *aged accounts receivable* report). This would be used by a single person (possibly the collections manager); the inputs and outputs are highly structured (sales records, aged accounts receivable report), and the information richness required is sparse (alphanumeric data).

On the other hand, the hardest system to develop and manage is one that addresses a situation at the upper right-hand corner of the cube: an application for many users from different organizations, where the task at hand is complex and ill-structured, and the information richness is very robust. Consider the example of a videoconferencing system designed to exchange blueprints of car components. The system would be used by designers from the car parts company and the car manufacturer, the exchanges of data are unstructured (conversations about a variety of topics requiring access to a variety of data), and the information richness would be robust since the system would need to manipulate video, audio, and text.

We now discuss how each of the three dimensions of the cube affects the choice of a development strategy.

FIGURE 7-1 The Information Systems Cube

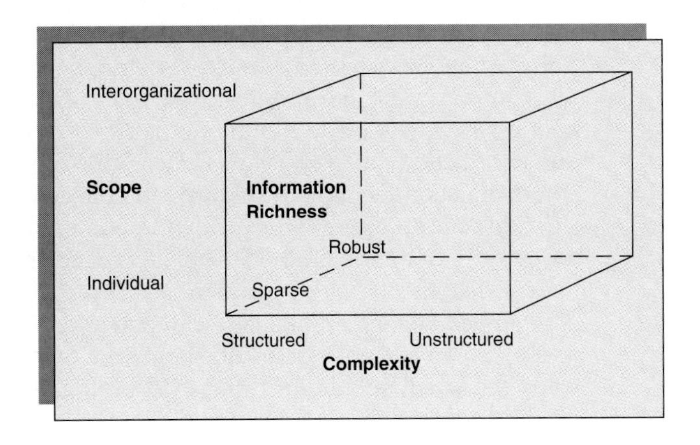

Application Scope. Application scope refers to the number of people the information system will support. Applications that support a single individual are, in general, much easier and quicker to develop than applications that support a large number of individuals. The primary reason is that the developer only has to consider the needs and desires of one person; there are no conflicts of interest, priorities, or preferences to deal with (remember the analogy of building a single-family home from Chapter 5). Also, quite frequently individual applications require little interaction with other information systems. If the only interaction is the extraction of data from an existing database, for example, then there is less concern for maintaining data standards and other system compatibility issues.

When the scope of the application moves from the individual to the workgroup, additional considerations come into play. Now the developer has to consider the needs and wants of multiple people, some of which may conflict (remember the analogy of building a condominium from Chapter 5). The issue may be simple, such as the display preferences of different members of the workgroup. Some people prefer to have information displayed in tabular (table) format, while others prefer graphical (chart) displays. How do we decide which to use? Can we accommodate both? Other more complex issues include the need for simultaneous access to data.

Task Complexity. Task complexity refers to the degree of structure in the inputs to, the outputs from, and perhaps to a greater extent, the decision processes of the required information system. A highly structured decision-making process is one where the decision can be broken into a series of sequential, predetermined, well-understood steps and where the decision variables are known and change in a predictable manner. One example is the inventory control task of reordering raw materials for a production process where lead times, prices, and demand are known and constant. An example of an unstructured decision-making process would be the selection of the body design for a new sport utility vehicle. For such a task, it is necessary to consider visual aesthetics, multiple functional issues such as air drag coefficients and internal cargo space, and so on. It would be impossible to establish a set of steps that would lead to the "optimal" output (vehicle body design), since the optimal output doesn't exist.

Thus, there is an inverse relationship between the structure of the task and the difficulty of developing information systems to support that task.

Information Richness. Information richness is a measure of the variety of data and the complexity of the information needed to support a certain task. Information richness is closely related to the complexity of the technology. Basically, the richer the information needed (e.g., video), the more complex the information and communication technology required to collect, analyze, and transmit it.

Consider an example involving the communication of alphanumeric data (the lowest level of information richness, i.e., sparse information) between two organizations: a manufacturing firm ordering raw materials from one of its suppliers. The communication can be handled with narrow bandwidth, twisted-pair wires, and the messages can be processed with standard computer capabilities, without having to worry too much about communication protocols and standards since the messages can be formatted into simple text files.

Now consider an application that accommodates contract negotiations between two companies. Since for negotiations face-to-face interaction is typically preferable—to enable each party to observe cues such as body language—an information system to support this task would include capabilities such as a videoconferencing or personal videoconferencing system (the next best thing to actually being there). Such a system would require more complex video and sound processing and transmission capabilities, to accommodate the higher information richness of this application (the information richness is robust). These additional capabilities increase the complexity of the technology involved, and hence, the complexity of the process to develop the application.

The Relative Complexity of Information Technology. The I/S cube is a useful starting point when trying to plan ahead for an information systems development project; but we need to consider one more dimension: the *relative complexity* of the information technology involved. A budget application requiring only an electronic spreadsheet on a personal computer will be much simpler to develop than a multimedia training program to be distributed on CD-ROM disks. Note, however, the importance of the term *relative* complexity. Relative to what? Relative to the expertise of the person or persons who will do the development. For example, someone who has spent years using multimedia authoring technology will find it much easier to develop the training program than someone who has used only word-processing packages in the past.

Roles in Information Systems Development. Regardless of the approach used to develop a new information system, certain roles must be performed. In the case of an individual application (such as preparing a budget for a manager), all of the roles might be performed by a single person. In very large, complex applications spanning multiple organizations and geographic regions, literally hundreds of people might be involved. The larger and more complex the application development project, the more specialized the roles. The more important of these are:

1. The **user**—the person who interacts with the system when it is completed. This role includes those individuals required to input data, as well as those who use the outputs from the system.
2. The **system analyst**—the person responsible for describing the existing system and defining the information requirements of the new system.

The complexity of technology is relative to the experience of the user. Photos courtesy of Strauss & Curtis/Offshoot Stock (left) and Frank Herholdt/Tony Stone Images (right).

3. The **system designer**—the person responsible for using the information requirements to generate detailed specifications for the new system.
4. The **programmer**—the person responsible for using the system specifications to write and test program code, and implement the new system.
5. The **database analyst**—the person responsible for defining the new data and databases when required and ensuring compliance with existing databases and data dictionaries.
6. The **project manager**—the person responsible for overseeing the system development project from beginning to end, including the postimplementation evaluation of the system.

You should note that these roles and titles evolved in the era of developing large-scale information systems, doing so in-house, and using procedural languages. Although titles such as programmer/analyst are still fairly common, individuals with that title today may just as commonly find themselves spending time using database languages on a personal computer to create quick prototype applications as they may be involved in developing a multi-user order fulfillment system. With the advent of end-user-developed applications, a title per se may not give you an understanding of the role that a person plays in developing an information system. Today, people with titles such as financial analyst or human resource specialist find themselves performing the roles of a system designer, system analyst, and programmer.

Given the large amounts of money, time, and other resources consumed in designing, building, and implementing information systems, **project management** has become a critical and difficult responsibility. Therefore, an important role is the one played by project managers. Project managers need to ensure that an appropriate development approach is selected, that project milestones are established and used to keep the project on schedule, that the project team has the appropriate set of skills, and so on. Traditionally, project managers came from the I/S department. More recently, project managers have been frequently drawn from the user community.

We now turn our attention to project management and the other activities that must be performed across the different phases of a project to ensure its success.

PROJECT MANAGEMENT

Managing large-scale information systems development projects is a very demanding task, and good project managers are highly sought after. The project manager uses various tools and techniques to try and keep the project on track; the goals are to have everything completed on time and within budget. These goals sound simple enough. However, estimates are that up to 80 percent of all information systems

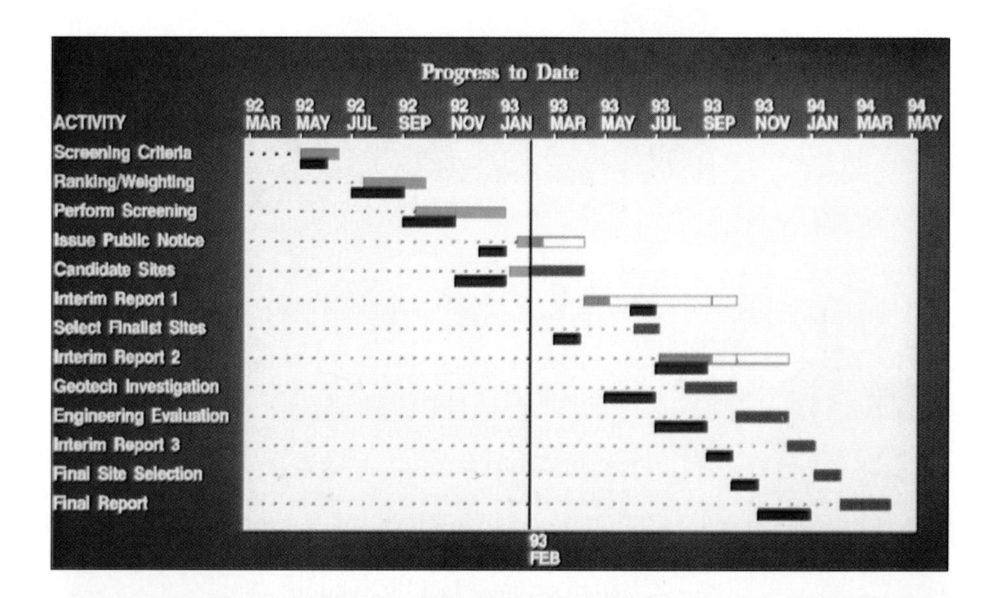

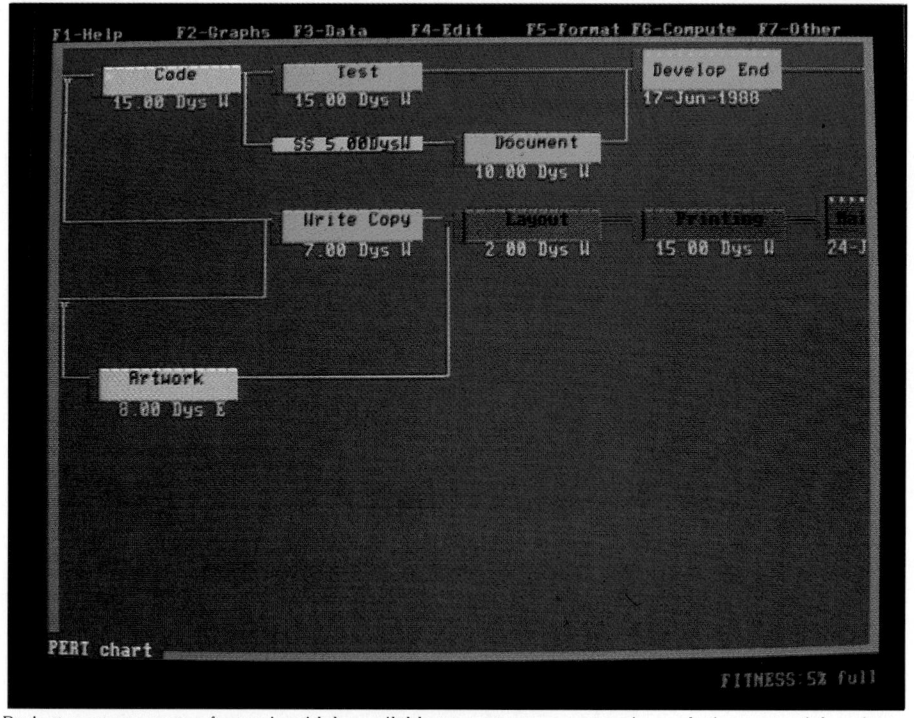

Project management software is widely available to support managers in analyzing potential project delays and their implications. Photos courtesy of Microsoft.

projects are finished late, or over budget, or both—and sometimes very much over budget and very late. For example, we previously mentioned the new international airport at Denver which opened in 1995, two years late and several billion dollars over budget, to a large extent because of a defective computer program that was supposed to manage and handle all the passengers' luggage.

Although there are quite a few different tools and techniques available for managing I/S development projects, they can be divided into two basic categories: integration tools and planning and control tools. Integration tools are communication devices that link the project team's work to the users, and also link the project team members to one another. Planning and control tools help structure the sequence of tasks and estimate the resources (time, money, people) needed for each task. These tools also help evaluate progress on the project, and indicate when and where corrective action is needed.

Let's assume, for example, that a company wishes to implement a new information system that will allow it to order replacement material directly from its suppliers, without contacting the suppliers by telephone or mail. The project manager has to determine in detail every step that will need to be completed, from determining the specific and measurable objectives of the new system, through the implementation and maintenance of it. The project manager may wish to use a Gantt chart, PERT chart, or some other tool to help plan the sequence of steps and measure progress against those steps. He or she will also need to maintain open and effective communication between the project team (systems analysts and programmers, and representatives from the suppliers' firms) and the users of the new system (most likely purchasing agents), perhaps having the users approve diagrams and output mock-ups (sample reports and screens) prepared by the project team members. It will also be important to ensure open communication within the project team, using facilities such as electronic mail and team meetings.

The type of project management tool is directly related to the type of information system being developed, that is, to the application scope, task complexity, information richness, and technology complexity involved. The larger the scope of the system, the more unstructured the task, the greater the information richness, and the more complex the technology (relative to the expertise of the developers), the greater the need for formal project management techniques.

Table 7–2 provides a way to estimate in advance how complex the development process will be, and also gives an assessment of the relative importance of project management. We can see from the table, that if the project consists of the development of a system to support an individual in performing a well-structured task requiring textual information only and of technology that is well known, then we don't need to have an experienced project manager overseeing the project to ensure its success. On the other hand, if the project consists of developing an interorganizational system to address a task that is not well structured, requiring information that includes video and sound and a technology that is not proven, then having an experienced and knowledgeable project manager becomes critical to the success of the project.

We now return to the process used to develop information systems. What we present is a generic systems development life cycle, with the assumption that we are considering a relatively major, enterprisewide system. Later, we will relax that assumption and consider the necessary modifications in the development life cycle for systems designed to support individuals and workgroups.

TABLE 7–2 I/S Development Strategies and Project Management

Application Scope	*Task Complexity*	*Information Richness*	*Technology Complexity*	*Complexity of Development*	*Project Management Expertise*
Low (individual)	Low (structured)	Low (sparse)	Low	Very low	Unimportant
			High	Low	Not critical
		High (robust)	Low	Low	Not critical
			High	Moderate	Relevant
	High (unstructured)	Low (sparse)	Low	Moderate	Relevant
			High	Moderate	Relevant
		High (robust)	Low	Moderate	Relevant
			High	High	Important
High (interorganizational)	Low (structured)	Low (sparse)	Low	Low	Not critical
			High	Moderate	Relevant
		High (robust)	Low	Moderate	Relevant
			High	High	Important
	High (unstructured)	Low (sparse)	Low	Moderate	Relevant
			High	High	Important
		High (robust)	Low	High	Important
			High	Very high	Critical

THE SYSTEMS DEVELOPMENT PROCESS

Information systems do not appear out of the sky; nor do development projects begin without some real or perceived need. The modification of existing information systems or the development of new ones is a problem-solving activity. As such, we can apply a rational decision-making approach to the **systems development process.** We first identify the problem or opportunity that we need to address (the purpose of the system); we then identify alternative ways to address the problem (different design alternatives); we decide on the best alternative (based on cost, ease of implementation, and fulfillment of goals); and, finally, we implement it. Although there are situations where a rational decision-making process may be overkill, it is always a good starting point.

The formal process of developing information systems is commonly referred to as the **systems development life cycle (SDLC).** The life cycle is a series of recommended steps, or phases, designed to reduce the risks of developing systems. Although the actual number of steps, and/or the titles given to each step, may vary from organization to organization, the general structure of the life cycle and content of the different steps are similar (see Figure 7–2).

FIGURE 7-2 System Development Life Cycle: Traditional and Problem-Solving Based

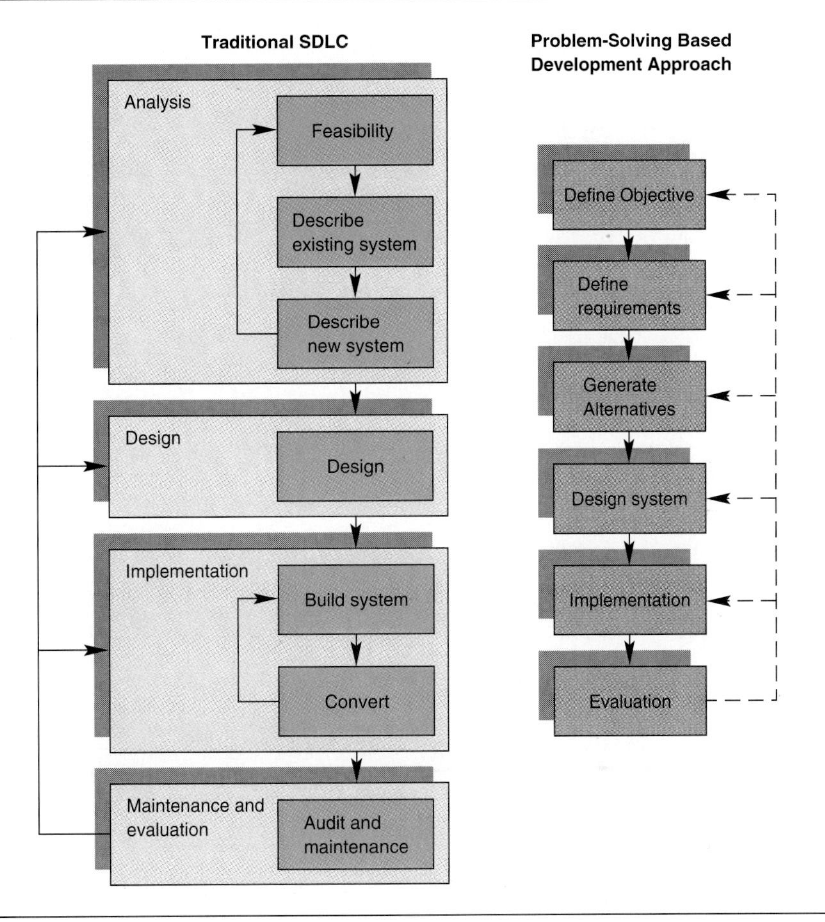

The process of following a formal SDLC methodology and using structured analysis and design tools (described in Appendix B) provides numerous advantages when developing information systems. Structured analysis and design tools support a formal, graphical, and modular approach to designing I/S.

The formal analysis provides the opportunity for the I/S specialist to gain a good understanding of the user area and activities. The structured system specifications are provided in graphical format; therefore, they are relatively easy to understand and facilitate communication among users and designers and among designers and programmers. The **modular program design** approach, by partitioning the programs into smaller, self-contained modules, allows for systems that tend to be brought on line more quickly (i.e., modules can be implemented without waiting for the whole system to be finished) and tend to be easier to maintain once the system has been implemented.

The structured SDLC approach had a tremendously positive effect on the systems development efforts up to the 1980s, but its usefulness has declined since then. There are still many situations where the SDLC or a variation of it can be employed productively. However, for small software projects (and there are many

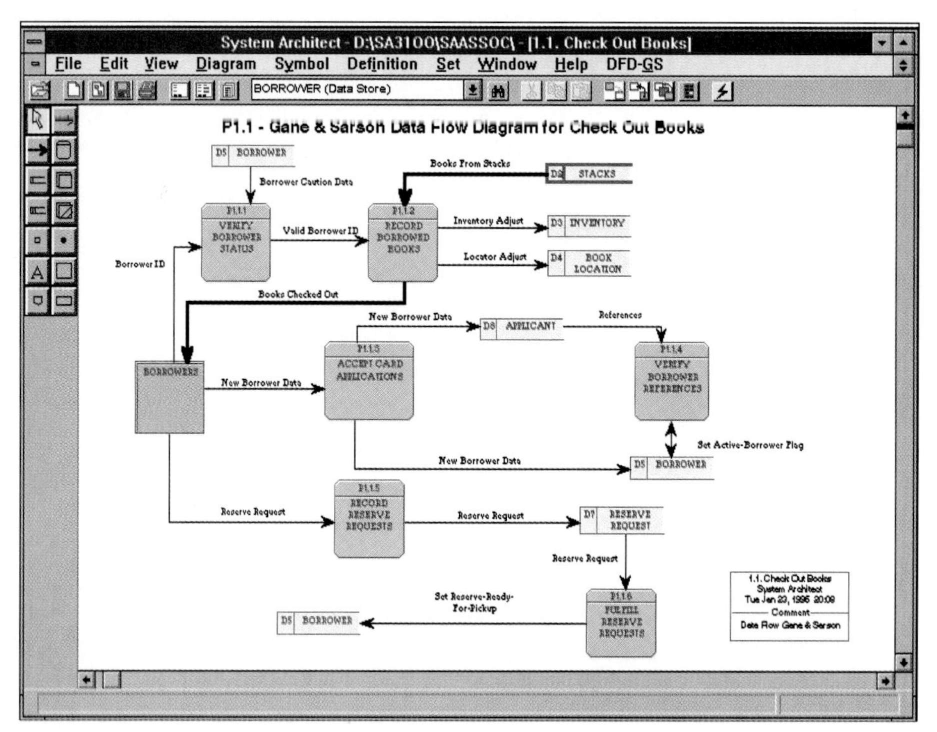

Specialists systems such as CASE tools help developers create new information systems. Photo courtesy of Popkin Systems, Inc.

more of these now than 10 years ago) the structured SDLC approach may not be appropriate, since the formality of the process can be very time consuming, expensive (I/S specialists aren't cheap, nor is the time of the users), and somewhat cumbersome.

One of the limitations of the structured techniques of the SDLC is that they tend to focus on the data *processing* required. Also, quite frequently there is an emphasis on how best to generate certain *outputs,* such as sales invoices or customer receipts. If the requirements are well defined and relatively stable, meaning that few changes will be needed later, this approach works well. A complementary but somewhat different approach is to focus on the *data* required for a certain task. This approach has been called **information engineering.**

Consider, for a moment, the Boyd's Construction Supply Company (BCSC). BCSC allows certain contractors among its customers to charge purchases to their account, and then bills them on a monthly basis. BCSC wants to use information systems for its record keeping. BCSC needs a program that will record all purchases by contractors, generate customer receipts, and assign the purchases to the proper accounts. BCSC also needs a program to record any payments made by the contractors, as well as a program to calculate the amount owed at the end of the month and to send bills to the contractors.

This type of application is relatively stable: the outputs are well-defined, and the processing required probably doesn't change very much. There could be some changes in business policies that could affect the programs, but these changes are usually not too frequent. For example, BCSC might decide to start charging interest on overdue accounts. This would require changing the program that generates the monthly bills to reflect the new corporate policy.

Now consider a different application which illustrates an information engineering approach. The marketing manager for BCSC wishes to focus her efforts on their contractor customers. She wants to know which contractors purchased the most supplies overall, or whether contractors' purchasing preferences are different than retail customers within each product category (for example, do contractors tend to purchase higher-grade, more expensive roof shingles?), or how sensitive contractors are to price changes, or some such information. As she comes up with new analyses and thinks of new questions she would like answered, her information needs change. The marketing manager's information needs change very frequently; she would be unable to tell an I/S specialist exactly what reports she needs, because she doesn't know herself in advance.

In this example, the *data* required to support the marketing manager are relatively stable (such as inventory data, purchase/sales records, and detailed contractor information), but the *output requirements* (reports) and *processes* required to generate those reports change frequently. In this application, it would be better to ensure that appropriate databases are developed and maintained, and then provide the marketing manager with appropriate access and development tools to query the databases. One of the critical design issues in this application is ease of use—the manager's time is too valuable to have her spend it trying to figure out how to get a simple report generated. The tools would include an easy-to-use database language (or report generator), and possibly an electronic spreadsheet. We would need, as project managers of the system, to ensure that the marketing manager has the proper training on how to use these packages, and access to expert support when required.

A development process following the structured analysis and design approach and using an I/S designer might help define an appropriate database for the marketing manager's application. However, the process would be too slow, given that the manager's information and reporting needs are fluid and changing. Having the manager apply user-friendly tools to fulfill her own processing needs would be an example of the end-user development mentioned earlier; the actual trial-and-error process she will likely employ to come up with a system could be described as prototyping.

The Approach

The environment for developing information systems has changed dramatically since the emergence of the structured techniques and the SDLC. First, the capabilities of information technology have greatly increased. Second, the organizational needs for information systems have expanded far beyond data processing and report generation; increased support for organizational communication is one example. Third, the development tools have improved substantially. No longer do we think of developing an information system exclusively in terms of writing computer programs from scratch using a procedural language such as COBOL or C. Finally, users are much more computer literate; most organizational members are more comfortable with information technology and have a better appreciation of its potential.

The organizational needs and information technology capabilities, including developmental tools, will continue to change and evolve. For this reason, suggesting a specific process of development for information systems is a futile effort. We prefer to offer a more generic development process, which can accommodate changes in technology. Although the roles, tools, and techniques may change, the guiding principles and concepts behind the proposed generic process will not. Our suggested process for developing information systems consists of the following six steps (as shown in Figure 7–2):

1. Define goals and objectives.
2. Define information needs (requirements).
3. Generate and evaluate alternatives.
4. Design the chosen alternative.
5. Implement and maintain.
6. Evaluate the performance of the system.

In a sense, this process is similar to the SDLC; the difference lies in the *way* activities are performed within the different phases and the range of these activities. Indeed, the generic process we propose is quite flexible. The development process addresses those instances when the use of structured techniques such as *data flow diagrams* and *structure charts* (see Appendix B) is appropriate, but it also addresses those instances when the decision is to buy a ready-made package from one of several vendors, each of which offers several packages. The problem solving–based process suggested here recognizes that the development process for a system to help a human resource manager prepare presentations should be vastly different than the process used to upgrade a bank's automated teller system. We now take a closer look at each of the six phases.

Define Goals and Objectives

The single most important step in any systems development process is to clearly define the goals and objectives of the new system and to relate those goals to the **critical success factors (CSF)** of the business. You can think of CSFs (a term coined by Jack Rockart, a professor of information systems at the Massachusetts Institute of Technology) as those activities and measures on which an organization absolutely has to do well to succeed—for example, safety in the case of an airline. CSFs can also be linked to the strategy of the company, such as being the low-cost producer, or differentiating their products, or obtaining a marketing niche.

Although defining goals may sound obvious, it is often difficult to do; and unfortunately, it is seldom done well. It is usually a good idea to start with fairly broad goals, and then try to identify very narrow, measurable objectives. If decision makers can clearly state and agree upon the goals and objectives, and measures for determining whether or not those goals and objectives have been achieved, the rest of the project will generally go much smoother.

Let's return to the BCSC example for a moment, and take a look at two different opportunities for information system projects. In the first, the marketing manager has a feeling that the company's contractor customers haven't been paying their bills as promptly as in the past, and that BCSC has written off some accounts where customers have failed to pay entirely. She is concerned that BCSC may be extending credit to customers who could become, or already are, bad debts, and she wants to check up on it.

For the second opportunity, we'll consider one of the situations described previously: the marketing manager wants more information about contractors and their purchases to help her plan more effective marketing efforts. Let's define the goals and objectives for these two systems.

For the first system:

Goal—Reduce the incidence of extending credit to high-risk contractor customers.
Objective—Obtain accurate credit and payment histories of contractor customers; establish and enforce company policies to reduce bad debt write-offs to a maximum of 3 percent of gross sales.
Relation to CSF—This is important because profit margins are slim, and increasing competitiveness is eroding the margins even further. The information system would reduce cost of doing business; the system is in line with a low-cost producer strategy.

For the second system:

Goal—Increase the volume of sales to contractor customers.
Objectives—Obtain accurate information on purchasing habits of contractor customers, and use this to develop marketing promotions; increase average annual sales to contractors by 5 percent.
Relation to CSF—This application is important because it will allow us to understand the needs of the customers better; it will allow us to service them better, increasing revenue from repeat business. The information system is in line with a differentiation strategy.

Notice that the objectives state not only what the user wishes the system to accomplish, but also what the department (or company) should see as a result of developing the system.

Define Requirements

This phase involves determining the **information requirements** for all major components of an information system, but the emphasis is typically on the outputs and inputs, the processes, the data, and the scale of processing. This determination of requirements might be considered part of systems analysis, using the terminology from the SDLC. Frequently, analysts will use diagramming tools to help document what the users want the new system to do. In some cases, the analyst begins by documenting how the existing system works in order to identify areas for improvement.

It is not unusual to begin the requirements determination phase by looking at the desired *outputs*; in other words, exactly what does one want this information system to produce? In the first example provided above, the primary output might be a report listing all contractors who have credit purchases outstanding more than 30 days. Furthermore, the marketing manager might want the report sorted by date, so that the purchases that have been outstanding the longest are listed first. Next, the marketing manager might decide that she would like to have all outstanding purchases for a single contractor grouped together with a subtotal, so that she can quickly see how much each contractor with outstanding credit owes BCSC. She might also decide to ignore those contractors who owe less than a certain amount (say, $1,000), and would therefore like the report to exclude them.

On the *input* side, it is necessary to identify exactly what *data* and information is required to produce all of the required outputs. To create a contractor report similar to the one just described, one would need to have access to all purchase and payment records for all contractor customers, as well as their outstanding account balances.

The *processing* requirements in this example are the steps necessary to take the inputs and create the outputs; this involves describing the logic or procedures involved. Note that at this point we don't necessarily have to decide exactly *how* the processing will take place (by a person, or a spreadsheet model, or a program embedded in a software package), but rather *what* processing is required.

The *scale of processing* refers to issues such as how many users will need to receive the outputs, how many will require access to data simultaneously, how much data will need to be stored, how frequently the process needs to be conducted, how much growth is anticipated in data storage and processing requirements, and so on. If BCSC has 20 contractor customers who average 1 purchase per month, the scale of processing required would be substantially different than a situation involving 20,000 contractor customers averaging 10 purchases per month.

The dimensions of the information systems cube can also help in determining the characteristics of the system. For example, the scale of processing is related to the *scope* of the information system in the information systems cube. Generally, the greater the scope of the system (e.g., an enterprisewide system versus an individual system), the greater the scale of processing will be.

The level of *information richness* required sometimes makes it harder to determine the specific needs of the user. Generally, the choices to present alphanumeric characters and simple charts are limited, but there is a much wider set of choices when the needed information includes graphics, video, and sound. The information richness of the application will also have an impact on the scale of processing (the higher the level of richness, the greater the scale of processing will be).

Finally, the level of *structure* in the task to be supported affects how the analyst will go about assessing the information requirements. If the level of structure is low (i.e., the task is unstructured), then the requirements may focus more on the inputs and tools needed (such as database software with report generators) than on the actual outputs (such as specific reports).

Note that the identification of requirements can be a difficult and sensitive procedure. The willingness and ability of the users to specify their needs is a function of their experience, knowledge, and motivation to think through the present and future information requirements of the task being supported. If we are trying to develop an expert system, for example, we need to somehow capture the expertise of a given individual or set of individuals. Those human experts obviously need to agree to cooperate; if they feel threatened by the thought of a computer system that will be able to make decisions at the same level they do, they may not cooperate. Furthermore, users may have difficulties verbalizing what their information needs are, particularly if the task is a new one or a constantly changing one. Finally, it is important for the analyst to differentiate between true requirements and current procedures. Too often organizations fall into the trap of simply trying to automate their current way of doing things, without first questioning the need for the specific job tasks and processes being performed. Before automating a given task and interviewing the people involved in that task to find out what their information needs are, the I/S designer should ask whether or not the task is necessary in the first place.

Numerous techniques can help determine information requirements. These techniques range from asking the user directly for his/her needs in a face-to-face interview, to developing prototypes and discovering what the preferences of the users are through trial and error (when the users cannot verbalize what their needs are). Usually, a combination of approaches is employed. Two very common techniques are interviews and document sampling (looking at existing reports, input forms, and so on to determine what data they contain). Questionnaires may be used when there are a large number of potential users. In some instances direct observation, where the designer(s) of the system watch the potential users as they go about performing their job functions, can be useful.

Each of these techniques has certain advantages and disadvantages. For example, questionnaires enable you to obtain information from a large number of people with a relatively small expenditure of time and money, but the information provided may be less detailed than the information one could get from a face-to-face interview, and it could also be biased information if only a few individuals respond to the survey. Typically, the two techniques are combined: the information systems specialist would send a questionnaire to all potential users and then perform face-to-face interviews with a selected, but representative, few. Table 7–3 provides a quick overviews of several information requirements determination techniques.

Remember that users, because they typically think that the more data they have the better off they are, will ask for anything that comes to mind when defining their information requirements. Having more data is not always better, however, and the analyst must always keep in mind the possibility of overloading the user of the system. The value of a report is not in the number of pages or tables it has, but in the way it affects decision making. Finally, in determining the information requirements for a system, the analyst must not forget to discuss with the users how the required data will be *collected* and how the analyses and conclusions will be *transmitted* to others.

Generate and Evaluate Alternatives

One common mistake in managerial decision making is the tendency for managers to implement the first workable solution they find rather than waiting to generate several feasible alternatives and then choosing the best among them. This tendency is also a common shortcoming of information systems development efforts.

One reason for this shortcoming in generating several alternative designs is what has been referred to as the **understanding gap.** On the one hand, we have the future users of the system, who understand their job tasks and what they need to do to fulfill their objectives but have a poor understanding of the different information technologies available to them and therefore cannot communicate their preferences. On the other hand, we have the information systems specialists, who understand the information technology very well but who have difficulty understanding the users' information needs and job requirements and may therefore fail to adequately communicate the capabilities and limitations of the various choices of information technologies to the users. In other words, the understanding gap is caused by the difficulty users have in specifying their preferences and by the difficulty analysts have in eliciting the needs of the users. The consequence of the understanding gap is that the analyst is unable to match the appropriate technology to fulfill the user requirements of the system.

Another reason the set of design alternatives is not always large is that when information systems specialists (whether internal to the organization or external consultants) are asked to recommend alternative configurations of hardware and software to address the information needs, they frequently choose an alternative from a narrow set based on their own familiarity. Also, many consultants and outside

TABLE 7–3 Comparison of Information Requirements Determination Techniques

Technique	*Advantages*	*Disadvantages*
Interviewing	Can obtain detailed requirements; provides instant feedback.	Time consuming; may receive biased responses; users may forget important requirements.
Questionnaires	Can obtain information from large number of respondents quickly.	Responses may be superficial, biased.
Document Sampling	Can be a good source of existing data and data-processing requirements.	May lead to incorporating obsolete or inappropriate procedures.
Observation	May reveal procedures and information needs not recognized or acknowledged by users.	Users may modify behaviors when they know they are being observed; time consuming.

vendors may have a conflict of interest; a representative from a hardware vendor is more likely to suggest alternatives involving one of the vendor's products, even if s/he knows that a competitor's product might be superior. On the positive side, this familiarity reduces the relative complexity involved in choosing the technology; but, on the negative side, it may omit possible solutions that have a better fit for the specific situation. One way to enrich the set of alternatives is to request proposals from a diverse group of information systems providers, which should result in a greater variety of solutions to choose from.

Choosing among competing design alternatives may range from relatively informal processes for very small applications to very formal processes for larger, more expensive information systems. In general, it is advisable to follow a rigorous evaluation and selection process. Even information systems that initially seem small and insignificant can have major repercussions down the road.

Once again we can use principles from a rational decision-making process to help guide the evaluation and selection process. The basic approach is a **cost–benefit analysis:** identifying the costs and benefits of each alternative, and then determining which alternative provides the higher net benefits. It is important to identify all the costs and benefits that will be incurred over the lifetime of the project. Since a dollar today is more valuable than a dollar a year from now (you could invest that one dollar and get a positive return on it, plus inflation will erode the purchasing value of that dollar over time), it is important to discount both positive and negative future cash flows to their current value (called a net present value calculation) so as to make the monetary assessment of the system's cost-effectiveness more accurate.

Although this may sound like a straightforward approach, in reality it is often difficult to implement. The biggest difficulty is that many of the benefits of an information system are hard to quantify. Even when the potential benefits are easy to quantify, they may be difficult to accurately forecast. Typically, the difficulty in assessing the benefits of the information system is related to the inherent structure of the processes being supported by the system: the more unstructured the process, the more difficult to define the benefits.

Nevertheless, it is very important to do as good a job as possible in estimating *all* costs and benefits. Monetary equivalents can almost always be estimated for those costs and benefits not measured directly in dollar terms. For example, one could argue that a new automated operator-support ordering system would have an impact on the morale of the employees answering the phone and taking orders, since the frustrations of taking the order by hand would be eliminated. How can we measure the impact of improved employee morale? We could assume that happy employees would be more productive, more pleasant to the customers, and that turnover and absenteeism would decrease. Could we assume then a 2 percent increase in customer retention due to the new system? A 5 percent decrease in labor costs? The exact figures are not crucial. It is the process of estimating and discussing the potential costs and benefits that is meaningful. As a rule, we advocate being conservative in cost–benefit analyses. It is usually wise to underestimate benefits and overestimate costs.

Many authors classify costs and benefits into tangible and intangible. We disagree with the definition of intangible that is commonly used in that classification. If a cost or benefit is truly intangible (by definition impossible to measure), then it should not be included in a cost–benefit analysis.

We like to classify costs and benefits on a continuum ranging from very easy to measure (tangible) to very hard to measure (intangible). The very-easy-to-measure costs and benefits are assessed on direct dollar amounts while the very-hard-to-measure costs and benefits are typically based on estimates and dollar equivalents. Dollars are used to estimate the value of a cost or benefit, such as an increase or drop in employee morale or the company's image; dollars, however, represent a proxy measure. Also, it is not unusual to represent costs and benefits with a range of values.

The *easy-to-measure costs* of each alternative are usually straightforward to list. These include costs of software licenses, computing hardware, information systems personnel (consultants, programmers, analysts, etc.), maintenance contracts, training costs, communications costs, and so on. The *hard-to-measure costs* include the time it will take employees to learn how to use the new system, the potential disruption to operations during the conversion from the old to the new, a potential drop in morale, and so on. Very often, the hard-to-measure costs are substantially underestimated.

The *easy-to-measure benefits* are those that can be quantified and expressed in monetary terms. If a new information system will enable a company to perform a required function such as inventory control with fewer people and lead to fewer stockouts, then the potential payroll savings and increased sales can be assessed in dollar terms and are therefore a tangible benefit. An improved company image would be another benefit, although harder to assess in dollar terms; nevertheless, it needs to be estimated (e.g., percent of repeat business and new business). Often the benefits are considered more in terms of cost avoidance than of cost reduction: if a new system will enable us to handle an increased volume of business with the same number of employees, then we can avoid spending money on increased salary expenses. Obviously, the expected or claimed benefits must be examined closely. For example, implementing an information system that displaces workers can lead to problems such as reduced employee morale.

The *hard-to-measure benefits* are more difficult to quantify, but it is important to avoid the temptation to simply list a number of potential "intangible" benefits without attempting to quantify them. It may be necessary to use proxies, estimates, and guesses. This type of subjective information is better than no information, since it provides some basis for decision making. Consider the expressed benefit of increased customer satisfaction for a new information system to track the servicing of automobiles at an automobile dealership. How can we quantify increased customer satisfaction? One way is to think in terms of generating more sales and increased service business through increased repeat business. If a new service tracking system will cost $50,000, how much increased business do we need to generate to pay for it? In other words, how much does the retention rate of customers need to improve to pay for the system?

We would obviously need to know more details on such aspects of the business as the average mark-up on new and used automobiles, the capacity and net revenue generated by the service department, and the total sales and service volumes. With this information, we could at least begin to associate some numbers with the benefit of an increase in customer satisfaction. We might determine that we would need to increase automobile sales by 3 percent and service visits by 5 percent over each of the next three years to pay for the system. How feasible is this scenario? That would be a question for managers within the dealership, but at least they would have something more tangible to work with.

In selecting alternatives, there may be additional considerations that are difficult to think of in terms of costs and benefits but are still very important. For example, when considering proposals from different consultants or vendors, some important considerations include the reputation of the provider, future compatibility with emerging technologies, and so on. Again, before committing to a given alternative one needs to assess the costs and likelihood of a vendor going out of business, or the system needing to be upgraded or changed, during the lifetime of the information system.

Once all the costs and benefits have been assessed, there are several criteria to select the best alternative. Three of the most common are the highest **return-on-investment (ROI),** the highest **net present value (NPV),** and the shortest **payback period** (the alternative that breaks even first).

Make versus Buy Decisions

In today's environment, it is unusual for organizations to build all of their information systems by themselves. There are so many software packages and programs available, that it is usually less expensive and time consuming to purchase one and customize it as necessary than it is to develop it internally from scratch. However, the *structure* of the decision situation will have an impact on the feasibility of finding a ready-made, packaged information system. The more unstructured, or unique, the decision process, the more likely it is that we will need to build the information system to support it in-house. Business Brief 7–1 gives an example of a company that, because of their specialized needs, decided to develop their systems internally.

The typical decision in manufacturing environments of making versus buying a certain part is very similar to the decision of building an information system internally or having external consultants build it. The first step in making such a decision is to determine whether or not ready-made software (also called off-the-shelf software) exists for the application we are interested in. If appropriate ready-made software exists, it is usually cheaper, easier, and faster to buy it rather than to develop it from scratch. If we determine that appropriate ready-made software doesn't exist, we can then decide to either build it ourselves or hire

BUSINESS BRIEF 7-1 DOWNHILL ALL THE WAY: SKI CONDITIONS IDEAL AFTER I/S INTEGRATION

After a long day of skiing, the last thing you want to do is hassle with a restaurant employee over a reservation or discover that your rental equipment must be returned earlier than expected. Despite their use of modern information systems technology, ski resorts often play host to logistical snafus. The problems stem from a lack of integration among various point-of-sale systems and back-office accounting packages, which makes the exchange of up-to-the-minute information difficult.

That's why Blackcomb Skiing Enterprises in Whistler, British Columbia, is carefully revamping all facets of its financial information systems using Progress Software Corp.'s Progress Application Development Environment, a fourth-generation-language (4GL) platform, and Progress RDBMS, an integrated database (management system). The result is that besides lessening the chance of its guests being inconvenienced, Blackcomb is better able to keep a tight grip on its labor scheduling and costs and overall cash flow in a highly changeable industry.

Blackcomb is a self-contained resort composed of the Blackcomb Mountain ski operations, 15 retail outlets, numerous restaurants, and many other businesses which serve the 1.6 million-plus skiers that visit the resort town of Whistler. "We are a service-oriented business, so labor is our biggest expense," explains David Creasy, controller for the resort. "Our business is very dynamic," Creasy adds. "Labor trends within the company can change from day to day."

Blackcomb evaluated several scheduling software applications in an effort to ease this management burden, but most programs were too rigid to easily accommodate its needs. "We didn't want to change our procedures to fit the software," Creasy explained. "We wanted software applications that could fit our procedures. So we decided to build our own payroll and scheduling systems from scratch."

QUESTIONS

1. Why do you think Blackcomb decided to change its information system in-house?
2. In making the decision, what other industries could they have looked at to determine if a suitable software package already existed?

SOURCE: D. Baum, "Blackcomb Ski Conditions after I/S Integration," *InfoWorld*, March 13, 1995, p. 64.

someone else to build it. If we have the expertise and capacity, we can proceed to analyze whether or not it makes financial sense to do it internally. If we do not have the expertise or capacity, or if it's cheaper to go outside, it will be necessary to ask external vendors for proposals to develop the system for us.

Table 7–4 provides a quick decision table for helping to determine whether to build a system internally or buy it from an external provider. The first question is whether the needs (system requirements) are unique (e.g., a system to visually identify the types of fish passing through a water conduit), or whether they are fairly common. The next consideration is how important the proposed system is to the organization (the business impact). The third consideration is whether the information to be processed and analyzed is proprietary or not (e.g., is it a trade secret?). A fourth consideration is the number of vendors who are qualified to provide this type of system. The final question is whether the system represents a part of the information and communication infrastructure for the organization. These last two considerations address the risk of becoming dependent on another company—a hostage—for some critical applications. Generally, it is better to create strategic alliances with one or more partners, companies that make a commitment to grow with you, than it is to just sign a contract for services with one vendor; and in the case of basic and critical infrastructure components, it is best to be responsible for them outright (e.g., a reservation system for an airline company).

TABLE 7–4 I/S Development Strategies: Make versus Buy

Needs	*Business Impact*	*Proprietary*	*Number of Vendors*	*Infrastructure*	*Strategy*
Common	Low	Yes	Many	Yes	Buy
				No	Buy
			None	—	Make
		No	Many	Yes	Buy
				No	Buy
			None	—	Make
	High	Yes	Many	Yes	Alliance
				No	Make
			None		Make
		No	Many	Yes	Alliance
				No	Buy
			None	—	Make
Unique	Low	Yes	Many	Yes	Buy
				No	Buy
			None	—	Make
		No	Many	Yes	Buy
				No	Buy
			None	—	Make
	High	Yes	Many	Yes	Alliance
				No	Make
			None	—	Make
		No	Many	Yes	Alliance
				No	Buy
			None	—	Make

Design the Chosen Alternative

After making a decision on which design alternative to go with, it is necessary to consider all of the necessary details for the new system. Designing an information system involves planning how the five components—software, hardware, data, people, and procedures—will interact once the system is implemented. Information systems design is more than just writing computer code. Typically, the design phase includes making changes to organizational procedures and tasks necessary to match the software that is either being built or purchased. This design phase also requires the identification of exactly what computer and communications hardware will be required, the determination of who will be responsible for interactions with the new system (entering data, querying the database, extracting reports). If the software is being written from scratch, we need to develop structure charts, program pseudocode, and so on (see Appendix B for examples).

Implement and Maintain

Once an alternative has been selected and details for each component of the information system (i.e., software, hardware, data, people, and procedures) have been determined, the next issue that needs to be considered is its implementation. Basically, implementation involves all the steps required to move from the existing system (whether manual or computerized) to the new one. There is no one way to implement a system; some approaches are better than others, depending on the situation. There are four general approaches to implementation: Parallel, pilot, phased (or piecemeal), and direct cut-over (or plunge).

The **parallel conversion** approach involves running both the old system and the new for a period of time, to ensure that there are no errors or problems with the new system. This approach is expensive and time consuming (employees are required to perform the same functions twice), but it has the advantage of reducing the risk of the new system being a failure. Unfortunately, the parallel approach to implementation is often not feasible because of its required redundancy.

The **pilot conversion** approach is where the new system is implemented in a subset of the organization first (an individual, workgroup, department, or branch office), and then it is disseminated to other sites if the implementation in the pilot is considered successful. This approach reduces some risks by confining the new system to a smaller target group, and allowing the debugging of the system without creating too much upheaval in the organization. It is important to choose the pilot site carefully and understand its characteristics to be able to learn what problems, if any, may occur when disseminating the system from the pilot to the whole.

A **phased** or **piecemeal conversion** approach involves the implementation of the new system in phases, allowing the organization to assimilate it little by little. This approach requires that the information system be modular. The approach has the advantage of introducing change progressively, allowing for changes and modifications (if needed) to be made as the implementation unfolds and is less overwhelming for the users. However, the realization of the benefits from the whole system is delayed.

Finally, the **direct cut-over** or **plunge** approach means pulling the plug on the old system and converting immediately to the new. Though this approach creates a sense of urgency and an attitude of commitment, since "there is no way back," it can create severe problems if the new system does not work as planned. A direct approach requires careful planning and the development of recovery systems. Table 7–5 summarizes these conversion approaches.

Regardless of the approach selected for implementation, new procedures will need to be developed and users of the new system will need to be trained. Depending on the type of systems, this might range from a brief hands-on demonstration to intensive, off-site training programs.

One of the critical success factors in introducing a new information system to employees is the elimination of all potential sources of **resistance to change.**

TABLE 7-5 Implementation Strategies

Strategy	*Advantages*	*Disadvantages*	*Risk Level*
Parallel	Easy to compare, safety net	Cumbersome, expensive	Low
Phased (piecemeal)	Low initial investment	Takes longer	Moderate
Pilot	Allows debugging of system	Difficult to find appropriate times to test, issues of transferability	Low
Direct (plunge)	No way back	No way back	High

Eliminating all sources of resistance requires more than simply providing adequate training. Resistance to the new system in users may be based on such things as fear of losing their job, having to learn a new job, or liking the old way of doing things better. Elimination of resistance to change among users requires identifying the sources of that resistance early on and developing measures to overcome them (e.g., training, incentives, explanations, reassurances, etc.). Involving users throughout the development process of an information system develops a feeling of ownership in the new system and facilitates its introduction. The strategy of implementing a system by removing the sources of resistance works better than the strategy of implementing change by increasing the pressure to change.

Another aspect to consider in the implementation phase of an information system is the physical aspect of installing the necessary communication media; it may be necessary to modify existing workplaces. Again, this might require considerable disruption to the current work environment, and plans are needed to keep the disruption to a minimum.

The implementation phase may also require converting existing data to new formats, and/ or using new processes for capturing and converting data. In some instances, such as going from a manual to an automated system, this can be a major undertaking. If employees are going to be asked to convert and enter data in addition to perform their normal duties, adjustments have to be made to their workloads and schedules. Often temporary employees are hired to convert existing data from one format to another.

Maintenance of an information system requires upgrading the system as required. In some instances, there may be errors in the software, training materials, or procedures that must be corrected. In other instance, the needs of the users may change (perhaps requiring different information or faster response) and the system will require modifications to match those needs. Maintenance is an ongoing activity during the life of the information system. It is the activity that ensures that the system continues to provide value.

Evaluation of Impact

Once the system has been implemented it is important to evaluate its performance (speed, reliability, accuracy, etc.) and the business impact it is having. Most I/S designers believe their task is over once the system comes on-line and implementa-

BUSINESS BRIEF 7-2 ARTCO OVERHAULS SYSTEMS FOR GREATER PRODUCTIVITY

Artco Inc. manufactures Arctic Cat snowmobiles, and Tiger Shark watercrafts, among other products. As recently as three years ago, Artco Inc. was experiencing a drag on its efforts to keep pace with demand for its products. One of the major problems was Artco's mainframe computer and information systems. The mainframe needed expensive upgrades every two or three years, and the user interface for the accounting, human resources, and operational systems was not user-friendly.

"Everything was cryptic. That was the biggest problem," says Ray Koukari, I/S Director for Artco. For example, in the shipping department, which sends out everything from the company's vehicles to its popular line of sports apparel and accessories, computer screens flashed only mysterious codes to communicate the critical information of which product needed to be shipped where. Department personnel were trained to memorize what all of the arcane series of letters and numbers stood for, a process that took six months. This arrangement made the crucial matter of moving products both expensive and difficult, notes Koukari.

But all that's changed now. The key to the turnaround was a $1.5 million investment in client/server technology, where the company downsized its equipment, replaced its database management system, and rewrote the key applications for running its design, sales, and manufacturing processes—that is, its business. It took 18 months to get the many applications up and running.

The result is both a system and a workforce that are more productive and better equipped to handle the additional workload that results from sales of a new all-terrain vehicle. The system has also helped Artco's recent moves to flatten its organizational structure.

QUESTION

1. Discuss the variables and methods you would use to make a cost-benefit evaluation of the revamping of Arcto's information system.

SOURCE: P. Wallace, "Artco Uses Client/Server to Gear Up for New Terrain." *InfoWorld*, March 20, 1995, p. 66.

tion is completed. However, an assessment of whether the system achieved its original goals should be an integral part of the systems development process.

Evaluation is a critical activity in determining if the system should continue to be maintained, replaced, or just retired. Evaluations of the impact of an information system should focus on whether or not the information system is contributing any value to the organization. Since there is always a learning curve to be climbed after the implementation of a system, in order for the conclusions of an evaluation to be meaningful, the first evaluation should occur only after that learning period is over. Evaluations should occur regularly and frequently after that; evaluation, like maintenance, is not a one-time activity but an ongoing one. Business Brief 7–2 shows the broad impact that a revamped information system can have on a business.

SUMMARY

The process of information systems development continues to change as new development tools and techniques evolve. Historically, information systems were developed entirely by technically trained specialists who wrote software programs using machine, assembly, and procedural (third-generation) programming languages. The development of such tools as electronic spreadsheets, database packages with nonprocedural languages (fourth-generation languages, or 4GLs), and visual and object-oriented programming languages has enabled the ultimate users of the systems to complete more of the development efforts (end-user computing).

The roles for many internal information systems specialists have evolved away from primarily system development, to:

1. Negotiating with and overseeing outside information systems consultants.

2. Developing and maintaining internal databases.
3. Establishing and maintaining corporate and work-group networks.
4. Evaluating, acquiring, and integrating new software products (operating systems, word processors, office communication systems, etc.).
5. Training and supporting internal customers.
6. Maintaining existing corporate information systems.

The roles played by people in the development and use of information systems include user, system analyst, system designer, programmer, database analyst, and project manager. Each of these roles may be performed by one or many people, depending on the situation.

The relative difficulty of the development process, and the importance of using appropriate techniques for managing the development project, can be anticipated by considering the application scope, the application complexity, the information richness, and the relative complexity of technology.

A generic process for developing information systems includes six steps or phases: (1) define goals and objectives, (2) define requirements, (3) generate and evaluate alternatives, (4) design the chosen alternative, (5) implement and maintain, and (6) evaluate. Today, an important decision in information systems management is whether to develop all parts of the system internally or with the help of an external vendor.

KEY CONCEPTS AND TERMS

KEY CONCEPTS

- The development process should be adjusted to reflect the type of system being developed. (223)
- The system development process is composed of six identifiable steps. (238)
- The development of an information system is essentially a problem-solving activity. (234)
- Because of the emergence of easy to use software development tools, nontechnical users are developing and implementing more and more information applications (end-user computing). (226)
- Because of the emergence of more and more commercial software, organizations are buying more applications rather than developing them. (244)
- Different I/S project situations will require a different approach and different type of leader to be successfully implemented. (233)
- Cost–benefit analysis of information systems requires the identification and qualification of all benefits and costs over the predicted life of the system. (242)

KEY TERMS

client-server configuration (227)
computer-aided software engineering (CASE) (225)
computer programs (223)
cost–benefit analysis (242)
critical success factors (CSF) (238)
database analyst (231)
direct cut-over (247)
end-user computing (224)
information engineering (236)
information requirements (239)
maintenance (248)
make versus buy decision (244)
modular program design (235)
net present value (NPV) (244)
object-oriented programming (225)
parallel conversion (247)
payback period (244)
phased conversion (247)
pilot conversion (247)
programmer (231)
project management (231)
project manager (231)
prototyping (224)
resistance to change (247)
return-on-investment (ROI) (244)
structured analysis and design (224)
system designer (231)
systems analyst (230)
systems development life cycle (234)
systems development process (234)
understanding gap (242)
user (230)

REFERENCES

Cash, J. I.; F. W. McFarlan; J. L. McKenney; and L. M. Applegate. *Corporate Information Systems Management: Text and Cases.* 3rd ed. Homewood, IL: Irwin, 1992.

Dewitz, Sandra Donaldson. *Systems Analysis and Design and the Transition to Objects.* New York: McGraw-Hill, 1996.

Gibson, M., and C. Hughes. *Systems Analysis and Design: A Comprehensive Methodology with CASE.* Danvers, MA: Boyd & Fraser, 1994.

Harris, D. *Systems Analysis and Design: A Project Approach.* Fort Worth, TX: The Dryden Press, 1995.

Keen, P. *Every Manager's Guide to Information Technology.* 2nd ed. Boston: Harvard Business School Press, 1995.

Reilly, N. B. *Successful Systems Engineering (For Engineers and Managers).* New York: Van Nostrand Reinhold, 1993.

Welke, R. J. "The Shifting Software Development Paradigm." *Data Base* 25(4), November 1994, pp. 9–16.

CONNECTIVE CASE: Intelligent Electronics

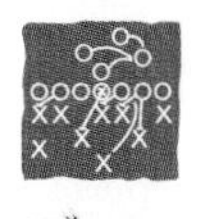

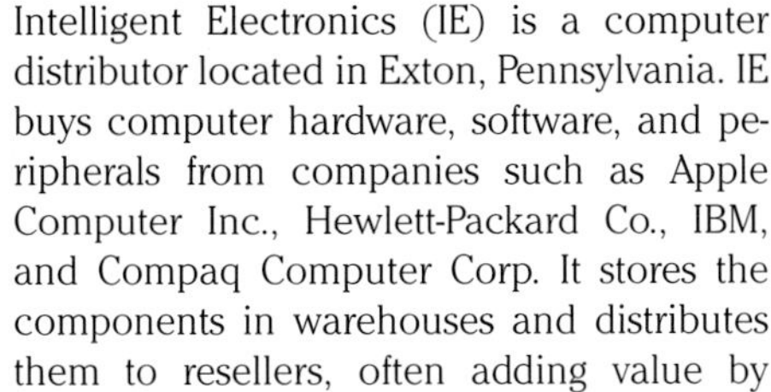

Intelligent Electronics (IE) is a computer distributor located in Exton, Pennsylvania. IE buys computer hardware, software, and peripherals from companies such as Apple Computer Inc., Hewlett-Packard Co., IBM, and Compaq Computer Corp. It stores the components in warehouses and distributes them to resellers, often adding value by creating custom-configured systems.

For years, IE has depended on a homegrown application for order processing and order management called the Intelligent Reseller Information System (IRIS). Based on a Hewlett-Packard 3000 host (mainframe) computer, it featured a character-mode user interface which resellers found difficult to use. IE decided to explore the possibility of moving to a client-server architecture, which would give the resellers more control, allow IE to provide a graphical user interface, and reduce operating expenses.

So began an ambitious client/server development project to simplify the order-entry process, add capabilities for automatic order tracking, and tie the ordering process more directly to the reseller's own internal business systems. The new client/server system was dubbed IQ Pro, and, like many projects of its type, it was publicized far and wide.

"Initially, we thought client/server was the right architecture for IQ Pro due to its ability to divide computing tasks among multiple locations—in this case, multiple reseller sites," recalls Brian Cunningham, the Chief Information Officer for IE. "We also thought that client/server would be the best way to achieve automatic order tracking."

The decision was made to go ahead, and the system was developed in-house. The developers were putting the final touches on the first production release of IQ Pro when Cunningham and other company officers began to have second thoughts about the new architecture. "Once we took a hard look at the ramifications of what we were attempting and started putting out feelers to our client user base, we realized it made better sense to capitalize on the system we had in place," Cunningham says.

There were three primary reasons for putting on the brakes. The first was the complexity of the new technologies they were using, based on Smalltalk (an object-oriented programming language). The second reason for questioning the efficacy of IQ Pro was the deployment costs for the resellers, especially the training costs and hefty equipment purchase requirements, because more CPU power would be required at their end to make the applications work. But what really tipped the scales against IQ Pro was work IE's resellers had already done. "Our resellers have invested a lot of time and effort into learning IRIS," Cunningham explains. "We have 2,000 customers out there who are accustomed to a certain type of system."

Working closely with Bonnie Lawson, manager of support services at IE, Cunningham and his I/S team began to evaluate alternative ways to accomplish many of the same benefits by IQ Pro using their existing, host-based system. They set the goal of making a series of incremental improvements to IRIS that would be easier to develop and require less upheaval among their reseller base.

Cunningham won't reveal just how much money was spent or how many development hours were consumed before IE pulled the plug on IQ Pro. "We were able to rebuild IRIS with the remaining IQ Pro budget," Cunningham says.

The moral of the story? Elegant solutions based on new technology often seem great in theory but are difficult to learn and expensive to deploy. "Any time you put in something brand new, there is risk associated with it—new architecture, new code, new platforms. There are so many unknown factors, so many intangibles that are difficult to foresee. In the end, it was really quite simple," Cunningham says. "We listened to our users."

Case Questions:

1. Consider the brief description of the original IQ Pro system development project. How closely did the process used at IE follow the process suggested in this chapter? What phases (if any) do you think might have been improved?
2. IE must have spent considerable time and money on the IQ Pro project, before scrapping it. Describe how they might have avoided some of these costs.

Source: David Baum, "Intelligent Electronics Learns the Pitfalls of New Technology," *InfoWorld*, January 29, 1996, p. 100.

IT'S YOUR TURN END OF CHAPTER MATERIALS

REVIEW QUESTIONS

1. What does the term *technology complexity* refer to in the context of choosing an application development strategy?
2. List the six phases of the systems development process.
3. Contrast goals and objectives, and explain the role of critical success factors in the definition of objectives.
4. Describe the tasks that need to be accomplished when determining information requirements.
5. What are some advantages and disadvantages of interviewing potential users to determine their needs for a new information system?
6. Describe the tasks that need to be accomplished when generating and evaluating alternative information systems.
7. Why is it sometimes difficult to complete a cost–benefit analysis of alternatives?
8. Describe the tasks that need to be accomplished during the implementation phase of the systems development process.
9. Describe why maintenance is an important part of the systems development process. In what ways can maintenance be reduced?
10. List at least four responsibilities (in addition to systems development) that are currently assumed by most information systems departments.

DISCUSSION QUESTIONS

1. Describe how the role of information systems departments changed from the 1970s to the 1990s with respect to the development of information systems.
2. Explain why it is important to estimate values for the costs and benefits of alternative information systems, even if the estimates are not very accurate.
3. Discuss the difference between using a parallel conversion strategy and a direct cut-over conversion strategy. Briefly describe a situation where a direct cut-over strategy might be preferable.
4. The chapter argues that the formality of project management techniques is related to the type of project. Briefly explain this argument.
5. Arguments have been made that end-user development of applications has made life easier for I/S departments, since it has removed some of their systems development responsibilities. Others have argued that end-user computing has complicated the situation for I/S departments, increasing their responsibilities. Comment on these arguments.
6. Some organizations have made the decision to outsource all of their I/S development projects, and rely completely on outside consultants and vendors to fill this responsibility. Comment on the advantages and disadvantages of using this approach.

GROUP ASSIGNMENT

As a group, contact a local organization (a retail sporting goods store, a clothing store, a doctor's office, a real estate agency, a car dealership, etc.). Arrange to meet with a manager in the organization who has had some experience with implementing an information system (e.g., a point-of-sale system or a customer database). Ask the manager to describe the process that his or her company followed. Don't worry about the details; try to focus on the overall process (when and how they decided a change was necessary, who decided to proceed, who was put in charge, how they identified potential vendors, etc.). After completing the interview, comment on how closely the approach described by your contact manager matched the prescribed process listed in this chapter.

APPLICATION ASSIGNMENTS

1. If you have access to a CASE tool, use it for this assignment. If not, use the drawing features of your word-processing package. Develop a diagram showing the primary interactions (information flows) between Boyd's Construction Supply Co. (BCSC) and their external environment (ORDER from CUSTOMER, PURCHASE ORDER to SUPPLIER, FILLED ORDER to CUSTOMER, etc.).
2. Use a database management system to open the ACME database that you can find by accessing the internet and locating the home page for this book. Use the DBMS to design an input form that could be used to enter data into one of the database tables. (This would be an example of prototyping an input requirement.)
3. Use a database management system to open the ACME database that you can find by accessing the internet and locating the home page for this book. Use the DBMS to design a report that could be used to retrieve data from one of the database tables. (This would be an example of prototyping an output requirement.)

CASE ASSIGNMENT: Great Sports!

Louis Pepin was getting another headache. As president of Great Sports! he believed in providing opportunities for senior employees to voice their concerns and raise important issues. The weekly Friday morning meetings served this purpose, but recently the discussion always seemed to focus on deficiencies in the methods used for handling finances or inventories, and today was no exception. Karen Finlay, the controller, wanted to hire another employee to help keep the accounting records current and to prepare some additional reports. Basu Sharma, who looked after the inventory, also wanted another staff member to help with record keeping. Louis, on the other hand, believed what they needed was a computer system and possibly a change in procedures.

THE BEGINNING

Three months after graduating from university in 1994, Louis Pepin still didn't have a job . . . at least not the kind of job he wanted. The obvious answer was to start his own company. Since he was living in Oregon, an area where sports and outdoor activities seemed to be a major part of people's lives, he decided to see if the market could support one more sporting goods store.

Obtaining the initial financing was difficult, but Louis managed to borrow some money and use it to encourage more investors. After renting the retail space, he purchased an initial stock of goods, hired an employee to help with sales, and Great Sports! was born. The first year was spent fighting fires, doing all of the day-to-day work of running the store himself. Louis had little time to forecast what products should sell, let alone keep track of what had sold and keep a reasonable level of inventory in stock. He also had to make time to do all of the bookkeeping, relearning the accounting he had conveniently forgotten after university courses had ended.

By the end of the first year, business was really beginning to pick up, but Louis could no longer handle all the work himself. He had found it necessary to add to the staff as the business grew, and had divided tasks and responsibilities. Karen Finlay was hired as the controller, and she looked after all bookkeeping and accounting functions. Basu Sharma was in charge of inventory.

At the end of the first year of business, Great Sports! carried over 200 items in stock and occupied 2,500 square feet. Gross sales topped $500,000. Because of the growth in business, Louis found that his functions changed somewhat: He now concentrated on purchasing to replenish stock, and also tried to keep track of trends to identify new items to carry. In addition Louis oversaw the sales staff, handled all marketing and advertising, and worked in sales when required.

TRACKING INVENTORY

Since Great Sports! was founded, the inventory records were kept in a ledger book, one page for each item carried in inventory. Inventory information included a description of the item, its product number, the name of the supplier, an entry including date for each sale and delivery, and a running balance of the number of items on hand. When one page got full, it was removed and replaced with a new blank page with the balance (final item count) from the last page carried over to the top of the new page.

Basu had taken over the job of maintaining inventory records. His job was to keep an accurate count of all items on hand, to advise Louis when items need to be reordered, and to restock the shelves with items from the storeroom when necessary. The procedure for maintaining inventory records could be broken down into five separate steps:

1. The inventory ledger was reviewed for accuracy once each quarter (every three months) when a physical inventory count was conducted. Each item in inventory was counted by hand. The balance on hand was compared to the total in the ledger. Discrepancies were researched and resolved, and any necessary adjustments made to the ledger.
2. Copies of all sales receipts were continually collected in a stock folder.
3. Once every two weeks, Basu took all the sales receipts from the stock folder and:

   a. Sorted them into order by type of sale—tennis racquets, hockey pucks, and so on.
   b. Tallied the amount of each item sold (how many).
   c. Recorded on each item's ledger page the amount sold and the current balance of items in stock.

4. When the balance on hand for an item was relatively low, Basu gave Louis a low-stock report so that he would know to restock the item (buy more). Louis prepared a purchase order and sent it out to one of the suppliers.
5. When the ordered goods were received, Basu took the bill of lading (the document identifying the contents of the shipment received) and recorded the information in the inventory ledger. The number of items just received was added to the prior balance to give the updated balance on hand.

CURRENT SITUATION

Business had continued to expand fairly rapidly. Louis had extended the hours of business to seven days a week: 9:00 AM to 9:00 PM Monday to Friday, and 10:00 AM to 6:00 PM Saturday and Sunday. Great Sports! now had over 800 items in stock, and gross sales had increased to over $1.5 million. There were four full-time staff members assisting Karen; two cashiers, one bookkeeper, and a clerk to handle personnel and payroll activities. In addition, the company employed six part-timers from the local high schools and the university.

Because 800 items were now being carried in stock, Basu was having trouble keeping inventory records up to date using the traditional manual ledger method. Far too many slow-selling items were being kept in stock, whereas some very popular items were almost always out of stock. Basu was spending his time stocking shelves and recording changes in inventory records, and had no time to review the records to forecast future sales or identify items that should be discontinued. A large amount of money was being tied up in inventory, and Basu believed that this money was not being spent wisely.

An additional problem was that some suppliers were much better than others in getting goods shipped promptly and with few errors. While it was possible for Basu to remember some of the better (or worse) suppliers, often he would find himself ordering from someone without really knowing how well they had performed in the past. It was also difficult to decide which supplier had the lower price on some items, without manually checking through supplier price lists.

Karen and Basu argued that Louis needed to hire at least one more full-time employee to record sales records and update the inventory records. If he wanted to start getting reports that would help forecast sales and make better decisions about inventory items and levels, they believed he would probably also need to hire another part-time employee. Although these positions would not require a great deal of education or experience, it would probably cost at least $25,000 per year for a full-time position once benefits were included. And if the business continued to grow, more employees would be required at a later time.

An alternative solution that Louis was considering would be to implement a computerized system to handle the inventory and accounting functions. He had decided to investigate this option, but wasn't really sure where to begin.

THE WISH LIST

Discussions with Karen revealed that she would expect a computer system to produce a substantial amount of useful accounting information and to take over the major burden of accounting-related processing activities. Basu said he would need a computer system to provide assistance in tracking the status of inventory as a whole and in restocking inventory. He believed that:

1. The system would need to allow him to quickly check on a terminal (or personal computer) the status of any item in inventory.
2. It would have to track inventory turnover (how quickly items are sold and replaced).
3. The following reports would have to be produced:
   a. Detailed inventory listings: two copies of each, about 30 pages daily.
   b. Inventory reorder report (low-stock item report): single copies, about two pages per day.
   c. Purchase orders: three copies, 80 columns wide, about 75 per week.

In addition, Basu believed that they would need to store the following kinds of computer files (Karen would need many more):

- Invoice files: both paid and unpaid invoices (about 5,000 invoices).
- Purchase orders: both filled and unfilled (about 500).
- Supplier information: about 50 suppliers.
- Inventory files: all the data on items that Great Sports! ordered, stored, and sold (item number, description, unit price).

Louis would also like a system that allowed recording of sales at the point of sale; that is, each cashier would need a computerized cash register that would automatically update the inventory files and sales records when a sale was made.

When the Friday meeting came to a close (two hours later than scheduled) Louis tried to sketch out his options. If he decided to go ahead with purchasing a computer system, he knew he would need some help. His exposure to computers in university had been minimal, and he hadn't worked much with them since. As he packed up for the day, Louis promised himself that he would find someone immediately to investigate his concerns—he was getting tired of these weekly headaches.

QUESTIONS

1. Assume you have been hired by Louis to assist with the new system project. Briefly work through the project phases—define goals, define requirements, generate alternatives, design and implement—making whatever assumptions are necessary. Use the chapter as a guide, and be as specific as possible. Don't just state what the steps are in the phases of the systems development process; try to complete the steps. For example, you will need to write a brief statement of goals and objectives for the situation at Great Sports!
2. (Assuming you have been assigned to complete Appendix A with this chapter.) Draw an entity relationship diagram and a database design (database tables with fields) for storing information about suppliers, invoices, and items. Assume that invoices list items that Great Sports! is purchasing from its suppliers, and that each invoice may list more than one item. Show how the tables will be related (how a link will be established between suppliers and invoices). Assume that suppliers have a unique supplier number, and that items for sale have unique item numbers; state whatever other assumptions you believe are necessary.
3. (Assuming you have been assigned to complete Appendix B with this chapter.) Draw a context diagram for the Great Sports! company, and also a context diagram for the subsystem of inventory control.
4. (Assuming you have been assigned to complete Appendix B with this chapter.) Draw a first-level (level 1) data flow diagram for the inventory control subsystem of Great Sports! Prepare a data dictionary entry for one of the data flows on your diagram.

MODULE II Case

DAKIN FARM (B): SAM'S EXPECTATIONS

Sam Cutting Jr., president of Dakin Farm, was looking back at the decision to replace the company's old methods and information systems used for processing customer orders: "Yes, it is safe to say that I had a lot of expectations for a new order-processing system. I also had a lot of questions. We weren't exactly sure what we were getting into when we started the change process. I only knew that we couldn't continue to operate the way we had been. That spring was definitely a time for making some major decisions."

THE COMPETITIVE ENVIRONMENT

The specialty food business was very competitive and was getting more so with each passing year. Larger national and international firms such as Hickory Farms had a strong brand name and used volume purchases of goods to lower costs. Such companies also had a very visible presence in the market; in many cases they operated retail outlets in shopping malls where customers saw them every time they walked by. This enabled the larger specialty food stores to pick up a lot of impulse buyers; for instance, customers who were desperately searching the mall for last minute Christmas gifts could stop in, select a basket of goods, and have it shipped to the recipient. On the down side, however, people receiving gifts from national chains might conclude that less thought and foresight went into selecting the gift.

The smaller regional and local specialty food companies typically tried to sell their products as being the best quality available. They relied on customers who were willing to pay a premium for the perception that their gifts were special in some way. Some of the smaller firms purchased goods that were in a "raw" form and then finished them in some way to differentiate their product from the competition. There was a limit, however, to how much of a premium customers would be willing to pay for the perception of higher quality.

Dakin Farm finished a fairly substantial amount of their products themselves. They purchased much of their maple syrup from local Vermont producers, but they also blended and packaged the maple syrup to achieve a consistent, high-quality product. By operating their own smoke house, Dakin was able to smoke meats using the company's choice of ingredients and this would ensure a high standard of product quality and a unique flavor. These and other procedures, such as ensuring all perishable goods were properly stored, and using and marketing "made-in-Vermont" products, were all part of Dakin's commitment to providing customers with the best quality possible.

Still, high-quality products were only one part of the equation. Other Vermont companies such as Cold Hollow Cider Mill had entered the mail order specialty-foods business and were also advertising high-quality made in Vermont products.

THE OLD SYSTEM

Dakin Farm operated two retail outlets, but it was primarily a mail order specialty food operation. Dakin had been experiencing problems with customer mail order processing. Everything about the process, from taking a customer order, picking the goods, packing the order, and sending it seemed to have inefficiencies. The system was not only inefficient, but also ineffective. The mail order system increased labor costs around heavy selling periods, could not handle the amount of orders during these times, and attributed (Sam Cutting believed) to the loss of return customers because of the time period between order and shipment.

Some of the problems stemmed from the computerized order-processing system which Dakin had in place. It had originally been designed for a different company, and then parts of it were rewritten to work for Dakin Farm. It was a batch system, which meant that orders were recorded on paper, held or "batched" during the day, and then entered into the computer system in batches. For several years Sam had searched for a new computerized mail order system, but he wasn't able to find anything which suited the company's needs.

Sam began talking with a friend, Alan Newman, about mail order processing systems. Newman was the founder of Gardener's Supply Company, and had also started another company named Seventh Generation. These mail order businesses were successfully using Nashbar mail order systems, which were developed and supported by a relatively large company. Nashbar, a sporting goods retailer, had initially developed the system for themselves, but had since sold the system to approximately 100 companies. Newman had demonstrated the system to Sam, who was extremely impressed with the functionality. Sam decided to use the Nashbar system as a benchmark in his search for a new mail order processing system for Dakin Farm.

THE NEED FOR CHANGE

Although Sam had a nagging feeling for some time that Dakin Farm needed to improve, the real impetus for change came from two separate but related incidents. The first was when Sam realized that during the most recent Christmas season, the company had to turn away business: When customers called during the final days before Christmas, the Dakin employees told them they couldn't guarantee that the orders would arrive on time because it was taking so long to process and ship the orders. That led many customers to cancel their orders and call a competitor who could guarantee delivery.

A second incident occurred about two months later when Sam visited another mail order company. As he observed the company's order-processing operations, Sam asked the owner a few questions from which he discovered that the employees were able to process, pack, and ship almost five times as many orders as the Dakin Farm employees during a shift.

Sam concluded that even though the Dakin Farm employees worked hard, their work procedures were inefficient and the information systems support they received was inadequate.

In March, Sam formally hired Alan Newman as a consultant to help redesign the customer order process and to recommend new information systems for Dakin Farm. The plan was to have a new process and system implemented later the same year. Because of the seasonal nature of the business (approximately 90 percent of Dakin's business was completed during the five-week period before Christmas), it was absolutely essential that the systems be fully operational by October. This would allow some time for employees to become familiar with new systems and procedures and to make any necessary adjustments before the heavy season started.

Sam knew that he was beginning a major change that would involve far more than buying a new computer. Newman would also be involved in plans to restructure and renovate the packing room and packing processes, which comprised a complementary effort to streamline the packing process. New procedures would need to be developed for employees who took customer calls—both for taking orders and responding to follow-up requests. Virtually every employee's responsibilities and job tasks would change, and for some the changes would be substantial.

VISION OF THE NEW OPERATIONS

Although it was too early to know the details, Sam and Alan did have a vision of what they were trying to accomplish. Under the proposed new system, calls coming in to the store would be answered by a Customer Service Representative (CSR) located at a workstation in the mail order office. The CSR would have either a dumb terminal or personal computer connected to either a minicomputer or a PC server at this workstation. If the customer had purchased a product before, the CSR would query the database by their name, credit card number, or phone number, and the computer system would bring up the customer information (address, previous purchases, sent to whom, etc.) onto the screen. If the customer was making a first-time purchase, the CSR would type in the name and address. The CSR would type the order and enter the information into a file in the computer system. The orders would then be printed out in the redesigned packing room.

The packing room needed to be redesigned to save time and effort in the picking and packing process. Picking involved reading the orders and locating the items from wherever they were stored, and ideally, the pickers wouldn't travel far to collect the items needed for each order. Packing involved placing the items in a shipping box, making sure that the items were packed for safe transport, providing special packing for breakable goods as needed. The packers would also attach a mailing label, which came as part of the printed packing list, to the package. The new system would allow the packing slips (orders) to be printed out in any sequence, so that the packers could query the unfilled orders file by item and pack similar orders in sequence rather than packing several different types of orders one after another.

After an order was packed, it would be prepared for shipment and placed in cold storage to await pick-up by the shipping company. The package had to be weighed and recorded so that the shipping company would know exactly what they were picking up and where it was going, and Dakin Farm would need a record of all outgoing shipments so they could track them if necessary. The cost of shipping was determined by the weight of the package and the destination.

EXPECTATIONS

Sam hoped that a new system would offer substantial benefits for three of Dakin Farm's major business functions: customer service, operations, and marketing.

Customer Service

The new on-line capabilities would greatly improve the efficiency of the customer service order entry time. Also the new system would contain all pertinent information about customers in a database, and provide it to the CSRs on-line. This would allow the CSRs to better answer any customer questions.

Also, Sam wanted a function which would enable the CSRs to quickly access a product information screen by pressing a "hot key," which would contain a technical description about a product. The CSR could read anyavailable information about a product to an interested customer directly from the information screen. Another feature Newman suggested was to have the system prompt the CSRs to try to sell products which were complementary to a product that had been ordered by the customer. This process (called "upselling") would be expected to increase average order size.

When asked about the customer service features, Sam responded, "Our company is very customer oriented. It has to be or we won't survive. Anything we can do to make interactions with our customers a more positive experience is something we should do. I would expect a new system to enable us to provide significantly better service to our customers, measured by everything from the length of time it takes us to answer the phone when they call to the quality of the information we provide them about our products and their orders."

Operations

Sam had very high expectations for improving the efficiency of the existing operations. He hoped that the new system would integrate three existing operations processes: the mail order process, credit card verification, and mail manifest. One goal was automatic verification of any credit card purchase, so that only orders for approved purchases would be printed to the packers, thereby lowering the risk of bad debt accumulation. The mail manifest (which calculates the amount of postage needed for an order) would be improved because the new system would show the phone operator the approximate weight and cost of shipping on-line as the order was being taken. This would also improve customer service because it would allow the customer to know the full price (order total plus shipping costs), of their purchase immediately. And the increased efficiency of phone time per customer would allow the CSRs to complete more calls in one day, decreasing the number of calls they could not answer during busy seasonal periods. This could also decrease the number of CSRs needed during peak business times.

During the summer months, the number of mail orders was quite low; typically Dakin Farm would ship 80 to 90 packages per day. Yet by late October, Dakin would receive as many as 500 orders per day, and by late December this could increase to 1,000 orders. Since Sam wanted to double sales over the next 10 years, he wanted to be able to handle volumes of 2,000 or even 3,000 packages per day—but the existing mail order and packing operations could barely handle 1,000 packages. Hiring additional CSRs and packing staff helped, but these individuals had to be trained and so were not as productive as full-time staff. Also, during the hectic Christmas season the workers worked long hours in attempts to meet demand, but productivity decreased as they became physically and mentally worn out. This situation had caused Dakin to turn away approximately $50,000 worth of orders during the most recent Christmas season.

Along with the new mail order system, Sam expected that the planned changes in the packing room would improve the operation of the packers, making the process more accurate and more efficient. Before the orders on file would be printed in batch mode after they were verified and could be printed out in any sequence. But the new system, combined with a new packing room layout, could dramatically increase the number of orders which could be packed in one day as well as the timeliness of the procedure. With these new improvements, the system was expected to shorten the time from order to shipment and from order to payment.

The decreased delivery time was also tied in with customer service: the sooner the customer received an order the happier they would be and the greater the chance they would order from Dakin Farm in the future. Also, with the new system temporary employees hired during the busy holiday seasons would not need as much training as they previously received. With the automatic upselling functions and the on-line technical product information given by the computer, the training costs could be reduced.

Marketing

Sam believed that a new system should also be able to efficiently produce sales and marketing reports and distribute marketing materials (brochures, etc.) from mailing lists generated from files of customer purchases. With the current operations, it was difficult to get accurate and timely information to help him develop an effective marketing strategy. Currently the CSRs were asked to write down where the customer heard of Dakin Farm and whether or not they had ordered from Dakin in the past. This information was then tabulated manually from the paper slips, which was very time consuming. The accuracy of the data was also suspect, since during busy periods the CSRs might be tempted to skip these questions or make up answers.

Advertising was expensive, and Sam wanted to ensure that he was getting the most out of his advertising dollars. If he was able to determine, for example, the amount and type of orders resulting from an advertisement in *Gourmet* magazine, that would help significantly in preparing his marketing strategy for the next year. Sam expected a new system to provide him with much more accurate and timely data concerning the source of orders, allowing him to analyze the data as necessary. He also expected a new system to allow him to easily segment his customer database so that he could direct different marketing efforts (such as brochures offering specials) to a subset of customers.

In addition, if the system contained "upselling" prompts during on-line order entry, it could be an effective way to tell customers about additional or new products, hopefully increasing their "impulse" buying and increasing the average dollar amount of orders.

MAKING THE DECISION

Sam wanted to reach a decision concerning a new computer system as soon as possible. He believed that the company was losing sales and profit because of the ineffectiveness and inefficiencies of the current mail order system. There were three areas where he believed a new system could pay for itself within a short time period:

1. Reduced labor costs.
2. Increased sales (by being able to handle heavy seasonal orders).
3. Increased customer retention.

Sam knew that moving to a new system would not be without expense or risk, however. In addition to the obvious costs of hardware and software, the company would need to train all existing employees on the use of a new system. Also, if a system was not installed and completely operational during the busy season, the company could lose current and future sales. If a new system had any bugs or operational problems, or if it crashed completely, it could literally wipe out the company; their mail order business, which now represented over 65 percent of annual revenues, would be totally dependent on the new system.

Questions

1. Using the description of the new system as envisioned by Sam Cutting, discuss how the transformation process could be improved (you may wish to refer to the Dakin Farm (A) case at the end of Chapter 4 for a more detailed description of the order process).
2. In what ways could the new order-processing system for Dakin Farm provide feedback?
3. Describe the components of the new system as envisioned by Sam.
4. Describe the process you would recommend to Sam Cutting in moving from the existing situation to having a completely new operational system. Use the framework introduced in Chapter 7 to guide your response.

SOURCE: This case was written by Associate Professors William Cats-Baril and Ronald Thompson of the School of Business Administration, University of Vermont. The case is designed solely as the basis for discussion, and is not intended to illustrate either effective or ineffective handling of an administrative situation.

MODULE III Applications and Management of Information Systems

This module focuses on ways that I/T can influence the competitiveness of organizations. This module also introduces the risks facing organizations in the application of information systems and discusses ways to reduce those risks.

Chapter 8 provides an overview of business process management (including reengineering and continuous improvement), as well as an overview of the relationship between business process management and information systems.

Chapter 9 discusses the topic of using information systems to improve the productivity of individuals and workgroups. A working definition of productivity is offered, and examples are provided of information systems which improve productivity. The chapter also offers some cautions on the use of information technology by individuals.

Chapter 10 addresses the issue of the competitive use of information systems by organizations. Three frameworks are provided which help identify the types of information systems that can be used to support organizational strategies. The chapter also provides a few cautions on the competitive use of information systems.

Chapter 11 provides an overview of the management of information systems within organizations. The chapter identifies three general categories of risk, and suggests approaches for reducing those risks. The chapter illustrates the importance—and the commensurate difficulty—of managing information systems as a corporate resource.

CHAPTER 8 Business Process Management

CHAPTER OBJECTIVES

After reading this chapter, you should have a better understanding of the role of information technology in managing business processes. More specifically, you should be able to:

- View an organization as a set of processes designed to achieve specific organizational goals.
- Explain the meaning of reengineering business processes.
- Explain the concepts of continuous improvement and Total Quality Management.
- Describe Integrated Process Management (IPM), which views reengineering and continuous process improvement (total quality management) as complementary strategies for change.
- Understand the roles of information technology in process redesign
- Describe the relationship between process management and information systems development.

I hear the terms downsizing, reengineering, total quality management, and continuous improvement, and I'm a little confused as to the way these terms relate to each other.

And by the way, what is the role of information technology in all of this?

INTRODUCTION TO BUSINESS PROCESS MANAGEMENT

Earlier in the text, we briefly discussed some of the prevailing philosophies concerning the structure and management of organizations. We examined differences between business *functions* (accounting, production, marketing, finance) and business *processes* (customer engagement, order management, new product development). Today, more and more organizations are attempting to improve the efficiency and effectiveness of their operations by focusing on their **business processes.** We can label this focus **process management.**

In the 1980s, the overall global economy was growing at a robust rate. Organizations in most developed nations experienced growth, adding staff to match increased demand for their products and services. In the late 1980s and early 1990s, a global recession changed the situation dramatically—economic growth slowed, and many organizations (including governments) found themselves under pressure to reduce costs and improve their internal operations.

Many companies implemented two approaches to deal with those pressures: downsizing and reengineering. Both approaches try to increase productivity but do so by different routes. **Downsizing** (basically, reducing the number of employees) attempts to increase productivity by doing the same with less people; **reengineering** attempts to accomplish the same goals by reinventing the way things are done. Both approaches rely heavily on information technology to work. But the approaches differ in an important way. While downsizing is all about reducing costs, reengineering is about increasing customer satisfaction (sometimes through greater efficiency, although that's not its focus).

The basic concept behind reengineering, or more formally, **business process reengineering (BPR),** is to examine the way the business operates and look for ways to fundamentally and radically change those operations. Proponents of BPR argue that most organizations use processes that have, over time, become outdated and inefficient. They argue that those processes should be scrapped, and new processes designed from scratch. They suggest that the basic question that needs to be asked when reengineering a specific business process like billing, for example, is: If you were to invent the process to bill your customers without any constraints, what would that process look like?

Recently, some management theorists have argued that process reengineering efforts tend to focus too much on short-term gains, and that overenthusiastic managers have used BPR as an excuse to slash payrolls without giving sufficient thought to long-term goals and employee considerations.

Information technology and information systems play an integral role in many process-reengineering efforts. In some instances, it is the introduction of new technology that enables an organization to do something it was previously unable to. An example was the development of voice mail systems with menus of options for

Construction supply companies such as Boyd's need efficient inventory control systems to keep track of their supplies. Photo courtesy of Frank Siteman/Stock Boston, Inc.

customers. Consider the adoption of such systems by investment organizations. Previously, customers who were interested in obtaining routine information concerning their investments or investment options would call a customer representative, who would look up the desired information from a variety of sources. Now most of the larger firms offer extensive support through menu-based voice mail systems. By using a Touch-Tone telephone to access the system, customers can obtain the latest price quote and balance in their mutual fund, move their investments among funds, obtain historical performance information on other funds, and so on. This technology has radically diminished the need for customer service representatives, and has altered the role of those who remain.

One quick note on terminology before we proceed. Although business process reengineering includes the term *business,* it should be noted that the concepts of process improvement and reengineering apply equally to the private sector and the public sector, to both for-profit and not-for-profit enterprises. Also, the term *reengineering* may mislead you into thinking that the approach is based on a mathematical model or that it only applies to technical parts of the business. Although reengineering is the popular term to describe the act of creatively rethinking business processes, a preferable name would be business process *redesign.* We will continue to use the term *business process reengineering* for the sake of consistency, but we wish to stress that the concepts can be applied to all types of organizations and to all their aspects.

This chapter will expand upon a few guiding principles for process change:

1. Look at your business as a set of processes; each process fulfills at least one customer need.
2. Keep those processes simple.
3. Don't automate mistakes. Before you design an information system, make sure the process is performing well. If not, first change the process, then automate.
4. Don't confuse downsizing (which deals only with costs) with reengineering (which deals with customer satisfaction).
5. Centralize information (make it available to everybody that needs access to it) and decentralize decision making (make the organization more nimble).

FIGURE 8–1 Boyd's Construction Supply Company (BCSC)

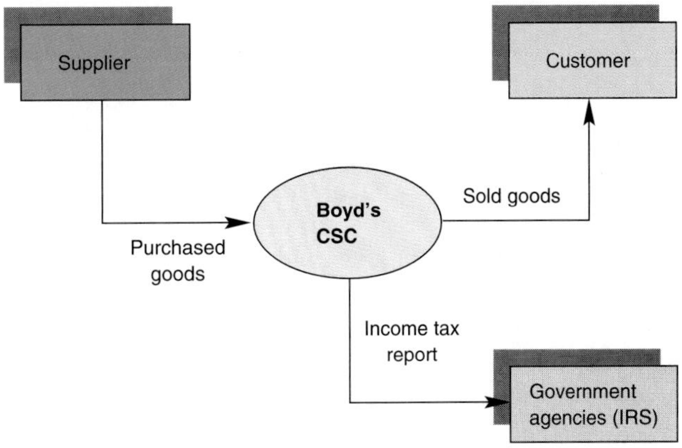

ORGANIZATIONAL GOALS AND BUSINESS PROCESSES

We have discussed earlier the importance of clearly stating specific business goals and measurable objectives before attempting to design information systems to help achieve those goals. It is not enough to recognize that the fundamental and very general goal is to respond to environmental changes in order to survive, and that a potential strategy is, for example, to be the low-cost producer in the industry. The key to long-term organizational success is to identify a set of processes that deliver an output that is needed by a given customer, and then to implement those processes in the most efficient way possible. From this perspective, it is possible to view an organization as a group of related processes cutting across functional areas. Each of these processes accepts inputs and creates outputs for a specific customer.

Consider the relatively small organization described in Chapter 7, Boyd's Construction Supply Company (BCSC). BCSC buys construction materials and supplies from a variety of suppliers. BCSC stores the goods in a warehouse, and distributes them as required to its retail outlets. BCSC is a relatively small, privately owned company, which means it doesn't have to prepare financial reports for stockholders. However, BCSC does have to report its income to the Internal Revenue Service, and it also needs a variety of information for internal decision-making purposes (e.g., purchasing and marketing decisions).

At a high level of abstraction, we could consider BCSC as a single business process, accepting materials and supplies from suppliers and producing sales (sold goods) for customers (see Figure 8–1). As a by-product of its operations, BCSC also produces an income tax report which is output to the IRS. (For simplicity we have ignored many other inputs and outputs, such as purchase orders from BCSC to suppliers.)

Some of the important managerial concerns for BCSC are the specific characteristics of the inputs and outputs and the process that transforms the inputs into outputs. BCSC's management should be asking: How readily available are the inputs (construction materials and supplies)? Are the inputs acceptable in terms of cost, quality, quantity? Can we obtain suitable inputs when we need them? How are our sales doing? What is the acceptance of our product or service? Is our market share increasing or decreasing? Are our customers satisfied with our products and service? How effective is our internal distribution system? Can we get the right materials to the right outlets when needed? Are we able to operate our retail outlets as efficiently as our competitors?

As you can see from the types of questions that management needs to ask, it is possible to break the overall organization into subsets or subsystems. Similarly, we can break down the overall business process (sales) into a series of overlapping subprocesses (acquisition, customer engagement, distribution). The advantage of looking at an organization from a business process point of view is that, because processes cross departments and functions, it facilitates the understanding of how different individuals within the organization need to interact to fulfill a customer need.

Also, since every process must by definition have an output, it must also by definition have a customer either internal or external to the company. (If the output of a process does not have a customer, then that process should be eliminated.) Thinking about and measuring organizational performance in terms of customer satisfaction implies delivering on the outputs the customers expect, which in turn implies delivering on the processes needed to generate those outputs. A process perspective encourages management to:

- See every aspect of the business as customer driven.
- Make employees responsible for the whole process rather than for just one task in it.
- Focus on *how* work is done rather that on *what* is done.

In other words, a process perspective encourages management to analyze not only the product or service being provided to the customer, but the process of doing business with the customer (e.g., ease of ordering, tracking of order status, billing, handling complaints, etc.).

Let's take a closer look at one business process for BCSC: the process of acquiring inputs. Figure 8–2 shows a diagram (a data flow diagram—described in more detail in Appendix B) of how the process works. The acquisition process is performed by a group of purchasing agents, reporting to a purchasing manager. The group receives a daily purchase request from each of the company's three retail outlets. Each request lists details of the items that the inventory manager of the specific outlet believes need to be replenished. The purchasing group combines the three purchase requests to determine the total amount of each item needed and to take advantage of any bulk order discounts that are available.

The members of the purchasing group then check their supplier-product files to see which suppliers can provide each item, and examine details such as the supplier cost, the minimum order size, the delivery time required, and so on. Using this information, they determine the best order details, and generate purchase orders to send to each of the suppliers who will be involved. The process of determining the purchase orders can be time-consuming as the purchasing agents have to go through details on different suppliers for a very large number of items each day.

Once the purchase orders have been prepared, they are sent (by courier) to the suppliers. A copy of each purchase order is sent to the distribution center, where it is filed for future reference; when the supplies are delivered to the distribution center the goods received are compared with the goods ordered to ensure that the correct materials and supplies were received. A copy is also sent to the accounting office, which needs to know how much money it needs to pay once an invoice is received from the supplier.

FIGURE 8–2 Boyd's CSC Acquisition Process

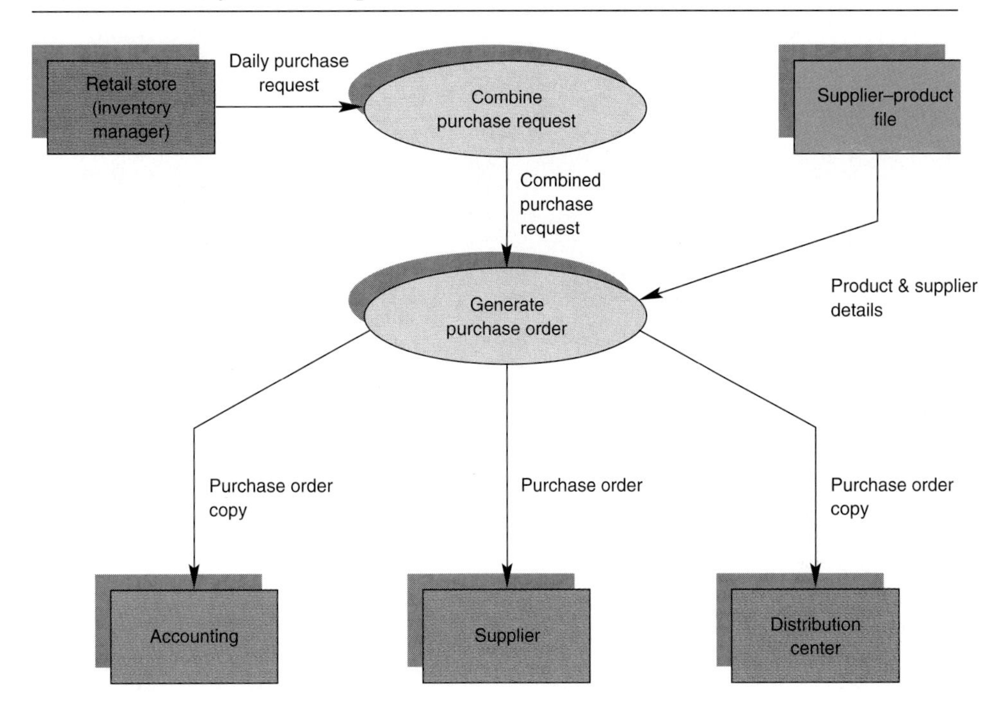

The BCSC acquisition process worked adequately for many years, but now staff members are feeling a need to improve it. Customers are complaining more often than they used to when they are unable to find a product on the shelf or in stock; even worse, they take their business elsewhere when they aren't satisfied. The acquisition process is simply too slow and inaccurate; the inventory managers have to spend a lot of time checking inventories, or else they have to make do with estimates of their needs.

This example illustrates how one process affects another. The purchase requests are the primary output of the inventory management process, and also the primary input for the acquisition process. Any problems the inventory management process has in generating accurate, timely purchase requests is going to affect the acquisition process. Also, the use of courier services for transmitting requests and purchase orders, although faster than regular mail, is still much slower than the electronic transmission that most of BCSC's competitors use. To provide better service to its customers, and hence remain competitive, BCSC needs to improve its existing acquisition process.

REENGINEERING AND CONTINUOUS IMPROVEMENT

The term *business process reengineering* gained widespread popularity with the publication of the book *Reengineering the Corporation,* by Michael Hammer and James Champy. Process reengineering had already been taking place in many organizations, but the popularity of the book brought BPR into the mainstream of business management considerations. Hammer and Champy defined reengineering

Many companies have instituted total quality management (TQM) and continuous improvement programs consisting or involving customers' opinions early in the design of products and services. Here, a group of potential customers evaluates a care before it does into full production. Photo courtesy of Chrysler Corporation.

as "the fundamental rethinking and redesign of business processes to achieve dramatic improvements in critical measures of performance such as cost, quality, service, and speed" (p. 32). Others have used such phrases as "strategic change projects" or "breakthrough innovation focused on customer needs" when describing reengineering.

The original concept of BPR from many advocates was that it should involve major changes to the organization. A successful BPR project involves a radical, not incremental, improvement.

A separate movement from BPR had involved ongoing corporate efforts based on philosophies of **continuous improvement** and the closely related **total quality management (TQM).** A primary distinction between BPR and these other philosophies is that continuous improvement tends to take a long-term, incremental approach while BPR tends to be short term and discrete (one-shot) projects. A second difference is that BPR tends to be driven from the top down, with much of the work done by consultants or specialists from outside of the company. TQM and related continuous improvement programs are typically run with strong input from the workers, using more of a bottom-up approach.

Recently, many organizations have begun to view BPR and TQM as complementary, rather than competing, approaches. They are thinking in terms of business process redesign (BPD) and integrated process management (IPM), in an attempt to gain the benefits of both BPR and TQM. To gain a better understanding of these approaches, we will examine reengineering and continuous improvement in more detail. Before we proceed with a discussion of what exactly IPM is, we need to define the basic terms we will be using throughout the remainder of the chapter.

Quality. The definition of quality has changed over time. Thirty years ago the definition of quality was narrow and internally focused. Quality was defined by the

FIGURE 8–3 Business Process Redesign Includes Continuous Improvement and Reengineering Initiatives

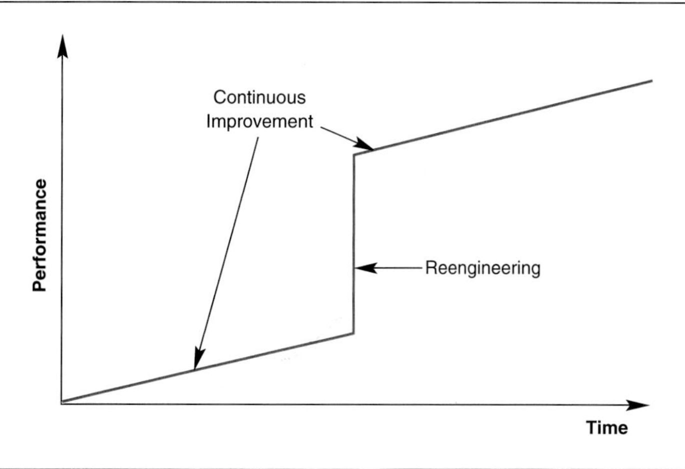

producer of the product or service (as a set of technical measures within a specific tolerance) and the view was that a certain number of defects was inevitable. Today, the definition of quality is almost entirely externally focused (quality is what the customer says it is) and the view is that total satisfaction of the customer is not only a realistic goal but a business imperative. Quality now encompasses not only technical parameters of a product and service but also how the product and service is delivered. Quality today is meeting or exceeding customer expectations at a price that represents value to them. Quality includes not only a product without defects but the on-time delivery of a product and service to a place convenient for the customer.

Reengineering. **Reengineering** is the fundamental rethinking and radical redesign of aspects of the business in order to achieve dramatic performance improvement. Reengineering efforts are typically a one-time initiative.

Continuous Improvement. **Continuous improvement** (and **total quality management**) are an ongoing commitment to excellence. They involve everyone within a company continually searching for *incremental* improvements in everything the company does.

Business Process Redesign. **Business process redesign (BPD)** is a fundamental change to how the enterprise operates. BPD has the primary goal of quality in everything that the enterprise does. BPD includes reengineering (one-time radical change to dramatically improve performance) and continuous improvement (continuous commitment to incremental betterment of performance). Figure 8–3 illustrates BPD in simple graph form.

EXAMPLES OF REENGINEERING

Before going further, perhaps some examples of business process reengineering efforts would help illustrate some of the concepts discussed so far. In 1988, CIGNA Corporation (a leading provider of insurance-related products) found its income had fallen from the previous year. As part of a new corporate strategic planning process, the chief information officer (CIO) started a review of how well the information systems department was supporting the strategic goals of the organization. The study revealed that sophisticated and expensive information systems were supporting an old organization. These systems have not changed the underlying processes and had not had the desired impact on the business.

The CIO decided to try BPR and looked for a division to volunteer as a guinea pig. The reinsurance group (CIGNA Re) signed on, and the project began in 1989. CIGNA Re was relatively small, employing only about 150 of CIGNA's 50,000 employees, but it offered complex products and services and was looking for improved information systems support. The division head was enthusiastic about the idea of reengineering the group; she believed that administrative expenses, product prices, and staff counts were all too high.

Over the next 18 months, CIGNA Re implemented new processes and cross-functional customer service teams in the administrative operations. By 1991, the division had downsized (reduced staff) by 40 percent. Operating costs were also down 40 percent, and an underwriting procedure that formerly took two weeks had been compressed into 15 minutes. A major change was a new culture that emphasized accountability and customer orientation. As an integral part of the reengineering effort, the division completely redesigned its information systems to match the new business processes. It reduced the number of information systems applications from 17 mainframe applications to 5 applications running on personal computers.

The reengineering effort at CIGNA Re did not happen without complications and problems. Nevertheless, the company learned a great deal from the experience; the CIGNA Re project was viewed as a pilot experiment for what has become a change in corporate culture at CIGNA. A reengineering group was formed, and numerous projects of increasing scope and complexity have been undertaken since then. To CIGNA, the institutionalization of reengineering means that reengineering is part of a company's operating style, and part of the way that its employees and managers think.

Business Brief 8–1 describes just how radical a pure reengineering strategy can be.

PRINCIPLES OF TOTAL QUALITY MANAGEMENT

One cannot speak about reengineering or process management without first acknowledging the influence of total quality management (TQM) on the managerial thinking of the 1980s. Indeed, TQM brought about a paradigm shift in management philosophy during the last decade.

The paradigm shift consisted of the following six changes in focus. First, the focus changed from selling a product or service to developing a relationship with the customer. The customer-driven corporation became a popular notion. It implies that the customer is at the center of all that the firm does. The customer is not an entity outside of the organization, but part of it. For example, customers are invited more and more often to help design products and add features to services.

Second, the measurements of organizational performance and success were expanded to include customer satisfaction measurements and not only financial yardsticks. Third, the supplier relationship changed from one of contention to one of partnership and strategic alliance (see Business Brief 8–2), and supplier selection changed to encompass issues of quality and synergy, not merely cost.

BUSINESS BRIEF 8-1 THE AX CAN BE SHARP: THE ULTIMATE IN REENGINEERING

As Ernest M. "Bud" Miller can attest, no one is safe in corporate reengineering—not even the engineer. Over the past several years, Mr. Miller, president and chief executive officer of Arvida, a real estate company, shuttered numerous regional offices, reorganized all departments, and reduced by half Arvida's work force of 2,600. In the process, he turned severe losses into strong profits.

But despite the years of trimming, Mr. Miller believed one intolerable layer of fat remained. So earlier this month, he resigned. "I couldn't justify me to me," said Mr. Miller, reached at a hotel in the Cayman Islands, where his family was "decompressing" in the wake of his surprise announcement. "I couldn't look at any one of the 1,300 people I let go and say I applied a different standard for me."

Mr. Miller, 52 years old, is forgoing a salary package that company sources say was in the "upper six figures" last year. The move eliminates one of the two senior jobs at the company. James Motta, the 38-year-old chief operating officer of Arvida, will become chief executive; Mr. Miller remains chairman through the end of the year.

Certainly, no one believes Mr. Miller—a former Marine with an MBA from Harvard University—will be on the street for long. For his part, Mr. Miller hopes soon he will be "helping a company restructure."

QUESTIONS

1. How difficult do you think it will be for Mr. Miller to find a new job?
2. If you were an employee at a company that hired Mr. Miller, how do you think you might respond to having him join the firm?

SOURCE: E. Thomas, Jr., "Re-Engineer Cut Corporate Fat, Then Fell On His Own Budget Ax," *The Wall Street Journal*, March 21, 1995, p. B1. Reprinted by permission of *The Wall Street Journal*,

Fourth, organizational structures were flattened by pushing decision making downward (empowering employees) and work was organized by process rather than by function. Fifth, the philosophy behind incentive programs changed from just performing work to improving performance and from recognizing individuals to recognizing teams. Finally, information went from being tightly controlled by a few managers to being openly shared throughout the organization.

It is also important to understand the principles underlying TQM. However, hundreds if not thousands of books and articles have been written on TQM. Most of them overlap in great measure; we have summarized their content into the following seven principles.

Quality is what the customer says it is. The customer is the ultimate arbiter as to whether you are delivering a quality product and/or service. Some critics of this view argue that often customers are unaware or have the wrong impression of the true quality level of a product or service. Therefore, these critics argue, it is not a good idea to give the customer the last say when it comes to quality. The fallacy of this criticism is revealed in the fact that it is the customers' impressions that determine whether they will ever buy from a specific firm, regardless of the "true" level of quality. The important point is that quality is both a tangible set of product/service characteristics and an image. Firms need to be aware of both levels: the tangible and the perceptual. Customer satisfaction is one of the most important measures of continuous and future organizational success. The implication for us, as students of management and information technology, is that customer satisfaction needs to be measured regularly, systematically, and consistently.

Think of yourself as the customer. Part of the problem most managers have in understanding the frustrations and complaints of customers resides in the fact that

BUSINESS BRIEF 8-2

DON'T GIVE AWAY THE FARM: MANUFACTURERS FARM OUT PRODUCT DEVELOPMENT

The next manufacturing revolution is under way, the U.S. companies are bringing airplanes, cars, even kitchen stoves to market faster and cheaper by leaning on their suppliers to help engineer and bankroll new projects.

This revolution goes far beyond the changes of the 1980s, when manufacturers attacked their high labor costs by shifting production to suppliers with lower labor costs. Now, manufacturers are slashing product-development expenses by farming out the tasks to suppliers—in essence, evolving from manufacturers to orchestrators that harmonize their suppliers' work.

Using this approach, Whirlpool Corp. is cooking up its first gas range without hiring engineers to create the gas burner system: instead, the design work is being done by Eaton Corp., a supplier that already makes gas valves and regulators for other appliance manufacturers. Whirlpool expects to get its new range to market several months sooner this way.

Under the old, "hierarchical" system, the subcontractors (such as Eaton Corp.) would simply have been given a product specification and then monitored. The new arrangement makes Eaton feel more a part of the team. It also allows the engineers at Eaton Corp. to use the expertise developed with similar products to design a burner for Whirlpool quickly and efficiently.

Chicago consulting firm A. T. Kearney, Inc., counsels companies to think long and hard before turning to suppliers for engineering help. "Before doing any of that, you've really got to look inside the company and say, 'What's the core thing we do and how do we distinguish ourselves from our competitors?' " says Tom Slaight, an A. T. Kearney efficiency expert. "If you give it all away, you pretty much have no edge in the marketplace."

QUESTION

1. Discuss the pros and cons of farming out product development efforts to subcontractors, as Whirlpool did with the gas burner system.

SOURCE: N. Templin and J. Cole, "Working Together: Manufacturers Use Suppliers to Help Them Develop New Products," *The Wall Street Journal,* December 19, 1994, p. 1.

those managers have never been customers of the processes they manage. A very good, and usually very sobering, exercise is for managers and employees responsible for a process to go through the process as their customers do. For example, the provost (chief academic officer) and president of a university should apply for admission to their own university and go through the entire application process. If you want to understand how customers see you, the best way to do it is to become one of them.

Customer satisfaction is impossible without employee satisfaction. It is difficult if not impossible for employees to interact with customers in a courteous and pleasant manner if they themselves are not treated accordingly. This is particularly true in businesses that are interaction intensive, like banks, hotels, airlines, retail sales, and the order-by-telephone businesses. Understanding how to keep employees satisfied is the first step toward providing quality products and services.

Improve continuously. Achieving total quality has been compared to a race without a finish. Customers' expectations of quality keep on increasing. There is always another aspect of the business that can be improved. TQM implies a constant commitment to improving all aspects of the firm. In doing so, two guidelines should be followed.

First, it's important to realize that "mistakes are treasures." Employees are usually not trying to make mistakes. No worker walks to his/her job thinking, "I am going to make lots of mistakes today." The systems and processes that are in place in a given

Satisfied employees generally treat customers better, which in turn improves customer satisfaction. Photo courtesy of Chip Henderson/Tony Stone Images.

organization are supposedly there for a good reason. So when a mistake occurs, it implies that something went wrong—that a system broke down, or that an employee did not know how to handle a given situation. Documenting, reporting, and analyzing mistakes is the most effective way to improve. A mistake is a treasure of information about an organizational breakdown. But in order to exploit that treasure of information, the mistake needs to be analyzed quickly. Unfortunately, in most organizations, information on mistakes tends to be repressed and delayed. If the source of the mistake is not addressed, there is no assurance that the mistake will not happen again. An important component of any TQM program is the implementation of a mistake collection and analysis system.

Second, it's important to realize that continuous improvement is impossible without having a *consistent* level of performance. Inconsistencies in performance are the number one enemy of customer satisfaction. From a TQM perspective, variations in quality are evil. Customers need to know what to expect when they walk into a restaurant, open a bottle of wine, or make a reservation on a flight. Variations in service and/or product quality need to be eliminated, and one very effective way to achieve consistency is to document procedures and enforce their use.

Therefore, to improve continuously a firm must document and eradicate mistakes, and eliminate inconsistencies. An effective twofold strategy to achieve this goal is as follows:

1. Review all procedures and make sure they are as simple and straightforward as possible.
2. Keep them that way.

Organizations need to resist the temptation to complicate processes and regulations as time goes by.

Leadership and accountability make quality happen. Quality in everything the organization does can only happen when top management demonstrates by example that quality matters to them. It is important to have the word *quality* in the mission statement, but it is much more important to use the word in conversations with employees. At the water cooler, in the cafeteria, on the parking lot shuttle, whenever the opportunity shows up, management needs to ask about quality, about customers' expectations being met, and about ideas on how to do better. Quality must be built into incentive programs and evaluation of performance formulas. TQM says that if you are going to talk about service routinely, you should also put your measures (of performance and rewards) where your mouth is.

The extent to which there is a strong shared vision of providing quality service and products is a measure of managerial leadership in establishing quality as a priority for the firm. A good example is the answer given by a janitor at a defense contractor, a manufacturer of helicopters, when asked whether he considered his job important or not. His response, as he continued sweeping the floor, was "I know that a clean environment contributes to a low defect rate. My cleaning of these floors contributes to keeping our helicopters flying and therefore minimizing loss of life."

Focusing on quality increases efficiency; focusing on efficiency often decreases quality. As stated above, process simplification and control, meaning consistency in performance, are key steps in delivering quality. Concentrating on doing things well by increasing the understanding of what contributes to problems eventually leads to doing things fast. By improving quality, that is, by understanding and simplifying procedures to create consistency, one improves efficiency. Remember, not all problems are equal in importance. TQM helps prioritize problems by stating that quality problems are more important than efficiency problems, and should be dealt with first.

In God we trust—everybody else better bring data. Quality management is a data-intensive process. Though anecdotes of great service or great disasters in service are powerful motivators of change, continuous improvement can only come through a systematic and regular assessment of performance. Improvement implies having targets and reporting progress in achieving those targets. Anecdotes by their nature tend to be extreme examples and as such tend to distort the view of the "average" level of quality being provided. TQM and business process redesign require the development of an information systems infrastructure that allows tracking internal performance measures (e.g., level of defects, cycle times, efficiencies, inventory levels) and external measures of effectiveness (e.g., customer satisfaction, market share).

EXAMPLES OF TOTAL QUALITY MANAGEMENT AND CONTINUOUS IMPROVEMENT

The productivity gains achieved with business process reengineering and corresponding information systems development efforts often come at a cost to the employees involved. Frequently, the largest gains are made by using new information systems to do more work with fewer people. Some organizations reassign the displaced workers to other positions. Others let them go. The employees who remain are often stretched thin as they attempt to do more with fewer resources. In many instances, this "doing more with less" has led to decreased employee morale and a counterproductive relationship between managers and workers.

Some organizations have attempted to change this pattern by actively soliciting input from employees, rather than mandating change from above. These companies are finding they can reap the benefits of process improvements by motivating employees to question and improve the way they work, without hiring consultants to tell them what changes are needed. An example of this approach occurred with the Canadian division of Merck, the large drug-manufacturing firm.

FIGURE 8–4 Integrated Process Management

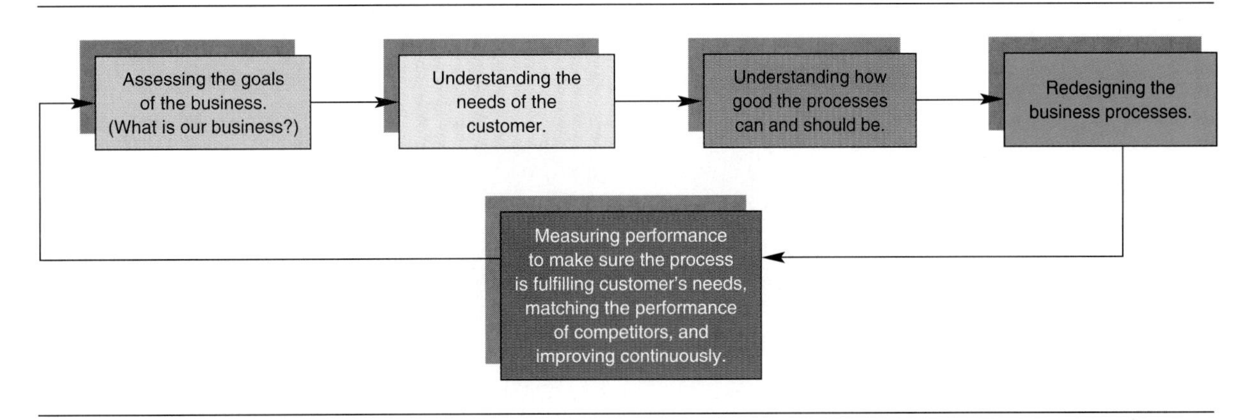

When Merck salespeople were brought together in small groups to discuss ways to improve their jobs, many complained of excessive reporting requests by managers. As the salespeople increasingly used computers to record sales data, managers were demanding more and more analytical reports. Some salespeople were spending nights and weekends crunching numbers. Others were hiding out at home during the day doing the reports, rather than traveling to visit their customers.

Merck followed up with small group discussions with the managers, who confirmed that many of the reports were never used or were only marginally useful. They were able to cut the number of reports by more than half, reducing the reporting time requirement for salespeople by a substantial amount. As a result, salespeople were able to make more sales calls, and were also able to maintain a better balance in their personal and professional lives.

This type of bottom-up approach is consistent with continuous improvement or TQM philosophies. The concept behind continuous improvement and total quality management is to have the workers, who really know their job tasks and responsibilities, suggest ways to improve them. In an organization that is committed to continuous improvement, employees at all levels are constantly looking for ways to do things better. This could involve anything from restructuring job tasks, to implementing improved information systems, to developing new products.

INTEGRATED PROCESS MANAGEMENT

Integrated process management (IPM) includes both reengineering efforts and TQM/continuous improvement initiatives. Earlier we introduced the term *business process redesign* (BPD) as a combination of BPR and TQM. The principle behind IPM is the constant review and assessment of critical business processes; IPM goes beyond BPD by designing and implementing systems for monitoring and assessing processes. The generic methodology consists of the following (see Figure 8–4):

1. Assessing the goals of the company. What is our business?
2. Understanding the needs of customers. What are the **order-winning criteria?** (The order-winning criteria are those the customer uses to decide what vendor to purchase from.)
3. Understanding how good the processes can and should be. What are the competition's performance levels?

FIGURE 8–5 Integrated Process Management Information System

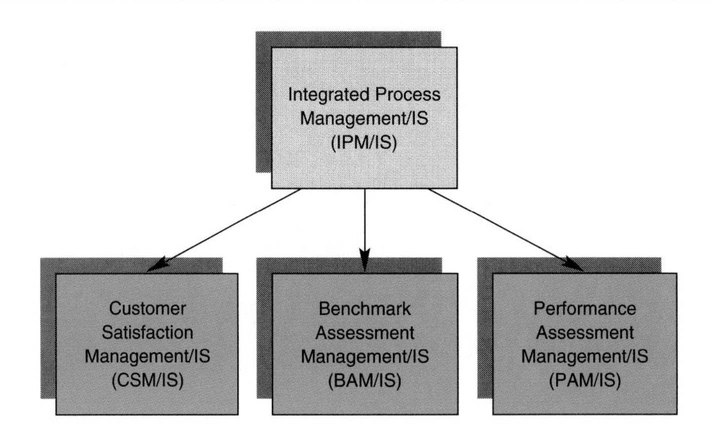

4. Redesigning the business processes. If we could start the process all over again, how would we organize it?
5. Measuring performance to make sure the process is (a) fulfilling customers' needs, (b) matching competitors' performance, and (c) improving continuously.

Therefore, Integrated Process Management (IPM) is a data-intensive approach to managing an organization with the goal of achieving excellence and 100 percent customer satisfaction. The success of IPM is dependent on the ability of a firm to understand what customers want, how competitors are performing, and how the firm is performing. Ideally, an organization should have the ability to monitor these variables. We refer to this information-processing capability as an **integrated process management information system (IPM/IS).**

An IPM/IS is an information system that allows a firm to continuously review its performance. There are three basic components to an IPM/IS: (1) a customer satisfaction management information system, (2) a benchmarking assessment management information system, and (3) a performance assessment management information system. (See Figure 8–5.) We discuss each of these components below.

The Customer Satisfaction Management Information System

Achieving high customer satisfaction starts with knowing what the customer wants. One way to do that is to elicit the customers' order-winning criteria (OWC)—the criteria used by customers to buy from one vendor rather than another. The common denominator to all business strategies is to keep customers coming back. For customers to come back, they must perceive the interaction with the company as satisfactory. Knowing what your customers want (i.e., what their OWC are), and delivering it to them, is what we call *listening to the customer's voice.* We believe that in order to listen to that voice you need to have a systematic way of collecting the thoughts, expectations, and evaluations of your customers. In other words, you need a **customer satisfaction management information system (CSM/IS).**

Customer Satisfaction: The Major Issues. Customers are the most important assets of the corporation. ("A company's only true assets are satisfied customers." Jan

Customer satisfaction has become the centerpiece of many companies' mission statements. Photo courtesy of John Curtis/Offshoot Stock.

Carlzon, former president, SAS.[1] "The three most important things you need to measure in a business are customer satisfaction, employee satisfaction, and cash flow. " Jack Welch, CEO, GE.) But, most corporations do not treat customers as such. Many tend to structure their processes in ways that facilitate internal constraints and preferences, rather than making the processes easier for the customer.

Customer satisfaction is the extent to which customers believe a product or service meets or surpasses their expectations. Customer expectations are set by a variety of factors including the performance of companies in other industry segments.

For most companies, listening to the customer's voice is difficult because a lot of their customers don't speak to them, though they speak to others. The average business never hears from 96 percent of its unhappy customers. However, unhappy customers do talk to other actual and potential customers about their experiences (Figure 8–6). The average customer that has a problem tells 9 or 10 people about it. In a study conducted by the U.S. federal government, researchers found that 13 percent of the customers that had a problem with a company shared it with 20 or more people. One important and promising result of that study was that customers who had complained to a company and had their complaint resolved told five people about the treatment they received.

The results of this study were replicated in a survey of 2,400 customers of IBM (Figure 8–7). In that survey, 84 percent of the customers who had purchased a computer and had no problem with it stated that they would purchase again from IBM, and 91 percent said they would recommend the product to others. As expected, a minority of the customers who had purchased a product and had a problem that had not been resolved to their satisfaction said they would purchase again from IBM (46 percent) or would recommend it to others (48 percent). The surprise in the survey was this: the highest percentage of customers who would either repurchase from IBM or recommend it to others came from those customers who had a problem with their purchase and had their problem resolved to their satisfaction (89 percent and 94 percent respectively).

[1]J. Carlzon, *Moments of Truth* (New York: Ballinger, 1987).

FIGURE 8–6 Impact of Customer Dissatisfaction

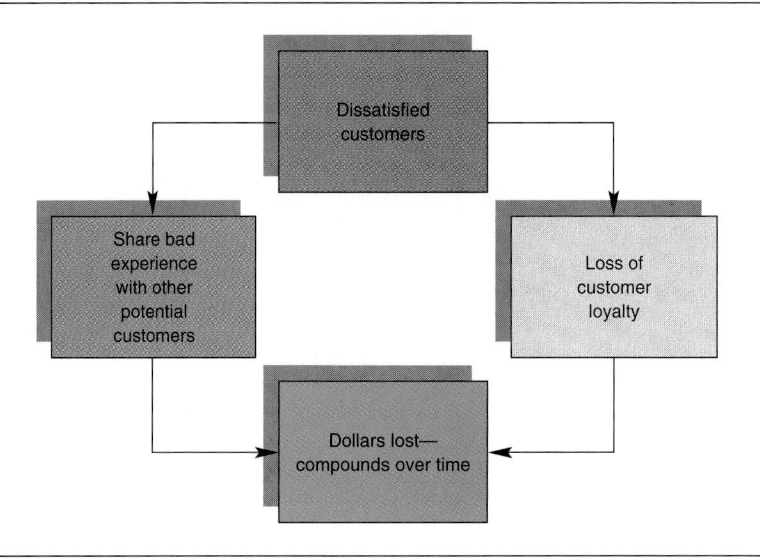

SOURCE: Adapted from IBM Rochester.

FIGURE 8–7 Tendency to Buy Again and Tell Others

Baseline Study of 2400 Customers

<table>
<tr><th>Customer Experience</th><th>Future Purchase</th><th>Recommend</th><th>Tell Others</th></tr>
<tr><td>No problem—satisfied</td><td>84%</td><td>91%</td><td rowspan="2">3</td></tr>
<tr><td>Problem—satisfied</td><td>92%</td><td>94%</td></tr>
<tr><td>Problem—dissatisfied</td><td>46%</td><td>48%</td><td>7</td></tr>
</table>

+ 1% of customer satisfaction = revenue opportunity = $257M

SOURCE: Adapted from IBM Rochester.

Why Losing Customers Is Expensive. The loss of a customer is an expensive proposition. Not only does that customer not come back, but other potential customers will know of the problem. Companies need to see a customer as a revenue stream over time and not only as a one-time transaction. Though a clerk at Taco Bell may think that alienating a customer is only costing the company a one-time sale (say, $3.50), in reality the cost may be much greater. Studies have shown that a Taco Bell customer is worth, over the lifetime of that customer, an average of $8,000. For Cadillac (the automobile manufacturer), the lifetime value of a customer is $355,000. Another study (Figure 8–8) has shown that if keeping a customer costs the company $1, gaining a new one costs $5, and regaining a disgruntled one costs $11.

FIGURE 8–8 Cost of Customer Loyalty

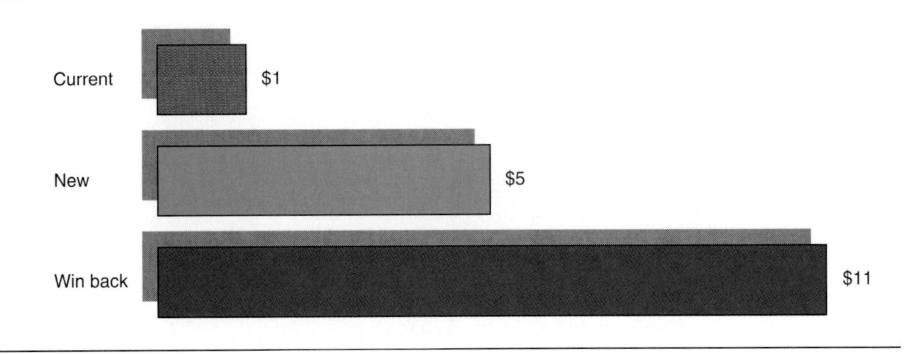

SOURCE: IBM Advanced Business Institute, "Organizing I/S," 1993.

FIGURE 8–9 Customer Interfaces

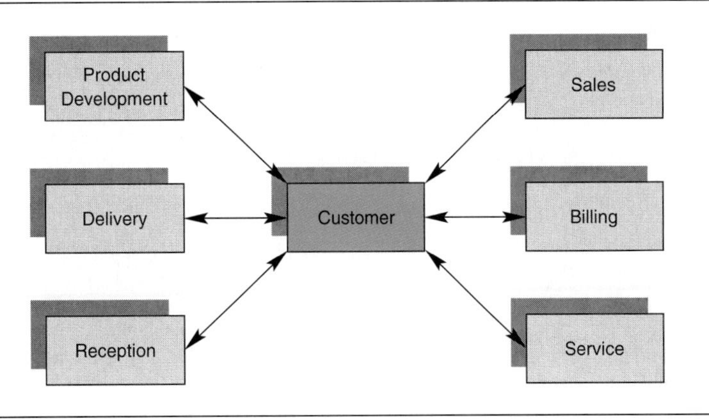

SOURCE: IBM Advanced Business Institute, "Organizing I/S," 1993.

One important conclusion from all these studies is that a complaining customer is an important customer and one that needs to be rewarded for coming forth. However, the attitude in most organizations is "to shoot the messenger" and to look at complaining customers as difficult and unreasonable. Companies need to realize that a complaining customer is one who is taking the time to point out a shortcoming of the processes the company uses in serving customers. Assuming that companies do not try to make mistakes on purpose, the information provided by a disgruntled customer is vital to improving those processes and ensuring that the mistake is not repeated. Also, when a disgruntled customer comes forward, the company has a chance to turn the problem into an opportunity by turning the customer from one that will disseminate bad publicity to one that will praise the company's recovery from a mistake. It is critical to build an information system to report on mistakes and to develop a policy to let employees know what to do right away to make the customer happy.

Why Keeping Customers Happy Is Hard. The difficulty of providing customer satisfaction is twofold. The first difficulty is that, as Figure 8–9 depicts, customer

FIGURE 8–10 Customer Retention Curve

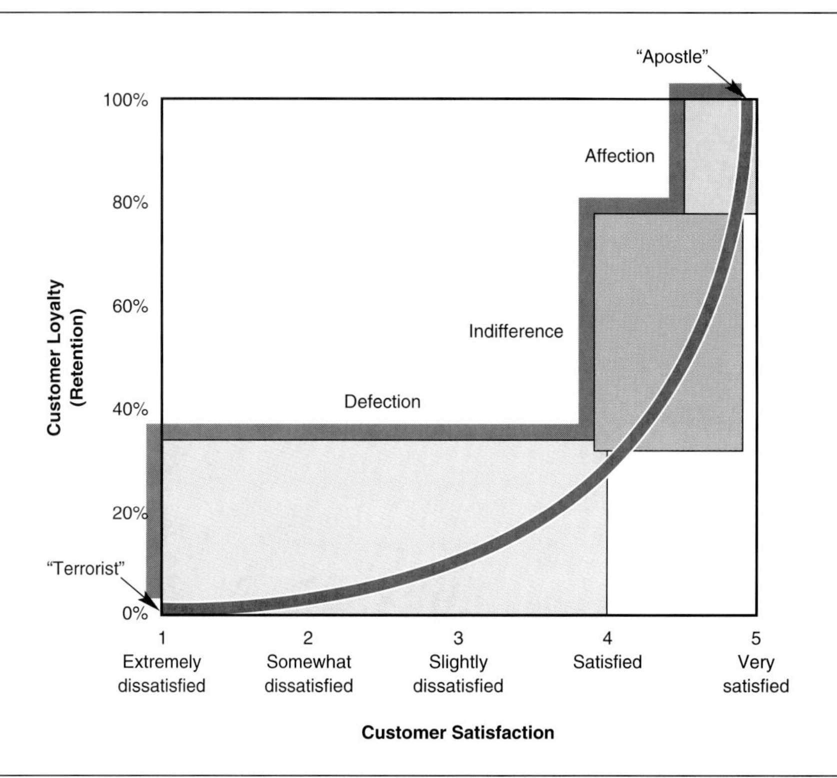

SOURCE: Adapted from Heskett et al, 1994.

interactions are many and varied. (As Jan Carlzon of SAS put it, "we have 50,000 moments of truth out there every day.")[2] In an average day as a customer in a hotel, you may interact with 8 to 10 different employees, each with a different level of education, training, and possibly, understanding of the company's policies. Making every single interaction with the customer a successful one is difficult.

The second difficulty in keeping customers happy is that customers are fickle. The curve shown in Figure 8–10 comes from a survey of over 250,000 customers of Xerox. What it shows is that in order to keep its customers (customer retention of 90 percent or better) a company needs to perform *consistently* at a level of 4.8 or better (out of 5). The notion of customer retention is often overlooked. Most managers are concerned with measuring the *quantity* of market share without assessing the *quality* of that market share. The quality of the market share, however, is quite possibly more related to long-term success than the actual quantity.

Development of a Customer Satisfaction Management Information System

The causes of customer dissatisfaction are 80 percent due to how the product or service is delivered to the customer. Only 20 percent of the causes are due to the product or service itself not meeting expectations. The implication is that *the difficulty of doing business with a company* is the major reason for customer dissatisfaction. This is an important implication, since the processes of interaction

[2]Carlzon, op.cit.

are under the control of management. A good customer satisfaction management information system (CSM/IS) should therefore measure not only the characteristics of the product but also the characteristics of the business processes used in delivering the product or service to the customer.

A CSM/IS consists of collecting, storing, and manipulating information to allow a better understanding of who the company's customers are, what they need and want, and how satisfied they are. A CSM/IS establishes the standard of service and quality that meets the expectation of the customers. Without that standard, trying to deliver quality is like participating in a high jump competition without knowing where the bar is that we need to get over.

Measuring customer satisfaction requires a measurement system that is ongoing, broad-based, multidimensional, and both proactive and reactive. The measurement system must be ongoing because, in order to pick up trends in changes of customer satisfaction, the system needs to collect data regularly. The more frequent the data collection, the earlier the system will pick up significant changes in customer satisfaction.

The measurement needs to be broad-based to ensure that the data are representative of all the relevant types of customers. The more broad-based the measurement system is, the better the understanding about what type of customer is satisfied. The customer satisfaction measurement system needs to include a variety of measures to be able to diagnose which features of the service or product are being appreciated and which are not.

Finally, the customer satisfaction management information system needs to include proactive and reactive measures of satisfaction. **Proactive measures** of customer satisfaction are measures that predict whether a customer is going to be satisfied or not and allow intervention to rectify a problem. **Reactive measures** of satisfaction describe the experience the customer had with the product or service.

For example, a proactive measure of customer satisfaction in the pizza delivery business would be the temperature at which the pizza leaves the store. Though it is not a measure of customer satisfaction per se, it correlates with one: the temperature of the pizza upon arrival. Knowing that the temperature of the pizza is low before it leaves the store gives employees a chance to intervene (e.g., reheat the pizza) and maximize the likelihood of having a satisfied customer at the end of the business transaction.

An example of reactive measure of customer satisfaction would be a course survey given to students at the end of a course. Such surveys tell whether students liked the course or not, and why, but do not provide an opportunity to change the course during that school term. Reactive measures of customer satisfaction are very important in that they provide actual data of customer satisfaction once the product or service has been used; but if satisfaction is low, reactive measures only leave the possibility to recover from—rather than avoid—having provided the customer with a bad experience.

A good customer satisfaction management information system will collect data on both proactive and reactive measures of satisfaction. Furthermore, a good CSM/IS provides feedback to managers in a way that they know what business processes they need to tinker with. An example of such a system is FedEx's performance assessment system. FedEx reports their Service Quality Index on a quarterly basis (see Figure 8–11). The index is based on 12 critical indicators of service quality (Table 8–1). The indicators have different weights. These weights reflect the extent of customer dissatisfaction, that is, the number of failure points that the company gets from a disgruntled customer. Notice that the indicators are clearly related to

FIGURE 8–11 Customer Satisfaction Ratings and SQI Trends

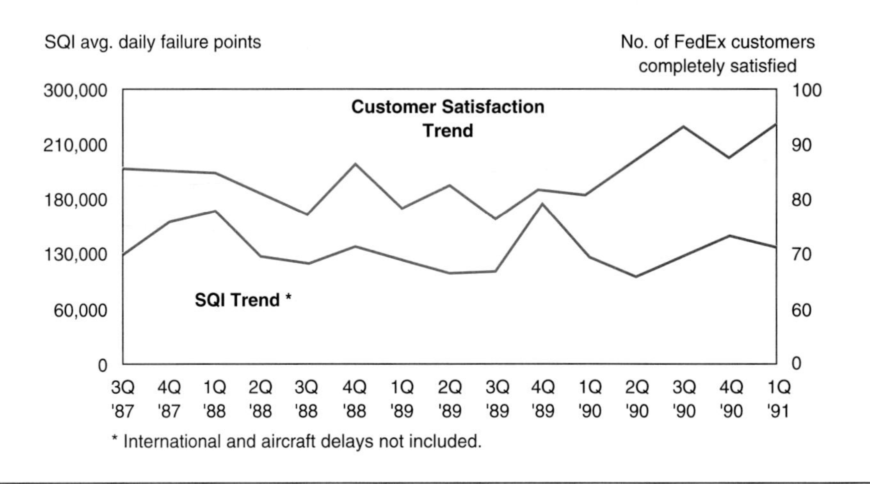

SOURCE: IBM Advanced Business Institute, "Organizing I/S," 1993.

TABLE 8–1 Federal Express Service Quality Indicators

Indicator	*Weight*
Abandoned Calls	1*
Complaints Reopened	5
Damaged Packages	10
International	1
Invoice Adjustments Requested	1
Lost Packages	10
Missed Pick-ups	10
Missed Proofs of Delivery	1
Overgoods (Lost and Found)	5
Right Day Late Deliveries	1
Traces	1
Wrong Day Late Deliveries	5

*All numbers listed in this column indicate the number of failure points given to the company by disgruntled customers.

SOURCE: IBM Advanced Business Institute, "Organizing I/S," 1993.

FedEx's business processes and that the index (the sum of all failure points accumulated in a quarter) is highly correlated with actual customer satisfaction.

Benchmark Assessment Management Information System

Another critical component of reengineering and TQM is the notion of **benchmarking.** A benchmark is something that serves as a standard by which given elements may be measured. Benchmarking is a continuous and systematic process for evaluating the products, services, and work processes of organizations that we recognize as having the best practices. In other words, we find out who is doing the best job in the industry, and compare ourselves with them.

Benchmarking establishes targets for organizational improvement. It allows organizations to define customer requirements and ways to fulfill them based on market reality. Benchmarking establishes not what is ideal in performing a process, but what is possible if a firm could be as good as the best firms performing that process. As such, benchmarking presents the need for change based on credible, unarguable data, and is an effective strategy to overcome internal resistance. Benchmarking allows for a reality check of how good the firm is and supports creative thinking about ways to match the performance of other firms.

Development of a Benchmark Assessment Management Information System

The first step in developing a **Benchmark Assessment Management Information System (BAM/IS)** is to decide what to benchmark and how to measure it. Are we interested in benchmarking results, overall performance characteristics, processes, or what? What are the relevant metrics (measures)? Some metrics to benchmark could include levels of customer satisfaction, intention to repurchase, satisfaction index, recommendations to others, perceived quality value, functionality, amount of paperwork, number of days to process an order, number of complaints, number of errors, days late in producing reports, or number of steps. The last question of this first step in designing a BAM/IS is: how often to collect the data?

The second step is to select **benchmarking partners.** We should choose partners on the basis of who our direct competitors are (to determine what we call the *best of breed* or the best in the industry) and also on the basis of who is known to be particularly good at a given process (to determine what we call *world class*). For example, L. L. Bean is known for its warehouse operations; EDS (Electronic Data Systems) for its information systems management capabilities; FedEx and Wal-Mart for their use of scanners and bar coding; USAA for document imaging and processing.

The third and last step is to develop the system to collect and compare data. Data can be presented as shown in Figure 8–12. The figure represents the performance of our company (labeled *Us*), the performance of the best company in our industry (best of breed), and the performance of the best company across industries on eight measures of customer satisfaction. These eight measures were identified by customers as being critical issues in their choice of vendors. Note that the only real company is "Us." The best of breed and world class profiles are created by collating the performances of the company that scores best on each measure. As such, the best of breed and world class profiles represent "virtual" companies having the attributes of the best performers on each measure. As soon as a gap in performance is identified (say, on measure M1 or M3), the BAM/IS should trigger an effort to investigate how to bridge that gap.

FIGURE 8-12 Identification of Performance Gaps through Benchmarking

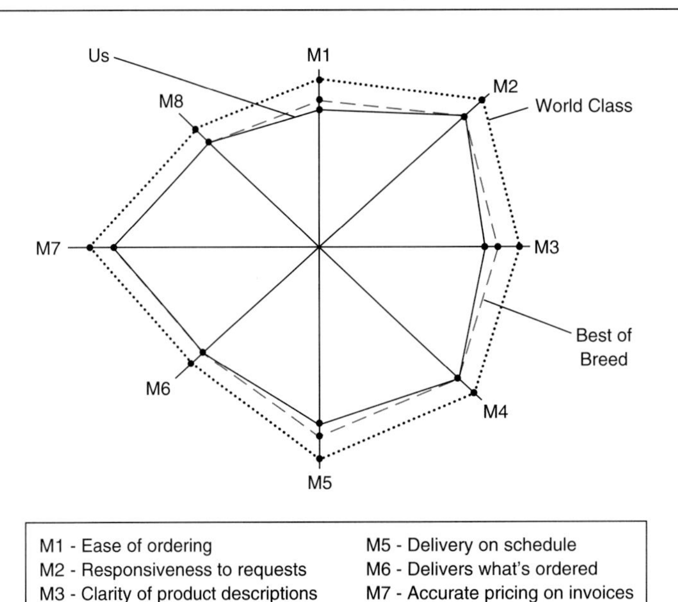

SOURCE: IBM Advanced Business Institute, "Organizing I/S," 1993.

Performance Assessment Management Information System

The third information system component to support integrated process management is a **performance assessment management information system (PAM/IS).** A PAM/IS consists of systematically collecting data on every critical factor of the business. The PAM/IS is like a control panel of a jet fighter. It should provide the pilot of the plane with the critical variables needed to fly the plane in an optimal fashion. In other words, PAM/IS is the control panel of the manager in charge of a business process. The PAM/IS combines measures reported in the CSM/IS and BAM/IS with measures of financial and operational performance. Another way of thinking about the PAM/IS is to look at it as the overall performance scorecard for a given business process. The PAM/IS calculates a performance score based on a series of differentially weighted measures. The PAM/IS should provide the manager with all the data necessary to know how customers (internal and external) feel about the process, its statistical characteristics (in control or not), its improvement rate, the performance of competitors and other benchmark partners on the same process, as well as a series of financial and accounting measures to help the manager allocate resources optimally.

In this chapter we have introduced terms to identify and describe information systems designed for specific purposes: IPM/IS; CSM/IS; BAM/IS; PAM/IS. These terms help differentiate between the objectives of these types of information systems; in reality, few organizations use these specific terms, even though they have information systems that perform similar functions.

For example, the concept of a performance assessment system is identical to that of an executive information system (EIS) which we introduced in Chapter 5. The term *EIS* is somewhat misleading, however, since it implies that the system is only used by executives. This was certainly the case when this type of system was first introduced and receiving considerable attention during the 1980s. As the systems matured, however, the performance information provided by them was made available to individuals at lower levels in the organization. For this reason we prefer the term *performance assessment system,* which is appropriate for a broader range of applications.

THE ROLE OF I/T

Information technology is a key enabler of business process redesign. Although our philosophy is "First think about the process, then think about the information system," it is sometimes important at the beginning of an engineering effort to be aware of how technology has changed processes at other organizations. For example, any firm that is thinking of reengineering their maintenance and after-sales service should be aware of the Otisline system at Otis Elevators. Any insurance company should be aware of the efforts by USAA to digitize and electronically store all its customer communications and do away with paper-based files. Any bank looking into changing their loan-giving process should be aware of the many examples of using expert systems in the industry to provide quick response to customers' requests. Any firm redesigning their sales processes should be aware of how Frito-Lay used custom-designed portable computers to redesign its process. Any company looking into establishing an EDI-based ordering system with its customers should be aware of the American Hospital Supply/Baxter story of establishing a clear value-added relationship for the system to work.

Therefore, I/T can not only help make a process better once it has been redesigned, but it can actually give you ideas on how to redesign the process. Technology can play several roles, including:[3]

Automational (eliminating human labor). A typical example is the more and more common use of automated telephone call distribution systems, instead of human operators, in telephone-intensive processes such as customer service.

Informational (capturing information to better understand the process). For example, operators in a paper mill use computer-based tools to capture information on resources and energy consumption and then use that information to optimize consumption levels.

Sequential (changing process sequence, enabling parallelism). One way that information technology can improve a process is by reducing the cycle time. I/T can allow some tasks to be performed in parallel, saving time. An example is checking a customer's credit while the customer is putting his/her order in.

Tracking (monitoring the physical location of objects). FedEx scans the package being delivered up to 10 different times in order to provide customers with the exact status of their packages. Satellite-based tracking systems enable trucking and railroad companies to know where their trucks and railroad car stock is at all times.

Analytical (improving analysis and decision making). Point-of-sale (POS) systems allow monitoring the sales performance of certain products. When these POS

[3]These roles have been adapted from Davenport (1993).

systems are integrated into inventory and production systems, "what-if" scenarios can be quickly developed to determine the most profitable product mix. Most of these scenarios can be developed automatically and reviewed almost instantaneously by the manager in charge. The ability to perform sensitivity analyses in fast-moving environments is one of the great contributions of information systems to decision making.

Geographical (coordinating processes across distances). Ford designed the 1994 edition of the Mustang in record time by coordinating its development electronically. Design teams in Detroit, Michigan and Milan, Italy exchanged drawings and manufacturing ideas as if they were sitting face-to-face. One of the important contributions of I/T is the shrinking of distance, making it possible for global companies to function in an integrated and efficient way.

Integrative (coordinating tasks). In bidding for contracts, a consulting firm may have to submit a proposal with input from several experts (e.g., legal, accounting, marketing, etc.). In determining whether to extend a loan, a bank officer may want to look at all the accounts (e.g., checking, savings, money market, mortgage) that the customer has with the bank. These are two examples where I/T supports processes that require highly coordinated tasks.

Intellectual (capturing and distributing knowledge and experience). I/T is becoming central in capturing and distributing knowledge in organizations. Airlines build databases on customer practices and preferences; large accounting firms develop expert systems on tax issues; utility companies implement expert systems to help recover quickly from systems failures. I/T provides the opportunity of leveraging the experience and knowledge of workers by centralizing and making that expertise available to all members of the organization.

Disintermediating (eliminate intermediate steps, intermediaries). Airlines selling tickets directly to customers, bypassing travel agents; drug manufacturers selling directly to hospitals, bypassing distributors; electronic markets allowing people to buy and sell houses directly, bypassing real estate agents, or to buy and sell stocks directly, bypassing stock brokers; trucking companies bidding for contracts, bypassing consolidators: all these are examples of the use of I/T in shrinking the distribution chain. This application of I/T not only reduces transactions costs, but also allows vendors to understand their markets better.

In general, one can think of I/T as a tool to facilitate three critical elements in achieving excellence in process performance:

1. The *monitoring* of process performance (on-line, real-time data to provide feedback to workers and managers on their progress toward achieving targets).
2. The *integration* of information from several sources to improve the process (using "800" help lines to discover new ways to improve products and services).
3. The *customization* of the process (micromarketing, mass customization).

PROCESS MANAGEMENT AND INFORMATION SYSTEMS DEVELOPMENT

We have described a method to redesign the business process which includes the following generic steps:

1. Define business goals.
2. Align process goals with business goals.

Before paving the cowpath, straighten it; before you automate, redesign! Photo courtesy of Leverett Bradley/Tony Stone Images.

3. Define process requirements.
4. Generate alternatives to change the process.
5. Design and implement the chosen alternative.
6. Evaluate and monitor.

This method follows the rational problem-solving approach: define purpose, establish goals, generate alternatives, choose best alternative, implement, evaluate. Not surprisingly, it is very similar to the method for designing information systems described in the previous chapter, since we use this same rational problem-solving approach to develop it.

Furthermore, developing information systems should not be viewed as a separate activity from business process management; since most business processes are supported by information and communication systems, the two need to go hand-in-hand. However, the sequence is important. One needs to *first redesign the process and then design an information system to support the new process.* One should avoid automating what are really unnecessary activities and procedures. In thinking about this relationship between redesigning business processes and developing information systems, it is always helpful to remember the saying, "Before paving the cowpath, straighten it!" (Before you automate, redesign!)

SUMMARY

Organizations attempt to achieve specific performance goals defined by customer needs. It is possible and desirable to view an organization as a set of interrelated processes designed to achieve these goals. Managing organizational processes is an ongoing activity, which may frequently be supported with the application of information technology.

Business process redesign (BPD) may take two major forms: business process reengineering (BPR), which focuses on short-term, radical change; and continuous improvement or total quality management (TQM), which involves constantly looking for ways to improve and is long-term in nature.

Integrated process management (IPM) involves designing and implementing information systems that support process redesign and ongoing process management. IPM is data intensive, involving the collection, analysis, and use of numerous process measures. Three main components to a system for IPM include customer satisfaction management, benchmarking, and performance assessment.

Information technology may be used in numerous ways to support processes and process improvement. Examples include automational (eliminating human labor), informational (capturing information to better understand the process), sequential (changing process sequence, enabling parallelism), tracking (monitoring the process), analytical (improving analysis and decision making), geographical (coordinating processes across distances), integrative (coordinating tasks), intellectual (capturing and distributing knowledge and expertise), and disintermediating (eliminating intermediaries or intermediate steps).

Final notes on process management: (1) view your business as a set of processes; (2) don't confuse downsizing with reengineering; (3) keep it simple; and (4) don't automate mistakes—before you design an information system, make sure you are familiar and comfortable with the process.

KEY CONCEPTS AND TERMS

KEY CONCEPTS

- An organization may be viewed as a set of processes designed to achieve measurable goals in the fulfillment of specific customer needs and desires. (264)
- Business process reengineering consists of radical improvements, typically with a short-term focus. (268)
- TQM and continuous process improvement consist of ongoing improvements with a long-term focus. (268)
- Integrated process management requires a set of information systems designed to support business process redesign (customer satisfaction, benchmark assessment, and performance assessment management). (275)

KEY TERMS

benchmark assessment management information system (BAM/IS) (283)
benchmarking (283)
benchmarking partners (283)
business process (263)
business process redesign (BPD) (269)
business process reengineering (BPR) (263)
continuous improvement (268)
customer satisfaction management information system (CSM/IS) (276)
downsizing (263)
integrated process management (IPM) (275)
integrated process management information system (IPM/IS) (276)
order-winning criteria (OWC) (275)
performance assessment management information system (PAM/IS) (284)
proactive measurement (281)
process management (263)
reactive measurement (281)
reengineering (263)
total quality management (TQM) (268)

REFERENCES

Carlzon, J. *Moments of Truth.* New York: Ballinger, 1987.

Caron, J. R.; S. Jarvenpaa; and D. Stoddard. "Business Reengineering at CIGNA Corporation: Experiences and Lessons Learned from the First Five Years." *MIS Quarterly* 18 (3), September 1994, pp. 233–50.

Davenport, T. H. *Process Innovation: Reengineering Work through Information Technology.* Cambridge: Harvard Business Press, 1993.
Hammer, M. "Reengineering Work: Don't Automate, Obliterate." *Harvard Business Review,* July-August 1990, pp. 104–12.
Hammer, M., and J. Champy. *Reengineering the Corporation.* New York: Harper Collins Books, 1993.
IBM Advanced Business Institute, "Organizing I/S," 1993.
Moad, J. "After Reengineering: Taking Care of Business." *Datamation,* Oct. 15, 1994, pp. 40–44.
Shellenbarger, S. "In Re-Engineering, What Really Matters Are Workers' Lives." *The Wall Street Journal,* February 1, 1995, p. B1.
Venkatraman, N. "IT-Enabled Business Transformation: From Automation to Business Scope Redefinition." *Sloan Management Review,* Winter 1994, pp. 73–87.

CONNECTIVE CASE: The Limited Curtails Fraud

With losses from credit card fraud nearing $4 million per year, The Limited Inc. decided to take action. In 1995 they implemented new procedures, supported with a new information system, which has allowed them to reduce the time it takes to review a fraud case from two hours to 20 minutes. The Limited spent about $800,000 on the new system, and has already seen a reduction of about 10 percent in fraud loss. That should work out to a savings of close to $400,000 on an annual basis. Officials also estimate that the company will save about $100,000 in annual training costs, since the new system is so much easier to learn.

The 40 analysts in the Credit Services Division of The Limited (which oversees credit operations for all 13 of the company's divisions, including Victoria's Secret and Abercrombie & Fitch) handle 27 million credit accounts. About 6 million new accounts are opened each year. Analysts perform two primary tasks: they review credit applications and decide whether to approve or reject them, and they research cases of fraud to find out how they occurred and how to prevent the same perpetrators from striking again.

Before the new system, analysts had to work their way through a hodgepodge of five different systems. They had to work their way through the databases, performing the searches by hand. To make matters worse, records of fraud cases were kept in handwritten files stored in manila folders. Ralph Spurgin, president of The Limited's Credit Services, asked the I/S staff to develop an automated system to reduce fraud.

One challenge was that the developers had to spend a long time working with fraud analysts to figure out how to automate their system, which had been largely paper based. "They really didn't have a process, so to speak," said Scott Crow, a senior programmer assigned to the project. "There was no existing system. But we had to build workflow into our system—we had to automate a process that just wasn't there before."

One goal for the new system was to automate the process of storing fraud case histories (that is, get rid of the folders), and also give the analysts quick access to relevant information on the existing systems. Another goal was to reduce the time spent training analysts on how to use the various systems. The new system, called Prevention Of Write-off (POW), reduced the time to review fraud cases dramatically. Equally important, the system cross-references files by criteria such as social security number. If someone who had defrauded The Limited previously tries to open another account with the same Social Security Number at a later date, the analyst will know.

A second part of the POW application has streamlined the process of reviewing applications for credit. The data in this component forms a kind of expert system based on information that analysts have gleaned from past cases. When an application comes in, the information is entered into an Oracle database management system, which checks it for errors or inconsistencies. Not only is the new application approval system much more thorough than the old procedures (it checks for possible fraud by the same person at previous times), it is also much faster than having the analysts reviewing files manually. Applications are now processed in about 40 seconds.

Case Questions

1. Describe the ways in which the fraud detection procedures used by credit analysts at The Limited have changed.
2. Would it have been possible to change the procedures to gain these same advantages, without also changing the information systems? Explain.

SOURCE: Daniel Lyons, "The Limited Curtails Credit Card Fraud in Retail Chain Stores," *InfoWorld,* January 1, 1996, p. 50.

IT'S YOUR TURN END OF CHAPTER MATERIALS

REVIEW QUESTIONS

1. What are two primary distinctions between business process reengineering and continuous improvement?
2. Describe the relationship between business process redesign and integrated process management.
3. What roles may information systems play in business process reengineering?
4. Why is it important to collect regular measures of customer satisfaction?
5. Why is it important to collect regular benchmark measures of the performance of other organizations?
6. What are some of the major issues in achieving 100 percent customer satisfaction?
7. List the principles of total quality management.
8. List the generic steps of integrated process management.
9. List the components of an IPM information system.
10. What roles can information systems play in business process reengineering?

DISCUSSION QUESTIONS

1. Review the Boyd's Construction Supply Company case described in this chapter. Describe how BCSC could go about improving its inventory control and ordering processes. Diagram the actual and the proposed processes. Using the list taxonomy of the roles that information technology can play in business processes, specify what roles I/T could play in the inventory control and ordering processes you have proposed.
2. Assume that BCSC wishes to pursue the possibility of implementing some type of integrated process management system. What features do you think would be most appropriate to concentrate on first? Why?
3. Comment on the expression, "The best customers are the ones you already have."
4. Comment on the expression, "Before paving the cowpath, straighten it" in the context of business process reengineering.
5. Comment on the statement, "We shouldn't try for 0 percent defectives; we should try to reach 100 percent customer satisfaction."
6. Develop a series of proactive and reactive performance assessment measures to determine the performance of an automobile dealership.

GROUP ASSIGNMENT

As a group, review the process of registering for courses at your institution.

- Draw the actual process.
- Generate a list of measures to determine the performance of the process.
- Proceed to benchmark the process with the registration process at other institutions.
- Develop a new process—be creative—and draw the new process.
- Prepare a PowerPoint presentation of the "before" and "after" processes and the measures you chose to determine the performance of the process.

APPLICATION ASSIGNMENTS

1. Access the Internet, locate the home page for this book, and open the file CHAP8.DAT. Take the data from Tables 1, 2, and 3, and produce a customer retention profile chart (customer satisfaction score versus percent repeat business). Comment on the customer behaviors that are exhibited by each pro-

file. Give an example of a product or service that could generate such a profile.

2. Access the Internet, locate the home page for this book, and open the file CHAP8.DAT. Take the data from Tables 4, 5, and 6, and generate a graph of the number of defectives over time. Comment on the shapes of the graphs; suggest reasons and possible events for the changes in those graphs.
3. Use the Internet to generate a listing of 10 companies offering TQM and reengineering services (consulting, courses, etc.).

CASE ASSIGNMENT: Lehigh Valley Hospital Gets a New Backbone

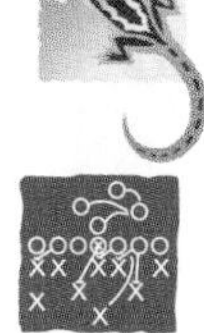

Time is of the essence. Nowhere is this adage more true than in the medical profession, where lost seconds can lead to lost lives, and even the most innocuous visit often turns into day-long drudgery. To contend with the demands of time, medicine has always been on the cutting edge of developing and using new technologies. But making a medical organization run more efficiently requires more than just the latest surgical tools or state-of-the-art devices: It requires better communication at every level, department to department, professional to professional, and professional to patient.

As the confluence of issues surrounding health care costs, quality, and availability has clogged the system with overcrowded hospitals, overworked nurses and doctors, and dissatisfied patients, many medical centers have come to rely upon technology to alleviate the congestion. One medical center that's had great success at both unclogging bottlenecks and increasing quality of service is the Lehigh Valley Hospital in Allentown, Pennsylvania. By changing the organizational structure, modifying business procedures, and revamping its network, the hospital has streamlined its operations, opened up new patient care opportunities for its staff, and has taken strides toward achieving what has always been its primary objective: to provide efficient, quality health care.

The hospital currently consists of two separate facilities and an I/S administrative center. One of the sites is an inpatient facility, and the other functions primarily as an outpatient clinic. This arrangement emerged over time as the hospital re-engineered their business operations to provide better services to patients. The outpatient clinic provided a separate place to handle less serious cases, thus allowing the inpatient facility staff to focus more closely on the needs of its patients. But as division between the two facilities increased, the differentiation of tasks at each created the need for better communication between the two sites.

One of the main catalysts for improving the telecommunications network was the growing need to have certain staff members, such as radiologists, at each site. Even though the facilities are transforming into their inpatient and outpatient roles, certain staffers who normally work at the inpatient site or in remote offices are often needed at the clinic to read X-rays and charts and to provide patient consultations. To handle the increased volume of network traffic, the hospital installed a new telecommunications network which provides a much larger bandwidth and less restrictive bottlenecks. The redesigned network allows clinic staffers to take X-rays and other tests at their site and transmit them to remote offices for reading and diagnosis. After the final phase of the upgrade is completed this summer, the hospital should be able to deploy even more sophisticated applications, such as videoconferencing, across the network.

Questions

1. Discuss the relationship between the change in business processes and the change in telecommunications at Lehigh Valley Hospital.
2. How could Lehigh Valley Hospital use its new telecommunication network to interact with the physicians in the community that send patients to the hospital?
3. Once Lehigh Valley Hospital has the ability to store and transmit images and video through its network can you think of applications that could
   - Enhance its standing as a research and teaching institution?
   - Be an efficient provider of health care (i.e., lower its costs)?
   - Increase patient satisfaction?
   - Create new business opportunities (i.e., increase revenues)?

SOURCE: Luc Hatlestad, "Hospital Upgrades ATM Network to Overcome Bottlenecks," *InfoWorld*, March 4, 1996, p. 65.

CHAPTER 9 Personal and Workgroup Productivity

After reading this chapter, you should have a better understanding of how information technology can be used to improve the productivity of individuals and workgroups. More specifically, you should be able to:

- Define productivity in terms of efficiency, effectiveness, and quality.
- Compare the productivity for organizations, individuals, and workgroups.
- Understand the difficulties of measuring productivity, including the need for breaking goals and functions into clearly defined tasks.
- Describe the use of I/T to support a variety of personal and workgroup tasks.
- Provide some warnings on I/T use by individuals (health risks, computer addiction, other ethical concerns).

Assuming that I buy the argument that information technology can help organizations, exactly how can it help me?

INTRODUCTION

Throughout this book we have made the argument that the appropriate use of information technology and information systems can improve the productivity of individuals, workgroups, and organizations. In previous chapters we have not used the term *productivity* directly. We have spoken of improving communications and decision making, of improving the flexibility and efficiency of business processes, of improving the quality of the products and services we deliver, of best fulfilling the needs of our customers, and of increasing organizational responsiveness. All of these goals, however, are related to the general concept of productivity.

We have discussed the concepts of competitiveness and responsiveness mostly from an organizational perspective, but it is equally important to understand them from an individual and workgroup perspective. Since an organization is made up of individuals and groups, by improving their performance it is possible to improve the performance of the organization as a whole. Also, a very large number of firms are quite small (many consisting of less than 10 people), and for them, increasing organizational productivity is identical to increasing individual and workgroup productivity.

In this chapter, we will focus on the ways information technology can improve the productivity of individuals and workgroups. We begin with a discussion of productivity for individuals and workgroups, and then move to examples of tasks and activities that are performed regularly by these individuals and workgroups. For each task or activity, we examine one or more examples of information technology that can be used to support that task. The chapter ends with a few cautions on the use of I/T by individuals and workgroups.

PRODUCTIVITY OF INDIVIDUALS AND WORKGROUPS

Productivity is a complex concept, meaning different things to different people. Typically, when issues of productivity are raised, there is some discussion of **output-to-input ratios:** how many inputs are required to produce a certain number of outputs. In a manufacturing setting, productivity measures are used extensively. Take, for example, a manufacturing plant that produces blue jeans. The denim is cut according to predetermined patterns, either manually or by a specially designed machine; sewing machine operators then perform the steps necessary to piece together the jeans. The steps might include these: (1) stitch together the inseam running from left cuff to right cuff; (2) stitch on the front pockets; (3) stitch on the rear pockets; (4) attach the zipper fly; and so on.

In this type of manufacturing environment, management can develop measures of productivity fairly easily. For example, let's assume that we have 10 people who perform step 1, stitching inseams. A fairly obvious measure of productivity would be to count how many inseams each of the 10 employees stitch together during an eight-hour shift. In this productivity measure, we are comparing the ratio of outputs

The days of the bloated business are over.

Ballooning costs. Bulging warehouses. Is your business growing in the wrong places? Let GE Information Services relieve some of the pressure.

We help you reduce swollen inventories and take the bulk out of your business, so you can be faster in your markets, more responsive to your customers and more attractive to your shareholders. We enabled a major electronics manufacturer to cut supplier cycle times from 6 days to 1 and slash warehouse space requirements by 50%. Another client has increased salesforce productivity, allowing salespeople to double the amount of "face time" they can spend with clients and prospects.

GE Information Services works with thousands of the world's best known businesses to help reduce costs and improve profitability. Our business productivity solutions can help you expand where you really want to—in your marketplace.

Productivity. It's All We Do.[SM]

GE Information Services

For more information, please call 44 (0)1932 776157, or write GE Information Services, INS House, Station Road, Sunbury-upon-Thames, Middlesex TW16 6SB, United Kingdom. Find us on the Internet at http://www.ge.com/geis.

Trademark of General Electric Company, U.S.A., not connected with the English Company of a similar name.

0902.222

Information technology has become the principal vehicle to improve productivity. Photo courtesy of GE Information Services.

(number of inseams sewn) to inputs (time). If we wanted to improve productivity, and this was the only measure we used for it, one approach would be to pay employees a bonus based on the number of inseams sewn over a given time period (each shift, each week, etc.).

This type of productivity measure focuses on **efficiency:** producing the maximum outputs with the fewest inputs in the shortest time. But what about **quality?** If an inseam isn't sewn properly, it will open when the customer wears the pair of jeans or possibly after a few washings, creating a dissatisfied customer. For that reason, the blue jeans manufacturer also has employees who check the inseams to make sure they are sewn correctly, and reject any that are inadequate. What if one employee sews more inseams than anyone else, but he also has the highest reject rate? Should he still receive the highest bonus? Obviously not. In this situation, it might be appropriate to subtract the number of rejects from the total inseams sewn before calculating the bonus pay.

As a matter of fact, low quality brings about a drop in efficiency not only in terms of less acceptable output, but also by consuming more resources to produce the same amount of acceptable output (since resources that would have generated more production have to be directed to rework of the defective parts). Now imagine for a moment a manufacturing environment where every worker produces no defects. In such an environment we could do away with all the quality control tasks and personnel, leading to even greater efficiency. In general, it is imperative to include quality measures in assessing productivity.

Another important component of productivity is the concept of **effectiveness.** Efficiency means doing things right; effectiveness means doing the right things. Consider the blue jeans manufacturer for a moment longer. Assume that we are able to motivate employees to work efficiently at a high level of quality within our manufacturing facility, so that we produce strong, low-cost blue jeans. Will that ensure that customers will buy them in sufficient quantities for our firm to be competitive and successful? Not necessarily. What if the predominant style suddenly reverts to tight, hip-hugging bell bottoms and we are still producing boot jeans? It is possible to have a process that is efficient and with high quality, and still not be effective. Being effective means fulfilling a specific customer need, and productivity measures need to address this issue.

Let's consider another example to illustrate the notion of productivity and the difficulties of finding appropriate ways to measure it. Suppose you are a member of the human resources department of a large consulting firm. One of your department's functions is to hire employees, and you have a budget for performing that function. One measure of productivity for the department's hiring group (a workgroup) could be the number of dollars spent per employee hired. This would be an efficiency measure, relating the outputs (hired employees) to inputs (dollars spent).

Similar to the sewer of inseams, however, not all outputs of the process are acceptable. What happens when someone you hire doesn't make it through the three-month probationary period, and has to be let go? Or when someone else decides s/he doesn't like all of the travel involved with the job, and quits? Most likely, you will have to replace that individual by going through the recruiting process all over again, interviewing more candidates, spending more money. Even if a large percentage of the new hires remain for a long time, it would be difficult to determine how much of their success can be attributed to the hiring process and how much to the work of the existing consultants who train and mentor them.

Worker productivity is usually measured on some criteria for efficiency and quality. As the job becomes more service-oriented, measuring productivity increases in difficulty. Photos courtesy of Siemens (left), B, Daemmrich/Stock Boston, Inc. (center), and Tony Stone Images (right).

Measuring Productivity

Evaluating the productivity of the hiring group would probably be much more difficult than evaluating the productivity of the sewing machine operator. When we are dealing with service environments rather than manufacturing facilities, with executive rather than clerical and support levels in the organization, or with groups rather than individuals, it becomes much more challenging to determine exactly what productivity is.

Consider the job of a university professor. Is it possible to compare two professors and evaluate them in terms of productivity? First, we would need to identify the outputs of a professor: number of courses taught, number of students in each course, number of books and articles published, number of committees served on, and so forth. Then we could consider the inputs, including factors such as hours worked and the availability of research and teaching assistance. This assessment would help us evaluate efficiency. Of course, we would need to make some judgments concerning the effectiveness and quality dimensions of productivity: how well prepared are the students who complete the courses to continue their education or to enter the workforce? How effective have the publications been in advancing the knowledge and understanding within the professor's field of expertise? These are not easy questions to answer, which makes evaluating the productivity of a professor a difficult task.

By now you may be asking: If it is so difficult to measure productivity, how can we possibly hope to improve it through the application of information systems? Although it may be difficult at times to come up with precise measures of productivity, the process of determining the effectiveness, efficiency, and quality measures of an activity is in itself useful. The process will make us more aware of the three components of productivity and, it is hoped, help us avoid the tendency to focus too much on efficiency measures just because they are easier to evaluate.

For example, although we may have difficulty determining if one professor is more productive than another, we might at least agree on some important areas to evaluate them; perhaps effective teaching and research, and useful service to the university and the community. Next, we need to define what we mean by effective research and education and useful service. We could then begin to specify activities within these broad areas, such as delivery of classroom presentations and the

Since group interactions and decisions require more communication and more complex decision-making processes, the information technology to support groups needs to have different features and capabilities. Photo courtesy of Tony Stone Worldwide.

preparation of research manuscripts for submission to academic journals. These activities could be further broken into more detailed **job tasks.** The preparation of a research manuscript might involve reading previous studies and generating testable hypotheses, accessing a database of relevant data, using statistical techniques to analyze the data and test the hypotheses, and then preparing the written manuscript for submission (with appropriate diagrams, tables, etc.). Once we have defined the specific tasks and agreed upon specific measures to assess what productivity means for each task, it becomes much easier to recommend appropriate I/T to support these tasks, and hence, improve the productivity of the professor.

In addition to looking at the functions of individuals, we need to consider workgroups—groups of people working together for a common purpose. A university professor is part of a group of individuals associated with a specific department or school, such as an Accounting Department or a School of Business. The group has certain **group functions** to perform, including hiring new faculty members, deciding if a junior faculty member should receive tenure, and initiating a new graduate program or terminating an old one. When we consider the productivity of the group, we still look at aspects of efficiency, effectiveness, and quality. The difference, however, is that we are trying to evaluate and support the entire group instead of a single individual. This support usually involves bridging distance and time.

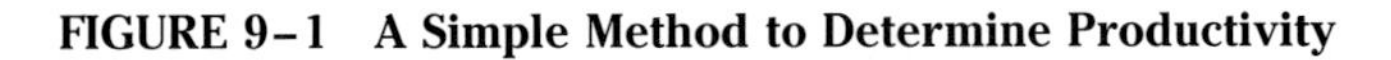

FIGURE 9–1 A Simple Method to Determine Productivity

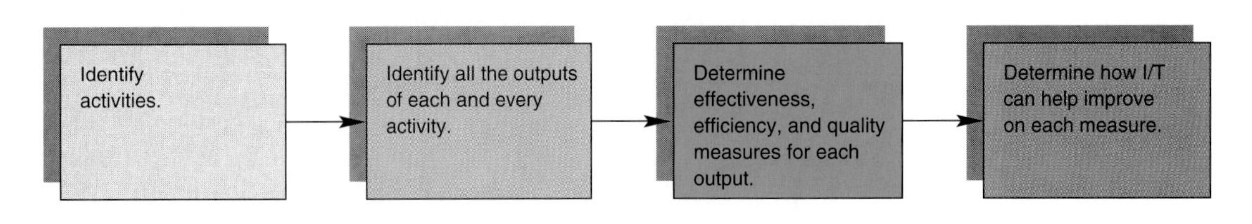

Of course, having access to appropriate information technology by itself, though it may improve efficiency, will never guarantee improved productivity. Productivity, particularly in service-oriented activities, often depends on factors such as the motivation and skills of the individuals involved in delivering the service. We should always focus first on what we are trying to accomplish—that is, on the tasks that contribute to the products and services that our customers are demanding—and then look for appropriate technologies to support those tasks. If we automate a task without determining whether the task is needed in the first place, what we may accomplish is being very efficient at making mistakes or at producing products and services that are not needed—in other words, being very efficient at being ineffective.

Individuals and groups that focus too much on the technology rather than on the requisite task or process tend to get hung up on trying to learn all the details of a specific information system, whether those details are relevant to their needs or not. ("I've learnt everything there is to know about this hammer; now I'm going to go out and cut a board in half with it.") By focusing on the tasks first, we can avoid the common mistake of wasting a great deal of time and money trying out new technologies that hurt rather than help our productivity, however defined.

So before plunging into a new technology to improve efficiency, first determine whether the task you are "improving" is needed. (Does the task contribute to our effectiveness as an organization? In other words, is the task fulfilling a customer need?) Also determine whether efficiency, typically a measure of cost, is the only relevant measure of performance on that task. (What is most critical to our customer in our performance of that task: cost, flexibility, quality, response time?) Figure 9–1 shows a simple method to deal with matching information technology to productivity improvements.

PRODUCTIVITY AND I/T IN GENERIC MANAGERIAL TASKS

In previous chapters, we have stressed the importance of some generic managerial tasks. Though managerial tasks and activities are dependent on the goals that have been set, the industry involved, and other factors, there are some relatively generic activities common to many individual jobs and group activities. These activities include ensuring the availability of inputs, the flexibility of the transformation process, the acceptance of outputs, and the accuracy of communications. As we indicated in our discussions of productivity, too, it is important to dig beneath the surface of such generic tasks and examine the specific activities needed in a given job. That is, we need to determine exactly what specific business processes, information, decisions, and communications are required to perform the job.

For example, when we discussed the management of the transformation process, we argued that three important considerations in evaluating the process

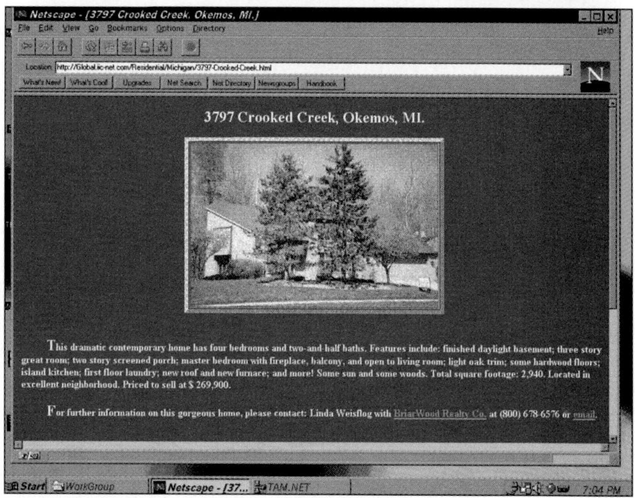

A real estate agent needs information about homes listed for sale to help match these homes to the needs of potential buyers. Information technology can make that match easier by sifting through large databases and showing actual pictures and videos of the houses. Photos courtesy of John Curtis/Offshoot Stock (top) and Microsoft (bottom).

were its *efficiency* and *flexibility* and the *quality* of the produced outputs. Take a claims processor for an insurance company. She receives an insurance claim as an input and produces a processed claim and check, or claim rejection notice, as an output. We need to consider how many inputs (e.g., time and resources) are required to produce the outputs, how easily the process can be changed to match changes in the environment (changes in regulations, or types of claims), what the customer expects (e.g., turnaround time), what we consider a high-quality job (claim charge to the right account, check sent to the right address, etc.) and so on.

When we discussed decision making, we said that we are interested in determining how *effective* the decisions being made are. For example, if a purchaser for a women's clothing retailer makes decisions concerning what styles of swimsuit to stock for a new season, we want to know how effective those decisions were. We could ask questions like: What percentage of the swimsuits were sold at the original retail price, and what discounts were used to sell the remainder? How quickly did the inventory turn over?

For the communication-based activities, we can return to our discussion of the communication dyad (in Chapter 4). A communication dyad consists of a sender, a message transmitted through some medium, a receiver, and feedback. Our goal should be to transmit the message with as little distortion or noise as possible, and also to reduce information overload for the receiver.

When considering individuals and workgroups, we can list a set of generic and specific managerial activities that affect productivity: Information acquisition and processing, analysis and control, forecasting and simulation, document management, presentations, inter- and intragroup communications, managing personal and group schedules, creativity and idea generation, and project management. We now discuss each of these activities, and the role of information technology to improve productivity for each one.

Information Acquisition and Processing

Most jobs require getting access to the right data at the right time, and then processing that data to help perform a function or to make a decision. If a potential client calls a real estate agent and asks how many homes are currently available that might be suitable, how can the agent respond to the request? After clarifying what "suitable" means (e.g., acceptable neighborhood, price range, minimum floor space, minimum number of bedrooms, preferred home style), the real estate agent will want to complete a search as quickly as possible.

One option for the agent is to consult a printed listing of all residential homes that are for sale; but if these listings are updated weekly, the information might be out of date. Although supplemental daily listings are also distributed, homes that have been sold will still appear in the master list. Also, searching through the book and checking for listings that match the criteria established by the customer will take some time. Although the listing is sorted by neighborhood and by price, it will still take too long to find the subset of homes that satisfy all criteria.

Another option would be to provide the agent with access to a computerized database of all home listings, with the ability to search the database by a set of criteria. With this type of information system, he would enter the desired neighborhoods, the price range, and the other relevant criteria. The retrieval system (a computer program developed using the database management system software) would then search the database and return a list of all homes that satisfied the criteria. Assuming that the computer hardware and software are adequate, it should be possible for the system to provide the information much faster than by looking at a printed list. This fast retrieval may allow the agent to continue the conversation with the customer, helping the agent to serve the customer better and make a sale.

Notice that the type of information system appropriate for this situation is entirely dependent on the application. The database management system is specifically designed for situations where it is necessary to track and monitor something, such as homes listed for sale. An electronic spreadsheet package wouldn't have worked as well. Also, note that the system described for the agent contains both an information-accessing component and an information-processing component. In many information systems it is difficult to separate the two, since much of the processing that takes place is somewhat transparent (not obvious) to the person using it.

Many job tasks requiring access to data and information involve interaction with a database, although the actual type of database may differ drastically. Consider the

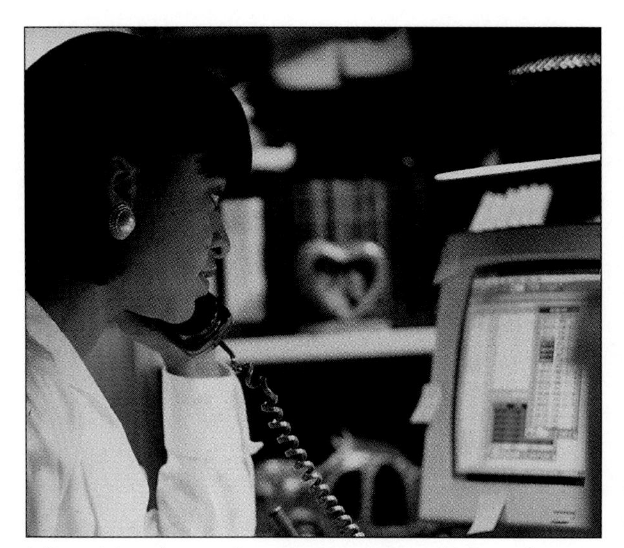

A financial analyst needs access to a variety of information sources and also needs appropriate tools for data analysis. Photos courtesy of Tony Stone Worldwide.

job of a financial analyst. Her task is to follow a small number of companies within a specific industry (e.g., automobile manufacturers) to try and predict how their stock prices will act (increase or decrease, by how much, over what time period), and this type of prediction requires access to a variety of data. She will probably want historical records of the company stock quotations, which she can obtain for a fee from a commercial database provider.

The analyst might also be looking for records of products shipped, raw materials purchased, orders taken, and so on. Most of this information is also available, and can be accessed electronically for a fee (or from hardcopy listings, for free). If she is looking for fast-breaking news that might influence the companies or the industry, she might be willing to pay to tap into a news service such as Lexis-Nexis, which provides current articles from a variety of news sources around the world. Another source might be rumors garnered from monitoring discussions on the Internet, or even intuitive responses to recent advertising campaigns. Notice that there is a cost associated with information. For many of the data sources, a fee must be paid. Even when the analyst is able to do without fee-based sources, she has to spend time collecting the data. Her time isn't free; and every hour she spends looking for and collecting data is one hour less to conduct her analysis and generate her recommendations.

Workgroups also need to access and process data in the performance of their job tasks. Consider the customer response groups at Hewlett-Packard. When customers call Hewlett-Packard's technical support for assistance, there is no guarantee that they will be speaking with the same engineer with whom they spoke the last time they called. Having ready access to a history of all previous service reports for a specific customer helps the engineers to respond faster to serve the customer. This is where the Hewlett-Packard customer service call database comes into play. The engineer taking the call types in the customer's identification number, and immediately has access to all the relevant information on the customer. When the call is completed, the engineer adds the call report to the database. The data are accessible to all Hewlett-Packard technical support engineers around the world.

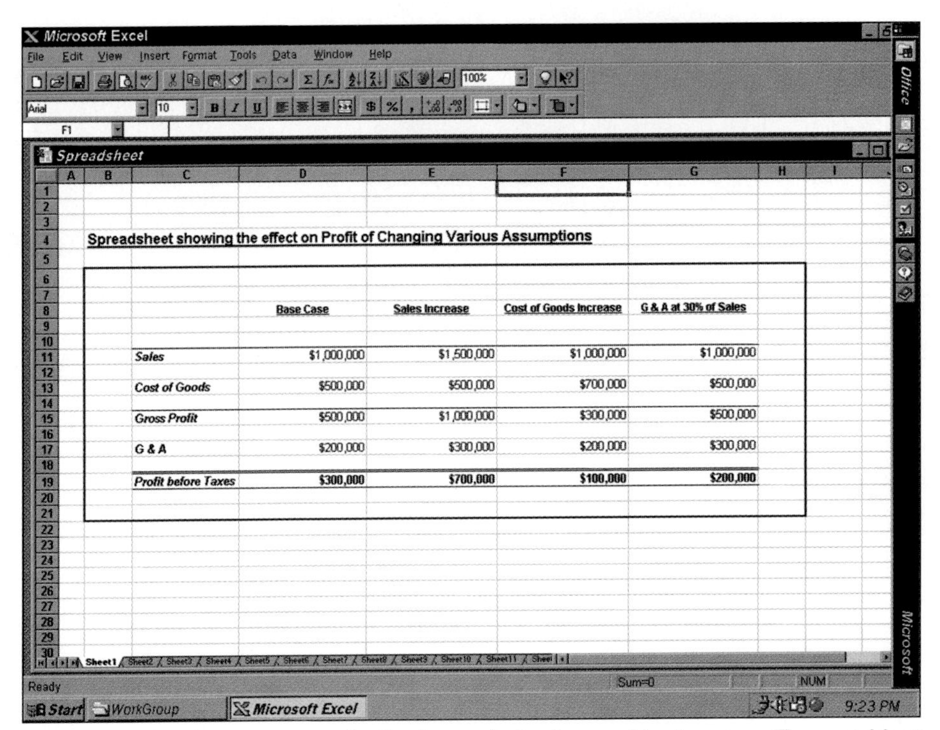

Spreadsheet showing the effect on Profit of Changing Various Assumptions

	Base Case	Sales Increase	Cost of Goods Increase	G & A at 30% of Sales
Sales	$1,000,000	$1,500,000	$1,000,000	$1,000,000
Cost of Goods	$500,000	$500,000	$700,000	$500,000
Gross Profit	$500,000	$1,000,000	$300,000	$500,000
G & A	$200,000	$300,000	$200,000	$300,000
Profit before Taxes	$300,000	$700,000	$100,000	$200,000

A financial budget is a common application for an electronic spreadsheet program. The spreadsheet program allows you to change assumptions quickly to check several scenarios. Photo courtesy of Microsoft.

Analysis and Control

After our financial analyst has pulled (downloaded) stock quotes or market data from a database, she then needs to "massage" it to make some sense of it, in preparation for making a decision. This is a task where an electronic spreadsheet might come in handy. The analyst could develop a spreadsheet model that proposes mathematical relationships between orders, purchases, sales, and stock prices. By altering one or more of the variables, she would be able to see, for example, how a decrease of 5 percent in sales might affect the stock price.

It isn't surprising that a person holding a job title with the word *analyst* in it would be required to perform data analysis. **Analysis,** however, is an important component of many job tasks. Most managers and owners of small companies control budgets. The task of preparing a budget for a department, a business, or, for that matter, an individual, is essentially the same. On one hand, it is necessary to include all anticipated income, and on the other it is necessary to identify all anticipated outflows (expenditures). Some expenditures might be fixed, such as rent or mortgage payments; others might be more discretionary, such as advertising.

Budgeting is another type of analysis task well suited for the capabilities of electronic spreadsheets. By storing the budget as a spreadsheet model, the manager or owner can input the actual revenues and expenditures as they occur. By comparing the actual flows to the planned, a manager can develop a sense of how to control the financial resources of the department, company, or individual. If salary expenditures are higher than planned because of unexpected overtime costs, and revenues remain flat, it might be necessary to cut expenditures somewhere else, perhaps in advertising. When the relationships among the different variables that

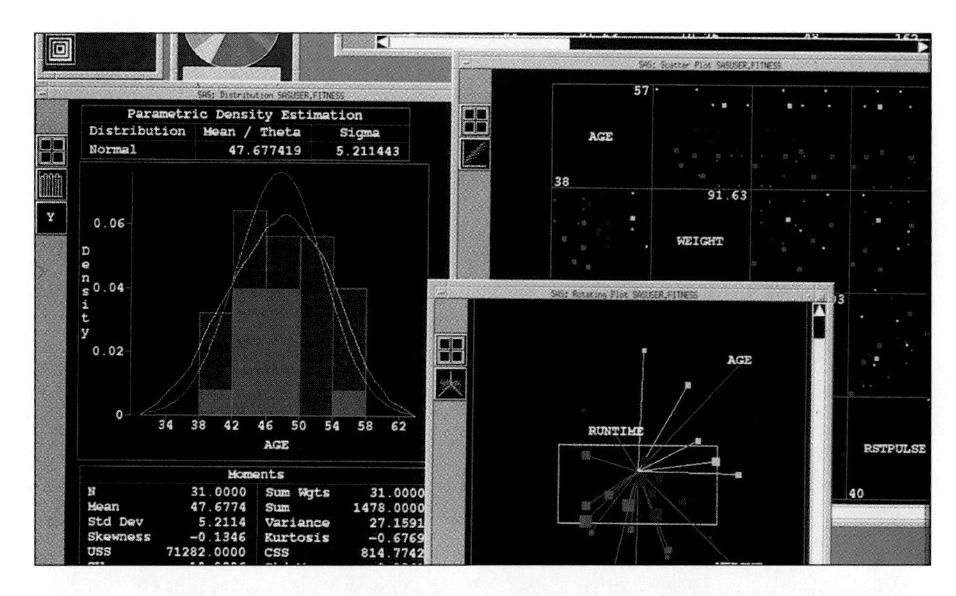

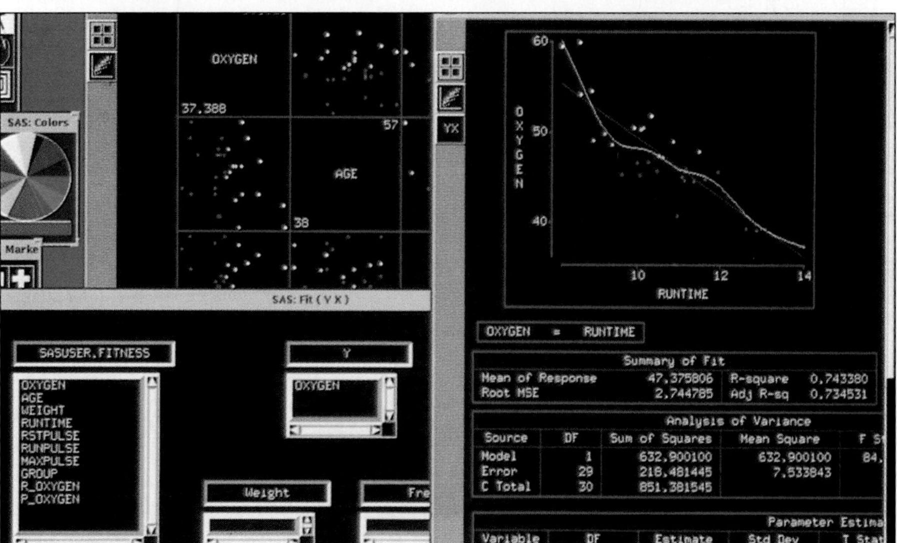

Specialized software is available for numerous applications. These screen shots show some of the functions available on SAS, a popular package used primarily for statistical analysis. Packages such as SAS have numerous functions that make the analysis and display of data much easier. Photos courtesy of Comshare Executive Systems, Inc.

drive the budget are readily available, the decision-making process of what and where to cut is much more efficient and effective.

Not all data analysis is performed with a simple spreadsheet. Complex financial-planning models are frequently completed with more sophisticated financial modeling software such as Interactive Financial Planning System (IFPS). Trends in data might be investigated using statistical analysis software. Although spreadsheet software provides some statistical analysis capabilities, more advanced data management and statistical analysis techniques require more specialized software, such as Statistical Analysis Software (SAS). Even more specialized software is available for very specialized functions; although spreadsheet software is used by millions of individuals worldwide, a package called Partial Least Squares (PLS) designed

Some people are great forecasters and some know how to use magic; for most of us, however, computers are a great help in making predictions about the future. Photos courtesy of Russ Schleipman/Offshoot Stock (left), Bettmann Archives (center), and Frank Siteman/Stock Boston, Inc.

specifically for academics conducting research in the social sciences is only used by several hundred. If an off-the-shelf spreadsheet package will handle the data analysis needs, great; if not, it is usually possible to find a tool suitable for the task.

For workgroups, analysis and decision-making tasks involve the use of spreadsheets and statistical analysis software. In some instances, it also makes sense to combine the analysis tools with communication tools (discussed in more detail later) which enables the group to work on the analysis in an interactive, "live" environment using packages like Lotus Notes.

Forecasting and Simulation

Let's return to the financial analyst for a moment. After preparing her spreadsheet, which shows relationships between some variables and the stock performance in the past, the analyst turns to her real need: making predictions for the future. She might decide to plot trends over time, and then project those trends into the future to obtain price quotes under different scenarios. This would be a simple, quick, but perhaps not very effective method of forecasting.

Forecasting is another generic task, common to most jobs in most organizations. Still, though critical, forecasting is a difficult art. Fortunately, some science has been applied to the art of forecasting, and forecasting software is available.

One important approach to forecasting is the use of **simulation.** As the name implies, with simulation techniques the idea is to simulate reality by creating **scenarios,** views of the world based on a set of specific assumptions. Again, software is available to run numerous scenarios, allowing the user to input different parameters and see what effect they have on the simulated outcome. The usefulness of the simulation model depends on how closely the outcome of the simulation model reflects the outcome of real situations.

Document Management

Communication is an integral part of all jobs in an organization. One important component of communication is the preparation and management of documents. Although the term *document* generally carries the connotation of something printed on paper, more recently the word has been used to include a much broader array of stored information structures. Under this broader definition, a document could be a

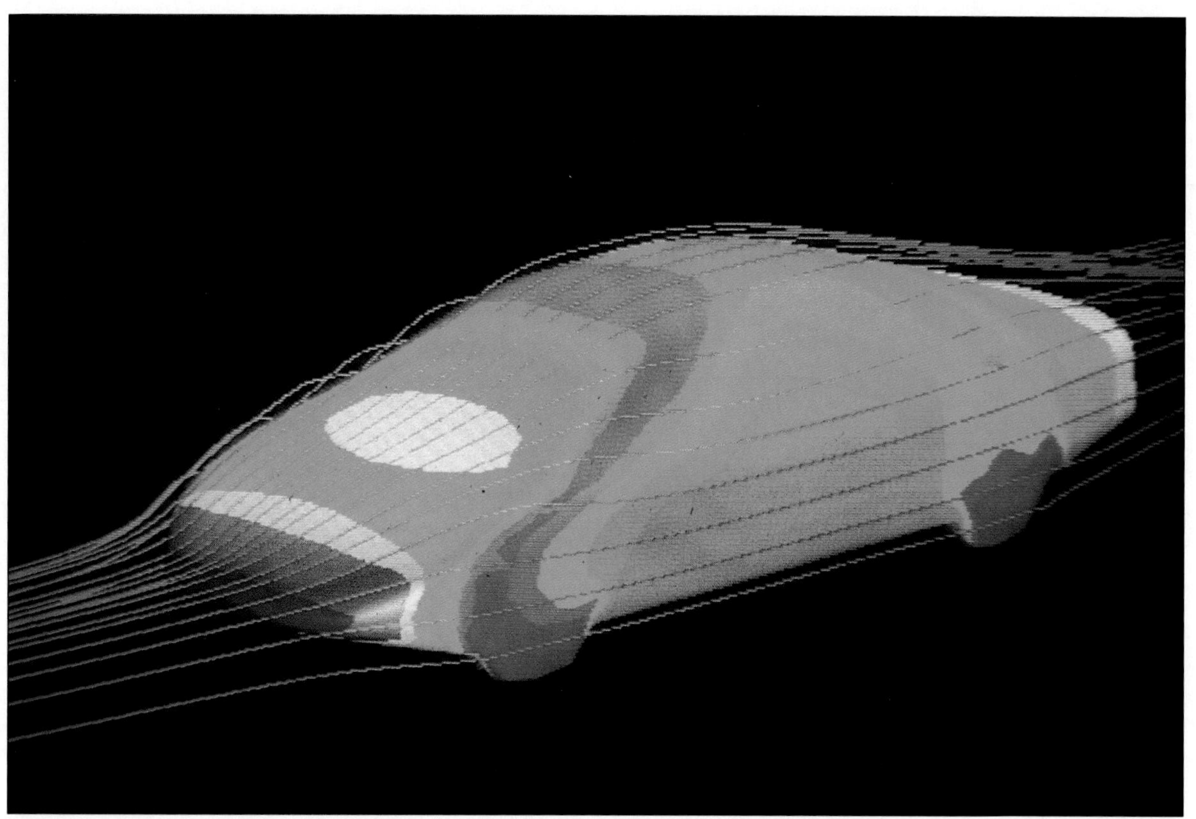

Computer-aided design (CAD) systems allow us to test products before they are manufactured—saving time, materials, and money. Photo courtesy of Hank Morgan/Rainbow.

research report prepared with a word-processing package and stored on a magnetic hard disk of a personal computer, a video clip stored on a CD-ROM disk, or a photograph and attached sound bite stored on a home page on the World Wide Web of the Internet. Regardless of the form it takes, a document must be created, stored, manipulated, retrieved, and transmitted. In short, many job tasks involve **document management.**

Let's return again to the real estate agent. Assume that the agent knows that his potential client has a home that has to be sold before a new one could be purchased. If the agent can persuade the client to list the existing home with him, he could substantially increase his income by collecting a commission on the sale of the old home as well as the purchase of the new. To try and win his client over, the agent might offer to complete a market study to provide a realistic estimate of what price the existing home should be listed at. To do the market analysis, the agent checks his database to find comparable homes that have recently sold in the same neighborhood and then uses a spreadsheet model to make adjustments to the price on the basis of features such as the age of the home, the landscaping, the available views, and the number of bedrooms.

Once the agent has completed his market study, he wants to provide it in a format that will impress the client. If the agent were to give the client a handwritten note with a range of prices, he probably wouldn't make a very positive impression. If, on the other hand, he provides the client with a professional-looking document with an introduction explaining the process used in the market study, a description

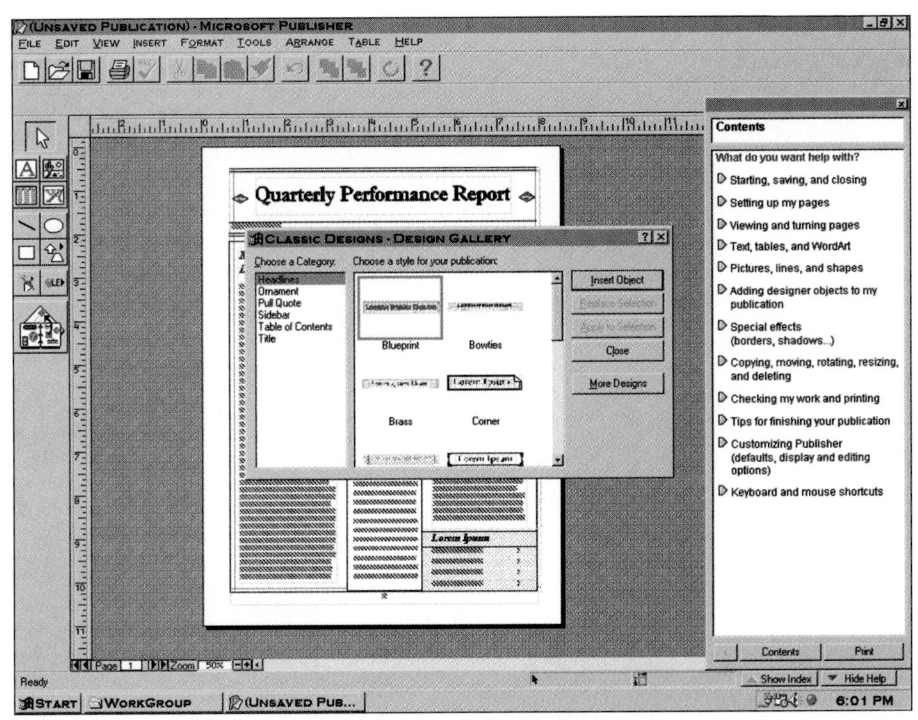

Specialized software is available for document management. This image shows a desktop publishing system used for creating nonstandard documents. Professional presentation of reports is a critical aspect of conveying the message. Photo courtesy of Microsoft.

and color photograph of the client's home and the homes used in the comparison, a table showing the features used in the comparison and the reasons for adjustments, and the final recommended price range, there is a much higher likelihood that the agent will get the listing and later collect his commission on the selling price of the home. In preparing his report he should consider the preferences of the customer (e.g., if the customer is a "numbers person," the report should have detailed information on how the price comparison was made) and the best way to present the report (i.e., the medium) to minimize the possibility of distortion.

The technology to produce that type of document is readily available. Most popular word-processing packages allow the user to import graphical images, including photographs that have been scanned in with the use of an image scanner. Although a camera that stores photographs as digital images could be used, a regular film camera and scanner would suffice. Color printers are relatively inexpensive, making the output of a professional-looking color document a quick and relatively inexpensive option.

Document management is one area where a large number of options are available, and making intelligent choices about those options can be difficult. In choosing among the options, the concept of information richness comes into play. Will the documents need to contain text only? Tables and graphs? Sound? Still images? Moving images? The issue of permanence needs to be considered: Is the document a one-shot deal that won't need to be stored? (This type of situation is uncommon; usually at least some type of backup is preferred.) Who needs access to the document, and how best should it be accessed or transmitted?

FIGURE 9–2 Components of an Imaging System

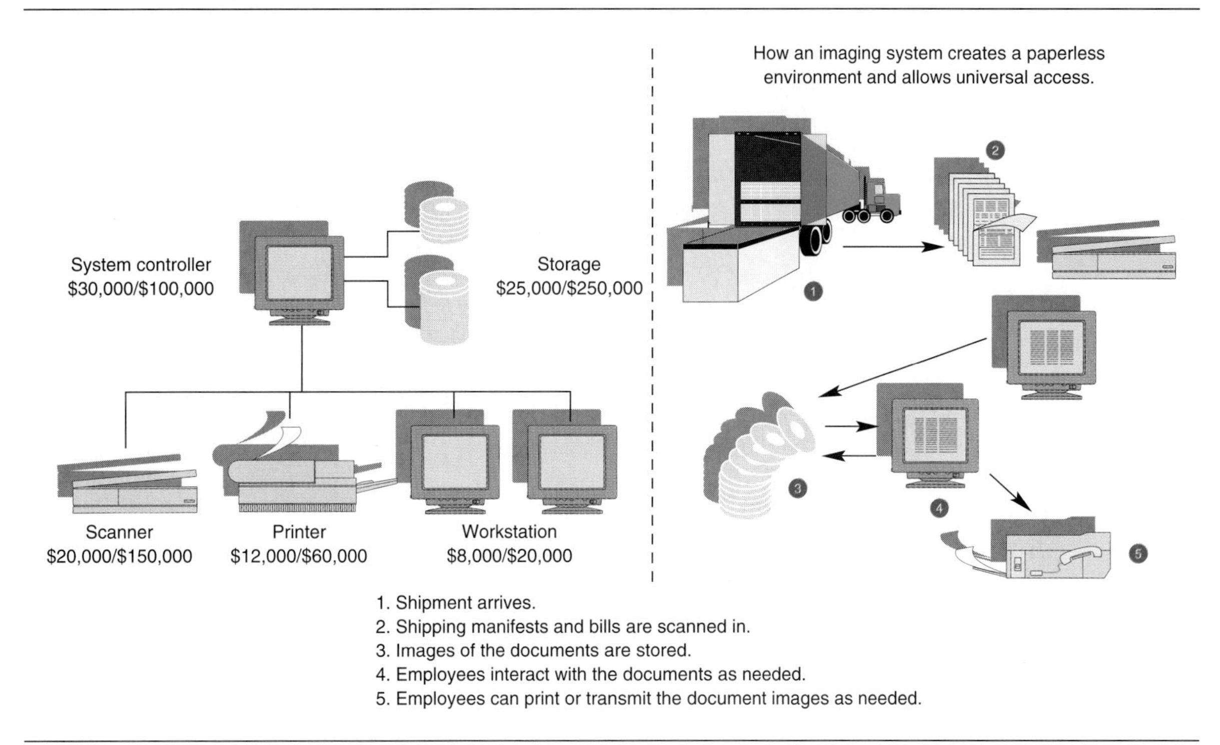

SOURCE: Adapted from *Information Systems: A Problem-Solving Approach,* Third Edition, by Kenneth C. Laudon and Jane Price Laudon, 1995, pp. 526–7.

Let's return to the financial analyst. After reaching her predictions on the future stock prices of the companies she follows, she needs to communicate this information to her boss. One way to accomplish this is through the preparation of a report containing her predictions and support for them, including a synopsis of her analysis. What happens if the analyst prepares her report, but before delivering it by electronic mail, she discovers new data that should be incorporated into her analysis? In this environment, it might make sense for the analyst to use integrated software which allows "dynamic" linking between her word-processing software and her spreadsheet software. That way, when she makes a change in the spreadsheet it is automatically updated in her word-processing document.

Managing documents in a workgroup environment adds a few complications (e.g., several people in different parts of the world contributing data to a report), but existing technology helps address these. Using word-processing and other document creation application software on a network, for example, allows members of a workgroup to share access to documents while they are being produced. Members of the group can grant and revoke access to others on the network, they can modify and store documents created by other group members, and so on.

With shared image-processing systems, group members can treat an electronic document as if it were a paper one (Figure 9–2). Consider the function of processing student applications to a university. One approach is to pass the paper application from person to person and department to department, with each person performing their specialized task and assessment. This sequential processing can be ineffective and inefficient—if one person gets behind, the entire process gets bogged down. Another approach is to scan the application into an image-processing

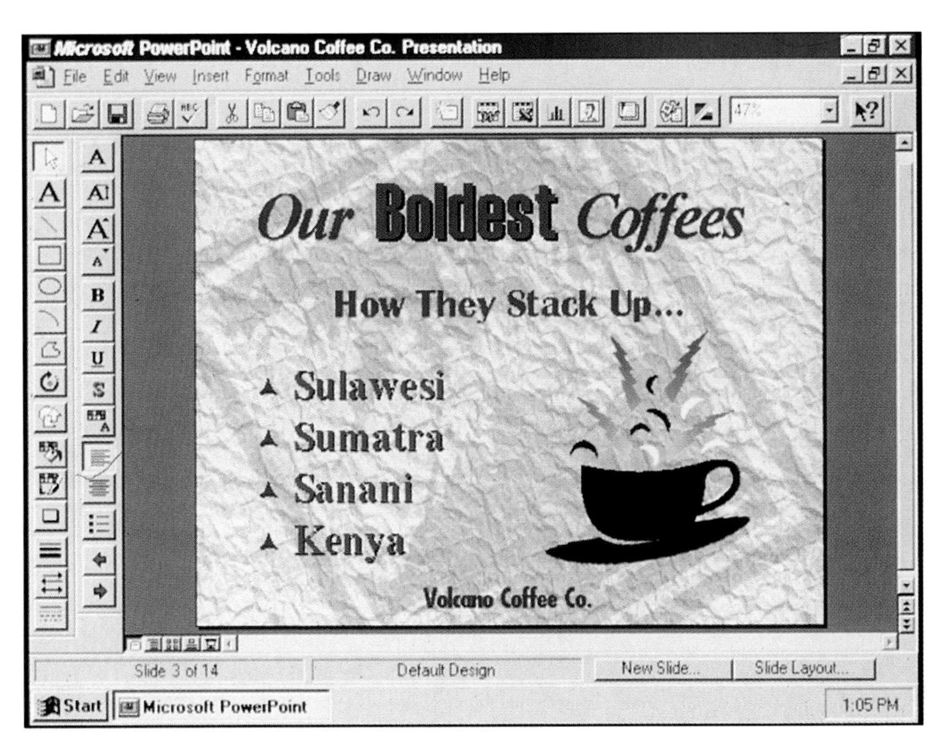

Presentation tools such as Microsoft's PowerPoint are commonly used to enhance presentations. Photo courtesy of Microsoft.

system, which allows group members to retrieve the document in any order, make notes on it, record their assessment, and then store it back in the application database. The use of the image-processing system can improve the efficiency and effectiveness of the application process quite significantly; of course, it is important to determine up front whether the benefits from these improvements exceed the costs of acquiring and operating the image-processing system.

Presentations

No matter how good an idea is, it usually has more of an impact if it is communicated effectively. One of the most powerful methods of communicating ideas is through a **presentation;** or perhaps we should say that presentations have the potential to be very powerful. On the flip side, they have the potential to be boring or even total disasters. Here again, information technology can help to improve the quality of performing this task.

Let's assume that the analyst's boss manages a mutual stock fund which invests other people's retirement funds in the hopes of gaining above average return on their investments. Furthermore, the financial analyst's boss received her report and read it. He isn't convinced of the accuracy of her predictions, and asks her to make a presentation to himself and another colleague who will be involved in the decision of whether to invest a very large sum of money based on her recommendation.

Once more, the analyst has numerous options on how to conduct her presentation and what (if any) support tools to use. Flipcharts, whiteboards, overhead transparencies, slide projection systems, and video are just a few obvious ones. Assume that the analyst also has at her disposal a projection system hooked up to a personal computer; the personal computer is equipped with a presentation software package allowing her

Communication among members of a group can be achieved through a variety of means. Photos courtesy of Tony Stone Worldwide (left), Motorola (center), and Tony Stone Worldwide (right).

to generate a relatively sophisticated presentation if she so desires. Using the presentation package, the analyst could quickly prepare a series of slides and arrange them into a slideshow presentation format. She could practice her presentation, and the system would record how long she spends discussing each slide. She could even include some sound and animation to liven up the presentation a bit.

Just because the analyst has access to the presentation system, doesn't necessarily mean she should use it. Her boss might be an informal, roll-up-the-sleeves and cut-to-the-chase type who dislikes flashy presentations. On the other hand, he might appreciate her efforts, and she might be able to use the presentation package to help communicate more effectively. It depends very much on her audience, as well as on what message she wants to communicate. One of the attractive features of the presentation package, however, is the ability to obtain prompt feedback and be able to change the format quickly.

Intra- and Intergroup Communication

The need for individuals to communicate within a workgroup (intragroup) and with individuals or groups outside their own (intergroup) is an integral part of many tasks and activities. One of the difficulties in workgroup communications is that often the group members are in different time and geographic zones. The I/T options to support group communications are numerous. Telephones, voice mail systems, fax machines and fax modems, electronic mail, electronic bulletin boards, list services, newsgroups, courier services, postal services, written memoranda . . . the list goes on and on. As technology continues its advance, the options increase and also merge somewhat. For example, personal videoconferencing (where individuals use specially equipped personal computers and telecommunication lines to see and hear each other through their personal computers) is a viable option that really didn't exist several years ago. The Internet can be used for voice conversations, competing with commercial telecommunications carriers.

Given the number of options, it becomes even more important to consider the goals and objectives of the communication before selecting among the alternatives.

For example, if workgroup members need to communicate effectively during an important decision-making process and they want to ensure that all have an equal say, they might decide that a group decision support system with anonymous voting capabilities would be appropriate. For example, a group of executives for a financial service company might need to decide whether to enter a new market. Using this type of group decision support system, each person's vote has equal weight, and less assertive group members are not intimidated by more vocal ones.

If the need is to transmit information rapidly among a widely dispersed and not very closely knit group, perhaps a list service on the Internet should be considered. Once a message is sent through the list service, all members who have subscribed will receive the message the next time they sign on and check their incoming electronic mail. An example here might be a group of researchers interested in the human genome project, which is attempting to map all genes within humans. Each time a new discovery is made, the information could be broadcast throughout the world to all interested parties through an Internet list service.

If the need is to share information within a workgroup where all members have ready access to electronic mail, then perhaps electronic mail and a distribution list would be appropriate. A department head might wish to inform all members of her department that the organization is considering new policies on the confidentiality of E-mail messages. Most likely the group members have a predefined list (a distribution list) of all appropriate department members; after composing a message (using either her word-processing software or the E-mail package) informing the group members of the proposed changes and inviting their responses, she uses the E-mail system to deliver the message to the electronic mailboxes of all departmental members on the list.

The software that is used to support workgroups, which is called **groupware,** not only helps established teams work more efficiently but also allows ad hoc teams to be formed quickly and work cohesively sooner. Figure 9–3 shows examples of how groupware can support the work of established and ad hoc teams.

Managing Personal and Group Schedules

An important part of improving one's own performance or enhancing the productivity of a workgroup is effectively managing time. If an individual performs only one task repetitively, such as in some manufacturing environments, time management is relatively straightforward. For most people, however, our personal and professional lives are full of a variety of tasks and commitments. Most managers spend a great deal of their time in short, disjointed communication activities like telephone calls and meetings. Keeping track of all the commitments can be a real headache, and doing it poorly can have very detrimental effects on efficiency and effectiveness.

At one time most managers had a personal secretary to manage their schedules for them, and certainly many executives still rely on administrative assistants to perform scheduling and "gatekeeping" roles. More and more, however, professionals are required to look after their own schedules, and I/T continues to emerge to assist them. One of the more common tools is scheduling software which can be used in a stand-alone fashion (accessed and used by only one person), or in a network environment for workgroups. In addition to booking meetings with others, the software allows the user to book recurring events (e.g., Monday morning program reviews) or ancillary resources (e.g., meeting rooms, presentation systems). When implemented for a workgroup, the scheduling software can simplify tasks such as scheduling meetings with multiple participants, by checking each person's (and resource's) schedule to find the next available time when all are free.

FIGURE 9-3 Groupware Assists Teams

1. Participants use groupware to set up a conference and share the document to be edited.

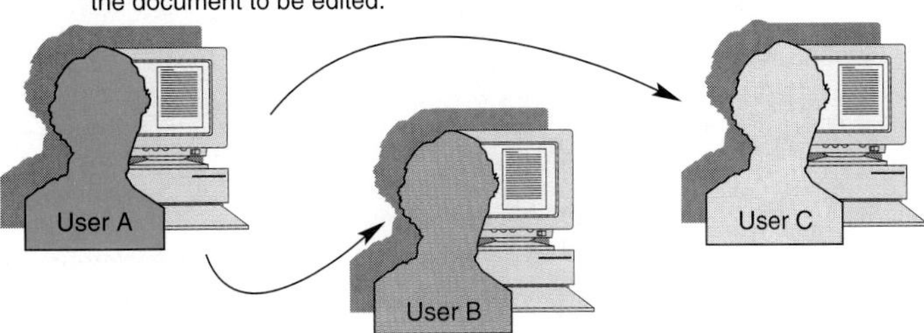

2. Any participant can make changes to the document. Each participant's computer displays the changes as they happen. If participants are in different locations, they can discuss changes to the document over the phone.

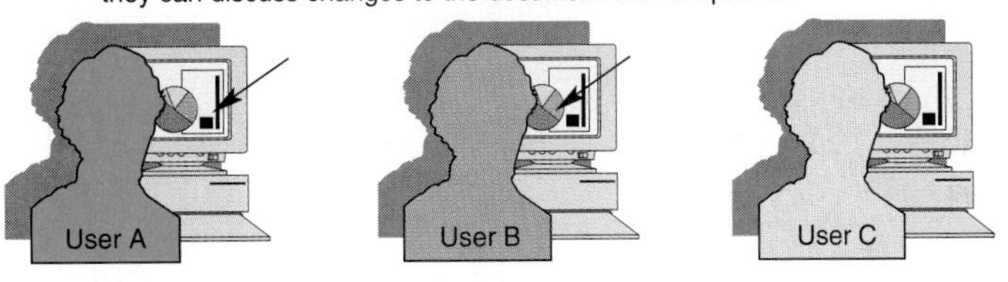

3. At the end of the conference, participants can save a copy of the final version.

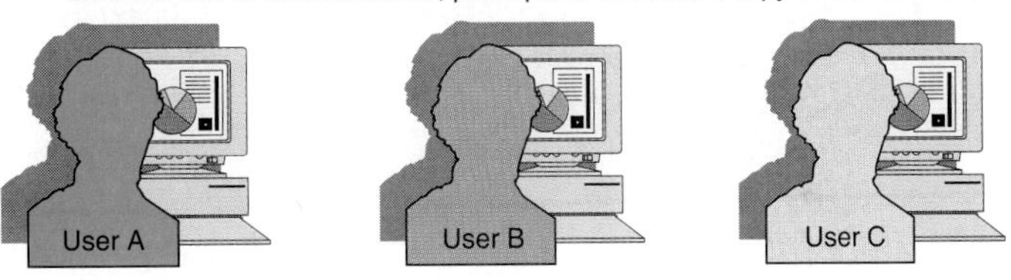

SOURCE: Adapted from *Information Systems: A Management Approach,* by Steven R. Gordon and Judith R. Gordon, 1996, p. 308.

Scheduling software can also help in environments where individuals tend to work outside of the office. For salespeople who are constantly on the go, or telecommuters who do much of their work at home, it is possible to connect to the Local Area Network (LAN) where the schedule is maintained (by laptop or notebook computer, or possibly with a personal data assistant system equipped with a modem) to check their schedule and update it if necessary. That can save a lot of telephone calls and missed appointments.

Like most information technology, scheduling software is not the answer for every situation. If people do not use the system regularly or keep their schedule current, then the software won't help. Some individuals are not particularly keen on having their schedules available for everybody in the office to see. Often the success or failure of the use of scheduling software is a "top-down" issue. In a hierarchical environment, the boss can exert pressure for all members to use it. In a collaborative environment, peer pressure is really the only recourse. Obviously, for individuals it becomes an issue of personal choice.

Creativity and Idea Generation

Although we have defined productivity in terms of efficiency, effectiveness, and quality, a fourth dimension might be considered as well; **creativity.** Creativity may be a somewhat nebulous concept—hard to define though easy to recognize—but it

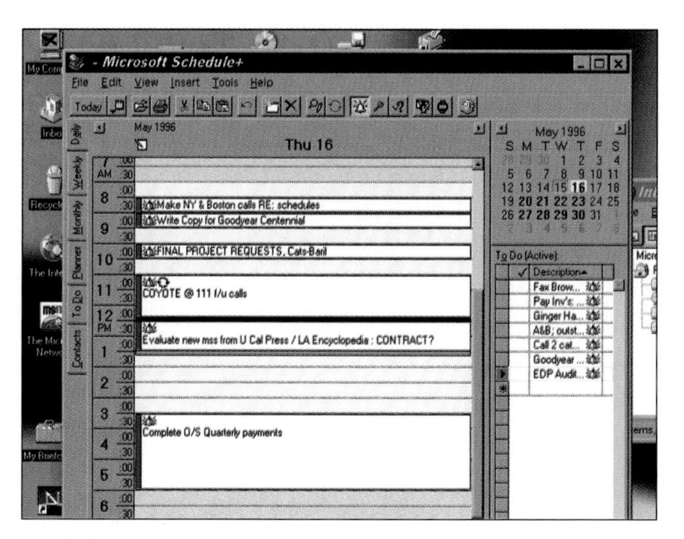

Scheduling systems can improve scheduling for individuals and groups, if every individual is willing to open their calendars for others to see them. Photo courtesy of Microsoft.

is an important component of many job tasks. Creativity is linked to the notion of idea generation. Research has shown that the likelihood of a good idea being generated (i.e., a creative one) is correlated with the number of ideas generated. Therefore, providing managers with the necessary tools to help them generate ideas may also help their creativity.

Let's revisit the real estate agent, who wishes to maintain an ongoing relationship with all of his previous clients in the hope they will call him when they decide to move again. He might consider using a desktop-publishing package to create a newsletter that he sends on a regular basis, perhaps biannually. The desktop-publishing software provides additional features beyond those available in the agent's word-processing package, giving him the choice of more options and therefore helping him think of alternative formats in the design of the newsletter and the use of it as a marketing tool. The agent could use one of the features in the package to develop a home page on the World Wide Web, inviting individuals who are thinking of moving into the area to browse through a database containing videos and pictures of houses for sale and information on schools, entertainment, and other pertinent local information.

Incidentally, note that different types of information technology and information systems are often used together for a specific application. The names and addresses of the agent's clients could be stored using his word-processing package, or a database management system, depending on the additional uses he might have for this data. He could then use a database file to print mailing labels for the newsletter.

Desktop-publishing software is only one example of information technology used to enhance a creative process. Within the world of entertainment, the use of I/T is enhancing, and in some cases changing, the creative process. The popular 1995 movie Toy Story was the first full-length animation film to be completely computer generated. Taking this approach further, the merger of film concepts with computer games has created an explosion of entertainment possibilities. Just having access to the technology doesn't ensure a successful product will emerge, however. Since the film industry specialists come from a different culture and speak a somewhat different language than the computer game developers, the original merger of the two wasn't quite as smooth as some had anticipated (as illustrated in Business Brief 9–1).

BUSINESS BRIEF 9-1 CULTURAL DIFFERENCES: HOLLYWOOD CLASHES WITH SILICON VALLEY

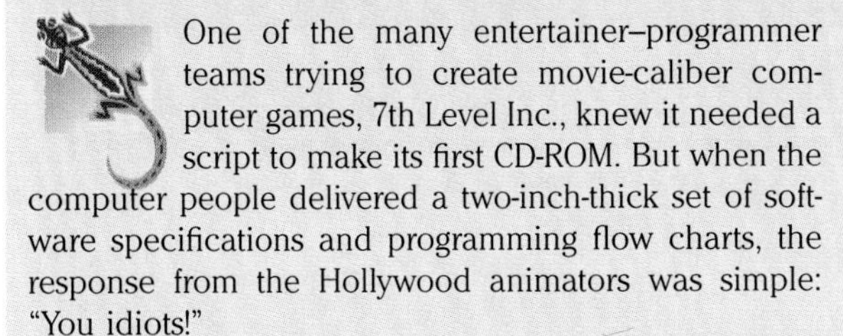

One of the many entertainer–programmer teams trying to create movie-caliber computer games, 7th Level Inc., knew it needed a script to make its first CD-ROM. But when the computer people delivered a two-inch-thick set of software specifications and programming flow charts, the response from the Hollywood animators was simple: "You idiots!"

"There was a lot of pain," says George Grayson, 7th Level's chief executive and president. And the pain didn't go away when the Hollywood types took the lead on 7th Level's second title. Programmers received reams of scenes, gags and video clips, without a clue how to put them together for the CD-ROM disk. "We were speaking different languages," says Scott Page, a former rock musician and 7th Level cofounder.

The bottom line, though, according to several multimedia companies, is that Hollywood directors, accustomed to wielding creative control over their projects, have to cede that power to computer programmers. "The most important guy is the programmer," says Silicon Valley veteran, Tom Zito, whose Digital Pictures Inc. was the first company to produce full-motion video games with real actors. "It's a totally different business," he adds, "and Hollywood hasn't figured that out yet."

QUESTION

1. Currently it appears that technical specialists (i.e., computer programmers) need to play a large role in the merger of movies and video games. Do you think this will always be the case? Why?

Source: S. McCartney, "Hollywood, Silicon Valley Team Up—and Clash," *The Wall Street Journal,* March 14, 1995, p. B1. Reprinted by permission of *The Wall Street Journal,* © 1995 Dow Jones & Company, Inc. All rights reserved worldwide.

For musicians, synthesizers and other specialized systems provide enhanced capabilities to create, store, manipulate, and distribute music. Some musicians have begun to bypass large record labels, preferring to start their own or to deal with smaller labels that allow them greater artistic freedom and a larger percentage of the royalties. Part of their ability to do this can be attributed to information technology which has drastically reduced the cost of making, recording, and distributing music. Some musicians provide music clips on the Internet so that potential customers can sample their music and order it directly.

Entertainment is only one of many realms where creativity is valued. The development of an effective marketing campaign requires creativity, and nowadays, information technology that manipulates sound and images is frequently employed. Creativity is also a component to many decision-making tasks; the comment that someone found a creative solution to a challenging problem is often (though perhaps not often enough) heard.

Project Management

Finally, a generic and very common activity is the management of projects. **Project management** means allocating the necessary resources (people, equipment) to successfully achieve the goals and objectives of a given initiative. A project consists of a series of activities. Some of these activities can be performed in parallel while others must be performed sequentially. Some activities are "critical," or on the "critical path"—meaning that if they are delayed the whole project is delayed—while others are not. Keeping track of the activities, deadlines, and deliverables, and allocating personnel to them, is a complex task particularly if the project manager has more than one project to oversee.

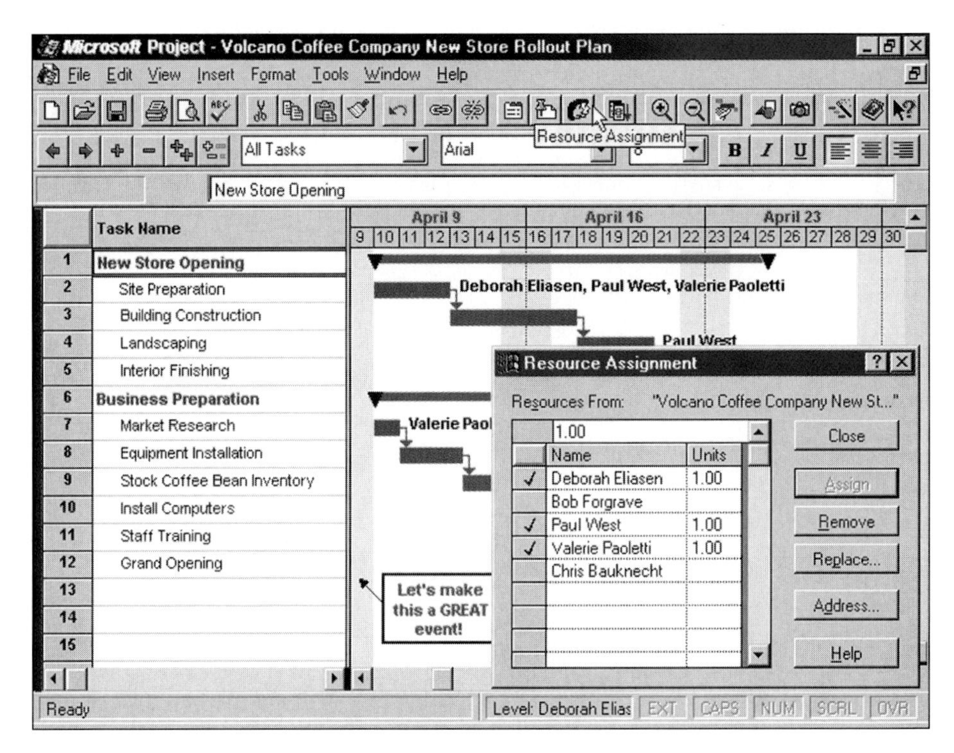

Project management systems can save substantial amounts of money by helping managers to better track, monitor, and control several projects at once. Photo courtesy of Microsoft.

A variety of software packages are available to support managers in controlling and managing projects. These packages help project managers identify the different activities, create relationships between them, enter deadlines and resource requirements. The packages then, by using traditional project management techniques like **critical path method (CPM)** and **project evaluation and review technique (PERT),** identify the critical activities and suggest ways to cost-effectively reduce the duration of the project. These packages allow managers to track and monitor progress, reminding them of deadlines and delivery schedules whenever the computer is turned on.

We close this section with a quick reference to the notion of being responsive to customer needs. Productivity is after all a function of how well we fulfill the customer's needs and how many resources we use to do so.

All the information technology and information systems mentioned in this chapter can be related back to this concept of achieving greater productivity by being more responsive. The real estate agent's market survey document (prepared using an image scanner, a personal computer with a word-processing package, and a color printer) was prepared to respond to a perceived need of a potential customer. The data collection, analysis, and presentation performed by the financial analyst was for the benefit of her customer: her boss. In a broader sense, her customers also include the individuals who invest money with the mutual fund company; they are entrusting their retirement savings to the mutual fund manager, who will make decisions based on the analyst's recommendations. The use of the commercial databases, spreadsheets, statistical analysis forecasting packages, word processing, and presentation systems are all in response to perceived customer

TABLE 9–1 Examples of Using Information Technology for Job Tasks

Task	*I/T Example*
Accessing information	Database and document management systems
Analyzing information	Electronic spreadsheet, statistical analysis software
Reporting information	Word processing, database management system
Developing forecasts	Forecasting software, groupware
Presenting information	Presentation software, groupware
Communicating information	Electronic mail, electronic bulletin board
Scheduling	Scheduling system, groupware
Generating ideas and alternatives	Idea generation system, groupware
Controlling activities	Decision and control system
Managing projects	Project management software

needs. Hewlett-Packard's technical support engineers need to answer customer calls and complaints as quickly and effectively as possible. The accessible-from-everywhere database containing the histories of customer calls enables them to do that.

Individuals and workgroups perform numerous processing, decision-making, and communicating tasks. Information technology may be used to support those tasks to improve the individual's or workgroup's productivity. Table 9–1 lists examples of information technologies to be used for different tasks.

NEGATIVE IMPACTS OF I/T ON PRODUCTIVITY

Information technology, like any other technology, has its good side and its bad side. In the following section of this chapter we consider the negative impact of technology on *individuals,* while in the next chapters, we will identify some of the *organizational* risks and vulnerabilities in the use of information systems. As the use of technology increases in organizations and homes, these risks are becoming larger and more prevalent. For organizations, the legal and productivity ramifications of inattention to the impact of I/T on human psychological and physical health can be devastating.

Health Risks

We can describe one type of risk under the general category of health problems created by concentrated computer use. As people spend more time using personal computers (workstations, computer terminals, home computers), potential health risks begin to come into play. One is that of injury from repetitive stress; some evidence suggests that persons using a keyboard for several hours per day may suffer stress injuries that can result in the loss of some or all of the use of their hands. Staring at a computer screen for long hours can cause eyestrain and headaches. Other evidence has suggested that the emissions from video monitors may adversely affect pregnancies, causing some pregnant women to miscarry. Improper seating

Persons using a keyboard for several hours every day may suffer stress injuries that are painful and can be disabling. Photo courtesy of Bonnie Kamin.

posture can lead to back strain and other back problems. These health problems usually lead to higher employee absenteeism, lower morale, and lower productivity.

All of these risks can be reduced, and as the health risks are discovered computer manufacturers generally respond by improving their products. The science of designing and arranging the tools people use so that their interaction will be efficient and safe is called **ergonomics** (see Figure 9–4). An example is the development of specialized keyboards—rounded, with a greater separation between the groups of keys normally accessed by each hand. This keyboard design allows users to keep their hands in a much more natural position, which tends to reduce the strain on the wrists, tendons, and finger joints.

Computer manufacturers can only address a subset of the issues, however. Many organizations have also implemented policies to help reduce health risks to employees, such as requiring pregnant women to fill jobs that require minimal computer use and limiting the time slots (such as two hours) that employees can use keyboards before taking mandatory breaks. These policies are deemed necessary to avoid potential losses from injuries (both from lost productivity, and from possible legal liabilities—see Business Brief 9–2).

Addiction

There are other risks involved as well. Some researchers are concerned about the potentially addictive features of emerging technologies. They argue that the advancements of multimedia hardware, coupled with advancements in entertainment software and the interactive capabilities of the Internet, have resulted in an environment that some individuals get hooked into and find difficulty leaving. Just as an alcoholic or drug addict prefers his or her artificial environment to the real one, so does a computer addict. The impact of this addiction on productivity is serious.

Consider the case of Scott, a 33-year-old Toronto musician. About 10 years ago he was between jobs, and having a few emotional problems. Each night after dinner he would head off to his room, turn on his computer, and load a game called Lode Runner. "At first, the idea was to beat my friends' scores," he recalls, "but I got better

FIGURE 9–4 Ergonomic Considerations in Use of a Workstation

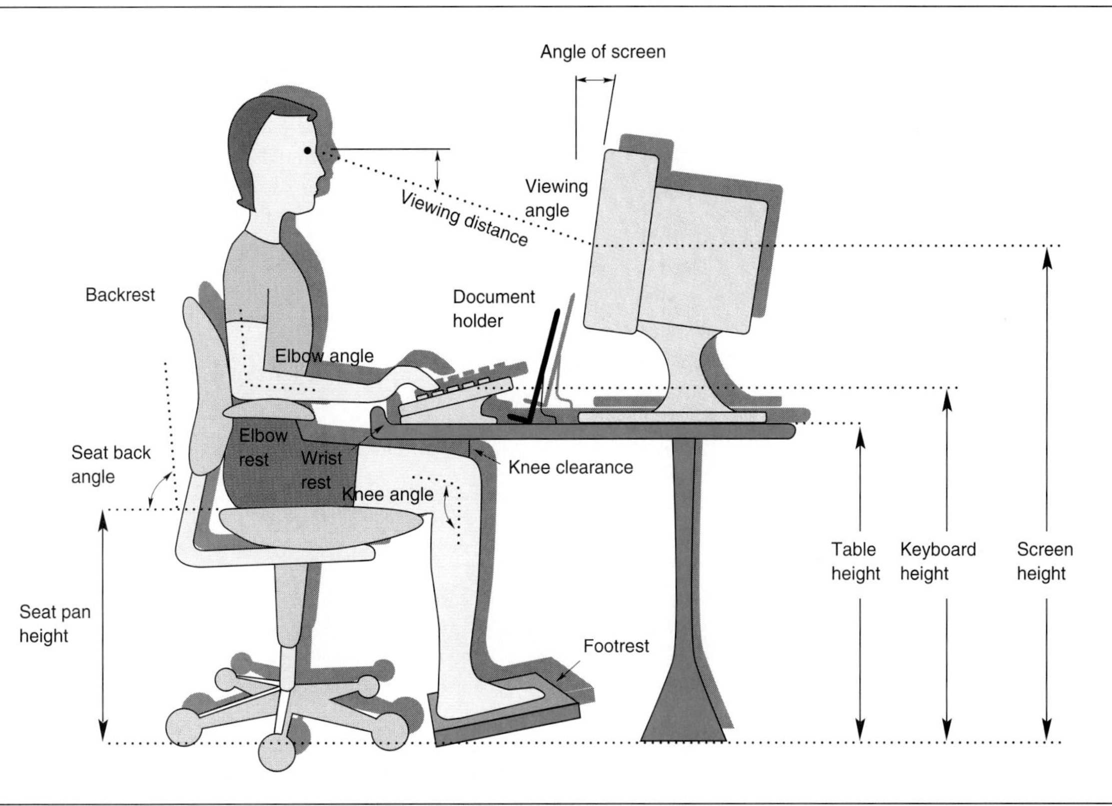

SOURCE: Adapted from Information Systems: A Problem-Solving Approach, Third Edition, by Kenneth C. Laudon and Jane Price Laudon, 1995, p. 333.

at it and began playing it more." In a couple of weeks, he was playing Lode Runner every night until 2:00 A.M. After three months, Scott realized he had a problem. "I thought, like, Wow- you could spend your whole life in here," he explains. He went cold turkey, quitting for good. And now, although he has a computer at home, he has no games installed on it—the allure would be irresistible. "Sure," Scott adds, "you can say, Who would want to waste their time with a bunch of zeros and ones? But you're not rational when you're on these things, and you get drawn into this different world."

Others discount the computer addict notion, preferring the notion of love or infatuation. Consider the MUDS (multi-user dungeons or dimensions) and similar environments that exist on the Internet. Users from around the world can access the environment, which allows them to assume an identity and develop their own personality characteristics. The player instructs the character to search the "world" looking for treasure or fulfilling a quest, and in doing so they encounter other players' characters and begin talking, fighting, even making virtual love with them. The argument has been made that when someone is in love, they can learn a lot about themselves. When someone is "seduced" into a virtual community or environment, they can also learn a great deal about themselves. According to this line of reasoning, what appears to be an obsession may in fact be a healthy process, as Business Brief 9–3 describes further.

Nevertheless, there are a sufficient number of horror stories to suggest that the obsession has a negative impact on at least some individuals. The most glaring example was that of Steven Robertson, a Scottish airman who killed himself after

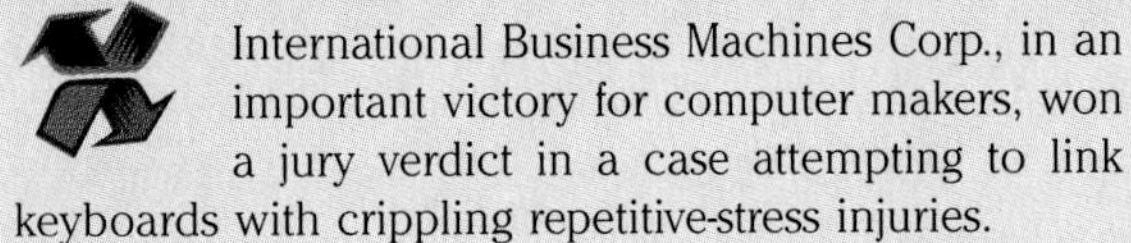

REPETITIVE STRESS INJURY: KEYBOARD VENDOR WINS SUIT

International Business Machines Corp., in an important victory for computer makers, won a jury verdict in a case attempting to link keyboards with crippling repetitive-stress injuries.

The closely watched suit in state court in Hastings, Minn., was considered an important test of whether juries would be swayed by new evidence indicating that some keyboard makers failed to warn consumers even though they knew that their own employees had been injured after using their keyboards. The case was the second to go to trial out of thousands that blame keyboard makers for wrist, back, and neck injuries. The only other case to go to trial was decided in favor of the manufacturer, Compaq Computer Corp., in 1994.

The new evidence apparently failed to move the jury. After deliberating only a few hours, it concluded that IBM had no obligation to provide a warning. The jury also found that IBM didn't do anything wrong in designing the keyboard. "IBM remains steeled in its position that these cases ought not to be cases," said Michael Cerussi, a lawyer with the firm Cerussi & Spring, who represents IBM. "Why should a manufacturer of a piece of office equipment be required to place a warning on it?"

QUESTION

1. Have you ever experienced soreness from using a keyboard extensively? How do you plan on avoiding injuries such as repetitive stress syndrome?

SOURCE: E. Felsenthal, "IBM Wins Jury Verdict in Case Seeking to Link Keyboards and Stress Injuries," *The Wall Street Journal*, March 9, 1995, p. B14. Reprinted by permission of *The Wall Street Journal*, © Dow Jones & Company, Inc. All rights reserved worldwide.

amassing $31,000 in debts to "feed his addiction" to computers. Less dramatic but equally disturbing examples of the negative side of obsessive use include adolescents who exhibit totally dysfunctional social skills, undergraduate students who spend 80 hours per week in cyberspace and flunk out, and adults whose personal relationships (including marriages) fail.

The vast array of services, products, and games offered on the Internet are increasing the lure of, and the time spent, surfing it. The amount of time that people can spend just "looking around" the Internet is such that an increasing number of companies, concerned about the impact on productivity, have established policies limiting its use by employees during work hours.

Distractions

Although computer addiction may seem more of a risk for younger users, a similar risk has emerged for users of all ages. From the dawn of time, people have been **multitasking:** trying to do several things simultaneously so they don't "waste" time. The proliferation of new technology—from laptop computers to speaker and cellular phones, electronic mail and voice mail, portable radios, portable televisions, personal digital assistants—makes it possible for almost anyone to multitask all day long.

For some people, this is not a positive development. Psychologists say that although it is possible for the human brain to process two or more tasks simultaneously, only one of the tasks will command sharp attention. This limited attention span leads to risk of traffic accidents as people talk on their cellular phone and look at portable computer screens while they are driving. Increased multitasking also adds even more stress to already stressful lives, causing *reduced* productivity and many stress-related illnesses.

BUSINESS BRIEF 9-3 BREAKING THE HABIT: ARE COMPUTERS BECOMING ADDICTIVE?

With the advent of the Internet—and with the explosion in such technologies as CD-ROM—interactive games and simulations of reality have become more sophisticated, more exciting, more fun. For some users, the computer's siren song has never been so loud.

But is it addictive? The expert jury is still out. "There is no recognized phenomenon of computer addiction," says Dr. Arthur Herscovitch, a psychologist at the Winnipeg based Addictions Foundation of Manitoba. But he suggests that many people may have the potential for a pathological computer habit, similar to addictions to alcohol or gambling—or, for that matter, to television. "With the increase in the amount of stimulation available through computers now," Herscovitch says, "I can see the possibility of addictions developing."

Sherry Turkle, a psychologist at the Massachusetts Institute of Technology in Cambridge, suggests that what might appear to be an obsession may in fact be a healthy process. Turkle is particularly interested in MUDs (short for "multi-user dungeon" or "multi-user dimension") and MOOs (for "MUD, object-oriented"). First developed in England in the mid-1980s, MUDs are virtual communities that exist only on the Internet.

Some of the tens of thousands of MUD users, who tend to be young males, spend as much as 80 hours per week playing their cyberspace persona. But if other parts of life—like studying and working—do not suffer, the computer time might actually be beneficial to some people, Turkle says. "Some adolescents go through six months or a year of extensive use, but then the characters and experiences have offered them a way to work through personal issues," she adds. "Then, they're ready to go on to RL"—the mudders' term for Real Life.

QUESTION

1. Do you know anyone who appears addicted to computer systems? Do you think computer addiction is a real threat? Why or why not?

SOURCE: Joe Chidley, "Seduced by the Siren Call of Computers," *Maclean's,* March 27, 1995, pp. 50–51.

Consider David Johnson, a stockbrocker and radio and television commentator. He operates from a setup "worthy of NASA's mission control." Using a headset phone to free his hands, Mr. Johnson can work brokerage computers, check news wires, listen in on his firm's internal radio network, and watch both CNN and CNBC, all while leaning over a pair of boom-mounted microphones for his different radio programs. His problem: "I have a bad habit of talking into the wrong mike."

Indeed, being distracted can mean putting the wrong number in a spreadsheet or clicking on the wrong E-mail address and sending the boss an embarrassing message. For many, the constant juggling of multiple responsibilities can have a detrimental effect on their decision-making ability, on the effectiveness of their communications, and on their productivity in general. As with the physical health issues, the computer addiction phenomenon and multitasking beg for the observation of that old adage, "All things in moderation."

What can we take with us from this discussion of the potential negative impact of information technology on individuals? Simply put, this is an area too often overlooked or downplayed by many organizations. When organizations look to improve business processes through reengineering projects, for example, they often bring in the human resource specialists relatively late in the project. In many cases, task design specialists are not consulted at all, resulting in the development of job tasks that can lead to many of the health risks described. The obvious solution is to make task design (examining the requirements for interacting with information systems) and ergonomics (human engineering) an integral part of process reengineering and continuous improvement efforts.

SUMMARY

The productivity of individuals and workgroups may be improved through the use of information technology. Dimensions of productivity include efficiency, effectiveness, and quality. Productivity may be difficult to measure, especially when dealing with service rather than manufacturing environments, with workgroups rather than individuals, and with jobs at higher organizational levels with multiple responsibilities and less tangible outputs. Nevertheless, it is imperative to identify the objectives of every task in a given job, and the measures of performance on those objectives, if we are to succeed in improving the productivity of individuals in those jobs.

Information technology can improve the productivity of individuals in performing generic tasks like information access and processing, data analysis, control, forecasting, and simulation. Information technology is a critical component of achieving efficient and effective communication. Communications tasks include document management, presentation, and other intra (within) and inter (between) group communications. I/T may also be used to manage individual and workgroup schedules, to enhance creativity and idea generation, and to help manage projects.

The use of information technology by individuals brings certain risks. The health risks include such aspects as repetitive stress problems from using keyboards, eyestrain and pregnancy difficulties from monitors, and back and posture problems from improper seating. Ergonomics, the applied science of human engineering, seeks to redesign and rearrange the things people use so as to avoid these health problems. Additional risks include notions of excessive multitasking and computer addiction, where individuals become obsessed with computer use to the detriment of other aspects of their personal and professional lives.

KEY CONCEPTS AND TERMS

KEY CONCEPTS

- Productivity can be measured through considerations of efficiency, effectiveness, and quality. (295)
- Job responsibilities and functions can be broken into tasks for which clearly stated goals and objectives can be established. (297)
- Information technology can be used to improve the productivity of individuals and workgroups as they complete tasks and fill responsibilities. (300)
- The use of information technology by individuals can lead to health and other risks, which need to be monitored and addressed. (315)

KEY TERMS

analysis (302)
budgeting (302)
creativity (311)
critical path method (CPM) (314)
document management (305)
effectiveness (295)
efficiency (295)
ergonomics (316)
forecasting (304)
group functions (297)
groupware (310)
job task (297)
multitasking (318)
output-to-input ratio (293)
presentation (308)
productivity (293)
project evaluation and review technique (PERT) (314)
project management (313)
quality (295)
simulation (304)
scenarios (304)

REFERENCES

Chidley, J. "Seduced by the Siren Call of Computers: Have Today's Sophisticated Computers Become Addictive?" *Maclean's*, March 27, 1995, pp. 50–51.

Jessup, L., and J. Valacich. *Group Support Systems: New Perspectives*. New York: Macmillan, 1993.

Kirkpatrick, D. "Here Comes the Payoff from PCs." *Fortune Magazine*, March 23, 1992.

McCartney, S. "The Multitasking Man: Type A Meets Technology." *The Wall Street Journal*, April 19, 1995, p. B1.

Nelson, R. *End-User Computing: Concepts, Issues and Applications*. New York: John Wiley and Sons, 1989.

CONNECTIVE CASE: Another Day . . .

Enrique opened his eyes as the sound of classical music filled his bedroom. As the volume of music slowly increased, the lights came on and increased in intensity to match. A light sleeper, Enrique rose from the bed and headed for the shower. The temperature in the bedroom was 62° Fahrenheit, as always.

After showering, dressing, and finishing his breakfast (orange juice; cold cereal with milk; toasted bagel with cream cheese; coffee, black) Enrique headed into his home office. His workstation was on power standby; he activated it and connected to his company's network. He skimmed over the 23 new E-mail messages quickly. The messages were sorted in terms of priority; there didn't appear to be anything urgent, so he would deal with them later. He did notice one message concerning his 9:00 A.M. meeting; he sent a quick reply asking the sales manager who had sent the note to forward the revised schedule to him.

Next Enrique opened the company's Executive Information System. His master screen—displaying a map of the world—showed one potential problem: a red light was blinking in Madrid. Enrique spoke slowly and clearly. "Show me Madrid." The map faded and was replaced by a split screen displaying bar charts of the Madrid facility's sales and production figures for the previous day. On the other half of the screen was a message indicating that the Madrid facility was 10 percent below its target output level for the past 24 hours.

Glancing at the time in Madrid displayed at the bottom of the screen, Enrique used the mouse to toggle to his E-mail system and composed a quick note to the Madrid plant manager. He then toggled back to the Executive Information System, flipping through screens and checking for any surprises in the current statistics for all of the company's five manufacturing facilities. Just as he was finishing this daily routine, his workstation beeped and announced in its precise voice, "You have a new message from Les in Madrid. It says 'I have a small problem at this end. Let's talk.' "

Knowing that the plant manager was in his office at the plant (he would have indicated otherwise), Enrique responded to the workstation. "Close Executive System. Open resource screen. Open videoconference. Connect to Les in Madrid." Enrique watched the screen carefully to ensure his instructions were understood and followed. The workstation made the connection, and a view of Les's Madrid office appeared in a window in the top right corner of Enrique's screen. "Hey Les," Enrique said, "Are you there?" Les appeared in the window as he replied, "Sure Enrique. I'm here."

"What's the problem?" Enrique queried. As Les explained the situation, Enrique subconsciously checked Les's body language and demeanor. Les appeared somewhat agitated, but not overly so; Enrique decided to go with the plant manager's suggestion for dealing with the slipped production numbers before he had heard all of it. If Les had been really concerned, he would be much more nervous.

Ending the conversation and disconnecting the videoconference, Enrique put the workstation on power ready and headed for his car. Before leaving the house, he checked the intelligent security and climate control systems, and set them for the day. Driving through his neighborhood on the way to the office, Enrique switched on his voice-activated car phone. "Call Mary Jean," he commanded. In a few seconds the connection was made and his sales manager Mary Jean Bendo was on the line. "Hi Enrique. What's up?"

"I just wanted to check with you before the nine o'clock meeting. Is the presentation ready?" Enrique inquired.

"You bet. Have you checked the revised agenda yet? I sent it to your E-mail account, along with the revised presentation," Mary Jean responded. "I suggest you focus on the new cost estimates in the cost/benefit analysis; the assumptions are included in the updated spreadsheet, which I've attached as well."

As he continued the conversation, Enrique glanced quickly at the automobile's traffic-control screen in the dashboard. The system was warning of traffic congestion ahead, so he turned at the next intersection and used a different route to reach the dock station right on time for the 7:30 ferry. Once he was safely parked on the ferry, Enrique powered up his wireless personal data assistant (PDA), glanced quickly at his schedule for the day, and then opened up the revised meeting agenda Mary Jean had sent. Next he viewed the revised presentation, and then accessed the updated spreadsheet file to see where the new costs had originated from. . . .

Case Question

1. The vignette describes an individual who seems to use information technology quite extensively in his personal and professional life. To what extent do you believe this scenario reflects reality? Discuss some of the pros and cons of emulating Enrique's approach to improving productivity.

IT'S YOUR TURN END OF CHAPTER MATERIALS

REVIEW QUESTIONS

1. What are the three main components of productivity?
2. Discuss differences between efficiency and effectiveness. Use an example (not from this book) illustrating the difference.
3. Discuss differences between effectiveness and quality. Use an example (not from this book) illustrating the difference.
4. Why is it sometimes difficult to measure productivity?
5. Identify a type of business software application commonly used for information access.
6. Identify a type of business software application commonly used for data analysis.
7. Why might someone choose to use a desktop-publishing system rather than a word-processing-package to create certain documents?
8. In what ways could a document-imaging system help a workgroup improve their efficiency and effectiveness?
9. Identify a type of business software application commonly used for presenting ideas to an audience.
10. What types of information technology are commonly used for communicating between individuals and groups?

DISCUSSION QUESTIONS

1. This chapter provided an example of breaking the research responsibilities of a professor into distinct tasks. Identify ways information technology could be used to improve the productivity of a professor completing these tasks.
2. Think carefully about the major education and/or job responsibilities you have. Select one, and identify as many distinct tasks and activities as you can. (Use the discussion of the research responsibilities of a professor as an example.) Now identify some ways you believe information technology could be (or is being) used to improve your productivity with respect to these tasks.
3. This chapter identified three major categories of potential downsides to the use of information technology by individuals (health issues, potential computer addiction, distraction). What other cautions might be raised concerning the use of I/T?
4. Some people have argued that telecommuting provides a great way for people to enhance their personal lives, by giving them more control over their schedules. Others argue that it simply means the employee spends more time working, since they always have access to necessary information and information-processing capabilities. Comment on these arguments.
5. This chapter has discussed numerous types of I/T that can be used by individuals to improve their personal and workgroup productivity. It also pointed out some overlap between software products (e.g., word-processing packages can do some desktop publishing; electronic spreadsheets have some statistical analysis capabilities). Comment on the implications for (1) how much effort is required to remain competent in using necessary I/T tools, and (2) how to decide what tool is appropriate for a given job task.
6. The argument has been made that the increasing capabilities of information technology are leading to a situation where some people are trying to become *too* productive; as a result, an increasing proportion of workers are experiencing increased stress levels, which actually reduces their productivity. Comment on this argument, and potential implications for the future.

GROUP ASSIGNMENTS

1. (For those with access to a group scheduling system, such as Microsoft's Schedule+ running on a network.) Individually, enter your schedules for the following week. Next, use the scheduling system to schedule a meeting for all group members at the next available time slot. Comment on the efficiency of using this approach, when compared to using a telephone to schedule a similar meeting. As a

group, prepare a brief position paper discussing the pros and cons of using scheduling systems in a workgroup environment.

2. Individually, use a word-processing package to prepare responses to the questions for the Connective Case at the end of this chapter. Next, select one group members' responses. Have that individual send his or her responses by E-mail to a second group member. Once the second group member has incorporated his or her responses, s/he should pass the revised file onto the third member. Continue until all members have had an opportunity to revise/modify the file. As a group, compare the initial responses to the final ones. Comment on the efficiency and effectiveness of using this approach to collaborative work. Suggest alternative ways that this type of group assignment could be completed, and discuss pros and cons.

APPLICATION ASSIGNMENTS

1. Use a project management software package of your choice to create a critical path for the project activities listed under the directory CHAP9 in the file PROJ.DAT that you can find by accessing the Internet and locating the home page for this book.
2. Use a spreadsheet program of your choice to analyze the performance of the two stocks listed in the file STOC.DAT that you can find by accessing the Internet and locating the home page for this book. Produce a one-page memorandum recommending which of the two stocks to buy. Use as many features of your package as possible to justify your recommendation.
3. Use a word-processing package or desktop-publishing package of your choice to produce a one-page newsletter to your friends about the events of the last two weeks in your life. Be creative.

CASE ASSIGNMENT: Pollution Solutions (A): Too Much to Do . . .

Pam Linton, owner and CEO of Pollution Solutions of Vermont (PSOV), was making a list of some of the things she wanted to get done the next day, before leaving her office. She had just finished a very busy day, and tomorrow didn't look any better. She found herself thinking, yet again, that most days she had so much paperwork, so many phone calls, meetings, and other distractions that she just wasn't able to get to her more important responsibilities.

. . . And No Time to Do It

First on Pam's list was the report that she and her sales manager Craig Senzel needed to put the finishing touches on for one of their major customers. Although PSOV's waste-tracking system was able to print out the relevant information, it wasn't in the format that Pam wanted to use on a customer report. One way of building trust and long-term relationships was to not only provide waste generators (customers) with accurate and timely information, but to present it in a very professional format. The word-processing package that PSOV used was not directly compatible with the DataBase Management System that had been used for the development of the waste-tracking system. This meant that although most of the data could be imported into the word processor, some of it had to be reentered and all of it needed quite a bit of formatting and manipulation to result in a report that Pam felt was acceptable.

Another item on Pam's list was to make sure that all employees were aware of the latest Environmental Protection Agency (EPA) regulations. She knew that ignorance was no defense against violations of EPA or Department of Transportation (DOT) regulations. If any of her employees failed to act on the new regulations, Pam could be held liable.

PSOV subscribed to a service that sent a weekly bulletin alerting companies to new regulations that could affect them. To share this information, each employee was required to read the bulletin (even though much of the information might not pertain directly to PSOV). Pam might also need to meet with the employees directly affected by major changes, and obtain their suggestions on how best to reach compliance. It might require changing their job procedures and/or modifying the waste-tracking system to record and process additional information.

Pam had received a bulletin with a major new EPA regulation in the mail today, and she wasn't too happy about it. The change only gave companies 30 days to come into compliance, and she didn't believe that was a reasonable length of time. If only she'd had more warning of the impending regulation, PSOV could have begun preparing for the regulation before it was passed. Pam knew that all EPA deliberations were available from the EPA department on an electronic bulletin board, and she had heard that it was possible to link up through the Internet to see what potential changes were being discussed. Unfortunately, she had only recently obtained the hardware and software necessary to allow PSOV to tap into the Internet, and no one within the company seemed to have the time to learn anything about it.

Pam glanced down at her desk calendar to check the next day's schedule. Her secretary managed her appointments, but Pam also made commitments on her own that sometimes conflicted with those set by the secretary. Basically, there were three copies of Pam's schedule; the one her secretary kept, the pocket calendar Pam kept with her, and the master schedule kept on Pam's desk. All three were kept manually, and sometimes coordinating her schedule was a headache.

Pam got thinking about her day, and had recollections of spending time tracking people down to try and give or receive information. She recalled popping her head into her employees' offices, checking in the lab, making phone calls only to get busy signals, and generally wasting too much of her precious time. She couldn't help thinking that there had to be a better way for the employees within the office to communicate. Ideally she would like better communications with all employees, including the waste handlers who went out on the jobs and lab specialists who worked part of the time at PSOV's facility and part of the time at customer sites.

Another issue she needed to deal with was the response time of the waste-tracking information system. The employees had been complaining that it was taking too long to get responses to their queries; instead of answering customer questions immediately, they now frequently had to tell the customer that PSOV would return their call in a few minutes. This had led to some problems where follow up calls were delayed, leaving the customer somewhat dissatisfied.

Craig Senzel, who managed the computer network, had raised the issue with Pam. His suggestions were to consider buying a faster file server for the local area network, or possibly to bring in their software consultants to see if they had other ideas. The consultants had previously mentioned the possibility of rewriting the programs for the waste-tracking system using a different DataBase Management System, to improve the response time and also to make the programs easier to modify in the future. They had indicated that it would be a fairly major undertaking, however.

Pam also got thinking about a large job that PSOV wanted to bid on. The deadline for bids was fast approaching, and she and Craig would have to hustle to get it ready on time. Preparing a bid was a complex process; there wasn't a lot of room for error. If the bid was too high, they wouldn't be considered for the job. If it was too low, PSOV might get the job, but it might also end up losing money on it. In the past she and Craig had used a Lotus spreadsheet package to prepare a bid, basically starting from scratch each time. Lately Pam had been thinking that there should be a way of using the information gained from previous jobs to help prepare new bids.

She had also been considering making more formal presentations to prospective customers; in the past it was a matter of dropping off the written bid and encouraging the potential customer to come to PSOV to audit their facilities and procedures. The audits had tended to be somewhat informal; a tour of the facility, answering any questions. Given the current environment—increased competition, more knowledgeable, price sensitive customers, and more sophisticated competitors—Pam believed that anything PSOV could do to help win and keep customers was important. She wondered if a more formal presentation as part of the customer audit might help build the type of trust and confidence in PSOV which she knew was essential.

As Pam packed up for the day and headed for the parking lot, she was still thinking of what the next day would bring. More phone calls, more busy work, more distractions; she wondered when she would have time to sit back and think more about the future directions for the company.

Questions

1. Use ideas presented in this chapter, and from other sources if you wish, to suggest ways to use information technology to improve Pam Linton's productivity (efficiency, effectiveness, quality). Make (and state) any reasonable assumptions (for example, concerning the presence or absence of any existing information or communication technology).
2. Repeat question 1, only now consider the office employees of PSOV as a workgroup, and provide suggestions for them.

Source: This case was written by Associate Professors Ronald Thompson and William Cats-Baril of the School of Business Administration, University of Vermont. The case is intended as a basis for discussion and is not meant to illustrate effective or ineffective handling of an administrative situation.

CHAPTER 10 Competitive Uses of Information Technology

After reading this chapter, you should have a better understanding of how information technology may be used to improve the competitive position of an organization. More specifically, you should be able to:

- Understand the concepts of competition and the use of competitive frameworks to identify potential uses of information technology.
- Describe specific uses of I/T to increase the effectiveness of decision making.
- Understand how I/T can be used to improve communications (reduce distortion, reduce information overload, improve communication among organizations).
- Understand how I/T can be used to improve a firm's operations (accelerate business processes, increase flexibility).
- Understand how I/T can be used to improve the availability of inputs (from suppliers) and the acceptance of outputs (by customers) and to enhance the products or services offered by the firm.
- Understand how I/T can be used to improve environmental scanning, feedback and feedforward, control systems, and early warning systems.
- Give some cautions on using I/T for competitive purposes.

Okay, you've convinced me that individuals and groups can benefit from using information technology. But can a company actually gain a competitive advantage through the application of I/T?

INTRODUCTION

Organizations compete for customers, for access to raw materials, for access to new markets, for the rights to develop new products. Not-for-profit organizations compete for donations and grants; political parties compete for votes; government agencies compete for funding from general fund budgets. Competition is a part of everyday existence for most organizations, and, when viewed from a longer term perspective, it is a fact of life for all organizations. Within this competitive environment, many organizations have successfully used information technology to help them compete.

In this chapter, we provide a formal introduction to organizational competition. We also discuss ways to use specific frameworks to identify appropriate applications of I/T that help organizations compete better. We illustrate these frameworks with numerous examples of the use of information systems to help organizations compete more effectively by improving organizational decision making and communications, by improving organizational operations and responsiveness, and by improving supplier relationships and customer satisfaction. The chapter closes with some cautions on the use of I/T for strategic purposes.

UNDERSTANDING COMPETITION AND STRATEGY

Organizations can use numerous different strategies for competing, such as being the low-cost producer, differentiating their products and services, or carving a market niche. We have suggested that many companies now attempt to combine these strategies as much as possible since their customers are becoming more demanding. You may also recall that we used the examples of Burger King, Dell Computers, and Saturn to illustrate the strategy of mass customization (i.e., quickly customizing products for a large number of customers). At this point we would like to examine competition and strategy in more detail.

It is important to note that competition is a fact of life; there are very few organizations that have the luxury of operating without competition. When a monopoly (an organization that has no competition) or near monopoly does occur, it usually does not last for long. Consider cable television companies within the United States, for example. The way the industry was structured, individual cable companies acted as virtual monopolies within a set geographic boundary; no other cable company could compete for customers within an established territory. This allowed the cable companies to provide whatever services, products, and prices they wished (within some limits); customers had the choice of either subscribing or not, but they had no choice among cable service providers.

This situation began to change with the development of personal satellite reception systems and with the lobbying efforts made by other industries (such as the telephone service providers) to deregulate the cable television industry. As

Even monopolies such as the U.S. Postal Service eventually weaken. Photo courtesy of Bonnie Kamin.

customers began to have a wider choice of options, they also began to demand better products, services, and pricing from the cable television providers. The initial response by the cable television industry was a marketing campaign to try and improve the industry's image, hoping to convince consumers to ignore the other products and services becoming available, but eventually they were forced into more competitive pricing and programming.

To provide a more formal look at competition, we examine three well-recognized concepts and frameworks:

- Order-winning criteria.
- The value chain.
- The five-force model.

Each of these can be used to help analyze and understand the position of an organization within its environment, to help define an appropriate strategy, and to determine how information technology can help in sustaining a given strategy.

Order-Winning Criteria. The concept of **order-winning criteria** (OWC) is simple but powerful OWC are the factors (criteria) used by a customer in deciding to put an order with one vendor rather than another, to stay in one hotel rather than another; to go to one restaurant rather than another; to buy one car rather than another, and so on. OWC tries to explain the decision-making process of customers. How do customers choose one product or service over another? What are the more important features or factors in making that choice? How do customers trade one factor against another? Listing the OWC that make customers order from a specific firm helps determine whether a second firm can compete with that first firm, and how.

For example, assume that a company finds out that the order-winning criterion for a potential customer is delivery time; the customer expects to receive its purchase (e.g., component parts) within a week and is willing to pay a premium to get that speed of delivery. At this point the management of the company supplying the parts can determine whether they can compete for that business (is there any way we can fulfill the customer's one-week delivery time requirement?) and what

Understanding how consumers make purchasing decisions helps companies design their products and services. Photo courtesy of Bonnie Kamin.

the implications are for future investments (should we spend resources to speed our processes to match the expectation of that customer and possibly others?).

The Value Chain. The purpose of all organizations is to create value for the customer (give customers something they like or need and that they cannot get from anybody else); products and services succeed when they provide more value to customers than the competition's. Value, from a customer's point of view, is a combination of features (quality, service, availability, ease of ordering, order-cycle time) and price. A firm's **value chain** is the series of activities performed to create the value that customers pay for. The value chain approach consists of identifying what activities within the firm add value to the product or service being offered to the customer. Organizations should concentrate on those activities and processes through which they unequivocally add value; these are the activities that can provide a competitive advantage to the firm. If an activity being performed adds no value to the customer, it should be re-evaluated or outsourced.

Although the initial focus of the value chain analysis was to look exclusively at the internal operations of an organization, more recently the analysis has been broadened to include suppliers and customers. The rationale is quite simple: If a firm is able to work with suppliers and customers to reduce costs and increase value to the customer, the firm will be able to improve its competitive position. This analysis often leads to redistributing some activities (e.g., quality control of component parts will be performed exclusively by the [illegible]ers) and outsourcing others (e.g., hiring one of the overnight package delive[illegible]ies to handle distribution of products).

Figure 10–1 shows a possibl[illegible]n for a manufactured product across three firms (supplier, manufacture[illegible]ner). The primary activities performed by the supplier include (*a*) develo[illegible]product, (*b*) producing, (*c*) selling, (*d*) delivering, and (*e*) providing **after-s[illegible] service.** For the manufacturing firm, the primary activities are essentially the same; the only difference is that the product is moved further through its production cycle. For the customer firm, the primary

FIGURE 10–1 The Value Chain

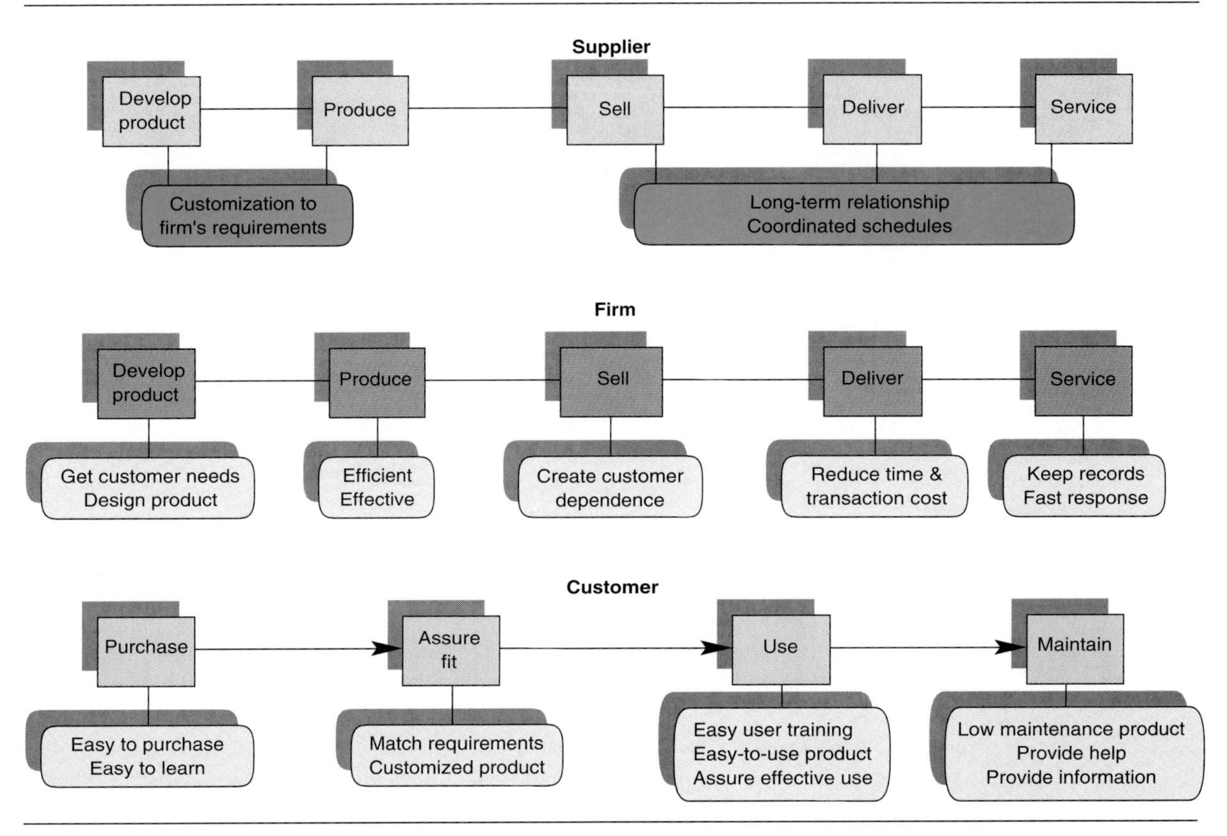

SOURCE: Adapted from Steven Alter, *Information Systems: A Management Perspective,* Reading, MA: Addison-Wesley, 1992, p. 12.

activities related to the product include (*a*) purchasing, (*b*) assuring fit, (*c*) using, and (*d*) maintaining. During each of these activities, there are opportunities for the manufacturing firm to increase value to the supplier and customer. For example, the firm may work with its supplier(s) to customize the inputs that the firm will be purchasing (e.g., Ford working with the producers of door handles for its automobiles).

The value chain can be used very effectively to explore areas in which I/T can provide a competitive advantage. For example, a firm can ask the following questions: How can we help the customer purchase our product? (One possibility might be providing access to a database containing all of the products, with prices and delivery lead times.) How can we help our customer use and maintain our product better? How can we better coordinate our production schedule with our suppliers to increase product availability and reduce the time is takes to fill an order? By examining each component of the value chain from the supplier's product development to the customer's maintenance, a firm can usually identify ways to add value to the customer. Many of these opportunities come about through the use of information technology.

Let us caution you on the use of value chain analysis as it is portrayed in Figure 10–1. The figure gives the impression that the primary activities within the firm can

FIGURE 10–2 The Five-Force Model (Competitive Forces)

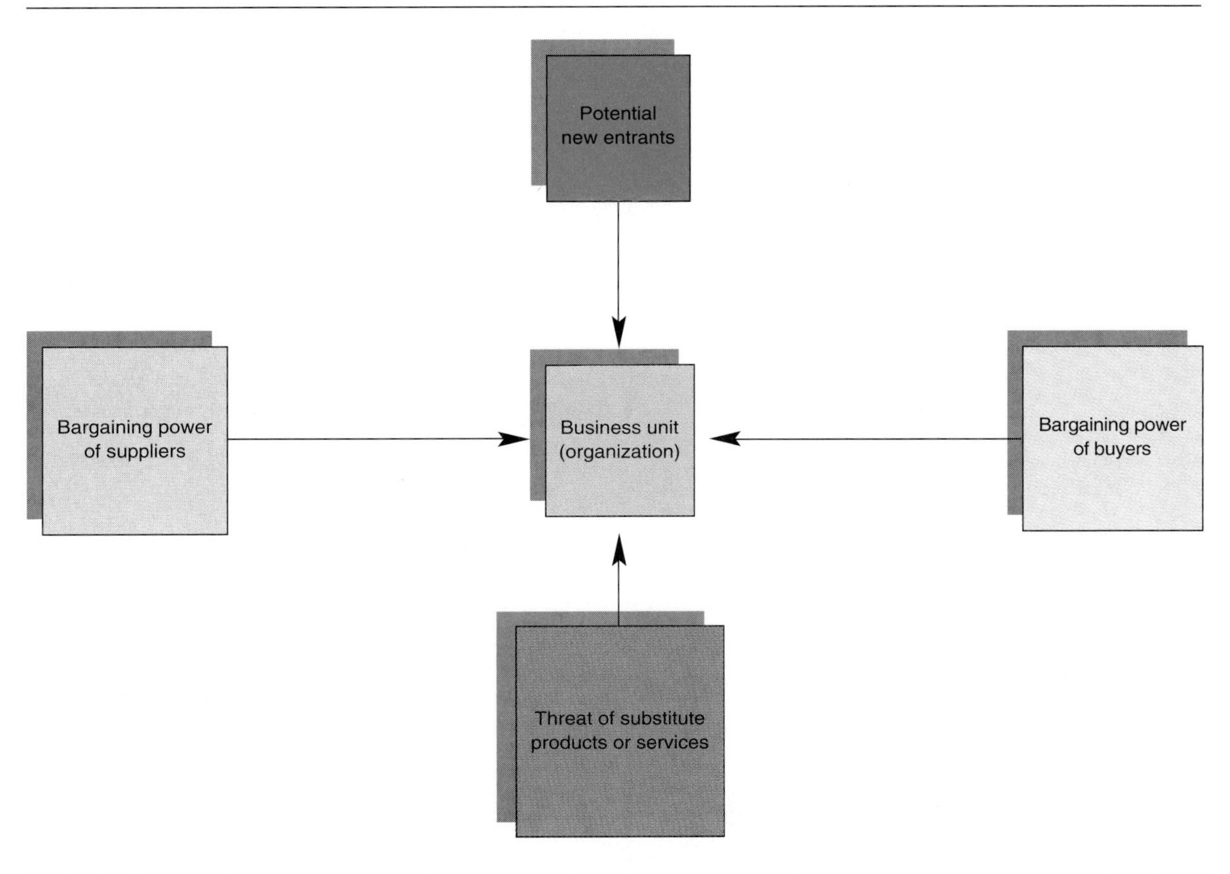

SOURCE: Adapted from Porter's (1980) Industry and Competitive Analysis. The fifth force is the rivalry among existing competitors.

be viewed as a series of sequential steps. This type of segregation of activities can lead to the type of functional organization structure we discussed earlier (in Chapter 3). It would be easy to envision a structure that contains separate departments for research and development, production, sales, distribution, and service. We have argued previously (and we repeat the argument here) that this type of functional segregation may lead to serious problems (e.g., local rationality, losing sight of customer needs, inefficiencies). An organization should not be developing new products without explicitly considering—during design—how they will be produced, distributed, and how the customer will be using them. The value chain can be a catalyst to viewing and structuring the organization as a series of processes designed to keep the customer happy.

The Five-Force Model. The **five-force model** is a framework that provides a way to assess the competitive forces that can influence an organization's strategy. This model was originally introduced by Michael Porter (1980) and has since been modified and extended by others. The model suggests that the state of competition within an industry depends on five basic forces (see Figure 10–2):

TABLE 10–1 Implications of the Five-Force Model

Force	*Implication*	*Potential Uses of I/T to Combat Force*
Threat of new entrants	New capacity Reduced prices	Provide entry barriers Economies of scale Switching costs
Buyer's bargaining power	Prices forced down High quality; more services Competition encouraged	Buyer selection Switching costs Product differentiation
Supplier's bargaining power	Prices raised Reduced quality and services (labor)	Selection Threat of backward integration
Threat of substitute products or services	Potential returns limited Ceiling on prices	Improve price/performance Redefine products and services
Traditional intra-industry rivals	Competition Price, product Distribution and service	Cost-effectiveness Market access Differentiation Product, services, firm

SOURCE: Adapted from Cash et al. (1992).

1. **Supplier's bargaining power** (the leverage that suppliers have over you in setting, among other things, delivery schedules and quantities, price, and standards).
2. **Buyer's bargaining power** (the leverage that customers have over you in setting, among other things, delivery schedules and quantities, price, and standards).
3. Threat of **new entrants** into the industry segment (the possibility of companies not previously in your market entering the market).
4. Threat of **substitute products** or services (the possibility of a new technology, product, or service making your product or service obsolete).
5. Positioning of traditional intra-industry rivals (the **rivalry intensity** among existing competitors).

By examining the five forces that shape competition, management can develop strategies to address each of them. For example, the threat of substitute products or services in the cable TV industry (such as the threat of small, digital-based USSB television satellite systems from RCA competing with cable television providers) can have the effect of putting a ceiling on the price that the cable companies can charge and can also limit their potential sales and profits. Strategies to manage the threat of substitute products include (*a*) improving internal operations to reduce costs and subsequently reduce prices to customers (improve the price-to-performance ratio) or (*b*) redefining products and services.

Table 10–1 provides an overview of the implications of the five forces as well as potential ways that an organization might use I/T to respond to these forces. The responses to competitive forces take the form of low-cost leadership, product or service differentiation, and/or focusing on a market segment or niche.

The concepts of order-winning criteria, the value chain and the five-force model help managers in a firm assess the impact of information technology on the strategy of the firm. One approach is to consider the following questions:

1. *Can I/T build barriers to entry?* This question asks whether I/T can make it harder for new competitors to enter the firm's market. For example, investing in a new computer-aided design/computer-aided manufacturing (CAD/CAM) system shortens the time to develop a prototype for a machine tool for a customer from three weeks to three days and will redefine customer expectations for delivery time. Any competitor that wants to be part of this market will have to match that performance and, therefore, will have to make the investment in CAD/CAM technology. This investment, because it raises the "ante" to enter the market for competitors, constitutes a **barrier to entry.** In the overnight package delivery business, delivering by 10:30 A.M. has become a competitive requirement. If a company does not have the capability of delivering that early they should not enter the business. The 10:30 A.M. standard has become a de facto performance entry barrier.
2. *Can I/T build in switching costs?* This question addresses ways to increase the dependence of the firm's customers on its products and services. Management should be encouraged to think of ways to link the customer into the firm's operations so that the customer will find switching to another supplier difficult. Such difficulties are known as **switching costs.** Clearly, the linkage to a vendor needs to have a specific value for the customer. For example, imagine the machine-tool manufacturer that we discussed in point 1 attaching an electronic device to its machines so that when one of its machines is in need of maintenance or repair the device signals the manufacturer's computer center over a telecommunications network. As soon as the message is received, the problem with the machine can be diagnosed, the most appropriate mechanic can be identified and dispatched, and the machine can be serviced without the customer ever becoming involved. This type of service, ensuring a minimum of downtime for the customer, generates customer loyalty and makes it less attractive for customers to acquire machines from, and/or enter into service agreements with, other vendors.
3. *Can I/T change the basis of competition?* In industries where competition is intense, the **basis for competition** tends to be price. Competing on price can be a bruising proposition. In those industries, I/T offers firms opportunities to compete effectively either by dramatically increasing productivity (e.g., staff reductions, higher machine efficiencies, lower inventory levels) or by adding features to their products and services, thereby changing the basis of competition from a low cost producer approach to a product differentiation one (e.g., better and faster service, more flexibility in ordering).

   Continuing with the example of the manufacturer of machine tools presented earlier, imagine that competition from the Far East has been pushing prices down. The manufacturer is starting to feel a serious pinch in its profit margins. The choice at that time for the firm from an I/T point of view could be to (*a*) spend resources to increase its efficiency in managing inventories and therefore lower costs or (*b*) spend resources to make the "call-home" maintenance device system described in point 2 available worldwide, thereby competing on an overall price basis (i.e., a price that bundles the machine and the post-sale service together). The former would be an investment in I/T to bolster the position of the firm within the existing basis of competition, while the latter investment would help change the basis of competition.

4. *Can I/T change the balance of power in supplier relationships*? Think of the following examples: Airline reservation systems have bypassed travel agents by developing frequent flyer programs; global electronic markets, where customers post requirements on a "billboard" (e.g., the need to transport 500 tons of bulk mineral from one country to another) and then wait for electronic bids to be made, have changed what used to be slow-changing, regulated industries (e.g., transportation); just-in-time inventory systems have given customers the ability to require suppliers to deliver the needed parts more often in ever smaller quantities. Each of these examples has changed the **balance of power** (i.e., the dependence) in supplier-customer relationships. Sometimes I/T can strengthen suppliers vis-à-vis customers; sometimes the reverse takes place. Interactions across organizations offer a great area of opportunity to develop a competitive advantage with I/T.
5. *Can I/T generate new products*? Not only can I/T support the faster delivery of better and cheaper products, but sometimes I/T can help the strategy of the firm by generating products on its own. For example, Nashbar, a catalog retailer of sportswear, created software for its own use and later decided to sell its software to other catalog retailers that were not direct competitors. The package supports a salesforce, allowing salespeople to sell more merchandise (e.g., adding software features helps a salesperson remind a customer buying a pair of running shorts that a matching T-shirt is available) and to sell it more efficiently (e.g., total purchases are computed faster, leading to shorter telephone waiting times for customers and, therefore, higher satisfaction). There are years in which American Airlines makes more money from its global reservation system (called SABRE) business unit than from flying airplanes. Supermarkets sell the data collected throughout their point-of sale (POS) systems to a variety of marketing companies.

INCREASING THE EFFECTIVENESS OF DECISION MAKING

All important management activities can be viewed from a decision-making perspective. For example, improving the transformation process involves making decisions about how to structure job tasks to make the most efficient use of available production equipment, how to organize the equipment to minimize the movement of raw materials and work in process, and so on. The way to improve management, therefore, is to focus on (and improve) the decision-making process.In the following sections we provide some specific examples of how I/T can improve decision making and then move on to the use of I/T to support organizational communication.

Automating Decisions

Many decisions are highly structured and can be automated. For example, it is a relatively straightforward task to develop a computer program that will calculate the amount owed an employee and generate a paycheck. The program requires certain input data (such as the hours worked and the rate of pay), decision rules (if the hours worked are greater than 40, then overtime pay needs to be calculated), and output instructions (print a paycheck and also update a payroll file for further report requirements).

Computers can use the knowledge of experts to help managers make better decisions. Here, an IBM programmer gave the world chess champion a very tough battle. Photo courtesy of Corbis/Bettmann Archives.

Automating decisions through the use of information technology can help streamline the internal operations of an organization. It can also improve communications among and within organizations. For example, many organizations accept credit card payment for their goods and services. To reduce the possibility of bad debts, the purchase amount is usually approved by the issuer of the credit card before the sale is completed. Not long ago, it was necessary for the retailer to call the credit card company; a representative would then examine the customer's record to determine if the purchase should be approved. Today, the information is transmitted electronically, automating the decision to approve or disapprove a sale. This process has reduced the cost to the issuer of the credit card, speeded up the approval process, improved communication between the retailer and the card issuer, and ultimately improved the service to the cardholder (customer).

Supporting Complex Decisions

Most management decisions are not highly structured—a structured decision is one in which the necessary inputs, the method to process those inputs, and the specific outputs are all well known—and cannot be completely automated. An entire branch of management theory and practice, termed **management science,** has evolved to bring more structure to unstructured decision-making situations. Even when the situation is very complex, it is usually possible to use information systems to support, rather than replace, the decision-making process.

Management science is based on the application of **mathematical models** and draws fairly heavily on the use of statistical analysis. Examples include the use of statistical regression analysis (to identify empirical relationships), simulation and spreadsheets (to develop a variety of potential solutions by varying assumptions), and optimization models (to generate a "best" solution when resource constraints exist.)

When the m cal model fits well with the real problem, it may be possible to full the decision. When the fit is less than perfect, it is necessary to cc se of the model with the judgment of a human decision maker. In Chapt entioned that the term *decision support system* (DSS) is often used to de information systems that address unstructured decision situations. Most decision support systems use management science models to develop what-if scenarios to help managers better understand the ill-structured situation they face.

Earlier in the book we described how American Airlines uses management science models to help schedule flight crews. The problem was how best to schedule 21,000 flight attendants and nearly 11,000 pilots on 681 airplanes in 201 cities, which could generate between 10 and 12 million possible solutions. There is no perfect solution to this problem. When you consider overtime costs, labor contracts, holiday preferences, and so on, the problem actually has more than one dimension. By coming up with the "best" solution for one dimension (such as reducing overtime pay), another dimension (such as holiday preferences) will be compromised. By applying management science modeling techniques, American Airlines was able to reduce wasted crew time and save $40 to $50 million per year.

Augmenting Knowledge

Humans have limited information processing capabilities and use shortcuts when analyzing a problem under pressure. One important role of information systems is **augmenting knowledge** to help us make better decisions. **Expert systems** are information systems that have been designed to capture and use the expertise of human decision makers. Two of the earliest examples of expert systems were DENDRAL, which was designed to predict the molecular structure of unknown molecules, and MYCIN, which was designed to aid physicians in the diagnosis and treatment of meningitis and bacteremia infections.

PROSPECTOR was another early expert system, developed in the late 1970s at Stanford Research Institute. It was designed to provide consultations to geologists in the early stages of investigating a site for ore-grade deposits. In 1980, as a test, PROSPECTOR was given data supplied by a group that had terminated exploration of a site at Mt. Tolman in Washington State in 1978. PROSPECTOR suggested that a previously unexplored portion of the site probably contained an ore-grade porphyry molybdenum deposit. Subsequent drilling confirmed the deposit. Thus, PROSPECTOR became the knowledge-based system to achieve a major commercial success. This fueled sh of development efforts that led to a proliferation of expert systems for nume organizations and applications.

Expert systems use different techniques in providing suggested solutions to the problems posed to them. Most use a structure that includes a separate database of previous cases (*knowledge base*), a group of if-then rules that are evaluated in a given sequence (*inference engine*), and an interface for the user to interact with the system (*dialogue structure*). As new expertise is gained, the knowledge base and inference engine can be updated by having a human input new rules and new cases to the knowledge base. Also, most expert systems have facilities to explain their reasoning consisting of printing the sequence of rules used to analyze the problem (so the human user can verify the logic being used).

Other approaches have also been used for expert systems, however. One that has recently gained a great deal of popularity is based on the neural structure of the human brain, and is referred to as a **neural network** or *neural net.* This type of expert system uses a different approach to gain expertise.

Consider, for example, the problem of deciding who should be approved for credit when a credit card application is received. The system accepts matched pairs of inputs (personal information such as age and income) and outputs (credit behavior) for existing customers and then looks for patterns in the data. Over time some relationships become stronger than others. In this way the expert system "learns" by associating specific variables to specific behaviors, and "infers" relationships, which can then be used to make credit approval decisions in the future. This type of expert system is being used for numerous applications, from selecting stocks on the stock market to providing vision systems for robotics. There are weaknesses, of course. If the input data are missing important examples, the inferences made by the system may be less than optimal. Fortunately, it is often possible to supply "hints" to the system, which helps speed its learning. One example was the IBM computer program "Deep Blue" that took on (and barely lost to) world chess champion Gary Kasparov.

Centralization of Data, Decentralization of Decision Making

In Chapter 1, we described how Charles Chaser, a line worker for Chesebrough-Ponds, decided to schedule more production of their Rose Awakening nail polish. This is an excellent example of using centralized data to facilitate decentralized decision making. Previously, any decisions concerning how much to produce, and when, would have been made by a production scheduling manager. To respond quickly to changes in their environment (such as increased demand for Rose Awakening), Chesebrough-Ponds decided to give more decision making responsibilities to line workers. Giving someone the responsibility is not sufficient by itself. It is also necessary to provide them with the information they require to make decisions.

IMPROVING ORGANIZATIONAL COMMUNICATION

Organizational communication is similar to organizational decision making in that it is pervasive and influences all aspects of management and organizational operations. You may recall that in Chapter 4 we argued that two general strategies to improve communication are to (*a*) reduce distortion and (*b*) reduce information overload. Information technology can play an effective role in supporting both strategies.

Reducing Distortion and Information Overload. To illustrate, let's continue looking at the Chesebrough-Ponds situation. In the case of Charles Chaser, he needs to have access to information such as (*a*) the current inventory level of all products he is responsible for, (*b*) the desired inventory level, and (*c*) production capacities and schedules. This is where the centralized database and organizational communications come into play. By storing the data in a central database and providing access to all individuals who require that data, there is less need to duplicate, manipulate, and transmit data. This arrangement reduces the possibilities of intentional and unintentional communication distortions, such as delaying the transmission of data. It also reduces the possibility of overloading one individual (a production scheduling manager).

Business Brief 10–1 illustrates how I/T support of internal communications and workgroups is a hot issue and a great commercial opportunity.

BUSINESS BRIEF 10-1 INTRANETS—THE HOTTEST MARKET IN COMMUNICATIONS

Microsoft, MCI Communications, and Digital Equipment are teaming up to address one of the hottest markets in communications: data networks linking employees within companies, called intranets. The three companies are expected to announce plans to develop and market an integrated package of communications services and products for corporations. The offerings are expected to include high-speed Internet access, electronic mail and groupware—software that allows employees of a company in different locations to collaborate.

The pact continues a frenetic pace of alliances driven by the increasing popularity of the Internet. The MCI/Digital/Microsoft team poses a direct challenge to AT&T, which has moved aggressively into Internet services and whose partners include IBM and Netscape Communications, two of Microsoft's bitter rivals.

Corporate data communications is a huge prize. Many companies are rushing to set up intranets, a low-priced alternative to proprietary networks that uses the technology of the Internet's World Wide Web. At the same time, intranets provide security so that data belonging to a particular company are available only to its employees.

Among the popular uses for intranets are projects requiring collaborative work by employees in different locations, the internal posting of marketing and product information, as well as the distribution of employee-benefit information. Sales of intranet software are expected to reach $1.2 billion in 1997, industry analysts say. "This stuff is hotter than hot," says Paul Callahan, an analyst at Forrester Research in Cambridge, Massachusetts. "Over half of the Fortune 100 companies will be up and running with intranets by the end of the year."

The latest collaboration is expected to combine MCI's network connections, Digital's experience in installing and managing large data networks, and Microsoft's software, including its Windows NT server operating system, along with Microsoft's electronic-messaging program, called Exchange, and its Web software. MCI is expected to take a leading role in marketing the new products and services, which will initially be aimed at the U.S. market.

The agreement builds on existing partnerships between Microsoft and MCI and between Microsoft and Digital. Earlier this year, MCI and Microsoft agreed to market each other's products, including the on-line service, Microsoft Network, to business and residential customers worldwide. In August, Microsoft and Digital formed an alliance aimed at large computer customers, under which Digital is installing networks that use Windows NT–based computers. Digital also said it would install and support Microsoft Exchange Server messaging software.

In the latest alliance, Digital may include the technology behind Alta Vista, a popular program for searching for information on the Internet, as well as its data-security software for keeping hackers out of corporate networks. The computer maker recently found a new "connectivity software" unit, headed by former Lotus Development executive Ilene Lang, to focus on new products and services to help businesses access information across and between enterprises.

The alliance seems largely targeted at outflanking AT&T, which has networking partnerships with companies that include Novell Inc. and Lotus, which was bought by IBM last year. AT&T originally planned to offer Lotus's popular Notes groupware program as part of a proprietary service, but it recently abandoned that approach in favor of a looser Internet-based collaboration. MCI is particularly interested in winning contracts to handle corporation's intranet business, analysts noted. "These phone companies are rapidly expanding into areas that are way outside of their core areas," says Jeffrey Kagan, an Atlanta telecommunications consultant. "Anything and everything that address businesses' communications needs are in play."

QUESTIONS

1. Why do you think intranets are so "hot"?
2. Do you believe that the three companies that are partnering in this venture have the necessary expertise to make intranets work? Why or why not?

SOURCE: Audrey Choi and Don Clark, *The Wall Street Journal*, April 8, 1996, p. B4. Reprinted by permission of *The Wall Street Journal*,

Communication among Organizations. Organizations, like individuals, need to communicate among themselves. Some of this communication is formal (such as an order to purchase goods) and some informal (such as conversations among executives at a social gathering). Communication among organizations can suffer from the same problems that affect communication among individuals. Therefore, I/T can play a useful role in supporting not only intraorganizational (within an organization) communication but also interorganizational (between organizations) communication as well.

The term **interorganizational system** (IOS) is generally used to describe a networked information system used by two or more separate organizations to perform a joint business function. Some IOSs are highly automated, requiring very little human intervention or interaction. For example, when a manufacturing firm runs low on a certain type of raw material, they may have an IOS that automatically scans the supplier's prices, stock levels, and delivery conditions and then automatically places orders to replenish the stock of raw materials.

A very well-known example of the use of an interorganizational system was the one developed by American Hospital Supply (AHS). AHS provides supplies to hospitals and related health centers. They developed a system that allowed their customers to select and order goods from AHS directly from a computer terminal (which was supplied by AHS). This reduced the time and paperwork required of the hospital purchasing agents, making their tasks much quicker and easier. The system gave AHS a big advantage over their competitors, as purchasing agents began to order AHS goods without even looking at competitor's products (the system increased the switching costs).

To facilitate interorganizational communications with information systems, it is necessary to have standards for data transmission. The term **electronic data interchange (EDI)** is commonly used to describe such standards, although some people use EDI in a broader sense to encompass the information systems and standards. During the early phases of EDI and IOS growth, numerous incompatible standards and protocols co-existed, forcing organizations to write additional software programs to translate from one set of standards to another.

IMPROVING OPERATIONS

In our discussion of General Systems Theory in Chapter 2, we stressed the importance of having an operational process (we refer to it as the transformation process) that is efficient (using the least amount of resources to achieve a high level of output) and flexible (being able to change quickly to meet changes in demand). There are numerous ways that information systems may be used to improve the efficiency and flexibility or the transformation process.

Accelerating Business Processes. Information technology is being used in numerous ways to transform the way organizations conduct their internal operations. Something as simple and common as a word-processing system can be used to effectively speed up a repetitive process. For example, many legal documents such as wills, proposals, and contracts have standard paragraphs that are used in slightly different combinations. Rather than retyping each applicable paragraph for each individual will (or other document), a word-processing system can be used to "cut-and-paste" and speed up document production substantially. More advanced legal document preparation systems include a knowledge base that compiles the appropriate paragraphs for the user, speeding the process up even more.

Business Brief 10–2 illustrates how the Russell Corporation has used information technology to completely transform its production processes. Instead of having people sort, cut, and sew fabric, they are using specialized tools built around information technology. The good news is that the company is able to produce better quality clothing faster and at a lower cost; the bad news is that fewer workers are needed, and many workers lost their jobs. Even the bad news may be good in the long run, however. Working in a textile factory can be a hot, dirty, undesirable job; you might want to watch the movie *Norma Rae* for a better understanding of what a factory is like. If the workers who were replaced by the computerized machines were able to learn new skills, they hopefully found more desirable jobs elsewhere.

Increasing Flexibility. Benetton, the clothing manufacturer and distributor, receives information from their retail outlets immediately after each item is sold. This enables them to dye-to-order and to switch their dyeing process to match demand. The increased flexibility in their manufacturing process enables Benetton to keep much smaller inventories and retail outlets than most of their competitors, enabling the company to reduce costs (rental on retail and inventory storage space, losses from inventory that doesn't sell) and improve their competitive position.

IMPROVING SUPPLIER RELATIONS AND CUSTOMER SATISFACTION

The availability of inputs (supplies) and the acceptability of outputs (products and services) are critical success factors for the survival of the organization. From a competitive perspective, our emphasis on the input side can be broadly described as *supplier relations* and on the output side as *customer satisfaction.* Within these broad categories, there are many opportunities for using information technology to improve the competitive position of the firm.

Matching Customer Demands: Improving the Product or Service. Customers are demanding high quality, innovative products, competitive prices, and excellent customer service. Dell Computers supplies customized personal computers to customers within five days. Dell employees also actively search the Internet for customer comments, helping them determine customer preferences in a timely fashion. Dell provides 24-hour, toll-free hot lines, which allow customers to call with any questions. These are all ways that Dell is using information technology to improve customer service. Business Brief 10–3 describes how some companies have turned to the Internet to support their customers.

Information technology is also frequently used to improve the product, by adding one or more "information components." Consider an automobile, for example. Information technology can be included in the anti-lock brakes, anti-theft system, active suspension, traffic and navigation system, and so on. Intelligent buildings contain systems for security and environment controls, including temperature and lighting. Even some bottles for prescription pills contain embedded microprocessor chips that record each time the cap is removed. By placing the pill bottle over a modem, the information is transmitted to the drug manufacturer, who can ensure that the patient is taking their medication at the prescribed time.

Information technology enables companies to speed up their processes to compete more effectively. Photo courtesy of Silicon Graphics.

IMPROVING ENVIRONMENTAL SCANNING

One important component of organizational responsiveness, is the need for effective feedback and feedforward systems. **Feedback systems** help monitor internal processes (to ensure efficient operations) and/or customer sales (to ensure the products are still in demand). **Feedforward systems** are useful for scanning the environment in an effort to keep current on relevant changes such as new competitors within the industry or new products (which could replace those already available).

Feedback systems have three basic purposes. They help managers (*a*) use resources more effectively, (*b*) better align parts of the organization with company goals, and (*c*) improve the collection of data for strategic and operating decisions.

The Chesebrough-Ponds case demonstrates the use of early warning systems, which is one type of control system. Charles Chaser was warned of a potential shortage before it became a crisis and was able to take corrective action. Benetton also uses a sophisticated feedback system that informs them immediately as each item is sold in one of their retail stores around the world. By getting this highly accurate information in a timely manner, decision makers working for Benetton are notified immediately and can take appropriate corrective action if need be.

BUSINESS BRIEF 10-2 I/T CAN TRANSFORM OPERATIONS: WHERE'S NORMA RAE?

"Where's Norma Rae[1]?" Executives at the Russell Corporation have heard the question so many times that it has become a running joke. Visitors to the Alabama apparel giant expect to find legions of unskilled workers toiling over 19th-century sewing machines, but they are surprised to discover something quite different: pristine textile mills where lasers cut fabric, robots sew seams, and seeing-eye computers sort fabric by color.

Russell chairman Eugene Gwaltney gambled on the proposition that you don't have to make high-tech products to operate high-tech factories, and the bet has turned Russell into the nation's largest supplier of athletic uniforms—tailor to Major League Baseball and a fashion player on college campuses. The 91-year-old company has spent more than $500 million in the past five years to automate its plants. This investment has certainly paid off. Since 1983, Russell's profits have more than tripled, from $27 million to $82 million. At the same time, the cost of production has shrunk from 69 percent of sales to 66 percent.

QUESTION

1. Use the value chain to illustrate how the Russell Corporation is using information technology to be more competitive.

---

[1]Norma Rae was a union worker that protested the inhumane conditions in the textile industry of the southern United States.

SOURCE: *U.S. News & World Report,* December 6, 1993, pp. 49 & 50.

Benetton receives retail information from their outlets immediately after each sale, allowing them to dye their sweaters to order to match demand. Photo courtesy of Benetton.

BUSINESS BRIEF 10-3 CUSTOMERS TURN TO THE WEB TO SOLVE PROBLEMS

A year ago, 80 percent of customers with questions about Macromedia software products phoned a customer representative. Today, only about 20 percent do so. The others access Macromedia's site on the World Wide Web for the information they need.

Macromedia is the beneficiary of what could be a major revolution in customer service. By putting information on the Internet's Web, companies can make it a cheap, fast, and effective customer service tool. "The Web is making an enormous change," says Macromedia chief executive Bud Colligan.

Hewlett-Packard's computer product support division now gets 1 million customer questions per month via its site and other electronic means compared with 600,000 by telephone. Last year, it got more phone calls than Web visits. Personal computer maker Acer America put in a Web site in June. Now, 10 percent of its customers use it for answers to technical questions. That number is growing 20 percent a month.

Computer and software companies lead in using the Web. Their customers have PCs, which are needed to access the video- and audio-rich Web. According to WebTrack, 63 percent of computer companies have Web sites compared with 9 percent of retailers.

But other industries are coming along. Customers of banking giant Wells Fargo can check account balances via its Web site. Fidelity Investments lets customers order mutual fund prospectuses. Federal Express customers can track their packages. The Internal Revenue Service launched its site in January. At last count, taxpayers downloaded 25,000 forms and publications a day.

As more people access the Web, more firms are expected to increase sites' customer service features. "Consumers will come to expect it just like they expect 1-800 numbers," says Mark Muchnick of Credit Card Network.

The benefits for companies include the following:

- *Lower costs.* "If customers can go to a Web site and answer a question themselves . . . money is saved," says Linda Glenick of Microsoft's Answer Point, its customer support Web site. Microsoft won't say how much it expects to save. Acer expects savings of at least 10 percent a year.
- *Customer education.* Once customers access a Web site, they find information they weren't initially seeking. Informed customers are happier customers, companies say.
- *Better service.* Many companies and customers believe the Web provides better service. "It is usually faster than calling," says Mark Kennedy, an engineer at Symantec. "And I don't have to deal with the frustration of knowing more than the person I get on the line."

QUESTION

1. In what industries do you think this type of Internet-based customer support system works best? Does not work? Why?

SOURCE: Julie Schmit, *USA Today*, April 8, 1996, p. B1.

CAUTIONS ON THE COMPETITIVE USE OF I/T

Investments in I/T do not always pay off. Although the examples in this chapter have all described uses of I/T that have given a competitive advantage to the firms that implemented them, it is important to caution you that it is not always as easy as it appears. Sometimes investments in I/T provide short-lived competitive advantages that cannot be sustained. These short-lived advantages can be due to technological obsolescence, to systems that change the basis of competition to a company's disadvantage (e.g., lowering rather than raising entry barriers, eroding the leverage on suppliers), or to misreading the needs of a market. Consider the following examples.

Systems can become too powerful for their own good. For example, the American Airlines reservation system (named the SABRE system) and its yield management features has been credited with putting out of business People's Express, one of the peskier, no-frills competitors in the airline industry in the 1980s. However,

American Airlines created an information system (SABRE) that has provided them with a competitive advantage. Photo courtesy of Tony Stone Worldwide.

the success of American Airlines in making life miserable for those competitors who did not have a national computerized reservation system brought American Airlines some aggravation of its own. American Airlines and United Airlines (which has the second largest reservation system—the Apollo system—as measured by the number of travel agent installations) were sued by 11 competitors for unfair practices. The suit claimed that United and American were, among other things, biasing the display of flight information and fares. The U.S. government intervened and, through the Civil Aeronautics Board (CAB), ordered changes in the systems. Pressure has continued to build for United and American to give up their systems. An industry-wide system run by an agency such as CAB or a consortium of airlines is being proposed. United and American Airlines have been forced by CAB and the Federal Aviation Agency to redesign the screens in their systems to provide "bias-neutral" presentation of flights (i.e., screens where the flights are shown by time of departure rather than by airline).

Bad timing. FedEx spent close to $200 million dollars to build the necessary telecommunications infrastructure to introduce Zapmail. Zapmail was a fax service whereby FedEx would pick up the material to be "zapped" from the customer, fax it to another FedEx site, and then deliver it to the recipient. The idea was good. The timing was awful. Soon after the introduction of the service, fax machines dropped in price dramatically and became a fixture in every office. FedEx pulled the plug on Zapmail and wrote the investment off. Another example of bad timing was Chemical Bank's push into home banking. Introduced with great fanfare in the early 1980s,

Chemical's product misread the demand for such a service, and Chemical lost an estimated $100 million on the venture.

Waking up a giant. Sometimes developing an I/T alliance with a supplier or a customer can threaten a larger, more established competitor. The response of that competitor may be to invest in a similar system and use its size and leverage to set the standards for future versions of that system. For example, Wal-Mart was not the first to implement computerized ordering systems. However, when Wal-Mart decided to implement electronic data interchange (EDI) with its suppliers, it was able to dictate the protocol and communication standards because of its size. Vendors that had moved earlier (such as Gillette) were forced to redesign their EDI systems to conform to the standards used by Wal-Mart.

Cultural issues matter. Sometimes ideas that work very well in a given country do not work as well in others. The success in France of the home-based computer service Minitel (see the case at the end of Module IV) spurred American companies (Sears, IBM, and some telephone companies) to develop similar systems. Minitel was introduced initially as an electronic telephone directory at a time when installation of telephone lines in France was exploding. Telephone books were obsolete within six months of being printed. Telephone assistance could take up to 15 minutes. Minitel, which was offered free of charge, addressed a real need and was quickly accepted across all segments of the population. If the electronic telephone directory gave everybody a reason to use Minitel, it was the slightly erotic, and very French, "chat" services that propelled Minitel as a consumer success. In North America, services such as America OnLine and CompuServe were very slow to be accepted by consumers. Their market penetration rates through the mid 1990s were a fraction of Minitel's penetration in France.

Another example of a failed transference was the attempt of Hong Kong to develop a system similar to Singapore's Tradenet. Tradenet is a system that allows shipping companies to clear customs extremely quickly. Since Singapore is competing to become the major trans-shipping port in Asia, Tradenet is a critical piece of Singapore's strategy. The system was developed in a centralized fashion with all standards being set by the government. Given the cultural and political environment of Singapore, the development and acceptance of those standards were quick and smooth. When Hong Kong tried to implement a similar system, the development of the system got bogged down in discussion about who should set the standard, who would run the system, and so on. Five years later the Hong Kong system has not been implemented. The idiosyncratic characteristics of an environment need to be understood before a copycat system is attempted.

Vulnerability to system's failure. As the strategic importance of I/T increases, so does the vulnerability of the firm to a crash of the system. For example, the dependency on I/T of the airline, retail, and financial services industries, to name just three, is such that companies in those industries could not survive more than a day or two without their systems. I/T in these industries is such a strategic necessity that substantial managerial time and resources are spent ensuring that the systems are reliable. However, as the strategic necessity increases so does the vulnerability of organizations to a system crash. Companies that become dependent on I/T for their operations must develop, as part of their strategic planning process, the necessary security mechanisms to protect their systems and the necessary contingencies and plans to recover from a crash of the system. We explore this increase in vulnerability in more detail in the next chapter.

Too Much of a Good Thing. Once a system is successful, most competitors will attempt to copy it. The result sometimes can be alienating for the customers. For example, take marketing through direct mailings. In an effort to streamline their

BUSINESS BRIEF 10–4 ADDING THE PERSONAL TOUCH: HAPPY BIRTHDAY TO YOU

It may not be celebrated as a national holiday, but it's a pretty big deal around here. Happy Birthday from the Claridge Casino Hotel, Atlantic City.

A growing number of companies are investing millions of dollars to build databases that enable them to figure out who their customers are and what it takes to secure their loyalty. Direct marketers have long been in the vanguard of database users: catalogs, record clubs, and credit card companies have always needed their customers' names and addresses to do business with them. But database marketing is now moving into the mainstream, as everyone from packaged-goods companies to auto makers have come to believe that, in the fragmented, fiercely competitive marketplace of the 1990s, nothing is more powerful than knowledge about customers' individual practices and preferences.

Consider the dilemma of a busy casino. In the old days, the pit boss kept notebooks on frequent players. Periodically, he would pick a name from the notebook, telephone the high roller, and offer a free room for the weekend. Today, with thousands of visitors trooping through on any given day, "It's virtually impossible to get to know people on a first-name basis," says Robert M. Renneisen Jr., CEO of Claridge Hotel & Casino Corporation.

Now, the casino's computer keeps tabs on visitors who use its frequent gamblers card and sends out offers every day. Claridge's Comp-Card Gold, which offers discounts and tips on upcoming events, has 350,000 active members. They get offers ranging from $10 in coins for slot machines to monogrammed bathrobes and door-to-door limo service. "It's made us more efficient," says Renneisen. "We can target our dollars directly to customers who justify the costs."

QUESTION

1. What order-winning criterion does Claridge's information system meet?

SOURCE: "Database Marketing: A Potent New Tool for Selling," *Business Week*, September 5, 1994, pp. 56, 59.

marketing efforts and personalize their products and services, many organizations have begun collecting and using information about their customers. Rather than sending mass mail-outs of catalogs and brochures to every address, companies are searching through databases of information to identify those individuals who are most likely to be responsive to their advertising message (see Business Brief 10–4). Typically the information in the database is collected when a sale or other transaction is made; another source is customer lists that are sold from one company to another. Lists of households and potential consumers have become so widespread that anyone can now purchase them on CD-ROM disks from a variety of retail software vendors.

The collection and use of information concerning customers (and potential customers) has obvious benefits. Marketers are able to make more effective use of their marketing resources, while consumers (theoretically) can be spared some of the "junk mail" that holds no interest for them. In reality, the practice of selling customer lists has led to a proliferation of telephone and mail advertising. It has also made it very difficult for individuals to maintain their privacy. Business Brief 10–5 illustrates this issue.

Technology versus Management of Technology. Information technology used to be the great differentiator when computers were very expensive and powerful and when user-friendly, packaged software was not widely available. Twenty years ago

BUSINESS BRIEF 10-5 I/T AND PRIVACY: YOU CAN RUN, BUT YOU CAN'T HIDE

For years, Lisa Tomaino kept her address secret. She and her husband Jim, a policeman, wanted to make it as hard as possible for the crooks he had put away to find out where they lived.

But last year, Lisa had a baby. So much for her big secret. Within six weeks, she was inundated with junk mail aimed at new mothers. The hospital had sold her name and address to a direct-marketing company, and soon she was on dozens of other lists. Efforts to get off them proved fruitless. "It was a complete violation of our right to privacy," she declares.

But vendors of marketing data argue that any intrusion of privacy from selling lists is offset "by the significant potential gain to consumers from the special offers and products offered by direct marketers," says Harry Gambill, president of Trans Union Corporation, a Chicago-based credit bureau. The industry has largely staved off regulation by convincing the U.S. federal government that it can police itself.

As marketing techniques become more sophisticated, the privacy of the Lisa Tomainos of the world will grow increasingly difficult to protect. And marketers will do everything they can to make sure remaining anonymous doesn't get any easier.

QUESTION

1. Have you ever been in a situation where you felt information systems were being used in a way that violated your privacy? As a consumer, how far do you believe a company should be able to go in their goals of micromarketing?

SOURCE: Mark Lewyn, "You Can Run . . . ," *Business Week*, September 5, 1994, pp. 60, 61. Reprinted by special permission, copyright © 1994 by The McGraw-Hill Companies.

one could talk about the "haves" and "have-nots" of technology. Today information technology, both hardware and software, is so accessible that companies have lost any fundamental ability to differentiate themselves with technology alone. Indeed, information technology today has become the great equalizer.

To differentiate themselves and compete more effectively, firms cannot rely anymore on technology alone. The competitive advantage is derived from *how* the technology is used. Today, the **management of technology** has become a critical issue in competing more effectively. The issue is not whether to invest in information technology or not, but where and how.

The great success stories on competitive uses of technology that have been reported in the literature (American Hospital Supply's customer-purchasing system; American Airlines' SABRE reservation system, with its yield management features; Otis Elevator's Otisline, with its remote sensing capabilities to minimize elevator downtime) have two characteristics in common. First, the technology used to implement those systems was far from being "rocket science." The technology was mainstream and well known at the time those systems were developed. What made those systems "new" was the way the technology was used to alter the basis of competition, the supplier's balance of power, and/or the value chain.

The second factor those success stories have in common is that the original source of advantage was eventually erased. Competitive advantage that is based only on technology can be quickly overcome by competitors. The sustainability of the competitive advantage when the advantage is based solely on hardware or software is low. The companies that have been able to sustain the competitive advantage originally achieved through technology are those companies that were spurred by the systems they implemented to develop new, faster, and better business processes.

SUMMARY

Although the level of competition may vary, organizations continually compete for resources and for customers. Competitive analysis frameworks help understand the forces that shape competition, and help identify ways to use information technology to improve competitiveness. Three such frameworks are the order-winning criteria, the value chain, and the five-force model.

Information technology can improve competitiveness in numerous ways. Five of these are (*a*) building barriers to entry, (*b*) building in switching costs, (*c*) changing the basis of competition, (*d*) changing the balance of power in supplier relationships, and (*e*) helping generate new products or services. I/T can also be used to increase the effectiveness of decision making by (*a*) automating structured decisions, (*b*) supporting complex decisions, (*c*) augmenting knowledge (with expert systems), and (*d*) decentralizing decision making by centralizing data.

Information systems can be used to improve organizational communications both internally and externally (through interorganizational systems). Information technology can help reduce distortion and information overload. An organization's transformation process may also be improved through the application of I/T. I/T can also accelerate processes and/or increase flexibility. Information systems can improve products or services, as well as environmental monitoring.

The use of information systems for competitive advantage brings with it certain risks and cautions. Systems may become too powerful, causing some type of retaliation by competitors or other external parties. If the timing is off, the systems may fail. Cultural differences can hinder the adoption and assimilation of information technologies. As organizations become more dependent on information systems, they also become more vulnerable when these systems fail.

We also must remember that technology alone does not provide a long-term sustainable competitive advantage. It is the way the technology is managed that gives firms a potential long-term edge.

KEY CONCEPTS AND TERMS

KEY CONCEPTS

- Competitive analysis (using competitive frameworks) can help identify appropriate uses of information technology. (329)
- Information technology may be used in numerous ways to improve the competitive position of firms. (332)
- Using information technology in a competitive mode can backfire. (343)
- The management of technology, not technology alone, is critical in achieving competitive advantage. (347)

KEY TERMS

after-sales service (329)
augmenting knowledge (336)
automating decisions (335)
balance of power (334)
barriers to entry (333)
basis of competition (333)
buyer's bargaining power (332)
electronic data interchange (EDI) (339)
environmental scanning (341)
expert system (336)
feedback systems (341)
feedforward systems (341)
five-force model (331)
interorganizational systems (339)
management of technology (347)
management science (335)
mathematical models (335)
neural networks (337)
new entrants (332)
order-winning criteria (328)
rivalry intensity (332)
substitute products (332)
supplier's bargaining power (332)
switching costs (333)
value chain (329)

REFERENCES

Abu-Mostafa, Y. S. "Machines That Learn from Hints." *Scientific American,* April 1995, pp. 64–69.

Hopper, M. D. "Rattling SABRE: New Ways to Compete on Information." *Harvard Business Review,* May–June 1990.

Ives, B., and G. P. Learmouth. "The Information System as a Competitive Weapon." *Communications of the ACM,* vol. 27 (12), Dec. 1984, pp. 1193–1201.

Mathur, K., and D. Solow. *Management Science: The Art of Decision Making.* Englewood Cliffs, N.J.: Prentice Hall, 1994.

Porter, M. E. *Competitive Advantage: Creating and Sustaining Superior Performance.* London: The Free Press, 1985.

Porter, M., and V. E. Millar. "How Information Gives You Competitive Advantage." *Harvard Business Review,* July–August 1985, pp. 149–160.

Olson, D. L., and J. F. Courtney, Jr. *Decision Support Models and Expert Systems,* New York: Macmillan Publishing, 1992.

CONNECTIVE CASE: Demco Uses I/T to Help Customers

Demco is a mail-order catalog company that manufactures and sells supplies such as book covers and tables for libraries, schools, day-care centers, and offices. They handle about 1,000 to 2,000 orders per day. The company operates in a mature market, where keeping customers happy is important. If the customer isn't satisfied with Demco, they don't have to look very far to find a competitor willing to take their order. "The heart and soul of our company is really our relationship with the customer," says Mark Anderson, vice president of I/S for Demco.

Recently Demco decided to switch from a mainframe computer environment to a mix of client/server and local area networks. The rationale was to try and find a hardware platform that would support better software tools, hopefully allowing Demco to purchase or build software that was more in line with their needs.

Anderson and his group selected IBM's AS/400 for their hardware platform, and they then found generic software packages for functions such as payroll and inventory. They also purchased a new Computer-Aided Software Engineering (CASE) tool and a marketing database system so they could build their own order entry, customer service, and marketing applications.

The result has exceeded their initial expectations. The marketing database allows Demco employees to analyze customer buying habits, see which products are most in demand, plan the next catalog, and decide who to send it to. In the catalog industry, the response rate to a given piece of mail is a measure of its success. Since the marketing system was installed, Demco's response rate has doubled.

Now that the company's customer service applications all work together, any employee can handle any type of call. Previously, applications and employees were divided into such categories as order entry, fulfillment, returns, and accounts receivable. "With one telephone call and one contact with the customer, we can satisfy the customer's needs," Anderson says. That means less time on hold for the customer, less review and description of customer contact history, and better follow-up on problems.

Case Questions

1. What competitive strategy(ies) do you think Demco uses?
2. Briefly describe how Demco's new information system may help the company compete.

SOURCE: Cate Corcoran, "Demco Looks to AS/400 for Its Client/Server Picture," *InfoWorld,* February 19, 1996, p. 67.

IT'S YOUR TURN — END OF CHAPTER MATERIALS

REVIEW QUESTIONS

1. Define the term *order-winning criteria.*
2. List and explain the five forces that shape competitive strategy.
3. Explain the concept of "creating customer value."
4. Identify at least two ways in which an information system may be used to improve the decision making of an organization.
5. Identify at least two ways in which an information system may be used to improve the communications of an organization.
6. Identify at least two ways in which an information system may be used to improve the operations (the transformation process) of an organization.
7. Identify at least two ways in which an information system may be used to improve the environmental scanning capability of an organization.
8. Identify at least two ways in which an information system may be used to improve supplier and customer relations.

9. Give at least two examples of how I/T initiatives, started for strategic and competitive purposes, can backfire.
10. Define the term *management of technology.*

DISCUSSION QUESTIONS

1. What is the basic concept underlying the value chain? How can the value chain be used to help identify opportunities for using information technology?
2. Identify two possible order-winning criteria for a company selling microcomputer chips.
3. Comment on whether management of technology is more critical in sustaining competitive advantage than technology itself. Do you think that a company can sustain a competitive advantage with the use of information technology alone? Why or why not?
4. How does Dell Computer's order-processing system contribute to providing value to its customers?
5. Airlines have complained that American Airlines' reservation system SABRE gives American an unfair competitive advantage. What do you think?
6. Give three examples of companies that have used "run-of-the-mill" I/T in innovative ways to develop information systems to gain competitive advantage. Describe the systems.

GROUP ASSIGNMENT

1. Take a company of your choice and
   a. List the order-winning criteria in the industry.
   b. Do a five-force model analysis of the industry.
   c. Draw a value chain that includes the company, its suppliers, and customers; comment on how the company builds value.
   d. Investigate whether the company is using I/T to help its competitive position.
   e. Give examples of how the company could use I/T to deliver greater customer value and enhance its competitive position.

APPLICATION ASSIGNMENTS

1. Consider yourself part of the team developing strategy for Sears Roebuck and Co. and use a drawing software program to depict a five-force model of the retailing industry.
2. Get on the Internet to find five companies that provide customer support on-line through the Net (list their www address).

CASE ASSIGNMENT: Pollution Solutions (B): One Person's Waste . . .

Pam Linton, the owner and CEO of Pollution Solutions of Vermont (PSOV), looked up from her desk as her sales manager entered the office. "Hi Craig. What's up?" Craig Senzel settled into a chair as he responded, "I've been thinking more about the waste tracking system, Pam. Maybe you are right; maybe we should try to expand it or modify it and see if we can't find ways to get even more out of it."

THE INDUSTRY

The hazardous waste management industry involved a wide variety of services that were purchased by all types of organizations. More than 4,000 facilities in the United States treated, stored, or disposed of an estimated 275 million metric tons of hazardous waste annually in the United States, and the volume was growing. Companies in the hazardous waste management industry could be classified into international, national, and regional groups. International and national firms generally bid on very large contracts that required bonding—insurance against potential problems that was required to complete a multimillion (or billion) dollar job. The major players that competed in the New England area included Chemical Waste Management, a division of WMX (a multinational firm); Laidlaw, an international corporation (which also competed with regional firms); Cycle Chem, based in New Jersey; and Clean Harbors, which had grown from regional to national status. There were about 50 regional firms operating in the New England area.

The hazardous waste management industry was heavily regulated by federal, state, and even local government agencies. In an effort to reduce the generation of hazardous waste and to minimize the present and future threat to human health and the environment, the U.S. Congress enacted the Resources Conservation and Recovery Act (RCRA) in 1976. The Act was designed to set standards for generators (producers) and transporters of hazardous waste and for owners and operators of hazardous waste treatment, storage, and disposal facilities.

RCRA created a "cradle-to-grave" regulatory scheme to ensure that hazardous wastes were properly disposed of. It required the Environmental Protection Agency (EPA) to develop criteria for identifying hazardous waste, taking into account a number of technical features. A permit system had emerged as the key enforcement provision, and therefore, all transportation, storage, treatment, and disposal of hazardous waste required a permit, subject to certain allowances.

Criminal penalties under RCRA could be severe. For knowingly transporting hazardous waste to a nonpermitted facility or knowingly treating, storing, or disposing of hazardous waste without a permit or in violation of a permit, EPA imposed penalties of up to five years in prison and a fine of $50,000 per day. In addition, the Department of Transportation (DOT) adopted federal regulations governing highway routing, handling of hazardous materials, registration of shippers and carriers, registration of packaging and container product manufacturers, and so on. Violation of DOT regulations could lead to civil and criminal penalties of imprisonment for up to five years and fines of up to $25,000 per day.

THE COMPANY

Pollution Solutions of Vermont was founded in 1988 by Pamela Linton, who is also the sole owner. Ms. Linton spent about 25 years in the health care industry, but in the mid-1980s decided she wanted a career change. She was looking for an entrepreneurial challenge that would also provide an opportunity for her to feel good philosophically about what she was doing. Although she had no experience in the industry, she chose hazardous waste management.

PSOV started with three employees, a pickup truck, a box truck, and an 18,000-square-foot warehouse that was converted into a waste storage and treatment facility. The company had a bit of luck early on that helped them tremendously. A somewhat inexperienced employee learned of a fairly large job contract and put in a bid, without really knowing if PSOV could handle the job. The PSOV bid was accepted, and everyone in the company scrambled to get the work completed. They were successful, and the generator (customer) was quite satisfied. The large profit margin from the job gave the company some working capital, and the recommendation from their first large client gave PSOV the much-needed credibility to bid on similar contracts.

The founding of PSOV involved a complicated permitting process, and it took several years to come into compliance with all EPA and DOT regulations. Although their initial focus was serving the manufacturing and defense industries, the economic recession of the early 1990s forced them to shift work to include the automobile industry (automotive oils and lubricants, etc.) and government base closures. In the mid-1990s PSOV had to change again, and they broadened their customer base to include dry cleaners, hospitals, automotive body shops, households, small manufacturers, and so on.

Most manufacturers generated one or more kinds of hazardous waste. According to RCRA, they had 30 days to get the waste out of their plant and disposed of in a safe manner. PSOV distributed empty 100-gallon metal drums to the manufacturers and then picked them up when they were full (each pickup was called a job). PSOV transported the drums to their facility, stored them until they had enough for a full truckload (approximately 100 drums), and then transported them to a licensed landfill for disposal. In addition, the company could handle liquid waste with their liquid tank truck, provide environmental consulting and remediation, and also sell some environmental supplies. The drummed waste constituted approximately 75 percent of PSOV's sales.

Gross sales figures for the company had grown from $1 million in 1990 to $5 million in 1992, and the number of employees grew to 36. The company experienced a downturn in 1993, with sales dropping to $3 million, but then rose again to $4.5 million in 1995. Fluctuations in sales and number of employees (which stood at 20) were attributable directly to economic conditions and the growth of the industry.

The hazardous waste industry took off in the late 1980s when the manufacturing industry was booming. In the early 1990s, companies such as PSOV were courted by waste generators who were anxious to get rid of their wastes. As a result, many small companies entered the industry and intensified the competition. When the manufacturing industry experienced a recession, so did the waste management industry; there was less waste to manage and more companies fighting over a smaller customer base.

PSOV made a lot of money in a short time after it started operations; the profit margins were very high. With the increased competition, customers became more price sensitive, and profit margins dropped dramatically. Linton believed that customers were still willing to pay more for better service; since the customer was also responsible for any waste they generated (not just the waste management company), customers were generally still willing to pay more for a higher level of trust.

INFORMATION TECHNOLOGY

Because of the multitude of federal and state regulations and the severe penalties for violating them, it was critical for PSOV to keep track of numerous details for every drum of waste they took control of. Complying with the regulations resulted in the generation of a tremendous amount of paperwork. For example, there were eight copies of each Uniform Hazardous Waste Manifest (a document describing the waste, signed by the generator); each copy had to be sent to various parties involved with the disposal process. Since PSOV could be audited by the EPA or DOT at any time (without warning), their records had to be completely accurate and current to within the last 24 hours. In addition, most customers (waste generators) wanted to audit the PSOV facility and handling procedures to ensure that PSOV was in complete compliance with all regulations.

To help keep track of all the paperwork, PSOV bought a small computer and the dBase III database management system (DBMS) soon after they began operations. Since no one within the company had a great deal of computer experience, a local software consulting firm was hired to develop a waste-tracking system for PSOV using dBase III. Over the years the software company was hired to make numerous changes and extensions, and the system grew with the company.

By the mid-1990s, the tracking system was implemented with the most recent version of the dBase DBMS on a microcomputer-based file server (using an Intel-486/66 MHz microprocessor). The company had 10 workstations (personal computers) attached to the file server in a local area network, using Novell LAN software. PSOV was not technology driven; there was no information systems department. Craig Senzel, the sales manager, also managed the network. They modified the software when necessary; as long as it worked, they kept using it.

All relevant information was entered from the manifests and other documents into the tracking system, allowing PSOV employees to track each drum (or liquid waste job). The system was used to generate the required reports that were sent to federal and state agencies (including the EPA and DOT), as well as reports for customers. Pam Linton believed that PSOV's tracking system gave them an advantage over many of their competitors because of its detailed and accurate record of all waste transported by the company. According to RCRA, generators (of waste) have cradle-to-grave responsibility for their hazardous wastes, no matter who transports, stores, and destroys them. Organizations tended to be very careful about who they selected to handle their waste stream; a great deal of trust was required, and companies with a proven track record, high standards, and experienced employees were in demand.

Lately, however, the tracking system seemed to be getting very slow in responding to requests. Recently when Pam had been demonstrating the system, she typed in the manifest number for a drum. It took more than three minutes for the tracking system to search through its database and retrieve the information she requested. Also, Pam had learned of new software packages that had been developed for the hazardous waste management industry. She had checked some a few years ago and found that PSOV's provided better information since it had been tailored specifically to their needs. She believed their system was still better than those used by her competitors, but she wasn't certain.

Questions

1. What are the major order-winning criteria for PSOV?
2. Use the value chain to describe ways that information technology could be used to help add value to PSOV's customers (hazard waste generators).
3. Analyze the competitive position of PSOV within the New England hazardous waste management industry, using the five-force model.
4. Pam Linton believes that PSOV's waste-tracking system helps provide a competitive advantage. Using concepts from the chapter, describe how this is possible. Also discuss how sustainable you believe this advantage is, and why.

SOURCE: This case was written by Associate Professors Ronald Thompson and William Cats-Baril with the assistance of graduate student Christine Kindstedt of the School of Business Administration, University of Vermont. The case is intended as a basis for discussion and is not meant to illustrate effective or ineffective handling of an administrative situation.

CHAPTER 11 Information Resource Management

CHAPTER OBJECTIVES

After reading this chapter, you should have a better understanding of many issues that need to be addressed in the management of information systems. More specifically, you should be able to:

- Explain why information systems, data, and knowledge should be viewed as corporate resources that need to be carefully managed.
- Understand the need for defining responsibilities when organizing the roles and relationships within the information systems department.
- Describe cost and resource management, including the concepts of outsourcing and chargeback systems.
- Discuss how to manage emerging information technologies within an organizational setting.
- Provide strategies for minimizing the organizational risks related to information systems (competitive, operational, and ethical vulnerabilities).

I now realize that information systems are critical to organizational survival, so how do I go about protecting them?

INTRODUCTION TO INFORMATION RESOURCE MANAGEMENT

Throughout most of this book, we have stressed the potential for using information technology to have a positive effect on organizations and society. As with many powerful tools, however, the application of I/T needs to be tempered with caution. The positive potential is enormous, but the negative potential is equally large. Although we have mentioned some potential risks and problems arising from the use of information technology throughout the book, in this chapter we deal with these risks in a more formal manner.

We start the chapter by providing an expanded discussion of the Hopper Specialty Company, which we introduced briefly in Chapter 1. You may recall that Hopper Specialty purchased an inventory control system and subsequently experienced difficulties that almost put the company out of business. Among other problems, the computerized inventory system provided inaccurate information and slowed the processing of transactions rather than speeding them up. Hopper Specialty claims the inventory system cost them more than $4 million in lost sales and related expenses over several years, and it sued the vendor that provided the system to try and recover some of this money.

First, we use the Hopper Specialty case as an example of the type of problems that can occur when I/T is not managed carefully, and then we describe more general management issues that need to be addressed to control I/T projects. After identifying several important risks associated with the use of I/T, we provide general strategies that have proven successful in managing and reducing those risks. The chapter (and module) concludes with a brief discussion of how managing information technology fits into the broader context of managing organizations.

DOOMSDAY DEVICE: THE CASE OF THE HOPPER SPECIALTY COMPANY

To celebrate how his new computer would streamline his parts-supply business, Joe Hopper hoisted a circus-size tent, set up picnic tables, and barbecued enough beef brisket to feed a small town.

In 10 years, Hopper Specialty Company had grown from a small storefront into the biggest distributor of industrial hardware in northwest New Mexico, catering especially to oil and gas drillers. Now, in May 1988, NCR Corporation's highly touted Warehouse Manager computer package promised even better things to come. When up and running, the computer system would track the thousands of items in a huge inventory, keep prices current, warn when items were running low, punch up invoices in seconds, and even balance the books—all with only a few keystrokes. Particularly for drilling customers, who lose money every minute their equipment isn't working, anything that could get orders for parts filled faster would indeed be cause for celebration.

To mark the event, two NCR sales representatives were circulating at the party to extol Warehouse Manager. But unknown to Mr. Hopper, no one was celebrating back at NCR headquarters in Dayton, Ohio. Four months earlier, shortly after Mr. Hopper had placed his order, the $6 billion computer company had suspended sales of

A critical component of managing inventories in large storage warehouses is an effective information system. Photo courtesy of Tony Stone Worldwide.

Warehouse Manager so its engineers could work out critical bugs. And, coincidentally, two ominous internal reports on the product had arrived in Dayton the week of Mr. Hopper's party. They revealed that the computer package had been inadequately tested and was performing unexpectedly badly in actual business settings.

Computerized Disasters. The reports from the field foreshadowed the extraordinary problems Mr. Hopper would face as a product he had perceived as a miracle worker emerged as a virtual saboteur. And he wasn't alone: Of the roughly 40 Warehouse Manager systems sold by NCR, at about $180,000 each, not one ended up working as promised. More than two dozen lawsuits, including one filed by Mr. Hopper, resulted.

NCR, renamed AT&T Global Information Services after its 1991 acquisition by AT&T Corporation, now concedes that Warehouse Manager was a disaster and stopped selling it several years ago. "With this particular piece of software, we did not do a good job," says spokesman Mark Siegel. "We did not service customers well." But few are aware of the debacle; the company has settled many of the suits under provisions binding the parties to secrecy.

Meanwhile, customers such as Mr. Hopper are still digging out from the recordkeeping mess Warehouse Manager created. Their nightmare illustrates both the risks of marrying one's company to a powerful new computer system and how limited the available remedies can be when things go wrong. All this, however, was far from Mr. Hopper's mind in 1987 when he began discussing with NCR how an automated system of computer controls could improve his business.

Software Incompatibility. Mr. Hopper knew that several large computer vendors were selling packages aimed at inventory-intensive companies. What seemed to set Warehouse Manager apart was NCR's promise that all its crucial parts—the computer hardware, the various software components, and all the countertop terminals—would be serviced by NCR under one roof. And salespeople were pitching it as a thoroughly debugged package that was running smoothly at more than 200 firms.

In fact, although the Warehouse Manager software package was indeed a success at those 200 locations, it was working on an operating system made by Burroughs (now part of Unisys), not NCR. Through a licensing agreement, NCR had arranged to piggyback the application, developed by Taylor Management, onto its own operating system. Taylor would be responsible for converting the software and maintaining the final package. But how well this would work wasn't at all clear when Warehouse Manager became available in April 1987.

Most of the early indications, as evidenced by customers' letters to NCR, were negative. In August, a wood-laminating company in Franklin Park, Illinois, complained that it hadn't been able to place a purchase order in the five weeks since it had switched over to Warehouse Manager. The backlog was costing $2,000 a day. "We are shocked and dismayed at this crisis that NCR and its software vendor have created," wrote William E. Schierer, president of the company, E. Kinast Distributors Inc.

At Burgman Industries, a Jacksonville, Florida, supplier of heavy construction parts, company president John W. Shearer complained in December 1987 that corrupted files in his Warehouse Manager had infected his general ledger with inaccurate numbers. In one instance, a machine part that had cost him $114 was listed for sale at 54 cents. "This software is so unprofessional and is riddled with so many bugs that it may actually put us out of business," Mr. Shearer wrote NCR.

Who's to Blame? Moreover, despite NCR's promise of a "single-source solution," customers who called for technical help were bounced between NCR and Taylor Management. By mid-January 1988, it had become clear that Taylor's software and NCR's operating system weren't compatible. That's why NCR finally ordered a halt to further sales until an updated version of the application was developed by Taylor and tested by NCR.

Delays and Lockups. Hopper Specialty says it knew none of this. Despite the sales freeze, NCR began installing hardware and countertop terminals the following month for Hopper. During sales demonstrations, Mr. Hopper had been impressed that the terminals could punch up a customer invoice in a fraction of a second. But when Hopper Specialty actually switched on its new system in September 1988, the response time ranged from half a minute to several minutes, leaving Hopper's customers waiting in increasingly long lines. Additional delays were caused by 20 to 30 terminal lockups each day.

At Hopper, Warehouse Manager couldn't even be relied on to keep prices straight. A piece of industrial hose that should have been listed at $17 per foot showed up as costing $30 per foot. "Our counter people didn't know it was the wrong price by looking at it," says Charles Brannin, Hopper Specialty's general manager. "Customers would go ahead and pay it, and then we lost their business."

By far the most damaging problem stemmed from huge gaps between what the computer told Hopper Specialty was in stock and what was actually there. The Warehouse Manager might show 50 parts in stock, for instance, when, in fact, Hopper needed to order 50. Other times, it would show that items were on order when they were sitting on the shelf. The chaos seemed to feed on itself. Six times in two months during 1989, Hopper employees hand-counted every item in the building, only to find the tally didn't match what NCR's computer said was there.

Ms. Irwin, the office manager, began logging 14-hour days and coming in on weekends with her children to work out problems with the system. But she couldn't keep customers from taking their business two doors down, to Advance Supply &

Pump Company, which now boasted superior inventory and service. As Hopper Specialty's customer base eroded, it couldn't afford to carry as big an inventory. The shrinking inventory and confusion over what was in stock, in turn, further hurt Hopper's reputation for reliability. "The whole thing just snowballed," says Mr. Hopper.

Back at NCR, Taylor Management's new version of its software, Release.2, was billed as the answer to everybody's problems. It was an improvement, but it, too, turned out to be full of bugs.

The biggest blow came in April 1993: Hopper's largest customer, BHP Mineral International Inc., canceled its contract, worth $350,000 to $500,000 a year. Hopper's contract required it to fill 90 percent of any parts order from BHP, a strip-mine operator, within 48 hours. Increasingly, Hopper could barely meet half the quota. With the loss of BHP's business, Mr. Hopper found he had no choice but to start laying off employees and slashing health care benefits; today, 10 of the 19 people who were in place when Warehouse Manager was installed still have their jobs. Since 1988, gross annual sales have dropped to $1.9 million from $3.5 million, according to Mr. Hopper. Inventory now is so low that Hopper Specialty doesn't need a computer to keep track of it.

As for NCR, it is publicly contrite. Mr. Siegel, the spokesman, maintains that AT&T Global Information Services is assuming full responsibility for what went wrong with Warehouse Manager and is bending over backward to accommodate the needs of its customers. Of the more than two dozen suits that have been filed alleging fraud, negligence, or misrepresentation, about half have been settled. The plaintiffs were required not to discuss any aspect of their dealings with NCR.

But NCR's stance toward companies that don't settle has been far from generous. In Hopper's suit, filed in U.S. District Court in Albuquerque, NCR is relying on its so-called Universal Sales Agreement signed by Ms. Irwin, the Hopper office manager, to limit damages. Hopper claims Warehouse Manager cost it $4.2 million in lost profit, but the Universal Agreement caps damages at the cost of the computer. (The two sides don't even agree on that. Hopper says it spent $284,821 on the system; NCR says it was $184,567.)

In settlement talks for the case, the company offered Hopper discounts on future AT&T phone rates and held out the possibility of replacing Hopper's Warehouse Manager with a new computer system. But Mr. Hopper won't hear of that. "We told them," he says, "We don't want any more of your equipment."

Unfortunately, the Hopper case is not an isolated instance. Many organizations and individuals have experienced everything from small frustrations to outright business failures because of faulty information systems. In 1995, for example, many individuals were horrified to learn that the tax returns they had prepared using the popular TurboTax software package might contain errors and that the U.S. Internal Revenue Service held them responsible for any errors. Problems are not just limited to software products, either; shortly after the Intel company released its Pentium microprocessor chip, it was found to have flaws that could lead to improper calculations in certain instances.

INFORMATION SYSTEMS AS A CORPORATE RESOURCE

Throughout this book, we have provided numerous examples of organizations using information technology to their advantage. The moral of all these examples is simply that information systems (I/S) are a very important component in the success of many organizations. I/S should be considered a critical **corporate resource,** just as financial capital and human resources are.

The recognition that information systems should be viewed as an important corporate resource brings with it certain important implications, not the least of which is that I/S needs to be a priority for management. Organizations need to realize the importance of investing, developing, and managing an entire array of organizational information and communication systems. The management duties related to information and communication systems are complex and constitute a challenge for most organizations. These duties include integrating I/T into the strategy of the organization; implementing policies to determine which I/S projects should be funded and which ones should be abandoned; determining appropriate development methodologies; establishing responsibilities for ongoing I/S operations, security, and maintenance; and so on.

The Hopper Specialty case provides a good example of just how important an information system can be to the success and demise of a company. If the Warehouse Manager system had worked as the NCR salespeople claimed it would, it is highly probable that Hopper would still be successful and would be growing as they had in the past. Because of the faulty inventory system, however, Hopper employees were unable to provide satisfactory service to their customers. Not surprisingly, most of Hopper's major customers abandoned them and moved their business to competitors. The faulty system also provided inaccurate information, which hampered decision making, accelerating the downward spiral of sales.

DATA AND KNOWLEDGE AS CORPORATE RESOURCES

In this book we have focused primarily on information and communication systems, with less emphasis on the actual data and knowledge that are an integral part of such systems. In Appendix A we examine data management in more detail; here we introduce some important concepts of what information is and place them within the broader context of I/S management.

Data is central to the concept of information systems. Without data, a system has no reason for being. Indeed, the value added by information systems to an organization is derived from supporting the processing and transmission of, and access to, data. Moreover, poorly managed data can cause major problems for organizations in their attempts to respond to environmental changes and implement strategy. Part of managing data is the way you build your data architecture, that is, the way you define your data and the type of data you collect. Consider a few examples of companies that ran into difficulties because they had not foreseen certain uses of their data and built their databases in ways that created barriers rather than flexibility of use.

A major bank, in response to changes in the industry, wanted to shift its strategy to focus more on customers. The first step was to categorize its customers. However, the bank discovered that it was unable to determine how profitable individual customer accounts were, or even what its total business was with each customer, because its customer codes were not the same across branch offices or across lines of business (deposits, loans, etc.). This bank decided (maybe not even consciously) at one point in the past that it wanted to collect data on accounts rather than on customers.

A manufacturing firm with nine plants wanted to negotiate better purchasing agreements with its major suppliers, using bulk order discounts and electronic data interchange. The firm discovered they were unable to pool the data from the plants to find out how much it purchased of specific items from each supplier because the plants used inconsistent data formats. This company decided at one point in the

Although different organizational units perform different functions, it is important that they are able to share data and knowledge. Photos courtesy of Bonnie Kamin.

past that it made sense that each plant would have its own self-contained, standalone system and did not see the need for a set of common standards.

A large chemical company wanted to merge two operating divisions to reduce redundancies and, hence, operating expenses. The greatest obstacle to implementing the merger turned out to be the incompatibilities in data definitions and information systems in their accounting departments.

These brief examples help illustrate the importance of thinking about the company's data resources as an asset to be deployed and used in many different ways as the strategy of the company evolves. Organizations use different approaches in structuring their thinking about **data management.** Some tend to use a technical emphasis in their efforts, focusing on tools and techniques such as database management systems, data dictionaries, and the use of data modeling (such as entity-relationship models, which are presented in Appendix A). Other organizations emphasize organizational responsibilities, establishing database administration and data administration functions and administrative policies and procedures covering topics such as data ownership, access, and security. A third major approach is the use of top-down, business objectives–driven planning methodologies. These methodologies attempt to link business objectives to data collection and use.

Although managing data can be challenging, managing organizational knowledge is even more so. With data, we tend to deal with "facts": a customer address, the purchase price of an automobile, and so on. The process of updating those facts is more or less difficult depending on the business (e.g., banks usually have an easier time tracking the address changes of their customers than car companies do since the bank's customers have an incentive—their bank accounts—to let the bank know where they are). With **knowledge,** we are dealing with more nebulous concepts, such as the "best" way to interpret a patient's symptoms, the "best" way to interact with a customer when he is making a reservation, or the "best" way to deduct a business expense. These practices, policies, models, and experiences (i.e., knowledge) are actually what a company is all about, what makes companies different from one another, and what gives a company its basic capabilities. Trying to institutionalize those practices, rules, and policies in a knowledge base is a key strategic concern of organizations. The constant update of that knowledge constitutes one of the main challenges of management today. This challenge is particularly acute in knowledge-intensive industries where professionals can change firms quite easily and often.

Knowledge management is a critical corporate activity that requires careful attention. The ability to share knowledge and expertise can greatly enhance organizational effectiveness. Global consulting companies such as Andersen Consulting and Price Waterhouse have computerized systems that gather knowledge from their consultants and customers around the world and allow the consultants to share experiences and answer queries quickly and effectively.

Dell Computer walks their customers through a series of questions to determine their computing needs and matches those needs to the most appropriate computer configuration. These questions have been developed by a team of computer experts, but they are asked by a clerk with only a high school diploma, who reads the questions from a computer screen. Similarly, inexperienced lawyers, accountants, stockbrokers, elevator and car mechanics, and physicians can consult a knowledge-based system developed by experts in their fields. These knowledge-based systems accelerate organizational learning, minimize "reinventing the wheel" and making costly mistakes, and, more importantly, allow firms to serve their customers better.

Knowledge-based systems are not only for large companies. Consider the example of Spears and Company, a small company with fewer than 30 employees servicing the hoists and gasoline pumps within a medium-sized county. Bill Spears, the owner of the company, has been in the business about 20 years. Over the years, he has accumulated a great deal of knowledge concerning the quirks of numerous pumps his company services. Since Bill is unable to handle all of the service calls himself, he employs several service technicians, who have varying degrees of experience and expertise.

On one fairly typical service call, a technician was dispatched to a service center to fix a gas pump that wasn't functioning properly. When the nozzle was pressed, there was a slight sound of escaping air, but no liquid appeared. The technician went through a series of standard diagnostic tests but was unable to determine the cause of the problem. He called the company headquarters for assistance, but unfortunately Bill was out of town. After speaking with another technician, he tried some additional diagnostic tests, to no avail.

Four hours went by—during which several customers were inconvenienced by having to wait to pump gas and some business was lost when a few potential customers seeing a line at the pump decided to go somewhere else—before he was finally able to contact Bill. Bill immediately understood the problem. Bill had worked on that specific pump previously and knew that the fuel line from the underground fuel tank to the pump had been laid too close to the ground surface. When the temperature got too hot (as it was that particular day), the fuel in the line vaporized. The short-term solution was to use a water hose to soak the pavement over the line. As the water evaporated it cooled the pavement and the line beneath, allowing the fuel to flow once again. Bill recognized the need to share this type of expertise among all his employees, and he eventually contracted a computer services company to develop an expert system that captured the details of service calls and made the history (i.e., facts or data) and knowledge (i.e., the rules and practices) of servicing a particular pump available to all service technicians.

INFORMATION SYSTEMS PLANNING

Once the realization has been made that the company's data and knowledge are valuable resources requiring careful managerial attention, the first step in managing them is the development of information systems plans. These plans constitute a blueprint of the hardware and software the organization needs to implement to exploit (i.e., access, process, transmit, and share) its data and knowledge resources.

Technological changes make information technology planning an ongoing activity that is essential for the effective management of corporate data and knowledge. Planning documents need to be created and reviewed on a regular basis to ensure that the I/S plans continue to reflect the business assumptions that were made about the future (both internal and external to the organization) and about the technical capabilities of the required hardware and software.

I/S plans need to be driven by, and must be consistent with, the overall corporate business plan. Since the purpose of information systems is to support the business, the strategic direction of the business must be known before any meaningful I/S plan can be developed. The concept can be stated simply: First strategy, then information technology. However, in organizations where information systems are a major component of the organization's strategy, the I/S plan needs to be developed in conjunction with the corporate plan since we must remember that the implementation of an information system can take years.

A long-range I/S plan is usually created from a top-down perspective, and it typically attempts to answer the following basic questions:

1. Where are we? How are we doing?
2. Where do we want to go? What are our competitors doing? What are our customers asking for? (The answer to this question is crucial in determining how data will be organized later.)
3. How do we get there; that is, what is the role of I/T in enabling the necessary capabilities to deliver what customers want better than the competition?
4. When will it be done?
5. Who will do it; that is, do we have the skills and resources internally to deliver what we need by the time we need it?
6. How much will it cost? Does it make economic sense?

The flow diagram shown in Figure 11–3 (at the end of this chapter) provides an overview of the decision-making process to determine whether to develop and implement an information technology project and assess its impact. The first task is to assess whether the proposed project is aligned with the strategy of the business or not. If it is, you need to ask whether the business processes that are going to be influenced have been analyzed to determine whether, for example, we are talking about reengineering a process or just improving it under a continuous improvement initiative.

Once the scope of the project has been determined, alternative designs need to be developed. These alternative designs need to take into consideration, among other issues, the impact of new upcoming technologies, the potential for ethical abuses, and the strategies to recover from partial or total system failure. The cost effectiveness of these alternative designs needs to be assessed next. Assuming there is at least one alternative that makes economic sense, then the question is whether the organization has the necessary skills to actually design and implement the system. If the skills are not available internally, then an outsourcing arrangement can be looked into. An implementation strategy needs to be carefully developed to improve the likelihood of the system being accepted and used. Finally, an evaluation of the impact of the system has to be made on a regular basis to determine when the system should be improved and/or phased out.

As you can see, the process of managing information technology is time consuming and complex.

FIGURE 11-1 Organization of Information Systems Department Historical View—Mainframe Environment

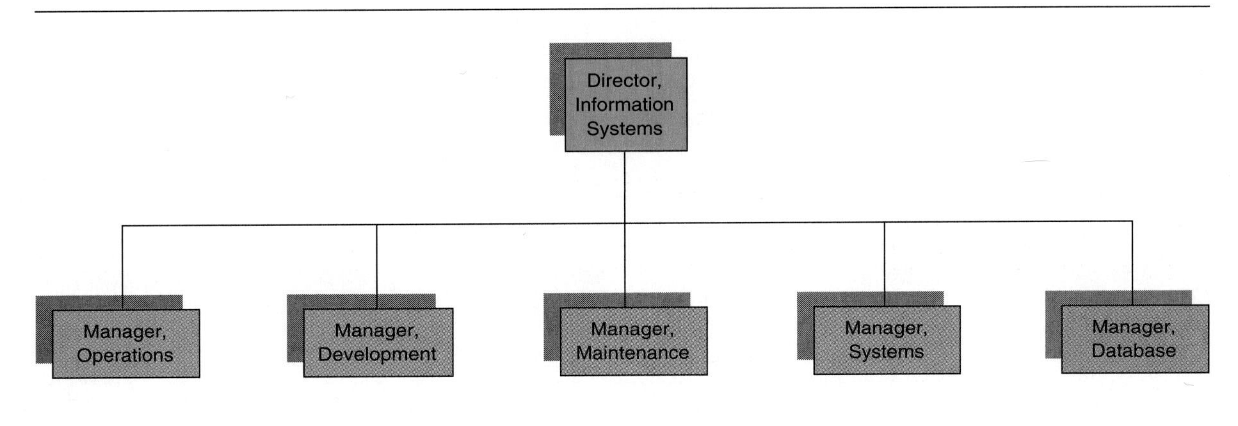

ORGANIZATION OF INFORMATION SYSTEM ACTIVITIES

Having made the point that it is very important for organizations to develop plans to effectively manage their data, knowledge, and information systems, we now turn to the issue of how to actually structure the required activities. However, since this is not a book that focuses on managing the I/S resources, what we provide here is just an introduction to the topic. Basically there are two major areas that need to be addressed: (*a*) deciding what information management functions and activities need to be performed, and (*b*) determining how best to organize the information systems specialists to perform these functions.

We have previously stated that many changes have occurred over the years in the processes used for developing information systems. Here we make the point that the ways in which organizations structure the management of their information systems activities has also evolved over time, and will most likely continue to do so. In the era of mainframe computers and specialized software developed in-house by I/S specialists, I/S departments were often perceived as being a group of technicians that were separate from the rest of the organization. Figure 11-1 provides a sample organization chart for an I/S department during this era.

Typically, there would be an I/S director who reported to second- or third-level management (such as a vice president of finance). Internally, the I/S department would be organized around four major internal functions:

- Development, containing programmers and analysts.
- Maintenance, containing mostly programmers.
- Operations, containing clerks who performed routine backups and batch program runs.
- Systems, containing programmers and other technical staff responsible for the operating systems and interfaces with program applications. If the organization had adopted the use of database management systems, there would also be an individual or group with specific responsibility for defining the database structure, the data formats, and so on.

During the early phase in the evolution of information technology and information systems, the communications technology for the organization (telephone

FIGURE 11–2 Organization of Information Systems Department Current View—Functional Organization

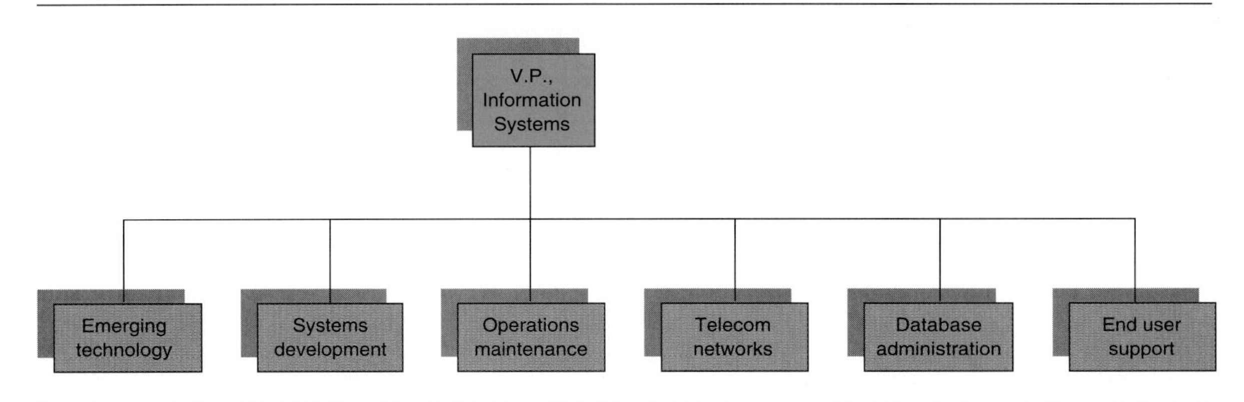

systems, etc.) and office systems (word processing, photocopiers, etc.) were typically under the control of separate groups. Furthermore, there was relatively little interaction between the I/S department and the other functional areas within the organization. I/S project requests were submitted by the user areas; the projects would be prioritized by the I/S department and completed as resources allowed. Users tended to have little understanding of I/S functions, and I/S specialists had little understanding of business operations.

As the information technology and I/S development methodologies evolved, so did the structure of the I/S departments. With the merging of communications, office, and information technologies, the responsibility for all three was merged and brought within the I/S group. As information systems became more important to organizations, the top I/S position was elevated to the vice president level or above [some companies created the position of **chief information officer (CIO),** reporting directly to the CEO].

The explosion of end-user computing, brought on by the expanded use of personal computers and easy-to-use software, made training and support of users in the development of their own systems much more important functions. As client server configurations started to emerge, the need to share databases increased the importance of data administration, elevating that function to a managerial level within the I/S group. To facilitate communications between I/S and the user departments, many organizations created the position of business analyst. The business analyst is someone who understands I/T but who works within a functional department to help define and address the I/T needs of the users in that department.

Another organizational structure innovation was the creation of the **information center.** Information centers were made up of I/S specialists who provided users with demonstrations, training, and support in the utilization of end-user computing and productivity tools. Information centers were created to provide users with a group of in-company consultants who would help them develop solutions to managerial information processing and reporting needs that could be implemented by the users themselves.

Figure 11–2 illustrates one alternative structure for organizing the I/S group. It is based on a fairly traditional structure with the addition of telecommunications and network support, end-user support (possibly an information center), an emerging technologies group (discussed later in this chapter), and a group that combines the functions of operations and maintenance. With this type of structure, there would need to be some overlap of responsibilities; for example, the end-user support group would need to coordinate their activities closely with the telecommunications and networking group since most of the end-user systems would be connected through local area and wide area networks.

The options to organize an I/S department are numerous and diverse. In organizations that have multiple business units, decisions need to be made concerning the level of decentralization of I/S responsibilities and resources. Once more, there is no single right or wrong answer; the appropriate degree of centralization or decentralization depends on the specific circumstances of the individual organization. The factors that need to be considered include aspects such as the need for sharing data between organizational units (do we share the same customers or suppliers?), the level of centralization of authority (do business units have complete control over all operations and decision making, or are all decisions made by the head office?), the opportunities for capitalizing on economies of scale, and so on.

The degree of centralization (or decentralization) of I/S responsibilities and activities is just one of the considerations when determining how to structure the I/S department. As mentioned previously, however, the first step is to determine exactly what functions and activities the I/S specialists should perform. In many organizations these functions now include the following:

- Developing a comprehensive I/T strategy.
- Documenting, operating, and maintaining the existing inventory of corporate hardware, software, and information systems.
- Setting standards for telecommunications and installing and maintaining local and wide area networks.
- Developing, maintaining, and protecting organizational databases and critical applications.
- Evaluating, acquiring, and integrating new hardware and software products (operating systems, workstations, productivity tools, office communication systems, etc.).
- Training and supporting internal customers (including defining their I/S needs).
- Developing procedures to negotiate with and oversee outside information systems consultants and vendors in the acquisition and development of new information technology and systems.
- Facilitating the transfer of technology across organizational units.

Once the specific activities and responsibilities have been defined, it becomes a much easier task to determine appropriate ways to structure and staff the I/S group. It is important to note, however, that the functions and responsibilities will continue to change as technology and business strategies change and will require new organizational structures as well. In some organizations, the I/S department is reviewed on an annual basis, and major structural changes being implemented every 18 months or two years are not uncommon. Business Brief 11–1 illustrates this concept in more detail.

Cost and Resource Management. There are numerous costs, both tangible and intangible, associated with an organization's information systems. As our society

BUSINESS BRIEF 11-1 CONTROLLED ANARCHY: USERS AND I/S SWITCHING ROLES

As personal computers become the dominant business computers around the world, companies are giving I/S departments more control over PC purchases while, at the same time, giving end users more authority over application development. This arrangement may sound paradoxical, but it's not. Networked PCs are driving the return to centralized control by I/S departments.

PCs are often thought of as being interchangeable commodities, but that's just not the case when you start hooking them together in large networks. "You cannot have many permutations of networking, protocols, and software and expect the system to behave in any predictable manner," says Richard Buchanan, senior analyst with Forrester Research Inc. Ironically, users are finding that to get the functionality they want out of the systems they've requested, the products must comply with corporate standards.

Southern California Gas Company is in the middle of a reorganization to make I/S more responsive to end users. The utility has moved application development out of an I/S department and into the company's five business units. It has also moved the I/T budgets into the business units.

However, a central I/S organization was retained to ensure that the utility doesn't end up with five systems that cannot communicate. This central group is responsible for Southern Gas's computing standards, which have been in place for several years. Ultimately, the CIO (chief information officer) is responsible for seeing that everything works together.

QUESTION

1. What are the pros and cons of giving users full control over the design, development, and maintenance of systems?

SOURCE: C. Corcoran, "The New IS: Controlled Anarchy," *InfoWorld,* March 20, 1995, pp. 61–62.

becomes more reliant on information technology, many organizations find that information technology and information systems consume an ever-increasing proportion of their overall expenses. Some observers, and many corporate executives, have publicly questioned whether the continually increasing investments have been balanced by corresponding benefits.

To control the costs and still manage to reap potential benefits, most organizations require that investments in information systems be justified in a manner that is similar to other capital investments. In previous chapters we described some of the costs that need to be considered when evaluating the costs and benefits of an information systems development proposal. These included factors such as hardware acquisition or leasing costs, software licenses and maintenance agreements, consulting and external development fees, and so on. In addition, all of the internal costs of running the I/S department need to be considered, such as the personnel salary and benefits and all ongoing hardware, software, and telecommunications costs. Some organizations also attempt to factor in the costs associated with end-user computing, such as the time "lost" when users are learning to use new applications and systems features.

The methods used to control costs vary widely from organization to organization. In some, very little effort is devoted to cost containment. These organizations view information systems as a necessary component of staying competitive and believe that attempting to accurately measure the costs associated with I/S is not worth the administrative cost and effort. At the other end of the spectrum, there are organizations that attempt to account and control all I/S-related expenditures. Business Brief 11–2 discusses this further.

BUSINESS BRIEF 11–2 NEW WAYS TO BUY NEW STUFF: IBM'S ELECTRONIC PURCHASING SERVICE

Coopers & Lybrand L.L.P. (C&L) implemented IBM's Electronic Purchasing Service, hoping to reduce the cost of ordering products and supplies for their offices by as much as 60 percent. The service is designed to streamline selection and acquisition processes, giving end users the ability to purchase their own computer and office supplies.

"With IBM's service we see an opportunity to exploit emerging technologies to save money, increase controls, build stronger partnerships with our suppliers, and meet the purchasing needs of employees throughout the firm," said Jeffrey L. Block, C&L's director of national purchasing.

The Electronic Purchasing Service allows users of OS/2- and Windows-based systems to browse, compare, and select products from electronic supplier catalogs and then route requisitions through a LAN for approval and electronic ordering. Orders are then submitted through the IBM Global Network using electronic data interchange (EDI). The service is integrated with C&L's Lotus Notes and cc:Mail systems to automate the workflow and messaging process with the ordering and approval process.

"Many companies still use paper processing that requires several weeks of waiting for approval and several more weeks for delivery," said Dave Cassano, vice president of IBM electronic commerce services. "Our system allows users to directly purchase supplies and have them routed for approval in one day."

QUESTIONS

1. What are the pros and cons of IBM's Electronic Purchasing Service?
2. What company policies need to be in place to address some of the disadvantages?

SOURCE: Karen Rodriquez, *InfoWorld,* February 20, 1995, p. 40.

One approach to cost control which has been widely adopted is the use of **chargeback systems**. The concept here is to calculate all costs associated with information systems, and then *charge* those costs *back* to the user departments on the basis of the number of employees in each department, the amount of computing resources devoted to each department, or some similar criterion. The idea behind chargeback systems is that they should make users more aware of the costs of information systems, providing them with valuable feedback that will help users decide whether they actually need some of the systems or enhancements they request.

Chargeback systems have many pros and cons. On the plus side, they can help users prioritize their I/S needs (since they need to pay for them) and also help I/S departments remain efficient and effective in their operations (since they now can be compared on "price" to outside vendors). On the negative side, chargeback systems can be costly and time consuming to implement, and they may stifle innovation by charging, and therefore discouraging, users for experimenting with new technologies.

Chargeback systems need to be adjusted as the organization moves through different stages of I/T sophistication and maturity. When an organization is experimenting with new systems and technologies, it may be better to relax cost containment efforts to encourage learning and innovation. As knowledge of, and expertise with, I/T spreads throughout the organization, more stringent cost controls may be necessary to focus efforts on productive uses of I/T and discourage excessive experimentation (see Business Brief 11–3).

BUSINESS BRIEF 11-3 KEEPING ON TRACK: CONRAIL ADDS CLIENT/SERVER

Conrail Inc. is putting its future in the hands of a small team of I/T executives who are helping to guide some of the most sweeping changes to take place at the railroad in the last 15 years. Using a combination of client/server and EDI (electronic data interchange) technology, Conrail launched an ambitious program to link its billing systems with a variety of other shipping organizations to streamline the number of bills customers must track.

This is particularly critical in an era characterized by trucking companies that now look to railroads—which ship items by the ton—as low-cost providers of interstate shipping services. Known within Conrail as the Flex-Flo program, these types of transloading activities are growing at a rate of 15 percent per year.

To help manage this business, Conrail needed a financial system that could be linked to both its customers and other shipping companies. The problem, however, was that Conrail's mainframe systems are not flexible enough to add the necessary new interfaces. So Conrail faced a dilemma: scrap the mainframes and go with client/server systems, or pass up a new business opportunity. Because Conrail spent years perfecting code for its control systems on the mainframe, scrapping them was not an option.

Instead, the company created an independent subsidiary to deploy client/server systems. "This is a compromise between technology and reality," said Tom Hoover, a business process engineer with the transloading division of Conrail.

QUESTIONS

1. What variables do you think Conrail used in assessing the cost benefit of scrapping the mainframes? Based on your list, do you think Conrail made the right decision?
2. Should Conrail have considered the possibility of outsourcing the client/server systems? Why or why not?

SOURCE: W. Pickering, "C/S Keeping Conrail on Track," *PCWeek*, March 20, 1995, p. 113. Reprinted by permission.

MANAGING INFORMATION SYSTEMS RISK

The use of information technology provides literally an infinite number of opportunities; we (as organizations and as individuals) are limited only by our imagination. With this potential, however, comes numerous risks and responsibilities, risks such as investing heavily in an information system that never delivers on its promised functionality; purchasing systems that "crash," bringing business operations to a grinding halt; or being sued by employees for breaching their right to privacy when auditing the use of the company's E-mail system. We have structured our discussion of **risk management** of information technology by classifying **risk** under three headings: competitive, operational, and ethical.

Competitive Vulnerabilities. Earlier in the book we provided examples of organizations that effectively used information technology to improve their competitive position or to respond to a competitive threat. In fact, we made the point in Chapter 1 that I/T could change the way organizations competed within an industry, could significantly alter industries, or even wipe out an entire industry. Let's consider another example for a moment. Have you ever thought of a career as a travel agent? Do you know anyone who works as a travel agent? Travel agencies demonstrate, to a large degree, the concept of **competitive vulnerability.**

If you think about it, travel agents basically deal with information. They act as a go-between, trying to match potential travelers with travel service providers. The

A travel agent's job is very information intensive. Photo courtesy of Bonnie Kamin.

service providers pay the travel agents a fee for their services, which enables them to continue operating. The travel agent needs to know what services are available (such as airline flight schedules, costs, seat availability) as well as what the potential customer wants (destination, price, time of day, dates).

Much of the information travel agents use (with the exception of customer preferences) is now available on commercial on-line information services, which potential customers can access directly. If a customer has access to an on-line service (America OnLine or CompuServe, for example), they can check the schedules and book the reservation themselves, bypassing the travel agent. As more potential customers sign up for this type of service and become comfortable with the direct use of on-line systems, the brokering power of the travel agent is reduced.

In early 1995, U.S. airlines, realizing the decrease in power of travel agents, decided to cut what used to be a percentage-based commission (10 percent) to a flat fee (maximum $50) for booking domestic flights. The travel agencies fought back, suing the airlines and claiming a violation of antitrust laws. Some travel agencies responded by starting to charge customers for their consulting time, similar to a doctor or lawyer. Still, most travel agencies found themselves in a somewhat precarious position, squeezed between airlines trying to develop direct access to flyers (through frequent flyer programs that would have been impossible to institute and manage without information technology) and computer-literate users making their own travel arrangements.

Operational Vulnerabilities. The Hopper Specialty case, discussed at the beginning of this chapter, provides a good example of what we mean by **operational vulnerabilities.** For Hopper, an efficient and effective inventory control system is essential for their internal operations. When the Warehouse Manager system failed (by providing slow response, inaccurate information, or completely shutting down), it had a very negative effect on Hopper's operations.

Another example of operational vulnerability is the customer accounts database maintained by a bank. If the computerized accounts database fails, the bank would be unable to process any transactions. Customers would be unable to make deposits or withdrawals, the bank would be unable to collect the interest owing to it from loans or pay any interest owing on deposits, and so on. Since a bank relies so heavily on the processing of information, it is very vulnerable to anything that interrupts its capacity to process and communicate information. Another obvious example of operational vulnerability is the reliance of airlines on their reservation systems.

As we have seen, some organizational operations rely completely on information systems. For other applications, the systems may be less important, and disruptions to the information system would result in less of a disruption to internal operations. Consider, for example, presentation software used by salespeople to prepare and deliver presentations to potential clients. If the computer system running the software fails, it is still possible to make a sales presentation—it might not appear as professional or be as effective as a sales pitch delivered with the system, but the operation (sales presentation) may still be completed (possibly using overhead transparencies created with a word-processing package or even drawn by hand).

The more information technology is assimilated into individual and organizational operations, and the more information systems are used to support and even automate job tasks and organizational functions, the more vulnerable individuals and organizations are to operational failures.

Ethical Vulnerabilities. **Ethical vulnerability** refers to the risks that a company has in collecting, using, and storing confidential and personal data. More and more companies are being sued by employees and customers for the improper release or use of information on who they are, what they do, and what they buy. Advances in information technology have allowed the generation, storage, retrieval, processing, and analysis of enormous amounts of information. This increased capability has been accompanied by an increased potential for ethical abuses. As with any tool, the more powerful it is, the more responsible one has to be in using it.

Companies collecting information on individuals have a responsibility not only for safeguarding it once they receive it but also to make sure that the information is accurate when they receive it. For example, people's lives can be affected dramatically by a clerk's mistake in entering credit information into a credit bureau's computer. The creation of large databases containing personal information from tax records to commercial transactions to medical and bank records has increased the likelihood of fraud. The use of telecommunications to send personal information (e.g., credit card numbers) through the airways and over networks with thousands of nodes has left open the possibility of abuse.

The dilemma of balancing the right to know versus the right to privacy is often faced in organizations where customer transactions are monitored closely (e.g., banking and stock exchange transactions, eavesdropping on reservation agents) and where employees use E-mail intensively (Business Brief 11–4 illustrates a case in point). Management needs to address this dilemma by drafting policies to protect the rights of the company and of the individuals, and it needs to understand that violations of these policies can lead to potential financial losses from lawsuits.

Another ethical dilemma is the balancing of improvements in productivity and efficiency versus dehumanizing the workplace. This dilemma is slightly different; it is not about the violation of privacy but about trying to offer employees meaningful and interesting jobs whenever possible. Information technology can enable the empowerment of employees at all levels of the organization by providing liberal access to the data they need to make decisions. Information technology can also enormously increase productivity. However, information technology can render certain activities highly tedious, and organizational efficiency is negatively affected by drops in job satisfaction (job dissatisfaction is accompanied by a drop in motivation and an increase in absenteeism and turnover).

BUSINESS BRIEF 11-4 FROM HER LIPS TO A THOUSAND EARS: A VOICE-MAIL TALE

The hottest tip on Wall Street in the past two weeks isn't about the next takeover or corporate coup—it's about The Message.

It comes from an unknown New York woman who had the misfortune to reach the answering machine of her lawyer friend Steven—or Stephen—instead of him. Her recorded message is a startlingly graphic, ribald review of the wild date she had the night before.

Whether her kiss-and-tell-all is real or well-crafted hoax, it has triggered a kind of chain letter meets gossip mill meets urban myth, an inevitable outcome when phone sex meets phone mail in the Digital Age. Stephen somehow copied The Message to his voice mail at work and forwarded it to a friend, who forwarded it to someone else, who forwarded it to still more users of ever more voice-mail systems. Those with voice mail who received it could copy it and send it to as many people as they chose.

In a matter of days, the woman's tawdry tale had circulated to hundreds of eager eavesdroppers—traders at Goldman, Sachs & Co., Donaldson, Lufkin & Jenrette, and other Wall Street firms; lawyers at white-shoe law firms; producers at CBS News and CBS Sports; executives at the Showtime and Comedy Central cable channels; entertainment types in Hollywood, and Beltway types in Washington, D.C.

It's easy to circulate a message within a company, but most rival brands of voice mail are incompatible with one another. To send The Message intercompany, people call up a friend's mailbox, then "conference in" to their second line to tap their own mailbox and play the message. And the beat goes on.

Most of the "forwarders" are, of course, men. On Wall Street, it seems, boys will *always* be boys. And because voice-mail systems let a sender tack a note to the start of a forwarded item, the Message often arrives with its own telltale litany of voyeuristic senders.

By the time one version reached this newspaper, 21 people had attached their personal introductions.

Therein lies the digital moral: Your private gossip can belong to everyone, anyone, when it can be digitized and diced and copied and forwarded, all in seconds with the press of a few Touch-Tone buttons.

Those who have heard The Message can't get enough. "It's great, it's just so classic. It's changed my life. It gets richer and richer every time I listen to it," says a female fan.

Many debate whether the woman's tale is simply too Penthouse Forum-ish to be true. Most men firmly believe it's real; some women think it's simply voice-mail-porn and question why any real woman would talk like that to a man. Other listeners don't much care.

QUESTIONS

1. Do you think there is an ethical dilemma here? If yes, describe it. If no, state why not.
2. Do you believe that the company where the message was sent to first is vulnerable to a legal suit?
3. Propose a set of policies to prevent this type of incident from happening again.

SOURCE: Adapted from Dennis Kneale, "From Her Lips to a Thousand Ears: A Voice-Mail Tale," *The Wall Street Journal*, June 2, 1995, p. B1. Reprinted by permission of *The Wall Street Journal*,

To address the potential vulnerability where information technology negatively affects the satisfaction of employees, management needs to remember that employee satisfaction should be a top priority and strategic objective since, in most businesses, customer satisfaction is difficult to achieve without employee satisfaction (and practically impossible in service-oriented companies).

STRATEGIES FOR MINIMIZING RISK

To address competitive, operational, and ethical vulnerabilities, we propose five broad-based strategies: the appropriate positioning of the I/T function within the organization, the development of an effective project management capability, the creation of a group to monitor emerging technologies, the development of a backup and recovery plan, and the creation of written policies to address ethical concerns. We discuss each of them in detail next.

Positioning the I/T Organization

One of the risks in managing I/T is the underfunding of a critically strategic I/T project because of a lack of understanding of its importance to the firm by the manager or management team overseeing the I/T function. Information technology is more strategically important in some industries than others and, within those industries, more critical to certain firms than others. The positioning of the I/T function within the organization [who (at what level?) and where (what functional area?) it reports to] should vary with the strategic importance of I/T to the organization. For example, the more strategic I/T is to the organization, the higher the reporting status of its director should be. The more dependent a critical success factor of the business is on I/T, the closer the I/T function should be to the department responsible for managing that critical factor.

For example, when Otis Elevators decided that they wanted to redeploy their I/T efforts toward after-sales service from the more traditional accounting applications, the firm moved the I/T function from reporting to the vice president of finance to the vice president of marketing. The proper alignment of the I/T function to the strategic goals of the firm, and therefore its placement in the organizational chart, is key in setting clear priorities, objectives, and performance measures for the I/T group.

Effective Project Management

Another common risk in managing I/T is the late delivery of information systems projects and/or the delivery of information systems with a reduced functionality from the one originally promised (e.g., the system response time is slower, or some reports are not produced). Many I/T projects (some estimates range as high as 80 percent) are late and/or over budget. The reason for this very poor record is, in part, the fact that managing I/S development projects is a very demanding task and, in part, the fact that organizations use the same project management approach for all applications. Not all projects are the same, and therefore, they should not be managed in the same way.

As projects increase in complexity (i.e., scope, complexity, information richness, and required technology), so will their risk of failure. Accordingly, as the project increases in complexity, the expertise of the project manager should be higher, the attention from management should increase, and the mix of management tools (e.g., number of reviews, type of budgeting, level of scheduling) used to manage the project should vary. This approach—managing projects in terms of their particular characteristics—focuses on the critical aspects of a given project and on the specific strategies to address them. This contingency approach to project management allows a better utilization of the I/T department resources and skills.

Managing Emerging Technologies

One of the risks created by I/T is the threat of **emerging technologies,** or the possibility of a competitor achieving a great leap in performance by using a new technology. For example, an insurance company gained substantial market share in the life insurance business by giving its agents portable computers before any of its competitors did so. Agents were able to give a policy quote to a customer within

Higher education, including library services, provides a good example of how the continuous change in information technology offers new opportunities and uses. Photos courtesy of Garth Falkenberg/Stock Boston, Inc. (left), Bob Kramer/Stock Boston, Inc. (center), and Tony Stone Worldwide (right).

minutes in a face-to-face meeting (by using a combination of portable computers and expert systems) rather than days (the agent needed to go back to the office and compute the policy on the firm's mainframe).

The rapid advances in information technology result in continual changes to an organization's environment. The possibility always exists that new technology will be developed that could pose challenges and/or opportunities for an organization, ranging from threats to its entire existence to the development of a slightly better way to service customers. For example, the explosive dissemination of fax machines made FedEx discontinue its Zapmail service and incur a loss of two hundred million dollars.

Throughout this book we have provided numerous examples to illustrate this constant technological flux; a quick glance at current newspapers or business publications will provide more. So many changes are occurring, and at such a rapid pace, that it is literally impossible for most organizations to keep current. For this reason, more and more organizations are adding an emerging technologies group to their I/S departments.

The responsibilities of the emerging technology specialists include the following:

1. Monitoring the environment for technologies that have some potential to help or hurt the organization.
2. Evaluate selected new technologies to determine how they might best be employed.
3. Assist in the adoption and assimilation of new technologies into the organization.

In smaller companies these activities might be performed by one or two individuals on an informal basis; in larger organizations the group might contain 10 or more specialists.

Consider the use of information technology in higher education. In 1975, most of the interaction between students and mainframe computers was for learning computer programming, and many of the systems used computer card readers as input devices. By 1980, access to computer systems by students was largely through the use of dumb terminals attached to minicomputers or mainframes. Use of computers was more widespread, with some word processing and statistical analysis being performed. In 1985 personal computers became available, and many institutions had small labs providing limited access to students. The personal computers were generally not networked and were used primarily for word processing, spreadsheet applications, and statistical analysis. By 1990 labs of networked personal computers were widely available, and many students also owned personal computers. High-end workstations with three-dimensional graphics capabilities were common in most engineering and computer science departments. Electronic mail was widely used, and library facilities were beginning to provide access to on-line searches of abstract databases and related information. Some computer display systems were being used in the classroom, primarily for demonstrating computer use.

By 1995, most students leaving high school had some familiarity with information technology, and for some it was considered a necessary tool. CD-ROM technology was widely available, both in computer labs on campus and on the personal computers being purchased by students and their families. Most educational institutions were providing access to the Internet, facilitating communication and information exchanges using a range of data and information. Library information systems had improved significantly, providing expanded options for computerized information search and retrieval, revolutionizing the way papers were researched, and raising brand-new copyright issues. Document scanners and improved document-processing systems had expanded the capabilities and expectations for student assignments. Presentation systems were being used widely by instructors and students. Videoconferencing systems were being used for distance education.

For individuals within these institutions of higher education, however, the continual transitions to new technology are not without problems. Many institutions lack the funds to continually upgrade their information technology infrastructures and face difficult choices on a regular basis: What component of the infrastructure do we upgrade first? When do we actually do the upgrading—before or after the introduction of a new generation of products? Even those institutions with sufficient funds find they run into difficulties; employees resist continually having to climb learning curves. (I finally figured out how to use this word-processing package, and now you want me to learn a new one?) Students purchase systems their first year of college that are outdated by the time they graduate (if not before), and professors need to adapt their assignments to a variety of software packages and versions.

Other difficulties facing higher education institutions in the implementation of I/T include the organizational culture—that is, traditional autonomy of instructors with respect to how and what they teach—and the decentralization of I/T responsibilities to academic departments. Indeed, some instructors sometimes resist changing their courses to accommodate the use of I/T. Also, the move to local area networks (LANs) takes the responsibility for maintaining the LANs away from the centralized I/T department in the university and puts it into the hands of the individual academic and administrative departments, often under the control of employees who do not have the training or expertise to adequately support the systems. This transfer of responsibility to people that do not have the necessary experience has resulted in frequent network crashes, apparently vindicating those who argued that too much reliance on I/T is not a good idea.

Furthermore, just having access to I/T does not mean it will be used appropriately or efficiently. Managers are dismayed when they find highly paid employees using personal computers as expensive toys, spending valuable time playing computer games and "surfing the Net." Inefficient uses of I/T are less obvious. For example, an employee who only knows a small subset of the features and functions of a specific application (such as a spreadsheet program) may take much longer to perform a task than they would if they better understood the available functionality of the software package.

The example of the uses of information technology in higher education is representative of what has happened in many other organizational contexts. The adoption and integration of new technologies is a serious issue that has to be continuously addressed. The management of emerging technologies is essentially the management of change within the organization. Although an emerging technology group can help, what is required for organizations to keep pace with new I/T and its uses is an organization composed of individuals who are all willing and able to continually learn.

Backup and Recovery Plans

Twenty years ago, few companies had a disciplined strategy for data and hardware backup. As recently as 10 years ago, many companies did not consider the cost of an I/T "disaster" worth the investment in a **disaster recovery plan** and the necessary backup facilities. As industries have become more dependent on computerized processes and data, recognition has increased that protection of these computer resources is a high management priority. Indeed, the disaster recovery industry today represents billions of dollars and is expected to grow at a 25 percent annual rate throughout the 1990s.

Why are so many companies developing disaster recovery plans? Next to personnel, a company's most important resource is information. Businesses are increasingly dependent on the uninterrupted flow of information, and thus, effective management of I/S resources is becoming a critical strategic factor in competition and customer retention.

In deciding how much to spend on its disaster recovery plan, a firm should have an understanding of the consequences of an interruption of information services. For example, the average company will lose 2 percent to 3 percent of gross sales within eight days of a sustained computer outage. Furthermore, the average company experiencing an outage of more than 10 days will never fully recover, with 50 percent going out of business within five years.

To many people, disaster recovery planning means planning for the restoration of mainframe operation following a disaster. Before, plans dealt primarily with replacing hardware and were often confined to the data-processing department of a company. Today, disaster recovery is concentrated around the recovery of all business systems, including personal computers (PCs) and local area networks (LANs), since an increasingly large percentage of vital business data are stored on PC hard drives and diskettes.

Experts now believe that effective off-site storage of critical data is the single most important determinant of successful business recovery following a disaster. However, off-site storage planning requires a multistage process, which includes the following:

- Analyzing and classifying data.
- Reviewing existing backup procedures.

Natural disasters are an all-too-common occurrence, and organizations need to protect their I/S resources against such disasters. Photo courtesy of Tony Stone Worldwide.

- Selecting a storage vendor.
- Formalizing the schedules for routine removal of data to storage.

If a company has no policy on records retention and classification, deciding what data belong in secure storage may be a Herculean task (especially with the proliferation of PCs and LANs). However, without a program to back up software and data, all the other logistics, strategies, and plans of disaster recovery are meaningless.

In developing a business-driven (as opposed to a data-processing) disaster recovery plan, a company must identify the functions that are critical to its mission and the applications that support those functions. Strategies for systems backup are based on an analysis of critical applications, minimum acceptable hardware configurations, number of users, and business function requirements. Critical applications are those that facilitate key business functions for which alternative performance methods are unacceptable or unavailable. Once these vital applications have been identified, the systems and minimal hardware configurations necessary to support them can be designed. Also, a list of the personnel needed to operate the business at emergency levels needs to be defined.

The need for disaster recovery planning is usually self-evident to I/T professionals but less so to general managers. Convincing management to shoulder the costs of a disaster recovery capability can often be a greater challenge than the technical problems posed by the plan itself. One of the issues in convincing management is the difficulty to cost justify such a plan. Although the costs of facility damages (e.g., hardware, office equipment) are easy to assess and the costs of rebuilding the system can be approximated quite closely, the costs of lost data, lost business, and loss of customer goodwill are difficult to assess.

There are a variety of strategies for backing up the information systems capabilities of an organization. Some of these are discussed in the following paragraphs.

Replacement. A **replacement strategy** is no more than "making do" until a new or comparable mainframe and/or network can be installed. Once installed, I/S personnel would load software and data that have been backed up on a regular basis, and users would frantically input interim data until they are up to date. This can be an effective plan in an environment where there are no critical (to business survival) systems.

Cold Site. A company-owned off-site facility without a mainframe or main information processing machine that is able to serve as an alternate data-processing center is known as a **cold site.** It is not used (as such) until disaster strikes. When disaster strikes, a new mainframe computer is moved to the site. This alternative also assumes the business can wait for the replacement to be operational. There are two variations on the cold site strategy: the joint cold site, which is identical to the cold site except that a number of businesses share costs through leasing the same facility, and the mobile cold site, where the facility is moved to the customer's location.

Reciprocal Backup Agreement. Two companies with similar hardware configurations (with spare processing capacity) agree to backup each other's critical applications in a **reciprocal backup agreement.** If disaster strikes company A, company B would allow A to restore its applications on B's hardware. Problems include the possibility that both systems are affected by the same disaster, disruption of the accommodating mainframe's applications, and mutually agreeable testing time.

Service Bureau. A software vendor who offers emergency processing services is a **service bureau.** Such vendors typically market this service to companies without their own computer systems and software (user terminals are installed in client offices, and jobs are submitted to the vendor CPU via data communications).

Hot Site. A freestanding, fully equipped data-processing facility to which one or more companies (with compatible hardware) subscribe is known as a **hot site.** Machine time is available to subscribers to test recovery procedures.

Redundant System. An identical operational data center (hopefully, in a different geographic location) is known as a **redundant system.** This strategy ensures full recovery (provided both facilities are not destroyed), but it is also the most expensive.

After deciding to undertake a disaster recovery plan, the company must determine whether to develop the plan in-house or to rely on **outsourcing** (hire an outside firm or consultant to perform this task). There are both advantages and disadvantages to outsourcing. The choice is highly dependent on the available resources and expertise within the company.

A critical aspect of disaster recovery is an emergency management plan that provides for the top-down coordination of recovery tasks and that identifies a disaster recovery coordinator. The disaster recovery coordinator needs to designate the personnel in charge of implementing the recovery activities and tasks, work with

BUSINESS BRIEF 11-5 A FRENCH BANK'S TRIAL BY FIRE

Although a fire destroyed its $300 million headquarters in Paris last weekend, Crédit Lyonnais was able to resume operations within a few hours.

Had it been unable to do so, industry analysts said, the loss of trading and goodwill could have been worse than the loss of the building itself. Following bombings at the World Trade Center in New York and in the City of London, companies have become acutely aware of the need to have back-up facilities.

Many Crédit Lyonnais dealers moved into a back-up trading room outside Paris, and others went to London. Others of the more than 2,000 staff moved into another building owned by the bank across the street.

Not everything went smoothly. Because it had nowhere for them to work, the bank told several hundred employees to stay home for six days. They demonstrated at the gutted building, fearing they would not be paid. But an agreement was reached to pay employees their full salaries.

"The name of the game is to have a contingency plan," said Alex Cheeseman of Hongkong & Shanghai Banking Corp., which was hit by a bomb in London in 1994. "Always imagine that the worst-case scenario is worse than you think. We would never have thought of a 1,000-pound bomb taking out half a mile of city."

A bombing in 1993 made it acutely aware of security, so the bank was prepared for the 1994 explosion and ended up by losing nothing except its physical premises. All computer data were backed up at another location. Valuable documents were locked in fireproof safes.

Planning for a disaster, she added, means setting priorities and making sure that staff know what to do. The first priority is to re-establish telephone connections, something that Crédit Lyonnais quickly had in hand at a building across the street from its former headquarters. Customers are understanding and supportive at first. Mrs. Cheeseman said, but they expect everything to be back to normal within 10 days.

U.S. banks are required to have disaster plans. "We have had a lot of horrible natural disasters—hurricanes, earthquakes," said John Hall, a spokesman for the American Bankers Association. "It's essential that banks have recovery plans in place because so much else depends on their being up and running from the start."

The main unanswered question at Crédit Lyonnais was whether damage was caused by fire or water to the 7,000 strong boxes in the basement of the bank, many of which are thought to hold paintings and art works. Although the vault is buried under tons of rubble, Jean Peyrelevade, the bank's chairman, said it seemed that the fireproof strong boxes were undamaged.

QUESTION

1. What lessons can the Crédit Lyonnais learn from the disaster?

SOURCE: Adapted from Barry James, "A French Bank's Trial by Fire," the *International Herald Tribune,* May 11–12, 1996, p. 13.

functional and business processes managers and teams, and identify the sequence of recovery tasks (see Business Brief 11–5). Another key element in ensuring a plan's validity is to test it. Testing also serves as a training exercise and helps to reveal any shortcomings with the plan. The best way to check the readiness and effectiveness of the personnel, programs, and plans is to do a surprise simulation of a disaster.

In determining what a given company's recovery requirements are, a business must determine its **window of vulnerability** (the length of time a business can survive the loss of its critical applications). Industries have varying degrees of strategic dependence on information systems that correlates with the duration of their maximum allowable downtime. One cost-justification strategy is to assign a dollar value to an hour of downtime (e.g., hourly wage multiplied by the number of users plus any lost business during that hour) and compare it with the costs of running the disaster recovery plan. For example, spending $50,000 on a recovery program that brings all critical systems back within 24 hours for a business that loses an estimated $12,000 per day may not be cost effective.

BUSINESS BRIEF 11-6 A CLEAN BILL OF HEALTH: IBM'S I-WAY IMMUNE SYSTEM

Computer viruses once spread slowly, via tainted diskettes. But over the Internet, a virus can infect millions of PCs in hours. Now, IBM has devised a software "disinfectant" modeled on the human immune system.

Each subscriber to IBM's AntiVirus system—mainly administrators of local area networks—will have a LAN-monitoring PC that acts like a vigilant white blood cell. When the PC spots a virus on the LAN, it whisks the infected file off to computers at IBM's research labs. If the computers recognize the virus, they will zip back an antidote. Beginning next year, when a new virus crops up, they will be able to "culture" it and use artificial intelligence programs to concoct a cure. Says AntiVirus head Steve R. White, the system can "detect new viruses better than our human experts."

QUESTION

1. Antivirus software is one effective way of defending the integrity of the data and software programs of a company. What are others?

SOURCE: O. Port, "IBM's I-Way Immune System," *Business Week*, International Edition, April 8, 1996, p. 59. Reprinted by special permission, copyright © 1996 by the McGraw-Hill Companies.

Phoenix Home Life Insurance combined data center operations and business considerations in its disaster recovery plans. Its goal was to bring back critical applications within a couple of days and then to recover and add applications as space and resources permit. Managers at Hallmark Cards analyzed whether a redundant data center would be worth the speed-to-recovery cost. They concluded it was not strategically necessary, realizing that systems could be down for up to a week and that data could be lost on a given day. They opted for a hot site, backing up critical applications with a system management facilities software package.

Disasters are not all due to natural causes (i.e., earthquakes, floods, fires). Companies have to protect themselves from vandalism, terrorism, and internal sabotage. A major source of computer systems failures is the **virus.** Computer viruses are computer programs that take over the operating system of the host computer and create havoc by generating commands to destroy or modify data and instructions. Viruses are transmitted electronically by downloading information from networks (e.g., the Internet) or from using data or programs stored on an infected diskette. Many companies are developing and implementing stringent policies to reduce the risk of infection. A whole industry has sprung up in the last few years to develop antiviral products that counteract a variety of viruses. Viruses are becoming increasingly intelligent and are able to mutate just like biological viruses; fortunately, the products aimed at neutralizing viruses are also increasing in sophistication (as described in Business Brief 11–6).

Establish and Enforce Written Policies on Ethics and the Use of I/T

When social and ethical issues are addressed, one important consideration is obviously the application of prevailing federal and state laws and statutes. For this reason, most organizations use legal advice to interpret laws and determine how to comply with them. Being aware of and in compliance with laws is important, but it certainly won't cover all issues. First, many laws related to social and ethical issues are ambiguous and often open to various interpretations. Second, the continuous development of new technologies and applications of technology affects existing

TABLE 11-1 Ethical Concerns in Data Management

	Data Storage	*Data Transfer*	*Data Transformation*
Access rights	What customer and employee data should we collect? How long should we store it? Who owns it?	Who can see it? Who can profit from its use? Should permission be obtained to use it?	What data recombinations are permitted? Who profits from employee developed applications?
Stewardship responsibilities	How is accuracy verified?	How do we prevent unauthorized access?	How is alteration or recombination controlled?

SOURCE: Adapted from Cash et al. (1994).

laws and social mores on an ongoing basis (e.g., consider the ethical issues that have been generated by surrogate motherhood). It takes time for society to develop a position about an ethical dilemma and to become aware that there is a deficiency in the law (if there is one); it takes even longer for a law to change. Because of this lag in laws catching up with moral values, organizations need to develop corporate policies to handle situations in which existing laws are vague or inadequate.

The responsibilities of organizational management concerning ethical issues can be broken into two broad categories; **information access** and **information stewardship.** The fundamental issue concerning *information access* is, who owns data created by or about individuals? In the United States, the law on ownership is ambiguous. For example, under current legal interpretation, when a customer makes a credit card transaction, the information about the transaction is owned by the credit card company. With that interpretation, the credit card company has the right to grant or revoke access to the information; for example, they can sell customer lists to third parties without the explicit consent of the customer.

Another issue is that of the recombination of data. Recombination means taking data from two different sources and combining them to form new information, in a way that was not originally intended. For example, combining data from income tax returns with data from records of divorced or separated parents who have refused to pay court-ordered child support allows authorities to concentrate on those who have the ability to pay.

Information stewardship involves additional responsibilities that fall on the organization (or individual) that stores, transfers, or manipulates data concerning other individuals. Here we are interested in such questions as, who is responsible for maintaining the accuracy of the data, and who should profit from information systems applications developed by employees? Under current U.S. law, an organization has the right to monitor their employees or to monitor electronic mail messages carried over systems provided by the organization. Employee medical histories are considered personal, however, and the employer has to guarantee their confidentiality. Table 11-1 lists some typical questions that management needs to address when considering ethical issues.

Some of these access and stewardship issues can be addressed through the implementation of information systems. For example, data accuracy can be improved through various error-checking features of database management systems and enhanced through even more specific software used for data entry. Data accuracy can also ensure data security and make tampering impossible or at least

TABLE 11–2 How Managers Address Ethical Issues

Stakeholder analysis	Identify all parties with a stake in the issue. Who will be affected by this data access decision? What are the consequences to each party of data access and disclosure?
Goal-based analysis	Select the option that promises the greatest good for the greatest number. Assess costs and benefits, including noneconomic factors (happiness, general welfare).
Rights-based analysis	Identify and/or articulate specific legal, institutional, and human rights to privacy, free speech, and other information-related values. Identify specific data storage, transfer, and transformation decisions that could violate those rights.
Duty-based analysis	Identify basic ethical duties, such as honesty, fairness, and doing no harm. Does this action violate any fundamental ethical duties? Are there alternative actions that do not do so?

SOURCE: Kallman and Grillo, 1996.

traceable. In many cases, however, it is necessary to supplement the programs with human procedures and audits.

Consider, for example, a bank that provides certificates of deposit (CDs) for customers. Assume that the bank records the pertinent information on a written form and that, at the end of the day, an employee enters data from the CD input forms into the information system that maintains data related to CDs. The bank wants to ensure that there are no errors (unintentional or otherwise) with these data; they could lose money if, for example, a $10,000 CD was inadvertently entered as $10,000,000. For that reason, a different employee checks the data on the input forms against a listing of all the new CDs that were created. To further reduce the possibility of error (or fraud), the bank will have someone else randomly select transactions (such as the issuance of new CDs) for auditing. The bank employees will be required to produce documentation to prove that all aspects of the selected transactions were correct and completely documented.

As mentioned before, one important way for organizations to reduce vulnerabilities related to social and ethical concerns is to establish, and enforce, corporate policies that address these concerns. For example, a company might establish a policy that states that no information concerning an employee (even telephone number and address) will be released without the employee's consent, unless the company receives a court order to do so. Furthermore, these policies need to be clearly communicated to all employees. Having a corporate policy that states that electronic mail should not be used for personal communications will not be effective unless everyone within the company is aware of it and unless audits are performed regularly. The policies need to be clear and consistent and must apply to all employees equally.

Earlier in this book we introduced a framework that could be used by managers to help address ethical issues. The framework involves four different perspectives that can be adopted to view an ethical dilemma: stakeholder analysis, goal-based analysis, rights-based analysis, and duty-based analysis. Table 11–2 provides a brief description of each. From the perspective of managing information systems, it is important to note that information systems are inherently flexible; they can be built and modified to support and reinforce organizational policies and culture. Once

FIGURE 11–3 An Overall Management Approach to I/T Development

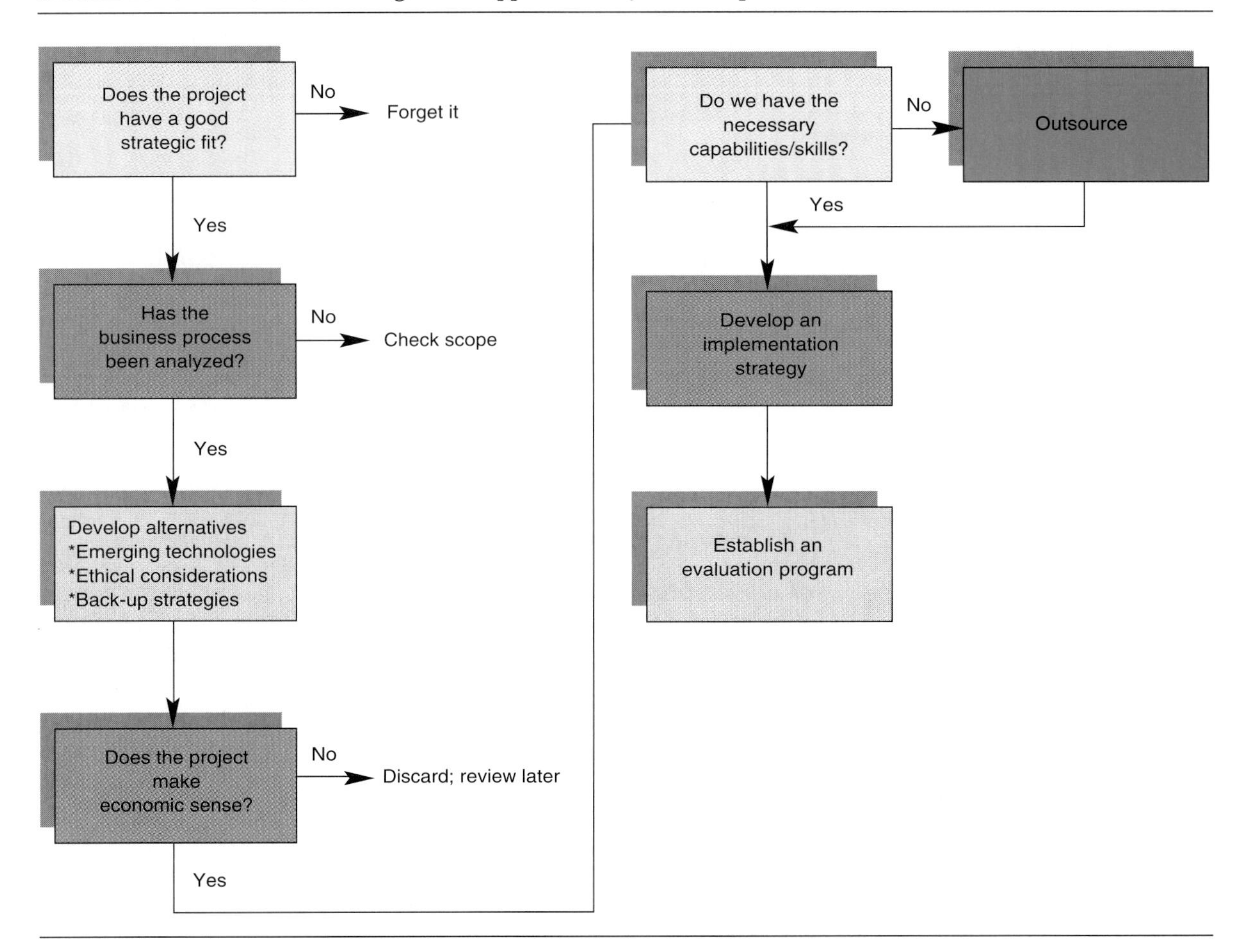

again, first we need to decide what we are trying to accomplish (e.g., reduce vulnerabilities from ethical and social concerns) and then decide how best to use information systems to accomplish those goals.

An Overall Management Methodology

The concepts described in this module of the book can be synthesized into the flowchart shown in Figure 11–3, providing us with an overview of the responsibilities and process of managing the information systems function.

The first question that one needs to ask when considering whether or not an information system should be developed is whether the system is aligned with a business goal. If there is no strategic fit, then the project should not be considered further. If the project is considered to be aligned with important business goals, then the second question to ask is whether the business process, of which the system will be a part, has been analyzed for improvement. If the answer is no, then the project scope should be reviewed to make sure that the system to be developed will not constrain future changes in the process. If the answer is yes (i.e., the information system will be supporting a business process that has been analyzed and possibly redesigned), then one can proceed to develop alternative designs to implement the system.

The alternative designs need to include backup and recovery contingency plans and capabilities. These alternatives are first reviewed using ethical criteria and then put through a financial analysis using return on investment (ROI), net present value, and payback criteria. The alternatives that are financially viable are then analyzed in terms of whether the organization has the expertise, capabilities, and skills to develop them. If the answer is no and the organization does not have the necessary expertise, then outsourcing should be considered. If the decision is to go ahead with the project, whether internally or externally, then an implementation strategy needs to be agreed upon. Finally, an evaluation program needs to be in place to make sure that the goals of the system are achieved and continuously improved.

SUMMARY

As organizations become more dependent on information systems, they also become more vulnerable to systems problems and failures. Hopper Specialty Company illustrates a typical problem system . . . a warehouse management system that was full of errors. Although the system didn't crash completely, its poor performance caused Hopper Specialty to provide poor service to their customers, and eventually the company suffered a severe decline in sales.

Information systems are important corporate resources. Organizations need to consider and treat data, knowledge, and information systems with the same care and attention they show to other corporate resources, such as employees and financial capital.

The functions performed by the information systems department differ from organization to organization; there is no standard structure. The key to determining an appropriate structure is to first determine the important functions, roles, and responsibilities that I/T has to fulfill and then determine how best to organize those responsibilities. Because of the dynamic nature of the information systems field, organizations need to review the I/S department structure on a regular basis and modify it as necessary.

Organizations encounter numerous risks with respect to information systems and information technology. These risks can be classified under the headings of competitive vulnerabilities, operational vulnerabilities, and social and ethical vulnerabilities. Several general strategies to address these vulnerabilities include (*a*) the proper positioning of the I/S organization within the overall organizational structure; (*b*) the effective project management of I/T projects; (*c*) the identification, integration, and management of emerging technologies; (*d*) the development of detailed backup and disaster recovery plans; and (*e*) the establishment and enforcement of written corporate policies on ethics and the use of I/T.

KEY CONCEPTS AND TERMS

KEY CONCEPTS

- Information systems are an important corporate resource, requiring close managerial attention. (358)
- Planning for information systems needs to be consistent with corporate business plans. (362)
- Clear plans and policies are essential for reducing organizational vulnerabilities associated with information systems. (379)
- Organizational vulnerabilities associated with information systems can be classified into competitive, operational, and ethical vulnerabilities. (368)

KEY TERMS

chargeback system (367)
chief information officer (364)
cold site (377)
competitive vulnerability (368)
corporate resources (358)
data (as a corporate resource) (359)
data management (360)
disaster recovery plan (375)
emerging technologies (372)
ethical vulnerability (370)
hot site (377)
information access (380)
information center (364)
information stewardship (380)

knowledge (as a corporate resource) (360)
knowledge management (361)
operational vulnerability (369)
outsourcing (377)
reciprocal backup agreement (377)
redundant system (377)
replacement strategy (377)
risk management (368)
risk (368)
service bureau (377)
virus (379)
window of vulnerability (378)

REFERENCES

Berman, K. "Crisis Planning Critical to Survival, Bank Expert Say." *Business Insurance*, February 1989, p. 25.

Butler, J. "How to Stay in Business when a Disaster Strikes: Data Center Disaster Recovery Extending to Schemes for Recovering the Business Systems Management." *Software Magazine*, August 1992, p. 48.

Cash, J., R. Eccles, N. Nohria, and R. Nolan. *Building the Information-Age Organization: Structure, Control, and Information Technologies.* Burr Ridge, IL: Richard D. Irwin, 1994.

Gentile, M., and J. Sviokla. "New Guidelines for Dealing with Data." *Information Technology Quarterly*, Summer 1990.

Geyelin, M. "Doomsday Device: How an NCR System for Inventory Turned into a Virtual Sabateur." *The Wall Street Journal*, August 8, 1994, p. 1.

Goodhue, D., J. Quillard, and J. Rockart. "Managing the Data Resource: A Contingency Perspective." *MIS Quarterly*, vol. 12 (3), September 1988, pp. 373–92.

Kallman, E., and J. Grillo. *Ethical Decision Making and Information Technology: An Introduction with Cases.* 2nd ed. New York: Mitchell McGraw-Hill, 1996.

Kantor, J. *Managing with Information.* 4th ed. Englewood Cliffs, NJ: Prentice Hall, 1992.

IBM Midrange Users Newsletter, published by IBM's Branch Office.

Toigo, J. W. *Disaster Recovery Planning: Managing Risk & Catastrophe in Information Systems*, New Jersey: Yourdon Press Computing Series, 1989.

CONNECTIVE CASE: Pollution Solutions (C) When It Rains . . .

Pam Linton, CEO of Pollution Solutions (PSOV), held her head in a gesture of pure frustration. "What are we going to do?" she asked rhetorically.

THE SYSTEM

Pollution Solutions had spent years in developing their waste-tracking system; it had grown with the company, being modified as needed. At this point the company had come to rely quite a bit on the system; it contained all relevant information on their customers and, more importantly, all hazardous waste materials they had transported, treated, or disposed of.

PSOV was required by law to have an "operating" record of all hazardous waste transactions with which they were associated, and the record had to be current to within 24 hours. If an inspector from the Environmental Protection Agency (EPA) or the Department of Transportation (DOT) conducted a surprise audit and found that PSOV was not in compliance with their operating permits, PSOV could be heavily penalized. The penalties could range from a notice of violation to being forced out of business. Heavy fines and prison sentences were also feasible.

THE CRASH

Late last night, a disaster occurred. During a thunderstorm, lightning struck (literally); the power surge heavily damaged PSOV's computer systems. As Pam surveyed the damage with her sales manager, Craig Senzel, she had a terrible sinking feeling in the pit of her stomach. The computer system appeared to be completely inoperable. They were unable to get any kind of response from it; not even a blinking light on the screen of the main server.

Pam turned to her sales manager. "Craig, please see what you can do with this. Call the store where we got the hardware and see what they can suggest. If this system is dead, maybe we can rent one or something for a while until we decide what we are going to do. Do you have copies of the software and data?"

Craig looked somewhat sheepish. "I've got copies of most of the stuff, Pam, but they aren't very current. I think we have made some changes to the programs since I last made copies. Maybe our software consultant will be able to help. I'll call him right away. I'm afraid we are going to have to recreate some of the data, however. I don't think we have made any backups for the last two weeks or so. We'll have to dig through our paper records and recreate the electronic files."

Pam nodded her head. "Okay, you start working on getting replacement hardware and getting the programs running. I'll organize the office staff to start pulling the files and getting everything ready to input once the system is up and running again. We'll also have to put some manual procedures in place for our current transactions, for the time being."

"Craig, we've got to get moving on this. If we get audited before we get the system running again, it could be rough. We could probably recreate everything with our paper copies, but it would be a real hassle, and it certainly wouldn't look very professional. Also, if any customers call, stall them. We obviously can't have any customer audits until we have the system running again." Pam paused for moment. "I suppose this means we won't be able to perform any of our office functions, like updating the general ledger, as well."

"I'm afraid so, Pam. We're pretty much shut down."

Pam turned to head back to her office. "If we survive this, Craig, I want to make certain that nothing like this can ever happen again."

Case Questions

1. Discuss the vulnerabilities faced by PSOV demonstrated by this case.
2. Describe in detail what your suggestion would be to Pam Linton to avoid a similar situation in the future.

IT'S YOUR TURN — END OF CHAPTER MATERIALS

REVIEW QUESTIONS

1. Identify and briefly describe two competitive vulnerabilities faced by organizations. How would you suggest that an organization reduce their vulnerabilities in this regard?
2. Identify and briefly describe two distinct operational vulnerabilities faced by organizations. How would you suggest that an organization reduce their vulnerabilities in this regard?
3. Identify and briefly describe two distinct social or ethical vulnerabilities faced by organizations. How would you suggest that an organization reduce their vulnerabilities in this regard?
4. What factors should be considered when determining the structure for the information systems function within an organization?
5. What are the different recovery plan options?
6. What are some of the issues facing an organization when managing knowledge?
7. What are some of the challenges facing an organization when managing emerging technologies?
8. Describe the steps that need to be followed in developing an information systems plan.
9. List the strategies that organizations can implement to minimize the risks posed by the use of I/T.
10. Describe the importance of each step in the overall I/T management methodology presented in this chapter.

DISCUSSION QUESTIONS

1. The Hopper Specialty Company argues that it was the Warehouse Management system that caused a decline in their business. Take the side of the software vendor; present an argument for other factors that could have caused this decline.
2. Explain what a chargeback system is. Provide a list of pros and cons of using chargeback mechanisms. When should they be used?
3. Give three examples each of the types of data, knowledge, and information systems that should be considered as precious corporate resources for a bank.
4. Give an example of an industry or a company (other than the travel agent example given in the text) that is highly vulnerable to changes in I/T.

5. Give an example of an industry or a company that would be hurt significantly by the loss of their I/T capability for a couple of days.

6. Describe three computer viruses that have attacked computer systems in the last few years.

GROUP ASSIGNMENT

Identify and contact a company of your interest (preferably in your community) that uses information technology to support its operations. Interview a manager about the impact of their I/T system crashing. List the actual costs of recovering the system, for example, the costs associated with bringing a new system in or a technician to fix it, the impact on customer goodwill, the effect of lost sales, and so forth. Describe the backup systems (e.g., who backs up what, how often, and where it is stored) and recovery plans of the company. Suggest improvements if possible (or draw some plans for them if they do not have any).

Create a three-slide computer-driven presentation. One should describe the impact on the business of losing their I/T capability; the second slide should present the policies and strategies the company has in place to recover from a crash or disaster; the third slide should present your suggested improvements.

APPLICATION ASSIGNMENTS

1. Go to a computer store and get information about various antivirus systems. If possible, try three different antivirus systems. Write a short essay describing how they compare (how they work, how fast they are, how many viruses they can deal with, etc.).

2. Do a computerized bibliographical search on litigated cases of breach of privacy and information technology since 1990. Create a graph describing the number of cases per year since 1990.

CASE ASSIGNMENT Disaster Recovery at Vermont Mutual

Wednesday morning, March 11, began as a normal day in Vermont's capital, Montpelier. Soon thereafter, normalcy went out the window. At about 8:30 A.M. Sheryl Crowley, manager of IS operations at the Vermont Mutual Insurance Company, was driving to work. She found that two of the three bridges that provided commuter access to Montpelier were closed. Sheryl crossed the last bridge to find that water had risen to cover her car's tires. As she entered Vermont Mutual's parking lot on State Street, she was immediately notified by the public security officer to move her car to higher ground. When she returned to the building, some cars in the lot were flooded and floating, and the basement of the building was taking water in. The company's minicomputer, an IBM AS/400, was located on the first floor.

When she entered the building, the operations staff had already powered the computer down and moved all of their computer backup tapes to the second floor. In an effort to keep the water from entering the computer room, the staff piled boxes of paper at the computer room entrance. The water was rising so quickly they had to move to the next floor and were promptly told that they had to evacuate. Within two hours, State Street became a raging river.

THE COMPANY

Vermont Mutual Insurance Company was a medium-sized business employing approximately 200 people and was located in Vermont's state capital of Montpelier. The company was established in 1828, and in 1904 they acquired the Northern Security Insurance Company. Vermont Mutual was licensed in 13 states and served customers with a field organization in the New England states, as well as in South Carolina, Virginia, and Tennessee.

The main products Vermont Mutual offered to its customers included homeowners' insurance, liability insurance for commercial businesses, inland marine insurance, and insurance policies for personal items such as jewelry, tools, and cameras. In addition, Vermont Mutual introduced a new insurance policy called Personal Line, which provided dwelling insurance for people who rented their buildings out as apartments or business space. They also offered a guaranteed rate on some policies for three years, which exceeded the industry norm of one year.

IMPORTANCE OF INFORMATION SYSTEMS

For many of the end-user departments, the service and support of the information systems department (ISD) was essential to their daily operations. For example, the policy assembly supervisor used the AS/400 minicomputer and the high-speed laser printer for automation of all business pertaining to customer policy forms and mail-outs. Without the computer support of ISD, the policy assembly department would not be able to operate. Other areas would be adversely affected as well. Three of the most critical business functions that would be affected by loss or downtime of IS were billing, customer service, and policy administration. Billing to agents and customers was completely automated on the AS/400. Any interruption in the system would prevent billing of services provided by Vermont Mutual, which would restrict (or stop) cash flow to the company.

Highly reduced customer service was an additional problem that would be caused by an interrupted or damaged system. The database, which contained information about all customers and their insurance policies, was on the AS/400, and it would be difficult (or impossible) to answer demanding questions about claims and billing. Policy administration was equally affected, where provision of quotes on premiums to field agents was a much slower process when calculated manually. Each of these business functions was critical to the operation of Vermont Mutual, and significant cash flow problems and loss of current and potential customers could result if ISD was temporarily shut down or information was lost.

THE FLOOD

The events surrounding Montpelier's flood can be summarized as follows. An ice jam blocked the Winooski River and caused it to erupt over its banks during a rainstorm Wednesday morning, March 11. This caused extensive damage and disruption in the state capital's downtown area. Water got as high as six feet during the day on Montpelier's State Street, soaking cars up to their windshields and covering parking meters and park benches. It was the worst flood in the city since the devastating flood of 1927. Estimates of damage to businesses and personal property were into the tens of millions of dollars. Most business in the State House on Main Street came to a halt, and the State Legislature was not called into session. Fortunately, there were no serious injuries reported.

Flood waters began to recede shortly before dark on Wednesday, but not before knocking out an iron railroad bridge in the center of the city. Part of the ice jam that had plugged the Winooski River broke the iron bridge in half. The force of the water and ice left the steel rails bent and twisted and splintered the wooden ties. This appeared to be the flood's parting shot. Soon after the bridge broke, the Winooski River flowed freely, and the water that had been rushing down State Street all day began to subside.

By about 6 P.M., the center of State Street was no longer under water. Parking lots, lawns, and other areas that had been flooded were littered with huge ice chunks or debris that had been carried from upstream. The North Branch, which converges with the Winooski in Montpelier, had dropped 8 or 10 feet by 6:30 P.M. City officials, concerned about continuing safety hazards and potential looting, imposed a curfew on the downtown district Wednesday evening.

THE AFTERMATH

It was only in the early hours of March 12, around midnight, that a crew of Vermont Mutual employees were allowed to enter their offices to assess the damage and start pumping water from the basement. The water that had risen to a depth of one foot in the computer room had receded. Not only had their disk drives and CPU been under water, but all of their company forms were soaked and ruined. Backup of all applications and data was done daily, and luckily their backup tapes had been moved to the second floor or were already stored off-site. The AS/400 was a potential loss, and the Xerox laser printer was damaged beyond repair.

The decision looming ahead was to either repair the damage or replace everything. Crowley notified the vendor, IBM, to find out what the procedure was at this point. Since they leased the equipment, it was determined that the equipment would be replaced. A replacement system was put on order that Wednesday by the IBM representative. The IBM plant in Rochester, New York, began building a new AS/400 on Friday and worked three shifts around the clock.

In the meantime, Vermont Mutual transferred its operation to a Quality Inn nearby. Although they did not have a computer, all information was taken down manually to be entered into the computer when it was up and running. Telephone lines were temporarily set up to accommodate clients and agents. A team was assigned to clean up the damage caused by the flood. They began preparing the site so that work could be resumed at their headquarters on State Street as soon as possible. Accessories and supplies were reordered promptly to make sure the IS department could start running as soon as the new AS/400 was ready. The computer paper supplier had orders placed in advance for Vermont Mutual. They were able to ship new forms immediately, so there was no downtime as a result of lost forms.

On Monday, March 16, IBM completed the new AS/400 and was ready to ship. The system was shipped that night and arrived at the Burlington, Vermont, airport on Tuesday, March 17, at 12:55 P.M. The system was then delivered by truck to Montpelier. Three chief engineers had everything assembled and operational by 8:00 P.M. Vermont Mutual's information systems programming and operations staff worked around the clock to rebuild and restore applications and data. By Thursday afternoon, March 19, they were in partial production, with most of their users back on the system.

When the system was reloaded, only one application was missing. When the application was restored, it was discovered that two weeks of data were lost and had to be recovered manually. The loss was apparently due to a programming error by a staff member in one of the backup program procedures.

Sheryl commented, "The days spent cleaning up with our staff and other departments created a camaraderie that might have taken years to develop." Concerning their recovery, "100 percent recovery will be a process lasting for the next several months." She stated, "Even though we're 95 percent recovered today, the last 5 percent may take some time. You need to make sure that your backups are as good as you think they are and that you have a recovery plan that will really work in the event of any type of disaster. We have learned a lot from this experience."

DISASTER RECOVERY PLAN

Prior to coming to Vermont Mutual, Crowley was director of IS at Gifford Medical Center. Although uninterrupted IS operation was critical to the functioning of the hospital seven days per week, 24 hours per day, Gifford Medical had no disaster recovery plan in place. During her tenure at the hospital, Crowley had pushed unsuccessfully for the implementation of a disaster recovery plan. Vermont Mutual also had no disaster recovery plan in place, although Crowley had raised the issue repeatedly. The perception seemed to be that the resources required for recovery would be better spent on improving existing capabilities. Vermont Mutual had analyzed the possibility of a "hot site" location to test their recovery plan twice a year at a cost of approximately $1,200 per month for 24-hour access, or a flat rate of $9,000 per year for monthly access.

Even with the imperative need for information technology in the daily operations of their departments, most of the users had no understanding of the importance of a disaster recovery plan for the I/T function. This was reflected in the answers received in a survey taken by the I/S department. The questions covered such topics as critical user applications, allowable downtime, and end-user risk assessment of an I/T disaster.

LOOKING AHEAD

Friday afternoon, March 20, after an exhausting and emotional week, Sheryl looked back at the events over the last few days. Even though Vermont Mutual did not have a disaster recovery plan, IBM's service and support agreement put them back in business less than a week after the flood. Sheryl now had to consider what should be done to prepare Vermont Mutual in the case of future disasters.

Questions

1. What kind of plan should be prepared to make sure Vermont Mutual would not be caught off guard by fire, flood, or any other unforeseen circumstance?
2. How could Sheryl Crowley make the implementation of the plan happen?

SOURCE: This case was written by Associate Professors William Cats-Baril and Ronald Thompson of the School of Business Administration, University of Vermont. The case is designed solely as the basis for classroom discussion and is not intended to illustrate either effective or ineffective handling of an administrative situation. Jon McLean, Jean-François Morin, Pat Orlando, and Laurie Ouellette contributed to an earlier version of the case.

MODULE III Case

DAKIN FARM (C): KEEP LOOKING FORWARD

Sam Cutting Jr., president of Dakin Farm, stopped smiling while describing the crash. "It was one of the worst experiences of my life. It got so bad that I started to think the unthinkable . . . that we might lose the company and put all of our employees out of work. If the system had been down even one day longer, I honestly don't know if we would have survived."

REDESIGNING OPERATIONS

In March of the previous year Sam hired Alan Newman, a friend and owner of two successful mail order companies, as a consultant to help redesign Dakin Farm's internal operations and their order-processing information system. The plan was to have a new system implemented later that year, before the busy Christmas season arrived. After an initial search, Newman focused his efforts on two different companies offering similar mail order processing systems; they were Total Order Processing Systems (TOPS), and Nashbar. The two different systems operated about the same and had the same basic functions. Newman was also involved in plans to restructure and renovate the packing room and change current procedures—a complementary effort to streamlining the picking, packing, and shipping processes.

Efforts to decide on a new order-processing system and to redesign operations proceeded in a somewhat parallel manner. Sam had established two broad general objectives: improve efficiency and increase capacity. He wanted to expand capacity by about threefold (from the current 1,000 orders to at least 3,000 orders)—and do it without hiring more staff. In addition, he wanted to provide customers with immediate response to inquiries and reduce delivery of orders from the current several days to a maximum of two days.

As Sam and Alan Newman reviewed the picking, packing, and shipping processes, they discovered numerous possibilities for improvement. The first was to bring the goods to the pickers rather than the reverse. Under the old system, the pickers would retrieve the next order and carry a "tub" (a plastic container about the size of a laundry basket) through the retail store collecting items from the shelves. If necessary, they would also go into the smokehouse storage area to pick up smoked meats and cheeses and into the sugarhouse storage area to pick up maple syrup containers. They would carry the full tub back through the retail store to the packing room, leaving it for the packers. Along the way they might chat with other employees or with customers in the retail store. Pickers often complained of sore backs and frequently scraped their knuckles as they passed through the several doors between the packing room and the sugarhouse.

Alan suggested building a storage area that would contain all necessary goods (or at least a vast majority of them) to reduce the walking. The ideal arrangement would be a series of backloading, refrigerated units with glass doors that would allow pickers to simply open the door and select the appropriate item. The stock of goods would be replenished from the back of the units so that no interruptions in the picking process would be necessary. He also recommended a thigh-high conveyor system; the pickers would leave the tubs on the conveyer, select the necessary goods, and then pass the tub along the conveyor to the packers. A further improvement was to have the goods stored in duplicate, on either side of the conveyor; two pickers could then work simultaneously without getting into each other's way.

Changes in the packing room were also planned. Currently the packers shared a long table that contained the necessary packing materials. As a new tub (order) was received from the pickers, they would retrieve the necessary size of packing box and packing and wrapping materials (ribbons, bows, etc.) and then pack the box. During this process they were constantly getting in each other's way as they moved back and forth between the packing table and the box and materials storage areas. Once the box was packed, they carried it to the conveyor belt, which carried the packed order to the basement. Here another employee weighed the package and entered it into the UPS manifest computer, which recorded the information for use by UPS and Dakin Farm.

Alan and Sam came up with several recommendations for improvement here. First, the packers would each be given a separate packing station that would be stocked with all the needed materials. Second, the conveyor system from the picking storage area would pass by each of the packing stations and continue to the mailing station, so no employee would have to lift or carry the tubs or packages. The packers would pull the next tub off the conveyor, pack the order, remove the address label from the picking list, and apply it to the completed package. Third, since the new information system would incorporate the UPS mailing manifest, the packed goods would proceed on the conveyor from the packing stations into the storage cooler in the basement.

The storage cooler would be redesigned so that the conveyor would run right through it. Alan also suggested attaching an expandable, flexible end to the conveyor and putting this end piece (about 30 feet long) on wheels, which would make loading the packages from the storage cooler onto the UPS truck much easier. The flexible conveyor would be wheeled out to the truck, and the packages would be transferred from the cooler to the truck with only minimal lifting and carrying.

THE NEW MAIL ORDER PROCESSING SYSTEM

Along with the planned changes to internal operations, Sam and Alan identified numerous requirements for a new order-processing information system. For example, the system had to be on-line (orders would be processed as they were received, not batched until later) and maintain customer and purchase records in a central database. It had to offer fast response time and allow the user to toggle to product information when needed. Most of these requirements had been identified earlier when Sam informally prepared his "wish list" for a new system.

COMPARISON OF THE TWO SYSTEMS

Once the two best-looking systems (TOPS and Nashbar) were identified, the next step was to evaluate them and select one. The TOPS firm had already given Sam cost estimates and details of their proposed system as follows:

- $39,000 up-front cost for hardware and software.
- $195 per month for software support.
- New specific customization for Dakin would be an additional cost; the charges would be $500 per month for 12 months (rather than a one-time fee).
- Upgrades made to the basic code of the complete TOPS system would be made free of charge by the firm.
- The system would run on a minicomputer with 7 dumb terminals, upgradable to 12.

The Nashbar proposal was somewhat different, even though features provided by the software were fairly similar:

- Estimated software price of $25,000.
- Estimated hardware price of $25,000.
- Service support 7 A.M. to 9 P.M. seven days a week, at an estimated cost of $200 per month.
- The system would use a personal computer server running 7 PC terminals, upgradable to 12.

Under both system options, the program code (software programs) would have to be modified. The software packages had a shell of modules oriented toward businesses the size of Dakin Farm, but they would need to be adjusted, depending on the specific functions desired for the company. With Nashbar, the cost of modifications was included in the total cost of the software.

Alan Newman had chosen these two firms based on comparisons of systems he had looked at over the years and, most importantly, the fact that these companies had installed numerous systems and had reputations for reliability. Alan and Sam checked references provided by TOPS and Nashbar, and all were quite positive. Alan also contacted a few clients of the two companies who were not on the reference lists, however, and discovered some minor concerns about the stability of TOPS. Two companies that used the TOPS system mentioned that TOPS seemed to have a fairly high turnover with their staff and that every time they contacted TOPS for system support they had to speak with a different individual.

On the positive side, the clients of both TOPS and Nashbar were quite pleased with the systems and the customization that had been performed for them. The TOPS system would likely take more customization, but Sam had been assured by the TOPS sales representative that if TOPS was given the contract and work began by June 1, TOPS could guarantee that the system would be completely operational and installed by October 1. Nashbar also guaranteed this timetable but anticipated they could have the system installed by August.

COST-BENEFIT ANALYSIS

To help decide which system (if either) should be purchased, Sam decided to perform an initial cost-benefit analysis. The two systems that were being considered, TOPS and Nashbar, were comparable in their functionality; the fundamental difference between the two was the hardware architecture. They both addressed the problems of the current system, had approximately the same capacity, and provided benefits in the same areas.

TOPS provided the hardware and software for $39,000 up-front, with another $6,000 spread over 12 monthly payments; they would also charge $195 per month for support. General improvements to the package were included in the initial Nashbar price. Nashbar's software was available for $25,000, and Alan Newman anticipated the hardware would cost about $25,000 also. The monthly charge for support had not yet been provided but was expected to be comparable to the TOPS price of about $200 per month. The initial cost of either system would include a one-week training program to be conducted by the vendor. The vendor would be responsible for the installation of the hardware and software and the conversion of the data files.

Both systems would also require Alan's time to be increased to 15 hours per week for three months to help Sam manage the project. The total estimated cost for his involvement was about $10,000. In terms of supplies and overhead, the ongoing costs should remain about the same. A minicomputer was currently in use, so the TOPS system, which was minicomputer based, would not increase these costs significantly. With the personal computer–based system from Nashbar, costs might be decreased since PCs were easier to maintain and repair and were less expensive to operate. In addition, PCs do not demand any special facilities for operation.

Although most of the benefits to be derived from the new system were common to both systems under consideration, there were several that were specific to a PC-based system. The changeover in technology from minicomputers to PCs could maximize the investment in hardware since they could be employed for other purposes as well. Also, Nashbar provided a support hotline with extended business hours and fast, easy problem resolution via modem.

Because of the low capacity of the current system, Dakin Farm had to turn away more than $50,000 of business during the previous Christmas season. The new system (either one) should be able to handle all orders. Sam believed that a conservative estimate of the return of lost gross sales would be about $30,000. The upselling feature, which would prompt the customer service representative (CSR) to sell products that complement the order, could lead to larger orders and increased sales. The database could also generate mailing lists for specific promotions and could "flag" customers that were due to order (based on historical sales). These features and special functions of the new system could not only facilitate increased sales but could also contribute to increased customer satisfaction and retention. No customer's order would need to be turned away because of system overload. Furthermore, the orders could be tracked quickly and easily, avoiding the paper trail that currently took days to sort.

While the costs were very specific for each of the systems, many of the benefits discussed were less tangible and difficult to quantify in terms of dollar savings. With this consideration, Sam completed a quick payback analysis and believed that a two-year payback would be acceptable for the size and scope of this project. After considering the results of the cost-benefit and payback analyses, Sam decided to go with the Nashbar proposal. Although the features and costs were fairly similar, Nashbar offered more stability, better customer support, and a longer window of time between implementation and the start of the busy Christmas season.

IMPLEMENTATION

Once all decisions and plans had been made by Sam and Alan, the actual implementation began. Subcontractors were hired to expand and modify the picking and packing areas; install the picking coolers, storage cooler, and conveyor systems; and modify and expand Sam's office. The construction project was completed in August, only a few weeks behind schedule. Sam acted as the project leader for all construction and physical alterations, while Alan acted as project leader for the implementation of the Nashbar system.

Since the Nahbar system was purchased and not developed in-house, the vendor was responsible for many of the initial implementation activities. The preliminary software construction and testing had already been completed by Nashbar; however, they needed to work with Alan and Sam to modify the system for Dakin's needs.

The technical details of implementation were completed by the vendor with the assistance of Alan Newman. The software was customized for the special reporting needs of Dakin Farm. Inventory files, technical information files for each product, and upselling reference files were built. Data files from the current system were imported into the new system and modified as necessary to produce the production files. This customization and the transfer of data took longer than anticipated; for example, many of Dakin's records had to be updated before they could be entered.

Since the company still needed the old system during installation of the new, the new system was first installed in a portable trailer for testing and training. Alan Newman and representatives from Nashbar conducted the final testing of the system during installation. No new personnel were hired to operate the new system; Kim (the office manager) was trained to become the primary operator and troubleshooter. A one-week training program was conducted for all CSRs, and the new work procedures were documented. Although the delays in customization and conversion pushed the cut-over date from August to late September, the new system was completely operational before the busy season began. With the expectation of being able to increase sales, Sam installed toll-free (800) telephone lines and increased his advertising.

THE CRASH

By December, the new information system and changes in procedures were reaping major benefits for Dakin Farm. Although everything wasn't going completely according to plan, in general their initial high expectations were being met. A much higher volume of orders was being processed more efficiently; the system was working.

On Friday, December 10, disaster struck. In the middle of one of the busiest days of the year, the new order-processing system died. The office manager, Kim, tried desperately to get it running again, but to no avail. The customer sales representatives were told to continue to accept orders and write them manually (going back to the old way), but they could no longer promise customers such fast turnaround and delivery. Sam called Nashbar and explained that he needed help right away. They promised to send someone as soon as possible.

By Saturday morning the phones were still ringing, and the manual orders were beginning to pile up. The CSRs needed more time to complete an order, and they weren't able to provide the kind of service the new system had allowed. For example, they were no longer able to tell customers how much the shipping costs would be on their package, nor were they able to verify credit card orders. Basically they had to revert to the old system, but, since they were unable to create invoices or mailing labels, they could only take orders, not fill them. Late Saturday the Nashbar representative arrived and began diagnostic checking on the system. He worked on it through the night, but by Sunday morning the system was still dead.

All day Sunday Sam paced nervously in the mail order office, where the phones kept ringing while the Nashbar representative worked on the order-processing system. As the orders continued to pile up (now totaling in the thousands), Sam told the CSRs to tell customers that they might not be able to guarantee Christmas delivery. He knew that it was going to take some time to process the backlog of orders even when (or if) the system was operational, and he didn't want to risk a situation in which Dakin was unable to fulfill its promises. Late Sunday afternoon, the Nashbar representative was successful in getting the system operational again.

Now the employees began a desperate battle against the clock. All of the backlogged orders had to be entered into the system, even as new orders continued to come in. Sam managed to hire three temporary staff members who had some experience with systems similar to the one used by Dakin, which helped somewhat. The pickers and packers worked around the clock; all six packing stations were manned continuously. It took four solid days of frantic, desperate work at full capacity, 24 hours per day, to get the backlog of orders processed and caught up. At that point, all of the employees were exhausted; most had been working too much overtime, and they still had to face 10 more days of heavy volume before Christmas. Somehow they pulled it off; in the end they had not turned away any orders.

LOOKING AHEAD

Several months passed after the crash of the order-processing system, and changes continued to occur. One of the first was that Sam made sure the company had a backup and recovery plan in place, to guard against potential disaster from any future system crash. Sam believed the system had paid for itself during the first Christmas season after installation, but that didn't mean Dakin could just be content to continue operations as usual. Sam continued to look for new ways to modify and expand the order-processing system to provide even more features and enhancements. He felt quite good about the order taking, picking, packing, and shipping processes; internal operations seemed to be working quite well. Now he wanted to concentrate more on marketing.

For example, Sam had been exploring the possibility of offering service to businesses, rather than just to individual customers. He had noticed that some companies would call and have Dakin send 15 to 20 gift packages at one time (to major clients). Sam's idea was to make this easier for them by having Dakin keep a record of all gifts sent by the organization—who they went to and what each person received. Dakin could then contact the client company in advance of the next special occasion and offer to send different gifts (of approximately equal value) to the previous year's recipients. He believed that companies would want this type of service, and it could open up a whole new market for them.

Sam also believed it might be time to explore new ways of using information technology to deliver their marketing messages. Postage costs for mailings continued to climb, as did advertising costs in the outlets he normally used. Recently Sam had seen a demonstration of a CD-ROM that had numerous products and retailers represented, and he thought it might be something to investigate. He had also seen some of the advertising and order-taking possibilities over the Internet and wondered if that was something he should check into. Whatever direction(s) he chose, however, Sam knew that Dakin Farm couldn't afford to sit still and let the competition bypass them.

Questions

1. Use suggestions from Chapter 8 to analyze the changes to the order taking, picking, packing, and shipping processes described in this case. Would you rate the change effort as successful or unsuccessful?

Do you have any recommendations for how the changes could have been improved, or do you have any suggestions for the future?

2. Analyze the Dakin Farm situation using Porter's five-force model from Chapter 10. Do you believe that the new order-processing system gives Dakin Farm a competitive advantage? Why or why not?
3. Identify managerial vulnerabilities from the Dakin Farm case, and evaluate the methods used to address these vulnerabilities. Make (and state) any necessary assumptions.
4. Discuss the potential usefulness of the suggestions for using information technology for marketing applications that are mentioned at the end of the case. If we consider these (CD-ROMs, Internet) as emerging technologies (for Dakin Farm), how would you recommend managing them?
5. Think back to the many examples provided throughout this book. Can you identify any other ways Dakin Farm (or its employees) might consider using information technology to improve their competitive position, communications, or decision making?

SOURCE: This case was written by Associate Professors William Cats-Baril and Ronald Thompson of the School of Business Administration, University of Vermont. The case is designed solely as the basis for discussion and is not intended to illustrate either effective or ineffective handling of an administrative situation.

MODULE IV Information Technology and Society

This fourth and final module examines aspects of information technology that go beyond organizational use. The two chapters in this module discuss issues that have far-reaching influences on numerous aspects of human society.

Chapter 12 introduces the concept of electronic commerce and describes how some organizations use information technology to facilitate their internal operations and interactions with their customers. The chapter also discusses various aspects of the Internet, including how it is being used as a vehicle for fostering electronic commerce. Going beyond organizational and commercial considerations, the chapter also addresses numerous societal issues arising from the rapid growth of Internet use.

The final chapter of the book, Chapter 13, raises numerous questions about the role of I/T in society. The topics range from implications for education and entertainment, to implications for the world ecology. Unlike many of the preceding chapters, the objective in Chapter 13 is to raise questions, not answer them. As you read through the material, you might consider whether information technology has opened a Pandora's box of social alienation, or whether it is a panacea bringing humans into a new era of prosperity and happiness.

CHAPTER 12 Networks and Electronic Commerce

CHAPTER OBJECTIVES

ELECTRONIC COMMERCE

NETWORK SERVICE PROVIDERS

THE INTERNET

- Introduction to the Net
- World Wide Web and Web Browsers
- Commercial Opportunities
- Open Market, Inc.

INTERNET ISSUES

HISTORICAL AND PRACTICAL VIEW OF THE INTERNET

CLOSING COMMENTS ON THE NET

SUMMARY

KEY CONCEPTS AND TERMS

REFERENCES

CONNECTIVE CASE: STUDENTS OFF-CAMPUS RENTALS

IT'S YOUR TURN

- Review Questions
- Discussion Questions
- Group Assignment
- Application Assignments
- Case Assignment: Banking on the Net

After reading this chapter, you should have a better understanding of electronic commerce and public networks, especially the Internet. More specifically, you should be able to:

- Define and provide examples of electronic commerce.
- Describe network service providers.
- Describe how the Internet can be used for commercial purposes.
- Discuss relevant issues related to Internet use (security, censorship, etc.).
- Provide a description of the Internet, including navigation and search facilities.

The Internet has received a great deal of hype, but is it really going to have much effect on organizations?

ELECTRONIC COMMERCE

Today, many of the more powerful and dramatic uses of information technology for **electronic commerce** are those that link multiple organizations. The concept of using information systems to transcend organizational boundaries is certainly not new; what has changed is the extent to which these **inter-organizational systems (IOS)** are being used.

One common form of IOS used for electronic commerce is the application of **electronic data interchange (EDI).** EDI involves the electronic transmission of common business transactions, such as purchase orders and invoices, between business partners. For example, Ford, General Motors, and most other automobile manufacturers use EDI to order parts from their suppliers. If parts manufacturers wish to compete for Ford's business, they have to agree to implement EDI and use it for much of their business correspondence.

The benefits of EDI, when compared to alternatives such as sending paper forms through the U.S. Postal Service, are quite substantial. EDI reduces the transmission time, it reduces errors caused by transcription or data entry, and it significantly decreases the time and labor required to manage the data related to business transactions. On the negative side, standards are still being developed that could ensure greater compatibility among EDI systems. Since different companies, industries, and countries developed their EDI standards independently, many EDI systems need to be modified before they can communicate with each other.

Electronic commerce can take many forms besides EDI. Some companies are using information technology to facilitate extensive working arrangements with other organizations. These arrangements may involve simple transactions, contractual agreements, or even complex partnerships. As an example of a partnership arrangement facilitated by the use of I/T, consider the Calyx & Corolla company.

Calyx & Corolla was founded in 1988. The vision for the firm was to provide high-quality, fresh cut flowers by direct mail. Rather than try to build up its own distribution system, Calyx & Corolla entered into a partnership with Federal Express (FedEx). FedEx handles all of the business logistics, while Calyx & Corolla maintains the customer databases and marketing. Calyx & Corolla also entered into arrangements with American Express and MasterCard, who handle all of the credit authorization and payment systems. Finally, Calyx & Corolla also created partnerships with independent flower growers.

All of these relationships are supported with sophisticated information systems; Calyx & Corolla is linked electronically to FedEx, to American Express and MasterCard, and to the flower growers. When Calyx & Corolla receives a telephone order from a customer, the credit card information is verified electronically with American Express or MasterCard; the order is transmitted electronically to one of the growers; and the pertinent information is also transmitted electronically to FedEx. FedEx picks up the flowers and delivers them to the customer; American Express or MasterCard charges the amount to the customer's account, and transmits appropriate payments to FedEx, Calyx & Corolla, and the grower (see Figure 12–1).

FIGURE 12–1 A Partnership Arrangement—Calyx & Corolla

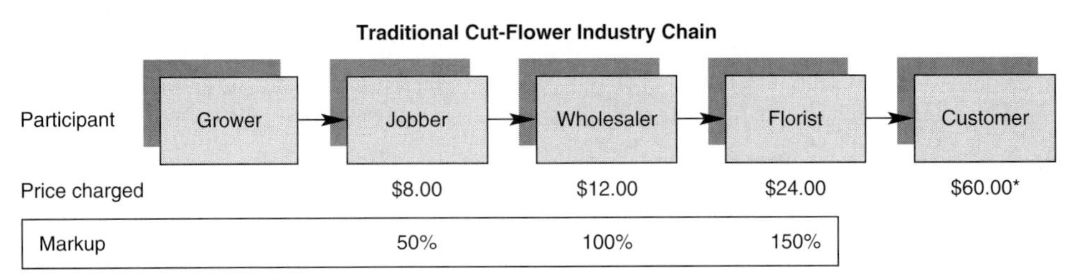

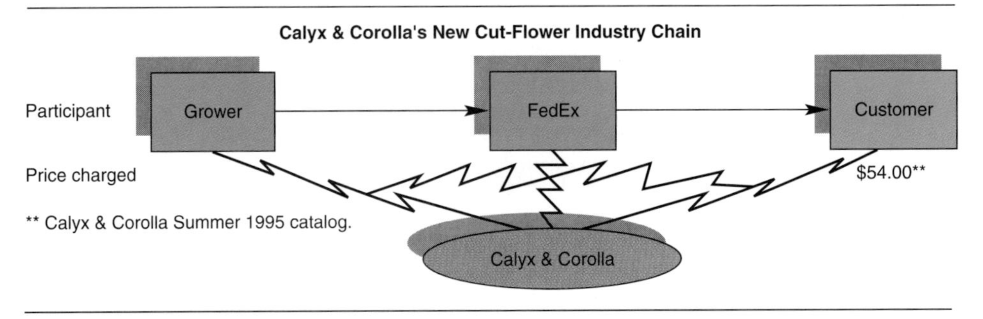

SOURCE: Applegate and Gogan, 1995a.

In essence, Calyx & Corolla operates as a virtual organization. Rather than handling distribution internally, it outsources it to FedEx; similarly, it avoids the need to keep track of customer charges and payments, by outsourcing the payment function to MasterCard and American Express. By transmitting the orders directly to the growers, Calyx & Corolla also avoids the need to carry any inventory. In this arrangement, all parties benefit: the growers, the credit card companies, FedEx, Calyx & Corolla, and the customers.

The increased interest in electronic commerce and technology-enhanced relationships has led to a number of important trends; these are listed in Table 12–1.

NETWORK SERVICE PROVIDERS[1]

Network service providers are organizations that charge customers fees for the right to tap into their networks and to access the services they have available. The most common providers (at time of writing) in North America include America OnLine (4.5 million subscribers), CompuServe (4 million), Prodigy (1.5 million), and the Microsoft Network (.5 million). These companies provide services such as checking airline schedules and reserving seats, electronic mail, access to information databases, and so on. Typically the customer uses a modem and telephone line to connect to the service provider's network, and pays (1) a flat monthly fee, (2) extra fees for some special services, and (3) any applicable telephone charges.

[1]The topics we cover in this chapter are in a state of constant change. For example, at time of writing, Prodigy was up for sale, and CompuServe was adding 700,000 new subscribers each quarter. The material presented here represents the situation in 1996. For an update on this information, see the Web site for this book: http://www.irwin.com/mis/catsbth.

TABLE 12–1 Trends in Using Information Technology to Support Electronic Commerce

1. Managers are choosing to source an increasing number of products and services outside the firm, often creating virtual organizations as they do so.
2. Within virtual organizations, many independent companies are increasingly specialized. Like Federal Express, they are becoming experts at performing their critical steps in a process.
3. Relationships among firms are becoming more complex, and they often blend transactional, contractual, and partnership elements.
4. The technology's growing capability to simultaneously manage product/market complexity and speed of response is enabling firms to bypass costly channel intermediaries and link directly to suppliers and customers.
5. There is an increasing separation of the physical flow of goods and services from the flow of information. Those capturing information in a form that can be packaged and delivered can significantly enhance the value of products and services.
6. Firms (such as American Airlines) that were able to achieve proprietary control (individually or in partnership) of both the information systems and the network channel upon which they are delivered have assumed the powerful position of channel manager within their industries.
7. With the rise of low-cost, third-party network providers, the cost of establishing and managing inter-organizational systems has decreased, threatening the sustainable proprietary advantages that can be gained through ownership of electronic market channels.

SOURCE: L. M. Applegate and J. Gogan, "Electronic Commerce: Trends and Opportunities," Harvard Business School, Note 9-196-006, August 1995.

The competition between service providers is very strong. The introduction of the Microsoft Network (MSN, which coincided with Microsoft's introduction of the Windows 95 operating system in 1995) put additional pressure on the other service providers, since Microsoft priced its initial monthly rate at about half that of the competition ($5/month instead of $10). Microsoft's intent was to rapidly build a large client base, and then use its considerable resources to develop MSN into a leading network service provider.

Although network service providers generally saw rapid growth in the number of subscribers during the early to mid-1990s, profits did not follow. One of the biggest factors was not so much competition among service providers, but rather the rapid growth of the Internet and more specifically the World Wide Web (from 1994 to 1995, the number of users went from one to eight million, and the number of business sites on the Web went from 1,700 to over 20,000). Figure 12–2 illustrates the growth in Internet use. Once service providers began offering access to the Internet in response to the insistence of their customers, the subscribers began to wonder why they needed a service provider. Although new subscribers continued to sign on, many more experienced subscribers defected to lower cost providers who only provided access to the Internet.

Another problem facing on-line service providers was the defection of many of the media companies which had previously been paid to set up electronic newstands. The media company (such as Sports Illustrated) would provide information content that was accessed only through the on-line service provider. These companies decided to bypass the on-line service providers to set up shop directly on the Internet. As the migration continued, the service providers were forced to pay

FIGURE 12–2 Growth in Internet and On-Line Service Providers

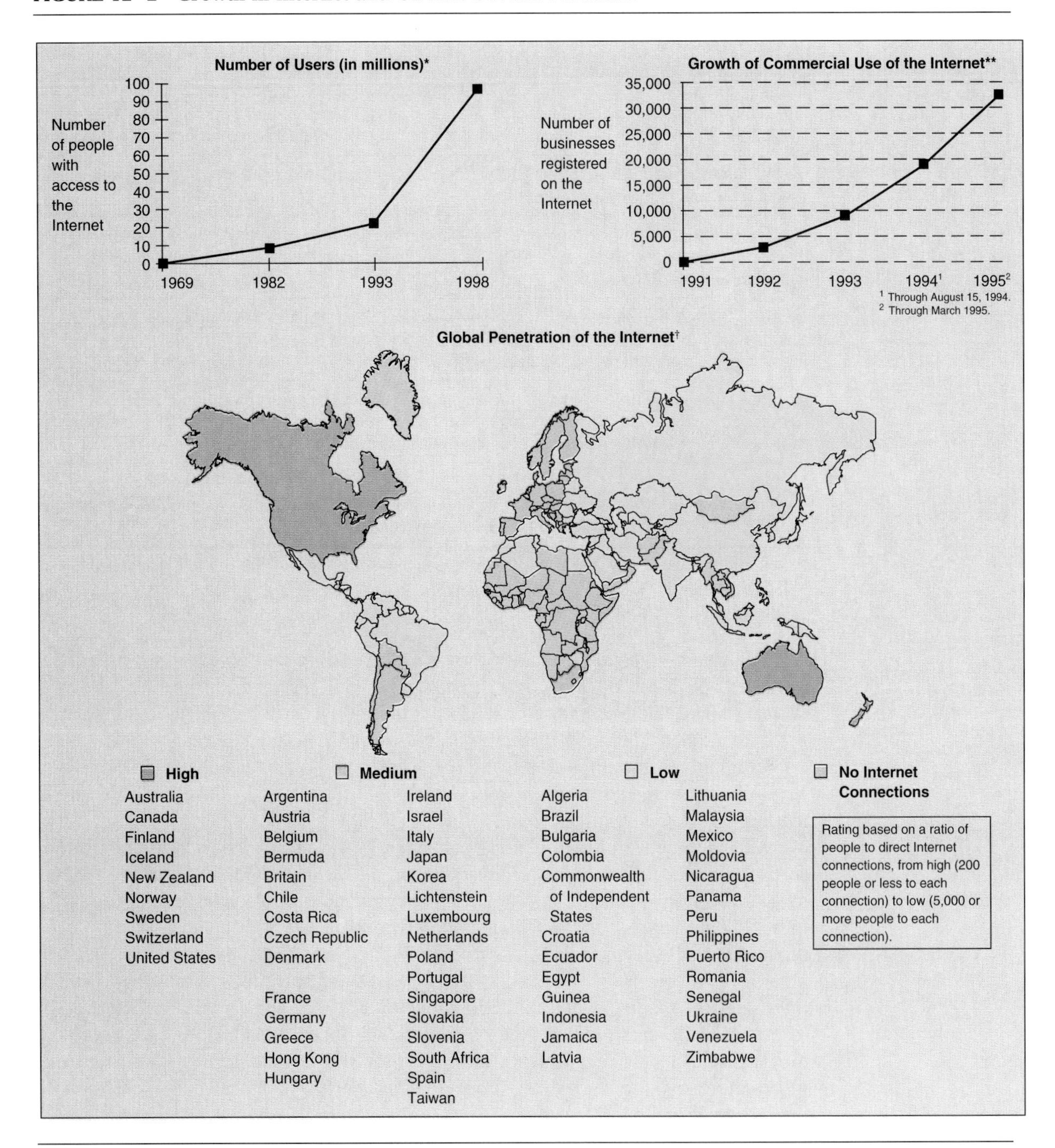

SOURCE: *Adapted from *Internet Business Advantage,* 1995.

**Adapted from *Internet Letter,* Vol. 2, No. 5, Feb. 1, 1995.

†Adapted from *Time Magazine,* Spring 1995.

more for the remaining information content, even as they were forced to continue dropping prices to try and attract new subscribers.

The on-line firms' earnings were also hurt by the huge investment required to embrace the World Wide Web. CompuServe spent $100 million to buy Spry Inc. for its WWW browser software, only to end up licensing a rival product. America Online bought a browser company for $41 million, but then abandoned it when they licensed the Netscape browser. Microsoft paid $130 million for Vermeer Technologies to get a beachhead in the development of a Web browser.

THE INTERNET

This section of the chapter is intended to provide a brief introduction to the Internet, and to introduce many important issues that have arisen concerning Internet use and potential use. The intent is *not* to provide a how-to guide; for details on how to use different features of the Internet, we have listed sample references at the end of the chapter. Other references can be readily obtained from almost any bookstore or library. If you are unfamiliar with the Internet and the use of many other Internet features, you may wish to review the material in the "Historical View of the Internet" section at the end of the chapter.

Introduction to the Net

The **Internet (Net)** has been described as a "network of networks" or as a "loose collection of related computer networks," both of which are accurate. Although initially a system used almost exclusively by the defense department and academic researchers, it has evolved rapidly into a mass communication media that may significantly change the way many organizations conduct business.

There is no central body to govern or control the Internet; some access providers attempt to monitor usage to some extent, but in general, any attempts to develop usage guidelines or standards are voluntary. The Internet has been described as the "last true frontier," where anything goes. This has led to many important issues, ranging from the security of computers connected to the Internet to considerations of the privacy of individuals using Internet services. As with any frontier, the wide open, lawless environment can't last forever. As its use became part of the mainstream, some of society's norms and rules for behavior began to be applied. On the other hand, the capabilities of the Internet continue to expand as new information technologies and applications are developed, raising even more operational, ethical, and societal issues.

To understand by analogy how the Internet operates, first consider the fact that each site (organization or individual) connected to the Internet operates independently, with no overall governance. Assume for a moment that there were no international governing bodies (such as NATO or the World Trade Organization); no federal governments or monarchs; no state or provincial governments. Instead, picture a world where each city, town, or family living in a rural area operated independently. Any given site (city, town, individual) could choose to connect to another site by building a road.

If you were to travel to one site, you would be subject to whatever laws or societal norms were in place. You would be able to take advantage of educational or entertainment opportunities existing at that site (museums, etc.), or you could choose to travel to any other site that was connected by a road. Some sites might

BUSINESS BRIEF 12-1 ON-LINE GOVERNMENT INFORMATION: PLENTIFUL, IF NOT ALWAYS USEFUL

Many breathless new stories have touted the Internet as a vehicle for bringing government closer to the people. After a look at what Uncle Sam has dumped out in cyberspace, however, the public may decide to keep its distance from the new electronic democracy.

A short trip down the information superhighway leads to one of the more popular Federal sites on the Internet, the electronic Consumer Information Center. Now, instead of stuffing a few dollars into an envelope and waiting for a pamphlet to arrive in the mail, computer users can download from the center's electronic bulletin board such titles as *Get Hooked on Seafood, Glove Box Tips,* and *Backyard Bird Problems.* Or there's the report on the "Process for Manufacture of Nonbleeding Maraschino Cherries," which computer-savvy cherry makers can find at the National Technology Transfer Center site.

When deciding what information to put on-line, departments and agencies are hardly selective. "They put out so much information that virtually anybody can find something useful," says Bruce Maxwell, author of a book entitled "Washington Online: How to Access the Government's Electronic Bulletin Boards."

QUESTION

1. It appears that governmental agencies are making a wide variety of information available electronically. Briefly discuss the usefulness of some of this information, using concepts such as information overload. How important would indexes and electronic search mechanisms be for making use of on-line government information?

SOURCE: Amy Schatz, "Government Information On-Line Is Plentiful, If Not Always Useful," *The Wall Street Journal,* March 22, 1995. Reprinted by permission of *The Wall Street Journal,*

have a great deal for you to explore, and might have excellent services to help you find everything. Others might have very little of interest, or might provide little assistance.

The same is true of Internet sites. Each operates independently, with no overall governance. Site administrators may elect to add or delete services without warning, leaving **links** (roads) that lead nowhere or services with few connections. If you are dissatisfied with the service, you may appeal to the site administrator (the "town mayor"), but there is no higher authority to appeal to if you are still dissatisfied.

The Internet is used for a wide variety of applications in education, research, information exchange, business, and entertainment. (Business Brief 12–1 gives a quick sampling of the federal government's offerings.) Because it grows so rapidly and is subject to so little control, however, it is a very unstable environment that can be frustrating to use. You might find something of great interest one day, and the next day it no longer exists or you are unable to access it.

This instability causes some concerns for potential users, especially organizations wishing to conduct business over the Internet. Scott McNealy, the CEO of Sun Microsystems, argues that the Internet needs to mature in several ways before its true capabilities come close to matching all of the hype. "The [information] superhighway is a combination of everything that is out there. The Internet is the dirt track. Telecommunications companies and the cable and satellite providers are building the freeways. But you need the equivalent of the U.S. Department of Transportation and the Highway Patrol to make it work for business."

The Internet can be a positive factor for both individual productivity and organizational competitiveness. On the negative side, Internet use can have many unanticipated side effects, such as lost productivity while employees waste time running into dead ends or retrieving useless information. Nevertheless, most users find that the benefits of tapping into and "surfing the Net" exceed the costs.

World Wide Web and Web Browsers

Most people consider file transfer protocol (ftp) to be the "first generation" Internet navigation technology, gopher the second, and the **World Wide Web** (**WWW,** or the **Web**) as the third.[2] The Web is a subset of the Internet, which uses a set of standard commands for defining objects such as text, sound, and images. Web browsers are software programs which enable the user to migrate from site to site on the Web, accessing the various text, sound, and image objects. Using hypertext and hypermedia links, a Web user can access text, graphics, sound, still images, and full-motion video images. The Web was originally developed at CERN (the European Center for Nuclear Research in Switzerland) to enable scientists to share research data and collaborate on new products. Because of the rich variety of information available on the Web with **Web browsers,** many Internet users stick with the Web and ignore other Internet features.

Hypertext is what gives the Web one of its more compelling features: the ability to jump from one "page" or document to another. If you are viewing one document and you see a "hot" topic that interests you, the hypertext feature of the Web enables you to jump to another document, wherever it may be physically located (it can be in a computer that resides in a different country altogether). The concept of **hypermedia** gives the Web a second compelling feature: the ability to access rich information sources (sights and sounds) rather than just text.

The most common Web browser is Netscape, used by over 80 percent of Internet users. The Web browsers each have their strengths and weaknesses, and support different features. At one point it was not unusual for a Web user to have more than one Web browser, although many have now standardized on Netscape. Also, many popular application packages (Microsoft Word, WordPerfect, etc.) have a Web browser as part of their functions.

By adding a graphical user interface and providing access to sounds and images, the Web moved out of the realm of "techies" and into the mainstream of everyday computer users. As more people got connected and began using Web browsers to surf the Net, more and more organizations began to see the potential for expanded commercial applications. There was also a sense of "keeping up with the Joneses," both by individuals and by organizations. The prevailing philosophy was, If everyone else is using the Web, we should too.

Another innovation that fueled Web growth was the development of easier-to-use languages for developing material to be stored on the Web. Initially, anyone wanting to set up a **home page,** or **node,** on the Web and to store material that could be accessed by other Web users had to learn a special programming language called **HyperText Markup Language (HTML).** HTML provides a series of commands enabling a user to store material using a standard format that can be accessed by most Web browsers. Unfortunately, HTML has numerous limitations and is not all that easy for some end users to learn.

---

[2]If you are unfamiliar with ftp, gopher, listservs, newsgroups, etc., see the "Historical View of the Internet" section toward the end of this chapter.

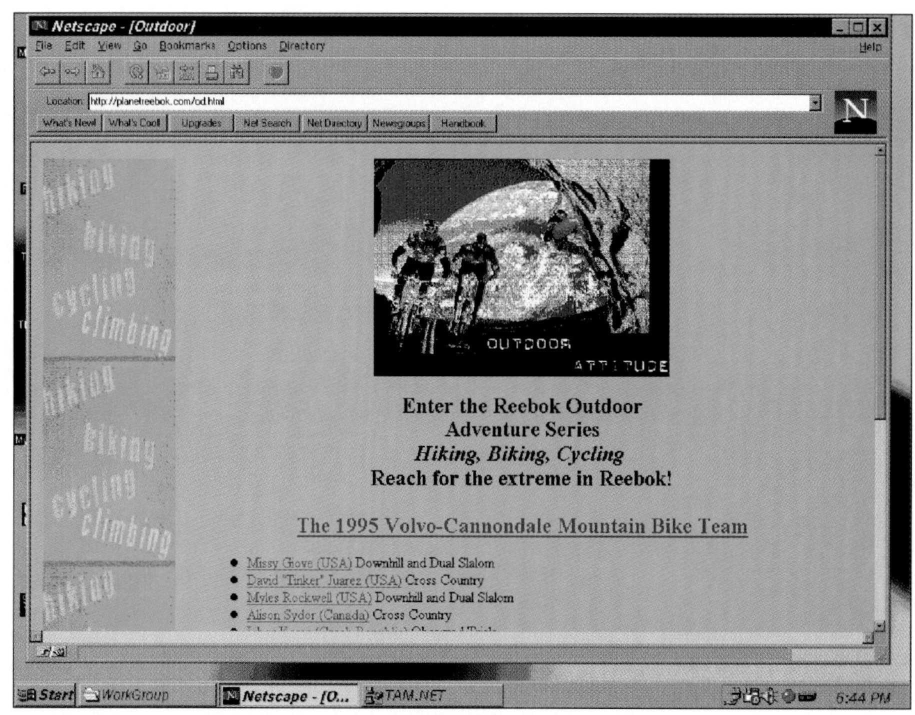

Web browsers are used to retrieve text, images, sound, and video from Web computer sites. This site offers a variety of products and itineraries for climbing, hiking, and cycling.

As more individuals and organizations developed home pages and tried to put their material on the Web, the limitations of HTML became more apparent. Several companies worked to develop better approaches; one of these was termed *Hot Java,* introduced in 1995 by Sun Microsystems. Java is an object-oriented programming language designed specifically for Web programming. Objects, referred to as "applets," created with Java are more dynamic than those created with HTML, allowing users to add animation, for example. Since Java is compatible with HTML, material created with Java can still be accessed using other Web browsers. Since its introduction, the use of Java and similar facilities for creating applets (objects which contain live data) has expanded rapidly. Sun Microsystems has continued to introduce new Internet development products, such as Java Workshop, Java Joe, and Internet Workshop. In early 1996, Microsoft announced its plans for Internet development tools, hoping to become a leader instead of a followers in this rapidly expanding area. Microsoft also went head-to-head against a consortium of companies called the Object Management Group (OMG), which were attempting to establish standards for transferring applets across the Internet.

At the same time, Oracle, developer of a very popular commercial database management system, has also attempted to take advantage of the growth of the Internet. Oracle has introduced several software programs which would allow a company to link external customers to their databases using the Internet and Internet tools. At the same time, Oracle introduced programs for enabling internal customers to link to databases using intranets, which are internal company networks that are designed using Internet tools.

Rather than describing additional features of the Internet in detail, we now move on to describe commercial opportunities offered by the Net.

The HTML code on the left was used to generate the Web page on the right. Photo courtesy of Jon Leland/Communication Bridges.

Commercial Opportunities

When the Internet started to become widely popular, numerous organizations jumped right in to try and take commercial advantage of this popularity. Initial attempts typically involved using the Net as a broadcast medium for sending marketing messages. Companies would send the message over as many list services (listservs) as they could locate. This met with limited success. Most of the initial Internet users resented attempts to commercialize the network, and the companies that posted the messages were "flamed" unmercifully: they received many derogatory E-mail messages from angry Internet users.

The next approach was to store information on a Web site, providing the Web user with product (or service) information and encouraging them to contact the company with orders and payment method. Typically, this meant having the user call the company and give their order and credit card information over the telephone. A further advancement was to develop software connected directly with banks and credit companies, enabling electronic payment and authorization directly over the Net. Most users were reluctant to transmit their credit card or other payment information over the Net, however, for fear that this information would be stolen and bogus charges run up on their credit account. In reality, by 1996, providing credit card information over the Internet was safer than providing it over a public telephone line.

In the retail sector, the Internet's impact could be immense. Levi-Strauss developed a system that would allow Web users to call up the company's home page, enter their exact measurements, and order a custom-made pair of jeans. The jeans are made to order in a computerized factory and delivered to the customer's door within days. At time of writing, this system was being trial tested.

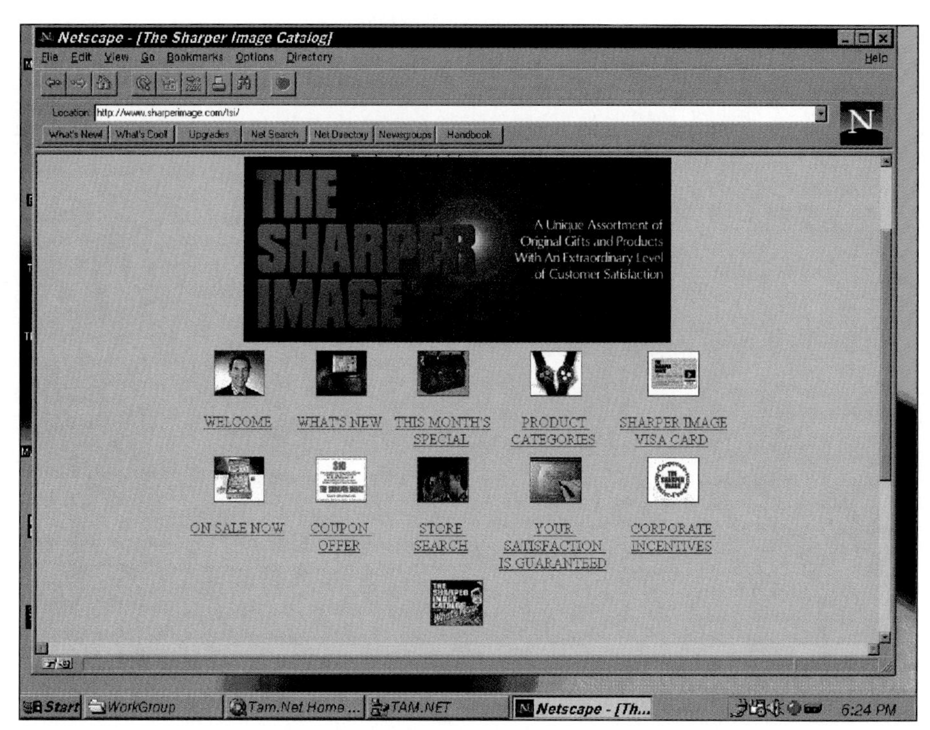

Retailers such as The Sharper Image offer shoppers a wide variety of products at low prices, accessible from any computer that is hooked into the Internet.

CUC International, Inc., of Stanford, Connecticut, runs a Web site called Shoppers Advantage that offers deep-discount prices on more than 250,000 brand name products, from highchairs to home theater packages. Web users simply click on an image of a house to find the product they want—microwaves, for example, are in the kitchen—and then check off the features they want. Provided they have paid a $65 annual membership fee and have phoned in a valid credit card number, they can complete their purchases by clicking on an image of a shopping cart and moving to the checkout screen. The goods are shipped directly from the manufacturer, which spares CUC the cost of operating a network of stores and warehouses. The company's 1995 revenues were over $1.4 billion. Another company that has a highly visited Web site is The Sharper Image.

The perceived lack of security on the Internet was a major hurdle to the advancement of commercial uses, but as the security and capabilities continued to improve, the commercial applications also continued to grow in number. One important breakthrough was when the U.S. Department of Commerce allowed the Internet software company Cybercash Inc. to export its electronic-payment software. The Cybercash software used a strong encryption method for securing information. Previously, the U.S. government had restricted the export of encryption software, for fear that it would hamper their intelligence efforts—they would be unable to monitor Internet transmissions for potential threats from terrorists or foreign powers.

Another type of commerce also grew rapidly: the selling of advertising space on the Internet, which is somewhat similar to the selling of advertising spots on television. The first major company to sell ad space was Time Warner, which initially charged $30,000 per quarter (three months) for ads in its Pathfinder service. Pathfinder is a multimedia newsstand accessed by several hundred thousand users

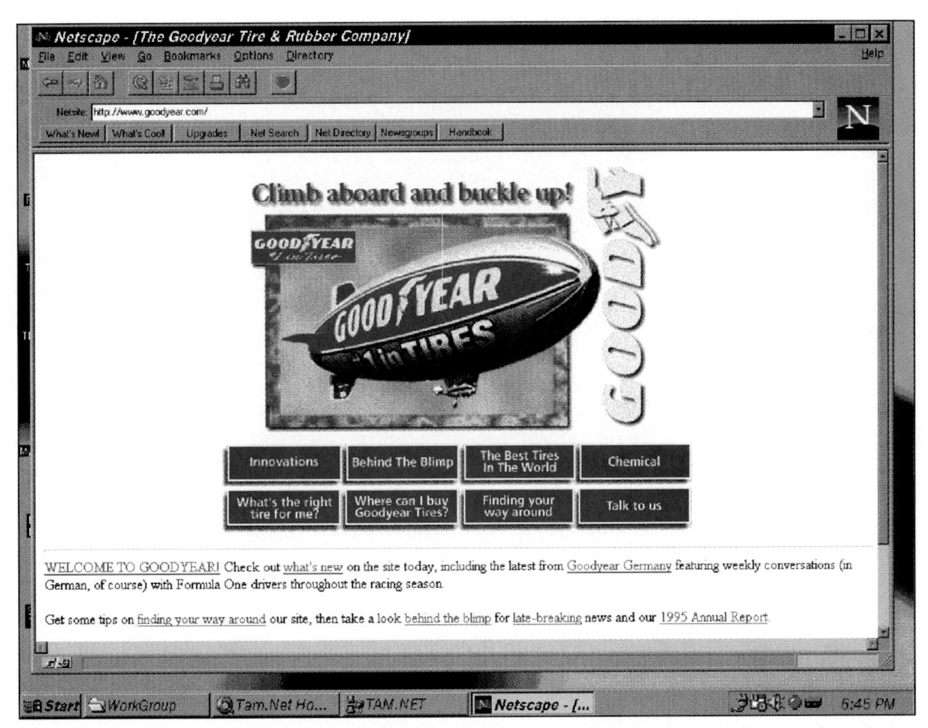

Many organizations use the Web as an electronic billboard to advertise their products and services.

weekly (one of the more popular items is the *Sports Illustrated* swimsuit edition). Time Warner's Elektra Entertainment Group has sound clips, music-video clips, and band tour schedules on Pathfinder. Time Warner monitors access to the ads, and provides the subscribing company with statistics on the number of times users access the service and what they look at.

According to WebTrack Information Services, a New York City–based market research firm, ad spending on the Web totaled at least $12.4 million in the last three months of 1995 alone. The company identified more than 250 active Web advertisers, with budgets for the quarter ranging from $5,000 to, in the case of AT&T, $567,000. That was still a tiny drop in a large bucket compared with ad spending in other media, but significant, given the short time the Web had been available to advertisers.

Commerce on the Internet raises many questions beyond the issue of network security. For example, two companies set up on-line betting programs in Caribbean countries to avoid U.S. laws that bar interstate gambling from home. The cyberspace casino developed by Canadian citizen Warren Eugene initially allowed only blackjack, and users played with play money. Later he offered blackjack with real money, but also kept the play money option (so U.S. government wiretappers couldn't tell which players were actually gambling). Mr. Eugene argued that, as a Canadian citizen whose business is in a foreign country (the Turks and Caicos Islands), he was not subject to U.S. law. Numerous questions surround cyberspace gambling, such as the potential access by children and addicted gamblers. Some people believe that cyberspace gambling will never become a major feature of the Web without some type of governmental oversight and regulation; after all, if a gambler wins big, it would be very easy for the casino to disappear into cyberspace—without paying off the debt.

BUSINESS BRIEF 12-2 ON-LINE PUBLISHING: WILL IT HELP SAVE THE TREES?

Newspaper publishers are a little nervous these days. Readership of major American daily papers appears to be in a long, slow decline, especially among younger people, who prefer looking at images on screens to reading words printed in ink on dead trees. At the same time, the cost of those dead trees—the paper—has surged.

So the publishers are experimenting with electronic newspapers, available on the major commercial on-line services or the Internet. Scores of papers are on-line, from small local weeklies to large dailies. None of these interactive editions is a big economic force yet. It's still a pain to browse through a large paper, and to read long stories, on a screen. For those activities, dead trees win hands down.

All four of the country's premier newspapers, the nationally influential papers other editors read most closely, will be on-line; the *New York Times, The Wall Street Journal,* the *Los Angeles Times,* and the *Washington Post.*

The Wall Street Journal entered the fray with a limited edition called *Personal Journal.* This wasn't a full-blown interactive newspaper, but a targeted search-and-retrieval system that quickly downloads to a user's computer news and market statistics that are updated throughout the day. Users select in advance any regular *Journal* features, plus specific company coverage they want to see. The user also can specify stocks or mutual funds whose prices should be retrieved. *Personal Journal* then downloads the material and constructs an electronic minipaper.

QUESTION

1. To what extent do you think on-line publishing of newspapers will replace the printed versions? Do you think many readers will cancel their subscriptions to printed newspapers and subscribe to on-line versions instead? Why or why not?

SOURCE: W. S. Mossberg, "Newspapers Go On-Line to Save the Industry and a Few Trees," *The Wall Street Journal*, March 23, 1995.

Another commercial use is to bypass commercial telecommunications firms and set up an internal communication network over the Internet. Software is available that allows an organization to use the Internet communications network, rather than the much more expensive commercial options. This type of application is growing in popularity because of the low cost relative to commercial communication networks, but concerns of performance, reliability, and security continue to be raised.

Although new commercial efforts are continually being attempted over the Internet, not all of them succeed. In some situations, would-be entrepreneurs or corporate marketers jump in without knowing what they are getting into. In others, the timing might be off—perhaps a marketer providing a service before a large enough segment of society is ready for it. When dealing with a very new and rapidly changing environment such as the Internet, it is difficult to monitor or anticipate changes.

The article excerpted in Business Brief 12–2 describes the experimentation by newspaper publishers with on-line publishing.

Open Market, Inc.

In spite of the uncertainties, many organizations and individuals are using the Internet effectively. One such example is a young organization called Open Market, Inc. Founded in 1994, Open Market, Inc. (OMI) of Cambridge, Massachusetts,

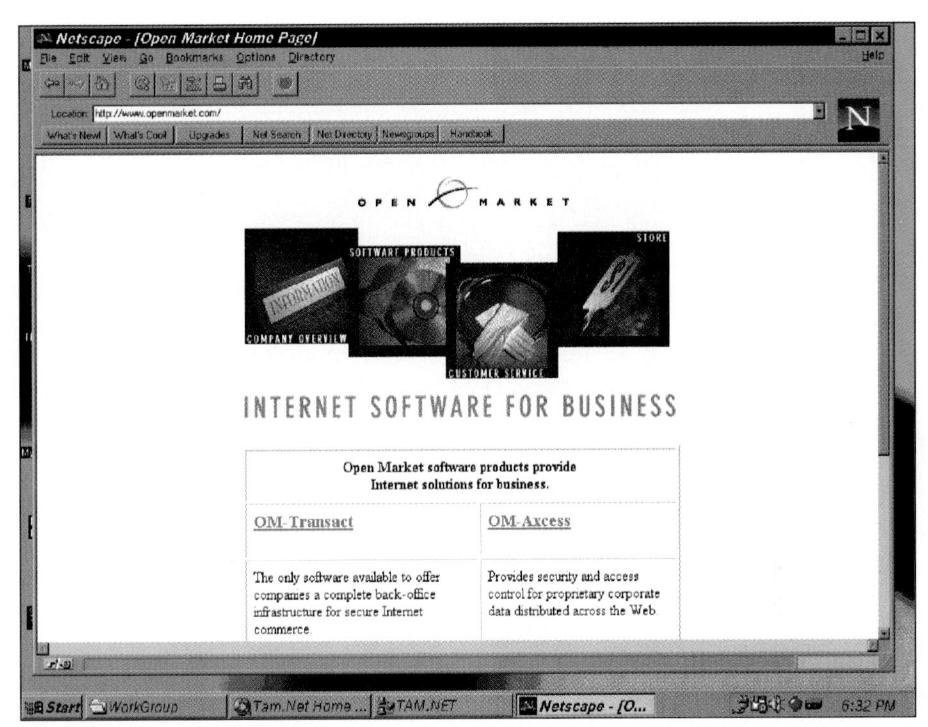

Open Market uses the Web as a place to advertise, as well as the primary vehicle for selling its commercial products and services.

develops and markets software products, services, and industry-specific solutions that enable businesses to tap the potential of the Internet and World Wide Web.

Open Market received its initial funding in the spring of 1994, and officially launched its first products in October of that year. David Gifford, a computer science professor from the Massachusetts Institute of Technology (MIT), started the company. He persuaded Shikhar Ghosh, a former consultant and later CEO of Appex, Inc., to join Open Market as CEO. Gifford acted as the chief scientist, and they hired Larry Stewart (a Ph.D. from Stanford who had worked at the Xerox Palo Alto Research Center and with Digital Equipment Corporation) as chief technology officer. By October 1994, Open Market had 12 employees, each with a broad set of responsibilities but no formal job titles.

The mission for Open Market was to "create an end-to-end infrastructure that enables businesses to buy and sell products and services in the global electronic marketplace." To illustrate how this mission was applied in practice, consider the relationship Open Market established with Mead Data Central, the providers of the Lexis/Nexis news and legal information services. Lexis/Nexis had been almost entirely subscription based, serving only large customers who could afford substantial monthly fees. Mead asked Open Market to put its services onto the Internet, making them available to small companies and individuals. Open Market developed a system that allows individuals to download information from Lexis/Nexis over the Internet, paying a small usage fee (say, $1.50 for an article) rather than a monthly subscription. The system was successfully implemented, and has been accepting payments since November of 1994.

Other major clients for Open Market have included Time Warner, Advance Publications, First Union Corporation, Banc One, and Hewlett-Packard. Although some relationships involved the development of sophisticated, proprietary systems (such as the $1 million system developed for Mead Data), Open Market has also provided relatively low-cost alternatives for smaller companies wishing to gain a presence on the Internet. Its Merchant Solution package, introduced in the Fall of 1995 at a price of $20,000, allowed a merchant to run its business over the Web. It included electronic store-building tools, commerce-enabling tools to allow real-time credit card processing, and other marketing tools.

Open Market has used numerous ways of ensuring the security and confidentiality of information passing through its systems. The company belongs to every major group involved with creating standards for electronic commerce, and supports every major security standard.

From its modest beginnings in 1994, the company grew rapidly. By the summer of 1995, it had 80 employees, and annual revenues were projected to be about $5 million. In late October of 1995, Open Market leased a much larger office space; it had grown to about 150 employees. Twenty days later, Gary Eichhorn (a veteran with experience at Hewlett-Packard and Digital Equipment) came on as CEO, while Shikhar Ghosh served as Chairman. At that point, the company had increased to over 170 employees.

Open Market continued to grow and create new Internet-related products and services. It teamed up with Sequent (a hardware vendor) to demonstrate its new Web server software, introduced in early 1996. The combination of Sequent's hardware and Open Market's software set new records for processing speed and the number of simultaneous dial-up lines the system could handle.

Although the company's original intent was to grow to about 300 employees and then stabilize, the combination of rapid growth and the unpredictable nature of the environment it operated in made planning very difficult. Despite conscientious efforts at strategic planning, Open Market decision makers discovered early on that they needed to be very flexible and able to shift focus to new products and services as the needs developed. For this organization, constant change is definitely an acknowledged way of life.[3]

INTERNET ISSUES

The intense interest on the part of a diverse array of organizations and individuals has fueled a rapid expansion of applications on the Web, as well as an explosion of serious commercial and social issues. For example, one major question that needs clarification is whether the Net is a broadcasted medium like radio or television, or more like a bookstore. With radio or television, there are a limited number of government-issued licenses, and the holders of the licenses have responsibility for controlling the content of their broadcast—and just in case they don't, a federal agency, the FCC, has overseeing power and the ability to fine them. The listener or viewer has little say on what is presented in the broadcasted programs. He or she is a passive recipient of the material. With bookstores, the content of products is unregulated, and the customer actively chooses what to browse, what to be exposed to, and what to purchase. We discuss some of these issues here.

---

[3]For an update on Open Market, see its home page (http:/www/openmarket.com).

Many organizations limit physical access to their computer systems. Here an employee uses a handprint recognition system to gain entrance to a computer room. Photo courtesy of Photosynthesis Archives.

Security. Computer security experts have battled computer hackers for decades; the Internet has added another dimension to this battle. The variety of resources available on the Net has lured more and more individuals and organizations to connect their computers to take advantage of the opportunities present. But once connected, these computers become vulnerable to "hackers" or "crackers" (malicious hackers) who wish to damage information systems (for example, by spreading computer viruses) or who wish to steal organizational resources.

Computer break-ins have been reported at companies such as General Electric, Sprint Corp., IBM, and Citibank. Many other organizations that have experienced computer break-ins don't report them, fearing the resulting publicity might damage their corporate image. Tsutomu Shimomura, a senior researcher at the San Diego Supercomputer Center, reported one such break-in: hackers broke into his computer electronically, seized control of it for a day, and stole copies of his files. Unfortunately, his experience is not uncommon.

In 1995, the Canadian Department of Finance was set to release the national budget to major banks and other financial firms on computer diskettes. One hour before the release was scheduled, it was discovered that the disks (which had been scanned for viruses) contained a potentially lethal computer virus. It was removed in time, but the virus came close to infecting the computer systems of many major Canadian financial institutions. The virus was one of a new type, known as polymorphic, which make detection difficult by changing slightly each time they replicate.

Many parents wish to restrict their children's access to potentially offensive material on the Web, and software has been developed to help them do so. Photo courtesy of Woodfin Camp & Associates.

In a recent demonstration, a 22-year-old math/computer science student at the University of Waterloo in Canada showed how a hacker can gain control of computer resources. Ian Goldberg was given the challenge of breaking into a Local Area Network. He responded by writing a "sniffer" program—in about 40 minutes—that allowed him to monitor activity within the LAN. The sniffer program enabled Goldberg to detect that one user was playing a game; another was typing an E-mail message. Then someone started to log on to the system. "There it is," said Goldberg, pointing at the screen. "There's the user ID—and there's the password." Armed with this information, Goldberg could log into the LAN and have access to all of the resources that the user had. If the hacker using the sniffer program was patient enough to capture the ID and password of a high-level network user (a system administrator or top-level executive), it could be the key to other users, other networks, other secrets.

Sniffer programs were apparently used by Kevin Mitnick, the 31-year-old American who allegedly stole more than $1 million worth of data and 20,000 credit card numbers through the Internet. This type of activity has apparently increased. The Computer Emergency Response Team, which monitors security issues throughout

North America from its base at Carnegie Mellon University in Pittsburgh, reported an increase from 32 intrusions in 1989 to over 2,300 in 1994. And these were only the *reported* computer intrusions; as mentioned, many go unreported. A survey conducted by the accounting firm of Ernst & Young in 1994 indicated that more that 50 percent of the 1,271 North American companies surveyed had experienced financial losses in the previous two years related to information security.

On the positive side, network administrators at most organizations are sharing information on new viruses and break-ins over the net, enabling one another to address potential security breaches quickly and effectively. As soon as a cure for a virus is found, for example, the cure is distributed through newsgroups and listservs to any interested party connected to the Net. Also, many law enforcement agencies are developing more computer expertise, and are working to share knowledge and expertise more quickly and readily. Still, the boom in computer hacking has led to a boom in computer security, and the use of thumbprints, voiceprints, or retinal scan technologies (in addition to user IDs and passwords) is becoming more widespread.

Censorship. The fast-growing nature of the Internet has led to a constant battle between advocates for free speech and individuals concerned about the widespread dissemination of material that is deemed by some members of society to be unacceptable for public access (child pornography, hate literature, etc.). Some Net users argue that there should be no censorship; if someone isn't interested in a certain topic (such as how to create a bomb to destroy a government building), they don't need to access it. Others point out that the Net isn't completely passive; material deemed offensive by some users can be transmitted (through E-mail, listservs, etc.) and stored so that a user has no choice but to be exposed to it.

Some government officials in several countries have supported taking steps to censor everything that is transmitted over the Net. The Canadian Association of Chiefs of Police recommended that the Canadian federal government make it a criminal offense to distribute pornography over computer networks. In Singapore, authorities announced plans to establish a "neighborhood police post" on the Internet to monitor and receive complaints of criminal activity, including the distribution of pornography. In the United States, a bill was introduced by Senator James Exon (Democrat, Nebraska) that would outlaw the electronic distribution of words or images deemed "obscene, lewd, lascivious, filthy, or indecent." Germany has laws that make providing access to child pornography and racist literature a crime.

This censoring and punitive approach raises a number of secondary issues, the most obvious being the question of who determines what should be classified as "obscene" or "undesirable." Since the Internet is truly international, the norms and laws concerning undesirable material differ significantly from one country to another, and even within countries, adding another wrinkle to the problem. Also, some observers point out that (1) if pornography is not illegal, then the transmission of pornography over computer networks should not be illegal, and (2) the amount of pornographic material on the Internet is so small, relative to the total, that it isn't worth trying to regulate it.

A different approach has been advocated by some private firms, who argue that the user should control what information they view, not a government. This has led to the development of software "filters," designed to detect material deemed offensive by the user and then filter it out. For example, a software program developed by SurfWatch Software Inc. allows users to block sexually oriented material. The software contains the Internet addresses of sites that have sexually explicit material, and blocks a user's attempt to access those computers. This could be used by parents wishing to block this material from their child's view.

One of the limitations to this approach is that it keys on the names of the files and directories (such as .pornography or .pedophilia), rather than on the content of the files. Those wishing to distribute this type of material can still do so by continually changing the location of the files, and by establishing coded file and directory names. This means that the vendor of the filtering software has to constantly monitor the Internet to update the list of sites their software will block, and then distribute the updated list to all users of their software.

Along similar lines, some lawmakers advocate making owners of Internet newsgroups register them and have the content rated (similar to a movie rating). Users would also have ID codes based on their age, and underage users would not be able to access restricted Internet sites.

Critics of attempts to regulate the content of material on the Internet argue that it boils down to an issue of free choice; the users should have the option of choosing what they wish to access, just as they do in a library or a bookstore. Many believe that the calls for regulation are overreactions from people who don't actually use the Internet, or even attempts by politicians to use the issue to their personal political advantage. Nevertheless, it appears that as the capabilities of the Internet expand, the issue of censorship will most likely continue to be a contentious one.

In one of the first related court cases in the United States, a New York state judge ruled that Prodigy, the on-line service provider, was responsible for the content of its subscribers' electronic mail messages. In effect, the judge ruled that Prodigy could be held liable because it functions "more as a publisher than merely as a passive conduit of information." The ruling was appealed, and the case was watched closely by the on-line information industry. On-line providers argued that they couldn't be responsible for what subscribers make publicly available; they contended that, like a bookstore or library, they exercised no control over the content of the subscribers' messages.

Intellectual Property Rights. The capability of widespread transmission of a rich variety of information sources over the Internet has led to some rather thorny property rights issues. For example, the Disney Corporation is very careful about how they control registered Disney images, such as cartoon characters from their popular movies. With the Internet, it is technically possible (and relatively easy) for someone to digitize a Disney image or video clip and store it for anyone else to access or use. It is also possible to alter the images in any way; Disney characters can be changed from friendly to fierce, from innocent to lewd. Since high-quality sound can also be digitized and transmitted, vocal artists can find that their recordings have been copied and stored on the Net. Books can be scanned and stored on Net sites, bypassing publishers and authors' royalties.

Much more subtle issues than outright theft emerge as well, however. What happens if someone accesses a file from the Internet (perhaps a shareware program), modifies it somewhat, and then sells it? How much alteration is necessary before the rights of the original owner no longer apply? Although laws exist to counteract activities such as outright theft, the laws seem to lag behind many other potential uses of the technology.

Additional Applications. As more people become familiar with the Internet and start using it, the types of applications are limited only by people's imaginations. Distance education, interactive entertainment, "virtual" family reunions . . . the list is endless. Some tourists tap into the Net for travel tips from others who have gone before them. Allen Noren toured the Baltic Sea region by motorcycle after planning the entire trip using the Internet. "I never opened a guidebook," he commented. Browsing electronic bulletin boards and newsgroups on the Baltics and Russia, he found out how to ship his motorcycle and buy fuel on the black market. (An Internet user in the Baltics gave him the name of an elderly Estonian who sold gasoline siphoned from a nearby pipeline.) On-line services can be used to book airplane tickets and hotel reservations, and there exist numerous commercial packages that can plot and print out maps and itineraries.

Steven Spielberg spearheaded another interesting application, in conjunction with four technology companies. The Hollywood director's Starbright Foundation helped link bedridden children with serious illnesses around the world. The children can use videoconferencing systems to speak with family members and other patients, and to play with children at other hospitals. The children can create animated characters to represent themselves as they interact in virtual worlds, which can be especially therapeutic for those who don't wish others to see them (such as chemotherapy patients or others whose illnesses affect their appearance). Some early studies suggest that such electronic diversions sharply reduce the need for painkilling drugs. The companies involved in the project hope to use the experiment as a way to advance their commercial applications.

A cruder but somewhat similar application was first tested in June of 1995. The first movie made for and distributed over the Internet opened with little fanfare and only a few thousand viewers. The film, entitled *Party Girl,* was viewed using software that allows for two-way video and audio transmission over the Net. The sound came through loud and clear for those users with good speakers, but the video quality left something to be desired—somewhat grainy and jerky. Nevertheless, this initial test of a concept, not unlike the first "talking picture," paved the way for many further advancements.

HISTORICAL AND PRACTICAL VIEW OF THE INTERNET

In the late 1960s the U.S. Department of Defense, and more specifically its Advanced Research Projects Agency (ARPA), created an experimental network connecting computers over telephone lines. This experimental network developed into ARPA-Net, which allowed scientists, researchers, and military personnel at diverse sites to communicate using electronic mail or through real-time conversations.

As ARPANet expanded, other networks with a limited focus were born. MILNet catered primarily to military personnel; NSFNet was for researchers and scientists working with the U.S. National Science Foundation; Bitnet for researchers and teachers at educational institutions around the world; and there were others. In the 1970s, ARPANet developed a protocol (a set of rules for communication) enabling other networks to connect to ARPANet. The Internet (internetwork system) was born in the early 1980s when other networks began to connect up to ARPANet, and it has grown rapidly in coverage and capabilities since that time.

Initially, networks such as Bitnet and ARPANet were paid for by the U.S. government. As their popularity spread and the networks matured, other organizations (such as universities) were asked to pay to connect to the network. The institution would pay a flat fee to connect, and then individuals affiliated with the institution could use network facilities without any additional charges. These "connect fees" were too expensive for most individuals or small companies, however, so Internet service providers emerged to fill the demand. The service

Software such as CuSeeMe, when combined with appropriate hardware, enables people to use the Web for personal videoconferencing. Photo courtesy of Charles Gupton/Stock Boston, Inc.

providers paid the connection fees and maintained Internet links, and then charged individual subscribers access fees. These Internet service providers included the primary on-line service providers (Prodigy, CompuServe, America OnLine) as well as many specialized firms. In this way Internet access became economical for individuals and smaller organizations, and the resulting growth in access and usage was explosive.

Names and Addresses. To help navigation throughout the Internet, every *host* (site) computer has a unique address (a *domain* address), and every person using the Internet has a username and domain address, which refers to their host address. This enables people to send and receive messages over the Net; without a unique address, the messages would never get to the correct receiver.

Consider the address "smith@bus.emba.ugm.edu" for a moment. The username is "smith"; the domain name consists of everything after the @ sign, or "bus.emba.ugm.edu." Typically, the rightmost level of the domain name indicates the type of organization (for those within the United States) or the country (for those outside of the United States). In this case, "edu" indicates an educational institution. The second one to the left might indicate the organization ("ugm" is the University of the Green Mountains), the third might be a department ("emba" or Engineering, Math and Business Administration), and the fourth a specific computer used by the department ("bus" is the imaginative name for the Business Administration computer). Domain names have as many segments as are required to uniquely identify the host computer.

In the United States, there are several types of suffix (ending) of the host domain name. Examples are:

.com	Commercial organizations
.edu	Educational institutions
.gov	Government organizations and departments

Organizations in countries other than the United States generally use a two-character suffix that indicates the country, such as:

.au	Australia	.mx	Mexico
.ca	Canada	.pl	Poland
.jp	Japan	.ru	Russian Federation

Electronic Mail, Newsgroups, List Services. One common use of the Internet is **electronic mail (E-mail),** while newsgroups and listservs are also popular. With E-mail, you can send messages to, or receive messages from, any other person who has an Internet address. It is also possible to send messages to multiple individuals at the same time, providing the E-mail software on your host computer supports that feature.

E-mail works roughly like ordinary "snail mail" (postal service), in the sense that you compose a message and send it to an address; if the address you used was correct and there are no unforeseen problems in the delivery process, the message should be received. The major difference is that with E-mail, the message is composed and transmitted electronically (or through some compatible channel or combination of channels, such as microwave or satellite transmission). If you send a message to an incorrect address, it is usually returned with an error message attached, such as "hostname not found" or "username not valid for this host."

Mailing lists or **list services (listservs)** are established to distribute messages to individuals with a common interest, such as golfing or French cuisine. Users can subscribe and unsubscribe to the listservs as they wish; membership is voluntary. When a member sends a message to the listserv, it is automatically distributed to everyone who has subscribed. If you belong to a listserv, all messages sent to the listserv will show up in your electronic mailbox.

Usenet **newsgroups** are also established for users with a common interest, but these work differently than listservs. You can think of a newsgroup as a forum for an electronic discussion; you can read the discussion that has taken place, and add your own opinions if you wish. The major difference from listservs is, instead of the messages coming to you, you go to the discussions. Newsgroups are similar to bulletin board systems (BBSs), special interest groups (SIGs) and electronic forums.

Telnet and FTP. Telnet is a feature (and an Internet command) allowing you to access computers that are connected to the Internet. Once connected, you become a **client** of the computer and it becomes the **host**. While connected, you can use the information located on the host computer, just as you can on your own computer. To establish a Telnet connection, you need to have an account on that computer. In addition, many computer sites allow you to log in as a guest in order to use some of the programs and information available.

Once you have connected to a host computer site, you may want to obtain copies of some of the programs or files stored at that site. Millions of files, stored on

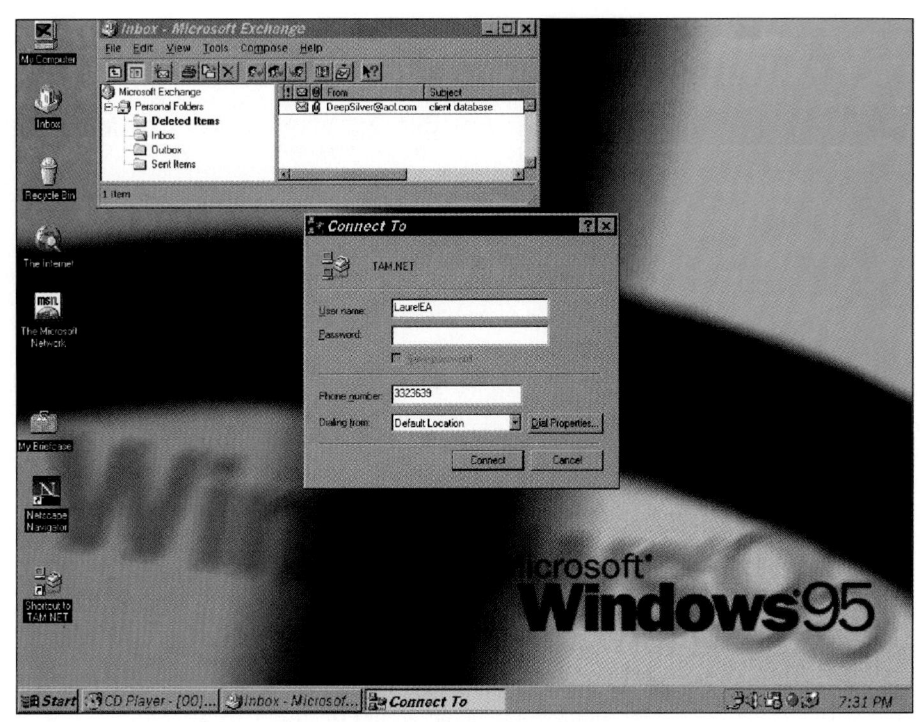

Many people use E-mail on a daily basis. Here a user checks her E-mail using Microsoft's Exchange mail system.

individual computers connected to the Internet, are free for the copying. These include shareware programs, books, maps, graphical images, sound bites, and much more. You can transfer the files from the host site to your computer using **file transfer protocol,** or **ftp.** Sometimes ftp sites are referred to as *anonymous ftp sites*, meaning that anyone is welcome to connect and get information.

Retrieving files using ftp requires you to first locate the file, and also to determine what type of file it is. Files may be stored in a variety of formats; the two most common are ASCII (text) or binary. ASCII (American Standard Code for Information Interchange) files can be produced or read by most common application software packages, such as WordPerfect or Excel, while binary files can only be read by the program used to create them. Sound files and graphic files and programs are usually stored in binary format. Files can also be compressed so that they require less space for storage and are easier to transmit. Copying a compressed file, however, requires that it be decompressed before it can be used (this issue is discussed in most "how-to" manuals).

Gopher, Archie, and Veronica. Before you can copy a file you need to find it, and finding files on the Internet is generally easier said than done. To help users locate files, numerous utility programs have been developed. One of these is **gopher,** which is a menu-based system that allows the user to search Internet sites for everything from weather reports to jokes. The gopher utility "goes for" the information you have requested from a gopher site.

As the number of gopher sites increased around the world, it became more and more difficult to locate and access them. To help address this problem, researchers at the University of Nevada developed **veronica,** which some people claim stands for "**v**ery **e**asy **r**odent-**o**riented **n**etwide **i**ndex to **c**omputerized **a**rchives." Veronica is basically an extension to gopher; it searches the titles of files in gopher servers around the world, and creates an index. Through a gopher menu choice that accesses veronica, you can then perform a keyword search on this index.

Another utility program that helps locate files is named **archie.** The archie program, developed at McGill University in the early 1990s, is designed to catalog all ftp files available on the Internet. Archie logs in to virtually all ftp sites, scans the list of ftp files, and then updates an indexed database. The database contains information such as the filename, file size, type (i.e., binary or ASCII), and a brief description.

Wide Area Information Server (WAIS). Archie and veronica do a good job of searching indexes of ftp sites and "gopherspace" for *titles,* but they don't search the *contents* of documents (files) within databases. There is a utility program, however, that does. When you give **wide area information server (WAIS)** a word or words to look for, it searches through WAIS server databases connected to the Internet for documents containing the search parameters (key words).

WAIS arose through a combined effort of three companies: Apple Computer, Dow Jones, and Thinking Machines Corporation. WAIS is supported by librarians and follows a standard defined by the American National Standards Institute (ANSI). This ensures that common standards will be applied when documents are indexed, making retrieval more consistent. In addition to simple keyword searches, WAIS allows you to enter multiple words, as well as logical operators (such as *and, or,* and *not*). The WAIS indexing and retrieval standard can be applied to many things besides text, such as graphical images and sounds.

Not all databases connected to the Internet are indexed according to WAIS standards, which means that a search using WAIS will only include a subset of Internet databases. For those sites that are WAIS-indexed, however, it provides a powerful tool for locating and retrieving information. Assume, for example, that you want to search for articles containing the word *Newtonian.* WAIS consults the indexes of the WAIS databases you specify to satisfy your search request; the indexes point to the database items (the source documents) containing that word. When an article is located, its title is displayed on your screen. If you desire, you can then review the article.

Interactive Activities. To this point we have only discussed one-way interactions on the Net; sending mail, accessing databases, retrieving images of weather maps, and so on. The Internet can also be used for interactive activities, which many people view as a major opportunity for future applications.

There are several ways to interact with other people on the Net in a real-time environment. You can use a Chat feature, which enables you to carry on an open discussion with multiple people on a channel. You can also establish a link to one other person and use Talk to carry on a conversation. Both Talk and Chat are really interactive electronic mail; instead of sending messages that wait in "mailboxes" to be retrieved, users type messages back and forth in a real-time setting. Note, however, that these are text messages and not the sound of a person's voice.

The introduction of software and hardware to carry on voice conversations over the Net has expanded possible uses significantly. Although users experience problems with the quality of the sound over some telecommunication lines, and can experience delays over long distances, the introduction of voice conversations over the Net has provided a low-cost alternative to public telephone utilities. If two users (say, one in Hong Kong and the other in Atlanta) both have the appropriate software

BUSINESS BRIEF 12-3 THERE GOES THE CYBERHOOD: INTERNET PIONEERS ABANDON WORLD THEY CREATED

As the masses get plugged into the Internet, some of the original inhabitants are fleeing, including scientists and scholars who made it such a valuable resource.

As early as 1982, Allan Schiffman used to tune into the electronic bulletin boards on the Internet every day to keep up with leading-edge discussions in his field of data encryption. Until a few years ago, he could get through a dozen topics in a half-hour or so of reading each day. But as the Internet population grew, he found increasing numbers of nonexperts flooding the bulletin boards with irrelevancies. He finally dropped the on-line discussion groups six months ago. "The sludge got pretty intolerable," says Mr. Schiffman.

"I wouldn't trust anything on [the newsgroup for computer architecture] unless I personally know the source," says Michael Slater, publisher of the *Microprocessor Report.* When he turned to the Intel newsgroup last year for updates on bugs in its Pentium chip, he found the group flooded with baseless assertions, Pentium jokes, and "hundreds if not thousands of messages beating on Intel," he says.

"I hate to sound undemocratic, but if you're going to have valuable discussion, you have to limit it to people with valuable knowledge," Mr. Slater says. "The beginners can have their beginners' group."

No one keeps statistics, but James Bizdos, president of RSA Data Security Inc., says that "the very best people are being chased off" the Internet. A 20-year Internet veteran, Mr. Bizdos used to spend up to three hours a day cruising through bulletin boards but stopped when the novices started drowning out the experts. Mr. Bizdos gave up on the Usenet altogether and, in its place, has gone back to conferences and print publications as sources of information.

Mr. Schiffman of Terisa Systems has his own way of dealing with the problems in the data-encryption newsgroup: he has a subordinate wade through it, and report back with the useful stuff.

QUESTION

1. One of the supposed advantages of the Internet is the facilitation of sharing ideas. This brief suggests that some individuals who may have a great deal to contribute to a discussion are choosing not to. What are some implications if this trend continues? Can you suggest any ways to address this situation?

SOURCE: Julie Chao, "Internet Pioneers Abandon World They Created," *The Wall Street Journal,* June 7, 1995, p. B1.

and hardware, and they establish a link over the Net, they are able to speak to each other without paying the long-distance fees. The further addition of real-time video transmission has expanded the information content of conversations from sound-only to sound and video, providing the capability of using the Net for personal videoconferencing.

Another form of interactive activity on the Net is the ever-expanding area of interactive games and entertainment. There are a multitude of games being played on the Net at all times. These range from simple two-person, information-sparse settings such as chess matches, to multi-user, multidimensional, information-rich environments such as dungeon games. As the technical capabilities of the Net continue to expand—addition of three-dimensional imaging to full-motion video, for example—the quality and sophistication of the games and other interactive activities continues to increase.

CLOSING COMMENTS ON THE NET

The potential for the Internet seems unlimited, and the growth in the number of sites, the number of users, and the amount of material is truly incredible. But quantity and quality are two very different concepts. On the downside, although there is more material available every day, some critics charge that most of it is at best interesting to a very small number of people and at worst totally useless—what some people call *cyberdreck*. Individual home pages are cluttered with pictures of favorite pets or toilets, newsgroup discussions are dominated by individuals who are poorly informed of the issues they are attempting to discuss, and some initial attempts at commercial use are clumsy and almost embarrassing for both the user and the advertiser. Business Brief 12–3 describes some of the problems.

Some early Net users argued that the Internet should be totally independent, with no commercial use. Others argued that without the development and use of systems for payment of services, the quality of material will only continue to decline. As systems are developed where users are required to pay to access material, they soon discover what is worthwhile and what isn't. The useful material will grow and flourish, the successful applications will expand and prosper. The less useful material (which no one is willing to pay for), will simply sit on the Net like a book that no one ever looks up or uses.

It looks like the second argument has won. For the Internet to expand, flourish, and provide its many potential benefits, commercial applications are necessary. Furthermore, attempts to rigidly control the content of everything on the Internet would unnecessarily restrict its development, and would prove virtually impossible to police. As with other means of communication in our society (such as television), certain abuses will undoubtedly occur. With a larger percentage of society tapping into the Net, however, society's norms should begin to relegate the abuses to lesser roles.

SUMMARY

Information technology is increasingly being used for electronic commerce. Many types of electronic commerce involve the use of interorganizational systems (IOS), which link two or more organizations. Often, electronic data interchange (EDI) is used to electronically transmit common business documentation, such as purchase orders and invoices. In more extreme cases, virtual organizations are created where different companies focus on different aspects of operations (marketing, distribution, payment), and information technology provides the communication links among them.

On-line network service providers such as America OnLine charge users for access to information products and services. They also provide access to the Internet, and are increasingly coming under competitive pressure from the Internet itself. The service providers argue that they are able to give users a much more structured environment, while more experienced users argue that the added benefits are marginal at best.

The Internet, and especially the World Wide Web portion of the Internet, continues to see explosive growth in the content and number of users. In addition to the typical user features, the Internet is now being used for many commercial applications. As payment systems mature and users become more comfortable with the notion of doing business over the Internet, this trend will most likely continue.

The rapid growth of Internet use has raised many issues. These include security and confidentiality of information, censorship, and intellectual property rights. The Internet technology also lends itself to a wide variety of applications, which seem to expand on a very frequent basis. The Internet is still very much like an adolescent—somewhat gangly and clumsy, full of good intentions and mischief, and growing very fast—and predicting how it will evolve is an impossible task at this time.

KEY CONCEPTS AND TERMS

KEY CONCEPTS

- Electronic commerce is a growing reality for many organizations. (397)
- Information technology is the backbone for electronic commerce, including the use of electronic data interchange and the Internet. (399)
- As with any powerful new technology, the Internet holds the potential for dramatic changes (positive and negative) to societal as well as commercial applications. (400)

KEY TERMS

archie (419)
client (417)
electronic commerce (397)
electronic data interchange (EDI) (397)
electronic mail (E-mail) (417)
file transfer protocol (ftp) (418)
gopher (418)
home page (403)
host computer (417)
hypermedia (403)
hypertext (403)
HyperText Markup Language (HTML) (403)
Internet (Net) (401)
interorganizational systems (IOS) (397)
link (402)
list service (listserv) (417)
newsgroup (417)
node (403)
veronica (418)
wide area information service (WAIS) (419)
Web browser (403)
World Wide Web (WWW, Web) (403)

REFERENCES

Applegate, L. M., and J. Gogan. "Electronic Commerce: Trends and Opportunities." Harvard Business School, Note 9-196-006, August 1995.

———. "Paving the Information Superhighway: Introduction to the Internet." Harvard Business School, Note 9-195-202, August 1995.

Financial Times Review, Information Technology, May 3, 1995.

Maclean's, "Crime in Cybercity." May 22, 1995, pp. 50–59.

Maclean's, "Plugging Into the Internet." January 29, 1996, pp. 28–35.

Salmon, W. J., and D. Wylie. "Calyx & Corolla." Harvard Business School, Case 952-035.

Wall Street Journal, "The High Road on the Highway: Helping Sick Kids Play Together." May 10, 1995.

Wall Street Journal, "New On-Line Casinos May Thwart U.S. Laws." May 10, 1995.

Wall Street Journal, "Cybercash Gets Clearance to Sell Product Abroad." May 8, 1995.

Wall Street Journal, "Time Warner Sells Ads in Cyberspace Via Its Pathfinder Service on Internet." May 10, 1995.

Wall Street Journal, "Home Banking: Will It Take Off This Time?" June 8, 1995, pg. B1.

Wall Street Journal, "New Software Filters Sexual, Racist Fare Circulated on Internet." May 15, 1995.

Wall Street Journal, "Web Trap: Internet's Popularity Threatens to Swamp the On-Line Services." January 18, 1996.

Wall Street Journal, "AOL, Netscape Are Discussing An Alliance." January 22, 1996.

SAMPLE INTERNET HOW-TO REFERENCE GUIDES

Bradley, Julia Case. *A Quick Guide to the Internet.* Albany: Integrated Media Group, 1995.

Salkind, Neil J. *Hands-On Internet.* New York: Boyd & Fraser, 1995.

Wyatt, Allen L. *Success With Internet*, New York: Boyd & Fraser, 1995.

CONNECTIVE CASE: Students Off-Campus Rentals

Pete Dixon provides a good example of how the potential of the Internet is changing how some organizations conduct business. In August of 1995, the 32-year-old computer consultant from Kitchener, Ontario, spent several frustrating hours helping his younger brother, a community college student, find an apartment in nearby London, Ontario. "It ticked me off that we had to keep searching through the papers and driving around to student housing centers," he recalls. "I knew it didn't have to be that way."

Five months later, Dixon launched his digital-age alternative: a site on the Internet's World Wide Web that enabled students at 59 Canadian Universities to hunt for housing on-line. Dixon's plan was simple: allow student's free access to the service, while charging landlords for listings. In that sense, Internet SOCR (Students Off-Campus Rentals) is a 1990s version of the classified advertisement section. But the Web makes it possible to search for listings by price range, number of bedrooms, proximity to public transit, and so on—even down to whether the landlord allows pets. The results appear on the screen in seconds, and service is accessible from any Internet-linked computer anywhere on the planet.

One of the interesting aspects of this is how little it cost Dixon to get his business running. For competitive reasons, he doesn't want to discuss actual numbers. But it is certainly a fraction of the cost of, say, a doughnut franchise. Including the purchase of a computer and software, a reasonably attractive Web site might cost $6,000 to $8,000; after that, expenses tend to depend on the amount of traffic.

Dixon uses other technology to help hold costs down and improve operational efficiencies. Landlords who want to place an advertisement are able to call a 1-800 number and be connected with a computer that uses voice-recognition software. Based on the caller's area code and exchange, the computer then sends a pager message to the nearest available of Dixon's service representatives (he hires students on a commission basis, after interviewing them on-line). The local representative then phones the landlord, takes down the information, and enters it into a computer. When the landlord wishes to cancel the ad—rates are $60 per month—he or she need only phone the main number again and punch in a special code. "Everything's so automated, we're actually wondering if we'll need anyone in the office," says Dixon.

Case Question

1. Analyze the competitive position and strategy of SOCR, and identify the relevant issues you believe Pat Dixon should be aware of.

SOURCE: Ross Laver, "The Next Frontier," *Maclean's*, January 22, 1996, p. 38.

IT'S YOUR TURN — END OF CHAPTER MATERIALS

REVIEW QUESTIONS

1. What does the acronym EDI stand for? Briefly describe the functions of EDI.
2. What does the term *electronic commerce* refer to? Provide an example of electronic commerce.
3. List three on-line network service providers. What are some common products or services offered by an on-line network service provider?
4. What features of the World Wide Web caused it to grow in popularity so rapidly?
5. Briefly describe three opportunities for using the Internet for commercial purposes.
6. Why is security a concern on the Internet? Who is responsible for maintaining Internet security?
7. What are some of the basic issues underlying concerns about censorship on the Internet?
8. Why are intellectual property rights a concern for users of the Internet?
9. Briefly identify several potential applications for the Internet.
10. How quickly are the on-line services growing, relative to the use of the Internet?

DISCUSSION QUESTIONS

1. This book has stressed the importance of communication in the functioning of an organization. In what ways can the Internet be used to facilitate (or impede) organizational communication?
2. One important component for effective decision making is access to appropriate information. In what ways can the Internet be used to facilitate (or impede) the acquisition of information for decision making?
3. Throughout this book we have stressed the need for organizational responsiveness to environmental changes. In what ways can the Internet be used to facilitate (or impede) organizational responsiveness?
4. Now consider the Internet as part of the environment in which organizations operate. In what ways can the Internet influence the organizational environment?
5. The adoption and use of many new information technologies raise ethical dilemmas for organizations and individuals. List several such dilemmas arising from the use of the Internet.
6. Comment on the statement, "There is no such thing as a completely secure computer system."

GROUP ASSIGNMENT

1. Individually, allocate a total of 45 minutes to complete the first part of this assignment. Use a Web browser to access the Internet, and then locate information on five master's programs in business administration at U.S. universities, one in each of the following areas: (*a*) Northeast, (*b*) Southeast,

(*c*) Midwest, (*d*) Southwest, and (*e*) Northwest. Try to locate the number of students in the graduate program, the entrance requirements, and the average GMAT score.

After 45 minutes, compare your list with those of your group members. Comment on the different search strategies that each chose, and how successful they were. As a group, go to your University library, and try to discover the same information without using the Internet. Comment on the efficiency and effectiveness of using the Internet for this task.

APPLICATION ASSIGNMENTS

1. Locate the Web page for this textbook. Download the latest statistics on the subscriptions for On-Line Service providers. Paste that information to a PowerPoint slide, and comment on the winners and losers in terms of market share.
2. Use a Web browser and search engine on the Internet to retrieve information on "laptop computers." Modify the search by adding "Compaq, laptop computer." Describe any differences you note in the results. What implications might you draw from this for general information retrieval using Web search engines?
3. Retrieve the home page for this textbook. Next, use the "source" feature of your Web browser to display and then print a listing of the source HTML programming code which generates that page. Comment on how difficult you believe it would be to learn to program using HTML.

CASE ASSIGNMENT Banking on the Net

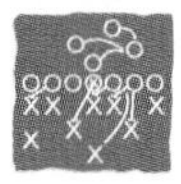

"Marty, I refuse to consider any option that places our clients' funds or financial information at risk," stated Simon Greenwood, president of Great Northern Bank (GNB). Martin Turgeon, vice president of client services, responded quickly. "But Simon, we need to have more of a presence on the Internet. Our competitors are expanding their Net services almost daily. If we don't join them, we could lose customers."

For almost 20 years, Simon Greenwood had guided the bank from his position of president and chief executive officer. Two months ago, however, Simon had announced his plans to retire the following year. Simon and the board of directors were looking for a successor, and three of the senior executives who reported to Simon were considered good candidates. One of these was Martin Turgeon, who had been with the bank for 10 years.

THE COMPANY

Great Northern Bank was located in the Pacific Northwest region of the United States, and had been in operation for well over 100 years. The bank had changed operations substantially over time, but tended to follow rather than lead in introducing new products or services. GNB was relatively small, with a regional focus. Although not located in a large urban center, GNB still faced stiff competition from both local banks and the branch offices of larger competitors.

Over the years, GNB had built a reputation for being somewhat conservative, but very safe. During the 1980s, many competing financial institutions had extended themselves to provide loans and mortgages to finance the growth that was being experienced at the time. GNB's conservative lending policies kept it from growing as rapidly during that period, but these same policies meant that GNB did not experience the same level of hardship during the subsequent recession. GNB offered its clients good, basic financial services and low-risk (and subsequently slightly lower-return) investment opportunities.

ON-LINE BANKING

The whole issue of home banking was somewhat tricky. Banks had been offering home banking services for quite some time, mostly using touch-tone telephones. Although a small number of customers took advantage of the limited services offered, many did not seem to use telephone or personal computer services for much more than checking balances in their accounts. Additional functions they could perform included tracking their accounts, making transfers, and paying bills electronically. Some banks also allowed customers to apply for loans or credit cards. Still, use by customers was limited.

When personal computers started outselling color television sets (in 1994) and personal-finance software jumped in sales, however, banks started watching carefully. The ill-fated attempt by Microsoft Corp. to buy the Intuit, Inc., software company (in 1995) made many bankers nervous, since this suggested that powerful nonbank companies such as Microsoft could try to compete in the home banking industry. Although home banking hadn't really taken off before, some observers believed that the time could be ripe. As a larger percentage of North American households obtained personal computers and homeowners became familiar with using on-line services and the Internet, the bankers felt that consumers might lose some of their hesitation about trusting electronic financial services.

To allow customers or potential customers to reach them electronically, banks (and competing nonbank institutions) basically had three options. They could develop their own proprietary systems, they could use systems offered by a commercial on-line service such as Prodigy, or they could use the Internet.

Many larger banks (such as Citibank, NationsBank and BankAmerica) had developed their own software and launched their own on-line systems nationwide. This approach was very expensive and resulted in the development of incompatible systems. A limited number of banks had signed on with commercial on-line services, but they found that only a relatively small percentage of customers seemed willing to sign on with the same on-line provider to access the bank. After all, on-line services were certainly not free; and many customers who subscribed to a different on-line provider were reluctant to switch.

THE INTERNET ISSUE

The explosion in Internet use, which really heated up during the mid 1990s, caught many bankers off guard. Although some jumped in quickly to try and be the first in the industry to take advantage of the "new" medium, most held back. The decision of whether to provide Internet services, and what services to offer, was not a simple one.

In 1993, only about 15 North American banks had registered addresses on the Internet. In 1994, 60 more went on-line, and three times that number in 1995. At first, most of the banks' Web sites were not much more than the Internet equivalent of roadside billboards, but soon some began offering some limited services. Several, including Capital One Bancorp, accepted credit-card applications over the Net. Canada Trust offered a discounted rate for customers who applied for car loans on-line, while Toronto Dominion Securities bank gave users daily financial market reports, allowed them to download software that could help write business plans, and suggested asset allocations based on the profile of the customer.

At Wells Fargo, the first step was to let customers access information about their accounts over the Internet. The hope was that once they got used to using the technology, they would feel more comfortable trying additional services such as paying bills and transferring money among accounts. But Wells Fargo didn't rely completely on the Internet; it also used the Prodigy system and had its own private network as well. Its approach was to try and offer whatever platform its customers wanted.

GREAT NORTHERN DILEMMA

For Martin Turgeon, getting a presence on the Internet seems essential. He firmly believes that any further delays could hurt. "We can't afford a private network," he claims. "And it looks like the Internet is going to continue to grow, while commercial services like America OnLine and Prodigy may grow, or they may level off or shrink. With systems like the Internet, customers don't have to physically go to a bank. They can do most of their banking without ever leaving their home, and I believe that more and more customers will choose home banking. If GNB doesn't offer that type of service, we're dead."

Simon Greenwood sees the situation differently. "Sure, a few banks have jumped in because they're afraid of missing the bandwagon. But despite recent efforts to provide hacker-proof security and standards, I don't trust it. Hackers still cause damage. If someone broke into our systems and altered or damaged any customer files, the negative publicity would kill us. We may lose a few clients, but I'm willing to bet that most are still more interested in security than on-line banking over the Internet. We offer sufficient on-line banking with our telephone service to keep them satisfied."

Questions

1. Put yourself in the position of a consultant hired by Martin Turgeon. Prepare a list of potential applications and services that GNB could provide over the Internet. Don't restrict yourself to those listed in the case.
2. Put yourself in the position of a consultant hired by Simon Greenwood. Prepare a brief statement presenting the merits and demerits of having GNB provide on-line banking services over the Internet.
3. Now put yourself in the shoes of Martin Turgeon. What additional information might be useful in deciding whether or not to push for putting GNB on-line? How (or where) could that information be obtained?

SOURCE: This case was written by Associate Professors Ronald Thompson and William Cats-Baril of the School of Business Administration, University of Vermont. The case is intended as a basis for discussion and is not meant to illustrate effective or ineffective handling of an administrative situation.

CHAPTER 13 Information Technology and Society

CHAPTER OBJECTIVES

After reading this chapter, you should have an appreciation for the diverse ways in which information technology is influencing our society. More specifically, you should be able to:

- Understand that information technology is having an impact across all areas of society.
- Discuss both positive and negative consequences of the use of information technology in these areas.
- Understand that while the opportunities from using information technology are tremendous, so are the potential problems.

The only constant in today's society is change, and information technology is driving it. Are you ready?

INTRODUCTION

In this book, we have focused primarily on information technology and management; in other words, the use of I/T in organizational settings and for organizational purposes. In doing so, we have alluded to some societal issues such as ethical dilemmas that arise in the use of information technology, issues like the right to privacy and freedom of expression.

As students of management, we need to concern ourselves mainly with managerial issues. As members of society, however, we cannot ignore the broader societal issues. Therefore, we would be remiss if we did not include in this book a discussion of the influence of information technology on society as a whole.

Breakthroughs in technology have led to major changes in society. Photos courtesy of Chip Clark/Offshoot Stock (top left) and (top center) Michael Holford Collection (top right), Photo Researchers (bottom left), Cray Computers (bottom right).

Information technology can help reduce pollutants released in the air. Intelligent sensors adjust temperature and the mix of gases to minimize pollution. Photo courtesy of Tony Stone Worldwide.

Throughout human history, there has been a very strong interplay between technological innovation and societal changes. From the development of the first crude tools to today's sophisticated systems, the adoption of new technology altered various aspects of society in dramatic ways. Historians differ in their interpretations of this interplay; some adopt a "hard determinism" stance, arguing that technology drives social change, while others view the interactions from a "soft determinism" perspective, arguing that groups select and organize technologies within a matrix of social conditions and cultural practices.[1]

Information technology has altered society in many ways, and in an exceedingly short time span. Indeed, the last couple of decades have had the highest rate of change in the known history of humankind—and the changes are far from over. Unfortunately, we do not have a crystal ball to enable us to predict with any certainty what lies ahead; we can only observe past changes and speculate on future ones.

In this final chapter, we offer few answers; instead, we raise questions and propositions for your consideration and reflection on the impact of information technology on our daily life. Also, we don't claim to have an exhaustive list of the important issues or possibilities. As you read this chapter, undoubtedly other issues will come to mind. Our hope is that by presenting this material, you will view information technology as holding the potential to facilitate strong and sweeping changes in many aspects of our lives. We also hope that with such awareness you may approach these changes in a proactive rather than a passive manner, and that in doing so you will become involved in making the world a better place to be.

ECOLOGY

The survival of the human species is dependent on the continued ability of the environment to support life. The state of the environment has become one of the most sensitive political issues of our time. Information technology has been playing

[1]See Smith and Marx (1994) for a series of 13 articles examining the interplay between technology and society.

BUSINESS BRIEF 13-1

BEAN ME UP, SCOTTY: THE SPACE AGE TOUCHES DOWN ON THE FARM

Big farm equipment manufacturers and suppliers are beginning to roll out farming systems that use satellite signals and other gizmos to measure the crop yields every few yards in their fields. Since the soil, moisture, and yield can vary widely in a field, the farmer uses the information to adjust the quality and mix of seed, fertilizers, and pesticides instead of spreading the same mixtures throughout the field, says the U.S. Department of Agriculture Research Service.

A Rockwell Corp. division later this month introduces a system that tracks yields in the field and builds a database so that the farmer can pinpoint trouble spots. Case Corp., in Racine, Wisconsin, and Deere & Co., in Moline, Illinois, are making their combines and other equipment more adaptable to the precision farming systems while testing their own systems.

QUESTION

1. Briefly describe some potential advantages of using this type of farming equipment. How quickly do you believe "precision farming" will spread? What factors might influence a farmer's decision of whether to use this approach?

SOURCE: *The Wall Street Journal*, June 8, 1995, p. 1.

a role by reducing environmental pollutants, monitoring environmental activities, and providing valuable information as input to policy-making processes.

For the purpose of reducing factory and industrial pollutants, information technology has been applied in numerous ways. By placing sensors in smokestacks, for example, companies are able to detect pollutant levels and adjust the temperature of waste-burning fires as required to remove the maximum amount of waste. Automatic sensors and monitors can also be set up throughout industrial production processes, helping to monitor and reduce wastes within the processes.

One major source of pollution of the earth is the heavy use of agricultural products such as chemical fertilizers, pesticides, and herbicides. In the past, these chemicals were applied somewhat indiscriminately, resulting in excess waste runoff which polluted underground water supplies as well as streams, rivers, and lakes. Proponents of the use of fertilizers have argued that without the chemicals, the agricultural industry would be unable to keep up with the increased food demands from a growing world population. Critics have argued that the resulting agricultural pollutants are killing the water supplies and that there are other means of increasing agricultural productivity.

Information technology brought about a compromise. The composition of the soil can change dramatically over very short distances; it is not unusual to find various soil compositions within one field. In the past, many farmers would take some soil samples, come up with an estimate of the average fertilizer needs given an average composition, and mix the appropriate chemicals for application over the entire field. Today, there are computerized fertilizing systems mounted on tractors that combine data from **global positioning satellite (GPS) systems** with the data from soil samples collected as the tractor moves through the field (see Business Brief 13-1). The data are analyzed on the spot and then the system mixes and applies custom amounts of fertilizer over each different type of soil within the field. This approach drastically reduces the amount of fertilizer used, which in turn reduces the resultant waste runoff (which makes environmentalists happy) and the costs (which makes the farmer happy). This type of system is still quite new, however, and is not being used very extensively.

Information technology helps monitor and model the earth's ecological systems, including weather patterns and the ozone layer. Photo courtesy of Ann Hawthorne.

Information technology is also being used in various ways to aid environmental resource management. Organizations such as the Environmental Systems Research Institute (ESRI) develop and implement systems, called **geographic information systems (GIS),** which are used for a variety of resource management activities throughout the world. These systems are tailored to specific needs, but generally focus on aspects of:

1. Society (cities, population density, political systems).
2. Social infrastructure (transportation, industry, power generation).
3. Resources (agriculture, land use, landscapes, soil, mineral resources, etc.).
4. Lithosphere (earthquakes, volcanoes, impact craters, etc.).
5. Atmosphere (air temperature, precipitation, solar radiation).
6. Hydrosphere (hydrographic network, surface runoff, water resources, etc.).

The types of applications for environmental systems vary substantially, and some are beginning to be quite comprehensive. For example, the country of Cyprus began a $12 million effort in 1995 to develop an integrated system to map the entire country. System administrators envision a single system for Cyprus that will automate all of its survey management business practices for land records management and fiscal/taxation accounting. The system will ultimately become the framework for

Geographic information systems (GIS) are helping cities to manage their resources better by creating interactive maps of their infrastructures. Photo courtesy of the U.S. Census Bureau.

other applications in areas including environmental, utilities, and transportation. The system will allow government agencies to monitor the effects of land sales and transfers, transportation and utility infrastructure developments, and so on.

Despite the potential for I/T to be used in ways to provide a positive influence on environmental management, there is obviously no guarantee that such uses will prevail. Despite good intentions on the part of many individuals and governments, the inherent tension between environmental resources and human consumption will continue. Many developing nations are more concerned with providing minimal living standards for their people than in preserving the environment—in effect, sacrificing longer-term resources to satisfy short-term needs.

GOVERNANCE

The lives and behaviors of human beings are governed, to a greater or lesser extent, by other human beings. Information technology can influence the scope and type of governance greatly.

The stereotype of the potential negative impact of information technology on the freedom of society was depicted by George Orwell in his classic book *1984*. Orwell described a stark society dominated in a ruthless way by the dictator "Big Brother" through electronic means. Many of the features used to control the lives of

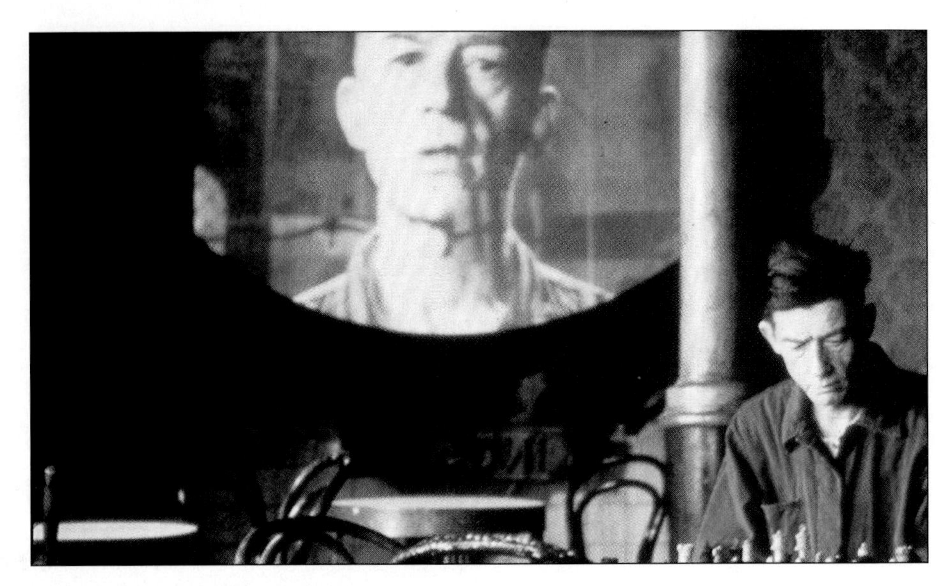

People have always feared the control that government might have in an all-electronic society. Photo courtesy of Shooting Star.

citizens in that society are technically feasible today, and some have actually been implemented on a limited basis.

In an Orwellian dictatorship, I/T would theoretically be used to monitor and control the activities of all citizens/subjects. Identification codes could be assigned to all people at birth, and all major events (educational achievements, medical history, work records, etc.) would be recorded. Citizens/subjects would be assigned to work details as needed, without their free choice. All reading material would be stored in an electronic database that would be censored regularly. Any deviation from the prescribed norm (such as writing electronic messages that criticize the dictator) could be detected and the citizen/subject punished.

Obviously, there is a dark side to an all-electronic world: the possibility of someone erasing, or changing, your identity and entire life by pushing a delete button is a perennial fear. More realistic but still worrisome is that someone will be able to snoop on you without your knowledge; and recent proposals of intelligence agencies like the FBI to expand their wiretap capabilities do not make people feel any more comfortable about the government gathering and centralizing personal information.

At the other end of the scale, many people have created visions of utopian democracies where, thanks to I/T, all citizens participate equally in setting policy for a country. This view proposes that it would be technically feasible to have all citizens vote electronically on all important issues rather than relying on elected or appointed officials to vote on their behalf.

In this view of governance structure, the role of government would be to propose legislation and to help carry out the "true will of the people," while the citizens would be responsible for making the actual decisions on proposed legislation. Citizens could even provide individual input on major decisions, such as suggestions for how to balance budgets for federal governments. (Business Brief 13–2 describes an experiment in this direction.) All government activity, including expenditures, could be recorded and provided openly and instantaneously to citizens, who could monitor government activity at their discretion.

BUSINESS BRIEF 13-2 THE FEDERAL BUDGET GETS WIRED: CITIZENS ON THE INTERNET CAN NOW PLAY SENATOR

Berkeley, CA: Taking interactive civic education to a new level, UC-Berkeley's Center for Community Economic Research (CCER) today demonstrated a new on-line National Federal Budget Simulator that lets anyone on the World Wide Web try their hand at balancing the budget. The simulation is located at http://garnet.berkeley.edu:3333/budget/budget.html

Going beyond the rhetoric and headlines of budget choices, this simulation allows Internet users to control a whole range of budget choices, submit a budget, and interactively see the changes in the federal deficit. Internet "Senators" can get into the nitty-gritty of controlling mass transit spending, weapons procurement, national parks allocations, and social welfare spending, and see results of cuts in all areas of the $1.5 trillion budget.

Additionally, Internet "Senators" are given interactive control of the $455 billion in "tax expenditures" in the federal budget. Some have called these tax deductions the largest hidden entitlements of the federal budget and this simulation demonstrates how adding them into the budget debate opens up far wider possibilities for balancing the federal budget.

The National Budget Simulator is part of the ongoing work of the Center for Community Economic Research to promote economic and civic literacy through interactive Internet tools. "The Internet has a lot of flash and glitz, but most of what is on the World Wide Web are cute toys," notes Dr. Anders Schneiderman, CCER's codirector. "This National Budget Simulator is one of the first tools on the Internet that really takes advantage of the interactive nature of the technology to enhance civic education."

QUESTIONS

1. To what extent do you think those responsible for setting the U.S. federal budget would be interested in viewing the suggestions of those using the budget simulator?
2. Of what benefit might the budget simulator be to those who decide to try it?
3. Do you think this might be a legitimate way for constituents to provide meaningful input to the governing process? Why or why not?

SOURCE: Press Release, Center for Community Economic Research, UC Berkeley, CA, May 30, 1995.

In some countries, efforts have been made to use I/T to make governance at least appear more open. In the previous chapter, we mentioned that although U.S. government departments and agencies have placed a great deal of information on the Internet, there are some who question the usefulness of the information. Also, the sheer volume of data can effectively hide useful information; there may be a nugget of gold in there somewhere, but who knows how to find it?

However, some agencies have created incentives for people to use electronic means to interact with them. The IRS has suggested that those individuals filing electronically may get their refunds (if they are due, of course!) sooner. Also, by making regulations available electronically, federal and state agencies argue that they are simplifying life for those businesses that are the target of those regulations. Rather than reading the whole Federal Register, for example, businesses can do electronic searches on keywords to identify aspects of legislation that affect them.

Some government leaders have been using interactive technologies to try and appear more connected with their constituents. In France, the Minitel system (discussed in the case at the end of this module) was used as early as 1988 by the then President Francois Mitterand to "discuss" issues with his citizens. In the United States, Vice President Al Gore went on-line by 1994 to answer concerns from taxpayers, and in Canada, the prime minister in 1995 (Jean Chrétien) participated in an interactive question-and-answer session with Canadians over the Internet. That

Government is using I/T to appear closer and more open to its citizens.

same year in the United States, President Bill Clinton had his commencement speech at Dartmouth College transmitted over the Internet, and today you can visit the White House and talk to the President by visiting the White House's home page on the Web.

At the international level, I/T can facilitate communication and cooperation between national governing bodies. Disseminating information to one hundred countries is just as easy as disseminating it to one. Information could be shared on whatever issues are necessary: trade, crime, and so on. The creation of a Europe that allows the free flow of people without internal borders (a concept that was implemented in 1995 among seven European countries) has been made contingent on the capability of European countries to share information on the legal status of all their citizens and strengthen the controls to keep track of non-Europeans who enter and live in Europe. This capability is being implemented as a huge information system to be accessible from all border posts and ports of entry in Europe.

International governing bodies such as the World Trade Organization will have the technical capability to share information and truly act internationally—assuming, of course, that national countries are willing to abide by international rulings. Although the information technology exists to facilitate international governance, it is questionable just how quickly and in what arenas countries will be willing to subject their short-term national interests for long-term, potentially more positive international interests. The latest problems with the European unification are a good case in point.

INTERNATIONAL RELATIONS AND POLITICAL POWER

It is relatively easy for one nation of humans to ostracize or condemn another when national perceptions are filtered through a lens of stereotypes and biases. It is much more difficult for one human being to support the condemnation of another nation when s/he has had personal communication and interactions with citizens of the other nation. Many of the problems experienced between nations are a result of misperceptions and miscommunications. To the extent that information technology fosters and facilitates communication between individuals from all nations, it holds the potential to reduce these misperceptions and miscommunications.

In the past, many people have relied on their government leaders to interpret the actions of other governments, and to develop responses to those actions. Government spokespeople disseminated information, through the mass media, to their citizens. Only a relatively small percentage of the population (especially in large countries such as the United States, Canada, or Russia) could actually use personal experiences, like those gained through extensive world travel, to interpret the messages disseminated by their government leaders. And, too, some governments have been quite successful at controlling the mass media in their country and hence controlling, misinterpreting, or hiding events they did not want publicized.

With the widespread use of information technology, these situations are changing rapidly. Although people may not physically travel much more than they did in recent years, many travel electronically and communicate with one another over the Internet and through other international telecommunications media; and they watch TV. As familiarity with individuals from various cultures and geographic regions increases, the misperceptions and misconceptions decrease. Also, as fax machines and electronic mail systems become commonplace, people take information dissemination into their own hands, making government control of information almost impossible.

Today, it is much more difficult for governments to conceal major events and policies from the rest of the world and their own citizens. For example, because of the extensive use of I/T in financial markets, these markets are now integrated around the world, allowing for 24-hour trading and facilitating the rapid movement of financial capitals. If financial analysts are wary of activities in one country, they must be offered a premium to leave capital there (i.e., by offering higher interest rates). This rapid movement of money around the world has taken some governments by surprise and limited the amount of flexibility to find policy solutions. This issue was brought home to the leaders of Mexico in late 1994 and early 1995, when their decision to devalue the peso led to a huge migration of funds that greatly impeded their ability to make or act upon internally generated policies.

Similarly, the government of Canada discovered (to their chagrin) that reactions by international financial markets to their internal policies actually placed very large restrictions on their policy options. For one thing, although they wanted to lower interest rates to stimulate the economy, leaders in the government discovered that the international markets demanded higher interests to compensate for the perception that the Canadian national debt load was way too high.

On a more political front, the freedom fighters in the 1989 Tiananmen Square protests in China used faxes and E-mail communication to spread information about

Information and images move so quickly around the globe that not even governments can stop them. Photo courtesy of AP/Wide World.

the confrontation and let the world know that the Chinese government's version of the events was not quite true. President Bush watched the bombs that he had ordered dropped on Baghdad during the 1991 Gulf War on CNN and got the TV report on the damage before he got the report from his generals. French citizens were able to read the account of President Mitterand's long and painful fight against cancer on the Internet a day after a judge had ruled that the book depicting the president's illness could not be published.

International relations and political power continue to be influenced a great deal by military strength, whether it be real or perceived. In this arena, information technology also plays a major role. In addition to the more obvious uses (such as intelligent weapons systems designed to hit very narrowly defined targets, which showed their devastating power and accuracy in the Gulf War of 1991), I/T is used behind the scenes for applications such as war-gaming.

These games are not for fun; intelligence-gathering systems feed data constantly into software that uses game theory approaches to predict outcomes to real or potential conflict scenarios. Within the United States, some military advisors have predicted that the application of information technology will become the predominant factor in balance-of-power situations, rather than traditional measures such as troop numbers and weapons stores.

POPULATION MOVEMENT

The industrial revolution meant fewer farm jobs, and more jobs in the cities. As a result, there was a massive migration of people from rural areas into urban ones. Cities expanded, while many rural towns stagnated, declined, or even disappeared. Cities grew to represent centers of society, and relatively few people made the reverse trek back to rural areas.

The growth of cities resulted in congestion, crime, and a host of problems which led to the development of large suburban areas surrounding the cities. Commuting

Information technology has revolutionized the capability of weapons and in so doing has changed military strategy. This computerized pilotless reconnaissance plane can fly over hostile territory for hours on end gathering intelligence without risking the life of a pilot. Photo courtesy of AP/Wide World.

became the norm for many professionals; live in the relatively safe suburb and drive (or use public transportation) to reach the job in the city. Eventually, many companies followed their employees, setting up satellite offices and then head offices in the suburbs. Many suburbs began to look more like cities, with office buildings, congestion, and so on.

As the Information Age flourishes, information technology is facilitating a potential migration back to rural areas. Many professionals are learning ways to earn a living that do not require being physically tied to an office or specific geographic location. More and more individuals are making the choice of where to live on quality-of-life criteria rather than proximity to a company office building. Many of these individuals telecommute to work. **Telecommuting** consists of staying home and "making it to the office" electronically. If telecommuting became the norm rather than the exception, the need for skyscrapers and multilane highways in our cities would diminish substantially.

Some rural towns and areas are discovering that with a good information technology infrastructure, they can successfully compete with larger centers when it comes to attracting potential landowners who can afford to pay property taxes and otherwise provide a positive contribution to the community. Just as the coming of the railroad brought life to rural communities during the 19th century, the coming of the I/T infrastructure can bring life to communities today.

Consider the largely rural province of New Brunswick in Canada. During the early and mid 1990s, New Brunswick invested heavily in information technology infrastructure. The provincial government persuaded major telecommunication companies to enter joint arrangements allowing New Brunswick to benefit from the latest in fiber-optic cabling, communication switching devices, and other technology. Once the infrastructure was in place, the provincial government went on the road, encouraging companies to relocate part or all of their business to New Brunswick. It offered a safe, clean living environment, a well-educated, largely

As long as you can connect to the information superhighway, you've got an office—even though it may be a virtual one. Photo courtesy of Robert Frerck/Woodfin Camp & Associates.

bilingual (French/English) workforce, and a sophisticated I/T infrastructure. The marketing efforts were successful, and the province experienced a significant influx of professional jobs and people.

Another example is illustrated by the experiences of Ainsworth, Nebraska. For years, travelers passing through were greeted by a billboard that said, only partly in jest, "Welcome to Ainsworth, the Middle of Nowhere." When a strong gust of wind blew the sign down, it seemed like an omen of change. While Ainsworth is far from the nearest interstate highway, it (and many other small towns) find themselves located right on the information superhighway. Ainsworth's public library boasts a two-way videoconferencing unit. Local ministers, hospital officials, a lawyer, and an insurance agent use it regularly. The Over-50 Club even squeezed in front of the set to discuss their arthritis with the staff of a nursing home in far-off Omaha.

During the 1980s, farm consolidations, plummeting land prices, and declining services drove many people out of rural areas like Ainsworth. During the 1990s, that trend has reversed. While some of the influx is caused by retirees or companies seeking lower-cost environments, information technology is exerting a pull of its own. "Every survey shows more people want to live in small towns than can find jobs there," says Calvin Beale, a senior demographer with the U.S. Department of Agriculture. "If you wire them, they will come."

Similar to the experiment in New Brunswick, the state of Nebraska invested heavily in I/T infrastructure. Some 6,700 miles of fiber-optic cable was laid, for example. State officials have used the systems to sponsor small-town experiments in telemedicine and distance learning. Which leads us to our next topics.

HEALTH AND MEDICINE

Medicine has long been known as a field that embraces and exploits new technology, and this trend shows no signs of slowing down. **Telemedicine** is one important example of how the application of information technology continues to advance medicine. By connecting patients to doctors electronically, a patient in a

BUSINESS BRIEF 13-3 KISS THAT OLD PATIENT LOGBOOK GOODBYE

For the staff at River Hills West Healthcare Center in Pewaukee, Wisconsin, the most dreaded chore used to be the paperwork. Each of the Center's 245 residents was receiving multiple doses of up to 15 different medications a day. Every time a doctor wrote a new order, it had to be transcribed by a secretary to a phone order, a pharmacy sheet, and several other patient forms. These all had to be checked by nurses and then entered into a three-ring binder. Each month nurses and secretaries spent about 64 worker-hours transferring records to new logbooks.

Since January, however, the whole routine has changed for about half the center's staff. Instead of transcribing orders, nurses write the first three letters of a drug's name on the screen of an electronic notepad called a CompuScriber. A list of choices appears on the screen, along with boxes to check off doses and time of day. Once these items are filled in, the device automatically zaps the information over a 900Mhz wireless link to the River Hills network server. Records are instantly updated, thus eliminating about five stages of paperwork. "To say it has made life easier is an understatement," says Assistant Director of Nursing Martha Kath.

At first, nursing staff had mixed reactions to CompuScriber, which CompuPharm, Inc., a division of GranCare Inc, of Atlanta, constructed from a Toshiba 486 notepad. But in just six months, two of the four units had made the switch at River Hills, which is run by GranCare. The remaining two should be on-line in the next couple of months. Next, they'll tap the system's vast data-processing powers. It can prepare everything from cost tables to lists of patients receiving specific medications.

QUESTIONS

1. Why do you think the new CompuScriber might have elicited mixed reactions from the nurses?
2. When we think of the application of technology to medicine, we often think of fairly exotic applications. How important are improved administrative systems, such as the one described, in today's healthcare environment? Why?

SOURCE: Neil Gross, "Kiss that Old Patient LogBook Good-Bye," *Business Week*, June 26, 1995, p. 108. Reprinted by special permission, copyright © 1995 by The McGraw-Hill Companies.

remote area can have access to a specialist who may be physically located on the other side of the earth. In addition to simple applications such as the sharing of records and X-ray images, current and future systems enable surgeons to conduct a surgical procedure from a remote site, for example. Business Brief 13–3 describes another angle of application in the medical field.

Information technology is also evident in medical expert systems that help diagnose illness and disease. By capturing the expertise of the world's top physicians and medical researchers into expert systems, this expertise can be translated into specific algorithms and guidelines that can be widely distributed and used by less-experienced medical practitioners all over the world. With the ever-expanding capabilities of the Internet, it would be technically feasible to provide access to these expert systems by end-users—that is, us. Did you hurt your back rollerblading? Try accessing a lower-back pain expert system for some self-diagnosis and treatment before contacting a medical practitioner. Some managed care organizations are starting to use E-mail systems to determine whether or not the patient should come in to the doctor's office and in some cases are even treating patients remotely.

Other popular applications are the use of computer-aided design (CAD) systems being used to customized implants for hips and knees. Instead of estimating by looking at X-rays what implant to use in surgery, orthopedic surgeons can now try for fit a variety of implants on an exact, computer-generated model of the hip or knee of the patient. This type of simulation can minimize the length of surgery (an important consideration for the elderly) and the rate of complications.

One project that provides an indication of the potential scope of application is that of the human genome project. This is actually not a single project, but rather a somewhat loosely coordinated research effort carried on by medical researchers in universities and private institutions in various locations around the world. The objectives of the project are to (1) identify all genes within the human body; (2) determine the relationships between defective genes and various human ailments; and (3) eventually use this knowledge to determine ways to correct the genes and prevent or cure the ailments. It is believed that defective genes could explain many human ailments, such as susceptibility to cancers.

The scope of this project is enormous, and the coordination effort required is mind-boggling. Scientists with varying motives and techniques are competing to identify and name tens of thousands of genes. Although there is currently no centralized database of genome research, some attempts have been made to develop databases that can share information. Also, some researchers have developed I/T that uses a "brute force" method for screening and identifying genes. They argue that this approach will be more efficient than the traditional, more intuitive research efforts. If this human genome project is successful to any significant degree, it could literally transform the practice of medicine as we know it.

The use of information technology to advance the practice of medicine raises numerous societal issues that need to be addressed. For one, many members of society do not support the concept of detecting defective genes, especially if no cure is known. They argue that someone who is predisposed to developing Alzheimer's disease, for example, gains nothing from having the knowledge in advance, or that people who know they may have a child with a predisposition to Alzheimer's disease may decide not to have that child.

Another issue is the depersonalization of medicine. Though medicine has become more and more technologically intensive, people still demand contact with a human (and humane) doctor and want to have specialists close by. Some people argue that the economics of medicine and the capabilities of information technology make telemedicine not only more efficient (less costly) but possibly better (higher and more consistent quality of care). Others argue that being sick is a scary experience for most people, and no matter how good telemedicine is, patients still want to be reassured by another human.

LEARNING AND EDUCATION

Lifelong learning is a noble goal for every human being, and education is the key to the advancement of society. Information technology has the potential to facilitate both. Unfortunately, I/T also has the potential to facilitate the dissemination of false information, impeding true learning and fostering political agendas on the part of individuals or organizations who are only interested in their own version of truth. And if access to and knowledge of I/T becomes a prerequisite for societal interaction and learning, it is easy to envision a division of society between those who have access to I/T and those who don't.

The application of information technology has rapidly expanded opportunities for **distance learning** and distance education. For example, since 1990 the University of Wisconsin has been teaching engineering courses to distance learners nationwide over regular phone lines. Each remote site connects via two phone lines: one for an open teleconference, and the other hooked to a modem and computer running a software program that creates a "virtual whiteboard" for all users on the network to share. This system is limited in many ways, not the least being that the

If you cannot go to the best universities, the best universities will come to you. The images and sounds from this class can be transmitted to distant students. Photo courtesy of Tony Stone Worldwide.

students can only see the whiteboard, and not the instructor or each other, but it offers the possibility for individuals to further their education even if they live in remote areas or need to stay at home (e.g., because of illness, small children, or a handicap). More recent systems offer television quality, two-way video in addition to on-line sharing of data and applications, but these are much more expensive to set up and maintain.

Another example is the Open University in Great Britain. The Open University has a physical home base but none of the students and few of its faculty are there; there is no campus, it is just an administrative hub. Few of the students have ever met any of the faculty or other students. However, its business school is already the largest in Europe. The Open University, in past years, used to run short residential summer schools on the campuses of other universities. This year Open University has gone totally virtual. The students participate from their homes or places of work via E-mail, mobile phone, and videoconferencing. The University has provided the mobile phone to students so that as they sit with their computers connected through a modem to the University's computer they can still converse with the faculty teaching the course.

Business Brief 13–4 provides a third example of distance-learning possibilities.

Also on the positive side, communication facilities such as the Internet provide a means for the wide dissemination of information. Individuals will be able to take on-line courses, pursue self-directed studies, and generally advance their level of education in whatever field they choose. Physical access barriers (such as the need

BUSINESS BRIEF 13-4 STANFORD PROFESSORS: ALIVE, AND IN COLOR

Some Silicon Valley engineers taking Stanford University's distance education courses are participating in Project Cardinal, an experiment that points the way to the information superhighway. Instead of going to videoconference rooms to watch Stanford's usual microwave broadcast, the students watch lectures on their computer desktops.

In one window, they see the professor's full-motion color video image, indistinguishable from that offered by cable television. There is none of the jerkiness we have come to associate with digital video over the phone wires, and students can resize the image at will. A second window carries data that the professor may want to share with his students, whether it's application software running on his computer or an image from an electron microscope. In future versions, students will be able to open multiple video windows and see each other.

QUESTION

1. Discuss some of the advantages and disadvantages of being able to receive a lecture through a personal computer monitor. Do you think this type of application could replace much of today's reliance on courses taught in classrooms? Why or why not?

SOURCE: J. Weiss, "Distance Learning," *Syllabus* 8 (3), November/December 1994, pp. 41–44.

to sit in an expensive-to-maintain lecture hall in front of an expensive university professor) could be reduced or removed. For those individuals with the desire and self-discipline required, self-directed education is already a reality and the opportunities keep on increasing.

In addition, the contents of the best libraries in the world are now available to anybody with a computer and a modem. These virtual libraries with electronic shelves and corridors are not as romantic as the stereotypical library with dark wood paneling and grey-haired, bespectacled librarians, but they are certainly more dynamic, user friendly, and mobile. When the war between Serbs and Croats in the former Yugoslavia destroyed the University of Dubrovnik's library, the international community provided the University with computer terminals linked to a host of foreign databases, giving the students access to better resources than they had before.

Today's age has been called the Information Age. The age when people can have access to information on everything, anytime. But what information will be available? Will cyberspace surfers be exposed to objective presentations of multiple viewpoints? Or will they encounter one-sided depictions of events reflecting the inherent biases of those who prepared the information?

This issue is not a new one. For example, the content of textbooks for primary and secondary education has been for years a major battleground across the country, with some individuals pushing for a "creationist" and some for an "evolutionist" view of the human race to be included in those textbooks. The first faction argues that book editors and publishers have been unduly influenced by liberal thinking and have provided a one-sided, Godless view of how humans appeared on the planet.

So the issue of what information to present is not new; it just has moved to a new medium—a medium that many people feel is accountable to no one. This lack of regulation makes people uncomfortable. Apple Computer was forced to reconsider their decision to distribute the CD-ROM title *Who Built America?* with their computers.

when they received complaints from some customers. These customers argued that the CD-ROM presented a very limited view of the development of America. Critics claimed there was almost no mention of any inventors, business leaders, or politicians; instead the material focused on the lives of "ordinary citizens, the poor, the minorities." Supporters argued that the disk was simply adding some balance to previous historical records, which provided limited coverage of the lives of most citizens. The developers of the CD-ROM refused to change any of the material, or to add other material, when Apple made that request.

From our perspective, the availability of material presenting alternative views should be welcomed; the use of information technology to promote biased viewpoints or to suppress objective ones should not. The key, however, is not censorship, but for consumers of information—including children—to develop critical thinking skills, and this should become a prime objective of educational institutions. Rather than focusing solely on the dissemination of knowledge, education today needs to focus on developing the necessary skills to access and search different sources of information and to critically evaluate what those sources say.

EMPLOYMENT AND ENTREPRENEURSHIP

In Chapter 1, we opened by commenting on the rapidly changing employment picture. We discussed how many organizations had reduced their layers of management and generally were asking remaining employees to do more with less. Unlike earlier applications of information technology, which focused on reducing manual labor (such as the use of computer-controlled robotics in manufacturing plants and the replacement of clerks performing routine accounting computations), later computer applications performed much of the reporting and analysis that had previously fallen on lower-level managers. This trend does not appear to be changing, even for companies that turned around their economic fortunes and began showing strong profits. In the past, many organizations were willing to add employees (and layers of management) in relation to their economic prosperity; the more profitable, the more layers could be added. This is no longer the case, as Business Brief 13–5 testifies.

The loss of blue-collar and midmanagement positions is only part of the story, however. The continued application of information technology in innovative ways is drastically influencing many service functions, reducing or removing entire job categories. The introduction of electronic devices that broadcast messages from the electric meters on homes reduced the need for human meter readers, putting at risk the jobs of the 35,000 meter readers in the United States. Information systems can accept loan applications and evaluate them, reducing the need for bank loan officers. The development of "intelligent" milking machines makes it possible to milk cows without human intervention. The examples go on and on. Figure 13–1 describes the changes in workforce percentages in several job areas.

Historically, job loss from technological advancement has always been offset by job gains. Although individual categories of jobs and workers might have been affected, the overall net effect for society tended to be neutral or positive. Many economists argue that the same will happen with our current transition phase: new jobs will be created as fast as old ones disappear.

Other, less optimistic observers argue that we are no longer in a temporary transition phase. Rather, the changes fostered by the application of information technology will continue to cause instability in the employment environment, with

BUSINESS BRIEF 13-5 THANKS, NOW GOODBYE: AMID RECORD PROFITS, COMPANIES CONTINUE LAYOFFS

Last week, Mobil Corp. posted soaring first-quarter earnings. This week, it announced plans to eliminate 4,700 jobs.

Companies argue that layoffs, in good times as well as bad, have become essential in an age of cutthroat competition. Procter & Gamble Chairman Edwin L. Artzt put it succinctly when his company began slashing 13,000 of its 106,000 jobs two years ago: "We must slim down to stay competitive. The consumer wants better value. Our competitors are getting leaner and quicker, and we are simply going to have to run faster to stay ahead."

But for employees, the latest layoffs, coming amid good times and fat profits, seem mean and arbitrary. It is the seeming relentlessness of the job losses that aggravates most. "Workers very definitely see this as a long-term trend that has little relationship to how their company is performing," says psychiatrist Reed Moskowitz, founder of a stress-disorder center at New York University. "Nobody feels secure."

For surviving employees, the pressure and the sense of instability can erode teamwork and trigger backbiting. People "are always looking over their shoulder," says Shawn Wyder, a systems analyst at the Summit, N.J., office of Ciba Geigy Corp. The pharmaceuticals division has eliminated some 800 jobs over the past two years, about 20 percent of its workforce. While no more are expected anytime soon, "it's still fresh in people's minds," Mr. Wyder says.

QUESTIONS

1. Do you believe there is any relationship between the application of information technology and the continued loss of jobs from some organizations? Explain briefly.
2. This business brief focuses on one side of the story—job losses. To what extent do you believe new jobs have been created through the application of I/T?

SOURCE: M. Murray, "Thanks, Goodbye," *The Wall Street Journal,* May 4, 1995, p. 1. Reprinted by permission of *The Wall Street Journal,*

no guarantee that any type of equilibrium will be reached. "The pace and intensity of technological advance are without historical precedent," says Robert M. White, president of the National Academy of Engineering in Washington. "The creation of new industries might not provide enough jobs fast enough to replace those lost as a result of technologically caused productivity increases." So, the long-term job-creating adjustments may never fully come.

In light of this "new reality" for employment, a larger percentage of the workforce has looked to more entrepreneurial efforts. With the continuing decline in costs of information technology, it is relatively inexpensive to set up a fairly well-equipped home office that can support a small—or not so small—business. In addition, the application of technology has opened many possibilities in the service sector (see the ad reprinted in Business Brief 13–6). Organizations are now paying others to perform tasks and accept responsibilities that were unheard of only a short time ago; people now make a living designing and managing the Internet home pages of other companies, for example.

Obviously, large organizations will not disappear. The laws of economies of scale will always hold true for some products and services, and large governmental bodies will always exist. Within organizations of all sizes, the need for employees who understand the I/T potential and who can use it to enhance their personal and organizational productivity will remain strong. However, the use of information technology may also tend to increase the use of virtual organizations and other temporary organizational and employment arrangements (contract work, for

FIGURE 13–1A White-Collar Occupations in the United States, 1900–2000

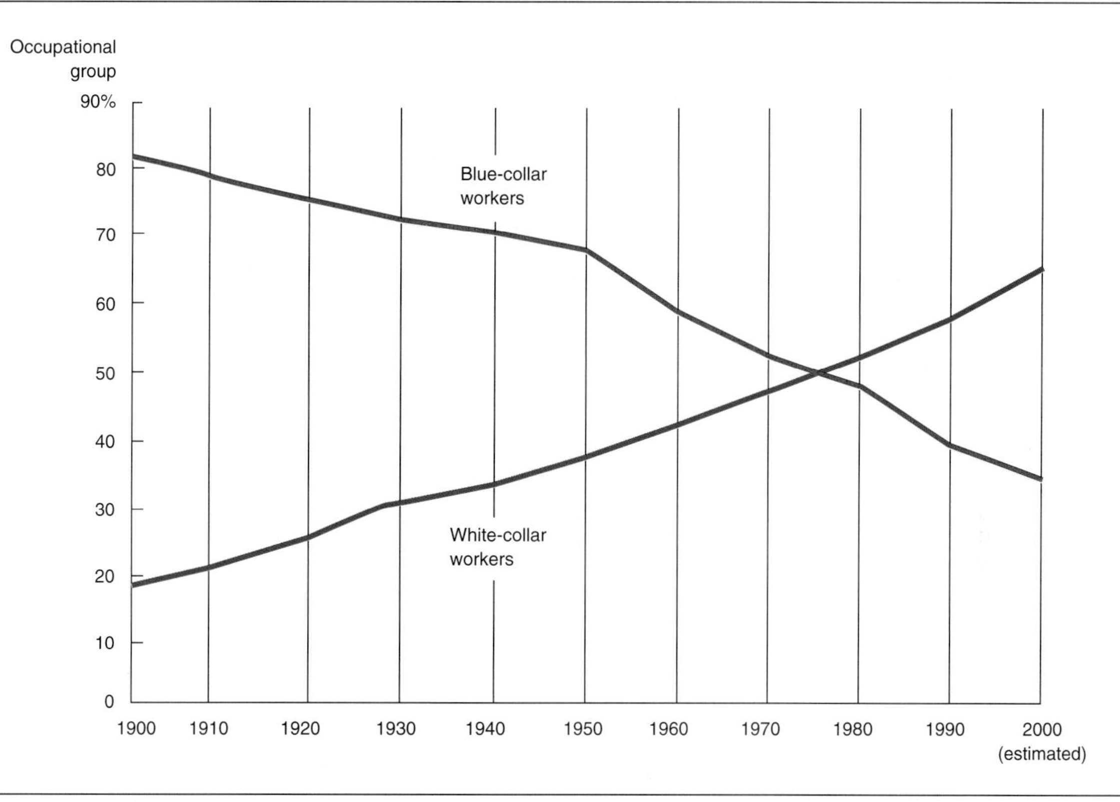

SOURCE: Vincent E. Giuliano, "The Mechanization of Office Work," *Scientific American*, September 1982, pp. 148–52.

FIGURE 13–1B Demand for Labor in the United States, 1960–2000

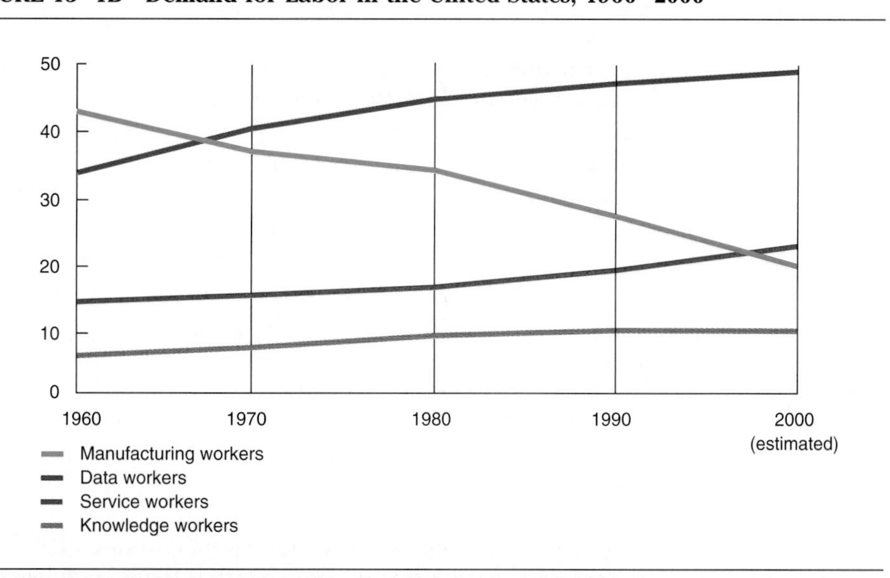

SOURCE: Edward N. Wolff and William J. Baumol, "Sources of Postwar Growth of Information Activity in the U.S.," C.V. Starr Center for Applied Economics, New York University, June 1987.

BUSINESS BRIEF 13-6 A BRIEF HISTORY OF OFFICING: I OFFICE. YOU OFFICE. WE OFFICE.

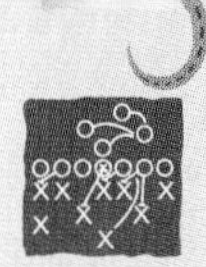

The office isn't what it used to be. That's because the way we think about the office is changing. (Uh, roger, Houston, we've got a paradigm shift.) More and more, the term *office* defines a state of activity rather than a place. Instead of adapting our lives to it, the office is becoming what we want it to be and what we need it to be. This is a good thing.

As long as the tools and the knowledge are available to make it work. And they are. At Kinko's. We have the equipment and expertise to help companies and individuals do a better job creating and producing documents. From reports to training manuals to proposals to presentations.

What's more, we're digital, and have an international videoconferencing network. With Kinko's, you have an office (noun), but only when you need to office (verb). That's why we're the new way to office. To learn more about what Kinko's can do for your business, visit our web site at: http://www.kinkos.com or call us at 1-800-2-KINKOS.

Office as a verb. "I office. You office. We office."

QUESTIONS

1. What are the pros and cons for a company that uses Kinko's as a branch office?
2. What are the pros and cons for an employee to use Kinko's as an office?

SOURCE: Kinko's advertisement, *The Wall Street Journal,* January 31, 1996. Reprinted by permission of *The Wall Street Journal,*

example), which will have a strong influence on the traditional employee/organization relationship. In this type of employment environment, most job positions should be viewed as temporary, or at least unstable. Already, in the European Common Market, half of the able workforce is in part-time or temporary jobs.

Virtual organizations allow for great flexibility and organizational responsiveness but create some managerial dilemmas. After all, the traditional management style has been to control and oversee employees very closely in both a physical and organizational sense. So managing people you actually don't see requires a new approach, an approach based on trust, accountability, and leadership. Also, creating an organizational culture and bonding among employees is difficult when they do not share a physical space.

For employees, virtuality is not as much fun as it sounds. Virtuality requires sometimes more formality rather than less. No more walking down the corridor to see a colleague for a spontaneous brainstorming session; telephone and videoconferencing sessions, two of the tools of virtuality, require a rigorous scheduling, in-advance arrangements, and being right on time. The human aspects of work—the gossip, the wink, the office politics, the joke, the slap on the back—that are for most people an important component of making long days of work tolerable, are lost.

This is an economy that has been called the *three I economy,* an economy where value is created through ideas, intelligence, and information. The challenge for governments is to make sure that as many members of society as possible are prepared to partake in this economy. The need is enormous for training and education to create a technologically literate population that can be gainfully employed.

LEISURE, ENTERTAINMENT, AND THE ARTS

Information technology has long held the promise of altering many nonemployment activities for humans, and that promise is being met. In sports and athletic activities, information technology is routinely used to enhance the performance of athletes.

"What is Art?" was the question of the 1960s when happenings were all the rage. Today the question is "What is Reality?" as computers recreate for us a world that is just as real, if not more real, than the real thing. Photo courtesy of Sam Ogden (top left), Tony Stone Worldwide (top right), and Strata Corporation (bottom left).

Cyclists can be custom fitted for bicycles, baseball players have their swings analyzed, swimmers use systems that monitor their body's oxygen-processing abilities, and so on. In leisure activities, the video game has crossed over to the personal computer, which is merging with the television. The application of computer graphics is blurring reality, as video is created and altered in ways such that humans can no longer detect what is real and what is imaginary. The creation of this type of reality, an artificial reality that seems so real that our senses believe it is true reality, is called **virtual reality.** Virtual reality simulations of flight (say, from the cockpit of a fighter plane), are startlingly real.

In the arts, information technology is being widely explored in exciting ways. Many musicians rely on I/T to enhance or even create their works. Some visual artists use information technology as the medium for their expression; others use I/T to try various concepts before moving to a more traditional medium such as watercolor or oil. It is not unusual to find university level art and music courses that focus entirely on the use and exploitation of information technology as an artistic medium.

On the walls of your house will be hung electronic frames. Electronic screens will be able to display whatever work of art you desire whenever you desire it. Feeling hyper? How about a modern expressionist like Jackson Pollock? Feeling religious? How about a Michelangelo? Feeling romantic? How about a French Impressionist like Monet? Or maybe you are not the artsy type and would rather have a poster of the latest swim-suited hunk or beauty? Or a landscape of a snowboarder surfing the Himalayas? You will be able to update and change your poster collection on command!

Given this background, one might assume that everyone will spend their leisure time in front of a video screen or interacting with information technology in some way. This doesn't appear to be the case. As the use of high technology goes up, nontechnology-based activities are also increasing in popularity. Some sociologists have called this the **high tech–high touch** connection: As society becomes more technologically oriented, people yearn for more human contact. Despite widespread predictions to the contrary, sales of books—the paper kind—are actually increasing, not decreasing. Golf is also increasing in popularity, and many people seem to have the attitude that "getting away from it (I/T)" is important. Although the applications of I/T to leisure activities increase daily, we advise that you don't try to throw your boomerang away just yet.

Virtual reality, virtual organizations, virtual friendships are here to stay. However, information technology has not replaced, and we trust will never replace, the need for people to belong, to chat and gossip, to relate, to be—in other words, human beings. Information technology has certainly brought, and will bring, tremendous benefits to society; but we need to make sure that technology is at our service, and not the other way around. Information technology is seductive. Let's remember that what makes us humans is not the ability to process information at blinding speeds and display it in all sorts of amazing ways, but our ability to love, to show compassion, and to help others. Let's make sure that we do not lose sight of that.

SUMMARY

Information technology is affecting all aspects of society. Society is being faced with virtuality (electronic realities and connections) in almost every realm: medicine, education, government, employment, to name a few. The challenges for society are many, and these include keeping a certain humanity in all the sea of technology and ensuring that the benefits of virtuality are offered to all, not only a favored minority.

The keys to satisfying and rewarding employment will include (1) a sufficient familiarity with I/T to exploit the opportunities it presents, (2) a commitment to life-long learning, and (3) an entrepreneurial mindset which constantly seeks new opportunities.

In an economy where value is created through ideas, intelligence, and information (what has been called the *three I economy*), the challenge for governments is to make sure that all members of society are prepared to partake in this economy by being technologically literate. The resources needed for training and education to achieve this goal are enormous.

Information technology offers limitless applications. I/T can have both a liberating and an alienating impact on society. I/T is here to stay; as members of society, we need to understand its power and limitations to use it wisely. Let's hope that we do.

KEY CONCEPTS AND TERMS

KEY CONCEPTS

- Information technology affects all aspects of society. (427)
- Changes in technology give a boost to productivity and usually increase the size of the economy and the number of jobs. (443)
- Information technology can have both a liberating and an alienating impact on the members of society. (433)

KEY TERMS

distance learning (440)
geographical information systems (GIS) (430)
global positioning satellite (GPS) systems (429)
high tech–high touch (448)
telecommuting (437)
telemedicine (438)
virtual reality (447)

REFERENCES

Business Week. "The Learning Revolution." (Special Report), February 28, 1994, pp. 80–88.

ESRI ARC News. "Integration of Cadastral, Survey and Fiscal Information: ESRI Announces Cyprus Countrywide GIS/LIS System Award." Summer 1995.

Smith, M. R., and L. Marx (eds.) *Does Technology Drive History?: The Dilemma of Technological Determinism.* Cambridge: MIT Press, 1994.

Trachtenberg, J. "U.S. History on a CD-ROM Stirs Up a Storm." *The Wall Street Journal,* February 10, 1995.

Zachary, G. P. "Worried Workers: Service Productivity Is Rising Fast—and So Is the Fear of Lost Jobs." *The Wall Street Journal,* June 8, 1995.

CONNECTIVE CASE: Internet Racial Hatred Case Investigated

The Mannheim (Germany) prosecutor's office is investigating CompuServe Inc. and Deutsche Telekom AG's T-Online service for inciting racial hatred, a crime in Germany, because they provide access to the Internet, where a Canadian neo-Nazi has set up a home page.

It is the second investigation in as many months by German prosecutors claiming that certain information distributed over the Internet violates German law and therefore should be censored. The first case, involving prosecutors in Munich and CompuServe, focused on user groups for child pornography and is still open. This new case again raises the issue of whether on-line access providers, such as CompuServe and T-Online can be held responsible for content placed by outsiders on the rapidly growing, and highly mobile, Internet. Experts say it's unrealistic to expect them to patrol the Net daily for offensive sites.

The investigation also comes days after a French Internet user posted the full text of a banned tell-all book by Francois Mitterand's doctor that reveals the extent of the former French president's battle with cancer. All these cases show the limits of government's traditional power to regulate information in borderless cyberspace.

In response to the Mannheim investigation, Deutsche Telekom, which has nearly one million on-line customers, barred access to neo-Nazi Ernst Zuendel's World Wide Web site. But CompuServe, which has 250,000 subscribers in Germany and more than four million worldwide, hasn't discussed following suit and most likely won't, said Marielle Boreick, a Munich-based company spokeswoman.

"We have no interest in disseminating child pornography or statements from left- or right-wing radicals," said a Deutsche Telekom spokesman, who learned of the neo-Nazi page for the first time Wednesday. But T-Online shouldn't be held responsible for Mr. Zuendel's electronic publications, he added.

According to the prosecutor's office, Mr. Zuendel is under investigation for distributing anti-Semitic propaganda through the Internet and propagating lies about the Holocaust. "As part of these proceedings, we are reviewing whether other companies have made themselves subject to prosecution by providing access," spokesman Wolfgang Kneip said.

Although the investigation is currently limited to two companies, many other companies, ranging from a joint venture between Bertelsman AG and America Online Inc. to a few hundred small firms, provide Internet access in Germany. The outcome of the investigation will show whether these companies also could be held responsible for the same reason, Mr. Kneip said.

The Mannheim prosecutor's office is investigating because it received information about Mr. Zuendel's Internet site, including documents that can be downloaded, from a citizen. Although Mr. Zuendel lives in Toronto, "because it's available over the Internet, it can also be called up in Germany," he said. "Then the scene of the crime is all of Germany."

The federal justice ministry in Bonn said it's not involved in either the Mannheim or the Munich case, but a spokesman described the two as "extreme cases" where there are strict German laws forbidding those activities. Several groups within the government are currently studying the issue of Internet content.

Case Questions

1. Do you think that CompuServe and Deutsche Telekom should be held responsible?
2. What do you suggest should be done (if anything) to avoid this type of problem in the future?
3. Comment on the difficulty for information services providers to respect censure laws that change from country to country.

SOURCE: From *The Wall Street Journal,* January 26, 1996, p. B13.

IT'S YOUR TURN — END OF CHAPTER MATERIALS

REVIEW QUESTIONS

1. Give an example of the impact of I/T on the ecological issues.
2. Give an example of the impact of I/T on issues of governance and government information.
3. Give an example of the impact of I/T on health care.
4. Give an example of the impact of I/T on entertainment.
5. What is a GPS system? What is a GIS? Give some examples of their use.
6. Define telecommuting.
7. Describe how a virtual university works. What are the pros and cons of getting a degree at such institutions?
8. Give two different approaches to keep off the Internet material considered to be offensive by some.
9. What is virtual reality?
10. What does the expression *high tech–high touch* mean?

DISCUSSION QUESTIONS

1. Do changes in technology (e.g., discovery of the wheel, the printing machine) generate changes in society, or the other way around (e.g., the Renaissance; the post-Victorian era)?
2. There is talk of giving every person in America a telephone number at birth—a telephone number that will stay with you until you die and that will not change no matter where you are or move to in the world. What do you think of this idea?
3. Can you think of any document (passport, driving license, credit card, birth certificate, school grades, etc.) that absolutely needs to exists on paper, rather than residing in some database somewhere?
4. The German government was investigating, in January 1996, CompuServe and Deutsche Telekom for providing access to the Internet where pornographic and racist information was being shown (described in more detail in the *Connective Case* in this chapter). Find out what has happened since then. How were the cases resolved? Do you agree with the verdicts and the policy changes?
5. Some people argue that computer-generated paintings and computer-generated art in general is not art. What do you think?
6. Today, having a connection to the information superhighway is permitting more and more people to work at home. This telecommuting has advantages and disadvantages. Make a list of both and comment on whether you personally would like to work exclusively at home if given the choice by your employer.

GROUP ASSIGNMENT

As a group, select one of the major areas introduced in this chapter (education, health, leisure, etc.). Split the group into two teams. One team should write a one-page memorandum on the potential negative influences of information technology over the next 5 to 15 years. The other team should write a one-page memorandum on the potential positive influences of information technology over the next 5 to 15 years. The memorandum should provide justifications for your predictions. Use, and cite, whatever resources you believe to be appropriate.

As a group, develop a set of recommendations and policies that need to be implemented today to make sure that the positive predictions occur while minimizing the likelihood of the negative predictions becoming reality.

APPLICATION ASSIGNMENTS

1. Using PowerPoint, or another package of your choice, create three charts showing: (*a*) the five most often visited Web sites (provide the number of "hits" for each); (*b*) the five most-asked personalities on the Net; and (*c*) the top five locations where Internet traffic originates. Produce one more

PowerPoint slide to present your conclusions on your findings in no more than three bullets.

2. Get to the Internet. Browse through some of the clothing companies that offer catalogs. Write a one-page memorandum to compare the experience of shopping electronically to the experience of shopping in an actual store.

CASE ASSIGNMENT 1: The Parable of the Pizza Parlor

Question: Why didn't the software agent show up at the party?

Answer: Because it had no body to go with.

This nerdy variant on the old Halloween joke about the skeleton neatly encapsulates some commonly expressed hopes and flip-side fears about the information superhighway—that it will inexorably replace transportation with telecommunication, face-to-face meetings with transactions in cyberspace and human secretaries and assistants with disembodied software agents. In reality, a robust infobahn is likely to produce a considerably more complex and subtle redistribution of functions among buildings, transportation systems, and computer networks. Let me illustrate this point with a homely story I call "The Parable of the Pizza Parlor."

Not so long ago pizza parlors were mostly found on Main Street. They had advertising signs out front to pull in customers, counters where those customers placed orders and handed over cash, kitchens where pizza was baked and an eating space containing tables and seats. All these components were wrapped up in one small building.

In the era of the automobile, a complete configuration emerged. The pizza parlor (by now perhaps part of a chain) did not rely just on its sign; it also advertised in the Yellow Pages and the mass media. It moved from Main Street to a location beside the highway, and it acquired a parking lot. Many customers now telephoned in their orders and had them delivered by car to their homes and offices. Transportation and telecommunication systems began to play significant roles in the pizza parlor's workings, and its architectural unity fragmented as consumption shifted from a single seating area to the many different locations where customers ate their delivered pizzas.

Main street began to die as the pizza parlor and other businesses left for more attractive sites. Soon the old, familiar Main Street was no longer the place where people went to hang out.

Sometime in the mid-1990s the pizza parlor went on-line on the World Wide Web. The street address turned into a network address, and the counter became a screen display that allowed a customer at any computer terminal to design a virtual pizza and pay using some form of digital cash. The kitchen transmuted into a nationwide collection of food preparation centers at locations carefully selected to provide maximum coverage of the market. Each order was automatically routed to the preparation point nearest to the customer. There the local kitchen produced and packaged the pizza, which was then delivered via a radio-controlled vehicle.

The old advertising signs gradually disappeared, and soon there was no newspaper or television advertising either. Instead, customers were attracted through graphic "storefronts" in on-line virtual malls and through network "Yellow Pages" listings.

The electronic pizza parlor, some future observer might note, was a big hit. Pizza suppliers reached a much larger market than before, and because customers now consumed the product at home, the suppliers did not have to build and maintain restaurant facilities in expensive locations.

The customers also liked the new setup; they could always get exactly what they wanted, quickly, reliably, and inexpensively. But they sometimes missed the atmosphere of the ramshackle old parlors, the conversations that unfolded there and the opportunities that the pizzerias afforded to get out of the house and feel like part of a local community.

The pizza parlor may seem like a minor institution, but this story illustrates a more general trend. Using sophisticated telecommunications, for example, office workers may now telecommute from home or simply rely on personal electronic devices to set up virtual workplaces anywhere. Retailers that combine on-line interactive catalogues with direct delivery from the warehouse can now compete with pedestrian shopping streets and automobile-oriented malls. And increasingly effective distance-learning and telemedicine systems are reducing the need to go to school or visit the doctor's office.

In short, cities will be transformed as the information superhighway develops. We will have to rethink the spatial relationships, transportation connections, and telecommunication linkages among homes, workplaces, and service providers. Housing will have to be reconfigured as a wide range of transactions that once took place elsewhere moves back into domestic space.

The weakening or disappearance of traditional gathering places will require the creation of different foci for community life—both physical places and on-line, virtual locations. Offices, hospitals, schools, and shopping centers will fragment and recombine in surprising ways as virtual transactions and telepresence relax traditional requirements of proximity. Perhaps reinvigorated local communities will cluster around restaurants, parks, and health clubs while also benefiting from strong electronic connections to the wider world.

This restructuring will take place on a massive scale. Depending on the design and policy choices we make in the coming years, it could produce more equitable access to services and economic opportunities, or it could yield electronically serviced islands of privilege surrounded by zones of disinvestment, unemployment, and poverty. The stakes are huge.

Cities will certainly not disappear as an increasing amount of human interaction shifts into cyberspace; they will evolve into complex hybrids of physical space and on-line locations. They will have places where you need a body to go and places where you don't.

Questions

1. Information technology is changing all aspects of society. List three positive changes and three negative changes in your daily life due to information technology.
2. As the world becomes more and more virtual, what are some of the issues that we need to worry about?

SOURCE: This social commentary by William Mitchell appeared in *Scientific American,* May 1995, pg. 112. Reprinted with permission.

CASE ASSIGNMENT 2: China Attempts to Build Cyber-Barriers

James Chu, a U.S.–trained computer scientist, is helping China to defend its sovereignty against an insidious threat: "barbaric information." Chu runs a small Hong Kong company called China Internet Corp. With backing from Xinhua News Agency, the mouthpiece of official China, Chu is pioneeering what he calls the "intranet," an insulated, but not isolated, corner of cyberspace.

The idea is simple, though the execution remains unproved. Using the latest filtering technology from Sun Microsystems, Inc., Chu aims to create a for-profit network within the Internet. Chinese users would have unlimited access to each other but only screened links with the world beyond. Says Chu, "We've eliminated what is undesirable and kept what is good."

Chu's comment depicts China's riposte to the information age. Beijing eagerly seeks the fanciest information hardware, but it fears much of the software. This paradoxical outlook has juxtaposed Physics professors at Qinghua University conducting video conferences over the Internet with colleagues around the world and broadcasting of American "Hunter" reruns on cable TV in Lanzhou—but the Meteorological Administration still forbids outsiders to predict the weather.

As a result, any involvement in China's information industry is a risky venture, especially for outside providers. Early in 1996, the Chinese government ordered Xinhua, the party's "throat and tongue," to restrict all foreign services offering economic information from abroad. Xinhua will decide what kinds of news and data can enter, who can receive it, and what share of the profits will accrue to Xinhua. Now, the State Council has started pondering similar restrictions on the Internet, where the Ministry of Post and Telecommunications is both gatekeeper and toll collector.

The clampdown has been accompanied by a burst of Maoist rhetoric. Jiang Zemin, China's president, reminded reporters this week of Mao Tse-Tung's advice to Chinese journalists: "You must be the engineers of people's minds."

WAR FOR CONTROL

China is determined to do what conventional wisdom suggests is impossible—join the information age while restricting access to information. In some respects, it is a battle long lost; China is awash in imported news and culture that only a few years ago would have been judged subversive. But China sees long-term profit from distributing news and information. And in that sense, the war rages on.

"The Chinese government is still far more sensitive to information than any other business, and that will continue," says Jim Rohwer, chief Asia economist for CS First Boston Inc.

The Chinese government's sensitivity hasn't prevented information services from becoming big business. Foreign wire services, such as those offered by Reuters Holdings PCL and Dow Jones-Telerate, sell services valued in the tens of millions of dollars to banks and traders on the country's fledgling securities and commodities markets. Star TV, a unit of Rupert Murdoch's News Corp., broadcasts sports and entertainment from a satellite and claims to reach at least 32 million Chinese households.

STAR ATTRACTION

Some 60,000 Chinese independent information businesses provide services valued at $1 billion, estimates

China's aptly named Economic Information Daily. Shanghai's Xinmin Evening News, a politically tame but offbeat tabloid, has displaced dogmatic rivals as the city's most popular daily. Hundreds of legal television and cable stations broadcast such a diverse mix of programs that the Ministry of Radio, Film, and Television spent eight months last year trying to document them all. Its verdict: Many stations have had "serious political lapses."

But while the Chinese have more access to news and entertainment from outside than ever before, restrictions on business haven't been rewritten since the early days of reform China, when authorities banned residential telephones. The Chinese bureaucracy moves slowly, often with the agility of an oil tanker, but it usually manages to exert control and exact revenues—whatever the medium or message.

China's jousts with foreign satellite television broadcasters are a case in point. Star TV offered the most obvious challenge: Its satellite casts a borderless beam from Turkey to Japan. Programming such as the BBC World Service Television and shows such as "Baywatch" have no counterparts in China. Shortly after buying Star, Murdoch publicly predicted that satellite television would contribute to the fall of totalitarian regimes.

China's response to Murdoch's sentiment involved the following actions: the government outlawed the sale of satellite dishes, launched a nationwide cable-laying plan to expand its own program offerings, and canceled one of Murdoch's Chinese publishing joint ventures. Now, CCTV, China's central television network, is launching its own satellite-based pay television service.

The strategy has paid off: Murdoch dropped the BBC newscast from Star's northern beam. Then he agreed to a $5.4 million information-technology venture with the People's Daily, helping the Chinese Communist Party's stodgy flagship newspaper into the electronic-publishing era. And now by some industry accounts, News Corp. is trying to forge a partnership between Star and the Chinese government, though no agreement has yet been reached.

China hopes the Internet will prove similarly pliable. In many ways, the Internet is a great boon to the country, even though there are only 50,000 Chinese users so far. The prospect of underfunded Chinese scientists freely probing databases around the world has appeal, as does the notion of businesses advertising and selling at low cost without traveling. "We should find a way for the Internet to work for our nation," says Jiang Lintao, an Internet specialist at the Ministry of Post and Telecommunications.

TOO MUCH OUTSIDE EXPOSURE?

China's scientists, who always seem to be strapped for funds, are the biggest fans of the Internet, especially its ability to allow two-way videoconferencing. Regularly, a group of scientists huddles in a room at the Institute of High Energy Physics, tucked away in the western outskirts of Beijing. Gathered around a color monitor, the scientists participate in a two-way video briefing with U.S. partners in a joint research project. In the past, China had to send scientists to the United States for such exchanges.

But Beijing keeps a close watch over such activity, because even though the Internet has proved its utility, it has also become a fluid medium for the two things China's authoritarian government most dreads: political dissent and pornography. Police blamed the Internet when they found "Sexual Fighter," a racy video clip, flashing on the screens of university students in Tianjin recently. Also, the Internet has become a means for the overseas Chinese dissident community to keep in touch with and send information to sympathizers in China. For example, when Wei Jingsheng, a leading democracy campaigner, was sentenced to a second long prison term late last year, the U.S.–based China Ness Digest E-mailed to its 40,000 Internet subscribers, including many inside China, the full text of Mr. Wei's "Fifth Modernization." That banned tract prompted his first incarceration 16 years ago.

Such breaches help explain Beijing's decision to suspend new Internet memberships, a move officially called "temporary" and attributed to "technical problems." In a meeting at which Premier Li Peng presided, authorities declared earlier this month that it was "imperative" to develop new Internet controls. Industry insiders say China, which has already bought some of the most powerful equipment available from U.S.–based Cisco Systems Inc. and Sprint International, ultimately aims to create a centrally administered monolithic Internet backbone that minimizes the threat posed by the Internet's amoeba-like structure.

BLOCKING ACCESS

Thus, James Chu is striving to develop an "intranet," or Internet "lite." On Chu's proposed network, which is backed by Xinhua but has yet to be seconded by China's top authorities, users will be able to set up their own home pages, trade information, draw on databases, or visit World Wide Web home pages to which gatekeepers grant access. Users can petition to open a channel to any outside Internet provider, which will be subject to review. "What we want is to make sure information doesn't violate China's laws," Chu says.

Chu is relying on firewall software from Sun Microsystems, which can selectively block access to Internet areas deemed unsuitable. He acknowledges that such filtering mechanisms aren't perfect; an aggressive user can always disguise information or photos, slipping them by censors. But with aggressive management, he says, Chinese authorities can make it difficult and risky to violate the restrictions. Herman Ho, a Hong Kong–based technician for Sun Microsystems, says his company's software can effectively filter unwanted information, but he cautions that it can't stop the determined hacker.

Other groups also believe China can create its own Internet subsystem. Information Highway Inc., a private company in Beijing, is cooperating with the telecom ministry to set up what it calls "Information Highway Space," a network modeled on the CompuServe service, but with guardrails to contain unwanted information. "The Internet is too independent. It doesn't meet Chinese special characteristics," says Jasmine Zhang, Information Highway's president.

The widely publicized move by Xinhua to rein in foreign economic news services is part of a similar effort to control information services. Until the 1990s, China had no capital markets, and Xinhua, its news agency, provided little real-time economic and financial news and data. Among others, Reuters and Dow Jones filled the gap as Beijing opened stock, bond, and commodity markets and started allowing banks and trading houses to hedge risks on markets abroad.

Information and markets became closely intertwined as companies like China National Cereals, Oils & Foodstuffs Import & Export Corp. (known as Ceroils), discovered. The country's monopoly trader of grain—one of the largest traders of its kind in the world—now "lives on Reuters," says Zhao Yang, a futures trader.

RUMORS OF DEATH

Now Xinhua is horning in on the lucrative business. Foreign media executives hope the agency will settle for a cut of their revenues. But Xinhua insists there is more to it. Rumors of the death of paramount leader Deng Xiaoping, which perodically shatter China's markets, aren't fit for news wires, agency officials say. Few expect Xinhua to whitewash stock prices. But the agency has set up a monitoring room to track news from abroad. It won't block incoming items but it has threatened to punish those who deliver "slanderous" news, a prospect that may chill coverage.

In fact, China already has its own economic news service, though it isn't owned by Xinhua. Yu Changli founded Newland Securities Investment Consultants Co. to offer an alternative to foreign wires. Yu claims that his service reaches 200 clients, generating $600,000 in annual revenue.

Yu predicts that China eventually will develop enough of its own news services that it won't have to depend on foreigners at all. "Foreigners don't have the feel of the Chinese people. They don't know what to publish and what not to publish," Yu says. As for Xinhua's crackdown on foreign news media, Yu says, "My only question is why didn't it come sooner?"

Questions

1. Do you think that China will succeed in limiting access to the Internet?
2. Do you think that other countries will attempt to follow China's lead?
3. If you were America OnLine or CompuServe, what strategy would you use to market your services in China?

SOURCE: J. Khan, K. Chen, and M. Brauchli, *The Wall Street Journal,* Wednesday, January 31, 1996, p. A1.

MODULE IV Case

THE FRENCH VIDEOTEX SYSTEM: MINITEL[1]

In the late 1970s, videotex[2] was an important fixture of the telecommunications landscape of most industrialized countries. Many national Post, Telephone and Telegraph (PTT) companies and commercial ventures started pilot videotex projects. Videotex was seen as one of the driving forces in the movement toward an information society. In 1982, there were at least 50 videotex projects in 16 countries of Western Europe, Japan, and North America.

A decade later most of those projects have failed. One noted exception is France's famous Télétel.[3] As of 1993, Télétel had over 6 million subscribers and 20,000 services, and handled close to 2 billion calls and 110 million hours of connection time a year. These statistics dwarfed, for example, the privately owned American systems Prodigy and CompuServe, which had, at that time, around a million subscribers each and two thousand services (nobody was talking about the Internet then). Britain's Prestel (150,000 subscribers and 1,300 services) and Germany's Bildschirmtext (250,000 subscribers and 3,500 services), which ranked second and third in the world during the 1980s, are today considered commercial failures, and their prospects for growth are not promising (Schneider et al., 1990).

What made Tététel such a success?

BACKGROUND

Information Technology and French Industrial Policy

In the mid 1960s, particularly after the American Congress denied a permit to export a large IBM mainframe computer to the French government, French political commentators started to voice concerns that France was falling behind the United States in information technology. Some predicted this would soon be an intolerable situation of technological and cultural dependence. For example, President Valéry Giscard d'Estaing stated that "for France, the American domination of telecommunications and computers is a threat to its independence in the crucially significant if not overriding area of technology and in the field of culture, where the American presence, through television and satellite, becomes an omnipresence." Similar concerns continued through the 1970s and influenced a central piece of the industrial policy of the country.[4]

In 1975, President Giscard d'Estaing asked two researchers (Messrs. Nora and Minc) to suggest a strategy to computerize French society. Their report became a best-seller and coined a new word, *télématique* (from telecommunications and informatique). It was proposed as the cornerstone of French industrial policy.

Télématique describes the merger of computers and communication technologies so as to create information-processing applications with broad societal impact. Nora and Minc predicted that eventually télématique would affect all aspects of society—education, business, media, leisure, and routine day-to-day activities. By increasing access to information, télématique was expected to decentralize government and business decision making, increase national productivity and competitiveness, and improve the ability to respond to an increasingly fast-changing environment.

The vision would require a new national communication infrastructure, a long-term strategy, and cooperation between the government and business sectors. One recommendation was for the Direction Générale des Télécommunications (DGT), as France Télécom was then named, to encourage cooperation among computer services companies and hardware manufacturers. Together they would produce the technical components of the required infrastructure. Another recommendation was for the DGT to implement a research program to develop applications to leverage the infrastructure investment.

Such recommendations are typical of French industrial policy. The strategy of having the government orchestrate and subsidize large technological projects by creating alliances among companies had been used frequently in the transportation sector (e.g., Ariane, Airbus, Concorde, TGV). The government has gone as far as "rationalizing" an industrial sector. Paul Maury, director of Minitel at France Télécom, put it this way: "This type of large industrial projects, or as we [French] call them, 'les grandes aventures', have always captured the imagination of French politicians."

The French Telephone System in the 1970s

In 1974, when Giscard d'Estaing became president of France, the French telecommunications system was very weak. Less than 7 million telephone lines served a population of 47 million. This was one of the lower penetration rates in the industrialized world and equivalent to that of Czechoslovakia. Customers waited four years to get a new line, and most rural areas were still equipped with manual switches.

President Giscard d'Estaing made the reform of the telecommunications infrastructure a top priority. In April 1975, the Conseil des Ministres (a cabinet-level meeting among the secretaries of all agencies) approved the president's program under the banner "Le téléphone pour tous" (a telephone for everyone).

Also in 1974, Gérard Théry took over as director of the DGT. At that time, the strategic direction of telecommunications technology was set by the Centre National d'Etudes des Télecommunication (CNET). The CNET was, and continues to be, the research and development arm of the DGT. The CNET was dominated by engineers whose responsibility and vocation was the design of new products. They focused on technical prowess and innovation.

Once the design of a product was complete, the CNET negotiated directly with the telecommunications industry for the development and commercialization of the product. The CNET engineers were constantly trying new technologies without a clear technological migration plan. This practice forced manufacturers into short production runs, made manufacturing economies of scale impossible, drove prices up, and made network compatibility difficult to achieve.

Théry changed the orientation of the CNET. The CNET adopted a more commercial and pragmatic attitude. The change in culture was difficult at first and led to a long and bitter strike. Eventually, Théry's vision prevailed, and a new relationship between the DGT and the French telecommunication manufacturers was forged.

A more commercial orientation at the CNET was realized by creating the Direction des Affaires Industrielles et Internationales (DAII) and by bringing an outsider in as its director. One of the principal functions of the DAII was to ensure standardization of equipment. The DAII invited bids not only from the traditional suppliers of the DGT (e.g., CIT-Alcatel, Thomson) but from others as well (e.g., Matra and Philips). To drive equipment prices down, the DAII announced that an important criterion in choosing suppliers would be their ability to export and acquire larger markets.

The government push toward standardization and export of equipment was partially responsible for lowering subscription charges, resulting in more than doubling the number of telephone lines between 1974 and 1979. By the late 1980s, the penetration rate was at 95 percent, one of the higher among the industrialized nations.

The transformation of the French telephone network from the "joke of Europe" to the most modern of Europe took some 10 years and a tremendous amount of resources. Indeed, from 1976 to 1980, the DGT was the largest investor in France, averaging around 4 percent of the total national investment in the country. The total cost of the transformation has been estimated at around FF 120 billion.[5]

TÉLÉTEL

A Strategy to Increase Telephone Traffic

The magnitude of the investment required to create the telephone network raised questions of how to maintain its expansion and how to recuperate the modernization costs. In early 1978, with the telephone penetration rate growing very quickly, Théry realized that telephone traffic alone would not be enough to pay back the investment in the telephone network and the public packet-switched network (Transpac). Théry asked the CNET to generate ideas for new services to increase traffic. These services would have to: (1) provide greater access for all citizens to government and commercial information, (2) benefit as many elements of society as possible, (3) demonstrate the value of merging computing and telecommunications, (4) be flexible enough to avoid quick technological obsolescence, and (5) be profitable.

Théry prepared a report for the Conseil des Ministres detailing six projects: the electronic telephone directory, the videotex, the videophone, the wide distribution of telefax machines, the launching of a satellite for data transmission, and the voice-activated telephone. The background for his presentation was the Nora and Minc report and the need, as perceived by Théry, to counter the threat of the American computer manufacturers capturing critical strategic markets if left unchallenged.

The Conseil des Ministres approved videotex and the electronic telephone directory. Three years after the successful launch of the "Le téléphone pour tous" campaign, "la grande aventure du Télétel" had begun.

Télétel: A Brief History

Work on Télétel began in the mid-1970s. The first prototype was shown at the 1977 Berlin Trade Fair. The British demonstrated at the show a very impressive operational videotex system. Théry realized he had to move fast. In late 1978, he persuaded the government to allow the DGT to pursue the Télétel project, and a test was set for December of 1979.

France Télécom initially made plans for just two applications: the development of an electronic telephone directory and classified ads. While the electronic directory service was a welcome innovation, the press and its powerful lobby generated a political furor over

EXHIBIT 1 Rate of Minitel Distribution

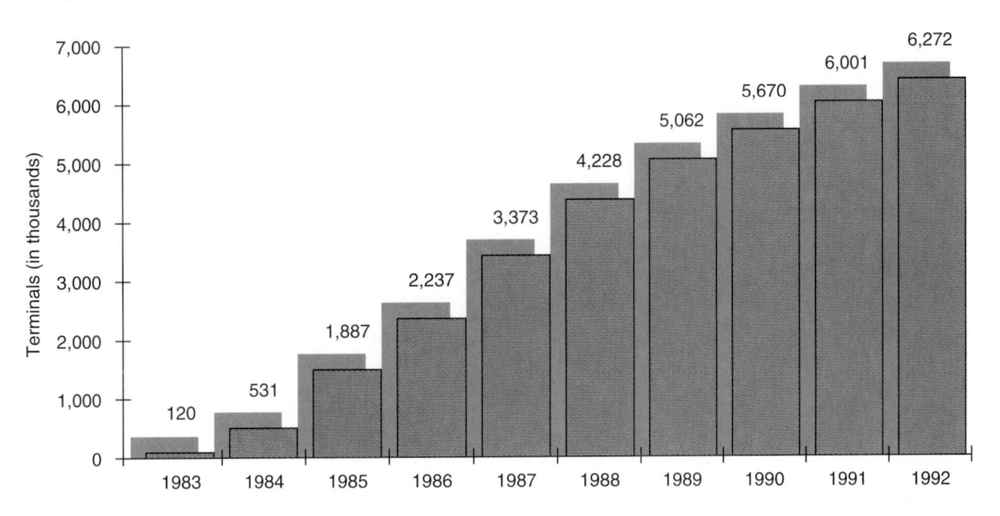

the government meddling in the classified ads business. The DGT dropped the classified ads idea and concentrated on justifying the videotex project on the electronic telephone directory alone.

With seven million new telephone lines added between 1974 and 1979, a telephone directory was obsolete before it was printed (and it was printed twice a year). Also, the cost of printing the French telephone directory had gone up so rapidly that in 1979 the paper telephone directory lost FF120 million. Between 1979 and 1984, another 7 million phone lines were expected to be installed. The cost of printing the directory alone was expected to double in five years, and the quantity of paper was expected to quintuple from 20,000 tons of paper in 1979 to a projected 100,000 tons by 1985. Directory assistance was hopelessly overloaded. It required 4,500 operators to provide a barely acceptable level of service. The number of operators needed in 1985 was forecasted to be 9,000. But the success of the electronic telephone directory required that a great majority of the subscribers be able to use it. To do so, subscribers needed to have access to an easy-to-use, inexpensive terminal.

DAII planners explored a scenario of distribution terminals free of charge to subscribers. They reasoned that with the cost of each paper telephone book being FF100 (and increasing), the FF500[6] cost of a dedicated terminal could be recovered in less than five years.[7]

The initial testing of the electronic directory began in July 1980, in Saint-Malo, a small town of 46,000 people in the county of Ille-et-Vilaine. The town was chosen for its size and proximity to the headquarters of the CNET where the electronic directory was developed. The actual videotex experiment started in Vélizy—a suburb of Paris with a representative socioeconomic profile and a good telephone network in place—in June 1981 with a sample of 2,500 homes and 100 different services.[8] After two years, the Vélizy experience showed that 25 percent of the users were responsible for 60 percent of all traffic, that a full one-third of the sample never used the device (this proportion of nonusers has remained constant throughout the dissemination of minitels), and that overall, households had a positive experience with Télétel. The experiment was considered a success in both technical and sociological terms.

In February 1983, a full-scale implementation of the electronic directory was started in the whole county of Ille-et-Vilaine. The county is made up of both rural and urban areas and is home to 250,000 people. In the opening ceremony, Louis Mexandeau, the new secretary of the PTT, exulted: "We are here today to celebrate the beginning of a 'grande aventure', an experience which will mark our future." François Mitterand had replaced Valéry Giscard d'Estaing as president of France, the left was now in power, but the rhetoric on the importance of Télématique to the future of the country and the underlying industrial policy were unchanged.

Soon after the successes of Vélizy and Ille-et-Vilaine, the voluntary and free distribution of minitel terminals began: There were only 120,000 minitels in France by the end of 1983, but over 3 million by December 1987, and more than 6 million by December 1992 (see Exhibit 1). Videotex services went from 2,000 in January of 1986 to 12,000 at the end of 1989 to more than 20,000 by

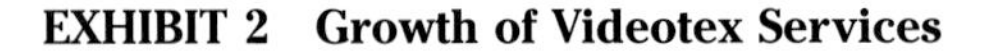

EXHIBIT 2 Growth of Videotex Services

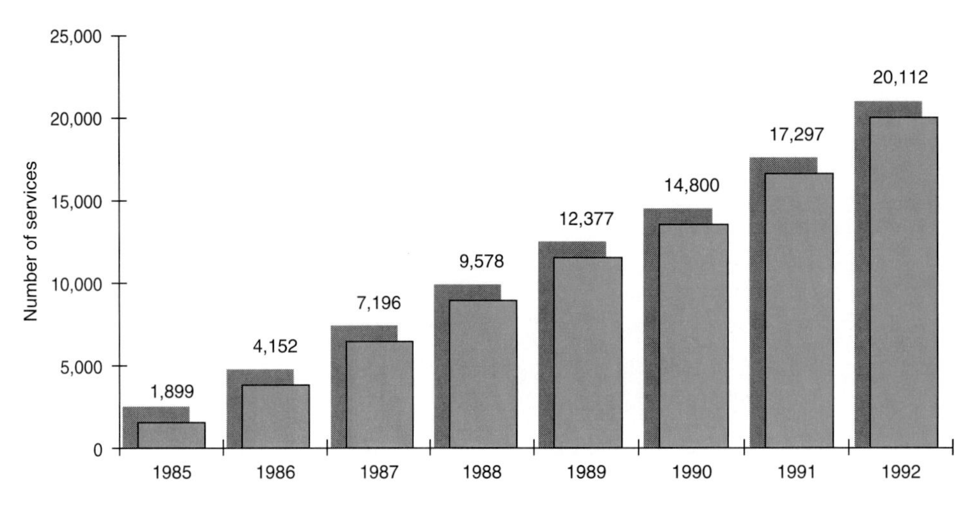

December 1992 (see Exhibit 2). Table 1 shows that traffic on the Télétel system and on the electronic telephone directory has steadily increased over the years. It is interesting to note, however, that the average monthly usage per terminal had gone down from 106 minutes in 1986 to around 90 minutes at the end of 1992. Indeed, the number of calls per minitel remained constant through that period and even showed a slight increase. The answer seems to be that not only the transmission rate is faster for the new generation of minitel terminals, but also that users are becoming more efficient and the system's interfaces friendlier to use, thus reducing the average length of a call by almost 20 percent. France Télécom's commitment to continuously expand and improve the system to match the increase in overall traffic can be seen in Table 2.

The Early Challenges

Télétel had to overcome four serious challenges in the early years. First, there were vicious attacks by newspaper owners, in particular by François-Régis Hutin, owner of Ouest-France, who saw among many philosophical reasons to stop videotex, a very pragmatic one. A government-run, videotex-based classified ads service was a serious threat to one of the newspapers' main sources of revenue. After a long fight, a political compromise was reached. The newspaper owners agreed to drop their resistance to the videotex concept in exchange for a say in the development of Télétel services, subsidies, and technical help from DGT to develop their own services, and a virtual monopoly on services for two years.

A second challenge came from politicians who felt the system could be abused by the state. They saw this new mode of information dissemination as a potential threat to liberty, and Télétel as the latest attempt of the state to manipulate information. Later, the rapid proliferation of "chat" (*messageries*) services, some of which range from the mildly erotic to the pornographic (*messageries roses*), brought criticism from both government and private groups who were concerned that the state was billing and indirectly subsidizing immorality.[9]

A third challenge was the early battle to establish an international videotex standard. The more advanced videotex system in the 1970s was the British system, Prestel. Prestel was based on the CEEFAX standard, which was different from the one being used by the French. The DGT, realizing that it was at a disadvantage, tried to have its own videotex standard recognized at several international forums. In a decision typical of the regulatory politics in Europe, the Conférence Européene des Postes et Télécommunications (CEPT) established in 1980 a European videotex "standard" with 10 variations! One of these variations was the French standard. The fact that this decision assured the incompatibility of the European videotex systems during the 1980s notwithstanding, the decision allowed the DGT to continue the development of Télétel as planned.

The fourth challenge that Télétel had to survive was the negative publicity created by the "crash of '85," the only system failure since its inception. The crash was the result of very heavy traffic of *messageries roses* services. The heavy traffic caused an overload of the Transpac switching system, and the network went down, generating considerable attention in the national press. The technical problem was easy to solve: the switching system was changed to handle higher volumes, and there has not been another crash since. The perceptual problem that Télétel was mostly about sex lingered much longer, slowed down Télétel's development, and, paradoxically, increased its international visibility.

TABLE 1 Télétel Traffic Statistics Including ETD* (1986–1992)

	1986	*1987*	*1988*	*1989*	*1990*	*1991*	*1992*
Total number of calls (in millions)	466	807	1,010	1,242	1,482	1,656	1,775
Total connect hours (in millions)	37.5	62.4	73.7	86.5	98.2	104.9	110
ETD connect hours (in millions)	6.0	10.0	13.2	16.4	19.9	22.0	23
Average number of calls per month	21.9	24.0	22.2	22.3	23.2	23.8	24.2
Average usage per month (in minutes)	105.9	111.3	97.0	93.2	92.4	90.2	87.6
Average call including ETD (in minutes)	4.8	4.6	4.4	4.2	4.0	3.8	3.7
Average call excluding ETD (in minutes)	6.3	6.2	5.8	6.5	5.5	5.3	5.1

*Electronic Telephone Directory.

SOURCE: Adapted from "La Lettre du Télétel," *France Télécom,* April and December 1992, and June 1993.

TABLE 2 Evolution of the Electronic Telephone Directory (ETD) and Videotex Networks (1987–1992)

	1987	*1988*	*1989*	*1990*	*1991*	*1992*
Number of access points to the ETD	58	72	78	82	86	88
Number of ports to the ETD	14,220	17,280	19,020	19,020	20,640	21,120
Number of information centers	31	40	42	44	47	49
Number of documentation centers	15	18	22	23	25	27
Number of videotex access points (VAPs)	43,160	49,611	50,500	53,000	57,000	59,500

SOURCE: Adapted from "La Lettre du Télétel," *France Télécom,* 1989–1991, 1993.

Overcoming these public controversies made Télétel stronger in the long run. Indeed, the political fury that Télétel generated in the period 1978–80, and later in 1985, led to a full and rich discussion on the issues of privacy rights, authority of the telecommunication agency, regulations of computer services, and the need to prevent the creation of a second class of citizens shut out of the information age. These discussions involved the president of France and the most notable political commentators and intellectuals in the country. They eventually created a broad national consensus on the use and limitations of the technology.

Today, Télétel is an integral part of the French lifestyle. A survey conducted by France Télécom in October 1992 indicated that 47.5 percent of the working population had access to minitels at home or at work. Another survey, conducted in 1992, showed that the system was used regularly by a broad cross-section of the population in a variety of ways. Table 3 shows that users are almost equally divided by gender, with 60 percent of the users being in the 25–49 years-of-age range. More than 55 percent of the users are executives or office and skilled workers. Calls for all professional applications represent 52 percent of the connect time. The proportion of calls to the electronic telephone directory represents more than 43 percent of all calls to Télétel but only 21 percent of the connect time. Interestingly, the most (in)famous calls of all, the calls to the "chat" services, represent only 6 percent of all calls but still make a significant 15 percent of the total connect time (Table 4).

Recent Developments

The line of minitel terminals has been expanded to include eight models with varying levels of intelligence

TABLE 3 Demographic Statistics of Minitel Users and the Overall French Population

	Minitel Users (in %)	*French Population (in %)*
Gender		
Male	49.8	47.9
Female	50.2	52.1
Age		
15–24 years	15.6	19.4
25–34 years	30.3	18.8
35–49 years	36.2	25.7
50–64 years	13.5	19.4
More than 64 years	4.4	17.7
Job Category		
Agriculture	4.4	3.4
Small business, handicraft, trade	10.8	6.0
Liberal professions, executives	23.2	11.1
Office and skilled workers	38.1	23.1
Nonskilled workers	15.3	25.2
Nonworking	8.2	31.2

SOURCE: Adapted from "La Lettre du Télétel," *France Télécom,* December 1991.

TABLE 4 Utilization per Type of Application in Percent of Connect Time and Percent of Calls (1992)

	% Time	*% Calls*
Business applications	23	19
Electronic telephone directory	21	43
"Chat" services (messageries)	15	6
Banks/stock market/insurance	11	12
Games/tests/astrology	8	5
Recruitment/training	9	6
Leisure/tourism/mail order	7	5
Transport/automotive	6	4

SOURCE: Adapted from "La Lettre du Télétel," *France Télécom,* December 1992.

and functionality (e.g., color screen, extended keyboards, compatibility with ASCII standards, service number memory). These second- and third-generation terminals are no longer free; they must be paid for or leased. More than 1.5 million had been installed as of June 1992. The latest model, which includes a color monitor and an expanded keyboard, sells for FF4,420.

The new generation of minitel terminals allows the user to prepare a message before placing a call, to monitor call set-up, and to switch between voice and text transmission during a call. They also serve as automatic answering devices with protected access. A portable minitel that can be used over the cellular telephone network is also available. ISDN[10] terminals have already been tested for the Télétel system. Numeris, as the integrated services digital network is known, had 150,000 subscribers at the end of 1991. An electronic mail service, Minicom, was implemented in 1991 and by December 1992 was carrying more than 5 million calls a year, and its volume was growing at a rate of 5 percent per month.

France Télécom is also experimenting with natural language interfaces for Télétel services. The Minitel Service Guide came on-line in 1989 with an interface that allows users to access the guide to minitel services using French, without the need for special commands or the correct spelling. This service averaged around 2 million calls a month in 1992. A new routing capability allows information providers to use several host computers under a single minitel access code. The new routing capability also allows the caller to access another service with Télétel without making a new phone call. Another product is the Télétel *a vitesse rapide* (fast speed), which opens a whole new series of potential products. It transmits at a rate of 4,800 bits per second instead of the usual 1,200 bits per second, thus making possible the transmittal of images and photographs.

TABLE 5 International Télétel Usage per Country in 1992

Country	*% of Total International Use*
Italy	42.0
Belgium	23.0
Switzerland	9.0
Luxemburg	7.0
Portugal	6.5
Andorra	4.0
USA	3.5
Germany	1.0
Ireland	1.0
Holland	1.0
Other (Spain, Britain, Finland)	2.0

SOURCE: Adapted from "La Lettre du Télétel," *France Télécom*, December 1992.

With the internal videotex market progressively being saturated and growth slowing down, France Télécom has made the international market a high priority. In 1989, France Télécom created Intelmatique—a division to sell videotex infrastructure and know-how. Recent clients included the Italian and Irish telephone companies. Intelmatique has also purchased 17 percent of the Dutch videotex operator.

Intelmatique markets the Minitelnet service that provides foreign users with access to the Télétel network. Télétel is now available in 27 countries and the service generated 287,600 hours of traffic in 1992, close to a 100 percent increase over 1990. Italy (42 percent of the traffic) and Belgium (23 percent) are the two major markets (see Table 5). The new service greets foreign users with a personalized welcome in their native language and utilizes the same multitariff billing scheme used on Télétel. Users have direct access to all the Télétel services, but the utilization of those services differs somewhat from the one in France.

Major efforts are currently being made to export minitel services to the U.S. market. A number of companies (e.g., US West) have established gateways with the minitel system. The Minitel Service Company, another entity of Intelmatique, was set up for the sole purpose of selling videotex know-how in the United States. France Télécom and US West launched a videotex service in Omaha, Nebraska, using French technology, and have signed a contract to offer an electronic telephone directory service in Minneapolis/St. Paul, Minnesota. Finally, US Videotel offers Télétel-based services to minitel owners connected to access points operated by Southwestern Bell.

There is a broad consensus in France that Télétel is a success from a social development point of view. Its positive impact on the technological literacy of the population is unquestionable. The primary concern about Télétel now is its profitability. But before exploring this concern, this paper describes some of the technical choices and characteristics that made Télétel so far the most successful commercial videotex system in the world.

GENERAL CHARACTERISTICS OF TÉLÉTEL

A comparison between the technical characteristics and policies that were used in implementing Télétel and those of the other commercial videotex systems explains to a certain degree the great success of Télétel and the rather tepid development of other government-owned systems and the more recently implemented, privately owned American systems. Videotex systems can be compared on four basic characteristics: (1) the terminal design and the strategy of terminal distribution, (2) the system architecture and other aspects of service delivery, (3) the billing system, and (4) the regulatory environment.

The Terminal Design and Distribution

Two arguments made it clear that Télétel's success was critically dependent on the development of an easy-to-use, dedicated, and inexpensive terminal for mass distribution. The first argument came from the British experience. In Britain, the high price of the chosen TV-based videotex configuration was a barrier to implementation. The second argument was that the Télétel investment would be paid back through increased telephone traffic and savings on the production of the telephone directory. The Vélizy experience had also established the need for a user-friendly terminal with an easy-to-use interface. The motto for Télétel became "Make it simple"—simple to install, simple to use, simple to manufacture.

In an approach typical of French industrial policy, the government, rather than the consumer electronic industry, decided on the specifications of the videotex terminals. The DAII opened the procurement of terminals to multiple vendors, and the promise of a production run of some 20 million terminals encouraged low bids.

The key decision on whether to distribute minitel terminals free of charge generated intense controversy within the DGT. On the one hand, some senior officers thought that a nominal monthly fee would recover development costs, while counteracting an attitude that "if it's free it cannot be very good." They also reasoned that once the system was distributed for free, it would be practically impossible to charge for it later without generating intense public resistance.

On the other hand, to distribute minitels on a free and voluntary basis gave it an aura of democracy; those who wished to have a minitel would not be impeded by its cost. It also made it easier for the mass public to try out the device and the services it offered. In what turned out to be a critical decision in the success of Télétel, it was decided that minitel terminals would be distributed free of charge.

The System Architecture

Another critical factor in the success of Télétel was the decision to implement the Télétel concept by interfacing the public-switched telephone data network. The subscriber was to be linked to the electronic directory or any other database via his or her telephone through a gateway—called a *videotex access point* or *VAP*—giving access to the public packet-switched network—called *Transpac*—to which the servers and host computers were to be connected.

This design approach had three basic advantages. First, Transpac charges are based on traffic (i.e., minutes of connect-time) and not on distance. The use of Transpac meant that any provider, independent of its geographical location, had equal access and costs to gain a national audience. Second, it established a common, standard protocol (i.e., the CCITT X.29) making connections to the system straightforward and relatively cheap (FF 100,000), which was crucial to attract service providers. Third, the networks were already in place, consisted of the latest technology, and could support a rapid expansion in the number of subscribers and providers.

More importantly, the decision of using the Transpac network kept the DGT from becoming an information provider. With the exception of the electronic directory, the DGT acted as a common carrier and was responsible only for the transmission of information and administration of the network. This is in contrast to the centralized solution offered by the British and German systems where British Telecom and the BundesPost provided the storage and structure of the databases. In Télétel, the storage and manipulation of information was left to the private information providers.

Building Télétel on a decentralized network and with an open architecture alleviated many of the "Big Brother" concerns of the press and politicians, and encouraged innovation in information services. With no government interference, a clear set of standards, and easy access to the network, the entry barrier to the information provider market was very low. The number of services exploded.

The Billing System

Another critical element in the success of Télétel is the billing system introduced by France Télécom in March 1984. The billing is done by France Télécom and not by the service providers. The system's name, *kiosk,* came from the newsstands where a variety of publications can be bought without leaving a record of what was bought or who bought it. The Télétel charges appear on the regular telephone bill as "minitel use" with no reference whatsoever as to what specific service was used.

The kiosk works as follows: when the connection to the desired service has been set up through the VAP, the VAP sends charging pulses to the subscriber's meter at a faster rate than the usual rate to cover the cost of using the Transpac network and the cost of the service. The Transpac network keeps track of the connection time and pays each provider as a function of that time. The billing system now allows the service providers to choose from eight levels of pricing.

The strengths of the kiosk concept are that it protects the anonymity of the users (important on both a financial and philosophical level), that it does not require passwords or payments in advance, that service providers do not have to worry about billing and its associated administrative costs, and that it allows differently priced services to be offered easily through a series of different numbers.

The Regulatory Environment

The monopoly that France Télécom had in the basic telecommunication services and the fact that it did not have the return-on-investment pressures of a commercial firm, provided Télétel with the necessary time to mature.[11] Infrastructure-based services like Télétel require a longer time horizon to assess and determine profitability. The regulatory umbrella that shielded Télétel in the early years appears to be one of the critical factors in its success.

Another component of the French regulatory environment that was important to the development of Télétel was the ability of France Télécom to subsidize ventures from its subscribers' revenue. Such subsidies are forbidden by American and British regulations. The subsidies allowed France Télécom to take a long and patient view on Télétel and helped amortize the free distribution of minitel terminals, which amounted to a cost of FF6 billion over 10 years.

There was one specific benefit of this protective regulatory environment. The ability to quickly implement changes to tariffs without going through a lengthy political process to justify them allowed France Télécom to respond quickly to changing market conditions. For example, there were many services that Télétel users could access and use without staying connected for very long. The user paid no fee because the tariff allowed free access. Because of the revenue-sharing arrangements with the service providers, however, France Télécom asked the regulatory bodies to charge subscribers a small access fee for every connection regardless of its duration. The request was barely scrutinized, and the charge was approved without debate.

Another benefit of the regulatory environment in France was the ability of France Télécom to run the kiosk billing system. The arrangement has come under fire on two fronts. First, the fact that the billing system results in the state (in the form of France Télécom) collecting fees for the distribution of services, which, in some instances, may be deemed pornographic, is seen by some as unlawful. Second, it has been suggested that even if it is not illegal, billing, which could be a very profitable stand-alone operation, should be a service offered by a third party and not by France Télécom. These criticisms have not stopped France Télécom from performing the billing.

The regulatory environment in Europe, with its myriad of standards and protocols, was good for Télétel initially because it served to protect the fledgling service from battering by competition from abroad. However, that same environment became a barrier to Télétel's penetration of other European markets. Indeed, it took almost 10 years to make Télétel available throughout Western Europe (Greece is the only country with no access). Finally, despite operating in a heavily regulated environment, France Télécom pursued on open network architecture and stayed out of the information services business with the exception of the electronic telephone directory.

The policy of decentralization and liberalization of services, contrary to the centralization policies in Britain and Germany, led to an explosion of services. Indeed, while in France the number of providers had grown steadily and the number of services today surpasses 20,000, in Britain the number has stagnated at around 1,300, and in Germany the number has not only stagnated but has actually declined to around less than 3,000.

EVALUATION OF TÉLÉTEL

For technologies like videotex, for-profit organizations predominantly use return-on-investment criteria to determine success. However, infrastructure projects like Télétel should not be analyzed exclusively on return on investment. The sociological impact needs to be assessed and evaluated as well. Measures of the success of technological adoption include (1) the rate of diffusion and growth, (2) the impact of the technology (e.g., number of users), (3) user satisfaction with the technology, (4) facilitating the performance of an old task or enabling a new one, and (5) the economic impact of the technology and its return on investment. Though measuring the nonfinancial (i.e., social, educational, and political) benefits brought by Télétel is difficult, the increase in technological awareness and literacy of society, for example, has to be factored in any cost/benefit analysis of the system. The next two sections discuss the social impact of the four criteria listed above and the financial assessment of the return on investment issues.

Social Impact

Through its 20,000 services the Télétel system offers information about entertainment events, train schedules, television and radio programs, jobs and classified ads, interactive games, backing services, grocery and home shopping, home banking, comparative pricing, and many other consumer services. Most services follow the same rules and command structures and the same multicriteria search process (e.g., a subscriber deciding on whether to go to the movies can search what films are showing in a given area, on a given topic, or starring a particular actor or actress), making it very easy for users to move from one application to another.

It is hard to assess the impact of Télétel on business because it varies by company size and industry sector. France Télécom estimated in 1990 that the overall penetration of the business sector was at least 30 percent and growing and that the penetration for large companies (more than 500 employees) was 95 percent. Indeed, some industries have been profoundly affected by Télétel applications. For example, the Telerouting system has influenced the transportation industry in France. Transportation companies have minimized the number of return trips when their trucks and moving vans are empty by posting the schedules of these return trips on minitel and matching them to requests from customers. The impact of these new electronic markets on the efficiency of transactions among firms is profound; these markets are not only restructuring how companies do business but are reshaping entire industries.

Almost every single bank has developed its own minitel-based home-banking system, allowing their customers to check the status of their accounts, order checks, pay utility bills, and trade stocks. Most retailers have also developed an electronic catalogue business, and although volumes are moderate at present, they are expected to explode as soon as payment can be done directly with the minitel terminal. Television stations run minitel-based surveys every night. Travel agencies, insurance companies, and consumer products companies have developed Télétel services.

Whether it is to be in greater touch with the client, to increase efficiency in distribution, to gain market share, or to develop videotex products and services, Télétel has become an important component of the business strategy of companies operating in France. Business-related volume represents today more than 50 percent of the overall Télétel volume, and while the overall volume increased by 5.1 percent in 1992, the utilization of professional services increased four times as fast.

From a social point of view, Télétel has had an impact in a wide variety of ways. For example, the success stories of the various Télétel chat services (*messageries*) range from relatives separated by World War II having found each other, to faster matching between organ donors and people in need of a transplant.

The anonymity that the chat services provide has encouraged the sick (e.g., cancer, AIDS patients) and the troubled (drug addicts, divorced, abused) to discuss their more intimate problems with others. Also, Télétel has played a role in helping individuals who have difficulty getting out and around (the disabled, the elderly) to shop, bank, and make reservations. Universities now use Télétel to coordinate student registration, course delivery, and examination results. Other services give students access to help from tutors at all times.

Télétel services have also been used in the political arena in innovative ways. During the last presidential election, a service allowed minitel users to exchange letters with the candidates. Any voter accessing the service could view the open letters and the politicians' replies. Another example is how the student unrest in December 1986 was followed by using minitel terminals. A service, sponsored by the newspaper *Libération*, allowed organizers to issue instructions to any minitel user to participate in various political activities without the mediation of a third party.

These examples illustrate how broadly Télétel has been used as a decentralized grassroots vehicle for the discussion of a variety of societal issues. This utilization is very much in keeping with the original vision of Télématique proposed by Messrs. Nora and Minc in 1978. Today, 34 percent of the population of France has access to a minitel either at home or at work. Furthermore, a recent survey conducted by an independent consulting firm found that 93 percent of all Télétel users are satisfied or very satisfied with the service, that 19 percent of all professionals using Télétel rate it "indispensable," and that 75 percent of users rate it "increasingly useful." Based on the number and variety of services being offered (from the original 145 in 1983 to more than 20,000 in 1993), the broad penetration of the service (an installed base of over 6 million minitel terminals and only 5 percent of the ones in homes not being used), the growth in connect time (from 14 million hours in 1985 to 110 million hours and almost 2 billion calls in 1992), and the high level of satisfaction of its users (only 1 percent of users declared themselves "dissatisfied"), one can only conclude that from a social point of view, Télétel has been a success.

Financial Assessment

There is a public perception, in part based on the free distribution of minitel terminals, that Télétel is another Concorde: a high-technology, money-losing proposition. A recent report from the state auditor general has stated that Télétel revenues have not covered its operating, depreciation, and capital costs and that as of the end of 1987 the deficit was FF 5.4 billion. The secretary of the PTT disagreed with that assessment, arguing that the analysis of the auditor took into consideration only the direct revenue generated by the telephone traffic but did not include all the other indirect revenues generated by Télétel.

Settling the argument is difficult for a variety of reasons. First, from a cost-allocation point of view, determining Télétel's share of the costs is a murky proposition. Indeed, it can be argued that Télétel is just a by-product of providing other telephone services, and therefore, little or no cost of the actual infrastructure should be allocated to it. Second, it is difficult to determine the indirect value-added to the French economy (e.g., greater efficiency of electronic markets). Third, France Télécom continuously introduces new products and services that affect previous cost-allocation and profitability calculations. Finally, France Télécom is not particularly forthcoming with the financial data surrounding Télétel.

The total investment in Télétel consists of the cost of the minitel terminals plus the costs of the gateways to the Transpac network (VAPs) plus the costs of ports to the electronic directory network. The following are approximate but noncontroversial figures describing the investment for France Télécom in Télétel as of 1989:

Minitel terminals	FF 6.2 bil
Electronic directory	FF 1.0 bil
R&D directory	FF 0.2 bil
VAPs	FF 0.6 bil
R&D (Télétel)	FF 0.3 bil
Transpac	FF 0.3 bil
Total	FF 8.6 bil

The official gross revenues from Télétel were approximately FF 5.8 billion in 1992. These revenues include fees from revenue sharing with information providers. That amount was close to FF 1 billion in 1992.[12] The revenues also include advertising, electronic directory usage above and beyond the free allocation, and rental and sale of minitels. The Transpac revenue generated by Télétel—FF 1 billion in 1992—is not included in the FF 5.8 billion. The additional revenues based on value-added tax from products, services, and increased employment spawned by Télétel should also be included but are difficult to calculate. The secretary of the PTT estimated that the total value-added of Télétel amounted to approximately FF 6 billion in 1988. Documents from a telecommunication consulting firm put the amount at FF 5.4 billion. Finally, cost savings from printing fewer telephone books (FF 147 million) and having less directory assistance operators must also be considered.

France Télécom claimed in 1985 that the break-even point for Télétel would be achieved in 10 years. France Télécom calculations in 1989 showed that the yearly revenue per minitel terminal was FF 432 and that the payback period was 5.7 years. The official version is that Télétel revenues and expenses were in balance at the end of 1989 and the system was expected to start showing a significant return on investment in 1992. A recent audit by Coopers and Lybrand for France Télécom has confirmed that the break-even point was reached at the end of 1989. The audit pointed out that Télétel will have made a profit of FF 4.3 billion from 1984 through the year 2000, equivalent to an internal rate of return of 11.3 percent.

On the basis of the numbers we have been able to gather and cross-reference (though they are practically impossible to confirm), we can conclude (1) that Télétel has reached an economic break-even point, and (2) that from a long-term economic point of view (say, 1978–2000), Télétel will possibly make a sizable profit with an overall return on investment of around 10 percent.

Senior officials of France Télécom view this type of accounting as premature and potentially misleading, since Télétel is a major infrastructure project for which profitability should be measured on a long-term basis and should not be the sole criterion of success. Still, France Télécom has become very sensitive to match demand and to create demand for new products.

The sociological evidence (rapid growth and adoption, impact on a large number of users, enabling new tasks to be performed, high user satisfaction) and the financial evidence (positive internal rate of return, profitability, creation of more efficient markets) supports the notion that Télétel is a French industrial policy success story.

Questions

1. What were the critical factors (political, sociological, technological) that contributed to the success of Minitel?
2. Compare the development and structure of Minitel in France to the development and structure of CompuServe, Prodigy, and America OnLine in the United States.
3. Describe in detail the hardware and software components of the Minitel system.
4. What impact do you think the internet has had and will have on Minitel?

---

[1]This case is an abridged version of the article, "The French Videotex System Minitel: A Successful Implementation of a National Information Technology Infrastructure," by W. Cats-Baril and T. Jellasi, which appeared in *MIS Quarterly* **18** 1, 1994, pp. 1–20.

---

[2]Videotex is a generic term for a computer-based, interactive system to access and selectively view text and graphics on a terminal screen. The content is usually organized into tree structures of pages that are selected from a series of hierarchical menus. Videotex systems typically offer a wide range of information retrieval, interactive and transactional services such as directory and reservations systems, financial reports, home banking, and shopping. Videotex was developed in Europe in the mid 1970s for consumer applications. Because of its consumer origins, videotex excels at delivering information to untrained or casual users. The user may use a dedicated videotex terminal or other access deliveries (e.g., personal computer). The primary objective of commercial videotex systems is the efficient delivery of value-added information and services to a maximum number of users profitably for both the system operator and the information providers.

---

[3]The system is popularly known as Minitel. In strict terms, however, minitel refers only to the dedicated terminal itself. Throughout this case Télétel is used when we refer to the whole system and minitel when we allude to the device.

---

[4]Although the "enemy" has changed and Japan is now the more commonly perceived threat, the policy is still very much in place today, as illustrated by the French government's decisions to save the consumer electronic companies Bull and Thomson from insolvency in 1991 and again in October of 1993.

---

[5]Though the exchange rate of the French franc (FF) has fluctuated in the last decade between 4 and 10 FF per American dollar (US$), its trading band is typically between 5 and 6FF/US$. The average value over the last decade has been close to FF5.15 per US$. By comparison, the U.S. government has been predicted to spend only $1 billion annually of the $200–400 billion expected cost of the American national data highway over the next 15 to 30 years (Wright, 1993).

---

[6]The cost turned out to be FF1,000. By 1989, the cost was FF 1,600.

---

[7]This break-even analysis was very conservative since it did not include the savings of slower growth in directory assistance costs.

---

[8]By comparison, the British television-based system Prestel had a field trial with 1,400 participants in 1978 and started commercial service in the fall of 1979. Full nationwide operation was established in March 1980. At the end of 1981, Prestel had only 1/10 of the users predicted for that time. The major reasons for this failure have been attributed to the late delivery and high prices of television monitors

(Prestel was television-based and needed a connection between the telephone and the television set), uncoordinated marketing, and bad quality of the databases.

---

[9]The chat services are very lucrative since both individuals "talking" pay for the "conversation," unlike a telephone conversation where only one party gets charged for it.

---

[10]ISDN (Integrated Services Digital Network) is capable of handling data, voice, text, and image transmission on the same line.

---

[11]France Télécom is directly accountable to the French government for all its ventures and is required to justify its fee structures. France Télécom, more so than other state agencies, is asked to demonstrate the viability of its investments and, therefore, is under some profitability pressures, mild as they may be.

---

[12]France Télécom takes a 30 percent fee on the revenue generated by information providers. Payments made by France Télécom to service providers for their share of Télétel revenues increased from FF278 million in 1985 to FF1.3 billion in 1987 to FF1.8 billion in 1989 and reached over FF2.5 billion by December 1992 (France Télécom, 1993).

Glossary

adhocracy An organization with a relatively flat organizational structure that can change quickly in response to perceived needs.

administrative model An organizational model in which decisions are made in an incremental fashion (*see also* rational model, political model).

after-sales service Assisting the customer after they have purchased the product (such as providing toll-free telephone help lines).

analysis A process of investigation, such as analyzing data to look for trends.

application generator A software package, often part of a database management system, used to quickly develop programs for specific applications.

application scope The number and type of people supported by an application, ranging from an individual to multiple organizations.

application software A software program designed for a specific purpose (such as accounts receivable or payroll).

archie A type of software program used to locate data and files on the Internet.

arithmetic-logic unit (ALU) The component of the central processing unit (CPU) that performs the arithmetic operations on data and decides what instructions to perform next.

artificial intelligence A science, and type of technology, whose goal is to develop computer systems that simulate thinking, seeing, hearing, walking, feeling.

augmenting knowledge Using an information system to enhance and/or expand the knowledge base of a human (*see also* expert system).

automating decisions Replacing a decision-making task of a human with a computer system (such as automatically reordering low-stock items).

barriers to entry Factors that make it difficult for a new organization to enter an industry (such as the need for a large amount of capital).

basis of competition Factor (or factors) that dominates the competition within an industry (such as price and features for personal computers).

batch processing An approach to processing in which data are grouped together and processed at some point after the original transactions occurred.

benchmark assessment management information system (BAM/IS) Means of tracking predefined metrics from an organization and comparing them with metrics from the best companies available.

benchmarking The process of comparing the organization against others, including the best companies available.

benchmarking partners The organizations selected for comparison purposes (could include the best in the industry and the best in the world).

biases Prejudgmental tendencies that prevent an individual from considering a situation without prejudice.

bit Binary digit; a 0 or a 1; the memory space required to store it.

boundary (of a system) The imaginary line separating a system from its environment; the line separates the variables over which the system has control and those over which it does not.

bounded rationality The realization that managers do not have an unlimited amount of resources and time to make decisions and that they have limited information processing abilities. Managers should make decisions that are good enough (see *satisficing*) rather than optimal ones.

budgeting Process of providing an itemized estimate of income and expenses.

buffer A mechanism for insulating the organization against changes in the environment (such as long-term contracts or inventories).

bureaucracy A type of organization characterized by an excessive concentration of power by administrators (*see also* standard operating procedures).

bus A set of conducting paths for the movement of data and instructions among the various components of the central processing unit.

business process An activity (or set of activities) that can be defined as accepting inputs and providing outputs for internal or external customers.

business process redesign (BPD) Changing a business process to make it more efficient and/or effective.

business process reengineering (BPR) The one-time radical redesign of a business process to achieve a dramatic improvement in performance.

buyer's bargaining power The relative strength in the relationship between an organization and its

by-exception-only (BEO) A management approach in which notice is taken only when a process goes outside of predefined standards.

customers (if there are few customers, the power generally rests with them).

byte A sequence of eight bits representing a specific character; eight bits are enough to identify each of the characters used in communicating (numbers, letters, punctuation). The term is also used as a measure of memory size.

central processing unit (CPU) Often considered the brains of a computer; controls all input, output, storage, and computations.

channel The means of communications; using a type of medium.

chargeback system A method for recovering the costs of running an information systems department by charging the costs to the organizational subunits.

chief information officer (CIO) The individual with the highest level of authority within an organization with respect to information systems.

client/server A computing environment in which central servers (usually minicomputers) are connected to user workstations (clients).

client/server architecture Computer system configuration consisting of clusters of devices (e.g., personal computers) or "clients" being served by a central computer or server. The clients request processing services from the server device.

closed system A system that does not have any interactions with its environment (no inputs or outputs; a truly closed system is unusual).

coaxial cable A transmission medium consisting of a relatively thick copper or aluminum wire, which has a higher bandwidth than a twisted pair line.

cognitive style The way in which a person accepts and interprets communication messages.

cold site A back-up and recovery site where data (and sometimes actual inactive computers) is stored. In case of a disaster that brings down the main site, the cold site cannot start processing data immediately.

communication The exchange of thoughts or information by some means (such as speech, writing, the use of signs).

communication dyad A model of communication involving a sender, receiver, a message traveling through a channel (or medium), and feedback.

communication network A series of linked communication dyads; the type of linking may take different forms (such as electronic mail or paper reports).

communication technology The hardware and software that allows computers to exchange data electronically.

competition The rivalry among organizations.

competitive strategy An organization can concentrate on low-cost production, product differentiation, and/or business innovation to help compete.

competitive vulnerability A situation in which an organization is exposed to competitive risks (such as a new entrant offering a new product).

complexity The number of variables, rules, procedures, and people involved in performing a task.

computer A physical device that accepts data, stores and executes a set of instructions, and manipulates the data to produce output.

computer-aided design (CAD) The use of computers for developing specifications for products or parts.

computer-aided manufacturing (CAM) The use of digital specifications (often from a computer-aided design system) to control production machinery.

computer-aided software engineering (CASE) Software programming tools that assist in the development of new application programs.

computer programs A set of instructions that control the operation of a computer.

computerized monitoring The use of a computer system to record human actions, such as counting keystrokes or recording details of telephone conversations.

content rationality Choosing appropriate and relevant information to solve a problem.

context diagram The top level in a set of data flow diagrams which depicts the boundary of the system, along with inputs from and outputs to external entities.

continuous improvement An approach in which employees constantly look for small (or large) ways to improve business processes.

control The exertion of influence over a person, group, or process.

control systems Systems used to control a business process (or part of a process); typically involves some type of feedback system.

conversion The process of moving from an existing information system to a new one.

co-opetition A situation in which organizations that are normally rivals decide to collaborate on part of their business.

corporate resources Factors (such as skilled employees or machinery) used by an organization in its ongoing operations.

cost–benefit analysis A type of formal evaluation in which estimated costs of an alternative are weighed against estimated benefits.

creativity The application of innovative approaches to decision situations.

critical path method A method used to find the shortest possible duration for a given project.

critical success factors (CSF) Those few things that an organization must accomplish correctly in order for it to survive and grow.

cultural differences Differences that are based on the cultural background of an individual and that can influence the communication between and among people.

customer satisfaction management information system (CSM/IS) An information system that captures metrics of customer satisfaction (such as repeat sales numbers or responses to questionnaires).

customized product A product that has been built to satisfy the desires of a specific customer (by allowing the customer to select among features).

data Raw facts that can be further processed into relevant information.

database Collection of data stored in a particular format to facilitate retrieval and analysis of that data.

database administrator (DBA) The individual or job position responsible for maintaining standards relating to the development, maintenance, and security of an organization's databases.

database design A technique used to identify an appropriate structure for the data to be stored in a database.

database management system (DBMS) A software package used to establish and maintain one or more databases; generally contains features for developing applications with input forms, reports, and processing facilities.

data dictionary A software program, typically part of a database management system, used to maintain information about data and objects used within the information systems of the organization.

data flow Depicts a movement of information between two objects on a data flow diagram; examples include a document, an electronic transmission of data, or a telephone call.

data flow diagram (DFD) A graphical representation of information flows within an organization (or subset); used as part of the analysis of information systems.

data management A set of activities and policies designed to protect and effectively employ an organization's data resources.

data model A graphical depiction of data entities and relationships for an information system or organization.

data store A symbol on a data flow diagram which depicts data at rest.

decision making The process of identifying a problem or opportunity and selecting among alternative courses of action.

decision support system (DSS) An interactive information system used in addressing semistructured decision situations.

decode The process of translating a message into a form understood by the receiver (*see also* encode.).

delaying Intentionally or unintentionally holding a message until it is late.

development methodology A series of steps and methods used to develop an information system.

development technique *See* development methodology.

direct access A method of retrieving data from files or databases in which a specific record is retrieved directly, without reading through multiple records (*see also* random access).

direct cutover A type of conversion (implementation) strategy in which an old information system is replaced with a new one all at once.

direct file organization A way of storing data in a file that allows a specific record to be retrieved directly using a key field.

disaster recovery plan A plan to allow a company to recover information-processing capabilities after a disaster harms, shuts down, or destroys its computer system.

disk density The amount of data that can be stored per track on a magnetic disk, CD-ROM, or diskette.

distance learning A learning experience in which the instructor and the students are not in the same geographical location.

distortion A change in a communication message (such as delaying or routing to the wrong recipient).

distributed processing A computer configuration in which processing of data takes place on multiple central processing units, which are (typically) geographically dispersed.

document management A set of activities (which may be supported by information systems) used to create, store, manipulate, and transmit documents.

downsizing The reduction in the number of employees and layers of management in a firm.

downward communication Messages passed from a supervisor to a subordinate (typically following formal lines of communication).

effectiveness Doing the right thing; making decisions and taking actions that help achieve defined goals and objectives.

efficiency Doing something right; usually measured as outputs divided by inputs.

electronic commerce A general term used to describe ways in which organizations employ electronic means to conduct business; often involves the use of EDI.

electronic data interchange (EDI) The use of standards and protocols for transmitting data from business correspondence (such as invoices) electronically.

electronic mail (E-mail) Computer-based messages that can be stored, manipulated, and transmitted electronically.

emerging technologies New information technologies that have not yet been widely adopted.

employee empowerment The process of giving employees at lower levels in the organization more responsibility and authority; generally requires providing better access to information.

encode Process of translating a message into a form that can then be transmitted to a receiver (*see also* decode).

end-user development The development of application programs by individuals whose primary responsibilities lie outside the information systems department.

enterprisewide system An information system that permeates an entire organization (such as an order-processing system for a mail-order company).

entity-relationship (E-R) diagram A specific type of data model used to depict the relationships among data entities.

environment Anything outside of a system (or organization) over which the system has little or no control.

environmental monitoring The process of scanning the environment for changes that could influence the system (organization).

environmental scanning The process of monitoring the environment of a firm to identify changes, opportunties, and threats.

environmental turbulence Instability or changes in elements of the environment that could influence the system (organization).

ergonomics The science of adapting technology, machinery, and work environments to people.

ethical vulnerability Any exposure an organization might have to issues that could violate moral principles.

ethics A system of moral principles.

execution The completion of a task.

executive information system (EIS) An information system that provides information and tools appropriate for decision making by top-level managers.

executive support systems (ESS) An interactive, user-friendly system which provides access to a variety of internal databases containing the operational performance information of a firm and external databases relevant to the business; also called *executive information systems (EIS)*.

expert system An information system that attempts to capture the expertise of one or more humans within a computer system; typically very narrow in scope. (*See also* augmenting knowledge.)

external entity An object on a data flow diagram which is outside the boundary of the system under investigation, but which serves as a source of data flow inputs or a recipient of data flow outputs.

feasibility study A formal analysis (often involving cost–benefit considerations) of the advisability of proceeding with a project.

feedback Information that is captured and returned to the system and then used to control a process or make a decision.

feedback quality (*See* quality of feedback.)

feedback systems Information systems that monitor and control the performance of a given process by comparing the performance of the process with a predetermined standard and set of tolerances, correcting the process if the measurement is outside those tolerances.

feedforward Information gathered about potential changes that could influence the system (organization).

feedforward systems Information systems that forecast and generate scenarios about the future.

field A group of characters that have a predetermined meaning. Examples include a first name or a telephone number.

file A set of related records.

file processing A method of data processing which stores and retrieves data in files (rather than databases).

file transfer protocol (ftp) A set of protocols used for transferring files between computer systems (used over the Internet).

filter A person or program whose purpose it is to stop unwanted messages from going to a receiver.

five-force model A competitive analysis framework involving new entrants, substitute products, rivalry among existing competitors, and bargaining power of customers and suppliers.

flexibility The ability to change quickly to adapt to internal or environmental changes.

forecasting The process of forming an opinion or prediction of a change in the environment, before the change occurs.

formal communication Communications that follow the formal reporting relationships and channels within an organization.

functional organization An organization that is structured around business functions (such as marketing and finance).

gender differences Differences based upon those between males and females and that can influence communications.

general systems theory (GST) A multidisciplinary theory of how a system (which includes organizations) interacts with its environment.

geographical information systems (GIS) Information systems used in producing maps and geographical modeling.

gigabyte One billion bytes; a measure of computer secondary storage capacity.

global positioning systems (GPS) Information systems that identify geographical coordinates by receiving signals from several orbiting satellites.

goal Something that the organization aspires to achieve; typically viewed as more general in scope than an objective.

gopher A software program used to help locate information on the Internet.

graphical user interface (GUI) A software interface that employs icons, buttons, and other images to initiate actions desired by the user.

group decision making Decisions made by more than one individual; no single person is ultimately responsible for the decision.

group functions Activities performed by groups.

group tasks Responsibilities of groups.

groupware Systems that are designed to facilitate collaborative group work and team building.

hardware The term used to describe the physical components of computer systems (*see also* software).

hierarchy A common type of organizational structure with positions ranked one above the other.

high tech–high touch A combination of advanced technology with old-fashioned materials and excellent service to give a warmer, friendlier feeling to the technology.

home page A page on the World Wide Web devoted to an individual, group, or organization.

homeostasis The process a system employs while trying to remain in equilibrium with the environment.

horizontal structure A type of organizational structure in which reporting relationships cut across functional disciplines.

hot site A back-up and recovery site where data and computers are stored and constantly updated to enable an immediate transfer of information processing capabilities. In case of a disaster that brings down the main site, the hot site can start processing data immediately.

hypermedia Software approach that uses links to combine several types of media (text, graphics, audio, video).

hypertext Software approach that uses links to connect text with other text.

Hypertext Markup Language (HTML) A type of scripting language used for creating pages on the World Wide Web.

I/S components Parts of an information system; includes a goal, data, information technology, people, and procedures.

I/S design The process and activities required to create a blueprint for a new information system.

I/S designer An individual responsible for developing the schematics for new information systems.

I/T architecture A blueprint and document summarizing the various information technology components in a firm, the way those components are linked, and the way they should operate together.

index-sequential file organization A way of organizing data in a file that attempts to gain the advantages of both sequential and direct file access.

individual support The use of information systems to support an individual worker in performing a variety of tasks.

inertia A characteristic of organizations that makes them respond more or less quickly to changes in their environment; the higher the level of inertia, the slower the responsiveness of the organization.

informal communication Communication that does not follow formal channels within an organization.

information Data that has been processed and has meaning to a user.

information center A support facility (containing development tools and staff) to help end users develop applications.

information engineering An approach for developing and managing information systems that focuses first on the structure of the data needed.

information flows The way and direction in which information and data move in an organization.

information needs The requirements for a new or revised information system which are determined as part of the development process.

information overload A common situation in which a receiver is unable to fully process all of the communication signals that are received.

information requirements Details that are identified as part of the analysis phase of a systems development project and that define the information needs of a system.

information resource management (IRM) A management concept that views information and information technology as valuable organizational resources requiring careful management.

information richness A term used to describe the form information takes, ranging from sparse (such as text) to robust (such as full-motion video with audio).

information stewardship The responsibility for maintaining the integrity and confidentiality of an organization's data resources.

information system A system composed of a goal, data, information technology, people, and procedures.

information systems cube A classification framework for information systems which has three dimensions: scope, complexity, and information richness.

information systems organization The way in which the reporting relationships for members of the information systems department are structured.

information systems support The use of information systems to help managers and employees perform their jobs.

information technology Technology that has the capability to accept, store, manipulate (process), and output data.

information technology infrastructure The combination of all information and communication technologies used by an organization.

input Information or data obtained from the environment that is necessary for the system (organization) to function.

input device Any means used to provide information into a computer system for further processing (such as a keyboard or bar-code scanner).

integrated process management (IPM) A management concept that includes a customer satisfaction management system, a benchmark assessment management system, and a performance assessment management system.

intentional distortion The intentional modification, routing, summarization, or delaying of a communication message.

international A perspective that encompasses multiple nations and world geographic and political regions.

Internet (Net) A loose network of networks that spreads around the world and is used by individuals and organizations.

interorganizational systems Those information systems that cross organizational boundaries (such as the use of electronic data interchange to transmit orders to a supplier).

interpersonal variables Factors that may influence communications between two people (such as gender or a superior-subordinate relationship).

job function A kind of action or activity normally associated with a job position.

job responsibility An activity or decision that has been defined to be under the purview of a job position.

job task A specific activity that must be performed as part of a job.

key A field used to uniquely identify a record within a file or database.

knowledge The realization that products and services become obsolete over time and that the real wealth of an organization is the experience and expertise of its employees.

knowledge base Within the context of expert systems, a term that refers to the collection of knowledge about a subject that is accessed by the system.

knowledge management The function of identifying and codifying relevant organizational knowledge (especially for expert systems).

lateral communication Communication between two or more individuals at the same organizational level.

law of requisite variety A law from General Systems Theory that states that for every possible action, there needs to be a reaction.

leadership The position or function of a leader.

limits on rationality Factors that preclude a rational decision-making approach from being used.

link Anything that serves to connect one part to another, such as a link in hypertext or from one Web page to another.

listservice (listserv) A facility that allows messages to be distributed electronically to all subscribers (usually over a local area network or the Internet).

local area network (LAN) A system that connects two or more computing-related devices within a relatively small geographic region (such as an office).

local rationality Process that occurs when a subset of a system (such as a department within an organization) pursues goals not congruent with those of the system.

machine language Internal programming language of a computer.

magnetic disk A data storage device consisting of a magnetized rotating disk.

mainframe A large computer used to support a large number of users, to build and store large databases, and to perform high-volume transaction processing.

maintenance The process of modifying and adapting a system over time after it has been installed to match changing needs.

make-or-buy decision The decision to purchase software from an outside vendor or to build it in-house; the decision to consider outsourcing other information systems operations.

management The group of people charged with major decision-making responsibilities within an organization.

management information systems (MIS) Information systems that provide information for managing an organization.

management science A systematic approach to solving managerial problems with mathematical models.

management of technology The recognition that technology plays an important role in a company and the set of actions and investments necessary to develop and maintain a technological capability to remain competitive.

mass customization A competitive strategy of customizing products for each of a large number of customers.

master file A file used to store relatively stable information about some entity.

mathematical models A set of equations and mathematical relationships that link variables describing a physical reality in a precise way.

medium (media) Anything that carries a message.

megabyte One million bytes; a measure of computer primary storage capacity.

megahertz (MHz) One million cycles per second; a measure of clock speed for the central processing unit of a computer.

menu-driven interface A software interface in which the user chooses what to do next out of a list of options displayed on the screen.

message Exchange of data between two or more individuals.

message content Meaning of the data being exchanged between two individuals.

microprocessor A single computer chip that integrates the central processing unit and memory.

million instructions per second (MIPS) A measure of the speed and power of a microprocessor.

minicomputer A mid-size computer typically shared by a small group of individuals working together in which common databases and programs are stored.

minimize distortion A strategy for maintaining a high level of quality of information in an organization by minimizing the likelihood of information being delayed or misinterpreted.

minimizing overload A strategy for maintaining a high level of quality in the analysis of information in an organization. Individuals who become overloaded (overwhelmed by the amount of the data they need to sift through) are more likely to make mistakes in processing information.

model An abstract, simplified representation of reality.

modem A modulator/demodulator; a device for encoding and decoding computerized (digital) data into analog data so that it can be transmitted over communication media (primarily telephone lines).

modifying distortion A strategy for changing the meaning of a message by actually modifying its content.

modular program design The separation of a system into a set of subsystems that can be developed and tested independently of each other.

monitor The screen of a computer system.

monopoly A market in which there is only one provider of a specific product or service; a market where there is no competition.

Mosaic A graphic-oriented software tool to navigate the Internet (*see also* Web browser).

multimedia Use of data, video, and audio in the same application.

multiplexer A device that allows several streams of data from different computers to use the same wire to send and receive data over a single telephone line for long-distance transmission.

multitasking The concurrent or parallel execution of different programs within the same computer.

natural language Language as it is spoken by humans; a computer interface that uses everyday words as its commands.

net present value (NPV) The present value of a series of future (positive and negative) cash flows emanating from a given project; the value of those flows needs to be discounted by the appropriate time value of money.

network management The process of monitoring a network's traffic and operations and making the necessary adjustments to use its capacity efficiently.

network topology A pattern of connections between the devices on a network (e.g., star); the structure or configuration of a network.

neural networks An information system that identifies objects or patterns based on examples that have been used to train it; the system learns by adjusting weights on links between a specified set of inputs and a specified set of outputs.

new entrants Companies entering a market for a first time; in setting strategy, it is important to consider not only traditional rivals but potential new entrants.

newsgroup A specialized type of electronic bulletin board in which subscribers can post and read messages.

node Any sending, receiving, or processing device in a telecommunications network.

noise Noninformative data that are attached to a message, disrupting the message and making the message harder to understand.

nonprocedural A programming language that enables the user to specify what the program needs to do without specifying all the steps (procedures) for doing it.

nonverbal communication The exchange of information between individuals without words (such as gestures, body language, eye contact, and style of dress).

nonvolatile memory Computer memory that keeps its contents when the computer is turned off.

object-oriented database A database used to store and manage data-processing objects.

object-oriented design A system design technique which incorporates the use of objects, rather than just data and processes.

object-oriented programming (OOP) A very flexible programming approach based on the concepts of object, classes, and inheritance that allows a programmer to develop computer routines that will work with multiple objects.

office automation systems (OAS) Information systems that facilitate everyday communications and data-processing tasks in offices and organizations.

on-line processing A mode of processing in which transactions are processed as soon as they are input into the system, rather than being stored for later processing.

open system A system (or organization) that has many and frequent interactions with the environment; or the use of nonproprietary industrywide standards that enables different computers from different vendors to "talk" to each other.

operating system Programs that control a computer system by executing a series of instructions to manage resources such as peripheral devices, disk space, and network access.

operational vulnerability The exposure of a company to an operational failure of the information systems.

order-winning criteria (OWC) The criteria that customers use to make a purchasing decision; the criteria that customers use to place an order.

organization A group of people brought together for a common goal.

organization communication output The exchange of information among individuals, departments, and divisions of an organization.

organizational responsiveness A measure of how quickly an organization reacts to a change in its environment.

organizational structure The blueprint depicting the formal reporting relationships within an organization.

output of an information system The data, in whatever form (paper reports, electronic messages), produced by an information system.

outputs of a system The product or service generated by the system; its reason for being; outputs need to be accepted by the environment for the organization to survive.

output device A device allowing the display of data and information.

output-to-input ratio The traditional way to calculate productivity.

outsourcing The process of providing contracts to outside vendors to operate and support the computer and telecommunications systems of a firm.

packet switching A technique for high-volume, high-speed data transfer based on splitting a message into small "packets", thereby sending them through a telecommunications link and then recombining them at its destination.

parallel conversion Simultaneous use of an old system and a new system during conversion.

payback period The length of time that needs to pass until the project breaks even.

peer-to-peer network Network architecture in which each workstation on the network can communicate directly with every other workstation on the network without going through a specialized server.

people A key element in the definition of information systems; includes users, designers, and operators of the information system.

perceived quality The perception of the customer of the quality of a product or service that is affected by, but independent of, the intrinsic or objective level of quality of the product and/or service.

performance assessment management information system (PAM/IS) An information system that monitors and evaluates performance on a set of predetermined criteria.

peripherals Input, output, and secondary storage devices of a computer system.

personal biases The shortcuts and heuristics that individuals use to understand data and make inferences.

personal computer (PC) Single-user computer; can be a desktop or portable model.

phased conversion A conversion approach based on implementing the new system for a subset of functions while continuing to use the old system for the rest of the processing.

pilot conversion A conversion approach that uses a trial system implementation on a small subset of users.

planning The process of deciding how the firm will deliver customer value (what services and products to offer, where, at what price); a process that determines who will be responsible for what in the delivery of a certain output at a certain future point in time.

platform The basic type of microprocessor or operating system or brand of computer that the information system uses.

point-of-sale (POS) system A transaction processing system that records the sale of a product or service and updates company records related or affected by the sale (accounting, marketing, inventory.)

political model A model that describes organizations as a set of coalitions, where people make decisions on the basis of maintaining power and influence. (*See also* administrative model, rational model.)

portability The ability of computers and other devices to be easily carried and moved around to be used in different places (home, office); also the ability to operate software on more than one computer platform.

postimplementation audit Evaluation of the impact the information system had compared with expectations; reviews the design, development, and implementation processes to understand what did and did not work.

primary memory The volatile semiconductor memory that the microprocessor uses to temporarily store data and instructions needed by the software programs being used; also called random access memory (RAM).

privacy The right of an individual to participate in decisions regarding the collection, use, and disclosure of personal information.

proactive Process of anticipating changes and acting in advance.

proactive measurement Measurement of a characteristic of a product or service that allows the firm to intervene and change the product or service before the customer interaction is over (the product or service has not already been purchased and/or consumed).

procedures Rules, policies, and methods for the development and operation of an information system.

process management The monitoring of the performance of a business process and the adjustment to the tasks in the process required to match changes in customer needs. If changes are gradual, then continuous improvement adjustments are considered; if the required changes are drastic, then reengineering is necessary.

process rationality The use of appropriate, relevant steps and methods to solve a problem.

product development The phase of manufacturing that converts general ideas and concepts about a product into a tangible good, product, or service.

product differentiation strategy A business strategy based on providing the customer with one or more features that make the product or service different from the competition's.

productivity The relationship between amount, quality, and timeliness of the output produced by a business, a business process, or an individual and the amount of inputs or resources (time, money, effort) the output requires to be produced.

productivity tools Software packages that help individuals perform certain tasks more efficiently (word processing, what-if analyses, scheduling).

programmable read-only memory (PROM) A nonvolatile semiconductor memory in which a set of instructions have been programmed.

programmer The individual who translates specific ideas and information needs into instructions that a computer can follow; person who codes, tests, and documents computer programs.

programming language The language or type of instructions used in coding a computer program.

project evaluation and review technique (PERT) A project management technique involving the calculation of the shortest, longest, and most likely durations for the project.

project management The activities directed at scheduling, planning, and organizing the necessary resources to design, develop, and implement an information system project on time and within budget.

project manager The individual in charge of delivering an information system with its full functionality on time and within budget.

prototyping An approach to designing information systems that consists of developing a "quick-and-dirty" model of the system to get early feedback from the user about the importance of various features.

purpose The ultimate objective or reason for developing an information system.

quality A set of performance features, including reliability, serviceability, promptness, pleasant delivery, and durability, that make a product or service desirable.

quality of feedback The timeliness, frequency, and level of detail and accuracy provided in the feedback.

random access (*see* direct access.)

random access memory (RAM) Semiconductor component of computers that temporarily stores data and instructions being used; typically, the contents of RAM are erased when the computer is turned off (i.e., it is volatile); also called *primary memory.*

rational decision making The process described by the rational model of decision making that implies a very well structured process based on the maximization of value, a thorough and comprehensive search for all information, and an exhaustive analysis of alternatives.

rational model A traditional model that explains how people should make decisions; an ideal model that assumes that the decision maker has the time to collect and analyze all relevant information. (*See also* administrative model, political model.)

reactive Process of waiting until changes occur and then acting in response to the change.

reactive measurement A measurement of a characteristic of a product or service after the customer interaction is over (the product or service has already been purchased and/or consumed).

read-only memory (ROM) Semiconductor component of computers that permanently stores data that usually consists of instructions controlling the operation of the computer.

real-time processing A form of computing in which the transactions are processed as they occur (as opposed to batch processing) and the data are updated immediately.

receiver One of the two components of a communication dyad (the other is the sender); the receiver is the recipient of a message sent by the sender and is defined by a set of personal characteristics and a position in the organizational structure.

reciprocal back-up agreement An agreement among two or more companies to develop a common back-up and recovery site and share the costs.

record A set of data fields that are treated as a unit because they are related to the same concept, thing, or individual.

reduced instruction set computer (RISC) A computer processor chip design that responds to relatively few(er) instructions as compared with the complex instruction set computer (CISC) design.

redundancy Sending a message more than once, from multiple sources, to ensure it is received; building a second information system as a backup.

reengineering The complete overhaul and redesign of a business process.

relational database A type of database structure which uses controlled redundancy to maintain relationships between tables of data.

resistance to change The normal phenomenon that occurs when people are faced with change. Resistance to change creates inertia in an organization and slows down its responsiveness.

responsiveness A series of organizational actions orchestrated by a firm to deliver what the customer wants, when the customer wants, and how the customer wants it; the act of having the firm predict and match changes in the environment as quickly as possible.

ring topology A network topology in which the nodes are directly connected to each other without a central computer node.

risk management The monitoring and evaluation of a system to minimize the negative impact of potential events that would cause the failure or degradation of performance of the system.

risks Possible events that will negatively affect the performance of the system.

rivalry intensity The amount of competition among existing firms in a given market segment.

routing distortion The sending of a message to the wrong location.

satisficing The practice of individuals to settle on an alternative that is "good enough" rather than to keep on searching for the "best possible" solution. (*See also* bounded rationality.)

scenarios Plausible situations based on a series of assumptions about the future.

scope Whom an information system supports, ranging from an individual to multiple organizations.

search A mode of actively scanning the environment to identify potential changes, opportunities, and/or threats.

secondary memory Data storage devices other than the primary storage (random-access memory) of a computer; examples are CD-ROMs, diskettes, tapes (video and audio) and hard-disk drives.

sectors A segment of a diskette or hard disk track created to facilitate the retrieval of data. Each track is divided into several sectors.

security The set of policies and actions that keep data and programs from being destroyed, abused, sabotaged, or used by unauthorized individuals.

sender One of the two primary components of a communication dyad (the other is the receiver); the sender sends a message to the receiver and is defined by a set of personal characteristics and a position in the organizational structure.

sensor A mechanism for capturing feedback information (such as a bar-code scanner that records the sale of products).

sequential access A data access method in which individual records within a file are organized in sequence and in order to read a record in a given location that all other locations before it need to be traversed. For example, the data is accessed on magnetic tapes using sequential access.

sequential file organization A way of storing data so that it must be retrieved in the order in which it is stored.

server A dedicated computer on a network that "serves" files, messages, and programs to a set of computers or users ("clients") on the network.

service bureau An outside vendor that sells computer services.

simulation A series of models that mimic reality; a method to test the effect of various events and changes in assumptions on the performance of a system.

software Programs (a set of instructions) that make a computer perform functions. (*See also* hardware.)

software interface The set and format of commands that allow users to interact with the software; can be menu-driven or a graphical user interface.

source Origin of data.

span of control The number of subordinates reporting to a supervisor.

stakeholder Individuals with a personal stake in a project or system.

standard A performance reference point.

standard operating procedures (SOP) Rules, policies, and methods that are to be followed by all members of an organization when faced by a particular customer request or event; the prevalent mode of operations of a bureaucratic organization. (*See also* bureaucracy.)

star topology A network topology in which all the messages among computers on the network go through a central computer node that serves as a switching mechanism.

strategic alignment The consistency between the purpose and objectives of a given information system and the strategic objectives of the firm.

strategic alliance An agreement between two or more companies involving the joint manufacturing, distribution, and maintenance of products and services.

strategic information systems (SIS) Information systems that support the strategy of a firm and give that firm a potential competitive advantage by affecting a critical activity in the value chain.

strategy An explicit (or implicit) intent for how to act (such as an organization intending to be the low cost producer).

stress A situation in which individuals feel pressure.

structured analysis and design An approach to describe and document the design and development of an information system using graphical procedures.

structured decision A well-understood decision in which there are problems and rules on how to address those problems.

structured design A technique for designing information systems which stresses the use of top-down, modular system and program structures.

structured English A way of describing procedures in a standard format which can be readily converted to program logic.

structured programming A technique for creating computer programs that stresses the use of self-contained modules that have few interactions.

substitute products/services A product or service offered by a company or set of companies to the customers of another company.

subsystem A component with a specific purpose but whose role is to interact with other components to maintain the viability of the system.

summarizing The act of abstracting relevant items of information from a larger set of data.

summarizing distortion The act of abstracting information from a larger set of data in a way that biases or changes the meaning of the original data.

supplier's bargaining power The leverage that suppliers have over a firm buying their products in terms of setting prices, delivery schedules, quantities, and types of products.

surveillance A mode of passively scanning the environment to make sure that events are within predicted ranges.

switching costs The costs associated with switching to a different supplier.

system Set of components that interact to achieve a purpose. In an organization, the components are the different departments that constitute the system; in an information system, the components are the different routines, procedures, data, people, and technology.

systems analyst An individual who serves as a "bridge" between users of an information system and its developers and whose function is to define the needs of the user.

systems development life cycle (SDLC) The stages making up the process of analyzing user requirements and then designing, developing, implementing, evaluating, and maintaining an information system.

systems development process An approach, such as the systems development life cycle, for analyzing, developing, and maintaining systems (usually supported by computer-aided software engineering tools).

tangible benefits Benefits that can be measured, preferably in monetary terms.

task complexity The number of variables and uncertainty associated with a specific task.

telecommunications Transmission of voice, data, and/or video from one device in one location to another device in a different location.

telecommuting Working at home and using electronic connections to "travel" or commute to the office.

telemedicine The performing of medicine through which the patient and the physician are in geographically different places.

time lag The time it takes for a system to realize that there has been a change in the environment requiring action, plus the time it takes for the system to match that change.

tolerance level The predetermined size of a variation around a standard that determines whether the variation is within an expected (tolerable) range and therefore whether to take corrective action; if the event is within the standard deviation, then no action is necessary.

topology (*See* network topology.)

total quality management (TQM) A set of principles that make quality and excellence the central purpose of any business process.

tracks Refers to the number of tracks or concentric magnetic bands on a diskette. Each track can store thousands of bytes.

transaction file A file used in batch-processing environments which contains transactions that have not been processed.

transaction processing system (TPS) Information system that collects and stores data about transactions.

transformation process The process of transforming (changing) inputs into outputs; the process of transforming (reinventing) a business process, an organizational purpose, and/or structure.

twisted pair Standard copper telephone line consisting of a pair of copper wires twisted to help minimize distortion of the signal by other telephone lines in the same sheath of cable.

unintentional distortion The process of changing the meaning of a message by mistake.

unstructured task A task that is poorly understood, in which one cannot specify a mathematical model to arrive at a solution, where it is not clear what information to use and how to use it, and/or where it is hard to determine whether that task is being done optimally or not.

upper CASE tools CASE tools which support the first steps in the development process focusing on analysis rather than implementation.

upward communication Messages and data that flow from a subordinate to a superior.

user friendliness A characteristic of information systems that makes it easy for novices to use and understand the system.

user interface The part of an operating system or other software package that allows the user to communicate with and control it.

value Something that customers want and are willing to pay for.

value-added network (VAN) A network that adds value by providing access to commercial and specialized databases.

value chain A set of processes a firm uses to create value for its customers.

veronica A set of tools that can be used to search for files and other resources on the Internet using gopher.

vertical structure A type of organizational structure which relies heavily on upward and downward communications; tends to be rigid and slow to change.

very large scale integration (VLSI) Technology that formed the basis for the fourth generation of computers.

videoconferencing system Teleconferencing in which participants can see each other through a television or computer screen.

videotex An interactive information service that is provided over telephone lines or cable.

virtual organization A cluster of organizations united by a series of electronic linkages.

virtual reality A very realistic, interactive simulation of reality.

virus A computer program that can "reproduce" itself and spread much like a biological virus, destroying information and disrupting and causing errors in the operations of other computer programs.

volatile memory Computer memory that loses its contents when the computer is turned off.

walkthrough A technique by which a user goes through a set of data flow diagrams in detail, ensuring no errors or misunderstandings remain.

Web browser A software program that resides on a client (user) computer that is used for navigating through the World Wide Web. (*See also* Mosaic.)

what-if analysis The process of questioning assumptions to develop a series of scenarios or possible situations.

wide area information service (WAIS) A system (and set of standards) used for searching files stored on databases connected to the Internet, using key words.

wide area network (WAN) Telecommunications network that geographically links separated locations two or more miles apart.

window of vulnerability The time period during which an organization is vulnerable to a given risk.

word size A given amount of data in bits that a computer can process at one time; the greater the word size the greater the speed.

workgroup Ad hoc or formal group of individuals who are in the same or different locations working together on a particular task.

workgroup support The use of information systems to support a team or group of individuals achieve a common set of tasks.

workstation A powerful, single-user computer; typically a desktop computer.

World Wide Web (also WWW, or Web) A set of hypertext links that permit easy navigation through the enormous and ever-expanding array of files, programs, documents, and videos available on the Internet.

APPENDIX A Data Management

INFORMATION REPRESENTATION

To be stored and processed by information technology, data and information must be recorded in a format that can be manipulated by the hardware and software. A **bit** is the smallest item (element) of data that can be processed by information technology. A bit is based on the binary numerical system and can take one of two forms ("on" or "off"; "1" or "0"). Bits are combined according to a set of standard codes into **bytes**, which represent alphanumeric characters and special symbols. Typically a byte consists of eight bits (depending on the code used). For example, the representation for the letter "z" in the common ASCII code is 10111010.

A **field** or **data element** is the smallest unit of data that has any meaning to humans and is composed of one or more bytes. Consider a typical organization such as a retail store. Examples of fields related to employees could be EMPLOYEE NUMBER, EMPLOYEE NAME, DEPARTMENT, and START DATE. Fields may also contain sounds or images, such as a photograph (this issue is discussed later in this appendix). A **record** is a collection of fields that contain information concerning a specific thing or event. For example, a simple personnel record for an employee might contain the four fields listed previously, such as "10121" (EMPLOYEE NUMBER); "Greenwood, Marie-Louise" (EMPLOYEE NAME); "Customer Service" (DEPARTMENT); and "07/01/1996" (START DATE). Typically the term *field* is used to describe the field name (i.e., DEPARTMENT) while the term *data element* is used to describe the contents of the field (i.e., Customer Service).

A collection of records that have the same fields is called a **file**. In the example just provided, the collection of all employee records would be referred to as the

FIGURE A–1 Data Hierarchy

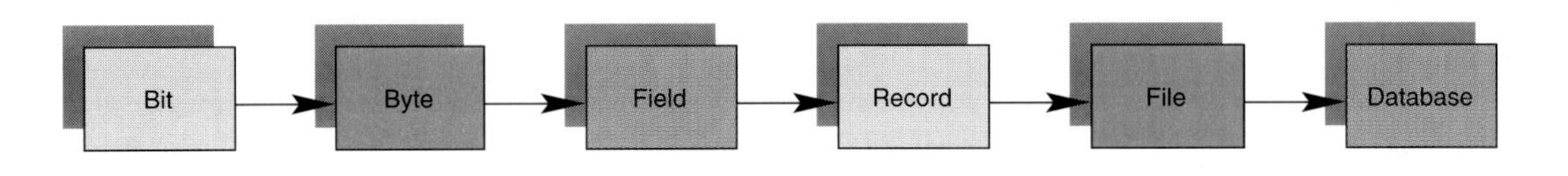

employee file. Records are usually identified within a file by a unique field, referred to as a **key**. In the previous example, the employee number would likely be the key. Since no two employees are assigned the same employee number, it is unique; if we provide a valid employee number, only one employee record will be retrieved. We can also be assured that if we supply the same employee number on two separate occasions, the same employee record will be retrieved each time.

A group of files that are related is referred to as a **database**. If we were to extend the previous example by adding information about employees' medical histories (employee medical file) and information about employees' benefits (employee benefit file), the combination of the three files could be the employee database. If each file within the database contains the employee number as a unique key (for example), it would be possible to combine information from the three files as required. Figure A–1 illustrates the relations between the terms introduced so far, in what is generally called the data hierarchy.

FILE ACCESS

There are two ways to access the records stored in a file (or stored in a database); either sequential access or direct access. Note that the term *random access* is sometimes used instead of *direct access*, although direct access provides a more accurate description. In **sequential access**, a specific record is located by starting at the beginning of the file and scanning each record, in turn, until the desired file is located. Picture an employee file that consists of folders containing individual information about each of 10,000 employees; to locate a specific employee record using sequential access, we would start at the first folder in the first drawer and flip through each one until we reach the folder we are looking for.

With **direct access**, we are able to shorten the search time by going directly to the correct folder (or at least close to it). The accuracy of the direct search method depends on the technique used by the software that stores and retrieves the records; some techniques are more detailed and precise than others. As a reasonable analogy, however, assume that we have a way to identify every possible folder location within the file cabinets. Let's make the further assumption that the employee number corresponds to the number of the storage location (cabinet number, drawer number, section number, etc.). By using the key field (employee number), we would be able to go directly to the exact location and retrieve the correct folder.

For computer files, the analogy of retrieving a folder from a file cabinet works reasonably well. For sequential access, the files are read in order until the desired record is retrieved. For direct access, a specific record can be retrieved without reading through the remainder.

FIGURE A–2 **File Processing**

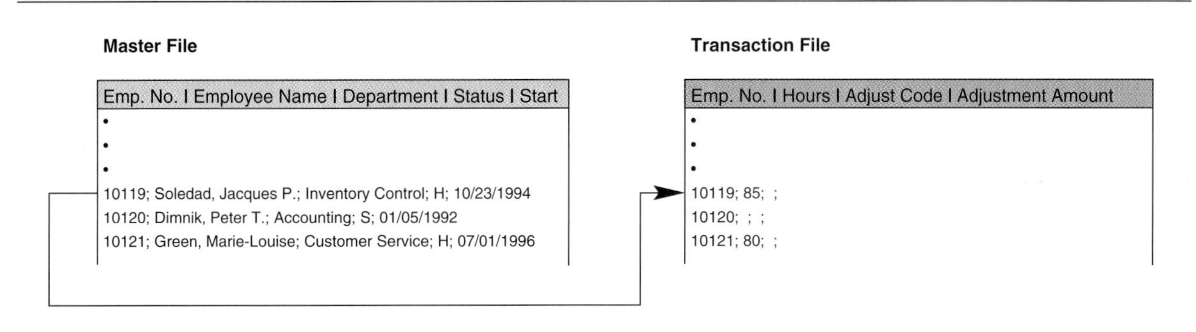

TRANSACTION PROCESSING

Organizations participate in events, such as the sale of a good to a customer or the hiring of a new employee. To maintain control of organizational operations and to obtain relevant information for decision making, it is necessary to record many of these events. In the terminology of information systems, a **transaction** is the record of an event. **Transaction processing** involves the use of human procedures and/or computer programs to store, retrieve, and manipulate these records of events.

Let us return to the example of employee records for a moment. When we hire a new employee, we need to record certain details about the employee and certain details about the event. For example, if the new employee decides she wants copies of her pay stubs mailed to her home address instead of receiving them at work, we need to record her address and her payment preference. If she wants her actual pay deposited directly into her bank account, we need her account number and bank identification code (of course, we also need her written authorization for the direct deposit on file). We need to record her official starting date, which will be used at a later time to determine her seniority status (if relevant), her pension calculations, and so on.

Now let us skip forward to the end of her first pay period, say, two weeks after she was hired. We have another transaction to be processed; the payment of wages earned by her (and by all other employees). To ensure that each employee receives the correct amount and that it is disposed of properly (i.e., a check issued or a direct deposit to the employee's bank account), we need to have a record of relevant information in the employee file. For employees who are paid on an hourly basis, we need to know how many hours they worked; for all employees, we need to know what adjustments need to be made to their pay (deductions for taxes, additions for bonuses, etc.).

To complete the payroll process, we need a **master file** that contains the basic (or stable) information about each employee: name, department, whether the employee is salaried or an hourly wage earner (status), and so on. We also need a **transaction file**, which contains information relevant to the most recent pay period, for example, the number of hours worked for hourly workers or any necessary adjustments to their base pay (see Figure A–2). In payroll processing, it is necessary to read the record of each employee from the master file and then use any information from the corresponding employee record (using the value of the key field as a comparison) stored on the transaction file. In a manual setting, a human (most likely with a calculator) would calculate the amount owed and write out a check. In an automated setting using an information system, a computer program would retrieve the relevant data from the master and transaction file, make the necessary calculations, and print the checks or create a file for bank deposits.

In the example shown in Figure A–2, a computer program would retrieve the record for employee 10119 from the master file and the record for employee 10119 from the transaction file. The program would check to see if the status was "H" (hourly worker). Since employee 10119 is an hourly employee, the amount owed would need to be calculated and either a paycheck printed or the information written to another file to be used for automatic bank deposit. Note that the master file illustrated in Figure A–2 also requires additional data fields, such as base salary or hourly wage rate; the figure is only meant to show how the key field (employee number) is used to match records from different files.

In what is commonly referred to as a traditional file environment, software programs (called file processing systems) are used to store, retrieve, and manipulate records within the files. In the example provided earlier, each employee record needs to be accessed during each payroll processing period. For this type of application, accessing the records on the master file and transaction file in sequential order, or **sequential file organization**, makes a lot of sense. For other applications, this is not true. When the new employee was hired, for example, we only needed to store a new record for her; there was no need to alter or use any other employee record.

If the employee file is stored in sequential order by number and the new employee is given a larger number than any previous employee, we would simply add her record to the end. If, however, we are storing the record alphabetically by employee name or using randomly selected numbers, we would need to read through the file and store the new record in the correct sequence. Similarly, removing an employee record would involve reading the file in sequential order until we reached the correct record, and then rewriting the entire file and omitting the deleted record. If we have 10,000 employees, this involves a great deal of reading and writing of files, which is time consuming and uses a lot of computer resources.

On-Line Processing. At this point we need to discuss the difference between batch and on-line transaction processing. The situation just described (payroll processing) is a good example of **batch processing**. All transactions relating to payroll (such as hours worked by a given employee on a given day) are batched (temporarily stored) during the pay period, and then they are processed all at once. Typically this involves entering the data from source documents (such as time sheets) into a file and then sorting the transaction file into the same order (i.e., alphabetical, ascending numerical, etc.) so that the transaction records can be processed against the master file. This approach works well for payroll, but it doesn't work for many other types of transactions.

Consider airline reservations, for example. If all ticket agents and travel agents were allowed to sell tickets for a specific flight without knowing how many tickets had already been sold, and if the tickets were batched and processed all at once, there is a very strong likelihood that many flights would be overbooked. For this type of application, on-line transaction processing is needed. In **on-line processing**, each transaction is processed as it occurs. When a customer requests a seat on a flight, the sales agent first checks a central file or database to ensure a seat is available. They then process the transaction, reserving a seat on the flight for the customer. (Most airlines intentionally overbook popular flights to cover for customers who don't show, but that is a separate issue.) **File processing** can be used to handle on-line processing, providing the file is organized using **direct** or **index-sequential file organization**. If a file is organized and accessed sequentially, it generally is too slow to use this approach for on-line processing.

File processing can lead to many difficulties. For example, consider a situation in which we wish to list all outstanding (i.e., not filled) orders for a specific customer and when we anticipate filling those orders (perhaps to respond to a query from the customer). Some of the information we need will be stored in the customer master file, some will be in the open order file, some might be in an inventory file, some in an outstanding supplier order file, and so on. To combine and extract the relevant information from the different files requires special programs and also requires reading through each file sequentially to select and match the relevant values in different key fields. This would be very time-consuming; if we have to go through the same process every time a customer wants to know what orders are outstanding and when they will be filled, we won't be able to provide this information in a timely fashion, and the customers will not be satisfied with our service. This type of limitation led to the development and widespread use of Database Management Systems (DBMSs) and database processing.

DATABASE PROCESSING

As organizations begin to use information systems for more sophisticated applications, they discover that one data element (such as a customer name) may be needed for many uses. They also discover that many applications require pulling data from numerous different files, combining and manipulating them in ways that were never anticipated when the files were originally designed. This is where a database environment, managed with a DBMS, comes into play.

A **Database Management System (DBMS)** is a software package designed to allow for the control and integration of multiple data records and files. The starting point for any DBMS application is the definition of the data, and every DBMS contains a *data definition language* that is used in conjunction with a *data dictionary* (part of the DBMS) that keeps track of every data field in the database, how they are formatted into different types of records, and how the record types are integrated. The data dictionary also keeps track of where the data fields are used (application programs, etc.), who has access to them, and so on. For simple applications, the software (the DBMS) keeps track of the data and how the data are structured and used with the database, and the user rarely needs to even know that the data dictionary part of the DBMS exists. In larger, more complex applications, the data dictionary is an important tool for the information systems specialists who manage the data.

A DBMS includes programs (called the *data manipulation language*) for retrieving and manipulating data, including the building of applications (such as transaction processing applications or reports). Most modern DBMSs have software features that make it relatively easy for a user to retrieve information for ad-hoc queries, produce reports, and even build simple transaction processing applications without needing to be a technical specialist. The common features most DBMS users interact with are input screens (for adding, deleting, and modifying data), ad-hoc queries and reports (for processing and retrieving information), and the database itself (the actual data).

FIGURE A–3 Sample Relational Database Model*

Customer

CustNo	C-Name	C-Address	C-Phone
101	ABACUS Computing Co.	345 Oak Dr., Smalltown ST, 00555	(555) 444-3333
102	Greenway Garden Center	24 Center St., Smalltown ST, 00553	(555) 434-5555
103	Cherry Blossom Gifts	988 Main St., Bigtown ST, 00463	(555) 545-4444
...			

Order

Order-No	CustNo	Order-Date	Order-Total
20245	101	3/7/97	4,502.35
20248	102	3/7/97	3,083.10
20249	101	3/9/97	2,306.23
20252	101	3/10/97	6,126.12
20255	103	3/10/97	1,879.13

*Field names in italics denote the key field for the table. Links between the tables are maintained by placing the key of the Customer table as a field in the Order table.

DATABASE ORGANIZATION

The most common way to organize data within a database is through the use of what is referred to as a **relational database** model. The relational model, which was developed in the 1970s, provides for easy-to-use interfaces between the users and the DBMS. For this reason the relational model has become the most popular, and it is here that we focus our attention.

With the relational data model, the data are logically organized into tables (or relations), which are essentially the same as the files we discussed previously (see Figure A–3). Another way to view a table is to think of an electronic spreadsheet, which has columns and rows of data. The columns represent data fields, while the rows represent records (or data occurrences). The difference here is that the tables within one database are all related, and the relationships are established and maintained by using key fields. For example, by storing the customer number (the key field for the customer table) in the order table (along with other pertinent data about orders), a relationship is maintained between customers and orders that allows us to match the order with the correct customer.

DATA MODELING

One of the more challenging and important tasks of setting up a database using a DBMS is deciding what data should be included and how the database should be structured. Typically, the term **data model** is used to represent a "blueprint" for the database, while the term **database design** refers to the structure of the tables.

FIGURE A–4a Entity-Relationship (E-R) Diagram

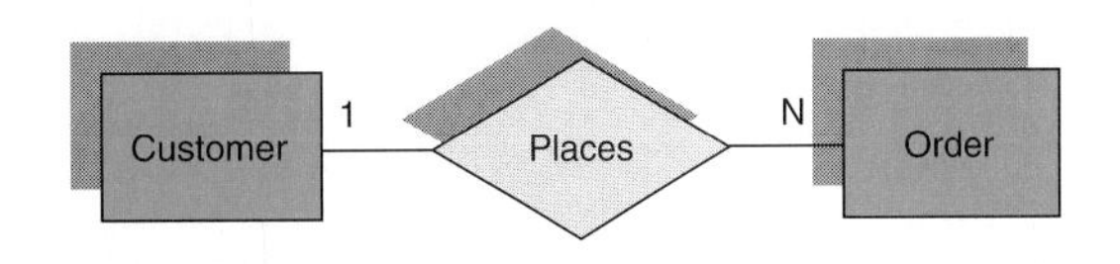

FIGURE A–4b Database Design

CUSTOMER (CustNo, C-Name, C-Address, C-Phone, . . .)
ORDER (Order-No, CustNo, Order-Date, Order-Total, . . .)

An **entity-relationship (E-R) diagram** is one common way of representing a data model. The term *entity* is used to refer to things about which we want to store information (customers, suppliers, orders, sales, employees, etc.). In an E-R diagram, a rectangle is typically used to represent an entity, and a diamond is used to represent a relationship between two entities. Figure A–4 shows an example of an E-R diagram; it also shows the database design for the customer and order example described previously.

Notice the "1" behind the Customer entity and the "N" next to the Order entity. This indicates the type of relationship existing between these two entities. There are three possible types of relationships; one-to-one (1:1), one-to-many (1:N), and many-to-many (N:M). In the example shown in Figure A–4a, the 1:N relationship indicates that for each customer, there may be many orders; however, each order is only associated with one customer. The type of relationship becomes important when deciding how to maintain relationships among tables. In this example, we placed the key of the "1" entity (CustNo) as an attribute in the "N" table (ORDER).

As mentioned, a data model (E-R diagram) is used as a blueprint to illustrate the entities that the organization needs to keep track of and the relationships among those entities. Identifying entities can be a challenge, depending on the complexity of the situation. An entity could be a thing (such as a product kept in inventory), an event (such as a sale or a purchase), or a role played by people (such as employee or customer).

When we create tables for the database design, there will be at least one table for each entity. For simple entities, there will be exactly one table. For more complex ones, there will likely be two or more. For example, the CUSTOMER entity will likely be simple; each customer will have one name, one customer number, one address, and so on. The ORDER entity could be different, however. It is quite likely that each order could have more than one product listed (see Figure A–5). If we try to store all of the information on an order form in one table, we will end up with a large number of fields that repeat. If we can have, say, 10 products on an order, we would have to have at least 10 separate product number fields (ProdNo1, ProdNo2, etc.). We would also need to repeat other information, such as the quantity of each product being ordered.

A better way to handle this situation would be to create a new table, say, ORD-PROD, that contains information about the combination of order and product.

FIGURE A–5 Sample Order Form

ABC CORPORATION
PURCHASE ORDER

Customer: Graehme's Graphics
Address: 123 Winding Brook
Any Town, USA 55555
Contact: Graehme Grey
Phone: (555) 555-5555

Date: xx/xx/xx

Order Number: 09341

Product Number	Description	Quantity	Price	Product Total
1003	Fontographer for Windows	3	258.98	776.94
1005	Primo Datapen OCR Scanner	1	299.88	299.88
1324	ScanMaster Plus	1	459.98	459.98
TOTAL:				1,536.80

Terms: net 30 days

By including the Order-No as part of the key, we will maintain a relationship between this table and the ORDER table:

```
ORD-PROD (Order-No, ProdNo, Quantity, Description, Price,
Prod-Total)
```

Notice that the key of this table includes *both* the product number and the order number. If we want to find out what quantity of product 1003 was included with order 09341, we have to use both. This is not true of Description or Price, however. These are characteristics of Product only and are independent of the order. In other words, if product 1003 shows up on 100 different orders, it will always have the same description (Fontographer for Windows). For this reason, we need to define a new entity, PRODUCT, and to create a new table for the PRODUCT entity. The ORD-PROD and PRODUCT tables would be added to the CUSTOMER and ORDER tables (see Figure A–4b) as part of the final database design:

```
ORD-PROD (Order-No, ProdNo, Quantity, Prod-Total)

PRODUCT  (ProdNo, Description, Price)
```

Creating a Data Model

The process of creating a data model requires identifying all entities and associated attributes (or characteristics of the entities, which will become fields) as well as the relationships between them. Assume we are trying to define a database design for Eastown Motors, a used car dealership. One approach would be to start by listing some obvious entities (CUSTOMER, VEHICLE, SALESPERSON) and then interviewing Samuel Balthazar (the owner) and his employees to see if they can identify others. This would be considered a "top-down" design; we start by identifying the major entities about which the organization needs to store data.

FIGURE A–6a Eastown Motors Data Model

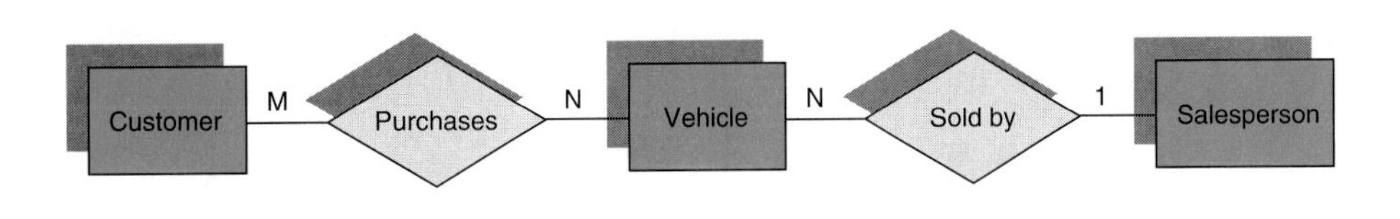

FIGURE A–6b Eastown Motors Database Design

```
SALESPERSON (SPNo, S-Name, S-Address, S-Phone, . . . )
VEHICLE     (VIDNo, SPNo, Make, Model, Year, List-Price,
            Sale-Date, Sale-Price, . . . )
CUSTOMER    (CustNo, C-Name, C-Address, C-Phone, . . . )
CUST-VEH    (CustNo, VIDNo)
```

Next we could try to determine what attributes (or properties) need to be stored about each entity, possibly through interviews. For example, we might determine that pertinent attributes of CUSTOMER include Name, Address, Telephone, and so on. After listing all potential attributes and grouping them with their entities, we could draw an E-R diagram showing the entities and relationships between them. One problem with this approach is that sometimes entities, attributes, or relations are omitted; occasionally employees forget about a business operation that may occur on an infrequent basis.

A slightly different (but complementary) approach would be to examine the different records and forms currently kept in Mr. Balthazar's office and then try to extract the relevant entities, attributes, and relationships from them. This would be considered a "bottom-up" approach, deriving the data model from the details of the current operations. For example, we could look at the Vehicle Inventory file (kept in a three-ring binder), and determine that a VEHICLE has a certain Make, Model, Year, and so on. We could then examine a customer record (currently kept in filing cabinets by each salesperson) to determine the CUSTOMER attributes required, such as Name and Address. One of the problems with the bottom-up approach is that it is difficult to anticipate desired changes to existing processes. In general, a combination of the two approaches is used.

Figure A–6a shows a simplified, first draft of an E-R diagram for the Eastown Motors database application. Note the N:M relationship between customers and vehicle; this indicates that a customer may purchase more than one vehicle and that a vehicle may be purchased by more than one customer (e.g., by a husband and wife). The next step is to transform the E-R diagram into a database design.

Moving from a Data Model to a Database Design

We showed (in Figure A–4a) that for a 1:N relationship, we need to place the key of the "1" entity as a field in the "N" table. In the example shown in Figure A–6a, we have a 1:N relationship between SALESPERSON and VEHICLE, which suggests that we need to place the key of SALESPERSON (SPNo) as a field in the VEHICLE table.

SALESPERSON (SPNo, S-Name, S-Address, S-Phone, . . .)

VEHICLE (VIDNo, SPNo, Make, Model, Year,

List-Price, . . .)

If we tried to maintain the relationship by placing the VEHICLE key (VIDNo) as a field in the SALESPERSON table, we would run into problems. Since a salesperson can sell many vehicles, it would mean we would have to add an undetermined number of fields to the SALESPERSON table, one for each vehicle sold. Although it might be physically possible to store the data this way, it would lead to numerous inefficiencies in data storage and difficulties in data retrieval.

Now let us consider the other relationship. For the moment, assume that the relationship between CUSTOMER and VEHICLE is 1:1; that is, a customer can only buy one vehicle, and a vehicle can only be purchased by one customer. If this were true, we could maintain a relationship between the CUSTOMER table and the VEHICLE table by either placing the CUSTOMER key (CustNo) as a field in the VEHICLE table, or by placing the VEHICLE key as an attribute in the CUSTOMER table. Either approach would work.

Since the relationship is N:M, however, it gets a bit more complicated. First, we need to create a table for the CUSTOMER entity (we already have one for VEHICLE). Next we have to maintain the relationship between CUSTOMER and VEHICLE, which is done by introducing a new table that contains the key fields of the other two:

CUSTOMER (CustNo, C-Name, C-Address, C-Phone, . . .)

CUST-VEH (CustNo, VIDNo)

This would allow us to associate more than one customer with a given vehicle or more than one vehicle with a given customer.

If we think about it, however, when we sell a vehicle to a customer there is actually more information we need to keep: date of sale, sale price, warranty conditions, and so on. Assume that we restrict the records in the VEHICLE table to those that are available for sale, but we also want to keep track of vehicles we have sold. In reality, we may have discovered the need for a new table:

SALE (VIDNo, Date, Price, . . .)

Now we have two tables (VEHICLE and SALE) that have the same key, VIDNo. This doesn't make sense; if they have the same key, they should be related to the same entity, and they should be combined into one table. On closer examination, however, are they really the same? A vehicle is available for purchase; a sold vehicle is not.

One approach would be to define two separate entities (VEHICLE and SVEHICLE), give them separate keys, and transfer a vehicle record from the VEHICLE table to the SVEHICLE table once the vehicle has been sold. A second approach would be to add the SALE attributes (date, sale price, etc.) to the VEHICLE table and leave the SALE attributes empty until the vehicle has been sold. The decision as to which approach to take could depend on such factors as how frequently we expect to access records about sold vehicles; for simplicity, we'll assume that we decide to use the second approach. Our database design (see Figure A–6b) would therefore be:

```
SALESPERSON  (SPNo, S-Name, S-Address, S-Phone, . . . )

VEHICLE      (VIDNo, SPNo, Make, Model, Year, List-Price,
Sale-Date, Sale-Price, . . . )

CUSTOMER     (CustNo, C-Name, C-Address, C-Phone, . . . )

CUST-VEH     (CustNo, VIDNo)
```

Testing and Implementing the Design

Once we have a database design to work from, the next step is to create a database (using whatever DBMS has been selected) and enter a small amount of sample data. Now we can start developing sample input screens and reports to determine if our design will allow us to provide the required output. If problems are encountered, (perhaps we discover more data fields that need to be stored), it is a lot easier to revise the database during this testing phase than after it has been fully implemented and all the data have been entered.

Prototyping is a term used to describe the iterative process used to try different report formats and input screens. Prototyping helps during the testing phase and during the transition to the final database design.

It is important to remember, however, that the data model (the E-R diagram), the database design, and all applications developed during prototyping need to be fully documented and modified whenever any changes are made. Although working with a database management system might lull you into thinking that changes will be easy, over time you will forget the instructions, menu sequences, and other procedures used to process the database. If the database is to be used by more than one person, the documentation is even more important.

Retrieving Information from a Database

The relational data model allows for certain logical operators (such as *join*ing two relations), which, in turn, allows for necessary data storage, retrieval, and manipulation operations. These relational operators are incorporated as part of the DBMS's data manipulation language; a common example is the **Structured Query Language (SQL)**, which is provided with many popular DBMS. SQL provides users with a set of concise but powerful data management commands. It can be used on all types of computer systems (personal computers, minicomputers, etc.) and has become somewhat of a standard for many relational DBMSs.

SQL is only one of many ways that data can be extracted from a database. Most DBMSs (Access, Paradox, Oracle, etc.) have their own query languages and report generators that can also be used to manipulate and retrieve data.

OBJECT-ORIENTED DATABASES

Traditional DBMSs were designed to handle sparse information composed of textual (alphanumeric) data elements. As advances were made in object-oriented programming and the need for richer information expanded, the capabilities of DBMSs needed to grow as well. For example, if a marketing firm wishes to keep track of all advertisement ideas and ad copy related to a specific marketing campaign, they need to store text, photos, sound, video, and so on. A manufacturing firm might need to store engineering drawings produced with a CAD (computer-aided design) system. These needs resulted in the development of object-oriented databases.

An **object-oriented database** can store and organize rich information structures consisting of text, graphics, sound, photographs, and so on. The data are treated as self-contained objects that can be stored, shared and manipulated. The object-oriented databases are designed to work with object-oriented programming languages, allowing for the reuse of objects and enabling the development of multimedia applications. A relatively simple example would be to include photos of employees in the employee database. When an employee record is retrieved, the employee photo (stored as a field) could be displayed on the screen or printed as part of the employee record.

DATA MANAGEMENT ISSUES

Chapter 11 of this book introduces a number of issues related to the management of organizational information systems and information, including security (guarding against unauthorized access), integrity (ensuring the accuracy of data), and importance (viewing data as an organizational resource). At this point we would like to briefly mention three additional issues that are related to data management and, more specifically, to database management systems: distributed databases, database interfaces, and disaster planning and recovery.

To this point we have discussed a database as if it were always a single entity contained on a single storage device (such as a hard-disk drive on a personal computer). In this environment, we may have one or more users accessing the database. If multiple users are involved, the software (either the DBMS or specially written programs) needs to handle issues such as concurrency control. For example, if two users want access to the same record at the same time, the DBMS has to have some type of protocol for allowing one user access and perhaps locking out the second user until the first is finished.

What happens if we have users at multiple locations who need access to the data? One option is to connect the users to the database with telecommunication lines. If we have a very large number of users spread over a large geographic area, however, this might slow down the access time substantially. Another option could be to create a distributed database by duplicating all or part of the database and allowing users at different locations to access exact replications of the database.

Duplicating (or replicating) a database raises a number of important issues, not the least being how to ensure that the data in all copies of the database are identical. If a user working with copy A of the database wants to change a data element (such as a customer address), all other copies of that data element must be changed as well. Somehow the DBMS software (or specialized computer programs) have to accommodate these changes. One of the advantages of replicating a database, however, is that a copy exists in case of an emergency. The copy can serve as a backup; if a single database is destroyed (by fire, mechanical failure, etc.) and no backup exists, the results could be disastrous.

Databases interfaces are also very important. Previously we used a generic term (data manipulation language) and also gave a specific example (SQL). In reality, a wide variety of methods are available for interacting with databases, and these methods are continually being refined and expanded. As an example, many people consider SQL to be very easy to use for simple queries but far too cumbersome for the average user when the queries become more complex. Having a senior executive spend hours trying to use SQL to retrieve needed information is not a very productive use of time. For that reason, natural language interpreters have been developed. These interfaces accept requests phrased similarly to "natural language" and convert the requests into SQL (or similar) commands which can be interpreted and recognized by the DBMS. For example, a user could type "Give me a list of all customers who are located in Atlanta" rather than remembering the SQL command "SELECT * FROM CUSTOMER WHERE CITY = 'Atlanta'."

Taking the notion of easier interfaces further, voice recognition and speech command systems attempt to interpret voice commands and retrieve the desired information. Rather than typing the command, the user speaks it. Although voice command systems continue to improve, they remain somewhat limited in functionality. Most have to be trained to understand the user, and most users have to be trained to use the voice command system effectively. Typically the user has to speak slowly and clearly, and often only a very limited set of commands can be used. As a result, some users experience hoarse voices and even some damage to their vocal cords. Nevertheless, voice recognition interfaces continue to improve and could represent an important part of database interface options.

One final, very important issue concerning databases is the need for effective disaster and recovery plans. Many organizations are very dependent on the information stored in databases; without it, they literally cannot continue to function. If a bank loses all the information concerning their customers (deposits, loans, etc.), they will be forced out of business. Because of this dependence, most organizations have detailed plans in place for recovering from a disaster (such as a fire, flood, or hardware failure).

SUMMARY

Computer systems are unable to read human language, so human-readable information has to be converted to computer-readable codes. Data and information are generally considered to be stored in a hierarchy, ranging from the smallest elements (bits) to the largest groupings (databases).

Computer files can be accessed either sequentially (one record at a time, in sequential order) or direct. Direct access is more common and is used with database management systems. Sequential access is typically used for situations in which the data do not need to be accessed frequently and where the needs are conducive to sequential access (such as running a payroll program to pay employees).

Transaction processing involves recording events (the sale of a product; the hiring of an employee; etc.) and then processing those records. Transaction processing systems record historical information and are focused on the details necessary to run an organization. All major organizational activities require that records be kept; transaction processing systems allow most organizations to do this.

Database management systems are used for many transaction processing applications and also for the reporting systems that use transaction data as their source of information. To ensure that the data are structured properly within a database, data modeling techniques may be employed. One such technique is referred to as entity-relationship diagrams, which are widely used.

KEY CONCEPTS AND TERMS

KEY CONCEPTS

- Information can be represented in human-readable and computer-readable form. (479)
- File access can either be sequential or direct; direct is more common. (480)
- Transaction processing involves recording events and processing those records. (481)

- Database processing is superior to file processing for many common applications. (483)
- Data modeling facilitates structuring data logically in a database design. (485)

KEY TERMS

batch processing (482)
bit (479)
byte (479)
database (480)
database design (484)
DataBase Management System (DBMS) (483)
data element (479)
data model (484)
direct access (480)
direct file organization (483)
entity-relationship (E-R) diagram (485)
field (479)
file (479)
file processing (483)
index-sequential file organization (483)
key (480)
master file (481)
object-oriented database (490)
on-line processing (482)
record (479)
relational database (484)
sequential access (480)
sequential file organization (482)
Structured Query Language (SQL) (489)
transaction (481)
transaction file (481)
transaction processing (481)

REFERENCES

Kroenke, D. and R. Hatch. *Management Information Systems* (3rd ed.). New York: McGraw-Hill, 1994.

Laudon, K. C. and J. P. Laudon. *Information Systems: A Problem-Solving Approach* (3rd ed.). Fort Worth, TX: The Dryden Press, 1995.

McFadden, F. and J. Hoffer. *Modern Database Management* (4th ed.). Redwood City, CA: Benjamin/Cummings Publishing, 1994.

McKeown, P. G. and R. A. Leitch. *Management Information Systems: Managing with Computers*. Fort Worth, TX: The Dryden Press, 1993.

Rob, P. and C. Coronel. *Database Systems: Design, Implementation, and Management.* Belmont, CA: Wadsworth Publishing, 1993.

APPENDIX B Systems Development Tools and Techniques

The process of developing information systems can be time consuming, complex, and fraught with error. The objective of any systems development effort is to implement and maintain a useful system that accomplishes the goals set for it and to do so in a timely, cost-effective manner. To help in the systems development effort, many methods, tools, and techniques have been developed.

DEVELOPMENT METHODOLOGIES AND TECHNIQUES

Systems **development methodologies** are comprehensive and attempt to cover the full range of the systems development life cycle (SDLC). As described in Chapter 7, the SDLC can be viewed as containing six major phases: (1) define goals, (2) define requirements, (3) generate and evaluate alternatives, (4) design the chosen alternative, (5) implement, and (6) evaluate and maintain. A complete development methodology should incorporate (1) step-by-step tasks for each phase, (2) individual and group roles to be played in each task, (3) deliverables and quality standards for each task, and (4) development techniques to be used for each task.

Many organizations purchase development methodologies from vendors (including some consulting firms). A methodology vendor such as Structured Solutions sells their methodology (in this case, STRADIS), which contains manuals, software, training and training videos, and consulting. The organization that purchases the methodology attempts to incorporate it into its systems development operation, using the methodology for future development projects.

Development techniques are approaches that apply specific tools and rules to one or more phases of the SDLC. Typically these techniques and tools are only applied to a subset of the development life cycle, and many competing techniques exist. There are also activities that cut across the phases of the SDLC, such as project management.

Many of the systems development techniques and tools are supported by information systems developed specifically for that purpose. This type of information system falls under the broad heading of **computer-aided systems engineering (CASE).** This appendix introduces some of the more common development techniques and briefly explains the role of CASE development tools. It closes with a discussion of the object-oriented approach to developing information systems, which is becoming a larger force in systems development and is slowly being used to enhance or even replace some of the earlier techniques.

Sample Case: Westward Ho. To help illustrate various development techniques, we will use a brief case description of a small retail organization, named Westward Ho. This company was started in 1995, and it specializes in western styles of clothing and accessories. The store is still relatively small; at the time of this writing there were six full-time and eight part-time employees. The company has strived for an up-scale image and is attempting to develop a niche market. Since most of the retail stores in the local area only carry lower-priced Western clothing as part of their total inventory, Westward Ho believes they can obtain a sufficient share of the market to survive and hopefully expand.

Very few automated processes exist at Westward Ho; all customer receipts, bills, rental and other payments, taxes, bank deposits, and purchase orders are handled manually. There is a personal computer with word-processing and spreadsheet software. Currently the spreadsheet is used to keep track of inventory; a column is maintained for the inventory category, the vendor's name and number, retail cost, markup percentage, sales price, and quantity on hand. Since there are more than 100 item categories in stock, the entire spreadsheet cannot be viewed at one time. Someone has to use the sales receipts and bills of lading to update the spreadsheet, which is time consuming and has a potential for errors. Also, the spreadsheet does not allow the owner to easily generate any reports (such as sales trends) or to easily answer ad-hoc questions (such as listing all items that have had fewer than 20 sales over the past month).

The owner of Westward Ho, Becky Carson, would like some help.

SYSTEMS DEVELOPMENT TECHNIQUES

One common technique for the analysis phase of the systems development life cycle is called data flow diagramming. **Data flow diagrams (DFDs)** graphically depict the flow of data through a system and also focus on the processes (or activities) involved. They can be used to describe the existing system and also to illustrate how a new system could operate. One of the advantages of DFDs is that they use only a few symbols, and are readily understood by clients of a development process as well as by information systems specialists. A DFD consists of a maximum of four types of symbols: (1) external entity, (2) process, (3) data flow, and (4) data store.

An **external entity** (which may be represented as a square) is outside the boundary of the system being studied. It could be a thing, a person, or another system. If we are examining the entire organization, common external entities would be Customer, Supplier, Bank, and so on. If we are examining a subset of the organization (such as the functions of the Receiving Department), external entities could also include other people, departments, or systems that are part of the same company but are outside of the area being investigated (such as Accounting, Shipping, etc.). An external entity is either the source of an input for the system being studied or the destination for an output being produced.

A **process** (which may also be represented as a circle) is a transformation of incoming data flow(s) into outgoing data flow(s). It may involve work or activities performed by people or through information technology. A process might split a complex input data flow into two or more output data flows. It might combine two or more input data flows into one output data flow. Another function could be to verify the contents of one data flow against the contents of a second data flow (or data store), without changing the physical content of the output data flow. A process might also reorganize incoming data flows by filtering, formatting, or sorting. The data is unchanged, but the structure is different.

A **data flow** can be considered a pipeline or conduit for data and information. It could take many forms, such as a sales receipt being passed from a sales clerk to a customer, a purchase order being transmitted electronically to a supplier, or a telephone call from a potential client. Data flows may also be data retrieved from or stored to a computer file, manual forms retrieved from or stored to files, or an entry recorded in a logbook or on a data sheet. All data flows must begin or end at a process and are named with nouns (verbs are not allowed).

A **data store** can be thought of as an inventory of data. Examples could include an index card file, a file cabinet of records, or a computer file or database. A data store might be an in/out box on someone's desk, a book or binder of tables or reports, a log sheet or ledger, or anything onto which entries are recorded. Some data stores are temporary (the data "rests" there for a short period of time), while others are more permanent.

Westward Ho: Operations

When merchandise is sold at Westward Ho, the employee who has been helping the customer writes up a sales receipt on a two-part form. One copy is given to the customer, while the second is placed in a file for later use. Daily cash, checks, and credit card slips are totaled by the store manager at the end of the day and then compiled into a bank deposit. The bank deposit is carried to the bank, and a copy of the deposit is given to the accountant. Twice a month Westward Ho receives a bank statement that they then reconcile against their bank deposit copies.

The sales receipts are collected at the end of the day, sorted by category, and entered into the inventory spreadsheet. This spreadsheet is used to calculate stock levels and determine what items should be purchased. A low stock list is prepared from the spreadsheet and given to the assistant manager (who handles all purchasing).

When items need to be purchased, a purchase order is prepared, and the original is sent to a supplier. Information about suppliers and the items they carry is contained in a binder. A copy of the purchase order is kept in an open order file. When the shipment of items is received from the supplier, it is accompanied by a bill of lading, which lists the quantity of all items in the shipment. The assistant store

FIGURE B–1 Westward Ho—Context Diagram

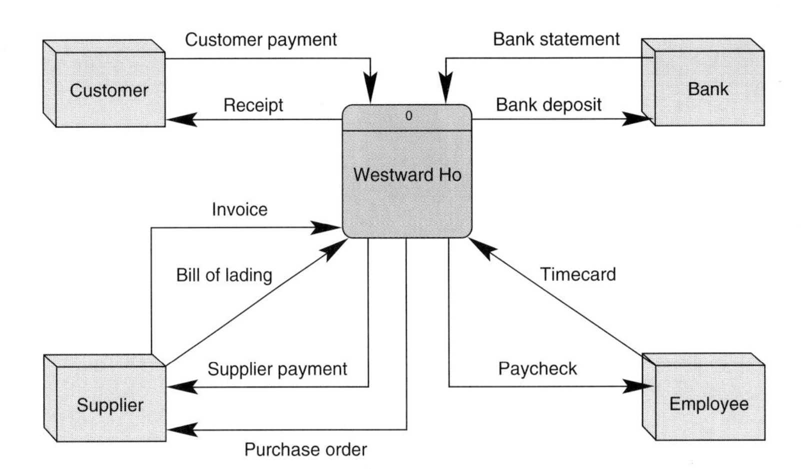

manager is responsible for entering the items received from the bill of lading into the inventory spreadsheet. She then pulls the appropriate purchase order copy from the open order file and checks it against the bill of lading to make sure everything ordered was received. The matched purchase order and bill of lading are then filed in a closed order file.

When a supplier prepares a shipment of items for Westward Ho, it also prepares an invoice (bill) which is sent through the mail (separate from the shipment). When an invoice is received, it goes to the accountant. The accountant usually pays the invoices and other bills twice a month, so she keeps the unpaid ones in an unpaid invoice file. Once an invoice has been paid, it is filed in a paid invoice file.

Employees keep track of the time they work on a timesheet, which has to be verified by the store manager or assistant manager. The accountant uses the timesheet and information from the employee file (which consists of file folders in a locked file cabinet) to calculate the amount owed each employee and to generate the paychecks.

Although Westward Ho engages in other activities (such as paying the rent on the retail space they lease), we will use the previous description to help illustrate some systems development techniques.

DFDs: The Context Diagram

The **context diagram** is the top level of the set of data flow diagrams. It may illustrate the primary interactions (inputs and outputs) for the entire organization or just for the area under investigation. Figure B–1 illustrates a context diagram for Westward Ho. The diagram does not include all interactions with the environment, but rather it shows a few of the more common and important ones. The procedure for drawing a context diagram involves (1) identifying all external entities that represent either a source or destination for information flows to or from the organization (or system), (2) identifying and listing major information flows to and from the external entities, and (3) drawing the context diagram with the organization (or system) as a single process, with the external entities connected to this process by the major information flows.

FIGURE B–2 Westward Ho—System-Level Diagram

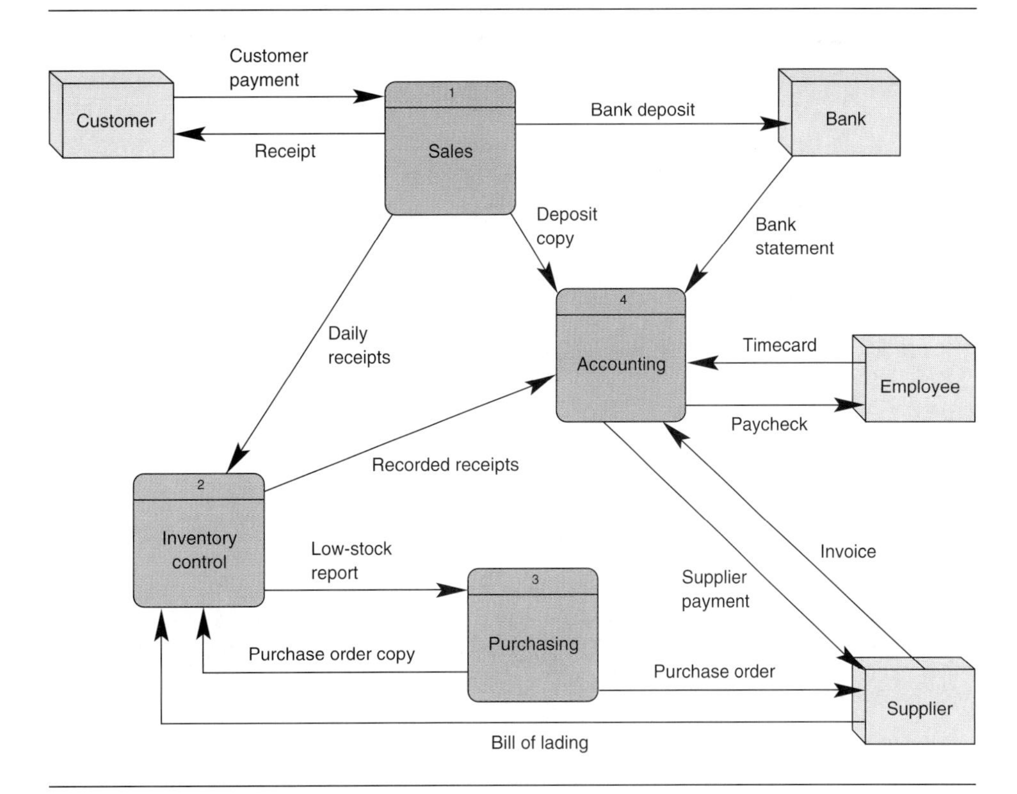

Notice that employees have been shown as being outside of the company. This may seem a little strange (since they work for Westward Ho), but actually it helps us show the interactions with timecards and paychecks. Also notice that there are no data stores on the context diagram. This is DFD convention; all data stores are assumed to be inside the main process (the company) and will show up on lower levels of the DFDs.

DFDs: The System-Level Diagram

Once the context diagram has been completed, the next step is to break the overall company (or system) into smaller subsystems. This is illustrated with a *system-level* (or *level one*) data flow diagram. Sometimes an organization chart is a good place to start. The procedure for developing the system-level DFD (see Figure B–2) is to start with the context diagram; all of the inputs, outputs, and external entities from the context diagram will also appear on the system-level diagram. Next, identify major departments or systems from the organization.

It should be possible to read the DFD by "walking through" the diagram. For example, a CUSTOMER (external entity) gives a CUSTOMER PAYMENT (data flow) to SALES (a process), receiving in return a RECEIPT (data flow). The DAILY RECEIPTS (data flow) are given to INVENTORY CONTROL (a process), and so on. If you were to write up a description of a **walkthrough** of the diagram, it should look fairly similar to the one provided earlier.

Note that the processes that appear on the system-level diagram do not have to appear on an organizational chart. For example, in Westward Ho the position titles are owner, store manager, assistant store manager, accountant, and sales representative. Although no one works in a "purchasing department" or has the title of purchasing manager, the purchasing function still takes place. This is where we can separate the physical description (*who* or *what program* does some activity) from the logical description (*what* activity is being performed). A DFD may be used to represent either a physical description of a system or a logical one. Typically we focus on the logical aspects.

Also notice that although the system-level diagram contains more information than the context diagram, it is still incomplete. For example, none of the data stores (such as the inventory file) have appeared on this diagram. Frequently data stores do appear on system-level (level one) DFDs; in fact, it could be argued that Figure B–2 should include the Open Order file data store, positioned between Inventory Control (process 2) and Purchasing (process 3), since both of these processes interact with the Open Order file.

The system-level diagram is also missing activities such as verifying the timecards from employees. These additional details would appear on lower level diagrams; this is one of the advantages of the DFD technique. It is possible to continue "exploding" the diagrams to reach whatever level of precision is necessary. Finally, Figure B–2 shows one possible system level DFD for Westward Ho. Other versions could be "correct" as well (such as splitting Inventory Control into two processes—Inventory Control and Receiving). Typically there is no "right" DFD; the goal is to generate a diagram that communicates the details of the organization or system as clearly as possible.

DFDs: Lower Level Diagrams

Assume that Becky (the owner of Westward Ho) has asked us to investigate the Inventory Control process in greater detail. The approach is to treat the Inventory Control process (process 2) as a process on a context diagram and explode it to a lower level. Each of the input and output data flows that interact with Inventory Control will also appear on the next level down. In addition, any processes that serve as sources of input data flows to Inventory Control or processes that serve as destinations for output data flows from Inventory Control will become External Entities to the Inventory Control process.

Figure B–3 shows one possible level two DFD for Inventory Control. Here the processes that interact with Inventory Control on the system-level diagram have been drawn as external entities, with their process numbers shown. Another option would be to leave Sales, Purchasing, Accounting, and Supplier off the diagram and just show the corresponding data flows (such as Bill of Lading from the Supplier). This approach makes it necessary for the reader to flip back to the previous diagram to see where the data flow comes from or goes to; hence showing the sources and destinations is usually preferred.

Diagramming Conventions

To help keep consistency among data flow diagrams, conventions have been developed for their use. A few of the more common conventions include the following:

FIGURE B–3 Westward Ho—Inventory Control Level Two Diagram

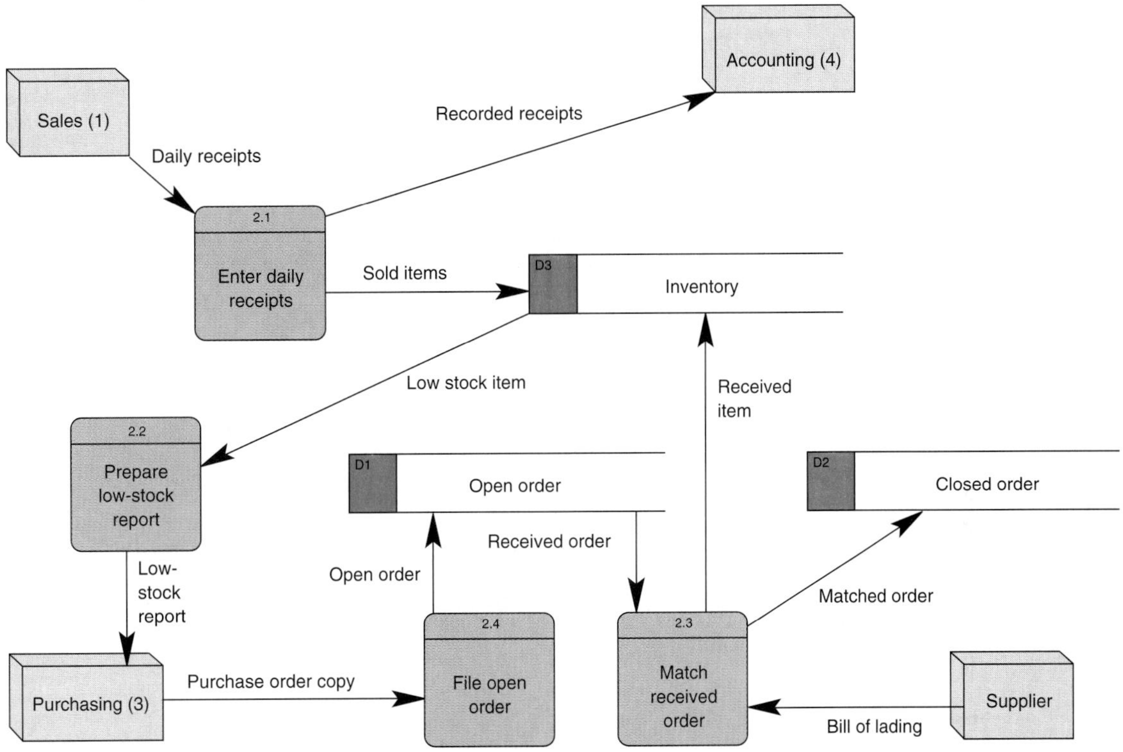

- All data flows must begin and/or end at a process (in other words, a data flow cannot go directly from one data store to another or directly from an external entity to a data store or between two external entities).
- No process may have only input data flows (this is sometimes referred to as a "black hole").
- No process may have only output data flows (this is referred to as a "miracle").
- The information contained on the input data flows to a process must be sufficient to generate the outputs.

Data Models and Data Dictionaries

The data flow diagrams illustrate the flow of information through the system and highlight the processes that need to be performed. Data modeling, using techniques such as entity-relationship diagrams (described in more detail in Appendix A), is another important systems development technique. Generally the data model and process models are developed together since they are closely related. Assuming that a new system will be implemented using a database management system, a database design (also described in Appendix A) would also be required.

To provide detailed descriptions of the data beyond that expressed with data models or a database design, **data dictionary** entries can also be used. Data

FIGURE B–4 Data Dictionary Entry—Data Flow

Data flow name:	Purchase order
Aliases:	P. O., order
Prepared by:	Joe Green
From:	Process 3.0, Purchasing
To:	External entity, supplier (original) Open order file (copy)
Description:	Two-part, carbonless, preprinted form (form 2021); prepared in response to a low-stock report

Contains elements:	Purchase order number
	P.O. date
	Supplier name
	Supplier number
	Supplier address
	Contact name
	Order total
	and 1 to 20 occurrences of
	  Item number
	  Item description
	  Quantity ordered
	  Item price
	  Extended price

dictionaries are generally provided as part of a database management system. The data dictionary (the term *repository* is also used) contains descriptions of the elements of the data flow diagrams, including external entities, data flows, and data stores. To illustrate, Figure B–4 shows a sample data dictionary entry for a data flow, and Figure B–5 shows an entry for a data element (which would correspond to a field in the database design).

Data dictionaries can also be used to record detailed descriptions of the processes on a data flow diagram. Typically these process descriptions take the form of pseudocode or **structured English**. Pseudocode and structured English are standard ways of representing procedures, which were initially developed to correspond fairly closely to structured programming (discussed later). Figure B–6 shows a sample of structured English.

Structured Design

Structured design is a technique for breaking up a large program (or a group of related programs) into a hierarchy of program modules. Each module is a group of instructions that perform some activity. When structured design is used with structured programming, each module in the design would be written using structured programming concepts.

One common form of structured design shows the hierarchy of progam modules as an inverted tree structure, with a single "root" (see Figure B–7). Following the concepts of structured design, the objective is to develop modules that are

1. Highly cohesive—each module should accomplish only one function.
2. Loosely coupled—modules should not be very dependent on other modules.

FIGURE B–5 Data Dictionary Entry—Data Element

Data element name:	Purchase order number
Aliases:	P. O. number, order number
Description:	Numeric, six digits in length Unique; used to identify data flow purchase order Sequential in ascending order (P. O. forms numbered sequentially)

FIGURE B–6 Process Description—Structured English

Process name: Prepare low-stock report
Process number: 2.2
Process description:

1. For each item in the inventory file:
   1.1 If the quantity on hand is less than the minimum quantity
      1.1.1 Subtract the quantity on hand from the maximum quantity to get the quantity needed
      1.1.2 Put the item number, description, and quantity needed onto the low-stock list
   Otherwise (quantity on hand is greater or equal to minimum quantity)
   1.2 Continue to the next item

FIGURE B–7 Sample Structure Chart (Structured Design)

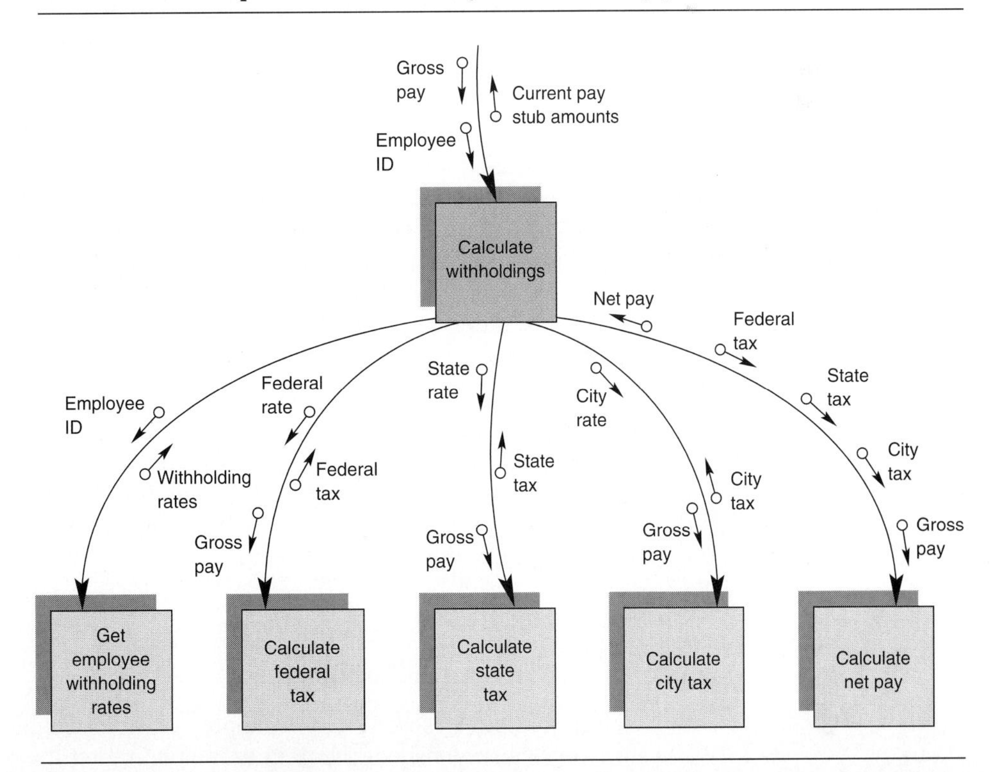

Structured Programming

Structured programming is a way of designing and writing programs that should be consistent and easier to maintain. The basic approach is to use a limited set of control structures within any program. It also suggests that a well-structured program should be read from top to bottom and should require minimal branching. The three basic control structures include the following:

1. Sequence—instructions that follow one after another.
2. Selection—branch to one of two or more groups of instructions based on some decision criteria (if-then-else or using a case construct).
3. Iteration—repeat a group of instructions based on some criteria (either repeat-until or do-while).

These three constructs can be repeated or nested within one another as required. To further simplify the systems that are developed, additional constraints include using only single entries and exits for interactions between program modules and using GOTO statements sparingly. Programmers frequently use program flowcharts or structured English (or pseudocode, which is similar) to help design a program before actually writing it. Figure B–8 shows the three constructs of structured programming, with the structured English equivalents. Structured programming can be viewed as a complement to structured design.

CASE Tools

To help speed the development process and to help ensure that high-quality, easy-to-maintain systems are produced, numerous software packages have been created. Examples include Visual Analyst Workbench (from Visible Systems Corp.), Excelerator (from Intersolv), and System Architect (from Popkin Software). These can be classified under the general heading of computer-aided systems engineering (CASE) tools.

CASE tools are generally designed to focus on either the analysis phase (these are termed **upper CASE** tools), or the design and implementation phases (**lower CASE** tools). The upper CASE tools allow the developer to quickly prepare data flow diagrams, entity-relationship diagrams, data dictionary entries, structure charts, and so on. Typically the diagrams and data descriptions are stored in a project dictionary (or repository), which helps provide consistency throughout the project development.

Lower CASE tools typically support the development of structure charts, prototype input screens and reports, process descriptions, and so on. Many also have the capability of actually generating programs (program code) in one or more popular programming languages (such as COBOL or C+) from the process specifications.

Recently some of the tools have been integrated and/or expanded to provide support for all phases of the systems development life cycle. Additional tools exist to support activities that cut across the different phases, such as project management and estimation of resource needs (mainly people) for completing each task. These tools continue to evolve, and their capabilities continue to expand, providing increasing support features.

Limitations of Structured Techniques

Let us return to the Westward Ho example for a moment. The employees of Westward Ho use a spreadsheet program to maintain their inventory records. Using

FIGURE B–8 Constructs for Structured Programming

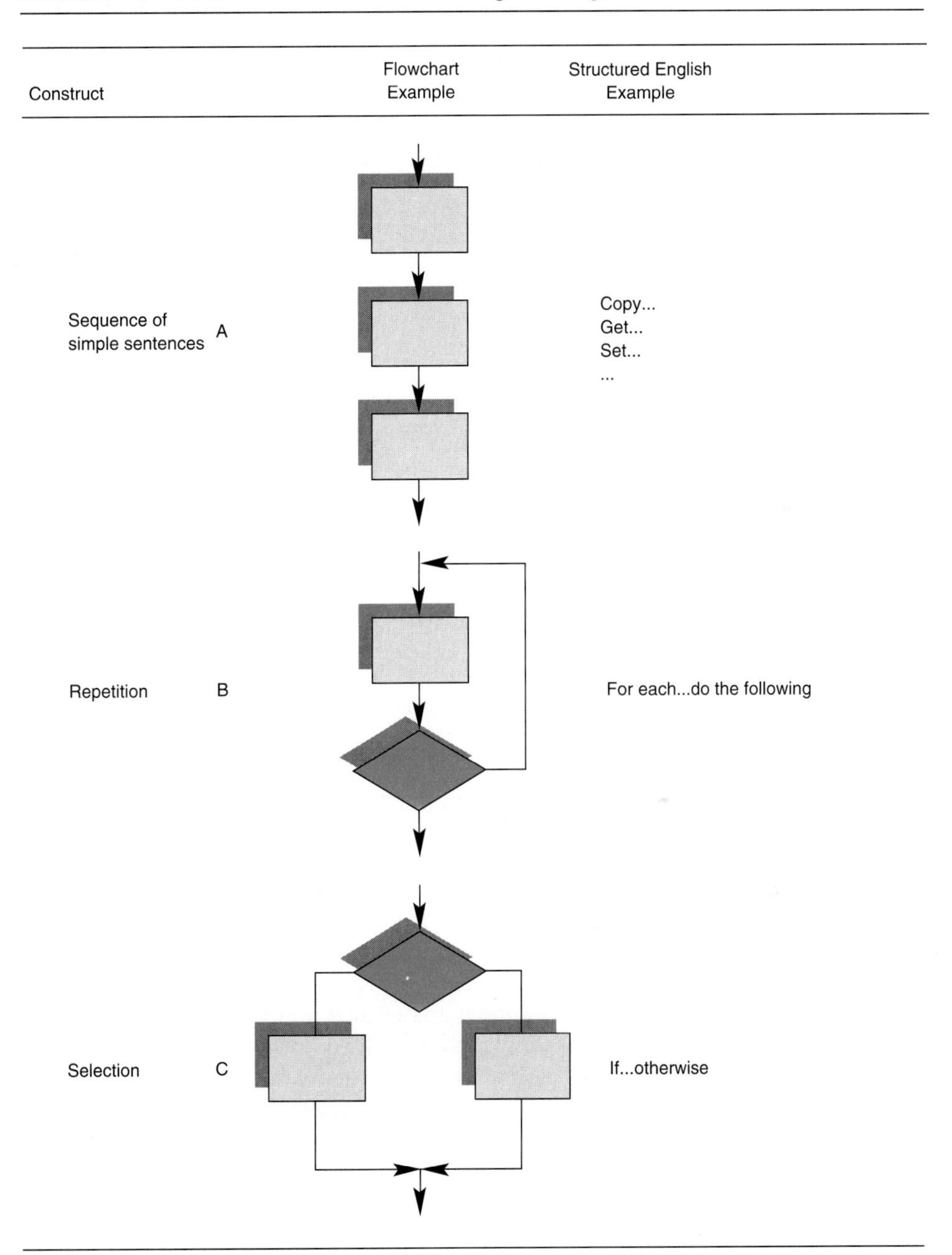

structured techniques, we could diagram the existing system in detail before examining alternative ways to improve it. This would probably be a waste of time, however. It wouldn't require a great deal of analysis to determine that a spreadsheet is not the best way to keep inventory records; a system based around the use of a database management system would be much superior.

Also, many systems have already been developed specifically for retail stores. It would probably take less time, be much less expensive, and much more effective to

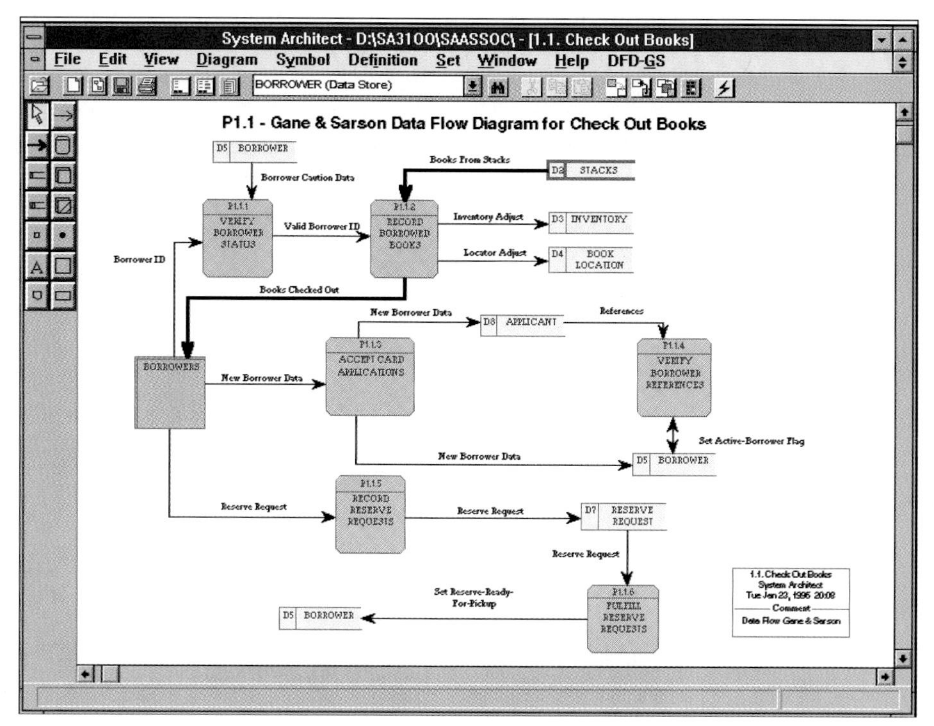

CASE tools help systems developers throughout the development process. Here Popkin's System Architect tool is being used to create diagrams and to describe data. Photo courtesy of Popkin Systems, Inc.

purchase a system rather than developing one either using programming languages or even a DBMS. Although it still makes sense to perform an analysis to determine information requirements before generating alternatives, it doesn't make sense to spend time describing processes that are going to be changed.

This illustrates one of the criticisms of structured techniques: They take too long and require too much paperwork. This has led to a greater use of prototyping, where application generators, report generators, and similar tools (commonly associated with database management systems) are used to produce "quick-and-dirty" mock-ups of a new system. The user typically works with the systems developer to define needs by reacting to a prototype and then having it quickly modified. This iterative process continues until the user is satisfied with the prototype, which may then either be implemented or rewritten using a programming language.

Dissatisfaction with structured techniques also led to the development of object-oriented approaches, which are discussed next.

OBJECT-ORIENTED TECHNIQUES

With the development of **object-oriented programming** languages and object databases, the use of object development techniques has begun to increase in popularity as well. Some people view the migration to an object-oriented approach as evolutionary, while others view it as revolutionary. Under this approach, an information system is viewed as a collection of objects. An object is a thing that exhibits certain behaviors and contains certain attributes.

Another important concept is that objects interact, both with other objects and with people. To interact with objects in an information system, the user tells the object to do something, and the object does what has been requested. With **object-oriented design,** the developer first defines the objects needed in a new (or revised) information system. If these objects already exist, they are reused. If they don't exist, the developer tries to select an existing object that is close to the one needed and then modifies the existing object as necessary. New objects are created from scratch only as a last resort.

As a comparison to structured techniques, an object-oriented development methodology would contain the following steps:

1. Object-oriented analysis (define the user environment and user requirements in terms of objects).
2. Object-oriented design (define all required components of the desired information system in terms of objects).
3. Object-oriented implementation (use object-oriented programming to select, modify, or create objects defined in the design phase and write procedures to interact with objects if necessary).
4. Maintenance and evaluation.

Object-oriented development is designed to improve the quality and flexibility of the information systems created, as well as the productivity of the development process. Since each object is small and self-contained, it reduces the complexity of systems development and makes systems easier to maintain. Also, since objects can be reused, productivity can be greatly enhanced. Not only is there less development time needed when objects exist, they are already proven, hence, less testing time is required. Maintenance is also much easier since a system may be modified by adding or changing objects rather than rewriting an entire system.

Object-oriented design is probably closest to data modeling concepts and techniques from structured development methodologies. Also, many of the structured techniques can be modified for use in object-oriented design. One major difference is that the object approach leads to a development methodology that relies heavily on creating building blocks (objects), which can be used and reused as often as necessary.

SUMMARY

The process of developing information systems can be time consuming, complex, and fraught with error. The objective of any systems development effort is to implement and maintain a useful system that accomplishes the goals set for it and to do so in a timely, cost-effective manner. To help in the systems development effort, many methods, tools, and techniques have been developed.

One common technique for the analysis phase of the systems development life cycle is called data flow diagramming. Data flow diagrams graphically depict the flow of data through a system and also focus on the processes (or activities) that are involved. They can be used to describe the existing system and illustrate how a new system could operate. One of the advantages of DFDs is that they use only a few symbols and are readily understood by clients of a development process as well as by information systems specialists. A DFD consists of a maximum of four types of symbols: (1) external entity, (2) process, (3) data flow, and (4) data store.

A set of data flow diagrams is leveled, starting with the most general diagram at the top (the context diagram). Each subsequent level provides increasing detail concerning the process(es) under investigation. Generally the data flow diagrams are supplemented with data dictionary entries, which describe the components of the DFD (the data flows, etc.). Structured English or pseudocode are frequently used to describe the processes.

Structured design is a technique for breaking up a large program (or a group of related programs) into a hierarchy of program modules. Each module is a group of instructions that perform some activity. When structured design is used with structured programming, each module in the design would be written using structured programming concepts.

To help speed the development process and to help ensure that high-quality, easy-to-maintain systems are produced, numerous software packages have been created. These packages can be classified under the general heading of computer-aided systems engineering (CASE) tools.

With the development of object-oriented programming languages and object databases, the use of object development techniques has begun to increase in popularity as well. Some people view the migration to an object-oriented approach as evolutionary, while others view it as revolutionary. Under this approach, an information system is viewed as a collection of objects.

KEY CONCEPTS AND TERMS

KEY CONCEPTS

- Tools and techniques are available to help in the development of information systems. (493)
- DFDs are a graphical tool used to depict the requirements of an information system. (494)
- Data flow diagrams consist of multiple levels, each one showing greater detail. (497)
- Structured techniques (design and programming) are based on the principle of breaking complex packages and programs into smaller modules. (500)
- Object-oriented development techniques are increasing in popularity. (504)

KEY TERMS

computer-aided systems engineering (CASE) (494)
context diagram (496)
data dictionary (499)
data flow (495)
data flow diagram (DFD) (494)
data store (495)
development methodology (493)
development technique (493)
external entity (495)
lower CASE tools (502)
object-oriented design (504)
object-oriented programming (504)
process (495)
structured design (500)
structured English (500)
structured programming (502)
upper CASE tools (502)
walkthrough (497)

REFERENCES

DeMarco, Tom. *Structured Analysis and System Specifications.* Englewood Cliffs, NJ: Prentice-Hall, 1979.

Page-Jones, M. *The Practical Guide to Structured Systems Design* (2nd ed.). Englewood Cliffs, NJ: Yourdon Press, 1988.

Satzinger, J. W. and T. U. Orvik. *The Object-Oriented Approach: Concepts, Modeling and Systems Development.* Boston, MA: boyd & fraser publishing, 1996.

Whitten, J. L., L. D. Bentley, and V. M. Barlow. *Systems Analysis & Design Methods* (3rd ed.). Boston, MA: Richard D. Irwin, 1994.

Index